HISTORY, CULTURE, AND RELIGION
OF THE HELLENISTIC AGE

Second Edition

ANCIENT MEDITERRANEAN
WEST

ANCIENT MEDITERRANEAN EAST

Volume One

INTRODUCTION TO
THE NEW TESTAMENT

HISTORY, CULTURE, AND RELIGION
OF THE HELLENISTIC AGE

Second Edition

HELMUT KOESTER

WALTER DE GRUYTER
NEW YORK • BERLIN

ABOUT THE AUTHOR

Helmut Koester is John H. Morison Professor of New Testament Studies and Winn Professor of Ecclesiastical History at Harvard University, Editor of *Harvard Theological Review,* Editor of *Archaeological Resources for New Testament Studies,* and Chairman of the New Testament Board of *Hermeneia,* a continuing critical and historical commentary on the Bible.

Copyright © 1995 by Walter de Gruyter & Co., Berlin

Library of Congress Cataloging-in-Publication Data
Koester, Helmut, 1926–
    Introduction to the New Testament / Helmut Koester. —2nd ed.
      p. cm.
    Includes bibliographical references and index.
    Contents: v. 1. History, culture, and religion of the Hellenistic
age
    ISBN 3-11-014693-2 (cloth : alk. paper). —ISBN 3-11-014692-4
(pbk. : alk. paper)
    1. Bible. N.T.—History of contemporary events. 2. Bible. N.T.—
Introductions. I. Title.
BS2410.K613   1995
225.9′5—dc20   94-47576
                                      CIP

Manufactured in the United States of America

10 9 8 7 6 5 4 3 2 1

To the Memory of my Teacher
Rudolf Bultmann

Contents

§1 Historical Survey

§6 THE ROMAN EMPIRE AS THE HEIR OF HELLENISM

Illustrations

MAPS

PHOTOGRAPHS

CHARTS

Preface to the Second Edition

While the first American edition of this book, published more than a decade ago, was a revised translation of my German book, *Einführung in das Neue Testament,* this second edition of the first volume of the *Introduction to the New Testament* is no longer dependent upon a previously published German work. I thoroughly revised the text of the entire work, adding also several new chapters and updating the bibliography for all sections. I am grateful for the positive reception of the first edition and I have learned much from those reviewers who correctly observed that I am not an expert in all subject matters treated in this volume. Although I made an effort to correct a number of flaws, I still cannot claim to have accomplished more than providing, especially for the student of the New Testament, a useful introduction into the many complex aspects of the political, cultural, and religious developments that characterized the world in which early Christianity arose and by which the New Testament and other early Christian writings were shaped.

I am again indebted to my former student Philip Sellew, now professor at the University of Minnesota, for his advise and assistance. He carefully read and revised the entire manuscript and freely shared his knowledge of literature about the Greco-Roman world. Students and colleagues at Harvard University also made numerous suggestions for improvement. Without the encouragement and patience of my wife Gisela it would have been difficult to survive the long hours at the keyboard of my computer. My thanks also go to the staff of Walter de Gruyter, New York, for the congenial and expert efforts in the copyediting and production of the book.

Almost fifty years ago, I began my studies at the Philipps-University of Marburg, where I soon became fascinated by the lectures of Rudolf Bultmann, went to his seminars with fear and trembling, and survived his unforgiving criticisms and was revived by his faithful encouragement in my efforts to write a dissertation. What I owe to him is expressed in the continued dedication of this work to the memory of the unrivaled master in the art of interpreting the New Testament in its contemporary setting.

Harvard University,
Cambridge, Massachusetts,
October 1994

Helmut Koester

The concept of an "Introduction to the New Testament" in the form of a history of early Christianity in its contemporary setting, including a survey of the political, cultural, and religious history of the Hellenistic and Roman imperial period, stems from the predecessor of this book, the *Einführung in das Neue Testament* by Rudolf Knopf (revised edition by Hans Lietzmann and Heinrich Weinel) in the series "Sammlung Töpelmann" (now succeeded by "De Gruyter Lehrbücher"). Thus, the *Introduction* presented here in its English version does not aspire to be an "Introduction" in the technical sense nor a "History of Early Christian Literature" which treats the scholarship, date, integrity, and literary structure of each of the New Testament writings. To be sure, these questions are encompassed in the present work, but they are discussed within the context of a reconstruction of the historical development of early Christianity. My primary concern is to present the history of the early Christian churches, since it seems to me that the student of the New Testament must learn from the outset to understand the writings of the earliest period within their proper historical context.

It is obvious that this attempt to reconstruct the history of early Christianity requires one to relinquish some strictures of traditional introductions. I do not limit the discussion to the twenty-seven canonical books, but treat also sixty other early Christian writings from the first 150 years of Christian history, whether or not these writings are preserved fully or only in fragments. These non-canonical works are witnesses to early Christian history no less valuable than the New Testament. A historical presentation of these materials requires that clear decisions be made about authorship, date, and place of each writing; in other words, the results of historical-critical inquiry have to be consulted fully in each instance. I have also made an effort to discuss the problems in making such decisions. If these issues remain controversial with respect to some parts of the New Testament, they are even more difficult for non-canonical literature: traditionally scholarly debate has focused on the canonical literature, whereas the so-called "apocrypha" and other non-canonical writings have received only scant attention. Furthermore, quite a few of the latter have been discovered only recently, and their critical evaluation has just begun. Nevertheless, it is much better to advance scholarship, and thus our understanding, through hypothetical reconstruction than to ignore new and apparently problematic materials.

In view of the present situation of New Testament scholarship, it would be misleading to suggest to the students of early Christian history that they can expect largely secure results. The New Testament itself furnishes evidence that the history of early Christian communities was a complex process, full of controversies and difficult decisions. Understanding this process requires critical judgment as well as the construction of trajectories through the history of early Christianity. The recent discovery of even more early writings not only demands a basic reorientation of our views, but will also enable the student to appreciate more fully the depths and riches of this formative period, especially as it is seen in the context of the general history of the culture in which Christianity began.

The scope of this book does not permit me to base my entire presentation upon the results of my own research. There are many topics in my survey of the Hellenistic and Roman world on which the specialist will have better insights and judgment. I am not only indebted to the published works of many scholars, but also owe much to my students at Harvard University, who have enriched this book in its various stages of writing and re-writing with their suggestions and criticisms, and equally to my colleagues, from whom I have learned a great deal during the last two decades in seminars and in discussions. I wish to express my special thanks to colleagues and friends: to Klaus Baltzer, of the University of Munich, and to Frank M. Cross, Dieter Georgi, George MacRae, Krister Stendahl, John Strugnell, and Zeph Stewart, all of Harvard University.

This book is the author's own translation of the German *Einführung in das Neue Testament,* published 1980 by Walter de Gruyter, Berlin and New York. Only in a few instances has the text been changed; one chapter was added (§6.3d). However, a number of minor errors and a few major mistakes were corrected. For this, I am particularly indebted to Eckhard Plümacher's review of this book (*Göttingische Gelehrte Anzeigen* 233 [1981] 1–22) and to the extensive notes which he kindly made available to me.

The bibliography has been redesigned so that editions and translations of texts are quoted first in order to encourage the student to read further in primary materials. English translations of texts are cited in the bibliographies wherever available. I am grateful to my colleague Albert Henrichs of Harvard University for suggestions regarding the revision of the bibliography. The bibliography is not meant to be exhaustive, but is designed to emphasize what is, in my opinion, the most valuable and more recent material, and what will best lead to further study. I have, however, included the most important "classics" which are still basic guides for scholarship today. For further reference, the reader should consult the standard reference works: *The Interpreter's Dictionary of the Bible* (especially its recently published supplement), *Reallexikon für Antike und Christentum, Der Kleine Pauly, Die Religion in Geschichte und Gegenwart,* and *The Oxford Classical Dictionary* (specific references to these works are normally not given in the bibliographies).

The English edition (as already the German work) would scarcely have been finished in such a brief time without the patience and interest of my wife and my children. Numerous persons have given their help in the various stages of translation and production of this work: Philip H. Sellew (editing, bibliography), Jonathan C. Guest (editing, copyediting, and proofreading), Gary A. Bisbee (maps), Pamela Chance (typing), Robert Stoops and Douglas Olson (bibliography). I am very grateful for their expert and untiring help. Rarely does an author enjoy such experienced and congenial production assistance as I had from my friends Charlene Matejovsky and Robert W. Funk of Polebridge Press at Missoula, Montana. Their dedication, care, competence, and advice accompanied every step of the book's production.

Inter Nationes, an agency of the government of the Federal Republic of Germany in Bonn, made a major grant to offset the cost of assistance for this translation. Thanks are due for this generous help.

This book is dedicated to the memory of my teacher Rudolf Bultmann. He encouraged me more than thirty years ago to deal more intensively with the extra-canonical writings from the early Christian period. His unwavering insistence upon the consistent application of the historical-critical method and his emphasis upon the investigation of early Christian literature in the context of the history of religions must remain basic commitments of New Testament scholarship.

Harvard University
Cambridge, Massachusetts
May 1982

Helmut Koester

Abbreviations, Serial and Journal Titles

AAWG.PH	Abhandlungen der Akademie der Wissenschaften zu Göttingen. Philologisch-historische Klasse
AB	Anchor Bible
ADAI.K	Abhandlungen des deutschen archäologischen Instituts Kairo, Koptische Reihe
AHR	*American Historical Review*
AJP	*American Journal of Philology*
ALGHL	Arbeiten zur Literatur und Geschichte des hellenistischen Judentums
AnBib	Analecta Biblica
ANRW	*Aufstieg und Niedergang der römischen Welt*
APOT	*Apocrypha and Pseudepigrapha of the Old Testament* (ed. R. H. Charles)
APP	Ancient Peoples and Places
ASP	*American Studies in Papyrology*
AThANT	Abhandlungen zur Theologie des Alten und Neuen Testaments
ATLABS	American Theological Library Association Bibliography Series
BAR	*Biblical Archaeology Review*
BCNH.ST	Bibliothèque Copte de Nag Hammadi. "Section Textes"
BibOr	Biblia et orientalia
BJudSt	Brown Judaic Studies
BKP	Beiträge zur klassischen Philologie
CBQ	*Catholic Biblical Quarterly*
CBQ.MS	Catholic Biblical Quarterly. Monograph Series
CP	*Classical Philology*
CRINT	Compendia Rerum Judaicarum ad Novum Testamentum
EHS.T	Europäische Hochschulschriften. Reihe 23: Theologie
EPRO	Études préliminaires aux religions orientales dans l'empire romain
EtBib	Études Bibliques
EtJ	Études Juives
FRLANT	Forschungen zur Religion und Literatur des Alten und Neuen Testaments
GCS	Die griechischen christlichen Schriftsteller der ersten drei Jahrhunderte
GLB	De Gruyter Lehrbuch
GRBS	*Greek, Roman, and Byzantine Studies*
GTB	Van Gorcum's theologische bibliotheek
HAW	Handbuch der Altertumswissenschaft
HCS	Hellenistic Culture and Society
HDR	Harvard Dissertations in Religion
Hesperia.S	Hesperia Supplements
HHS	Harvard Historical Studies
Hist	*Historia, Zeitschrift für alte Geschichte*
HNT	Handbuch zum Neuen Testament
HSCP	*Harvard Studies in Classical Philology*

HSM	Harvard Semitic Monographs
HSS	Harvard Semitic Series
HTR	*Harvard Theological Review*
HTS	Harvard Theological Studies
HUCA	*Hebrew Union College Annual*
Hyp.	Hypomnemata. Untersuchungen zur Antike und zu ihrem Nachleben
IDBSup	*Interpretor's Dictionary to the Bible. Supplement*
JAL	Jewish Apocryphal Literature
JBL	*Journal of Biblical Literature*
JEA	*Journal of Egyptian Archaeology*
JHS	*Journal of Hellenic Studies*
JJS	*Journal of Jewish Studies*
JQR.MS	*Jewish Quarterly Review.* Monograph Series
JRomS	*Journal of Roman Studies*
JSHRZ	Jüdische Schriften aus hellenistisch-römischer Zeit
JSNTSup	Journal for the Study of the New Testament Supplement Series
JSOT Press	Journal for the Study of the Old Testament Press
JSPSup	Journal for the Study of the Pseudepigrapha Supplement Series
JSS	*Journal of Semitic Studies*
JTC	*Journal for Theology and the Church*
JTS	*Journal of Theological Studies*
KlT	Kleine Texte für (theologische und philologische) Vorlesungen und Übungen
LBS	Library of Biblical Studies
LCL	Loeb Classical Library
LEC	Library of Early Christianity
LHR	Lectures on the History of Religions, Sponsored by the American Council of Learned Societies
MAPS	Memoires of the American Philosophical Society
MBPF	Münchener Beiträge zur Papyrusforschung und antiken Rechtsgeschichte
MH	*Museum Helveticum*
MHGRW	Methuen History of the Greek and Roman World
Mn.Suppl.	Mnemosyne. Bibliotheca classica/philologica Batava. Supplements
NAWG.PH	Nachrichten der Akademie der Wissenschaft in Göttingen. Philologisch-historische Klasse
NHC	Nag Hammadi Codex
NHS	Nag Hammadi Studies
NovT	*Novum Testamentum*
NovT.Sup	Novum Testamentum. Supplements
NS	New series; neue Serie
NTDSup	Das Neue Testament Deutsch. Supplementband
NTOA	Novum Testamentum et Orbis Antiquus
NTS	*New Testament Studies*
NumenSup	Numen. International Review for the History of Religions. Supplements
ÖAW	Österreichische Akademie der Wissenschaften
OCT	Oxford Classical Texts
OTS	*Oudtestamentische Studien*
Ph.S	Philologus. Supplement
PMAAR	Papers and Monographs of the American Academy in Rome

PVTG	Pseudepigrapha Veteris Testamentis Graece
RAC	*Reallexikon für Antike und Christentum*
RB	*Revue Biblique*
RPS	Religious Perspectives (series)
RSR	*Revue des sciences religieuses*
RVV	Religionsgeschichtliche Versuche und Vorarbeiten
SBAW.PPH	Sitzungsberichte der bayerischen Akademie der Wissenschaften. Philosophisch-philologische und historische Klasse
SBLDS	Society of Biblical Literature Dissertation Series
SBLEJL	Society of Biblical Literature Early Judaism and its Literature
SBLMS	Society of Biblical Literature Monograph Series
SBLSBS	Society of Biblical Literature Sources for Biblical Studies
SBLSCS	Society of Biblical Literature Septuagint and Cognate Studies
SBLMS	Society of Biblical Literature Monograph Series
SBLSP	*Society of Biblical Literature Seminar Papers*
SBLTT	Society of Biblical Literature Texts and Translations
SCHNT	Studia ad corpus hellenisticum Novi Testamenti
SJ	Studia Judaica
SJLA	Studies in Judaism of Late Antiquity
SNTSMS	Society of New Testament Studies Monograph Series
SÖAW.PH	Sitzungsberichte der Österreichischen Akademie der Wissenschaften. Philologisch-historische Klasse
SQAW	Scriften und Quellen der Alten Welt
SQS	Sammlung ausgewählter kirchen- und dogmengeschichtlicher Quellenschriften
SSRH	Sociological Studies in Roman History
StHell	Studia hellenistica
StPB	Studia post-biblica
STRT	Studia Theologica Rheno-Trajectina
SUNT	Studien zur Umwelt des Neuen Testamentes
SUNY	State University of New York
SVTP	Studia in veteris testamenti pseudepigrapha
TF	Texte zur Forschung
TSJTSA	Texts and Studies of the Jewish Theological Seminary of America
TStAJ	Texte und Studien zum Antiken Judentum
TU	Texte und Untersuchungen zur Geschichte der altchristlichen Literatur
UB	Urban-Bücher
VT	*Vetus Testamentum*
VTSup	Vetus Testamentum. Supplement
WdF	Wege der Forschung
WUNT	Wissenschaftliche Untersuchungen zum Neuen Testament
YCS	Yale Classical Studies
Zet.	Zetemata
ZNW	*Zeitschrift für die neutestamentliche Wissenschaft und die Kunde der alten Kirche*

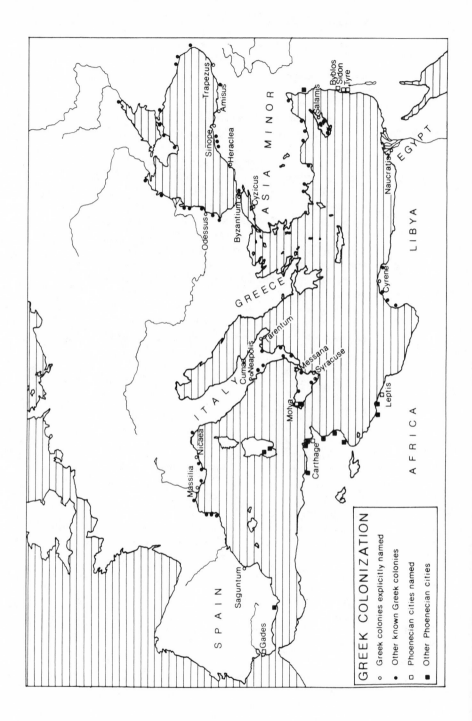

GREEK COLONIZATION

○ Greek colonies explicitly named
● Other known Greek colonies
□ Phoenecian cities named
■ Other Phoenecian cities

Trapezus
Amisus
Sinope
Heraclea
Byblos
Sidon
Tyre
Salamis
Cyzicus
Byzantium
Odessus
Naucratis
ASIA MINOR
EGYPT
LIBYA
GREECE
Cyrene
Tarentum
Cumae
Neapolis
Messana
Syracuse
ITALY
Motya
Leptis
Massilia
Nicaea
AFRICA
Carthage
SPAIN
Saguntum
Gades

Acknowledgments

Grateful acknowledgment is made for permissions to use a number of photographs in these volumes: to the Agora Excavations, Athens, Greece, for the photograph of the Library of Pantaenus Inscription (vol. I, p. 95); to the Fogg Art Museum, courtesy of the Sardis Excavation Office of Harvard University, for the photograph of the Synagogue of Sardis (vol I, p. 207).

Additionally, the author wishes to express his thanks for permission granted him to take photographs, also used in this volume, at the following institutions: the Archaeological Museum, Thessaloniki, Greece (vol. I, pp. 174, 188, 291); the National Museum, Athens, Greece (vol. I, p. 165); the Archaeological Museum, Verria, Greece (vol. I, p. 316); the Louvre, Paris, France (vol. I, p. 106); the Staatliche Museen Charlottenburg, Berlin, Germany (vol. I, p. 12); the Pergamon Museum, Berlin, Germany (vol. I, p. 21); the Museum für Kunst and Gewerbe, Hamburg, Germany (vol. I, p. 178); the National Archaeological Museum, Copenhagen, Denmark (vol. I, p. 7).

HISTORY, CULTURE, AND RELIGION OF THE HELLENISTIC AGE

The countries surrounding the Mediterranean Sea form the cradle of Christianity. To the east lay the centers of older cultures and empires: the Nile valley of Egypt; the lands of the Tigris and Euphrates, which were once the centers of Sumer, Akkad, Assur, and Babylon; Syria, Israel, and the Phoenician coast; and Anatolia with the Hittite and the Lydian empires. Further to the west, the Minoan culture that was centered on the island of Crete had long since been buried in the flood and under the ashes of the explosion of the Thera volcano (ca. 1470 BCE), leaving various Greek city-states as its heirs. What is usually called the "Classical" period, that is, the 5th and 4th centuries BCE, was characterized by rivalry between the Greek states and the Persian empire. It was this rivalry that ultimately, through the conquests of Alexander the Great, sparked the creation of the new culture of Hellenism. Through the Hellenization of Rome this culture expanded to include the western Mediterranean.

Christianity did not develop as a representative of merely one old local culture and religion, such as Israel's, but instead as part of the universal culture of the Hellenistic-Roman world. The dominant element of this new culture was Greek. The Greeks provided the unifying language, to which even Aramaic, the language of the formerly Persian east, and Latin, the language of the new political and military masters, had to take second and third place. Greek philosophy, art, architecture, science, and economic structures formed the bonds that held the various peoples and nations of the Roman empire together as parts of one single world, encompassing Mesopotamia and Syria in the east as well as Spain and Gaul in the west, Egypt and Africa in the south as well as Germany and Britain in the north. As the Christian missionaries carried their message throughout this world, they arrived as heralds of a Hellenistic religion.

The process that created this new culture, called "Hellenization," drew on different and often contradictory elements. National and ethnic interests of particular peoples sometimes clashed with the universalizing power of Hellenism. The cities were the backbone of this new world culture. Largely emancipated from local and ethnic peculiarities, they became links in a chain binding together the most important cultural, economic, and religious activities of the entire region.

Yet the individual city (*polis*) remained a potent symbol of utopian ideals. Although Stoic philosophers could talk about the entire inhabited world as the city of gods and human beings, each city still had to solve a variety of social, moral, and religious problems that were imposed upon it by worldwide economic and political developments. New religious and philosophical movements developed fresh ideals about the liberation of all human beings from traditional bonds, talked about the equality of slaves, and debated the notion of the emancipation of women. However, such ideals were often at odds with the established structures, which remained largely patriarchal and stayed closely tied to the institutions that guaranteed economic and social survival, especially for the large urban middle classes.

It was precisely in the Greek or Hellenized cities of the Roman Empire, and particularly in the structures of the urban middle class, that early Christianity's potential as a new world religion took shape. The social and religious formation of early Christian communities can only be understood within the context of this process. The early Christian writings that are still extant, including the literature of the New Testament, reflect this process in many ways. A historically oriented *Introduction to the New Testament* thus must begin with a consideration of the Hellenistic Age in order to clarify the dynamics of the world in which this new religion sought to find its own identity.

HISTORICAL SURVEY

1. GREECE AND THE ANCIENT MEDITERRANEAN
BEFORE ALEXANDER

(a) Hellenization prior to the Fourth Century BCE

The expansion of Greek settlements beyond the Greek mainland began many centuries before the conquests of Alexander. Aeolian Greeks settled on the northern coast of western Anatolia, with their center in Kyme, as early as the 12th or 11th century BCE. Ionian Greeks founded many cities in the central section of the Anatolian western coast, among them Smyrna, Ephesos, Priene, Myus, Miletos. Under the benign rule of the Lydian kings of Sardis during the 7th and 6th centuries BCE, these cities flourished and became leading participants in the founding of Greek cities in other areas of the Mediterranean. Miletos, the home of Thales, Anaximander, Anaximenes, and Hekataios, was in cultural terms the most significant city of the Greek world. Cities like these served as mediators for the influence of eastern thought on Greece and, in turn, contributed to the process of Hellenization of other parts of Asia Minor. When the Persians conquered all of Anatolia in the second half of the 6th century BCE, most of its western part and all the islands of the Aegean were Greek.

Greek colonies were founded in most other regions of the Mediterranean and the Black Sea, beginning as early as the 8th century. Miletos founded Greek cities on the coast of the Black Sea, including Sinope, Amisos, Trapezos, and Pantikapeion; it also established Naukratis, the only Greek colony in Egypt. Corinth founded such colonies as Syracuse in Sicily and Knidos, Phaselis, and

Bibliography to §1: Texts

Michael H. Crawford, ed., *Sources for Ancient History* (Cambridge and New York: Cambridge University Press, 1983).

Michael M. Austin, ed., *The Hellenistic World from Alexander to the Roman Conquest: A Selection of Ancient Sources in Translation* (Cambridge and New York: Cambridge University Press, 1981).

Roger S. Bagnall and Peter Derow, *Greek Historical Documents: The Hellenistic Period* (SBLSBS 16; Chico, CA: Scholars Press, 1981).

Stanley M. Burstein, *Translated Documents of Greece and Rome*, vol. 3: *The Hellenistic Age from the Battle of Ipsos to the Death of Kleopatra VII* (Cambridge and New York: Cambridge University Press, 1985).

Russell Meiggs and David M. Lewis, eds., *A Selection of Greek Historical Inscriptions to the End of the Fifth Century B.C.* (Oxford and New York: Oxford University Press, 1969).

G. H. R. Horsley, *New Documents Illustrating Early Christianity* (6 vols.; The Ancient History Documentary Research Centre; North Ryde, New South Wales: Macquarie University, 1981–91).

Soloi on the southern coast of Anatolia. Kyme (Cumae) and Neapolis (Naples) in southern Italy and Rhegion and Messina in Sicily were Euboian colonies. Other Greek cities in southern Italy were mostly founded by the Achaians (Sybaris, Kroton), while Tarentum was a colony of Sparta. Massilia (Marseilles) and Nicea (Nice) in southern Gaul and Olbia on the coast of the Iberian peninsula are foundations of the Anatolian city Phokaia; Cyrene and Apollonia in North Africa were established by settlers from the island of Thera. As early as the 6th century BCE, there was a network of Greek cities around almost the entire Mediterranean. The only areas left unsettled by Greeks were the Syrian coast and the western part of North Africa, both under the control of the Phoenicians.

Most of these new Greek cities were *apoikiai,* that is, founded by the emigration of part of the population of the founding city. A new colony would maintain political and economic ties with its mother city (metropolis), connections that often lasted for many centuries. Most colonies relied heavily on agriculture and were founded at first to address their home cities' overpopulation and social problems. Additional economic benefits soon developed—new markets were opened for the export of manufactured goods from the mother cities and for the import of raw materials and grain into Greece. In the course of time intellectual, cultural, and religious exchanges also developed, with lasting impact on the development of Greek culture.

In the following centuries, many of these colonies grew less dependent upon their founding cities, a tendency reinforced by political developments. In Asia Minor the rule of the Lydian kings was replaced by the more oppressive rule of Persian satraps, depriving both the mother cities and their colonies of some of their former freedom. But the primary factor contributing to the increasing independence of the colonies was economic. The new cities began to produce their own manufactured goods with the raw materials they had formerly shipped to their metropolis, which had initially supplied the finished products they needed.

Bibliography to §1: Comprehensive Studies of the Entire Period

W. W. Tarn, *Hellenistic Civilisation* (3d ed.; rev. by the author and G. T. Griffith; London: Arnold, 1952; reprint New York: New American Library, 1975).

F. E. Peters, *The Harvest of Hellenism: A History of the Near East from Alexander the Great to the Triumph of Christianity* (New York: Simon and Schuster, 1970).

Peter Green, *Alexander to Actium: The Historical Evolution of the Hellenistic Age* (Hellenistic Culture and Society 1; Berkeley and Los Angeles, CA: University of California Press, 1990).

Hermann Bengtson, *Griechische Geschichte von den Anfängen bis in die römische Kaiserzeit* (HAW 3/4; 5th ed.; München: Beck, 1977).

F. W. Walbank, *The Hellenistic World* (Cambridge, MA: Harvard University Press, 1982).

Bibliography to §1.1a–b

Roland A. Crossland, "Early Greek Migrations," in Grant and Kitzinger, *Civilization,* 1. 155–70.

John Boardman, *The Greeks Overseas: Their Early Colonies and Trade* (3d ed.; London: Thames & Hudson, 1980).

Idem and N. G. L. Hammond, eds., *The Expansion of the Greek World, Eighth to Sixth Centuries B.C.* (*CambAncHist* 3/3; 2d ed.; Cambridge: Cambridge University Press, 1982).

Edouard Will, *Histoire politique du monde hellénistique (323–30 avant J.-C.)* (2d ed.; 2 vols.; Nancy: Berger-Levrault, 1979–1982).

A. J. Graham, *Colony and Mother City in Ancient Greece* (New York: Barnes and Noble, 1964).

This development began in southern Italy and Sicily in the 5th century BCE, continued in the following century in the east, and was one of the main causes of the economic crisis of Greece in the 4th century.

(b) The Eastern Mediterranean before Alexander

In the two centuries before Alexander, the opposition between Greeks and Persians was the dominant political and economic factor in the eastern part of the Mediterranean world. Within a few years the Persians had been able to conquer Syria, Palestine, Egypt, and Asia Minor, including its Greek cities (an Ionian insurrection of 500–494 BCE failed). But the Persians' attempt to extend their rule to the Greek homeland did not succeed. The victory of the Greeks over the Persians left a deep impression on the Greek mind. The theme found manifold expression in Greek literature, in poetry and fiction as well as in political and scientific writings, and led to reflections about the fundamental differences between "East" and "West" that would remain significant for many centuries to come. The Greeks had successfully withstood the onslaught of an eastern superpower. A belief in the superiority of Greek education, Greek culture, and of the Greek gods formed not only the Hellenic mind, but also that of other nations, later including even the Romans.

Greece and Persia were indeed fundamentally different. Persia was a vast empire under the central administration of a Great King, who maintained his rule over large areas through military power, even though the various satrapies and dependent states retained their cultural and religious heritage. Greece, for its part, was a small and agriculturally poor country that was divided into a number of democratic, oligarchic, or aristocratic states. The kingdom of Macedonia, to the north, was just beginning to enter into the orbit of Greek influence. All these states existed side by side, their relations tense, rarely cordial, and often openly hostile.

The Greek city-states, divided but not altogether dissimilar, had developed, at least initially, an amazing economic power and extended their cultural influence far beyond their borders. Persia, even without the conquest of Greece, remained the only superpower in the eastern Mediterranean. Its empire, in spite of huge wealth that had accumulated in its capitals, lacked economic, cultural, and religious potency. In the western Mediterranean the long power struggle among Syracuse, Rome, and Carthage had barely begun.

(c) Greece

The golden age of Classical Greece during the time of Perikles came to a dreadful end in the thirty years of the Peloponnesian War (433–404 BCE). Though

Bibliography to §1.1c–d

A. R. Burn, "Historical Summary of Greece," Michael Grant and Kitzinger, *Civilization*, 1. 3–44.

J. B. Bury, *A History of Greece to the Death of Alexander the Great* (4th ed. rev. by Russell Meiggs; London: Macmillan, 1975).

N. G. L. Hammond, *A History of Greece to 322 B.C.* (3d ed.; Oxford: Clarendon, 1986).

Hermann Bengtson, ed., *The Greeks and the Persians from the Sixth to the Fourth Centuries* (New York: Delacorte, 1968).

Athens had to capitulate and recognize Sparta as the victor, both cities lost their position as the leading powers. The condition of the Greek states grew continually worse during the following decades. Political disunion increased; the country was torn by never-ending internal wars. Attempts to replace the former hegemony of Sparta and Athens by federal republics had no lasting success. Beginning in the middle of the 4th century, Macedonia, Greece's Hellenized neighbor to the north, asserted its dominance, but at the cost of more wars, culminating in the destruction of Thebes by Alexander (335 BCE). Even Macedonia, though powerful, could not establish a lasting peace. Disorders during the following period, often brought about by external powers, namely the Hellenistic empires and Rome, ended only when the latter established its rule over both Greece and Macedonia.

The economic situation worsened during the 4th century. To be sure, the process of industrialization that had begun in the 5th century continued. Through the employment of slave labor, industrial manufacturing increased its output of both consumer goods and of the weapons and other equipment of war, which were in ever-increasing demand due to continuous fighting. Shipbuilding was further developed (deforestation was a consequence). Banking expanded, but there was no corresponding growth in the Greek foreign market. Archaeological excavations have demonstrated that Syria, Egypt, and the Greek colonies on the coasts of the Black Sea and elsewhere in the western Mediterranean replaced the goods which they had formerly bought in Greece with their own products. Building activity in the Greek cities declined; major construction projects were often halted, only to be resumed in the time after Alexander or during the Roman period.

An impoverishment of the population of the Greek homeland corresponded to these developments. The lack of natural resources, minerals, wood, and arable land, was felt ever more strongly. These needs could not be satisfied through imports, because Greek exports, such as wine, olive oil, and pottery, could not balance the foreign trade deficit. Imported luxury items, such as gold, spices, perfumes, and incense for the temple cults, became so expensive that fewer and fewer people could afford them. At the same time, the total population increased, deepening the contrast between rich and poor and aggravating the unemployment problem. A large portion of the middle class slid into poverty. Banishment and confiscation of property, a consequence of the political turmoil, weakened both the middle and upper classes. With the decline of those classes of citizens that in the past had been the main support of the state, the armies became increasingly dependent upon the recruitment of mercenaries from the lower or unlanded classes. Greek mercenaries also served foreign powers, even before Alexander's time.

(d) The Persian Empire

The Persian empire was established by conquest during the second half of the 6th century BCE and comprised vast areas of different character. There were striking contrasts from region to region in the social and economic conditions of its multiethnic population. The eastern section, east of the Tigris River, including the Persian heartland (Persis) and Media as well as Baktria and Sogdia, mostly settled by people of Iranian ethnicity, was primarily rural. Independent farmers lived side by side with landed proprietors raising cattle and horses. The recruits for the Persian army came from these regions, while the families of the landed gentry supplied the officials for the administration. Further north, near the Caspian Sea and the Aral Sea, the inhabitants were nomadic tribes.

Immediately west of the Persian heartland the situation was completely different. At the time of the Persian conquest, no Iranian people were living in Mesopotamia or any further to the west. The ancient cultural centers of Babylon and Ur in Mesopotamia continued to exist under Persian rule, though their fortunes declined visibly after the destruction of the great Babylonian sanctuaries by Xerxes in 482 BCE. The priestly aristocracies retained a certain degree of economic power, but they were primarily dedicated to the preservation of the inherited legal system and the perfection of astronomical mathematics. Their influence upon the population diminished, especially since large numbers of immigrants (mostly Persians, Medes, and Israelites) settled in Babylonia. The highly developed agriculture of lower Mesopotamia continued to be a source of prosperity for this densely settled area with its numerous towns and villages, even though the Persian treasury and the large banks were the primary beneficiaries.

Assyria, to the northwest, had been sparsely populated since the collapse of its empire at the end of the 7th century BCE. The city of Assur still existed, but Nineveh was in ruins. Between the middle portions of the Euphrates and the Tigris were barren steppes. But Syria, stretching from the upper course of the Euphrates to the Mediterranean Sea, with its large populations of various ethnic origins, was one of the most vital parts of the Persian empire. In its interior were thriving centers of international trade, the caravan cities of Damascus, Aleppo, and Palmyra. On the Syro-Palestinian coast were the powerful merchant cities of the seafaring Phoenicians (Tyre, Sidon, Byblos, Berytos), which also provided Persia with its naval forces. With the exception of the insurrection of Sidon (350–344), Persian rule brought peace and prosperity to these countries, including the dependent temple states of Jerusalem and Samaria that had been reconstituted by the Persian kings (§ 5.1a).

Asia Minor was a mosaic of many different peoples with diverse economic and social structures. Hittite rule over Anatolia, once firmly established in the middle of the 2d millennium, had given way to the ambitions for independence of the Phrygians and Lydians as well as new immigrants from other parts of the Mediterranean (Karians and Lykians), although Hittite religious traditions continued to be influential. The coastal regions of Anatolia, especially along the Aegean Sea and the Black Sea, were tied to Greece through numerous bonds and had an important share in the culture, trade, and industrial production of the entire Mediterranean world. In the interior and the eastern regions, different forms of agricultural economy dominated, such as subsistence agriculture among primitive mountain tribes, and villages dependent upon ancient temples or large estates owned by Persian noblemen. Throughout Asia Minor, economy and trade were also linked by caravan roads.

Egypt, heir to one of the oldest of cultures, had always been ruled by a strong government with a centrally directed economy. The Persians did not change these structures, but tried to fortify their control through military colonies, such as the

Jewish colony of Elephantine in upper Egypt. When Egypt became independent again in 405 BCE, after more than a century of Persian rule, it returned without difficulty to the ancient pattern of administration. In this last period of autonomy, Egypt prospered until it was conquered once more by the Persians (343 BCE), shortly before the arrival of Alexander the Great.

The organization of the Persian empire involved a central government and regional administrations (satrapies), which were strengthened by standing army detachments but still enjoyed a certain degree of independence. Sometimes the satraps proclaimed themselves as semi-independent rulers, such as King Mausollos of Karia, who became famous through the building of his monumental tomb at Halikarnassos. The military units detached to the various satrapies were often composed of mercenaries, among whom both Jewish and Greek soldiers appeared. The Jewish military colony in upper Egypt is especially well known through the discovery of its papyri. Xenophon tells in his *Anabasis* about the employment of Greek mercenaries in a dynastic Persian struggle.

The Achaemenid Persian rulers made no attempt to impose their culture upon the people they ruled, nor did they try to bind their subjects to a state religion or royal cult. Economy and trade were strengthened, but more by default than through an active economic policy of the Persian court, which restricted its influence to the building of a "Royal Road" from the far east to the western port cities of Ephesos and Miletos, and through the maintenance of peace and security. The hoarding of immense amounts of unminted gold and silver by the royal Persian treasury became an ever-increasing encumbrance on the economy. There was no unified monetary policy, although barter trade was at least partially replaced by the monetary market.

In one respect the Persians created a bond of unity that continued to have its effects: they employed the Aramaic language, spoken by many nations of Semitic origin under their rule, as the primary medium of their administration (so-called Imperial Aramaic). Western Aramaic was the dialect of this language spoken in Palestine at the time of Jesus; from its eastern branch developed Syriac—the primary language of early Christian literature in the east—as well as Mandean.

2. ALEXANDER THE GREAT

(a) The Presuppositions for the Conquest of the East

The Macedonians, inhabitants of the wide river valleys of the Axios and Haliakmon, along with the surrounding mountains, were a nation closely related

Bibliography to §1.2

W. Lindsay Adams and Eugene N. Borza, eds., *Philip II, Alexander the Great, and the Macedonian Heritage* (Lanham, MD: University Press of America, 1982).

Bibliography to §1.2a

Paul Cloché, *Histoire de la Macédoine, jusqu'à l'avènement d'Alexandre le Grand (336 avant J.-C.)* (Paris: Payot, 1960).

Arnaldo Momigliano, *Filippo il Macedone* (Firenze: Monnier, 1934).

Marble Head of Alexander the Great
(Roman copy of a statue from Alexandria)
Alexander is presented with the characteristic ram's
horns of the Egyptian god Ammon-Re, whom the
Greeks called Zeus (cf. p. 10).

to the Greeks. Their language belongs to the family of Greek languages. But the Macedonians, different from the Greeks in many respects, played only a minor role in the Classical history of the Greek states. Macedonia's geography gave the country a different character: instead of the high mountains and narrow valleys which divide Greece into numerous units, Macedonia boasts of fertile coastal plains with large rivers, which make the more remote valleys accessible. Thus the mountains do not block access to the inland regions, as is the case elsewhere in Greece. On the other hand, ancient Macedonia lacked good natural harbors or cities that were primarily oriented toward the sea. It was self-sufficient economically, whereas the economy of the Greek cities was dependent upon foreign trade.

This unified geographical structure was reflected in the Macedonian political and social character. Its mostly rural population did not share the petty-state consciousness of the Greek polis, nor was there any movement from aristocratic to democratic government. The king was the commander of an army recruited from throughout the country, and although there were rivalries among the noble families concerning the royal office, the constant conflict between tyrannic, aristocratic, and democratic rule that haunted the Greek cities was unknown in Macedonia.

Beginning in the 5th century, Macedonia began to participate in the cultural life of Greece. Macedonian kings, even before Philip II and Alexander, favored this development. It is no accident that the famous Greek tragedian Euripides spent the last years of his life at the Macedonian court in Pella, where he wrote his famous *Bacchae,* and that Aristotle was the teacher of the young prince Alexander. Nonetheless, when the Macedonians assumed political leadership in Greece during the 4th century, this did not represent merely the transfer of power from one Greek state to another, but rather a momentous change to new political structures. Although the Macedonians were conscious of being the heirs of the Greek tradition when they took responsibility for the Greek mission to the world, this inheritance and mission now appeared in a completely new perspective.

The victory of Philip II of Macedonia over Athens and its allies at Chaironeia in 338 BCE, through which Athens lost its hegemony over Greece once and for all, marks the beginning of a new epoch. Demosthenes, the famous Athenian orator and archenemy of the Macedonians, was correct when in his memorial speech for the fallen soldiers he lamented the freedom and glory of Athens, departed forever. Yet Isokrates, then ninety years old, saw the signs of the times when he wrote to Philip: "Once you have made the Persians subject to your rule, there is nothing left for you but to become a god."

(b) Alexander's Conquest of the East

Alexander, born in 356 BCE as son of Philip II of Macedonia and Olympias, received a Greek education; one of his teachers was the philosopher Aristotle.

Bibliography to §1.2b

Johann Gustav Droysen, *Geschichte Alexanders des Großen* (Düsseldorf: Droste, 1966; first published 1833). The classic monograph and basis of all modern scholarship.

W. W. Tarn, *Alexander the Great* (Cambridge: Cambridge University Press, 1948; reprint Boston: Beacon, 1968).

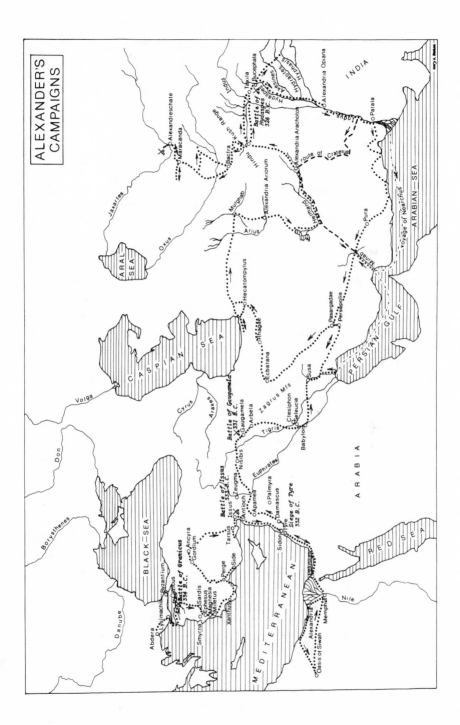

ALEXANDER'S CAMPAIGNS

When his father was murdered in 336, the army proclaimed Alexander king of the Macedonians. His first action was to complete the conquest of Thrace begun by his father, and then, confirmed by the Greeks as commanding general, he subdued the barbarian tribes north and west of Macedonia. In 335 he was forced to suppress a Greek insurrection; Thebes, the leading city of the revolt, was completely destroyed. Still in the same year, Alexander crossed the Bosphoros into Asia Minor, vanquished the relatively weak Persian army at the Granicus in 334, and liberated the Greek cities of Ionia from Persian rule in a triumphal procession.

The first decisive victory over the Persian king Darius III was won in 333 BCE at Issus, near the gateway leading from Asia Minor into Syria. An offer of Darius to cede the western half of the empire was rejected; Alexander would claim no less than the throne of the Achaemenids and control over the entire realm of the Persians. The rest of Syria and Phoenicia, Samaria, and Jerusalem were taken without major resistance; only the conquest of the old Phoenician city of Tyre involved a lengthy siege. Soon Egypt also submitted to Alexander without battle, and in the Libyan temple of Ammon at Siwa, Alexander was greeted as the son of Zeus-Ammon. The founding of the new city of Alexandria at the western end of the Nile delta became a symbol for a new cultural epoch. In 331 Alexander moved east across the Euphrates and won a final victory over Darius at Gaugamela, east of the upper Tigris. This opened access to the central regions of the Persian realm. But the conquest of the northeastern provinces, including Baktria (= modern Afghanistan), entangled the Macedonian army in protracted warfare. Finally, in the year 327, Alexander reached India (= modern Pakistan), but before he could advance to the Ganges river, his army forced him to turn back. Historians have evaluated the political significance of this expedition to India in different ways, as also the subsequent passage of Alexander's fleet through the Hydaspes and Indus rivers and on by the Arabian Sea to the Persian Gulf. However, these exploratory missions were a powerful stimulus, both for the development of Greek science and for the literary imagination, with effects that lasted for many centuries.

After a difficult return through the Gedrosian desert to the Persian heartland, Alexander tried to reorganize the immense empire he had conquered. If he failed in his efforts, it was due to not only the complexities of the problems created through his conquests, but also to certain difficult aspects of his own personality: his political meandering, often coupled with a want of moderation; his increasing unpredictability; the simultaneous alienation of the Persian nobility and of his Macedonian advisors and generals; and finally the ill-conceived policy of amalgamation of the Greco-Macedonian and Persian populations.

These last years of Alexander also seem to have witnessed the beginnings of

C. Bradford Welles, *Alexander and the Hellenistic World* (Toronto: Hakkert, 1970).

Guy Thompson Griffith, *Alexander the Great: The Main Problems* (Cambridge: Heffer; New York: Barnes & Noble 1966).

Ernst Badian, "Alexander the Great and the Unity of Mankind," *Hist* 7 (1958) 425–44.

Idem, *Alexander the Great: Collected Essays* (Chico, CA: Scholars Press, 1981).

the divine veneration of the ruler, although not all information about this process is reliable. It is well attested, however, that in the year 324 Alexander requested the Greeks to worship his deceased friend Hephaistion as a divine hero, and that Greek ambassadors appeared before Alexander wearing crowns fit for an audience before a god. Contrary to former views, it is recognized today that ruler cult did not derive from "oriental" concepts imported into Greek culture, but was a genuine development of Greek ideas about the presence of the divine in extraordinary persons. Egyptian ideas may have played some role in the formation of the concept of the divine king (§1.5a–d).

In the year 323 BCE, Alexander, not yet thirty-three years old, fell ill and died in Babylon, which he had chosen to become the capital of his empire.

(c) The Situation at the Time of Alexander's Death

At the time of his death, Alexander's empire was not threatened by any external enemies and was protected by a strong army, but the problem of the consolidation of this vast realm was unresolved. New Greek cities had been founded as colonies primarily serving the military defense and the civil administration; only later would these cities become significant culturally and economically. For the organization of the empire, the Persian administration was simply retained, with Greeks and Macedonians (and later in the east, Persians too) appointed as satraps and financial administrators. Military concerns predominated; the older Persian provinces were usually entrusted to generals, who were most unlikely to subordinate their personal ambitions to the common good of a new, united empire.

Immediate difficulties arose from the psychological effect of the news of Alexander's death. As soon as the report arrived, Greece rose up in arms and involved Antipater, the administrator of Macedonia in a difficult war. Greece was neither ready nor able to share responsibility for the new situation in the east which had been created by Alexander. To be sure, large numbers of Greeks emigrated to the new cities founded in the lands of the former Persian empire and thus played a decisive role in shaping the newly formed political units into "Hellenistic" states. But the old city-states of the Greek homeland never considered the new kingdoms of the east their own concern.

It proved disastrous that Alexander died without leaving an heir and successor. His son by the Baktrian princess Roxane was born after his death, and from the day of his birth was nothing but a pawn in various political intrigues. Alexander's younger brother Philip Arrhidaios was incapable of filling the dead king's shoes. The Macedonian army, by no means committed to the house of the king for better or worse, would readily give allegiance to whichever individual proved to be the most influential leader. Furthermore, the Persian auxiliaries, together with the Macedonian footguards an important part of the army, could not be expected to show special loyalty to the house of the foreign king.

Bibliography to §1.2c

Fritz Schachermeyer, *Alexander in Babylon und die Reichsordnung nach seinem Tode* (SÖAW.PH 268/3; Wien: Kommissionsverlag der ÖAW, 1970).

Silver Tetradrachma of Lysimachus

The obverse (above) shows the head of Alexander the Great with the horn of Zeus-Ammon above his ear. The reverse (a cast) shows the goddess Athena, seated with shield and snake, and holding winged Victory (Nike) in her hand, flanked by the inscription ΒΑΣΙΛΕΩΣ ΛΥΣΙΜΑΧΟΥ ("of king Lysimachus").

3. THE DIADOCHI AND THE FORMATION
OF THEIR EMPIRES

(a) Developments prior to the Death of Antipater

The battles that the successors of Alexander (= Diadochi) fought among themselves have been described in greater detail than is possible within the scope of this book. They illuminate the different forces and tensions at work in both the development and the decline of the Hellenistic empires. What happened during these decades began to shape the different regions of the eastern Mediterranean in ways that ultimately became significant for the geographical diversity found in Christian beginnings.

The decision about the succession of Alexander fell to the assembly of the Macedonian army in the temporary capital Babylon. The political center of gravity would never return to the Greco-Macedonian homeland. Perdikkas, who had already served under Philip II and held the position of commander of the royal guard (chiliarch), was confirmed in this office and remained in the east as regent of the Asian part of the empire. At the time of Alexander's death, Krateros, the most experienced of his generals, was leading the veterans back to their Macedonian homes. He was appointed "guardian of the royal interests," that is, he assumed responsibility for Arrhidaios, Alexander's brother, and for Alexander's yet unborn child, and he became commander-in-chief of the army in their name. Antipater was confirmed in his position as the *strategos* of Macedonia, where he was occupied with battling the insubordinate Greeks (the Lamian War).

An agreement was reached for a division of the former Persian satrapies: Antigonos Monophthalmos ("the one-eyed"), one of Alexander's longtime generals, received Phrygia, Pamphylia, and Lykia (i.e., the southern and central parts of Asia Minor); Lysimachos, another senior officer, took over Thrace; Eumenes of Kardia, a Greek distinguished as an administrator, became satrap of Cappadocia. Ptolemy, who belonged to Alexander's generation, his bodyguard and an excellent army officer, received Egypt. Ptolemy was the only one of this first generation of satraps who was able to hold on to his original satrapy, a feat due not only to his intelligence and cunning, but also to the isolated position of the

Bibliography to §1.3

F. W. Walbank, A. E. Austin, M. W. Frederiksen, and R. M., Ogilvie, eds., *The Hellenistic World* (CambAncHist 7/1; 2d ed.; Cambridge: Cambridge University Press, 1984).

Peter Green, *Alexander to Actium: The Historical Evolution of the Hellenistic Age* (HCS 1; Berkeley and Los Angeles, CA: University of California Press, 1990).

Edouard Will, "The Succession to Alexander," *CambAncHist* 7 (2d ed.) 23–61.

Paul Cloché, *La dislocation d'un empire: Les premiers successeurs d'Alexandre le Grand (323–281/80 avant J.-C.)* (Paris: Payot, 1959).

Hatto H. Schmitt, *Die Verträge der griechisch-römischen Welt von 338 bis 200 v. Chr.* (Die Staatsverträge des Altertums 3; München: Beck, 1969).

Hermann Bengtson, *Herrschergestalten des Hellenismus* (München: Beck, 1975). Contains biographies of Ptolemy I, Seleukos I, Demetrios Poliorketes, Pyrrhos, Ptolemy II and Arsinoë II, Antigonos Gonatas, Kleomenes III of Sparta, Antiochos III, Eumenes II of Pergamon, Mithridates VI, and Kleopatra VII.

country that he received. Ptolemy abandoned any thought of reconstituting the unity of Alexander's empire and concentrated all his efforts on strengthening his own position as a ruler of a separate kingdom. The primary interest of the other Diadochi, in contrast, was to reunite the whole empire under their own leadership—an aim not always motivated by selfish ambition alone. But this idea of a unified empire receded into the background during the wars of the following decades; building clearly defined separate kingdoms became the only concern. Another factor fueled the battles of the Diadochi: the maintenance of a connection with the Greek homeland proved to be of lasting importance for the Hellenistic kingdoms, as well as the control, for reasons both economic and symbolic, of at least some part of the old Greek territories. Conflict with the old Greek city states was unavoidable, as their striving for freedom was repeatedly frustrated.

Perdikkas, occupying the most powerful position during the first few years and supported by Eumenes, tried to establish the unity of the empire under his own leadership, with Babylon as his capital. He was defeated and killed when the other satraps formed an alliance against him. In a provisional settlement, Antipater became regent in his stead (321 BCE), and Seleukos, who had participated in the alliance against Perdikkas, received Babylonia as his satrapy. Antigonos Monophthalmos sought to expand his influence in Asia, but both Eumenes and Seleukos stood in his way. When Antipater died in 319, the settlement collapsed after lasting only two years.

(b) Events prior to the Battle of Ipsus

Before Antipater died, he appointed Polyperchon, an old, tested general, as his successor. However, Antipater's son Kassander, resentful at being passed over, revolted against this appointment, supported by Eurydike, a granddaughter of Philip II, who meanwhile had married Alexander's brother Arrhidaios. The powerful Antigonos Monophthalmos also joined with Kassander; only Eumenes recognized Polyperchon as regent, who in fact was quite incompetent and was expelled during the course of the ensuing wars. Eumenes, who had unselfishly supported the concept of the unity of the empire, was defeated and executed; Arrhidaios and Eurydike were poisoned by Alexander's mother Olympias, who had returned from exile. Seleukos, threatened by Antigonos, who was now the sole ruler of Asia, fled to Ptolemy, while Kassander established himself as ruler of Macedonia and Greece. A preliminary peace was agreed upon in 311 BCE. Kassander sealed this treaty by executing the young son of Alexander, now officially the king, along with his mother Roxane—both while held under his protection.

It appeared that a balance had been found among the rival Hellenistic kingdoms, each an economically viable unit. Asia Minor and western Syria together formed the most powerful kingdom under the rule of Antigonos, and also possessed the greatest share of world trade. Egypt, which for a time also controlled southern Syria and Palestine and the Cyrenaica, was able to strengthen its position. Seleukos had returned to Babylon in 312 and subjected the Iranian east to his rule; he also was able to reach an agreement with the Indian king Sandrocottus (Tchandragupta). In the west, Lysimachos ruled Thrace in relative peace.

Kassander of Macedonia was the master of Greece proper. But the balance of power was soon disturbed by the ambitious design of Antigonos, who for the last time tried to reconstitute the unity of the whole empire of Alexander the Great. It is questionable, however, whether the peace agreement would have lasted in any case, because Egypt and Babylonia/Persia had no direct access to the Greek homeland.

War started again when Demetrios Poliorketes ("the taker of cities"), son and coregent of Antigonos Monophthalmos, took Athens by a *coup de main*. This ended the last period of independent renewal of Athenian culture under the ten-year rule of the Peripatetic philosopher Demetrios of Phaleron, now forced to flee to Ptolemy in Egypt (307 BCE). Shortly afterwards, Demetrios Poliorketes defeated Ptolemy's fleet near Salamis on Cyprus and thus achieved undisputed maritime superiority. Encouraged by his son's achievements, Antigonos claimed the title of king for them both, thus emphasizing their claim to leadership in the attempt to reconstitute Alexander's empire. The immediate result, however, was only that Seleukos, Ptolemy, Lysimachos, and Kassander now also claimed the royal title for themselves, thereby instituting particularism.

In 305/4, Demetrios Poliorketes besieged Rhodos, but despite the employment of the most modern siege machinery he was unable to conquer the city, which was allied with Ptolemy of Egypt. (The rise of Rhodos to become a significant center of culture and trade continued without interruption from this time on.) Meanwhile the coalition of all the other kingdoms against Antigonos consolidated. In the battle of Ipsus in Phrygia (301 BCE) Antigonos Monophthalmos, almost eighty years old, lost his life and his kingdom. The last attempt to reconstitute the empire of Alexander had failed.

(c) The Consolidation of the Hellenistic Empires

The second cause for the wars of the Diadochi now assumed greater significance in this last phase of their military conflicts: neither the kingdom of Seleukos, now enlarged by western Syria, nor Ptolemaic Egypt had any share in the rule of the Greek homeland. The Thracian king Lysimachos had been able to add Asia Minor to his realm, including the Ionian cities, and the Macedonian king Kassander controlled the affairs of Greece unchallenged. But access to Greece was important for the other Hellenistic kingdoms. Their administrative services and their armies needed new supplies of manpower from the homeland, and their economies were closely intertwined with the Greek cities. Moreover, dominating Greece had considerable symbolic value.

The first to claim sovereignty over Greece, however, was neither the Seleucid nor the Ptolemy. Rather, Demetrios Poliorketes, the Antigonid who, after the death of his father, ruled over the eastern Mediterranean as the "Sea King," endeavored to gain possession of Macedonia and thus also control of Greece. Once more he conquered Athens (294 BCE), where he had earlier received divine honors: the Athenians had been the first to worship him and his father as "Savior Gods." Kassander of Macedonia, whose reign is marked through the city that he founded and named after his wife Thessalonike, had died in 298 BCE. Through marriage with Kassander's sister, Demetrios gained the Macedonian throne and with it control of Thessaly and major portions of Greece.

However, his ambitions carried him into the adventurous attempt to regain the Anatolian kingdom of his father. When Lysimachos, in alliance with Pyrrhos, the young king of Epiros who later became famous through his "Pyrrhic" victories over the Romans, invaded Macedonia, Demetrios left control of Macedonia to his son Antigonos II Gonatas and invaded Asia Minor. Yet, after some initial success, he fell into the hands of his son-in-law Seleukos (286), who kept him as an honored prisoner until his death three years later. Egypt could now secure its access to Greece by seizing the rule of the sea, extending its dominion over the Aegean islands and, after the fall of Lysimachos, over some coastal areas of Asia Minor as well.

Seleukos could gain access to Greece only at the price of war with Lysimachos. This exemplary administrator and successfull general, especially in his fight against the northern barbarians, had established a flourishing kingdom that controlled access to the Black Sea. After the demise of Demetrios Poliorketes and a war against his former ally Pyrrhos, Lysimachos also ruled Macedonia and Greece. A family conflict was the incident that triggered the war: Lysimachos had his son Agathokles executed, whose partisans fled to Seleukos. In the subsequent war Seleukos defeated and killed Lysimachos in battle on the Koroupedion near Magnesia-on-the-Maeander (281 BCE). Seleukos proclaimed himself king of the Macedonians and prepared for the conquest of Macedonia and Greece. For

MACEDONIA

(all dates are BCE)

Macedonian Rulers		Events	
359–336	Philip II		
336–323	Alexander the Great		
317–297	Kassander	316	Founding of Thessaloniki
	Antigonids		
294–287	Demetrios I (Poliorketes)	294	Founding of Demetrias
283–239	Antigonos II Gonatas	277	Victory over the Celts
		273–271	War with Pyrrhos
		267–261	Chremonidean War
239–229	Demetrios II		
229–221	Antigonos III Doson	222	Victory over Sparta
221–179	Philip V	220–217	Social War
		215–205	1st Macedonian War
		200–197	2d Macedonian War
179–168	Perseus	171–168	3d Macedonian War

168–149	Macedonia divided into four districts
149	Insurrection of Andriskos
after 148	Roman province of Macedonia
146	Rome defeats the Achaian League
	Destruction of Corinth

the last time, the idea of the reunification of Alexander's empire seemed briefly to be revived. But just as Seleukos prepared to set foot on European soil, he was assassinated by Ptolemy Keraunos, the eldest son of Ptolemy I of Egypt. Thus the last of the Diadochi died (the first Ptolemy had met his death two years earlier). But the Seleucid empire as well as Ptolemaic Egypt had reestablished their vital connection to the realm of the Greek homeland and hence to its economy and culture. The situation of Greece itself, however, remained in lasting confusion.

4. The Empires and States of the Hellenistic World prior to the Roman Conquest

(a) Macedonia and Greece

In cultural and economic terms, the first half of the 3d century BCE was the most significant period of the Hellenistic era. The Hellenistic kingdoms were governed by the sons of the Diadochi, all remarkable rulers: In Egypt, Ptolemy II; in Syria, Antiochos I; a little later in Macedonia, Antigonos II Gonatas. Greece itself, however, shared little in the fortunate conditions of the time. Before the middle of the 3d century BCE, a Celtic invasion brought destruction and war to Greece and parts of Asia Minor. With the exception of Pyrrhos' short-lived adventures in southern Italy and Sicily, political developments in the Helle-

Bibliography to §1.4

M. Cary, *A History of the Greek World from 323 to 146 B.C.* (2d ed.; London: Methuen, 1951).
Edouard Will, "The Formation of the Hellenistic Kingdoms," in *CambAncHist* 7 (2d ed.) 101–117.
Erich S. Gruen, *The Hellenistic World and the Coming of Rome* (2 vols.; Berkeley: University of California Press, 1984).
Grace Harriet Macurdy, *Hellenistic Queens: A Study of Woman-Power in Macedonia, Seleucid Syria, and Ptolemaic Egypt* (Johns Hopkins University Studies in Archaeology 14; Baltimore, MD: Johns Hopkins University Press, 1932).

Bibliography to §1.4a

F. W. Walbank, "Macedonia and Greece," in *CambAncHist* 7 (2d ed.) 221–256.
N. G. L. Hammond, G. T. Griffith, and F. W. Walbank, *A History of Macedonia*, vol. 3: *336–167 B.C.* (New York: Oxford University Press, 1988).
J. A. C. Larsen, *Greek Federal States: Their Institutions and History* (Oxford: Clarendon, 1968).
William Scott Ferguson, *Hellenistic Athens: A Historical Essay* (London: Macmillan, 1911).
W. G. G. Forrest, *A History of Sparta 950–192 B.C.* (2d ed.; London: Duckworth, 1980).
A. H. M. Jones, *Sparta* (Oxford: Blackwell, 1967).
Moses Hadas, "The Social Revolution in Third-Century Sparta," *The Classical Weekly* 26 (1932/33) 65–76.
F. W. Walbank, *Aratos of Sicyon* (Cambridge: Cambridge University Press, 1933).
Idem, *Philip V of Macedon* (Cambridge: Cambridge University Press, 1940).
Idem, "Macedonia and the Greek Leagues," in *CambAncHist* 7 (2d ed.) 446–481.

nistic east had taken little account of Rome and its steadily growing power. The interventions of Rome at the end of the 3d century came as a real shock with far-reaching consequences. Macedonia and Greece, much weaker militarily than the other Hellenistic kingdoms, were the first to be surprised by Roman interventionist politics, and they were no match for the newcomers.

After the assassination of Seleukos I, Ptolemy Keraunos took control of Macedonia, which Demetrios Poliorketes had left to his son Antigonos Gonatas; but in 279 BCE he was killed in battle against the Celts, who advanced as far south as Delphi and caused widespread devastation, but withdrew before the approaching winter and invaded Asia Minor instead. The anarchy left in Greece in the wake of the Celtic invasion, together with the weakening of Macedonian power, provided opportunities for new anti-Macedonian alliances. The Aetolians, a league of tribes settled in the mountains of central Greece who had distinguished themselves in the fights against the Celts, were the first to strengthen their position. In the Peloponnesos and elsewhere in southern Greece, Ptolemy II of Egypt encouraged an alliance of Sparta and other cities with Athens, where the pro-Macedonian government was toppled in 267 BCE. The Athenian politician Chremonides introduced in the Athenian demos (people) a resolution against the suppressers of the Greek cities, that is, the Macedonians.

Antigonos II Gonatas, who had clung to a small portion of his father's kingdom, had to bring all of Macedonia under his control and subdue those Celts who had settled in Thrace; he also had to face the new alliances of the Greek cities and to defend his position against Pyrrhos of Epiros (§1.4e), who was killed in a street battle (272 BCE). In the Chremonidean War (267–261) Gonatas took Athens after a long siege and prevailed over the army of the Peloponnesian cities. He then went on to defeat the Egyptian fleet near Kos, thus curtailing the Ptolemaic influence in the Aegean Sea and securing free access to Greece for much-needed grain imports. Antigonos Gonatas was not only an energetic ruler, but also a student of philosophy, whose teacher had been Zeno, the founder of the Stoa (§4.1d). Philosophers were welcome at his court, and in his political actions he strove to follow the principles of the Stoic teachings. In his long reign he strengthened the domination of Macedonia over Greece, though he experienced setbacks in the last years before his death (239 BCE): the leagues of the Greek states, once more supported by Egypt, renewed their efforts to achieve greater political independence; Corinth and Euboia gained autonomy, and there was a marked increase in Aetolian piracy.

Under the rule of Gonatas' son, Demetrios II, Macedonia was embattled by invasions of the Dardanians from the north and revolts by Athens and Peloponnesian cities. After his death, Demetrios' cousin Antigonos III Doson became regent in behalf of his young son. Doson reestablished peace under Macedonian dominion, but at a price. He could achieve his goals only by subduing Sparta, bringing to a premature end the social reforms begun by the Spartan king Agis IV and resumed by Kleomenes III. Thus Macedonia's drive for control prevented the strengthening of the social infrastructure of the Greek cities it wanted to rule. A second problem of Doson's reign was his inability to come to terms with Rome and its increasing power and influence. The aid of other Hellenistic states would have been required, since Macedonia alone was too weak. But neither the Ptolemies nor the Seleucids were willing or able to lend any support. On the contrary, the major Hellenistic states, Macedonia, Syria, Egypt, and later also Pergamon, continued to play the game they had played for a century, namely to hurt and weaken each other wherever there was an opportunity.

The question of Roman intervention in Greek affairs became a real issue during the reign of Doson's successor, Demetrios' son Philip V (221–179). The peace of Naupaktos, which ended the war of Macedonia and Achaia against Sparta and the Aetolians (the Social War, 222–217) was the last treaty the Greeks achieved without Roman participation. In the First Macedonian War (215–205), when Pergamon and Aetolia fought as Roman allies against Macedonia, which was in league with Rome's archenemy Hannibal of Carthage, Greece was still spared from military intervention of Rome, which was occupied then with its struggle in Italy against Hannibal's invasion in the Second Punic War (§6.1c).

But when Philip sought to take control of the Ptolemaic possessions in the Aegean, in accordance with the Egyptian partition treaty he had made with Antiochos III of Syria, Rhodos and Pergamon appealed to Rome (201 BCE). Rome, strengthened in its self-assurance by its victory over Hannibal, decided to intervene. A Roman army under T. Quinctius Flamininus, supported by Macedonia's bitter enemies, the Aetolians, defeated Philip at Kynoskephalai in Thessaly (197 BCE, Second Macedonian War). Philip's domain was restricted to Macedonia, and he was forced to surrender his fleet and pay a war indemnity. The Romans proceeded to punish the Spartan king Nabis, who had attempted to resume the social reforms of Kleomenes. After sending a large number of Greek works of art home to Italy, the Romans proclaimed the freedom of the Greek cities and withdrew.

Philip's son Perseus (179–168) sought to break the isolation of Macedonia imposed by Rome and established relationships with Bithynia, Rhodos, and Syria. He also tried to win the sympathies of Greece for the Macedonian cause. But Rome, seemingly offering its help, was already planning to crush Macedonia once and for all. Though Perseus defended himself well at the beginning of the war, he was defeated at Pydna by the Roman philhellene Aemilius Paullus (168 BCE). As an aftermath came the humiliation of Rhodos, which had sided with Macedonia. Although Rhodos had not engaged in open war with Rome, the Roman Senate, subject to the pressures of a strong business lobby, forced the island to relinquish its possessions on the mainland of Asia Minor and to accept severe restrictions in its trade, to the benefit of Roman-dominated Delos. The curtailing of Rhodian naval power soon backfired, because Rhodos had been the only force in the eastern Mediterranean able to control the pirates.

Rome's rule did not bring peace. A blacksmith named Andriskos, who claimed to be the son of Perseus, led an insurrection in Macedonia (149 BCE). After its suppression Macedonia became a Roman province. In 146 BCE the Achaian League went to war against Rome's ally Sparta. Roman emissaries were insulted in Corinth. After the defeat of the Achaian League the Romans completely destroyed that city. The site remained largely uninhabited until Julius

Caesar refounded Corinth as a colony and settled it with Italian colonists (44 BCE; see §6.3b). The country, now divided into the provinces of Greece and Macedonia, had suffered immensely. New miseries came through the wars of Mithridates with Rome at the beginning of the 1st century (88–83 BCE).

(b) Asia Minor

Only the western, central, and southern parts of Asia Minor were conquered by Alexander the Great; the northern and eastern regions remained on the fringes of Hellenistic domination. The collapse of Lysimachos' kingdom, situated on both sides of the straits leading to the Black Sea, allowed new independent development in the western regions. The rise of more localized power centers was encouraged by the decreasing strength of the Seleucid kingdom and the inability of Ptolemaic Egypt to maintain its control over the coastal areas of Ionia, Karia, Lykia, Pamphylia, and Cilicia including such important cities as Ephesos, Miletos, Xanthos, Phaselis, and Side.

PERGAMON

(all dates are BCE)

281–263	Philetairos	
263–241	Eumenes I	Victory over Antiochos I at Sardis
241–197	Attalos I Soter	Victory over the Celts
197–159	Eumenes II Soter	Karia and Lykia added to Pergamon
		Pergamon Altar for Zeus
159–138	Attalos II Philadelphos	
138–133	Attalos III Philometor	
133–130	Aristonikos	"Heliopolis" and freedom of slaves

As the power of the Seleucids and Ptolemies waned, Pergamon became culturally and economically the most important kingdom of Asia Minor. Philetairos, son of Attalos of Tios, a Macedonian nobleman, had been installed by Lysimachos as commander of Pergamon, but he deserted Lysimachos shortly before the latter's final defeat (281 BCE) and supported Seleukos. This led

Bibliography to §1.4b

H. Heinen, "The Syrian-Egyptian Wars and the New Kingdoms of Asia Minor," in *CambAncHist* 7 (2d ed.) 412–445.

George M. A. Hanfmann, *From Croesus to Constantine: The Cities of Western Asia Minor and Their Arts in Greek and Roman Times* (Ann Arbor, MI: University of Michigan Press, 1975).

Louis Robert, *Villes d'Asie Mineure: études de geographie antique* (2d ed.; Paris: Boccard, 1962).

R. E. Allen, *The Attalid Kingdom: A Constitutional History* (Oxford: Oxford University Press, 1983).

Reconstruction of Pergamum

This reconstruction shows the theater of the city, carved out of the rock of the mountain, above it the temple of Athena, behind the temple and to the left the famous library. On the right is the altar of Zeus in the center of a peristyle court and accessible by a large staircase. On the lower right a stoa flanking the entrance way to the theater.

to the establishment of a small principality, whose capital was the fortress and city of Pergamon, strategically situated on a mountain (333 m high) dominating the Kaikos valley in northwestern Anatolia. Philetairos' nephew Eumenes I (263–241 BCE) defeated the Seleucid king Antiochos I near Sardis and expanded the rule of Pergamon over the entire Kaikos valley and to the Aegean coast.

The reigns of the three successors of Eumenes I mark the century-long flowering and continuous expansion of Pergamon. Attalos I Soter (241–197), a cousin of Eumenes I, defeated the Celts, who had invaded Asia Minor after their raid of Macedonia and Greece, and who had since resettled in north-central Asia Minor (Galatia). Attalos I assumed the royal title and temporarily controlled all of Asia Minor as far as the Taurus mountains. He reached an understanding with Rome which he supported against Macedonia. The fame of Attalos and his successors was established through their support of the arts and scholarship and through their splendid buildings. Attalos' son Eumenes II Soter (197–159) made Pergamon a major world power, not without the blessings of Rome. The wealth and splendor of his rule achieved worldwide fame through the Library of Pergamon with over 200,000 volumes, the Altar of Zeus ("Pergamon Altar," now in Berlin), and such dedications as the Stoa of Eumenes in Athens.

The Attalids became the most significant patrons of Greek art and scholarship in the 2d century BCE. Attalos II Philadelphos (159–138 BCE) continued the building activities of his brother, still visible today in the Stoa of Attalos in Athens, rebuilt in its original splendor by the American School of Classical Studies. The southeastern expansion of the Pergamene kingdom is marked by the founding of the city of Attalia (today Antalya) in Pamphylia. The last king of Pergamon, Attalos III Philometor (138–133), died after a short reign and willed his country by testament to the Roman Senate. However, Aristonikos, an illegitimate brother of the last king, did not abide by the will, declared the freedom of all slaves, and announced the establishment of the utopian city of Heliopolis. Defeated by the Romans, he was brought to Rome and executed. In his territory the Romans established the new province of Asia.

Bithynia, a Thracian country in northwestern Asia Minor on the Propontis and the Black Sea, was able to maintain its independence even after the conquest of Asia Minor by Alexander the Great. The most important ruler in the 3d century BCE, Nikomedes I, founded the city of Nikomedia (264 BCE). He defended himself successfully against the Seleucid king Antiochos I and against Antigonos II Gonatas of Macedonia; however, he had called to his aid the Celtic tribes which were to remain the terror of large parts of Asia Minor, even after their forced settlement in Galatia. Nikomedes' successor Prusias I (230–182) founded the city of Prusa. It was this Bithynian king to whom Hannibal fled after his defeat by Rome. In order to avoid extradition, Hannibal committed suicide in Bithynian Libyssa, where much later the Roman emperor Septimius Severus—descendant of an African Punic family—erected a monument in his honor. In the decades following Hannibal's death Rome intervened repeatedly in the affairs of Bithynia, until it came under Roman control in 74 BCE through the testament of its last king.

In northern Asia Minor, the kingdom of Pontus, situated along the coast of the Black Sea, was ruled by Hellenized Iranian princes. Independent Greek cities (Sinope, Trapezos) had been established in its domain for many centuries. The first known ruler of the Hellenistic period was Mithridates II Ktistes (302–266 BCE), at first subject to Lysimachos, after 281 BCE he called himself king and successfully defended his independence against the Seleucids. Pontus had a mixed population of Greeks, Iranians, and remnants of older Anatolian nations, who were Hellenized only during later centuries. The Greek cities preserved their autonomy for a long time, but Sinope was conquered by Pharnakes I (185–170 BCE) and became the capital under his successor Mithridates IV. The kings of Pontus wanted to appear as the equals of other Hellenistic kings as is evident in their Greek surnames; these were later supplemented by Roman honorific titles that demonstrate the growing influence of Rome even in this remote area. Mithridates IV Philopator Philadelphos (170–150 BCE) called himself "Friend and Ally of the Romans," a title also assumed by his son Mithridates V Euergetes (150–120 BCE), who supported Rome during the Third Carthaginian War.

The Romans had no objection to further expansion of the realm of Pontus, but conflict became unavoidable in view of the aspirations of the most talented but also the last king of Pontus, Mithridates VI Eupator Dionysos (120–63 BCE). This Hellenized Iranian made himself the advocate of the Greek inheritance, trying to establish a Hellenistic empire in the east, which would halt Rome's imperialistic expansion; the result was decades of war during which Greece as well as the Greeks of Asia Minor were subjected to countless sufferings. Mithridates, the "Savior of the Greeks," began by conquering western Armenia (Armenia Minor), and thus became the master of northern and eastern Anatolia and almost all of the area bordering the Black Sea. In the first war with Rome, which now opposed any further expansion of the Pontian realm, Mithridates, enthusiastically hailed by many Greeks as the "New Dionysos," conquered all of Asia Minor and Greece (86 BCE). This liberation of the Greeks was accompanied by the murder of 80,000 Italians in Asia Minor (the "Asian Vespers") and the sack of the Roman-dominated island of Delos. The new freedom of the Greeks did not last very long. Sulla (§6.1d) defeated Mithridates in several battles and forced him to give up all his new conquests. Athens, the first Greek city to make an alliance with Mithridates, was demolished and plundered by Sulla's army. But the wars with Mithridates continued until Pompey (§6.1d) finally defeated this last Hellenistic kingdom and established a new order in Asia Minor according to Roman criteria of pacification (63 BCE).

Kappadokia, the easternmost district of the Anatolian highlands, at the upper course of the Halys river, became subject to Hellenistic rule under Alexander's successor Perdikkas. But it seceded during the latter part of the 3d century BCE under Ariaramnes, grandson of the last Persian satrap. Ariaramnes' son Ariarathes III assumed the title "king" in 225 BCE. Subsequently, Cappadocia remained on the fringes of Hellenistic influence, at times completely independent, at times subject to Pontus, until it was conquered by Pompey and became a vassal kingdom, later a Roman province which, together with Pontus, Galatia, and Paphlagonia, was administered by an imperial legate.

(c) Egypt

EGYPT

(all dates are BCE)

Rulers	Events
	332 Alexander in Egypt
	Founding of Alexandria
323–283/2 Ptolemy I Soter	ca. 300 Creation of cult of Sarapis
283/2–246 Ptolemy II Philadelphos	276–271 1st Syrian War
	260–253 2d Syrian War
246–222/1 Ptolemy III Euergetes	246–241 3d Syrian War
222/1–205 Ptolemy IV Philopator	219–216 4th Syrian War
205–180 Ptolemy V Epiphanes	195 Palestine comes under
	Syrian rule
180–145 Ptolemy VI Philometor	170–168 Antiochos IV in Egypt
170–116 Kleopatra II	
145–116 Ptolemy VIII Euergetes II	Greek scholars expelled
116–108 Ptolemy IX Soter II	
108–88 Ptolemy X	
88–80 Ptolemy IX (see below)	
80–51 Ptolemy XII Auletes	55 Roman garrison in Egypt
51–30 Kleopatra VII	48 Pompey killed in Egypt
51–47 Ptolemy XIII	Caesar in Egypt
	30 Marc Antony commits suicide

after 30 BCE Egypt Roman province

Egypt was more homogeneous geographically and economically than the other Hellenistic states, but the founding of Alexandria created a stark cultural contrast. The most emphatically Hellenistic city of antiquity was placed beside a country that remained mostly rural and was at most superficially Hellenized. Wars with other countries usually concerned Egypt's outlying territories in Syria, Anatolia, and the Aegean islands. Only in the latter part of this period did military conflict reach Egypt itself. Egypt's secure situation under Ptolemaic rule was the foundation of its economic wealth and prosperity and permitted Alex-

Bibliography to §1.4c

Eric Turner, "Ptolemaic Egypt," in *CambAncHist* 7 (2d ed.) 118–174.

Alan K. Bowman, *Egypt after the Pharaohs, 332 BC–AD 642* (Berkeley, CA: University of California Press, 1986).

Edwyn R. Bevan, *A History of Egypt under the Ptolemaic Dynasty* (London: Methuen, 1927).

E. van't Dack, P. van Dessel, and W. van Gucht, eds., *Egypt and the Hellenistic World: Proceedings of the International Colloquium, Leuven, 24–26 May 1982* (StHell 27; Leuven: Orientaliste, 1983).

P. M. Fraser, *Ptolemaic Alexandria* (3 vols.; Oxford: Clarendon, 1972; reprint 1984).

T. C. Skeat, *The Reigns of the Ptolemies* (MBPF 39; 2d ed.; München: Beck, 1969).

Alan E. Samuel, *From Athens to Alexandria: Hellenism and Social Goals in Ptolemaic Egypt* (StHell 26; Leuven: Peeters, 1983).

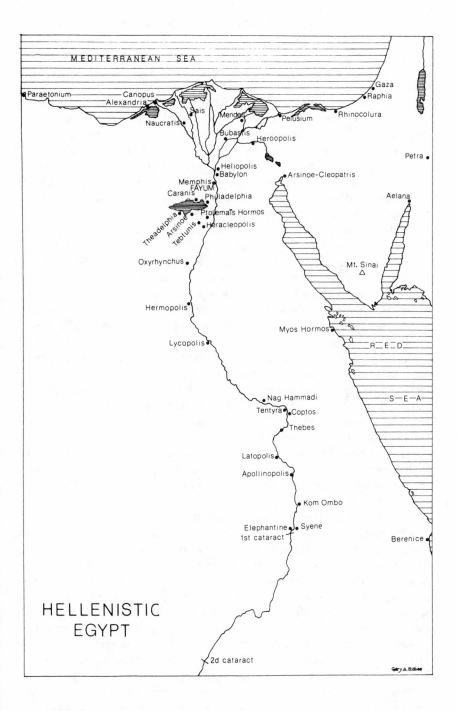

MEDITERRANEAN SEA

Paraetonium

Canopus
Alexandria
Sais
Naucratis
Mendes
Bubastis
Heroopolis

Gaza
Raphia
Rhinocolura
Pelusium

Petra

Heliopolis
Babylon
Memphis
FAYUM
Caranis
Philadelphia
Theadelphia
Arsinoe
Tebtunis
Heracleopolis
Ptolemaïs Hormos

Arsinoe-Cleopatris

Aelana

Oxyrhynchus

Mt. Sinai
△

Hermopolis

Lycopolis

Myos Hormos

RED

Nag Hammadi
Tentyra
Coptos
Thebes

SEA

Latopolis

Apollinopolis

Kom Ombo

Elephantine
1st cataract
Syene

Berenice

HELLENISTIC
EGYPT

2d cataract

Gary A. Bisbee

andria to become the center of Greek art and science during the flowering of Hellenistic culture (§3.2b).

Ptolemy I Soter ("Lagos," 323–283 BCE), first satrap and then king, laid the foundation. He established a Greek administration, which took over the lower ranks of the existing Egyptian system. Productivity increased, due to the transition to a monetary economy, which replaced the barter trade that had been customary in domestic transactions. At the same time, Egypt became a more active partner in Mediterranean trade. Ptolemy I also moved the capital from Memphis to Alexandria. Complete isolation from the rest of the Hellenistic world was prevented by its possession of southern Syria, Cyprus, the Cyrenaica, and several regions and cities of Asia Minor (Miletos, Ephesos, Karia, Lykia). Egypt also established a protectorate over the league of the Aegean islands—Samos, Lesbos, Thera, and parts of Crete.

The Hellenistic empire of Egypt experienced its greatest flowering under the rule of Ptolemy II Philadelphos (283/2–246). To be sure, the long series of Syrian Wars began during his rule, in which Egypt fought with the Seleucids over the possession of southern Syria, Palestine, and the Phoenician cities. For the time being, Egypt was able to defend these possessions; its cultural and economic influence remained unbroken over the areas inhabited by the nation of Israel. To the south, expeditions into Arabia and Ethiopia expanded the area of Ptolemaic dominance.

Philadelphos also improved the effectiveness of the administrative systems, the internal revenue service, geodetic surveys, irrigation, and the centralized regulation of agricultural production. In 278 Philadelphos divorced his wife Arsinoë I in order to marry his sister Arsinoë II, who had been married to Lysimachos and afterwards to Ptolemy Keraunos (§1.3c). Such a marriage was thought incestuous by Macedonian standards, but had considerable legal precedent according to Egyptian custom. Arsinoë II was the first great woman of the Hellenistic period who fully shared in the making of political decisions. Arsinoë and Philadelphos received divine honors during their lifetime as "The Brother and Sister Gods" (§1.5c).

Under Philadelphos' successor, Ptolemy III Euergetes (246–222/1), Egyptian power reached its apex. Euergetes was a skilled diplomat, successful in war against the Seleucids; he also protected Egyptian trade with a strong navy. In war with Syria he advanced as far as the Euphrates, but was unable to hold his Syrian conquests, other than Antioch's port city of Seleukia. Egypt's situation, however, began to deteriorate under Ptolemy IV Philopator (221–205). Although a victory over Antiochos III of Syria at Raphia in 217 BCE confirmed Egyptian rule over Palestine, Nubian kings in the southern regions of the Nile were able to establish an independent realm (206–185). Mediterranean trade, vital for the Egyptian economy, suffered severely during the Second Carthaginian War, and Egypt itself was tormented by repeated insurrections of the native population—a problem that the government was never able to solve. After Philopator's death, when guardians governed for his young son Ptolemy V Epiphanes, Antiochos III of Syria and Philip V of Macedonia made a partition treaty for the Egyptian possessions. Following the terms of this pact, Antiochos conquered southern

Syria and Palestine, which thus became a part of the Seleucid empire (see also §5.1b).

During the 2d century BCE, Egypt was torn by repeated struggles over succession to the throne, conflicts in which the sister-queens Kleopatra II and Kleopatra III played important parts. Several times the Egyptian empire broke up into its constituent parts of Egypt, Cyprus, and Cyrenaica. Attempts to reconquer southern Syria failed, instead enticing Antiochos IV Epiphanes to attempt to conquer Egypt; only Roman intervention forced him to withdraw and saved Egypt's independence. The process of Hellenization also suffered severe setbacks. Though Alexandria was the leading Greek city of its time, the countryside remained largely Egyptian since the Ptolemies had no interest in founding new cities in Egypt. Ptolemy VIII Euergetes II (170–164 coregent with his brother; 145–116 king and second husband of his sister Kleopatra II) expelled Greek artists and scholars from Alexandria. As a result, Rhodos and Pergamon achieved eminence as new centers of Greek culture and learning. Hellenized Egyptians began to play an increasingly significant role in the royal administration, replacing members of the Macedonian upper class. At the same time, Egypt lost its political independence and became a client state of the Romans, who had once before intervened to rescue Egypt from the threat of a Seleucid takeover and did not hesitate to interfere in its internal affairs.

When the victorious Pompey brought Anatolia and Syria/Palestine under Roman control in 62 BCE, Egypt still maintained its independence. A Roman garrison was established in the year 55 BCE, when the Romans restored Ptolemy XII Neos Dionysos (called "Auletes" = "the flute-player"; 80–58 and 55–51) to his throne. From that time Rome considered Egypt a possession. Pompey, after his defeat by Julius Caesar at Pharsalos (48 BCE), fled to Egypt, where he was murdered at the instigation of Auletes' son, Ptolemy XIII. This last Ptolemaic king of Egypt drowned in the Nile when the Romans attacked his camp (47 BCE). His sister and wife, Kleopatra VII, the last of the house of the Lagids, mistress of Caesar and later wife of Antony, had the political astuteness of the best of her family. When all her plans had failed, this last ruler of the Ptolemaic house chose death through the bite of a poisonous snake.

(d) The Seleucid Empire and Syria

The Seleucid empire encompassed an immense area, extending from Bactria in the east to Anatolia in the west. The dilemma of the Seleucid kings was to balance their security and defense with attention to internal problems and the economic development of their central provinces of Syria and Mesopotamia. Control of the important centers of trade and commerce on the Syrian coast, and

Bibliography to §1.4d: Texts

Kai Broderson, *Appians Abriss der Seleukidengeschichte (Syriake 45, 232–70, 369): Text und Kommentar* (Münchener Universitätsschriften: Münchener Arbeiten zur Alten Geschichte, Band 1; München: Editio Maris, 1989)

SYRIA

(all dates are BCE)

Rulers	Events
312–281 Seleukos I Nikator	312 Founding of Seleukia on the Tigris
	300 Founding of Antioch on the Orontes
281–261 Antiochos I Soter	275 Defeat of the Celts (273?)
	276–271 First Syrian War
	262 Defeated by Eumenes I of Pergamon
261–246 Antiochos II Theos	260–253 Second Syrian War
	256/55 Secession of Bactria
	247 Establishment of Parthian kingdom
246–225 Seleukos II Kallinikos	246–241 Third Syrian War
	240–228 Separate kingdom of Antiochos Hierax in Asia Minor
225–223 Seleukos III Soter	219–216 Fourth Syrian War
223–187 Antiochos III the Great	212–206 Anabasis of Antiochos
	195 Conquest of Palestine
	191/190 Defeat of Antiochos by Rome
187–175 Seleukos IV Eupator	
175–163 Antiochos IV Epiphanes	170–168 Conquest of Egypt
	168–164 Maccabean Revolt
164–139 Antiochos V, Demetrios I Alexander Balas, Antiochos VI	164–64 Hasmonean rule in Palestine
139–129 Antiochos VII Sidites	
126–96 Antiochos VIII Grypos	
	83–69 Tigranes of Armenia occupies Syria
	64 Pompey makes Syria a Roman province

thus of access to the sea routes in the eastern Mediterranean, was crucial. However, southern Syria, Palestine, and Phoenicia were in Egyptian hands. Wars with Egypt over the possession of these districts occupied the entire 3d century BCE. Once these disputed districts were under Seleucid control, it became evident

Bibliography to §1.4d: Studies

Domenico Musti, "Syria and the East," in *CambAncHist* 7 (2d ed.) 175–218.

Edwyn R. Bevan, *The House of Seleucus* (London: Arnold, 1902; reprint London: Routledge, 1966).

Hatto H. Schmitt, *Untersuchungen zur Geschichte Antiochos des Großen und seiner Zeit* (Historia, Einzelschriften 6; Wiesbaden: Steiner, 1964).

Alfred R. Bellinger, *The End of the Seleucids* (Transactions of the Connecticut Academy of Arts and Sciences 38; New Haven, CT: Connecticut Academy of Arts and Sciences, 1949) 51–102.

Glanville Downey, *A History of Antioch in Syria: From Seleucus to the Arab Conquest* (Princeton, NJ: Princeton University Press, 1961).

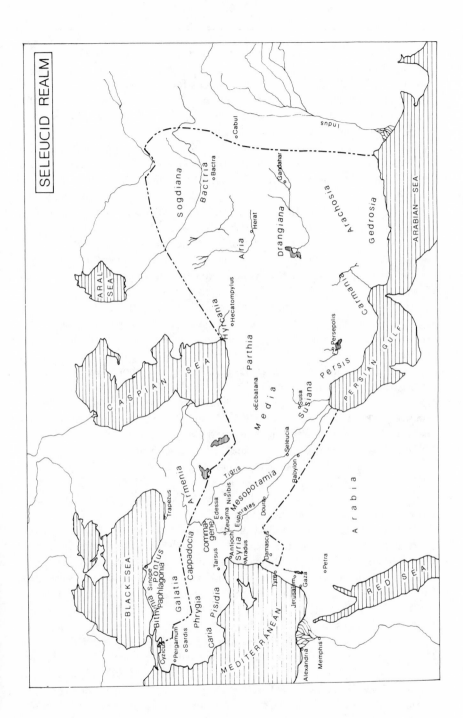

SELEUCID REALM

that the empire could not be defended against the rising powers of Parthia in the east and Rome in the west. Nor had the internal process of Hellenizing the many nations living under Seleucid rule been successful.

Antiochos I Soter (281–261; coregent with his father Seleukos I from 293) was able to vanquish the Celts and settle them in Galatia. But he had no success in the First Syrian War against Egypt (276–271), and he was defeated by Eumenes I of Pergamon (262). Antiochos II (261–246; coregent from 266), in alliance with Antigonos II Gonatas of Macedonia, regained some portions of Asia Minor during the Second Syrian War (260–253). He was murdered in Ephesos by his divorced wife Laodike. Under Seleukos II Kallinikos (246–225) and Seleukos III Soter (225–223) the Seleucid empire experienced its first major crisis. The Third Syrian War (also called "Laodicean War," 246–241), caused by dynastic problems, led to the temporary loss of large areas of Asia Minor and Syria and strengthened the Anatolian kingdoms (Pergamon, Kappadokia, Pontus). The king's brother, Antiochos Hierax, established himself as a rival king with Sardis as his capital, although he was finally defeated by Attalos I of Pergamon and was killed while fighting the Celts in Thrace in 226. The cousin of Seleukos III forced Pergamon to return some Seleucid territories in Asia Minor, but then also made himself independent with Sardis as his capital.

The difficulties that arose under Seleukos II had even more disastrous consequences in the eastern provinces. The satrap of Baktria, Diodotos I, seceded from Syria, relying on aid from the flourishing Greek cities and the Iranian nobility in his realm. This independent Hellenistic kingdom survived for many centuries until it was finally conquered by the Arabs in 642 CE. Around the year 200 BCE Baktria controlled a large realm, including Sogdia (its capital Samarkand is in modern Uzbekistan) and parts of northwest India (today's Pakistan), as well as parts of Chinese Turkestan. Even after the collapse of the Bactrian kingdom the influence of Greek culture survived for a long time, as can be seen in the region's architecture and coinage.

While the developments in Baktria posed no direct threat to Seleucid power, the rise of the Parthian kingdom meant the loss of the entire Iranian region east of the Euphrates River. The Parthians remained as a military threat to Hellenistic and, later, Roman expansionist aspirations. Horsemen from central Asia, they had conquered the satrapy of Parthia southeast of the Caspian Sea shortly after 250 BCE—thus they called themselves "Parthians." In their further expansion, they adopted Iranian ethnic and religious traditions and claimed to be the legitimate heirs of the Achaemenid Persian dynasty, but also incorporated elements of Greek origin. Both Aramaic and Greek were used as languages of their administration. They also confirmed the privileges of the Greek cities of their realm. It was as a Hellenistic power that the Parthians challenged Seleucid rule in the east. Arsaces I of the tribe of the Parni is remembered as the founder of the Parthian royal dynasty (the "Arsacids"). More is known about his successor Tiridates I (ca. 247-210 BCE) who consolidated the Arsacid rule over Parthia and neighboring Hyrcania, south of the Caspian Sea, and made further advances to the west, since the Bactrians prevented any expansion to the east.

Under Antiochos III ("the Great"; 223–187) the Seleucid empire recovered from its impotence. First, Antiochos turned against Egypt with some initial success, but was forced to give up southern Syria and Phoenicia/Palestine when he was defeated by Ptolemy IV at Raphia in the Fourth Syrian War (221–217). Antiochos then turned to Asia Minor, where he defeated and executed the disloyal viceroy of Sardis, Achaios (213). Antiochos was now ready for his great campaign into the east (the "Anabasis of Antiochos," 212–206). Armenia, Parthia, and Baktria were defeated and forced to recognize the supremacy of the Seleucid ruler as the "king of kings." Thus he succeeded at least temporarily in reestablishing Seleucid dominion over the east through a system of dependent vassal states.

As had been agreed in the treaty partitioning Egypt with Philip V of Macedonia, Antiochos occupied southern Syria and Phoenicia/Palestine as soon as the weakness of Egypt became evident after the death of Ptolemy IV in 205 BCE (Fifth Syrian War, 201–195). After Egypt ceded to him all its possessions in Syria, Asia Minor, and Thrace, Antiochos moved west with his army and occupied the straits leading to the Black Sea. However, when a call for help from the Aetolians enticed him to invade Greece, Rome decided that it should intervene. Rome defeated Antiochos at Thermopylae, twice scattered his fleet in the Aegean Sea, and followed him in his retreat to Asia Minor with an army under the leadership of the brothers Scipio (Africanus and Asiaticus). At Magnesia-ad-Sipylum Antiochos suffered a crushing defeat (190 BCE) and was forced to withdraw entirely from Asia Minor. Most of his former possessions on the subcontinent became Pergamene territory. The peace treaty of Apamea (188 BCE) demanded heavy war reparations from Antiochos, a burden that caused immense financial problems for his realm and severely impaired its stability. Antiochos was slain when he attempted to plunder the treasures of a temple.

Antiochos' successor, Seleukos IV Eupator (187–175), was assassinated by his chancellor. Seleukos' brother, who had spent fourteen years in Rome as a hostage, ascended to the Seleucid throne: Antiochos IV Epiphanes (175–163). The conflict with Egypt for southern Syria flared up once more in the Sixth Syrian War (170-168). Antiochos Epiphanes was able to conquer all of Egypt except for Alexandria. He was forced to return to Syria briefly (this is when he "plundered" the temple treasure of Jerusalem), but then invaded Egypt once more. However, in a suburb of Alexandria, the Roman ambassador Popillius Laenas encountered him and relayed a message from the Roman Senate; he drew a circle around the king with his cane and requested, before the king stepped out of the circle, an answer to Rome's demand that Antiochos return to Syria immediately and give up his Egyptian conquests. The king knew that prudence required him to yield. Shortly afterwards he died during a campaign in Armenia and Media.

Beginning with the Books of the Maccabees, Antiochos Epiphanes has been depicted as a tyrant who oppressed the Jews and whose ill-advised policies of Hellenization triggered the Maccabean War (§5.1c). However, he should also be recognized as the last Seleucid king who dreamt of recapturing the legacy of Alexander the Great—a united kingdom of the eastern Mediterranean, in which

Greek culture and tradition would provide the bond for the coexistence of many nations. He encouraged Jerusalem to join this Greek world and become the "New Antioch" with its temple of Yahweh/Zeus Hypsistos. He also spent large sums of money to revive the construction of the Temple of Zeus Olympios in Athens, a project that had been abandoned since the fall of the Athenian tyrants in the 6th century.

When Antiochos was crowned in Memphis as king of Upper and Lower Egypt, albeit as the guardian of his nephew Ptolemy VI Philometor, he took an important step towards reunifying the empire of Alexander. But two new powers had arrived on the political scene, Rome and Parthia. Rome's intervention against Antiochos IV in Alexandria only a few weeks after the defeat of Perseus of Macedonia at Pydna (§1.4a), and the successful expansion of Parthia under Mithridates I (171–138 BCE), reduced the Seleucid kingdom to the level of a petty Asian state. Inevitably, former client states seized the opportunity to fight for independence. Dynastic quarrels impaired the power of the Seleucid state after Antiochos' death—a symptom of the decline of Seleucid rule.

Palestine was under the authority of the Seleucids for only a few decades. The Maccabean insurrection resulted in the establishment of the Jewish state of the Hasmoneans, which lasted until Pompey's conquest of Syria. East of the Jordan, the ancient Arab state of the Nabateans was reorganized with its capital at Petra; not until 105 CE did Nabatea become the Roman province of Arabia Felix. In northern Syria, the satraps of Kommagene established their rule with the claim of descent from both the Achaemenids and the Seleucids; Antiochos I Epiphanes of Kommagene (ca. 69–38 BCE) created the spectacular cultic burial site of the divine king at Nimrud Dag.

The Parthians continued their westward advance after 160 BCE under Mithridates I, conquering Media and Babylonia and the Iranian countries to the south, the Persian heartland. Antiochos Sidites regained these areas for a brief period, but his army was crushed by the Parthians in 129 BCE. Meanwhile Armenia, ruled by a branch of the Parthian royal family, also rose to become an independent country. Further expanding its domain to the southwest, it temporarily controlled Cappadocia. In the year 86 BCE Tigranes I of Armenia conquered whatever was left of the Seleucid empire. Armenia's rule over Syria lasted until the appearance of the Roman legions under Lucullus in 69 BCE and Pompey in 64 BCE.

The successor states of the Seleucid empire, including some smaller domains that had been able to gain independence (e.g., Kommagene and Adiabene), were Hellenized countries that saw themselves as heirs to the Greek tradition, which they combined with their own national heritage. The Parthian rulers took over much of the existing Seleucid administration, and as they were Hellenized themselves, they had the right to appear as protectors of Greek culture. The Arsacid ruler Mithridates I (171–138 BCE) called himself Euergetes, Dikaios, and Philhellene. The political energies of Hellenism still lived on in these successor states of the Seleucid realm, as did most of its Greek cities. The Roman conquest marked the beginning of a new political era, but at the same time a renewal of Hellenistic culture.

(e) Sicily and Southern Italy

Greeks had inhabited Sicily and southern Italy (Magna Graecia) for centuries, but in the second half of the 4th century BCE they felt increasing pressure from Italic tribes—ultimately from Rome—and from the Phoenicians of Carthage. The only effective attempt to unite the Greeks of this area was led by Agathokles. His home was Thermae in western Sicily, where he was born ca. 360 BCE. He became a citizen of Syracuse, in 319/18 its *strategos* ("commander"), and in 317/16 absolute sovereign of that important Greek city. He first fought against Carthage in Sicily, but with little luck, and later without final success in Africa. Still, he did succeed in uniting the Greeks of Sicily. After making peace with Carthage (306 BCE) he assumed the title "king" (following the example of the Diadochi) and lent his support to the Greek cities of southern Italy in their fight against the Italic tribes. He died in the year 289 BCE without ever accomplishing his goal of establishing a united Greek kingdom in Sicily and southern Italy.

The expedition of King Pyrrhos of Epiros to Italy against Rome did little if anything to strengthen the situation of the Greeks of Magna Graecia. After a variety of experiences Pyrrhos had become king of the Molossians and leader of the Epirote league in northwestern Greece (297 BCE). After the death of Demetrios Poliorketes he was even proclaimed king by the Macedonian army. In 280 BCE Pyrrhos invaded Italy to support the Greek city of Tarentum against the Romans. The whole campaign was organized at great expense and was advertised as a Panhellenic war. Pyrrhos defeated the Romans in two costly battles ("Pyrrhic victories"). He advanced as far as the immediate environs of Rome, then went to Sicily and routed the Carthaginians almost completely from the island. But difficulties with the Sicilian Greeks, a last indecisive battle with the Romans, and his aspirations to the Macedonian throne prompted Pyrrhos to withdraw from Italy (275 BCE) without achieving any lasting results but leaving behind one significant inheritance: Rome never forgot the impression that Pyrrhos had made upon them; this decisively formed their image of the Hellenistic empires and their rulers as adventurous, dangerous, and expansionist.

In the following years the Romans rapidly conquered all of southern Italy and part of Sicily. Syracuse retained some degree of independence under king Hieron II (269/68–215) but was restricted to a narrow strip of land along Sicily's eastern coast and was compelled to pay tribute to Rome. In the first war with Carthage (First Punic War, 264–241) the Romans occupied most of Sicily, which became a

Bibliography to §1.4e

K. Meister, "Agathocles," in *CambAncHist* 7 (2d ed.) 384–411.

Moses I. Finley, *Ancient Sicily to the Arab Conquest,* in idem and Denis Mack Smith, *A History of Sicily,* vol. 1 (New York: Viking, 1968).

Erik Sjöqvist, *Sicily and the Greeks: Studies in the Interrelationship between the Indigenous Populations and the Greek Colonists* (Ann Arbor, MI: University of Michigan Press, 1973).

David Randall-MacIver, *Greek Cities in Italy and Sicily* (Oxford: Clarendon, 1931).

Helmut Berve, *Die Herrschaft des Agathokles* (SBAW.PPH, Jg. 1952 H. 5; München: Verlag der Bayerischen Akademie der Wissenschaften, 1953).

Idem, *König Hieron II* (SBAW.PPH, Abhandlungen n.F. 47; München: Verlag der Bayerischen Akademie der Wissenschaften, 1959).

Roman province in 227 BCE. During the last years of its independence, Sicily once more enjoyed a flourishing culture. But disorder following the death of Hieron II prompted Rome to intervene; Syracuse was conquered and incorporated into the province of Sicily. However, the Greeks of Sicily and southern Italy played a significant role in the mediation of Greek culture to Rome and thus decisively influenced the process of the Hellenization of Rome.

5. POLITICAL IDEOLOGY AND RULER CULT

(a) Basic Features of Hellenistic Political Ideology

In Egypt and Syria the Hellenistic kings claimed to be the legitimate successors of the Pharaohs and the Achaemenids, the rulers whose lands they had conquered. Indeed the Seleucids took over the Persian king's royal diadem, signet ring, and the sacred fire. But the legitimacy of these new dynasties in the eyes of their Macedonian and Greek subjects was not based on this sort of resumption of Persian or Egyptian symbols. Rather, the idea of absolute monarchy, which became a reality in the establishment of the Hellenistic rulers, was rooted in Greek beliefs about the lawful rights that an extraordinary individual could claim. In Greece such people had always been honored as heroes after their death, and poets had praised them as divinely inspired human beings. The philosophers spoke of the "man of wisdom," whose charisma and education would qualify him to become king. But in the common perception it was simply the "best person" who should be king. The philosophers generally taught that the king was in fact the best person, and that he could claim divine rights and divine kingship. Stoic concepts contributed the idea that the exercise of royal office on earth corresponded to Zeus' royal office in heaven. In the Hellenistic period philosophers went to great lengths to demonstrate that absolute monarchy was the best form of government.

Nonetheless, the Greeks, in contrast to the Egyptians, did not consider the state to be the personal property of the ruler, although it was understood that private interests were subject to those of the state. Everyone had to serve the state when necessary with provision of time, private possessions, or life. It is important to note that the Greeks would not have used the word "state"—a concept missing in Greek thought and language—they would have spoken instead about

Bibliography to §1.5a

F. W. Walbank, "Monarchies and Monarchic Ideas," in *CambAncHist* 7 (2d ed.) 62–100.

T. A. Sinclair, *A History of Greek Political Thought* (2d ed.; Cleveland: World, 1968).

Victor Ehrenberg, *The Greek State* (2d ed.; London: Methuen, 1969; reprint 1974).

Mason Hammond, *City-State and World State in Greek and Roman Political Theory until Augustus* (Cambridge, MA: Harvard University Press, 1951).

Erwin R. Goodenough, *The Political Philosophy of Hellenistic Kingship* (YCS 1; New Haven, CT: Yale University Press, 1928) 55–102.

Paul Veyne, "Greek Euergetism," in idem, *Bread and Circuses: Historical Sociology and Political Pluralism* (London: Penguin, 1990) 70–200.

the "polis" or the "commonwealth" (τὸ κοινόν). A king might receive divine honors, but the polis remained the possession of the citizens. In order for the Macedonian kings to control the affairs of the Greek cities, they were obliged to form alliances and leagues, reserving for themselves the right of presiding at the assembly.

An identification of the state (as distinct from polis or commonwealth) with the ruler is only conceivable where the land is the property of the king. This was the case in the Hellenistic empires of the east: the new countries were "lands conquered by the spear," over which the king possessed unlimited sovereign rights. Here his will was law. The inhabitants of these countries were simply subjects. The position of the Greek cities in these areas was somewhat different, because their inhabitants were citizens who possessed certain rights and privileges; but even these cities could not act against the king's will. It served their own best interest to render him special honors and thus express their recognition of him as absolute sovereign.

In Macedonia itself the situation was different. The office of the king continued to be understood as something legitimized by the people. Once the Antigonids had been recognized by the Macedonians as their rightful kings, they could count on the people's allegiance to the very end. Thus there was no basis in Macedonia for the development of a ruler cult; only Greek cities outside of Macedonia extended divine honors to the Macedonian kings. Even under Roman domination, Macedonia was reluctant to inaugurate a cult of the Roman conqueror or of the Caesar; rather, they preferred to honor them as their Roman benefactors.

It should be stressed that the royal cult took different forms in the various states of the Hellenistic world. This is later mirrored in the variety of the forms in which Roman emperors would be worshiped as divine.

(b) The Origin and Beginnings of Ruler Cult

It is not possible to trace the origin of the Hellenistic ruler cult to oriental concepts. To be sure, in Egypt the divinity of the Pharaoh had always been the unquestioned foundation of royal sovereignty. However, the Pharaoh's divinity was based on the office, while "the divinity of the Hellenistic ruler was based on

Bibliography to §1.5b–e: Texts

Grant, *Hellenistic Religions,* 64–70 ("Divine Honors Paid Antigonus and Demetrius").

Bibliography to §1.5b–e: Studies

J. Rufus Fears, "Ruler Worship," in Grant and Kitzinger, *Civilization,* 2. 1009–25.

Nilsson, *Griechische Religion,* 2. 132–85 ("Die Religion im Dienste der Könige").

Fritz Taeger, *CHARISMA: Studien zur Geschichte des antiken Herrscherkultes,* vol. 1: *Hellas* (Stuttgart: Kohlhammer, 1957; reprint 1978).

Christian Habicht, *Gottmenschentum und griechische Städte* (Zet. 14; 2d ed.; München: Beck, 1970).

Heinrich Dörrie, *Der Königskult des Antiochos von Kommagene im Lichte neuer Inschriften-Funde* (AAWG.PH 3/60; Göttingen: Vandenhoeck & Ruprecht, 1964).

Nock, "Notes on Ruler Cult I–IV," in idem, *Essays,* 1. 134–59.

Idem, "Deification and Julian," in idem, *Essays,* 2. 833–46.

his excellence" (A. D. Nock). Derivation of the Hellenistic ruler cult from Persian ideas is even less plausible. The Achaemenid kings practiced the oriental court ceremony, a ritualized demonstration that the king was elevated over all his human subjects; but the Persian kings were not considered gods. Any older concepts of the divine king had long since disappeared in the east by the time of Alexander's conquests. In considering the possible Greek background to ruler cult, one could compare the worship offered heroes. But hero cult was traditionally rendered to someone who had already died. Thus there is no direct connection between ruler cult and hero cult. A different development of Greek thought will explain the origin of the worship of the living king.

At the time of the crisis of the Greek polis at the end of the 5th and the beginning of the 4th centuries BCE, the philosophers were the first to advance the idea that only a divinely gifted individual would be able to reestablish peace, order, and prosperity. Plato, Xenophon, and Aristotle expressed this idea quite clearly, though each in his own way. They believed that education, charisma, and divine sanction were intimately related. Accordingly significant rulers and generals had on occasion received divine honors during their lifetime even before the rise of Alexander. In Syracuse, such honors were accorded to the dead ruler during the 5th and 4th centuries, and later to the living ruler as well, who was worshiped as a benefactor. The Spartan general Lysander, after his victory over the Athenians in the Peloponnesian War, received divine honors, voted for him by the Oligarchs of Ionia on Samos (404 BCE). A few decades later, Philip II of Macedonia was hailed as a god by the Athenian rhetor Isokrates.

Alexander at first understood himself as the imitator of his "hero" Herakles. It is not known when and how his self-conception changed. When he visited the oracle of Ammon in the Libyan desert, the priest greeted him in front of the temple as the son of the god Ammon Re. This was nothing extraordinary in Egypt because, after its conquest, Alexander had become the legitimate Pharaoh, and thus also the legitimate son of god by virtue of his office. Nobody knows what happened inside the temple. It is quite possible that at the time Alexander accepted that he was indeed the son of the god Ammon Re (whom the Greeks identified with Zeus), and this event could have inspired him to solicit tokens of divine veneration for himself (§1.2b). Nevertheless, ruler worship did not become an institution during Alexander's lifetime. His abortive attempt to introduce the customary oriental adoration of the ruler in Bactria in 327 BCE is no proof to the contrary, because this was simply an eastern court ceremony, not an act of divine worship. Alexander's letter to the Greek cities of 324 BCE, in which he demanded the return of the exiles, cannot be used as evidence, because only later sources report that in this letter Alexander requested to be worshiped as a god. Divine worship of Alexander seems to have been instituted by some Greek cities during his lifetime, though only sporadically. Another piece of evidence for such worship may be the Philippeion in Olympia, a tholos temple begun by Philip II after his victory over Athens at Chaeronea in 338 BCE and finished by Alexander. Chryselephantine statues of Philip II, his parents, his wife Olympias, and his son Alexander stood in this temple. Statues made of gold and ivory were normally reserved for images of the gods.

The Diadochi made no requests that implied divine worship of their own persons. Perhaps they were still too close to the overwhelming impact of the personality of Alexander. Nevertheless, they occasionally received such honors from Greek cities, even before they assumed their royal titles. Such honors were actually thrust upon them, most obviously when the Athenians greeted Antigonos Monophthalmos and his son Demetrios Poliorketes as Savior Gods. The cult of the dead Alexander was energetically promoted by the Diadochi. Eumenes placed the throne of Alexander in the tent that served as his council chamber. Alexander's body, which Arrhidaios wanted to transport to Macedonia, was seized by Ptolemy, who brought it to Memphis. It was later transferred to Alexandria, where a permanent cult for the dead king was established with all expenses paid by the government. Temples and sanctuaries dedicated to Alexander's worship are known to have existed, especially in the Ionian cities of Asia Minor; some of these may go back to his own time. But this worship of the divine Alexander, which continued in many places for several centuries, is not directly responsible for the Hellenistic ruler cult.

(c) Ruler Cult in Egypt

The divine veneration of the Macedonian king by the native population of Egypt was a matter of course from the very beginning. Such worship was due to him by virtue of his office. The traditional Egyptian ruler cult was simply transferred to the Ptolemies and later to the Roman emperors. For the Macedonians and Greeks in Egypt, the first step towards the institution of a ruler cult was the worship of Ptolemy I and his wife Berenike as Savior Gods, a practice instituted by the second Ptolemy after their death. Coins issued under the authority of Ptolemy I now changed the inscription on the reverse of the coin from "Ptolemy the King" to "Ptolemy the Savior" (σωτήρ). Other members of the royal family (including even a mistress) were also deified after their deaths. According to Greek custom, the building of a temple and the institution of a festival were a regular part of the establishment of a new deity. Ptolemy II decreed that the winners of the games in honor of these Savior Gods should receive the same honors as winners at the Olympic Games.

At a later date, Ptolemy II ("Philadelphos") also included himself and his sister-wife Arsinoë II as "Divine Brother and Sister" (θεοὶ Ἀδελφοί) in the worship of the divine members of the royal house. This kind of worship of the ruling king and queen during their lifetime transcended the limits of the traditional hero cult, but can still be understood as a Greek development on the basis of Greek presuppositions. The presentation of the two as gods on later issues of their coins proclaims the excellence of their rule rather than the virtue of their office. Alongside these factors, the traditional Egyptian worship of the Pharaoh as god probably contributed to the strong institutional development of the Hellenistic ruler cult under the Ptolemies. Ptolemy II and Arsinoë II may well have encouraged the people to worship the living king and queen as gods in order to unify their subjects in an activity that both Greek and non-Greeks could sanction. In its basic character, this ruler cult remained a Greek institution and did not differ from the ruler cult practiced in the Seleucid realm and occasionally elsewhere in Hellenistic kingdoms. It is characteristic that divine titles like "Savior," "Philadelphos," and "Benefactor" were shared by the kings of Egypt, Syria, Pergamon, and Pontus; on the other hand, they are just as characteristically absent from the titles of the kings of Macedonia.

A special development of the ruler cult in Egypt occurred under Ptolemy IV Philopator (222–204 BCE). He claimed to be a descendant of the Greek god Dionysos and had that god's ivy leaf tattooed on his body. According to a legend preserved in *3 Macc.* 2.28ff., he attempted to force the Jews of Alexandria to be tattooed in the same way. The expansion of the cult of Dionysos is clearly reflected in these traditions (§4.3f). Ptolemy IV appears on coins issued after his death wearing the radiate crown of Helios, the aegis of Zeus, and the trident of Poseidon; he is thus identified as the ruler of the sky, the earth, and the sea. There is also evidence of syncretism: in a dedication of a temple for queen Berenike II (wife of Ptolemy III) she is called "Isis, Mother of the Gods, Berenike." If "Mother of the Gods" is a reference to the Phrygian Magna Mater (§4.4.b), the appearance of an Asian deity in combination with Isis demonstrates the spread of syncretism at an early stage in the Hellenistic period. Identification of a royal personage with particular traditional deities became a typical phenomenon as ruler cult developed further in the Roman period (§6.5b).

In the 2d century BCE, especially after the loss of the Greek parts of the Ptolemaic realm in Asia Minor and the Aegean, the religious policies of the Alexandrian court show increasingly Egyptian features. The state assumed supervision of the synods of Egyptian priests. Kleopatra III, who died in 101 BCE, and later queens appeared in official proclamations under the name of the goddess Isis. The sacred marriage of Antony as New Dionysos with Kleopatra VII as New Isis was the natural culmination—as well as the termination—of the development of the Egyptian ruler cult. In the eyes of the west the celebration of Antony and Kleopatra as revealed gods was an un-Roman presumption, and Octavian used this argument successfully against his adversary. Nonetheless, features of this Hellenistic ruler cult would soon make a reappearance in the Roman cult of the divine Caesar.

(d) Ruler Cult in the Seleucid Empire

In analogy with the deification of the first Ptolemy after his death, the second Seleucid decreed that his father Seleukos I be worshiped as "Zeus Nikator." Very soon the cult of the living king was also introduced. However, there is scant evidence for a state cult in the Seleucid empire: direct testimony is much rarer here than for Egypt, which is so rich in papyrus finds. In the case of Antiochos III there is proof of worship of the king as a god while still living. A letter of Antiochos III requests that high priestesses should be named for his wife Laodike in all those cities in which high priests for the king had already been appointed; the letter reveals that high priests for the royal cult were already functioning under his predecessors. Seleucid ruler cult was closely associated with worship of Zeus and Apollo, the chief state gods of the Seleucid realm. This is evident at the famous sanctuary of Apollo in Daphne, near Antioch on the Orontes.

In addition, the Seleucids energetically promoted existing local cults. This was important for political reasons; the Seleucid empire included a large number of temple territories, which (like some of the Greek cities) possessed certain privileges of autonomy and were thus not subject to the ordinary administration of satrapies. Usually they were ruled by a high priest, as in the case of the Jewish temple state in Jerusalem, which came under Seleucid rule at the beginning of the 2d century BCE. Temple states could normally regulate their own affairs. Conflicts might arise if an attempt was made to introduce the cult of the state gods into these temples (for the conflict of the Jewish temple state with Antiochos IV Epiphanes see §5.1c).

(e) Ruler Cult in Pergamon and Elsewhere in Anatolia

The rulers of Pergamon were officially deified only after their death, though priests were appointed for their cult as soon as they assumed the royal title. Festivals and athletic contests were celebrated in honor of living kings. Priestesses served in the cult of the ruling queen. A most influential role in the establishment of religious institutions was played by Queen Apollonis, wife of Attalos I and mother of Eumenes II and Attalos II, who sponsored the renovation of the Demeter sanctuary in Pergamon. (This queen also appears together with her son Attalos II in the dedicatory inscription of the Stoa of Attalos in Athens.) A temple was built for her in her home city of Kyzikos, and altars, sacrifices, and hymns dedicated to her ("the goddess Apollonis Eusebes") are attested in several cities.

It was only during the brief reign of the last Attalid that a king received cultic honors comparable to the worship of the gods. He was not officially deified, but his statue was placed in the temple of Asklepios so that he would share his temple. Incense was to be burned for him every day on the altar of Zeus Soter, and his arrival was to be celebrated with festive processions and sacrifices by the entire population as if he were a god.

There is evidence that kings of other states of Anatolia, such as Bithynia and Cappadocia, received divine honors, at least after their deaths. One very impressive monument is the burial chamber (ἱεροθεσίον) of Antiochos of Kommagene (died before 31 BCE) on Nimrud Dag with its larger than life-size statues. This king called himself "Theos Dikaios Epiphanes," but the inscription on the monument makes a clear distinction between the gods and the king, who is venerated as a dead hero and has festivals held in memory of his birthday and his enthronement.

SOCIETY AND ECONOMICS

1. HELLENISM AND HELLENIZATION

(a) The Concept of Hellenism

In 1836 and 1843 J. G. Droysen published his innovative two-volume work on the "History of Hellenism" (*Geschichte des Hellenismus*), where he employed the term "Hellenism"—contrary to its earlier usage—to describe the amalgamation of Western and Near-Eastern cultures under the auspices of Greek education during the period from Alexander to the beginnings of Christianity. The designation of these centuries as the "Hellenistic" period has become widely accepted, though there are problems relating to this designation because the Hellenistic empires expired well before the beginnings of Christianity, as they succumbed to the onslaught of Rome in the west and of Parthia in the east. On the other hand, the cultural and religious impact of Hellenism went far beyond the Hellenistic period and remained visible for many centuries not only in the Hellenization of Rome and of many countries of the east, but also in the development of ancient Christianity.

Recent scholarship has also been more cautious than Droysen in describing the relationship of Greek and Near Eastern elements as amalgamation. To be sure, the contacts between the Greek world and other cultures were both close and intimate. There had already been a lively exchange between Greece and the east during earlier centuries. Greek colonization, the expansion of Greek economic power, and cultural exchange, especially of the Greeks of Ionia with the east, had long since led to a very intense and creative interaction of Greek and non-Greek elements. "Classical" Greek architecture and art, religion and mythology, science and philosophy would be unthinkable without this interaction. It remains problematic, however, whether this process, which intensified during the Hellenistic period, should best be described as "amalgamation" or as "combination." Alexander's attempt to unite the Greeks and the Persians into a new nation remained an unfulfilled dream. His successors insisted that they were first of all Macedonians and Greeks, and they made great efforts to promote the Greek element as the dominating factor.

It is advisable to use the term Hellenism primarily as a designation of the period that began with Alexander the Great and ended with the conquest of the east by the Romans. The most characteristic phenomenon of this period is the intensification of the process of "Hellenization," namely, the expansion of Greek language, education, and culture initiated by the establishment of Macedonian and Greek political dominion over the nations of the former Persian empire. Never was there any question as to which element would predominate. Even when Greek culture encountered Rome and fell under its political domination, the Greek element prevailed. Rome itself was deeply affected by Greek art, architecture, philosophy, and literature; the eastern part of the Roman empire remained essentially Greek, and the Greek language, culture, and Greek religion gained ground even in the Latin west. The developments of the Roman imperial period cannot be understood without Hellenism, and insofar as the Roman empire was Hellenized, it found its natural continuation in the "Greek" Byzantine period. Indeed, Christianity, which had its beginnings in the early Roman imperial period, entered the Roman world as a Hellenistic religion, specifically as the heir to an already Hellenized Jewish religion.

(b) The Greeks and the Nations of the Hellenistic Empires

The extent of the influence of the Greeks and the Hellenized Macedonians on the nations they governed differed from state to state and changed over time.

Bibliography to §2: Texts
see Bibliography to §1.

Bibliography to §2: Studies

W. W. Tarn, *Hellenistic Civilization* (3d ed.; rev. by author and G. T. Griffith; London: Arnold, 1952; reprint New York: New American Library, 1975). A very useful introduction.

F. W. Walbank, *The Hellenistic World* (2d ed.; Cambridge, MA: Harvard University Press, 1993). idem, ed., *The Hellenistic World* (*CambAncHist* 7/1; 2d ed.; Cambridge: Cambridge University Press, 1984).

Roger Ling, ed., *The Hellenistic World to the Coming of the Romans* (*CambAncHist*, plates to vol. 7,2; Cambridge: Cambridge University Press, 1984).

Especially for Economic and Social History:

Michael I. Rostovtzeff, *The Social and Economic History of the Hellenistic World* (3 vols.; Oxford: Clarendon, 1941). The most fundamental and comprehensive study, with rich documentation.

Jean-Philippe Levy, *The Economic Life of the Ancient World* (Chicago and London: University of Chicago Press, 1967). An instructive brief survey.

Moses I. Finley, *The Ancient Economy* (3d ed.; Harmondsworth: Penguin, 1992).

Bibliography to §2.1

Johann Gustav Droysen, *Geschichte des Hellenismus* (2 vols.; Hamburg: Perthes, 1836–43; reprint Basel: Schwabe, 1953). The first and classic treatment of the phenomenon of Hellenism.

Reinhold Bichler, *"Hellenismus." Geschichte und Problematik eines Epochenbegriffs* (Impulse der Forschung 41; Darmstadt: Wissenschaftliche Buchgesellschaft, 1983). A critical evaluation of the concept of Hellenism and its problems.

Moses Hadas, *Hellenistic Culture: Fusion and Diffusion* (New York: Columbia University Press, 1959; reprint 1968).

John Pentland Mahaffy, *The Progress of Hellenism in Alexander's Empire* (Chicago: University of Chicago Press, 1905).

Peyton Randolph Helm, "Races and Physical Types in the Classical World," in Grant and Kitzinger, *Civilization, 1.* 137–54.

Bibliography to §2.1b

J. K. Davies, "Cultural, Social and Economic Features of the Hellenistic World," in *CambAncHist* 7 (2d ed.) 257–320.

There were also variations in the policies of Hellenization from one ruler to the next. In the beginning, the Greek influence was slight, especially since the Diadochi did not continue Alexander's policies in this respect. Macedonians and Greeks formed the ruling class and occupied all the important positions in the administration and the army. The Greek populations of the newly founded cities and military colonies lived lives that were more or less separate from the native populations. The Greek cities enjoyed some autonomy in their own administration: they had their own gymnasia, to which only Greeks were admitted (§3.1), their own temples, in which primarily Greek deities were worshiped, and their own social life, which was characterized by the Greek system of associations. The native populations at first had little contact with these institutions; for them, Greek cultural predominance was expressed in the use of the Greek tongue as the official language of government and in trade relations with rapidly expanding Greek commerce and industry.

Local interactions with Greek culture, literature, morality, and religion evolved only gradually. "Syncretism" (§3.3a)—a substantial mixture of Greek and Near Eastern elements—can be observed first in the area of religious history. In the domain of the Macedonian rulers of Egypt, where syncretistic developments are most obvious, the term essentially means that Near Eastern deities and traditions appeared in Greek dress as early as the 3d century BCE. This phenomenon did not arise naturally from encounters between the different populations of the Ptolemaic domain. Royal initiative was instrumental in creating the cult of the Greco-Egyptian gods Sarapis and Isis (§3.4a). Typically, the legend about the origin of the Septuagint (§5.3b)—assumed to have taken place in Alexandria—ascribes the Greek translation of the Hebrew Bible to Ptolemaic initiative, although the real cause for this translation was the substantial Hellenized population of Israelites in Alexandria who actually used the Greek language even in their synagogue services.

The Hellenistic version of the goddess Isis, on the other hand, became very popular in the rest of the Greco-Roman world, but was never accepted by the native Egyptian population, who by and large stayed unaffected by Hellenization. There is no single formula that could describe the process of Hellenistic syncretism. Much depended on the degree of Greek learning among non-Greek populations, upon their social standing and economic success, and on the residual resistance to Greek, that is, "foreign" influence. Hellenism also includes an antithesis that is characterized by the differences between east and west and between barbarian culture and Greek education.

The antithesis was neither an irreconcilable opposition nor a stimulus for amalgamation, but rather a mutual fascination and stimulation in the political, cultural, and religious realms. In each sector the Greek element determined the

Arnaldo Momigliano, *Alien Wisdom: The Limits of Hellenization* (Cambridge and New York: Cambridge University Press, 1975).

Amélie Kuhrt and Susan Sherwin-White, eds., *Hellenism in the East: The Interaction of Greek and Non-Greek Civilizations from Syria to Central Asia after Alexander* (London: Duckworth, 1987).

shape of the antithesis. Political actions of the Greeks and Macedonians were strongly influenced by a desire to maintain some relationship to their homeland. Economy and trade followed Greek standards (the Attic standard of coinage was almost universally accepted; banks were in Greek hands), although many centers of business and trade shifted to places outside of the Greek homeland. Greek language and ideals of education dominated culturally, but the centers of education shifted to Alexandria, Pergamon, and Rhodos. In all this, the non-Greek contribution was present from the beginning but was not always immediately recognizable, since it made its appearance in Greek dress, using Greek language and Greek organizational structures. In many instances, non-Greeks were the instigators of new developments in Hellenistic culture; for example, Zeno, the founder of Stoic philosophy, was the son of a Phoenician merchant from Cyprus. Barbarians also organized their social structures according to patterns they learned from the Greeks. The establishment of the Phoenician merchants from Berytus/Beirut on Delos, for instance, is styled as a *thiasos* under the patronage of the Greek god Poseidon.

In the vast realm of the Seleucid empire the most effective element of Hellenization was the founding of numerous cities peopled by Greek and Macedonian immigrants. Some of these cities began as military colonies, but they had important functions beyond military service that aided the internal stabilization of the empire. The immigrants felt at home in new cities, and often named them after the cities of their origin (for example, Larissa or Edessa). The new settlers worked and fought not only for the king but also for their own security and prosperity. The Seleucid kings did not consciously pursue a policy of Hellenization, at least in the beginning, nor did they intend to create a national state of Greeks and Hellenized barbarians. They seem to have accepted the pluralism of the different nations, cultures, and religions in their realm as natural. However, in order to maintain control over their realm, they needed a strong presence of Greeks and Macedonians as a counterbalance to the centrifugal forces at work in their multinational kingdom. To some degree the Greeks became orientalized and many orientals became Hellenized, especially as they advanced in the service of the kings and came to participate more fully in the culture and economy of the new Greek colonies and the Hellenized older cities. Thus it happened that Jewish military colonists from Babylon who had been settled in the old Lydian capital of Sardis emerged as a thoroughly Hellenized, Greek-speaking synagogue community. Such developments came about more by chance than by design.

In Ptolemaic Egypt the situation was quite different. Egypt could boast of only two Greek cities, Alexandria and the older Milesian colony of Naukratis. The Ptolemies were not interested in founding new cities within Egypt itself, which meant that no means were provided for breaking down the differences between the Greek urban population and the native population of the countryside (the Jewish residents of Alexandria in this respect belonged to the Hellenes). Most of the native Egyptians did not learn Greek, although all official documents had to be written in the Greek—a task accomplished by appointed village scribes. Egyptian remained the country's spoken vernacular, which was to reappear as a literary language in the Coptic documents of the early Christian church. The frequent insurrections of the native Egyptian population that characterized the 2d century BCE were due to the failure of Hellenization in the rural areas outside of the city of Alexandria.

2. THE BASIC STRUCTURES
OF ADMINISTRATION AND ECONOMY

The Hellenistic states extended over large areas, encompassing millions of inhabitants of various nationalities. The vast size of their realms demanded a completely new concept of the state on the part of the Macedonian and Greek conquerors, whose traditional image of a political community was the city-state or the petty kingdom. Since there were no existing Greek models—even Aristotle had developed his theory of the state on the pattern of the polis community—the Hellenistic empires relied largely on the inherited Persian or Egyptian administrations. But this was not a simple transfer of power, as happened when the Persians ousted the Babylonians. The Greeks brought an advantage that no previous conqueror had possessed: a highly developed economy, including established monetary systems, which could be put to immediate use stimulating economic growth in the new realms. The economic horizon was further expanded by expeditions of discovery, such as the sea route to India, or an expedition into the Sudan. Furthermore, the conquerors introduced and developed an entity of social and political life still unfamiliar in the east: the Greek city. Outside of Egypt, the founding of numerous cities and the reorganization of existing cities created cultural and economic centers everywhere, to an extent that was previously unknown in the east.

(a) Greece and Macedonia

The old Greek cities gained few if any advantages from the new developments. All the Hellenistic kingdoms tried repeatedly to gain a foothold in Greece and thus carried their wars onto Greek soil. As a consequence, the Greek homeland sank more and more deeply into poverty. Greece was already disadvantaged with its poor agricultural and mineral resources. Even the demand for manufactured goods from Greece, which had increased at the beginning of the Hellenistic period, sank to new lows.

Bibliography to §2.2

Chester G. Starr, "Greek Administration," in Grant and Kitzinger, *Civilization*, 1. 631–47.
Michael I. Rostovtzeff, "The Hellenistic World and its Economic Development," *AHR* 41 (1935–36) 231–52.
Fritz M. Heichelheim, *An Ancient Economic History: From the Palaeolithic Age to the Migrations of the Germanic, Slavic, and Arabic Peoples*, vol. 3 (Leiden: Sijthoff, 1970).
Robert J. Littman, "Greek Taxation," in Grant and Kitzinger, *Civilization*, 2. 795-808.

Bibliography to §2.2a

F. W. Walbank, "Macedonia and Greece," in *CambAncHist* 7 (2d ed.) 221–256.
Richard M. Berthold, *Rhodos in the Hellenistic Age* (Ithaca, NY: Cornell University Press, 1984).

The gradual economic recession was not felt in the same way everywhere. Athens enjoyed moderate economic prosperity for a long period. Under Macedonian rule it was the major trade center and clearinghouse of the Macedonian kingdom. The level of Athenian cultural life also remained relatively high. Delphi continued to flourish as a wealthy center of religious life and retained much of its significance as the diplomatic capital of Greece. Both Athens and Delphi also benefited from building projects sponsored by the Hellenistic kings. The economic decline was most strongly felt in those cities that traditionally had only a small share of industrial production and trade. This was most evident in Sparta, where the decline was aggravated by the city's inability to solve its social problems. The ancient population of 8000 citizens had sunk to only 700 by the 3d century BCE, and most of the land was in the hands of no more than a hundred citizens. Reforms by the kings Agis and Kleomenes III were frustrated by the resistance of the oligarchs and were wrecked by outside military interference. It is unclear whether Sparta actually had a strong enough economic base to have sustained social reforms in any case.

The islands of the Aegean were not as involved in the continued warfare, but they were increasingly harassed by pirates and weighed down by the financial burdens of foreign occupation. Financial and economic troubles were felt quite strongly and were only partially alleviated by generous royal donations, as in the case of Samothrake and Delos. Rhodos, however, enjoyed a special position. On the basis of the island's rich agriculture and its possessions on the mainland of southwestern Anatolia, it maintained its independence, serving as a clearinghouse and host to many international trade agencies and as the most important port of transshipment in the eastern Mediterranean. In order to protect its trading interests the island maintained a strong navy, which had considerable success in controlling piracy, and Rhodos was quite willing to support other cities with its military power. Rhodian maritime law, which epitomized the traditions and experience of Greek seafaring, remained valid even into the Roman period. After a crippling earthquake of 227 BCE, Rhodos received aid for its reconstruction from many countries. Due to its wealth and a well-balanced system of social and political structures, Rhodos was one of the few Greek states to avoid social unrest in this period. Rhodos also became an important cultural center, next only to Athens and Alexandria; here such scholars as Poseidonios (§§3.3b; 3.4c; 4.1a) made their home. In spite of some setbacks when Rome began to dominate the east, Rhodos preserved its economic prosperity and cultural position in the Roman period.

Like Rhodos, and later at its expense, the small Cycladic island of Delos also enjoyed the status of an international trade and banking center. First dependent on the Ptolemies, then on Rhodos, Delos later came under a Roman protectorate. Trade relations with Syria were especially important. The island continued to prosper until its destruction by Mithridates VI of Pontus (§6.1d) in the year 88 BCE. Other islands were able to manage fairly well as long as they enjoyed a substantial agricultural base and some share of manufacturing industries; Kos, for example, developed its silk production. In these instances, the property-owning middle classes had a better chance of survival than their counterparts in the cities of the Greek mainland. But even here declining wages, an increased use of slave labor in farming and industry, and heavy tax burdens were indicators of economic recession.

(b) The Greek Cities of Asia Minor

The Ionian cities on the western coast of Asia Minor—Ephesos, Miletos, and others—remained autonomous in their internal administration, but were ruled in military and political affairs by Ptolemaic Egypt in the 3d century BCE. During this period, tax burdens were heavy, military personnel were quartered in the houses of citizens, and the cities were burdened with other obligations to the Egyptian army (maintaining their horses) and navy (shipbuilding). The economies of these cities were rebuilt only after the end of Egyptian rule, but even the subsequent Seleucid rule was troublesome. As Michael Rostovtzeff has written, "The Seleucids could not exist without these cities, and they were unable to live with them." Although the Seleucids continued to grant internal autonomy, the cities remained politically dependent and had to pay tribute. In addition, the citizens were subject to the usual royal taxes. In spite of occasional royal donations and favors (exemption from tribute or the gift of some building), the cities waited in vain for the "freedom" that had been promised ever since their liberation from Persian rule. Nevertheless, surviving documents as well as archaeological evidence of building activity during this period demonstrate that agriculture, industry, and trade brought a good deal of prosperity, which continued during the period of Pergamene rule over western Asia Minor. Economic ruin, aggravated through the wars of Mithridates of Pontus, came ultimately from Rome's mismanagement and exploitation during the first century of its administration. Later on, the Roman emperors intervened personally to restore the prosperity that these cities had once enjoyed.

The Greek cities on the coast of the Black Sea, such as Kyzikos, Byzantium, Heraklea, Sinope, and Trapezos, remained independent for some time and beyond the influence of any of the major Hellenistic kingdoms, though some were later incorporated into the kingdom of Pontus. All these cities were small territorial states with an agricultural base. Trading, fishing, and manufacturing conferred a modest degree of prosperity. The Greek or Hellenized cities on the southern coast of Asia Minor in Lykia and Pamphylia (Xanthos, Patara, Perge, Aspendos, Side) exchanged Ptolemaic for Seleucid rule. Finally, after a short period of Rhodian control, they gained their freedom, which they were able to maintain during much of the 2d and 1st centuries BCE. Rich agriculture and some trade brought benefits, but also attracted piracy, which continued to be a problem until Roman rule was firmly established.

Bibliography to §2.2b

David Magie, "Rome and the City-States of Western Asia Minor from 200 to 113 B.C.," in Calder and Keil, *Anatolian Studies*, 161–85.

A. H. M. Jones, "Civitates liberae et immunes in the East," in Calder and Keil, *Anatolian Studies*, 103–17.

K. M. T. Atkinson, "The Seleucids and the Greek Cities of Western Asia Minor," *Antichthon* 2 (1968) 32–57.

(c) The Kingdoms of Asia Minor

In Pergamon, the plan of the city, with its citadel, royal palaces, temples, theater, and gymnasia is still today a visible document of the Greek spirit; its aqueduct and water supply system are testimony to Greek technical ingenuity. The inspiration was partly supplied by Alexandria, partly by Athens or Epidauros (as in the rebuilding of Pergamon's Asklepieion). The increasing wealth of the kings of Pergamon is evident. Only a small territorial state at the beginning, it quickly secured its economic independence, boasting the rich wine and olive production of the Kaikos valley, sufficient resources in raw materials (wood, copper, and silver from the Ida Mountains), and its own port. The administration was fashioned according to the Egyptian model (§2.2d): a centralized system with an economy strictly controlled by the king. In the original area of the Pergamene realm, the capital was the only significant city. The countryside was divided into districts, which remained royal property, and was farmed by indigenous farmers or tenants (*klerouchoi*), who paid rent or tithes to the king. As elsewhere in Asia Minor, there seem to have been a number of major agricultural estates. Industry received royal subventions and was partly concentrated in manufacturing plants (especially for textiles and parchment) owned by the king. Export of these products and of the famed horses bred in Pergamon brought enormous wealth to the royal treasury, but little economic benefit to the population in general.

Bithynia, situated at the northwest corner of Asia Minor, was richly endowed by nature, boasting a productive agriculture, many forests, and quarries of precious stone and crystal. The free Greek cities on the Propontis and on the Black Sea (Kyzikos, Herakleia) made the Thracian inhabitants of the country dependent on Greek trade. The Thracian dynasty freed the country from domination by the successors of Alexander. Like other Hellenistic kings, they founded new cities (Nikomedia, Prusa) and appeared as patrons on Delos and in Delphi. Trade agreements with the Ptolemies and with Macedonia allowed them to gain their share of the trade and commerce. Bithynia remained independent until 74 BCE and competed with Rome in banking and in the slave trade.

Pontus, situated inland south and southeast of the Black Sea, boasted productive agricultural areas in its river valleys. In its eastern district it controlled the most important mining area of the ancient world, producing iron, copper, and silver. Exports went not only to Mesopotamia and Syria, but after the founding of the Greek cities on the coast (Sinope, Trapezos, ca. 630 BCE) also to Greece. Pontus and Kappadokia, which had been the centers of the ancient Hittite empire and then became the mainstay of the Iranians of Anatolia, were bypassed by Alexander, and the Seleucid kings were never able to bring them under their

Bibliography to §2.2c

H. Heinen, "The Syrian-Egyptian Wars and the New Kingdoms of Asia Minor," in *CambAncHist* 7 (2d ed.) 412–433.

Michael I. Rostovtzeff, "Pergamum," in *CambAncHist* 8. 590–618.

Idem, "Some Remarks on the Monetary and Commercial Policy of the Seleucids and Attalids," in Calder and Keil, *Anatolian Studies,* 277-98.

Esther V. Hansen, *The Attalids of Pergamon* (Cornell Studies in Classical Philology 36; 2d ed.; Ithaca, NY: Cornell University Press, 1971).

control. Thus the pre-Hellenistic structures of the society remained intact during the Hellenistic period.

Pontus had no urban culture. Large estates with villages controlled either by feudal lords or by temples (in which Iranian deities like Anahita were worshiped) characterized its social and economic structures. The royal family was originally Iranian, but had been Hellenized, and the kings made great efforts to obtain a due share of Hellenistic commerce and trade. An important step in this direction was the conquest of the Greek cities. Sinope was conquered in 183 BCE; it became the new capital of the country and reaped increasing profits from the growing wealth of the kings, who now controlled the export of ores and levied transit duties on the goods that arrived on caravan routes from Asia for shipment west. Merchants from Sinope were well-known figures in Greece, and later also in the western Mediterranean, wherever metals and ores were traded. At the end of the 2d century BCE, Mithridates V of Pontus was the wealthiest king in Asia Minor. His successor, Mithridates VI, made use of these rich resources to equip his army and navy for a war that seriously challenged Rome's control of the Greek world (§6.1d).

The Celtic Galatians, after their invasion of Greece and Anatolia in the 3d century BCE, had been resettled in the regions of ancient Phrygia. Galatians populated such cities as Gordion, Ankyra, and Pessinus, the home of the Magna Mater (§4.4b). Their nobles, wealthy and in control of the tribal organization, had established themselves as masters of large estates and marauding knights. Neither the indigenous population nor the Galatian lords were much influenced by the process of Hellenization. In the 2d century BCE, the Galatians attempted to gain a share of the Hellenistic economy and gain access to the Black Sea by conquering the Greek city of Heraklea. But Pergamon and Rome brought this to naught. The Romans devastated the country, triggering a terrible insurrection of the Galatians (168 BCE), which had to be quelled by Eumenes II of Pergamon. Only after these events did the slow process of Hellenization begin in the central districts of Asia Minor, especially under Roman vassal kings of the 1st century BCE. Like Galatia, Cappadocia also remained economically and culturally on the margins of the Hellenistic world.

(d) Egypt and Cyprus

Most of the Greek and Macedonian population of Egypt was concentrated in Alexandria. Except when employed as officials in the royal administration,

Bibliography to §2.2d

Michael I. Rostovtzeff, "The Foundations of Social and Economic Life in Egypt in Hellenistic Times," *JEA* 6 (1920) 161–78.

Eric Turner, "Ptolemaic Egypt," in *CambAncHist* 7 (2d ed.) 118–174.

Fraser, *Alexandria*.

Hugh MacLennan, *Oxyrhynchus: An Economic and Social Study* (Princeton, NJ: Princeton University Press, 1935; reprint Chicago: Argonaut, 1967).

William Linn Westermann, "The Ptolemies and the Welfare of Their Subjects," *AHR* 43 (1937/38) 270–87.

Roger S. Bagnall, *The Administration of the Ptolemaic Possessions Outside Egypt* (Leiden: Brill, 1976).

Greeks and Macedonians were scarce outside Alexandria, the older Greek city of Naukratis, the city of Ptolemais founded by Ptolemy I in upper Egypt, and some new settlements such as those in the Fayyum. The locals thought of these Greek officials as representatives of a foreign power. The king, his administrators, and to a certain degree other Alexandrians, were in complete control of the wealth of the country. Navy and merchant marine were stationed in Alexandria, and nearly all transfer of goods in the import-export trade took place there.

The Ptolemies administered the country according to the principles of a capitalistic state monopoly, taken over from the Pharaonic government. The economic expertise of the Greeks enabled them to refine this system and to apply it with more consistency, thereby intensifying production. On the other hand, the desire to exercise more control resulted in a bloated administrative apparatus that was ultimately self-defeating. Most of the agricultural land belonged to the king and was managed according to the directives of the central government. Stock farming, insofar as it was still in private hands and not confined to the royal ranches, was strictly supervised by the state; statistics listing every single animal and its acquisition and sale were collected annually. Bee-keeping and fishing were left in private hands, but a share of the proceeds had to be paid into the royal treasury. All rights of hunting, mining, and timber were vested in the royal administration.

Most manufactured goods, especially those destined for export, were produced by the royal industries; all raw materials were owned and allotted by the state. In addition, there were some factories owned by the temples, from which the kings may have originally learned their methods of monopolistic industrial production and its organization. Private production was restricted to the manufacture of simple articles for the indigenous population. The most important state monopolies were in the production of oil (several types of vegetable oil), which was sold at a strictly controlled price; textiles, especially linen (wool was manufactured privately); beer; salt; leather; and papyrus. Papyrus was produced for domestic use, including immense quantities for administrative use. It was also exported in bulk to satisfy the brisk demand from other countries.

Egypt was an active participant in east Mediterranean trade, especially with its possessions in Africa (Cyrenaica), southern and western Asia Minor (including Cyprus, which was ruled by the Ptolemies until the arrival of the Romans), and the Greek islands. While the Ptolemaic possessions in Asia Minor and in the Aegean were allowed to manage their own economic affairs, the partly Greek and partly Phoenician island of Cyprus was integrated into the system of state monopoly. Its copper mines were directly managed by the kings; Egypt itself possessed few mineral resources. Under the Ptolemies, Egypt made a strong effort to become economically independent. The wealth of the kings came largely from promotion of exports and restriction of imports (only lumber and ores had to be imported regularly). Southern Syria, Phoenicia, and Palestine, under Egyptian rule during the 3d century BCE, will be discussed below. The economic decline of Egypt, accompanied by increasing unrest and repeated insurrections by the native Egyptian population, began with the loss of its overseas possessions.

(e) The Seleucid Empire

Though it was impossible to enforce a unified economic system in the vast Seleucid realm, with its many nationalities and diverse economic structures, the Seleucids did institute a uniform administrative structure founded on their claim to be the legitimate heirs of Alexander and of the Achaemenids. The primary aim of the kings was to maximize income to maintain their expensive standing army, engaged in war most of the time, and to cover the ever-increasing expenses of the royal court and its officials. A centralized fiscal administration was therefore important, although there was no unified system of levies and taxes. The central government controlled the mints and monetary policies of dependent cities and principalities, making decisions about the export of those goods and manufactured products that were by right due to the king. Otherwise, the royal administration managed only the properties directly owned by the king (estates owned by his "house"). It is difficult to assess the actual size of these lands; they may have amounted to as much as half of the entire area ruled by the Seleucids.

The remainder of the land was owned and managed by the various subject vassal princes and cities. Since the kings could not rely on the indigenous populations to run the royal estates, Macedonians and Greeks were brought into the country as administrators. The numerous new cities founded by the Seleucids, settled mostly by Greeks, also served to stabilize the royal interests. Since cities governed their own affairs, they did not burden the royal administration, but strengthened the economy and created income in the form of taxes and tariffs. If they were also instrumental in furthering the Hellenization of the country, this was a secondary, and not necessarily intentional, result of their presence.

Some information is preserved about the royal estates in Asia Minor and Babylonia, but our information about the Seleucid empire is more meager than in the case of Egypt. The land of the numerous long-established temple states, especially in Asia Minor, was considered part of the royal estates, yet the priests continued to serve as administrators. The inhabitants of the villages belonging to these estates were serfs or, in many instances, temple slaves. There were also large estates owned by Persian noblemen or indigenous families. Some of these remained with their former owners; others were transferred to Macedonian noblemen, or else became the king's property and were administered in his name. In the villages connected with these estates the people were bondsmen or serfs, but rarely slaves. In Mesopotamia, the inhabitants of the temple territories remained free and retained their tribal organizations. While the kings interfered

Bibliography to §2.2e

Rostovtzeff, see under §2.2.c

Domenico Musti, "Syria and the East," in *CambAncHist* 7 (2d ed.) 175–218.

Getzel M. Cohen, *The Seleucid Colonies: Studies in Founding, Administration and Organisation* (Wiesbaden: Steiner, 1978).

Susan Sherwin-White, "Seleucid Babylonia: A Case Study for the Installation and Development of Greek Rule," in Kuhrt and Sherwin-White, *Hellenism in the East*, 1–31.

Fergus Millar, "The Problem of Hellenistic Syria," in Kuhrt and Sherwin-White, *Hellenism in the East*, 110–33.

little with the existing structures of Babylonia and Persia, they nonetheless could use the lands they owned to found cities and military colonies.

Southern Syria, Palestine, and Phoenicia, though governed by the Ptolemies for a century, had an administrative system rather like that of the Seleucids and quite different from that of Ptolemaic Egypt. The country was divided into hipparchies through which the kings exercised control, and there were tax farmers everywhere who looked after the royal interests—not only the collection of revenues, but also such matters as the registration of cattle. But various forms of limited self-government continued to exist, since the country was less uniform than Egypt itself. Several nations existed side by side with the partially Hellenized cities of the Syrian and Phoenician coast. Among these cities Sidon became the center of a far-reaching Hellenization; there were even colonies of Greek Sidonians in Palestine. The Ptolemies also granted a certain measure of self-government to temple states like Jerusalem and to sheikdoms like that of the Tobiads in Transjordan, as long as they cooperated with, or at times were even integrated within, the fiscal policies of the royal court of Alexandria. Here the people remained free and preserved their ethnic traditions but were required to pay an annual tribute. Similar arrangements were made with the coastal cities.

The Ptolemies founded Greek cities in this region, and thus promoted the process of Hellenization. Among these cities were Gaza and Ptolemais-Akko on the coast, Philoteria, Philadelphia (Amman), Pella in Transjordan, and several cities in Idumea. They were founded for political and military reasons. The primary aim was to prevent foreign invaders from building a base for attack on Egypt, and they were therefore equipped with fortifications. As the Zenon correspondence demonstrates, Greek merchants from Alexandria traded with both the coastal cities and the interior of Palestine and Transjordan; there Zenon, traveling through the country on behalf of his master Apollonios in the year 260/259 BCE, bought slaves and merchandise from the Nabatean caravan trade.

Little change came over this region with the transfer to Seleucid rule, except that the new subjects now gained direct experience of the difficulties that beset the Seleucid realm, especially its financial problems as it lost control over its far eastern and Anatolian possessions. The Seleucids reinforced the process of Hellenization as part of their effort to stabilize their increasingly shaky rule. These efforts, coupled with fiscal exploitation and outright temple robbery, had the unforeseen result of mobilizing the Jewish resistance against foreign rule.

(f) Taxes

Taxes were an important element of the administrative and economic policies of the Hellenistic empires. Direct taxes, levied on the whole population, un-

Bibliography to §2.2f

Aandreas M. Andreades, *A History of Greek Public Finance* (2d ed.; Cambridge, MA: Harvard University Press, 1933).

Henri Francotte, *Les finances des cités grecques* (Paris: Champion, 1909; reprint New York: Arno, 1979).

A. H. M. Jones, "Taxation in Antiquity," in P. A. Brunt, ed., *The Roman Economy* (Oxford: Blackwell, 1974) 151–85.

known in Classical Greece except in times of tyrannical rule, were customary in the empires of the east. They were usually levied only on those inhabitants of the cities who lacked full citizenship rights. Citizens might be asked to make contributions in exceptional circumstances, and wealthy individuals were expected to make voluntary payments on special occasions. All other taxes were indirect: customs duties, sales taxes, market taxes, and fees for the use of public facilities, such as port taxes. The Hellenistic kings further refined these systems of indirect taxation, but the huge expenditures of these vast empires, especially for maintaining the army and navy, required new sources of income. All conquered lands were legally owned by the king, and since income from agriculture (where labor was cheap) remained the primary source of wealth throughout antiquity, rents from the lease of agricultural lands and real estate taxes became the most important source of revenue. In order to maximize their income, the kings also used some direct taxes: head taxes, commercial license fees, and property taxes (including slaves, cattle, and buildings).

Similar systems of taxation were used throughout the Hellenistic kingdoms. Egypt had a central financial administration that collected taxes through state employees in Egypt itself. Tax farming was used for the Egyptian possessions in southern Syria, Asia Minor, and the Aegean islands. Wealthy people applying for a job as tax farmer went to Alexandria in person every year to submit their bids to the king. The highest bidder usually received the franchise. The story of the Tobiad Joseph, reported by Josephus (*Ant.* 12.169ff.), is a good example of this procedure. This system of tax farming was taken over by the Seleucids in Syria and later by the Romans.

Surviving sources testify to the heavy tax burden under Ptolemaic rule. The oppressive weight of the tax burden was due not so much to the high level of taxes as to the perfection of the system of collection, leaving no loopholes, and to exploitation by the tax farmers, who were also in the business of enriching themselves. Taxation under the Seleucids was less rigid. Established traditions and individual agreements determined the amount of real estate taxes and other revenues that cities, temple states, and tenants of royal lands had to pay. There was also considerable variation among the several satrapies; even within one particular satrapy the taxation was anything but uniform. It is difficult to determine how oppressive the taxes actually were. Tax levies do not seem to have been exorbitant, even in the case of the Jews (see 1 Maccabees 10 and 14), who objected not so much to the high level of taxes imposed upon them as to the principle of imposing taxes at all.

3. Society

(a) The Situation of the Indigenous Populations

It is impossible to make universally valid observations about the situation of the many nations that were ruled by the Macedonians and Greeks. In all regions of the east the indigenous people were subject to foreign rulers who—despite their propaganda of liberation—were uninvited and not necessarily preferable to previous masters. The lot of the indigenous populations varied greatly, depending on the different systems of royal administration and taxation, the availability of opportunities for Hellenization, and the differences between city and countryside.

The Egyptians under the Ptolemies were a social class strictly separated from the Macedonians, Greeks, and other immigrants (including many Jews). Nevertheless, native Egyptians did not become bondsmen of the king but retained their independence and freedom of movement within their district (*nomos*); under certain conditions they could move elsewhere in Egypt. They had their own courts, which adjudicated according to traditional Egyptian law. Though they were neither unemployed nor penniless, they constituted a class without privileges, totally dependent on their foreign masters, in whose wealth they had no share. Employment and income were determined by the king—no fundamental change from their former situation, though the rulers were now foreigners. Workers in farm and industry were strictly supervised, and what little income they did receive was subject to rigid taxation. In the case of default in debt payments, sale into slavery was a continuous threat. Even employees in the lower ranks of the royal administration (e.g., as the mayor or scribe of a village) were at the mercy of their Greek supervisors.

Greeks and Macedonians, speaking a foreign language and worshiping foreign gods, always remained foreigners as officials of an administration that was more efficient and demanding than that of their Pharaonic predecessors. At the end of the 3d and the beginning of the 2d century BCE the pressure of the bureaucracy increased. Further restrictions were imposed on possession of private property (even among the Greeks), and higher levels of service were demanded. The resulting riots and insurrections were intensified by general deterioration of the economy. The Ptolemaic administration was unable to control this unrest, despite bloody suppression and the kings' attempts to lend support to the cause of the indigenous Egyptians.

Repeated outbreaks of these insurrections were due not simply to the incompetence of the later Ptolemies; nor was it caused by the increasing political pressure of Rome. Nor is it likely that they arose simply from the Egyptians' desire to shake off this despised foreign rule. The primary cause was the centralized system of state monopoly, which imposed oppressive regulations on the native working class, but never granted a share in the proceeds of their labor. Not even in the later Hellenistic period, when many Egyptians had advanced to higher positions in the administration, and when many Greeks had become "Egyp-

Bibliography to §2.3

J. K. Davies, "Cultural, Social and Economic Features of the Hellenistic World," in *CambAncHist* 7 (2d ed.) 257–320.
Veyne, *Private Life*.

Bibliography to §2.3a

Horst Braunert, *Die Binnenzuwanderung: Studien zur Sozialgeschichte Ägyptens in der Ptolemäer- und Kaiserzeit* (Bonn: Rohrscheid, 1964).

tianized," would the unrest abate. The organization of the entire economy under a system of a centralized state monopoly finally led to depopulation of the villages, a decrease in cultivated farmland, and a national economic crisis. It was this system, designed to reap maximum profit from this fertile country, that ultimately resulted in nearly complete impoverishment of the indigenous working population.

In the Seleucid empire, the situation was completely different. The kings never tried to impose any unified economic system, nor did they attempt to assign a clearly defined social and economic status to the indigenous populations. On the contrary, newly inaugurated social structures, especially the Greek city, offered opportunities for social advancement that were often better than the inherited structures. Yet a large portion of the rural populations saw little change, because the Greek culture had little effect outside of the cities. Things also remained much the same in the tributary states and in temple territories with an autonomous internal administration. Foreign rule affected them primarily through military occupation, taxes, and tribute. In the older cities that had not been reconstituted as "Greek" cities, the inhabitants continued in their inherited vocations and occupations. They became Hellenized to some degree, more deeply in the west and at least superficially in the east.

The new cities, especially the large cities of Seleukia on the Tigris and Antioch on the Orontes, had mixed Greek and non-Greek populations. But since no one hindered the non-Greeks from moving into new occupations these cities transformed innumerable people into Greeks during the following centuries. Here the Seleucid empire created no social contrast between Greeks and non-Greeks. Other factors favoring the Hellenization process included increased mobility and economic opportunities. Large groups of the population could migrate, as is evident in the formation of Jewish diaspora communities in east and west. Greek culture and language were the means by which such groups could establish themselves in their new homes. Therefore the new institution of the Greek city proved to be particularly beneficial for the native populations.

(b) The Status of Greeks and Foreigners

Foreigners in Egypt, both Greeks and non-Greeks, constituted separate ethnic groups. They were subject to the same taxes as the native Egyptians and had to respect state monopolies. But foreigners had more rights than natives. Immigrants enjoyed a certain degree of self-governance, could organize (e.g., in gymnasium associations), and own real estate. Most foreigners had employment related to serving the king such as military service, administration, and supervising the economy, whether in agriculture or in factories operated by the state monopoly. Important positions in the civilian administration and the army were at first reserved for Macedonians and Greeks. Later on, Hellenized members of the Egyptian upper classes could also advance in the king's service. Some Greeks had other occupations, such as crafts, trade, or farming. But even the philosophers, scientists, and artists whom the king had called to the Museum could be removed at will, as actually happened in the 2d century BCE.

Foreigners were categorized separately in national *politeumata*, comprising a number of associations (cultic, professional, and gymnasium associations; see §2.3e). They had their own courts, which were allowed to use their own laws (e.g., Jewish law) as long as this did not create any conflicts with royal ordinances. All privileges were granted personally by the king and could be revoked. The associations were exclusive, and admission was supervised. To become a member of a Greek gymnasium association, for example, one had to pass a Greek language examination. Thus also children of the Egyptian upper class eagerly studied Greek grammar books, available everywhere, in order to pass these examinations.

Also in the Seleucid empire Macedonians and Greeks initially constituted the upper class, including the following groups: (1) the "house" of the king, that is, his family, friends and closest advisors; (2) the highest administrative officers and other members of the king's court, each with his own "house" and their subordinates, servants, and slaves; (3) independent Greeks, such as wealthy landed proprietors or wholesale merchants. From the beginning non-Greeks belonged to the second and third groups (Phoenician merchants, Iranian landed gentry and high administrative officers), but they were never very numerous. Everyone in these groups had various privileges and was likely very rich.

Macedonians and Greeks also served as officers and soldiers; lower-ranking public officials, especially those employed in the financial administration and the internal revenue service; owners of estates, farmers, and colonists; and in occupations typical of the Greek bourgeoisie, such as scholars, physicians, merchants, and craftsmen. Non-Greeks could be found in these privileged groups too, and as time went on, they came to dominate them. The kings strengthened and preserved these groups as a "Greek" middle class, not because they believed in the ethnic superiority of the Greeks, but because they relied on the strength of Greek education. It was a typical Greek idea that only education and training enable a human being to make an appropriate contribution to society. Even if some looked down on artisans as inferiors, what was needed for the large realms of the east was a great number of trained specialists (*technitai*) for numerous professions. Of course, there had always been specialists, especially in Egypt; but they had usually been recruited from restricted segments of the population, and entrance into those professions was a carefully guarded tradition. The Greeks alone had developed the concept of education and professional training as generally available opportunities, but the beneficiaries of this system had to adopt Greek ways. It is thus quite natural that the kings welcomed into these classes people who were willing to accept Greek culture (language, education, and professional training).

Demand for trained specialists in the Hellenistic kingdoms was considerable. The army and navy needed not only soldiers and sailors, but also craftsmen and artisans to build ships and construct and operate war machines. The royal administrations employed thousands of Greek-speaking specialists, accountants, financial experts, lawyers, scribes, and secretaries. These complex but usually well-functioning Hellenistic administrations, which bore little resemblance to their predecessors, were constantly concerned with training new generations of qualified professionals—always in notoriously short supply.

Many independent occupations achieved a high degree of professionalization in the Hellenistic period. There were physicians and lawyers; actors, dancers, musicians, and others with jobs related to the theater (organized in the professional associations of the Dionysiac *technitai*); professional athletes; and finally philosophers, scientists, poets, lawyers, and physicians. Some of these were in the employ of the kings (as in the Alexandrian Museum) or supported by private patrons; others had to earn their living as orators, wandering preachers, or else in private praxis. Egypt apparently had a public health service, but this is less certain in the Seleucid empire. Though it earned little respect and less remuneration, teaching became a widely practiced profession. The cities employed teachers for their schools, and wealthy people often hired private tutors.

All professions required a general education in elementary reading and writing in school and gymnasium. There were no professional schools. Philosophical schools and libraries did not educate people for particular professions. Rhetorical schools provided a "liberal arts" education without a professional specialization; their graduates might become orators or lawyers or architects. Schools for physicians were the only exception; otherwise, professionals were trained through apprenticeships. Theaters, for example, also served as schools for actors and dancers. Guilds and professional associations oversaw admission and training for particular jobs, and thus came to play a significant role in Hellenistic life. In fact, professional associations were the backbone of the large urban middle class and might include citizens as well as aliens and slaves.

(c) Slaves and Slavery

Various forms of personal dependence, servitude, and diminished legal status were by no means rare in the older cultures of antiquity. In the Hellenistic and Roman periods, slaves were offered for sale in large numbers and bought like any other goods. Certain types of agriculture and industrial production depended on

Bibliography to §2.3c: Texts

Thomas E. J. Wiedemann, *Greek and Roman Slavery* (Baltimore, MD: Johns Hopkins University Press, 1981). Anthology of 243 ancient texts illuminating all aspects of slavery.

Jo-Ann Shelton, *As the Romans Did: A Sourcebook in Roman Social History* (New York: Oxford University Press, 1988) 168–89.

Bibliography to §2.3c: Bibliography

Joseph Vogt and Heinz Bellen, eds., *Bibliographie zur antiken Sklaverei*, rev. by Elisabeth Herrmann with Norbert Brockmeyer (2 vols.; Bochum: Studienverlag Dr. N. Brockmeyer, 1983).

Bibliography to §2.3c: Studies

Moses I. Finley, ed., *Slavery in Classical Antiquity* (Cambridge: Heffer, 1968).

Keith R. Bradley, *Slaves and Masters in the Roman Empire: A Study in Social Control* (Tournai: Latomas, 1984; New York: Oxford University Press, 1987).

Keith Hopkins, *Conquerors and Slaves* (SSRH 1; Cambridge: Cambridge University Press, 1978).

William Westermann, *The Slave Systems of Greek and Roman Antiquity* (MAPS 40; Philadelphia: American Philosophical Society, 1955).

Veyne, "(Roman) Slavery," in idem, *Private Life*, 51–69.

W. Z. Rubinsohn, *Die grossen Sklavenaufstände der Antike. 500 Jahre Forschung* (Darmstadt: Wissenschaftliche Buchgesellschaft, 1993).

slave labor. Slave labor of this type was introduced into Greece around the 6th century and to Rome in the 4th century BCE. Since slavery in the Roman imperial period resembled that of the Hellenistic period in many ways, it will also be treated in this chapter.

The slaves of Classical Greece were usually non-Greeks. The wars of the Hellenistic period increased the supply of new slaves considerably. Many prisoners were taken on all sides during the wars of the Diadochi, the Hellenistic kings, and the Greek cities and leagues. As a consequence, large numbers of Greeks and easterners, many of them Hellenized, were sold into slavery. Another source of supply of new slaves came from the pirates who were increasingly active in the late Hellenistic period, systematically kidnapping people and selling them in the major slave markets. Often towns were attacked and the entire population sold into slavery. Piracy haunted the Greek homeland more than the areas in the east. When the Romans conquered Greece and Macedonia and subjugated the realms of the Hellenistic empires in numerous campaigns, immense numbers of prisoners fell into their hands, including many Greeks.

Slavery reached its peak during the last hundred years of the Roman republic (ca. 150–50 BCE). There were fewer wars of conquest during the Roman imperial period after Augustus, and so the supply of new slaves dropped noticeably. At the same time, manumissions of slaves increased in the imperial period, which in turn led to a marked decrease in the number of slaves. On the other hand, there were still ways to obtain new slaves: children of slaves remained the master's property, even if they were fathered by the master; abandoned children— exposure of freeborn children was not rare—could be taken as slaves; sometimes people sold themselves into slavery, either for economic reasons (to escape poverty) or to obtain influential positions.

The economic, social, and legal status of slaves in antiquity was very different from, and often far better than the status of the African slaves in the United States. In antiquity, slaves were by no means deprived of all legal rights; in the Roman empire, they had the right to retain property (though the master had no obligation to pay them wages) and to appeal disputes with their masters to the local governor or the city praetor in Rome. But all slaves' rights were limited, and some were only nominal. Slaves were admitted as witnesses in court, but only under torture. They could be beaten by their masters, or even executed. With the Roman emperors, the legal status of slaves was somewhat improved and humanized: abuse and killing of slaves without just cause became a punishable crime. Though slaves as a class were frequently despised as lazy, dishonest, or stupid, ethnic and racial prejudices rarely played a role in the institution of slavery.

The economic situation of slaves spanned a wide range, depending on their education, professional training, and abilities. Slaves employed in households were charged with the numerous jobs and services that an ancient household required—the better-situated ancient households were much more independent economically than they are today. Grinding corn, baking bread, sewing clothes, pressing oil, boiling soap, and other activities were carried out within the home itself. Slaves who performed these jobs were members of the household and would often eat together with their masters' women and children; the situation was different when the number of slaves increased considerably in the households of the very rich.

Numerous slaves were employed in farming, especially on the large landed estates of the Roman senatorial class, in manufacturing and industry, and in the mines. Work in the mines was dangerous and was sometimes assigned as punishment. While some of the major factories might employ a few dozen slaves, the operators of mines and estates often owned hundreds or thousands of slaves, especially when the establishment belonged to the state and was managed by royal or imperial administrators. In those instances important management positions were also open to slaves. When employed as managers and supervisors, slaves might acquire knowledge and skills that could prove useful after their eventual manumission. Slaves also occupied leading positions in the "house" of a king or an emperor, or in the household of wealthy merchants and businessmen. As the number of educated Greeks increased among the prisoners of war, more slaves could use their scientific, literary, or rhetorical training in employment as teachers, court poets, librarians, and high-ranking administrators.

In the Seleucid empire and in Egypt slavery played a minor role. Egypt knew an indigenous form of temple slavery (*hierodoulia*): slaves performed the more humble duties in the temples and were employed in factories and on agricultural lands owned by the temples; but these were of only minor economic significance. Among the Greeks and other foreigners in Egypt, only the king and a few wealthy citizens were rich enough to own slaves. The kings did not favor slavery and tried to restrict it as much as possible through the imposition of high taxes on slave owners. An edict is known from Syria that forbids serfs to be considered and treated as slaves. The Seleucid kings had no interest in reducing the subjects of their realm to the status of slaves. The institution of temple slavery continued to exist in some areas of Asia Minor, and the Seleucid kings themselves and some wealthy people employed slaves; but the economy at large, and especially agriculture, did not rely on slavery. The only Hellenistic kingdom in which slavery played a major role was Pergamon, where slaves were employed on royal agricultural estates, in factories, and major building projects (e.g., the royal library)—though the latter required some degree of technical skill.

Rome was much more dependent on slaves during the 2d and 1st centuries BCE. This was less the case for manufacturing and industry, in which slave owners usually contracted out their slaves for wages, of which they collected a proportionate share. Such slave labor was expensive. Slave labor could compete successfully with the free labor market only when the owner of a plant or business also owned the slaves he employed. Therefore this use of slaves remained relatively rare. On the other hand, the huge Roman agricultural estates could not have functioned without employing whole armies of slaves.

It was primarily in southern Italy and Sicily that the major slave insurrections took place, namely those of Eunus of Apamea (136–132 BCE) and Spartacus (73–71 BCE). During this period the Romans indeed employed a multitude of slaves, both in Rome itself and on the estates—the number of slaves in the city of Rome alone has been estimated at between 200,000 and 300,000—one-third of the total population! To what extent these slave insurrections were caused by social problems is difficult to determine. Agricultural slaves generally had a harder life than their urban counterparts. Religious and nationalistic motivations seem to have played a role. In Pergamon, where the situation of the slaves was comparable to that in Italy, the insurrection of Aristonikos (133–130 BCE) reveals some of the motivations for the insurrections. This was a revolt against Rome, which had just inherited Pergamon through the testament of the last Attalid. Aristonikos disputed the legitimacy of the testament, claimed to be the legal heir of the last king, and organized the rural population for struggle against Rome. He proclaimed an end to all slavery and called his followers "citizens of the state of the sun" (Heliopolis), thus drawing on some of the utopian and social-revolutionary ideas of his time (see §3.4e).

Opinions about slavery vacillated between acceptance, rejection, and indifference. Although condemnations of slavery are heard from philosophers and other social critics, slavery is rarely thought to warrant justification. Revolutionary demands for abolishing slavery are missing. The Sophists of the Classical period were the first to deny the right to own slaves. Stoics and Cynics emphasized repeatedly that slaves were human beings just like everybody else, possessing the same natural abilities and rights. The same philosophers, however, were never willing to criticize the institution of slavery from a fundamental perspective, but stressed that true freedom was independent of social status. Other voices argued that slaves were inferior "by nature."

The basic problem remained unresolved. Slaves were, on the one hand, human beings, and were expected to receive benefactions from their masters, be it money and gifts, or at least kindness, mercy and understanding. Masters who treated their slaves in an inhumane way might risk being murdered by their slaves (though in fact this was a very rare occurrence) or at least losing the respect of their friends—at stake was the masters' moral reputation rather than the well-being of the slaves. Slaves were expected to respond with devotion and good service. On the other hand, slaves were possessions, and could be discarded if they became useless. The human value of slaves depended on dutiful service, not on their natural human dignity.

Though often depicted as ignoble buffoons and even criminals, slaves could appear in comedy and literature with the same weaknesses or virtues as other people. In their dealings with each other, masters and slaves were depicted as having the same human obligations and deserving the same kind of respect. In religion, apart from civic cult, differences in social position were irrelevant. The Eleusinian mysteries accepted Athenian slaves as well as full citizens and initiated them into their rites. The new religions of Near Eastern origin, which were often brought to the west by the slaves themselves, acknowledged no differences in social status. Christianity was one of these religions. Though Christian slaves could be admonished to obey their masters, they served as presbyters and deacons in Christian churches.

Manumission of slaves was considered a good work, and one of the first rights that Constantine would later grant to the bishops' courts was the manumission of slaves. But neither Christianity nor other new religions advocated the abolition of slavery as an institution (even if a few church fathers indeed demanded just that).

Genuine social-critical ideas did not take root in antiquity, and the new religions did not regard the social position of slaves as an essential liability; and when they insisted on equality for slaves within their own ranks, they assumed the noblest traditions of Greek thought.

Although in late antiquity slavery was not outlawed altogether, it was at least severely restricted and had almost disappeared by the beginning of the Middle Ages. Many factors contributed to the diminution of slavery. Philosophical and Christian criticism played some role. But more important were changes in the economic structures, which no longer favored slave labor. Slavery became too expensive; dependent sharecroppers were more profitable. Increasing impoverishment of the average household and the gradual disappearance of the middle class, especially during the 3d century CE, made owning household slaves more and more difficult.

(d) The Status of Freedmen and Freedwomen

Former slaves would seem to be better off after manumission—at least if they could find suitable employment, which could be difficult for unattached women. Once slaves had been freed, however, their status of dependency did not end. There were some benefits. They would now receive a real name—as slaves they often had insulting names like "Lucky" (*Felix*) or "Useful" (*Onesimos*) or "First" or "Second." If the master was a Roman citizen, his slaves would gain the citizenship upon manumission. He might well set them up in business, such as shop-keeping, which they would run for their former master. Freedmen and freedwomen had the right to marry; however, the evidence of tomb inscriptions indicates that most preferred to live in continuing concubinage.

Manumission did not mean that former slaves could go wherever they liked and do whatever they wanted. They would no longer have legal obligations to their former masters; but the patronage system, especially in Roman society, still bound them to their master who now became the patron. As his client, the freedman had to pay daily visits to his new patron for a morning greeting, might receive a small sum of money in return, and could be asked to perform various services. The freed person was now even more closely bound to the master by the bond of gratitude. Powerful and influential people often used their freedmens' sense of obligation to employ them as agents in important business or political missions. Children of former slaves were in a strange legal position in Roman custom: children born to a slave woman who was subsequently freed legally became the slaves of their mother; and if a father bought his own son out of slavery, he became his freedman, not legally his son.

Bibliography to §2.3d: Texts
Shelton, *As the Romans Did*, 190–205.

Bibliography to §2.3d: Studies
Peter Garnsey, *Social Status and Legal Privilege in the Roman Empire* (Oxford: Clarendon, 1970).
Susan Treggiari, *Roman Freedmen during the Late Republic* (Oxford: Clarendon, 1969).
Sandra R. Joshel, *Work, Identity, and Legal Status at Rome: A Study of the Occupational Inscriptions* (Norman, OK: University of Oklahoma Press, 1992).

In Roman society, some freedmen became notorious for their wealth. But even if they had become Roman citizens, they were not accepted by the society of the freeborn as equals. Even a poor nobleman would sneer at a wealthy freedman, and the attempts of freedmen to exhibit their wealth were a constant topic of ridicule. Children born after their parents' manumission were considered freeborn and thus had a better chance of receiving an education and entering society without social stigma. A famous example is the poet Horace, the son of a freedman. Wealthy freedmen, however, remained a small minority. Thousands of freed slaves with little chance for independent economic survival relied on their client status. While they were slaves, the master was obligated to feed and clothe them, even if economic misfortunes meant that he could no longer offer them meaningful employment. Once freedmen and freedwomen lost their employment, or were without a patron, nobody was obligated to take care of them. The mass manumissions of slaves on an estate on the death of the master committed these people to the urban proletariat, which may help explain Augustus' severe limitation of this practice.

(e) The Position of Women

In all ancient Mediterranean societies women had limited legal standing and no political rights. The status of women was not uniform; in some Greek cities and in Egypt, women had certain rights of property and could testify in court. However, no traces survived of archaic matriarchal systems or of legal equality, as may once have existed in Bronze-Age Mykene and Crete. As a rule, women were subject to their fathers or husbands, and their domain was restricted to the house. In Greece, respectable women were excluded from the "symposia," the dinner and wine parties that formed the center of the social life of the citizens.

Bibliography to §2.3e: Bibliography:

Leanna Goodwater, *Women in Antiquity: An Annotated Bibliography* (Metuchen, NJ: Scarecrow, 1975).

Bibliography to §2.3e: Texts

Mary R. Lefkowitz and Maureen B. Fant, eds., *Women's Life in Greece and Rome: A Source Book in Translation* (2d ed.; Baltimore, MD: Johns Hopkins University Press, 1992).
Ross S. Kraemer, ed., *Maenads, Martyrs, Matrons, Monastics: A Sourcebook on Women's Religions in the Greco-Roman World* (Philadelphia: Fortress, 1988).
Shelton, *As the Romans Did*, 290–307.

Bibliography to §2.3e: Studies

Helene P. Foley, "Women in Greece," in Grant and Kitzinger, *Civilization*, 3. 1301–17.
Sheila K. Dickison, "Women in Rome," in Grant and Kitzinger, *Civilization*, 3. 1019–32.
Judith P. Hallett, *Fathers and Daughters in Roman Society: Women and the Elite Family* (Princeton, NJ: Princeton University Press, 1984.)
John Peradotto and John P. Sullivan, eds., *Women in the Ancient World: The Arethusa Papers* (SUNY Series in Classical Studies; Albany, NY: State University of New York Press, 1984).
Sarah B. Pomeroy, *Goddesses, Whores, Wives, and Slaves: Women in Classical Antiquity* (New York: Schocken, 1975).
Eadem, *Women in Hellenistic Egypt from Alexander to Cleopatra* (New York: Schocken, 1984).
Suzanne Dixon, *The Roman Mother* (Norman, OK: University of Oklahoma Press, 1988).

Marriages were arranged, and marriage contracts were negotiated between the groom (or his father) and the bride's father. Upon the death of her husband, a wife, together with all his property, was inherited by the male relative next in line, who was often required to marry her.

The Hellenistic period brought a number of changes. Greater mobility, the fact that households became less self-sufficient, and an increasing emphasis on education gave women more opportunities and more leisure, though probably only in the upper classes. Marriage was no longer always an economic arrangement between families, but could also be seen as a valuable opportunity for sharing a common life. In the Classical period, husbands had been advised to instruct their wives in the duties of the household; now a husband could teach his spouse liberal arts and philosophy. Women appeared increasingly among poets and prose writers, and the literature of the Hellenistic period no longer reveals the misogynist attitudes of its classical predecessors. In at least some cities (apart from Athens, which remained quite conservative in this regard) women might hold public office, own property, and run households.

There is much less information available about women in families of less wealth and lower social status. It seems that here distinctions in status and legal rights mattered little, at least for married couples. Men and women simply had to work together to make ends meet. Women would always have to share the work of farm and garden. Certain domestic skills, such as spinning and weaving, were traditionally required of women. Prostitution or other occupations of service to men were the lot for many unmarried women. Among artisans, married women might assist their husbands in their craft.

In Rome, at least as early as the late republic, women had more rights and privileges than in the Greek world. Wives could appear in public together with their husbands in the theater and at dinner parties. As a person *sui iuris,* a wife could manage her own and—in case of the husband's absence—also her husband's property, and could appear as a witness in court. Wives retained rights over all property that they brought into marriage. Divorce could be initiated by either partner. What was not acceptable was a woman in civic or military service. Any Roman women known to have exercised important political roles belonged to the aristocracy; such women would often exert their influence behind the scenes through their husbands or sons.

It was in the sphere of religious and cultic activity that women had the greatest opportunities. A number of priestly offices were traditionally reserved for women, such as the Vestal Virgins in Rome. Women could serve as *prytaneis* in Ephesos, the highest cult official of the city. Many female names appear in inscriptions of the high priests of the imperial cult in the provinces. Priestesses and other female officials appear especially in new cults of Near Eastern origin, particularly in Judaism and Christianity, where women are attested in such offices as president of a synagogue (*archisynagogos*), or as apostle (Rom 16:7), deacon, and president or patron (Rom 16:1) of Christian congregations. Under no circumstances, however, could a woman assume public political and voting rights. Where women did play significant roles, among the Ptolemaic rulers and in the Roman imperial house, where they also received the title "Augusta," this was due to dynastic prerogative and should not be cited as evidence for the general emancipation of women.

(f) House and Family

It is impossible to discuss all details of this topic, especially as regional and ethnic differences play a considerable role. But some of the basic features common to all societies of the Hellenistic and Roman imperial period must be described briefly. Household (*oikos*) and family were the smallest functioning cells of society everywhere. Both in the cities and in the rural areas, households were economically semi-independent units, which produced much of the necessary food and clothing from raw materials. The household included the master of the house, his wife, children, aging parents, unmarried relatives, as well as servants and slaves. Though the father as head of the household would be set apart in many ways, the rest of the family would share various responsibilities, eat together (including slaves, at least originally), and observe religious rituals.

In legal terms, the authority lay in the hands of the master, owner, and father of the family. In actual practice, managing the daily household chores, supervising female slaves, and educating the younger children were the responsibility of his wife, except in wealthier families, where the care of children was delegated to a nurse and a "custodian" (*paidagogos*). In middle-class and poorer families, father and mother shared most of the responsibilities equally; in the more affluent houses, master and mistress had little part in running the household and supervis-

Bibliography to §2.3f: Texts
Shelton, *As the Romans Did*, 18–167.

Bibliography to §2.3f: Studies
A. R. W. Harrison, *The Law of Athens*, vol. 1: *The Family and Property* (Oxford: Clarendon, 1968).
W. C. Lacey, *The Family in Classical Greece* (London: Thames & Hudson, 1968).
Beryl Rawson, ed., *The Family in Ancient Rome: New Perspectives* (London: Croom Helm, 1986).
Eadem, *Marriage, Divorce, and Children in Ancient Rome* (Oxford: Oxford University Press, 1991).
Keith R. Bradley, *Discovering the Roman Family: Studies in Roman Social History* (New York and Oxford: Oxford University Press, 1991).
Susan Treggiari, *Roman Marriage* (Oxford: Oxford University Press, 1991).
Suzanne Dixon, *The Roman Family* (Baltimore, MD: Johns Hopkins University Press, 1992).
John Clarke, *The Houses of Roman Italy 100 B.C.–A.D. 250: Ritual, Space, and Decoration* (Berkeley, CA: University of California Press, 1991).
Claudine Leduc, "Marriage in Ancient Greece," in Schmitt Pantel, *History of Women*, 235–94.
Sarah B. Pomeroy, "Greek Marriage," in Grant and Kitzinger, *Civilization*, 3. 1333–42.
Susan Treggiari, "Roman Marriage," in Grant and Kitzinger, *Civilization*, 3. 1343–54.
Valerie French, "Birth Control, Childbirth, and Early Childhood," in Grant and Kitzinger, *Civilization*, 1355–62.
Veyne, "From Mother's Womb to Last Will and Testament" and "Marriage," in idem, *Private Life*, 9–49.
Yvon Thébert, "Private Life and Domestic Architecture in Roman Africa," in Veyne, *Private Life*, 313–409.
Alexander Gordon McKay, "Houses," in Grant and Kitzinger, *Civilization*, 3. 1363–83.

ing their own children. In Rome, though fathers traditionally schooled their sons, parents who were wealthy enough to employ a wet-nurse sometimes did not bother themselves with raising their children. Cicero's "mother" tongue was Greek, the language he learned from his Greek nurse.

Much has been said about the patriarchal structure of the ancient family. To be sure, the Romans told grim stories of men exercising their paternal powers to punish, disown, or even execute wayward children. In reality, depending on their personalities, most male heads of households were not tyrannical rulers of family and household. Though the father had exclusive rights over property, including slaves, and judicial and financial authority even over adult children, the mistress of the house would normally exercise exclusive authority in domestic affairs, often had control of her own money, and might herself own some slaves. In post-Classical Greece, wives increasingly exercised their own rights in education, and in the buying, selling, and inheritance of property—even if the husband in some societies had to function as a cosigner.

Marriage, which was restricted to the freeborn, had little relationship to love. Marriages were arranged, often for financial reasons. In Roman society, either partner could initiate a divorce simply by moving out of the house, or by notifying the spouse. In Jewish Palestine, the situation may have been different: If Mark 10 reflects actual practice, only the husband had the right to divorce. In the middle and lower classes, divorce was economically difficult. But it was quite common in the upper class, and was rarely prompted by the infidelity of one of the partners—though adultery was often the pretext! Abortion was widely practiced, and unwanted children were usually exposed. Poor parents might arrange an adoption for their children, to ensure them a career or give them a better chance of an inheritance. Adopted children were often better cared for than physical offspring.

It is difficult to speak of private life in a Greek or Roman family, because there was little privacy, even less in the houses of the wealthy than in those of the less privileged classes. There was constant coming and going by slaves, friends, relatives, visitors, and clients. Husband and wife might even have trouble finding a place for private sex, because a slave girl normally slept in her mistress' room, while one or several slaves were always on call for their master. Tenderness and warmth between blood relatives was not considered important. A husband might have his most intimate personal relationship with a young slave, boy or girl, whom he kept as a concubine and page. The story of the boy Antinoos, who was the pet of the emperor Hadrian, is typical. A divorce or the death of the husband was not necessarily a disaster in wealthy families; the rich widow was the most attractive prospect in Roman society. Liaisons with wealthy widows are the sort of relationship that Ovid had in mind when writing his *Ars Amatoria*. In less affluent families, however, the relationship between husband and wife and between parents and children was more intimate. As a consequence, the death of the husband meant real trouble for the widow, unless she could remarry or return to her family.

The Stoics, and later the Christians, preached a very different morality of marriage, which reflects truly middle-class values: Husbands and wives should love and respect each other; the wife should be subject to her husband; and they should not divorce. Sexual relationships between adult men and boys were frowned upon. Sexual love—so agreed the philosophers, the Jewish teachers, and the Christians—should serve exclusively for procreating children. Abortion and exposure of children were forbidden. Children should obey their parents, and parents were obligated to love their offspring and care for them. From the beginning, Christian congregations considered it a primary duty of the community to care for widows and orphans.

(g) Wealth and Poverty

In the Hellenistic period, especially in the countries of the east, agriculture remained the primary basis of economic prosperity and one of the most important sources of income, for both villages and cities. Rural areas, with villages of free farmers, serfs working on large estates, or temple territories, accounted for some of the agricultural lands. Other lands were controlled by the cities. Originally owned by large groups of citizens they formed a basis for the economic prosperity of all inhabitants. Land use varied from subsistence farming to intensive grain production and seminomadic cattle herding. While people in rural areas were usually poor and often bound in servitude, they were not an impoverished proletariat. In the cities, however, impoverishment was a real social problem. Wherever a large segment of the city population lost its share in the land, the formation of a proletariat was the consequence.

The Greek cities consisted of essentially two classes. The upper class was formed by the established aristocratic families, who owned large estates from which they drew their wealth. (In the Roman period, these landowning families were more strictly defined as "decurions," that is, those who formed the city council [curia] and supplied candidates for political office.) The large middle class consisted of farmers, craftsmen, merchants, teachers, and various other groups of technitai (§2.3g). This group included citizens as well as foreigners (though the latter could not own real estate), free people as well as slaves. Some owned their own businesses, others worked for wages. The social stability of the cities, was tied closely to the well-being of this class. Impoverishment could result in the formation of a third class: a disenfranchised and unemployed proletariat, consisting of freed slaves without a patron, petty farmers who had lost their land to debt, widows and their children, and foreigners who failed to make a fortune.

In Greece itself, and perhaps to a certain degree also in the older Greek cities of Asia Minor, more land gradually passed into the hands of the small upper class. The middle class became increasingly dependent on wages, and the proletariat grew considerably. (This later occurred in Roman Italy on an even larger scale.) After an initial upturn, wages fell throughout the Hellenistic period and prices rose. While population remained steady, the number of available jobs

Bibliography to §2.3g: Texts

Shelton, As the Romans Did, 129–52.

Bibliography to §2.3g: Studies

Sandra R. Joshel, Work, Identity, and Legal Status at Rome: A Study of the Occupational Inscriptions (Norman, OK: University of Oklahoma Press, 1992).

decreased because of increasing economic difficulties and the rise of slave labor in households, agriculture, and industry, a trend that forced free laborers out of work. The contrast between rich and poor became more pronounced. Among the poor, free workers and indebted farmers were worse off than many slaves. Slaves were fed and clothed by their masters, whether or not they could be employed profitably. Slave holders in the Greek east who experienced economic problems often freed large numbers of slaves, thus adding to the unemployed proletariat; this was later prohibited by law, since it increased competition on the labor market and misery for the working class. Unrest, revolts, strikes, and insurrections of the urban working classes became a regular part of city life during the Hellenistic period.

In Greece, all revolts aimed at the redistribution of land were doomed to failure, not only because of the resistance of the rich; the country was naturally poor in arable land and mineral resources and suffered continual depredation and warfare until the Roman conquest. The methods of warfare were both cruel and economically devastating. Frequently half of the soldiers of a vanquished army were killed in battle. Captured soldiers were sold into slavery along with the civilian inhabitants of a conquered city to recoup the expenses of war. Whole cities were razed to the ground: Thebes was leveled by Alexander the Great, Mantineia by the Achaians and the Macedonians, and finally Corinth by the Romans. Profit by plunder became the primary purpose of warfare; the vanquished country was despoiled, its fields devastated.

Piracy, free-booting, and kidnapping were also commonplace in Hellenistic Greece. Not merely islands and coastal cities, but also the interior of the country suffered under this scourge. More than once a thousand or more people were captured in a single raid. Surviving sources from this period leave the impression that sacrilege, desecration of temples, and violation of the rights of asylum had become everyday occurrences. Warring parties often used pirates for their own purposes; Crete and the Aetolians were especially closely allied with pirates, and the Romans had no scruples about buying slaves from them.

(h) The Associations

The Hellenistic kingdoms as well as the Roman imperial government left a large space in the life of its citizens that was not regulated by the government,

Bibliography to §2.3h: Texts

Shelton, *As the Romans Did*, 308–23.

Bibliography to §2.3h: Studies

Nicholas R. E. Fisher, "Greek Associations, Symposia, and Clubs," in Grant and Kitzinger, *Civilization*, 2. 1167–97.

Idem, "Roman Associations, Dinner Parties, and Clubs," in Grant and Kitzinger, *Civilization*, 2. 1199–1225.

Franz Poland, *Geschichte des griechischen Vereinswesens* (Leipzig: Teubner, 1909).

Mariano San Nicoló, *Ägyptisches Vereinswesen zur Zeit der Ptolemäer und Römer* (MBPF 2; 2d ed.; 2 vols.; München: Beck, 1972).

Nock, "The Guild of Zeus Hypsistos," in idem, *Essays*, 2. 414–43.

Horsley, "A Fishing Cartel in First-Century Ephesos," in idem, *New Documents*, 5. 95–114.

nor did the administrations of the individual cities concern themselves with many matters that were important for the life of the society. While the officially recognized cults, public streets and buildings, weights and measures in the market place, and citizenship lists and taxation were controlled by the cities, many other significant societal infrastructures were left to the initiative of the inhabitants. Associations, who filled this void, became the most important structural element of city life. The gymnasia, centers for the physical and intellectual training of the young people, were sponsored by private associations, as were the various trade and manufacturing enterprizes. Associations also played a role in the welfare and social care of their members. In all instances, funds for these activities would be provided by wealthy members as benefactions. As long as benefactors were willing to share considerable portions of their wealth with other members, the functioning of many of these infrastructures of the cities was guaranteed.

The dinner party, always connected with wine drinking (*symposion* literally means "drinking together"), was the very center of social life in the Greek city. Groups that met regularly for *symposia* were defined by shared interests, such as particular forms of worship, professional bonds, neighborhoods, inherited descent, or political interests. Women were normally not admitted, except to amuse the gathered males as singers, dancers, or sexual partners. In some instances, women formed their own associations, usually related to ritual activity. It is difficult to imagine how anyone could play a political, social, or professional role in society, or for that matter have any fun, without membership in an association.

The Hellenistic period saw the greatest proliferation of associations. Though the Romans outlawed such groups in the late republic, associations and clubs remained an important social institution in the Greek east well into the Roman imperial period. While some private and religious clubs existed among members of the aristocracy, most belonged to the large middle class of the cities. These clubs permitted persons of different social and economic status to be united as equals in a common religious, economic, or social cause. Many of the associations of the Hellenistic cities were continuations of older Greek associations, but some continued native traditions of associations in Egypt and in the Seleucid countries. During the Hellenistic period associations grew increasingly independent of traditional political and social structures, and came to be based primarily on voluntary commitments.

Because of the great variety of associations and the considerable differences from place to place, their classification is difficult. Nor has the vast source material related to associations in the ancient world, though frequently consulted, undergone a systematic and comprehensive treatment in scholarship during the past eighty years. It is useful to distinguish (1) associations that fulfilled tasks for the whole community (especially gymnasium associations); (2) professional associations, guilds, unions, and cartels; (3) clubs serving social purposes; and (4) religious associations (*thiasoi*).

Almost all associations served multiple purposes. Gymnasium associations, for example, were organized to serve athletic and pedagogical functions as public institutions, but were also social clubs. Different associations might share much in common in their methods of organization. Social clubs and professional guilds could have religious features and be dedicated to, or named after, a certain deity. Sometimes this was a formality, at other times it implied a serious religious commitment. The character of our sources does not always permit clear distinctions. Musical clubs preferred Apollo as their patron deity, while guilds of actors and dancers of the theater were organized under the patronage of Dionysos. Later on Dionysos also became the most popular patron of social and dinner clubs. In other cases, such clubs might claim to be a *thiasos* dedicated to a local or foreign deity who was worshiped under the name of a Greek god.

The most important associations of communal life were the gymnasium societies. They appear wherever Greeks settled, were officially recognized and regulated by the authorities of the city, received subsidies, and possessed certain privileges, including the right to own real estate, buildings, and other property. Their presiding officer was the gymnasiarch, whose office was a "service" (*leiturgia*)—he received no salary and was expected to finance festivals and athletic competitions on special occasions out of his own pocket. Here, as in other associations, the benefactions of the rich, often in the form of lavish gifts to their fellow citizens, regularly handed out during common meals, served to lessen social envy and to soften the impact of economic inequalities. The primary purpose of the gymnasium associations was to build, equip, and maintain the gymnasia, and thus to advance the Greek education of the young. At the same time, the gymnasia served as "clubhouses" for various social events. Life in a Greek city would have been inconceivable without a gymnasium and its association.

There was a great variety of professional associations. Not all were supervised by the cities or by the kings; some were Hellenized guilds or unions formed by non-Greek residents. The associations of royal officials in Egypt were a continuation of an older Egyptian institution. Associations of craftsmen and merchants are in evidence in large numbers in the cities of Asia Minor, especially in the Roman period. Most likely they existed in the Hellenistic period as successors to even older native guilds. Professional associations were particularly important in view of the great mobility of the population; they offered accommodations and lodging to traveling colleagues and helped them find work and settle in a foreign city. This is the context of the depiction of Paul in the Book of Acts as able to find work in his profession of tentmaking when he moved to another city (Acts 18:1–3).

The guild of merchants from Berytos on the island of Delos is a typical example of this kind of association. They were organized as a *thiasos* of Poseidon and owned a large house, equipped with sanctuary and meeting hall, where Phoenecian merchants and their Roman counterparts could stay while conducting their business. Associations of Dionysiac *technitai,* which included in their membership anyone whose profession was related to the theater, were the most widely distributed. These associations occupied privileged positions and in some places were organized under royal supervision. Their members served as teachers, so that these associations also functioned as schools for actors, dancers, and musicians. It can be assumed that other professional associations exercised a similar control over vocational training, perhaps as part of their admissions structure.

Clubs serving primarily to encourage social fellowship existed in great numbers. In the upper class, philosophical discussions at dinner meetings were highly praised, and even prompted the production of a special genre of literature (the "Deipnosophists"). But good fellowship at regular dining and drinking parties was desirable in all classes of Hellenistic society—even if such parties would sometimes end with quarrels, rowdy processions through the streets, and the occasional lawsuit. Some associations wrote into their membership regulations that forbade members to take their quarrels to court (see also 1 Cor 6:6–7) and required that they be settled within the association. Social associations might appear under such names as "Club of the Young Men" or "Club of Seniors" and similar designations. Their sole purpose was to make all sorts of social gatherings possible, for example, for people from the same country or the same school. Such associations were popular among noncitizens and foreigners, who were excluded from the regular duties and opportunities of full citizenship.

Religious associations were primarily founded for gods and cults that were not sponsored by the political community and so did not have publicly recognized sanctuaries. They often became the vehicles for disseminating the new propaganda religions from the Near East (Sarapis, Isis, Attis, Men Tyrannos, Christ, and others). Many Dionysos associations were not purely social clubs, but serious cult associations; private Dionysiac mysteries must have been celebrated in houses, unconnected with the established temples of the god, which were usually found in close proximity to the theater. These religious associations normally admitted men regardless of their social class, especially slaves and foreigners, and often women too. Any of the members, even women or slaves, was allowed to occupy positions of leadership. The same liberality was evident in early Judaism and Christianity, which organized their communities on the model of such associations. This reveals a new, and in many ways utopian sense of community in which differences in social status had become irrelevant.

In the Roman imperial period, dining clubs and associations maintained their traditional roles; they may even have become the primary social infrastructure for those who were disenfranchised politically. In the upper classes, there was a new emphasis on the art of preparing the most sophisticated kinds of food and of providing congenial environments for guests. Though the extravagances of such dinners, especially when hosted by wealthy freedmen, became a topic of discussion in poetry and literature (see Petronius' "Dinner of Trimalchio" in his *Satyricon*), the normal life and regular meetings of most associations proceeded on a much more modest scale.

The Roman administration tried to regulate associations. Colleges of priests and public officials were supervised in their regular meetings. The most prominent of these were the associations of the *Augustales,* composed mostly of freedmen in the various cities of the empire. Subject to imperial or local oversight, they were charged with supervising various aspects of the cult of the Roman emperor. Other associations were either encouraged to request imperial or municipal recognition or were simply allowed to exist informally, as long as they were not thought to threaten public order. If professional associations, like those of bakers or shippers, promised to benefit the public, they might even receive privileges and tax exemptions. On the other hand, emperors were notoriously fearful of the possibly seditious activities and drunken bouts of associations. Funerary clubs, which guaranteed a decent burial for their members, were deemed to be among the most innocuous. Most suspicious were those that met at odd hours (Christians met early in the morning) and had leaders who were women and slaves. Pliny reports that he found female slaves holding offices in Christian churches (*Epist.* 10.96).

4. THE HELLENISTIC CITY

(a) The Founding of New Cities and Military Colonies

The eastern Mediterranean and the countries of the Fertile Crescent could boast of a very ancient urban culture, especially along the Phoenician coast and in Mesopotamia. Greek colonists had already founded new cities on the coasts of the Mediterranean and Black Seas. But Alexander and his successors initiated an unparalleled process of urbanization that would continue into the Roman imperial period and fundamentally change the social and economic structures of large areas that had previously been primarily rural.

The only exception was Egypt. There was only one truly ancient Greek city: the merchant city of Naukratis, founded by Miletos ca. 650 BCE. With its own mint and a famous faience industry it was the only place in Egypt open to Greek trade. The Ptolemies founded only one new city in Egypt, Ptolemais Hermiou in Upper Egypt, which became the center of Hellenism for the southern part of the country. Otherwise new settlements were attached to the major royal estates, which were held in fee by royal officials. Greek immigrants constituted their upper class (administrators, soldiers, and craftsmen); all the services were performed by native Egyptians. These settlements were not "cities" but living quarters for technocrats and soldiers. Nor did they function as places where Egyptians could adopt Greek culture and become Hellenized.

Alexandria "at" Egypt, however, founded by Alexander, and residence of the kings, became the symbol of the Hellenistic city for the whole Mediterranean world. Alexandria was unlike any other Greek city, since it did not develop under its own administration; it was the king's city. It quickly grew to a size much larger than any city of Greece or Ionia, and second only to the capitals of the

Bibliography to §2.4

R. E. Wycherley, *How the Greeks Built Cities* (2d ed.; London: Macmillan, 1967). This is the best and most readable general introduction.

F. E. Winter, "Building and Townplanning," in *CambAncHist* 7 (2d ed.) 371–383.

Richard Tomlinson, *From Mycenae to Constantinople: The Evolution of the Ancient City* (London: Routledge, 1992).

A. H. M. Jones, *The Greek City from Alexander to Justinian* (Oxford: Clarendon, 1940; reprint 1971).

Victor Tcherikover, *Die hellenistischen Städtegründungen von Alexander dem Großen bis auf die Römerzeit* (Ph.S 19/1; Leipzig: Dieterich, 1927).

Fraser, *Alexandria*, 1. 3-92.

Seleucid empire, Antioch on the Orontes and Seleukia on the Tigris. Alexandria was equipped with splendid edifices. A third of its area was occupied by a complex of royal buildings: the palace, the library, the Museum, the zoological garden, and the tomb of Alexander the Great. There were two magnificent boulevards, grandiose squares, lovely fountains, and great temples, of which the one dedicated to Sarapis was the most prominent.

The people lived in several distinct quarters, the largest being for the Greeks and for the Jews. The total population is estimated to have been at least half a million, possibly as much as a million. A small majority were free inhabitants, the rest slaves. Some were full (Greek) citizens; the other free inhabitants, including the Jews, were organized according to their own constitutions (*politeumata*), but were disadvantaged in various ways, especially during the Roman period. This social situation became the cause of much unrest, sometimes leading to bloody conflicts. As a trade center, Alexandria was the equal of other large cities of the eastern Mediterranean. As a city of the arts, sciences, and literature, however, it had no rivals during the period of the flowering of Hellenism.

The Seleucids, beginning with Seleukos I and continuing under his successors Antiochos I and Antiochos II, resumed Alexander's policies and made the founding of new cities an important part of their political program. If these new cities became the most significant element in the process of Hellenization, this was not necessarily the original purpose of their foundation. They were established primarily to protect important trade routes and military supply lines, to restrain the mountain tribes in the north and the Arab tribes in the south, and to defend against the Galatians in Asia Minor.

Quite a few of these towns were founded not as *poleis,* but as military colonies. The founding of a new polis was expensive and required the investment of considerable time and effort. Military colonies (*klerouchiai*) offered many advantages because maintaining a standing army of paid mercenaries could become expensive over time. Once soldiers were settled on royal lands that they could farm, they possessed a source of independent income, and a new bond was established with the country that they would have to defend in case of war. This policy also offered opportunities for Greek immigrants, since service in the Seleucid army would eventually give them a home and a farm of their own. Finally, more effective agricultural methods could be introduced in this way, and new areas opened up for agriculture. Even if military colonies did not enjoy the same privileges as the new "cities," they eventually fulfilled similar functions.

Among the hundreds of new cities and colonies, the foundations of the Seleucids included many cities of first importance: Antioch on the Orontes in Syria, the political capital of the realm; the important port cities Seleukia of Pieria and Laodikeia on the Sea; in Asia Minor, Thyatira of Lydia, Apamea Kibotos of Phrygia, and Seleukia and Antioch of Cilicia; in Mesopotamia, Edessa, Dura Europos, Antioch of Mygdonia, and, most important of all, Seleukia on the Tigris, the eastern capital. Only a few colonies existed in Persia and Media, but several fortresses were built, some as reconstitutions of older Persian cities, such as Seleukia on the Elaios, erected on the site of the ancient Persian Susa.

Over time, all these new foundations became "cities," although they had been founded differently. In a new polis the land became property of the city and was then transferred to citizens as their personal property. In military colonies the land allotted to the individual settlers remained the legal property of the king, although its use could be passed on through inheritance; it reverted to the king only when there was no heir. Other differences relate to the people who settled in these new foundations. In a military colony, the inhabitants were ordinarily Greek and Macedonian soldiers. In other instances, civilian immigrants founded daughter-cities of their home city. Others were created through *synoikismos*, that is, several villages and towns were united into a new city; in this case, and when a king transferred entire groups of people from one place to another in his realm for resettlement, the non-Greek population would predominate. In this way Jews from Mesopotamia were settled in Asia Minor (Josephus, *Ant.* 12.148). Finally, older cities were reorganized as Greek poleis, provided with new privileges, and given a new name (often the old name reemerged at a later time). In this way Edessa was refounded as Antioch, Nisibis as another Antioch, Ecbatana as Epiphaneia. Other older cities were Hellenized: Uruk-Warka became Orchoi; although it included within its walls a sizable Greek population, the administration remained in the hands of its original inhabitants.

Seleukia on the Tigris (not far from Baghdad) was founded by Seleukos I as the royal capital. As a new center for banking and east-west trade, the primary basis of its wealth, it took the place of the ancient city of Babylon. Its population is estimated to have been about 600,000. Even when Seleukia came under Parthian rule, it maintained some independence as a Greek city. It was finally destroyed during the campaigns of the Romans against Parthia, first by Trajan, and finally in 164 CE. Seleukos I also founded Antioch on the Orontes, which became the capital after his death. Antioch experienced its first flowering under Antiochos IV Epiphanes, was conquered by Rome in 64 BCE, and became a splendid metropolis and cultural center as the capital of the Roman province of Syria. This was the location of the first major Hellenistic Christian congregation. Though badly damaged by an earthquake and frequently embattled in the wars with the Sassanian Persians and in conflicts between the Byzantine empire and the Muslims, Antioch remained an important city into the Middle Ages.

(b) City Plans and Buildings

Plan and buildings of the Hellenistic city continued those of the Classical Greek city. Powerful walls were laid out according to the geographical features of the site and often enclosed an area larger than that occupied by the city proper. A centrally located agora was surrounded by stoas, law courts, and government buildings (*bouleuterion, prytaneion,* city archives). Temples could be situated near the agora or elsewhere in prominent places. A theater, on the slope of a hill, an odeion, and several gymnasia and fountain houses were other important features.

The city plan named for the architect Hippodamos had been used in Ionia as early as the 5th century BCE. The streets would be laid out at right angles, dividing the entire city into equal rectangular blocks, which were subdivided in such a way that all citizens received lots of the same size. Only public buildings and temples were permitted to occupy one or more of these blocks. Hippodamos had used this plan for the construction of Piraeus, Athens' port city, and Thurii in southern Italy; it became the basic pattern for the new Hellenistic cities and was also used in rebuilding cities in the Greek areas of Asia Minor, for example at Miletos, the home of Hippodamos, and in Ephesos and Priene. This last city illustrates the rigorous application of this pattern, even though the city was built on the slopes of a steep hill.

The new Hellenistic cities, when compared to the cities of Classical Greece, received a number of modifications which, though dictated by the Hippodamian plan, also reflected the changed social and economic situation. An acropolis, originally the fortified castle of the king, which a later democratic spirit adorned with temples, is frequently missing altogether in the Hellenistic cities. A fortified place within the confines of the city, which could also serve as a tyrant's strong-hold against the citizens, was discordant with the new citizens' view of their city. Thus, the acropolis disappeared, or was only superficially fortified, while the defense of the city was entrusted completely to the city walls. Their irregular circle enclosure could include large vacant spaces if this was advisable for defense. (This practice differed markedly from Roman foundations, where the walls of cities often followed the pattern of the rectangular Roman army camp.) The gates and bastions were built of hewn stone; the walls themselves consisted of two layers of dressed stones, enclosing an earth and rubble core, or were built of mud brick on a stone foundation. The walls were very strong, since they had to withstand the onslaught of highly developed siege machines; their construction therefore posed a considerable challenge to the energy and initiative of the citizens.

In the Classical period, the agora was of irregular shape and was left open to the major streets of the city and the residential quarters of the city. As the center of political and economic life, it was surrounded by market halls, administrative buildings, courts, and temples. In the Hellenistic period, however, the agora was built in a strictly rectangular form; surrounded by stoas on all four sides, it was closed off from the rest of the city. Thus the agora became one building usually with only two entrances, which in the Roman period were often decorated with impressive gate structures. In larger cities, a second agora was reserved for administrative buildings and temples, while the agora used for trade and shop-ping assumed the character of a mall. New stoas were built in all public places; older stoas were enlarged, often with two inside colonnades. As the center of city life and open to all people, they served various purposes: trade and relaxation, entertainment and talk, private or public debates, or the display of artwork. It was here that philosophers and missionaries would hold forth with their message and teachings.

Temples and other public buildings had to fit within the rectangular layout of the city streets. The most important temples were situated directly on the agora, as were also the *bouleuterion* (the meeting place of the city council) and the *prytaneion* (the magistrates' hall with the sacred hearth). Other major buildings could encompass two or three city blocks, and larger sanctuaries might even be situated outside the city walls, especially if ancient tradition demanded that they remain on a specific hallowed site (like the famous temple of the Ephesian Artemis.)

Whenever possible, the theater was also adjusted to the Hippodamian layout of the city. If the city wall enclosed a mountain or hill, its slope would be used for the auditorium. Later the Romans, masters of building in concrete, introduced theaters and amphitheaters in which the seats rose to an immense height, supported by artificial terraces and huge vaulted substructures. A stage building with a *proscenium* (raised stage) became a regular part of the theater during the Hellenistic period. The actors would play on this stage, although the originally diamond-shaped, then circular or semicircular orchestra would still be used in addition to the stage. The auditorium (*cavea*) and the stage remained two separate buildings, separated by entranceways from the right and the left (*parodoi*). In the Roman period the theater was conceived as a single building, closed on all sides. It was also the different tastes of the Roman period that resulted in rebuilding the orchestra into an arena that could be filled with water for the performance of small-scale naval battles.

Gymnasia are among those ancient buildings whose impressive ruins have survived. They were originally gymnastic fields surrounded irregularly by a few buildings; their most notable feature was a covered hall (*xysthos*), as long as a stadium, for running practice in bad weather. In the Hellenistic period, the gymnasia were constructed as well-designed architectural units. A rectangular field was surrounded by colonnades on all sides, allowing access to a number of rooms serving various athletic purposes (dressing, bathing, and anointing with oil), but also for social gatherings, lectures, and instruction, even as small shrines and libraries. Some of the gymnasia were of immense proportions. The harbor bath-gymnasium complex at Ephesos, built in the Roman period, included a gymnastic field of 200 by 240 meters.

Every major city also possessed a stadium, usually situated outside the city walls. The cities began to equip these stadiums with rows of stone seats (originally spectators sat on the grass of the sloped enclosure) and with semicircular rows at one end, which could be used as a small theater.

The houses of the Hellenistic cities were built according to a number of traditional types. The Hippodamian layout of the city, with its standard-sized blocks and subdivisions, determined the size of the houses. One might find two, four, or even more houses in each block of the city. Though the number of houses in each block was originally the same throughout, this egalitarian principle was often violated over the course of time. Wealthy citizens might acquire an entire block for their spacious homes. In cities that did not use the Hippodamian plan, the dwellings of the rich and the poor, spacious peristyle houses and small buildings, could be found side by side in various mixtures. Among the various types, the peristyle house was preferred by wealthy citizens: an open rectangular paved court, often covering an elaborate system of cisterns, was surrounded by porticoes on all sides, giving access to rooms of different size. While the rooms rarely had any windows opening to the street, their windows to the central court provided light and air. Houses with two (and sometimes even more) stories were not rare. The peristyle court could be covered with beautiful mosaics which, along with wall frescoes, decorated many of the rooms as well. Even poorer houses were built around a central court, though without a peristyle.

Further developments in the Roman period preserved most of the basic features of the Hellenistic cities, but also brought some characteristic changes. Two wide main boulevards, the *cardo* and the *decumanus,* consisting of a central wagon road, gutters and drains, and porticoed sidewalks, intersected at the town's center. Their architecture and decoration displayed the city's wealth. The agora took on the features of the Roman forum, becoming a structure that could be completely closed off by monumental gateways. Elaborate bath complexes were built, with several vaulted halls enclosing facilities for undressing (*apodyterium*), cold bath (*frigidarium*), warm bath (*tepidarium*), and hot bath (*calidarium*). Aquaeducts helped answer the increasing demand for fresh water, and artistic fountain houses replaced the simpler wells of an older period. City renewal of this sort began exactly at the time when Christianity was attempting to establish itself as a new religion in the major cities of the eastern Roman empire, as well as in Rome itself. By then urbanization had reached even such relatively remote areas as lower Galilee, the region of Jesus' hometown of Nazareth. Urban renewal, initiated by Rome, changed the social structures of almost all areas of the Mediterranean world and brought new jobs and a renewed prosperity to the older Hellenistic cities.

5. AGRICULTURE

(a) Agricultural Production and Its Setting

While urbanization was a significant development of the Hellenistic and Roman periods, the cities, whether they had been long established or were newly founded, maintained their character as regional centers and marketplaces for the surrounding villages and hamlets, where many people normally lived. Much agriculture and animal husbandry was "subsistence farming": its purpose was to provide for the needs of the city that controlled the region. As much as 70% of the population's nutritional requirement came from cereals, so most of the arable land was committed to growing grain. Wheat and emmer (a hard two-kernel wheat) was grown throughout the ancient Mediterranean. If the soil was poor, barley rather than wheat was the primary grain product. Next to cereals, vegetables, peas, beans, fava, and olives supplied what was needed. Produce and

Bibliography to §2.5: Texts

Shelton, *As the Romans Did*, 152–66.

Bibliography to §2.5: Studies

Dorothy J. Thompson, "Agriculture," in *CambAncHist* 7 (2d ed.) 363–70.

K. D. White, "Farming and Animal Husbandry," in Grant and Kitzinger, *Civilization*, 1. 211–45.

K. D. White, *Roman Farming* (London: Thames & Hudson and Ithaca, NY: Cornell University Press, 1970).

Peter Garnsey, *Famine and Food Supply in the Graeco-Roman World: Responses to Risk and Crisis* (Cambridge and New York: Cambridge University Press, 1988).

herbs came from private gardens or were brought into the market from nearby villages. Meat was not a staple of the diet. Cows and oxen (not horses) were used primarily as draft animals, while dairy products came from sheep and goats. Sheep provided wool for clothing. While beef and lamb were available occasionally, the primary source of meat was pigs.

The prohibitive cost of overland transport limited the export or import of agricultural products. Oil and wine could be exported, depending on available sea routes; larger quantities of grain products could be obtained from far away as long as there was direct access to the Mediterranean. For its everyday needs a city had to rely on its own food production. Only some of the largest cities, like Alexandria and later Rome, became permanently dependent on the import of large quantities of cereals from overseas—imports that could be secured only through generous royal and imperial subsidies.

All the countries of the Hellenistic empires included areas of rich agricultural production. Agriculture remained the primary source of wealth throughout the ancient period. If cities controlled agricultural areas that could satisfy the needs of their own population, special products suitable for export, like oil and wine, were additional sources of income. Greece possessed a highly developed agriculture and sometimes specialized in oil and wine production for export; but only a tenth of its area was suitable for farming, leaving it unable to produce enough staple food for its own population. The Greeks were therefore always dependent on imported grain, most of which came from Thrace and southern Russia.

Other sources of grain imports, namely Cyprus, Phoenicia, and the Cyrenaica, were in the hands of the Ptolemies during the early Hellenistic period, which meant that the Ptolemies controlled the Greek food market. By increasing their own grain production, they made Egypt one of the primary grain exporters of antiquity, a role that it continued to play in the Roman period. Access to the Egyptian grain market became vital for control over the entire Mediterranean realm. Egypt itself was self-sufficient in every aspect of its food production, but the fertility of its fields depended upon the Nile, its source of irrigation and fertilization.

The Seleucid empire encompassed the most diverse agricultures, ranging from nomadic animal husbandry to highly sophisticated irrigation systems for growing wheat, especially in Mesopotamia. Deficiencies could be corrected by regional trade within the Seleucid realm, but difficulties arose when agricultural areas were lost in the gradual dissolution of the empire. Rome was originally fully capable of providing for its own population. However, as many areas in Italy were converted to oil and wine production for the lucrative export trade, grain products had to be imported, especially for the needs of the growing masses of Rome's urban population.

(b) Innovations in Agriculture

The amount of land devoted to agriculture increased markedly during the Hellenistic period. Several attempts were made in Greece to drain swamps, a practice that is also attested for the Fayyum in Egypt. The Seleucids made similar efforts in Mesopotamia; technicians and engineers would be supplied by the king. Vacant and fallow areas were opened up for agricultural use by founding new cities. In other cases, land owned by the king was sold, leased, or given outright to new settlers to establish farms and estates.

Little is known from the Seleucid empire about improvements in agricultural methods or introduction of better machinery. Unlike the Ptolemies, the Seleucid kings made no attempt to centralize their economy. It is certain, however, that the Seleucids introduced many innovations—analogous to new methods put to use in Ptolemaic Egypt—especially on the farms cultivated by Greek settlers. But there was little change for the native farmers, the temple territories, and the estates that remained in the hands of their former owners. The Persians had already begun to acclimatize oriental fruit trees in Asia Minor, and the Seleucids probably continued those efforts. But Persian fruit trees like the apricot, peach, and cherry did not become established in the Mediterranean world until the Roman period, when they were introduced first of all to Italy. The situation was similar in the introduction of most citrus fruits.

Much more is known about Egypt. The Greeks introduced iron plowshares, hoes, and shovels to replace the traditional wooden tools. The wheel for raising water was introduced by the Ptolemies, permitting more effective irrigation than had been possible through the use of human water carriers. Machines for processing harvested fruits were either Greek inventions or Greek improvements of older tools. Several new kinds of produce were brought into the country by the Ptolemies, including apples, nuts, garlic, and several improved varieties of traditional vegetables. Egypt had few vineyards during the time of the Pharaohs; the popular national drink was beer. The Ptolemies expanded the vineyard regions and introduced grape varieties from Greece and Asia Minor. Egypt had always grown olives, but primarily for consumption as fruit. The Ptolemies encouraged oil production in order to meet the local demand for vegetable oil; import duties of up to 50% were charged for olive oil produced elsewhere. Sheep were imported from Asia Minor and Arabia to breed flocks that could produce better wool; the Greek residents of Egypt, accustomed to woolen garments from their home country, did not want to give up their traditional clothing. Pigs, horses, and donkeys were brought in from other countries for breeding purposes. At the same time, the kings introduced Egyptian produce to other areas of their domain. Typical Egyptian plants like beans, lentils, mustard, and pumpkins were established in this way in southern Syria and Palestine.

The kings of Pergamon followed the Ptolemaic-Egyptian example and actively engaged in planning and managing agricultural production. They were especially concerned with improving cattle breeds, in part in order to obtain skins for their parchment industry (see §2.6d). Their stud-farms became famous.

In spite of the great interest of Roman writers in describing farming methods, Roman agriculture followed Greek models and showed few if any innovations. The development of a large scythe to replace the sickle for harvesting grain seems to have been limited to Gaul and Britain. There is also evidence in Gaul for the invention of a grain harvester, drawn by a mule or ox; but it has not been successfully reconstructed on the basis of ancient depictions and descriptions. Roman interest in improving and propagating viticulture, especially in Gaul and

Germany, is well known. The Romans were also successful in improving graft-
ing methods and in introducing eastern fruit trees, such as the peach and the
cherry, and promoted the consumption of figs for their high nutritional and sugar
value. The contribution of Roman agriculture was its mediation of Greek and
Near Eastern foods and production methods to western and central Europe.

6. Manufacturing and Industry

(a) The Arts and the Social Status of Artisans

The artisan was the backbone of Hellenistic and Roman culture. All ancient art
media, from architecture to metallurgy, from pottery and painting to weaving and
dyeing, required an intimate knowledge of materials and highly developed skills
that could be acquired only with years of training. The knowledge of a craft was
handed down, usually in small workshops, from father to son and from master to
apprentice; the secrets were family traditions. In all crafts, much of the work
involved producing simple and sometimes crudely made items for daily use. But
there was also an astounding amount of work devoted to manufacturing items
that even today provide examples of the highest perfection in execution and
beauty.

Two facts about ancient artisans are most striking: there was little specializa-

Bibliography to §2.6: Texts

Shelton, *As the Romans Did*, 127–67.

M. M. Austin, "Greek Trade, Industry, and Labor," in Grant and Kitzinger, *Civilization*, 2.
723–51.

Keith Hopkins, "Roman Trade, Industry, and Labor," in Grant and Kitzinger, *Civilization*, 2.
753–77.

J. K. Davies, "Cultural, Social and Economic Features of the Hellenistic World," in *CambAncHist*
7 (2d ed.) 257–320.

Carl Roebuck, ed., *The Muses at Work: Arts, Crafts, and Professions in Ancient Greece and Rome*
(Cambridge, MA: MIT Press, 1969).

Engineering and Technology:

R. J. Forbes, *Studies in Ancient Technology* (9 vols., Leiden: Brill, 1944–64; some vols. revised,
1965–1971).

K. D. White, *Greek and Roman Technology* (Ithaca, NY: Cornell University Press, 1984).

Albert Neuburger, *Technical Arts and Sciences of the Ancients* (London: Methuen, 1930).

J. G. Landels, *Engineering in the Ancient World* (Berkeley and Los Angeles, CA: University of
California Press, 1978; reprint 1981).

Moses I. Finley, "Technical Innovation and Economic Progress in the Ancient World," *Economic
History Review* 2/18 (1965) 29–45.

Bibliography to §2.6a

Alison Burford, *Craftsmen in Greek and Roman Society* (London: Thames & Hudson, 1972). The
most readable and comprehensive introduction to this topic, with rich illustrations.

Eadem, "Crafts and Craftsmen," in Grant and Kitzinger, *Civilization*, 1. 367-88.

Sandra R. Joshel, *Work, Identity, and Legal Status at Rome: A Study of the Occupational Inscriptions* (Norman, OK: University of Oklahoma Press, 1992).

tion; and no fundamental distinction was drawn between the designing master-mind and the executing technician.

The lack of specialization is most evident in building and architecture. Work-shops were small, employing no more than two to five workers. Construction work on major buildings, such as temples, stoas, and law courts, would be farmed out to a large number of workshops, but not according to specialty; each workshop would be assigned one section of the building. Each artisan working on the project had to be skilled in working with stone, but also with wood for the scaffolding and the beams of ceiling and roof. He was both stonemason and carpenter. Even a knowledge of working with metal was required for fitting the iron clamps used to secure stones and column drums. The craftsman also had to master the arts of quarrying and constructing and operating machines designed for transporting and lifting building materials. The sculptor Pheidias, overseeing the building of the Parthenon on the Athenian Akropolis, also cast bronze statues and made the wood, gold, and ivory statues of Zeus in Olympia and Athena Parthenos in Athens. Pheidias was no exception. While a simple shoemaker or fuller was as a rule restricted to his particular trade, any distinguished artisan was able to work in several different crafts. Architects and sculptors were able to execute both arts, and many architects started their career as carpenters.

Antiquity made no distinction between the people who planned and designed a work and those who executed these designs. The building trade, in contrast to other crafts, required a master planner, due to the complexity of the construction of a temple or a ship. But the designing architects were at the same time stone-masons or carpenters, and the people designing foundries might have learned their craft as miners or metal workers. The ancient attitude is expressed by the fact that the same daily wages were paid to the master architect as to the masons and carpenters, although an architect's training was more demanding because he had to engage in theoretical studies of geometry, mathematics, and other sci-ences. In other crafts the artisan would manage all the stages of production, from obtaining the raw materials to finishing the final product.

In spite of the highly developed skills of the artisans, they did not occupy an honored place in society. Some were foreigners or slaves; but even those who had citizen rights were considered to be nothing but *banausoi*, people forced to earn their living by the work of their hands. Accordingly, they were not paid very well for their work, hardly more than unskilled laborers, even if they were well known for the high quality of their designs and products. Nonetheless, artisans were proud of their craft, cherished the tradition of their art, and often expressed their pride by signing their names to their works, whether it be a painted am-phora, a fresco, a mosaic, or a temple. Their works were indeed very much in demand, and many earned international fame.

Throughout antiquity there was a chronic shortage of skilled craftsmen, arti-sans, and architects. There were never enough skilled people to fill the demand, yet this lack never led to better pay or improved social status, which might have attracted a larger number of people to these professions. Other factors that discouraged people from seeking employment as artisans were the many years of training required and the difficulty and dangers of the work. When the apostle

Paul speaks of the way in which he earned his own living as "toil and sweat, working night and day" (1 Thess 2:9), he is describing the daily life of every ancient artisan. Miners were exposed to deadly fumes and to not infrequent mining accidents; tanners and fullers were exposed to poisonous chemicals, smiths to fire and sparks, and workers in construction had to do much of their work on high scaffolding, since the fluting of columns and the fitting of capitals and of the entablature decoration took place only after all the dressed stones were positioned. The crippled god Hephaistos was an apt image of the artisan.

(b) Mining and Metal Industry

The Hellenistic states had an enormous demand for metals, especially gold, silver, copper and tin (for the production of bronze), and iron. In previous times, gold had been collected from alluvial river deposits, such as the gold (actually electrum) of the Paktolos River responsible for the proverbial wealth of the Lydian kings. These resources were quickly exhausted. Deep-vein mines had been developed during the Classical period, especially for silver; the Laurian Mines of Attika and the silver mines of Thasos, which had been opened by the Phoenicians, are among the best known. Iron ore was found in many areas of Greece, especially in the Spartan mines in the Taygetos Mountains and the Athenian mines on Euboia and the island of Seriphos. For Macedonia, gold and silver ore came from the Pangeon Mountain near Philippi, and iron was available from Thrace. Iron ore deposits of Greece had already been exhausted by the Classical period, so the Greek cities were forced to import what they needed; gold and silver mines yielded only a limited supply. Finding new sources was therefore extremely important. Alexander the Great included prospectors in his army, who were charged with investigating new sources of ore.

In the newly conquered areas, many rich sources for metals existed and had been exploited for centuries. The Ptolemaic kings had access to gold and electrum at their border with Nubia, and to the copper of the Sinai (soon abandoned in favor of the richer resources of Cyprus), as well as to the iron mines of Lebanon. They suffered no shortages as long as they held on to their overseas possessions. The Seleucids controlled numerous sources of most ores and metals, scattered over their vast realm. But gold had to be imported from Siberia, and these imports reached no further than Baktria after the rise of the Parthians. The Seleucids were also cut off from silver in Asia Minor once they lost their western provinces. The kings of northern Asia Minor and Armenia controlled the mining of iron ore; thus the Seleucids were finally left with nothing but the copper and iron mines of southern Syria, which had formerly belonged to Ptolemaic Egypt.

Bibliography to §2.6b

John F. Healy, Mining and Metallurgy in the Greek and Roman World (London: Thames & Hudson, 1978).

Idem, "Mines and Quarries," in Grant and Kitzinger, Civilization, 2. 779–93.

T. R. Glover, "Metallurgy and Democracy," in idem, Greek Byways (Cambridge: Cambridge University Press, 1932) 58–77.

Rome found itself initially without any direct access to metals, because the Apennine Mountains of Italy lack ores. The acquisition of Sardinia in 238 BCE, after the First Carthaginian War, supplied iron, silver, and copper, and the conquests of Spain and Britain provided access to unlimited quantities of all necessary metals. Spanish silver permitted the Roman mint to issue as much as fifty metric tons of coinage annually.

The techniques of ancient mining are well known from the study of the mines of Laurion in Attika and the Roman silver mines of Spain. Mining galleries, branching off from the larger shafts, were never higher than forty inches; all the work had to be done while the miners lay on their backs. Ventilation and lighting (by torches and oil lamps) were poor. Huge quantities of ore had to be moved; one ton of silver might require the digging of as much as 100,000 tons of ore, equivalent perhaps to the annual workload of 1000 men. All ore had to be hauled out of the mine, often from a great depth (some Spanish silver mines were over 800 feet deep). Considering the manpower needed to drain underground water and the huge amounts of wood required for the refining process, it becomes clear that armies of workers had to employed, all working under horrible conditions with little reward. Free workers would normally not work in the mines. Slaves, prisoners, and convicts were employed instead, including Christians in later times. Sometimes the local population would be forced to work in the mines. Conditions changed only through legislation starting in the time of Hadrian in the 2d century CE, when the diminishing supply of slaves made it necessary to hire free workers and to improve conditions; miners had to be supplied with public bathing facilities, food, and clothing; teachers were invited to operate schools in mining settlements.

The methods of metallurgy were highly developed even before the Hellenistic period, especially in the countries of the Near East. Manufacturing was not industrialized, but remained in the hands of skilled artisans working in small family workshops. Some workshops specialized in the production of only a few items. Because of the great demand for war equipment, the production of weapons by smithies was the most important branch of this industry. Weapons were mass-produced and bought by the kings, and later by the Roman army, for storage in large arsenals. The best steel was produced in Asia Minor, but throughout antiquity India remained famous for manufacturing the best hard steel products. (What became known in the Middle Ages as "damask" steel was actually Indian steel imported through Damascus.) Household goods made of bronze were also mass-produced.

Demand for luxury items increased in the Hellenistic period and rose in the Roman imperial period as the tastes of the Roman aristocracy diversified. This gave new incentives to makers of artistic vessels in eastern workshops. Toreutics, that is, the art of producing decorated cups, plates, amphoras, and other vessels in gold, silver, and bronze, thrived in the east. Egypt's production of such vessels continued to flourish throughout the period, to meet both domestic and external demand. Their exports, however, had to compete with products from Syria, eastern Asia Minor, and Armenia, especially the famous workshops of the Chalybians on the southeastern shores of the Black Sea. Persian toreutic art continued to flourish and strongly influenced the Hellenistic toreutic style. In the Roman period very beautiful products also came from the cities around Mt. Vesuvius, from northern Italy, and from Gaul.

(c) Textiles

Textiles were ordinarily manufactured in individual households, mostly by women. Small workshops supplied local demand. Precious textiles and luxury clothing were produced in factories and exported. Manufacture of textiles relied on traditional methods that saw little change throughout antiquity. An exception was the invention of the vertical loom, originating in Egypt and introduced to Italy and Greece at the beginning of the Roman period. The books of the philosopher Bolos of Mendes (2d century BCE) about dyeing, with instructions for imitating precious dyes and textiles, were frequently copied and excerpted, demonstrating that there was an intense interest in dyeing clothes. Some of their material reappeared later in the pseudoscientific literature of alchemy.

Production of fine textiles differed from almost all other ancient crafts because here alone the primary suppliers were large factories employing dozens of people, often slaves and women. The countries of the east were the leading producers of textiles. The Greeks improved the production and distribution of wool to satisfy Greek demand in the east. Flax was grown in Egypt, but was rare in other countries. Fine-textured linen, known as byssos, in great demand and famous worldwide, was produced in the royal weaving mills and, as in former times, in temple mills. Its decorative motifs, however, were no longer Egyptian but Greek.

Other export articles included Egyptian and Babylonian carpets. Silk was imported from China, beginning at the time of Alexander the Great; it was processed in Phoenician factories before being shipped for sale to western countries. Silk production was developed on a small scale on the island of Kos. Silk products manufactured there in large factories, where female slaves did most of the work, were known as "Coan fabrics." The kings of Pergamon promoted methods for refining and improving textile production. Several cities of their realm produced carpets for export. Pergamon was especially renowned for its production of curtains and brocades interwoven with gold, manufactured in royal factories by mostly female slaves.

(d) Ceramics and Glass

Ceramic articles for daily use were produced and sold at local potters' shops. Artistically designed ceramic products were a specialty of several older Greek cities. The export of such articles was still important during the 3d century BCE. From Greece they were shipped all over the east, and from Sicily primarily to Egypt. Before long, pottery imitating Greek forms and decorations was produced in eastern countries. Egyptianized Greek forms were successfully exported by

Bibliography to §2.6d

Anita Engle, ed., *Readings in Glass History* (4 vols.; Jerusalem: Phoenix, 1973–74).

Egypt. Red-figured Attic ware, predominant in the Classical period, was replaced by black-glazed pottery without figurative design. Light-colored vessels with various decorations were also made in the Hellenistic period.

Expensive ceramic vessels were less in demand, because toreutic products had become more fashionable. Gold, silver, and bronze vessels with artistic reliefs decorated the houses of the rich everywhere. In imitation of popular toreutic products, ceramic vessels with decorations in high relief began to appear about 250 BCE. Near Eastern influence inspired the production of faience vessels (painted pottery with a glossy glaze). A new type of ceramic product appeared in Rome at the time of Augustus, the so-called *terra sigillata* ware. These cups and plates are thin-walled, with a layer of glossy clay, imitating vessels made of metal. They are unpainted though sometimes decorated in relief. Mass production of this earthenware was at first centered in Italy, but very soon spread to the provinces of Gaul, where the forms were influenced by local traditions of ceramic manufacture. Large quantities of exports from these workshops have been found as far away as Britain and Egypt. Local factories in Asia Minor, Syria, and Spain produced imitations of *terra sigillata* of a lesser quality.

Glass was rarely manufactured in Greece, though it was not unknown there. Most glass products came from Phoenicia and Egypt. Egypt had always been a center of glass manufacturing. The Ptolemies promoted this industry, particularly the production of luxury items (vases and bowls) and decorative pearls (as a substitute for precious stones), all designed for export. In the Seleucid empire the Persian tradition of manufacturing glass vessels with golden decoration was continued by the Syrians. All of these glass products were made by working and shaping molten glass as it congealed. Glassblowing was invented at the beginning of the Roman period and quickly revolutionized the manufacture of glass products. The new centers of production in Italy, Egypt, and Syria thus could make large quantities of inexpensive glass articles for everyday use. These were exported quite successfully.

(e) Writing Materials and Books

All sorts of materials were used for writing in ancient times: wood, stone, tablets of wax or clay, pieces of pottery (ostraca), and various metals (note the

Bibliography to §2.6e: Texts

Jenö Platthy, *Sources on the Earliest Greek Libraries with the Testimonia* (Amsterdam: Hakkert, 1968).

Bibliography to §2.6e: Studies

Mohammad A. Husayn, *Origins of the Book: Egypt's Contribution to the Development of the Book from Papyrus to Codex* (Leipzig: Edition Leipzig, 1970; reprint Greenwich, CT: New York Graphic Society, 1972).

David Diringer, "Greek and Latin Book Production," in idem, *The Hand-Produced Book* (New York: Philosophical Library, 1953; reprint 1974) 228–74.

C. H. Roberts and T. C. Skeat, *The Birth of the Codex* (London: British Museum, 1983).

Roberts, "Books in the Greco-Roman World and in the New Testament," in *Cambridge History of the Bible* 1. 48–66.

Frederic G. Kenyon, *Books and Readers in Ancient Greece and Rome* (2d ed.; Oxford: Clarendon, 1951).

copper scroll found near Qumran). But only animal skin (parchment or vellum) and papyrus, commercially produced, were widely used in the Hellenistic and Roman periods. The choice of skins or papyrus varied with the policies of the Hellenistic kings. Egypt possessed an industrial monopoly on papyrus, which it produced in large quantities and various degrees of quality, ranging from delicate luxury paper to rough packing material. Egyptian policies ensured that papyrus was exported at a good price. Sometimes other countries placed an embargo on importing papyrus. Syria did so for a while, as did Pergamon later, in the latter case to enforce the use of animal skins for writing. The Seleucid empire was self-sufficient in producing papyrus; the kings made their country independent of Egyptian imports.

Papyrus was made from the papyrus plant, found abundantly in the swamps of the Nile delta, and growing as high as five meters. Its stem with a diameter of about 5 cm was cut into lengths of about 30 to 50 cm. These were slit open lengthwise, and the soft pith was cut into thin strips laid out side by side on a firm support. A second layer was laid crosswise on top of the first. Pressing and hammering produced a firm papyrus sheet; the juice of the plant acted as glue. On the writing side, called *recto,* the papyrus strips ran horizontally; the other side, called *verso,* was usable but more troublesome, because here the strips ran vertically. Papyrus was therefore better suited for the production of scrolls, where only one side was used for writing, than for a codex, where the leaves were used on both sides. A few scrolls, called opisthographs, have writing on both sides.

Vellum and parchment are writing materials made from the specially processed skin of cattle, donkeys, horses, sheep, or goats. The most delicate parchment was made from the skin of newborn animals. The skin was not tanned, as in the production of leather, but was treated with chalk and water, cleaned of all hair, stretched, dried, and smoothed with pumice. As in the case of papyrus, quality varied. The introduction of special methods of preparing skins was ascribed to Eumenes II of Pergamon. The name "parchment" is derived from the Latin *pergamina (charta),* that is, "the paper from Pergamon." The elder Pliny relates (*Historia Naturalis* 13.21-22) that Eumenes intended to buy quantities of papyrus from Egypt in order to produce books for his new library; however, Ptolemy V of Egypt, jealous of this competition for his own library, imposed an embargo on papyrus exports. Eumenes, forced to seek a different writing material for his books, invented parchment made from animal skins. Though this story is most likely a legend, there is no doubt that Pergamon had a vital interest in its economic independence. The Attalids contributed substantially to the improvement of industrial production in general, and they produced parchment not only for their own library, but also for export.

The book format most widely used in antiquity was the scroll (Latin *volumen,*

Clarence Eugene Boyd, *Public Libraries and Literary Culture in Ancient Rome* (Chicago: University of Chicago Press, 1915; reprint 1966).

Tönnes Kleberg, *Buchhandel und Verlagswesen in der Antike* (Darmstadt: Wissenschaftliche Buchgesellschaft, 1967).

from *voluere* "to roll"). Several papyrus sheets were glued together until the customary length was achieved. In the case of parchment, the individual pieces were sewn together. The normal length of a scroll was 6 to 10 m, its average height 25 to 30 cm. Writing was done in individual columns of regular width, with an identical number of lines in each column and margins at the top and bottom as well as between the columns, where corrections and other *marginalia* might be written. Since there was a limit to the length of the scroll—to prevent it from becoming too unwieldy—the works of ancient authors were divided into books ("volumes"). The longer books of the New Testament would each fit on a scroll of average length. Only Luke's work had to be divided into two volumes, the Gospel and the Acts of the Apostles.

In the early Christian period the codex began to replace the scroll. A codex was less cumbersome than a scroll and could contain much more than a single "volume." To produce a codex, several sheets of papyrus were laid on top of each other and folded in the middle. The individual units were stitched together and bound, usually in leather. Ancient codices are described according to the number of folded sheets in each unit ("plies"); one therefore speaks of a two- or three- or four-ply codex. Since papyrus tended to break at the fold, this was sometimes reinforced with parchment. In a codex, the back of the papyrus (*verso*), usually left blank in scrolls, would also be used.

Christians may have been the first to produce codices, for both practical and liturgical reasons. Among the papyri from the 2d century CE, most codices are Christian, while all the scrolls and fragments of scrolls are Jewish or pagan texts. All surviving copies of New Testament books from the 2d to the 4th century CE are codices, even when papyrus is used as writing material, while the non-Christian literary papyri from the same period are usually scrolls. Although Christians relied on papyrus codices for several centuries, and others continued to consider the papyrus scroll the more distinguished form of a book, the parchment codex finally prevailed. It had distinct advantages over papyrus, especially the papyrus scroll: it was more durable and more serviceable, and one could write easily on both sides.

The economic policies of the Ptolemies were the most important reason for the lasting popularity of papyrus. Traditionally grown and used in Egypt anyway, papyrus was the inexpensive writing material for the countless records of the Ptolemies' administration: official correspondence, revenue lists, statistical materials, documents, and contracts. Promotion of the export of papyrus improved Egypt's foreign trade balance. Once papyrus had become fashionable, its predominant position lasted for centuries. It was probably the introduction of the codex, mostly by the Christians, that made parchment the preferred writing material, until this in turn was replaced by paper, introduced from China in the high Middle Ages.

Commercial production of books was known as early as Classical Greece. Writing shops (*scriptoria*) employed professional scribes who wrote from dictation, resulting in characteristic mistakes and corruptions of the text well known to text critics. Scribes were paid according to the number of lines they wrote in a given time period; more careful writing was expensive. In the later period slaves often worked in the *scriptoria*. In everyday correspondence a cursive script was used, in which groups of letters were combined in ligatures. In book production uncial letters, that is, stylized capitals written singly without ligatures but without spaces between words, were customary. Though none are preserved, all autographs of ancient literary works were written in cursive script.

The prices of books varied according to the quality of the writing material, the number of illustrations, and the expense of the binding. Illustrations in books are attested for the first time in the 1st century CE and were widely used in late antiquity, but were no doubt already in use in the Hellenistic period, for example, in textbooks for craftsmen. A picture of the author was also sometimes provided. Ancient book production flourished in the Roman age, the time when Christians also began to produce books.

7. TRADE, MONETARY SYSTEMS, AND BANKING

(a) The Most Important Trading Interests

Long-distance trade and monetary systems, designed primarily in the interest of foreign trade, were developed in the Mediterranean world by the 7th century BCE. The Greek monetary system spread over the entire region during the 5th century BCE. The trade of Phoenicians, Carthaginians, Etruscans, and Greeks stretched from the Atlantic Ocean to India. The conquests of Alexander brought fundamental change by making many nations parts of a single market. Trade among the different Hellenistic kingdoms had the character of domestic commerce, for which semi-autonomous cities like Athens, Miletos, and Rhodos served as the commercial centers. This large trading area, to which Rome would also come to belong, had external trading partners of completely different cultures and economic structures, although Hellenistic influences may have reached them occasionally. Foreign trade was with India, and later also with Parthia; with the people of the Arabian Peninsula, as well as the Libyans, Nubians, and Ethiopians in Africa; with the peoples Europe (Illyrians and Celts, and later also the Germans, and with the Scythians and the Sarmatians). Within the Mediterra-

Bibliography to §2.7

Fraser, *Alexandria*, 1. 132–88.

Bibliography to §2.7a–b

Peter Garnsey, Keith Hopkins, and C. R. Whittaker, eds., *Trade in the Ancient Economy* (Berkeley, CA: University of California Press, 1983).

Peter Garnsey and C. R. Whittaker, eds., *Trade and Famine in Classical Antiquity* (Cambridge Philological Society Proceedings, Suppl. 8; Cambridge, 1983).

M. M. Austin, "Greek Trade, Industry, and Labor," in Grant and Kitzinger, *Civilization*, 2. 723–51.

Keith Hopkins, "Roman Trade, Industry, and Labor," in Grant and Kitzinger, *Civilization*, 2. 753–93.

Lionel Casson, *Travel in the Ancient World* (London: Allen & Unwin, 1974).

nean trading area itself, Rome ultimately became dominant and was to play an increasingly significant role as a Hellenized commercial power.

The primary motivation for trade was to obtain goods and raw materials not available nearby, rather than to find export markets. During the Classical and Hellenistic periods, and to some degree in the Roman imperial period, war was an important factor in motivating trade. Armies consumed an enormous quantity of goods; weapons and clothing for soldiers had to be transported from work-shops, often hundreds of miles away. Raw materials such as wood for shipbuild-ing and iron ore could also be far removed. Most of the countries in question had direct or indirect access (through navigable rivers) to the Mediterranean Sea. Often goods had to be transported over long and expensive land routes, espe-cially east of the Mediterranean. In trade with foreign countries, the import of luxury articles predominated: precious stones and pearls, expensive textiles (silk and cotton), frankincense, ointments and cosmetic articles, rare woods and ivory. Food staples and other goods for mass consumption were traded only with nearby areas, transported over long distances only when river and sea routes were available.

Among the Hellenistic kingdoms, trading in foodstuffs and goods for mass consumption was very important in the beginning. The Greek cities needed grain, and in turn the Seleucids and Egypt bought large quantities of manufac-tured goods from Greece. But the kings were eager to make their countries self-sufficient in the supply of raw materials and widely used manufactured goods, especially weapons and textiles. Therefore, while trade within each of these kingdoms continued to flourish, their striving for autonomy became an obstacle to trade between these countries. Complete independence was never achieved. Egypt needed to import wood and metals, and the decline of the Seleucid empire resulted in an increasing demand for the imported goods necessary for everyday life. In general, trade among the various countries of the Mediterranean world tended to favor items of special value and quality: expensive wine, fine olive oil, ceramic and toreutic products of particular beauty, and expensive clothing. These items remained the mainstay of long-distance trade in the Roman period, espe-cially in response to an increasing demand by wealthy urban populations, even if longer land routes were involved in the transport.

The cities of Greece continued to require imports of grain, wood, and metals but experienced difficulties in increasing the volume of their exports. Greece's shortage in raw materials and foodstuffs became chronic. Some cities and islands were able to secure a share in Aegean trade. The Aegean Sea was the center of international trade during the 3d and 2d centuries BCE and lost little of its significance during the Roman period. The attempt of Ptolemaic Egypt to gain control of Aegean trade succeeded only briefly. Athens maintained its position as an important commercial center, Rhodos always played a leading role, and Delos, supported by Rome, gained great importance for a while. Ephesos and Miletos, temporarily under Egyptian domination, soon regained their traditional position as strong trading centers, a position they were able to renew with the support of Roman patrons.

Egypt's trade is well known from the discoveries of countless documentary

Warehouses on Delos

These warehouses, lining the shore near the ancient harbor of the island of Delos in the Aegean Sea, were built in III and II BCE. Because of its central position, Delos was used as a primary place for the reshipment of goods transported from the eastern parts of the Mediterranean to Rome. Awaiting reshipment, goods could be stored safely in these warehouses.

papyri. Egypt imported metals, lumber for its navy, horses, and elephants for its army. Gold, ivory, and elephants were shipped by sea from east Africa through ports on the Red Sea, occasionally also via Nubia and the Nile. Sometimes slaves were imported from Arabia, while tortoise shells, dyes (indigo), rice, spices, cotton, and silk came from India. Luxury foods like fine olive oil were also imported, despite high tariffs protecting domestic production. Egypt's main exports throughout antiquity were grain and papyrus. Some of the goods imported from India into the western Mediterranean passed through Egypt.

Much less is known about the trade of the Seleucid kingdom. Luxury items must have been as much in demand also here. The Seleucids would naturally profit from whatever trade in luxury items for sale in the west passed through their realm, although Egypt and the cities along the Black Sea were strong competitors. The rise of Rome and the unparalleled concentration of a wealthy urban population in that city shifted trade patterns. An immense demand for luxury items from the east was now channeled to the western part of the empire, bringing considerable profit to the commercial cities of the eastern Mediterranean. At the same time, Rome's insatiable appetite for imported grain required hundreds of merchant vessels to bring grain from Egypt and from the ports of the Black Sea. Once the seas had been freed from the bane of piracy by Pompey and Augustus, and after the conquests of Spain and Dacia, merchant fleets transported silver, gold, and iron in great quantities in order to supply the Roman mint and army.

(b) Important Trade Routes

The most significant trade routes were always those by the Mediterranean and the Black Seas, and the newly opened sea passage to India. The Romans called the Mediterranean Sea *mare nostrum* ("Our Ocean"). For trade with Africa and with the east, overland caravan routes were important, while river traffic played a minor role. The Nile, Euphrates and Tigris, and then later the Danube and the Rhone, were the only rivers used by merchants to any great extent. Trade routes were beset by numerous perils. Warfare threatened security; caravans, forced to traverse large deserts, were exposed to brigands and needed military protection, which at times they had to procure for themselves.

Land routes from the east terminated at different points on the Mediterranean or the Black Sea. From there the imported goods were transported by sea, with several transshipments before reaching their final destination. The northernmost caravan road ran north of the Caspian to the Black Sea (the Chinese silk road). It was not controlled by any Mediterranean power, gaining in significance once the troubles besetting the Seleucid realm made the southern routes more risky. Another road, much less used, running south of the Caspian Sea, had to pass through countries controlled by the Parthians, the Seleucids, and the kings of Pontus.

To the south were the ancient roads connecting India and Babylonia, a northern route through Bactria, and a southern route through Gedrosia and the Persis. In Hellenistic times, both routes terminated in Seleukia on the Tigris, the most important commercial city and point of transshipment in the east. As long as the Seleucids ruled the east, they maintained and secured both roads for military purposes. Reshipment to the Mediterranean Sea was difficult from here, since Egypt controlled the port city of Seleukia in Pieria for some time. Later traders would follow either the route that paralleled the course of the Euphrates and terminated in Antioch (the route by which Christianity later moved in its eastward expansion) or the road via Palmyra and Damascus to the cities of the Phoenician coast. The southernmost route used the sea passage from India to the Persian Gulf.

Further transport westward to the Mediterranean varied with the political situation. Merchants preferred the road that led from the Persian Gulf and across the Arabian peninsula to the Red Sea through the country of the Nabateans, or to Egypt via the Sinai Peninsula. As long as Egypt had good relations with the Nabateans and controlled the Phoenician cities on the Mediterranean coast, it profited considerably by this transit trade. Rome's control of this area through the establishment of the province of Arabia Felix was motivated by similar commercial interests. The Seleucids tried to detour goods arriving at the Persian Gulf to Seleukia, and later the Parthians intercepted goods from this route at the Persian Gulf. The wars of Rome with Parthia for possession of Mesopotamia were motivated in part by an attempt to control this important trade route. There was also some interest in maintaining a direct sea route to India around the Arabian Peninsula. Once the canal from the Red Sea to the Nile had been reopened, goods from India could be transported by sea from India all the way to Alexandria.

Trade in the western Mediterranean depended on sea routes. Among the Greek cities, Corinth led in trading with the west; when Caesar rebuilt Corinth, it became the most important transfer point. There were, of course, ancient ties between Carthage and its mother city Tyre on the Phoenician coast. This connection became important during the Hellenistic period, when new markets were created in the west for luxury goods from India and Arabia and when raw materials from the west were imported by the Hellenistic empires. Sulfur was exported from Italy, silver from Spain, and tin from as far away as Britain. These sea routes, however, were brought more and more under the control of Rome and were dominated by Roman commercial interests. The roads that the Romans built for military purposes very soon also served the expanding trade between the eastern Mediterranean world and western Europe.

(c) Coins and Monetary Systems

Before the time of Alexander the Great, the monetary system of the ancient world was chaotic. A variety of gold and silver currencies was in use, with no

Bibliography to §2.7c

Colin M. Kraay and Max Hirmer, *Greek Coins* (New York: Abrams, 1966).

Edward Allen Sydenham, *The Coinage of the Roman Republic* (rev. by Geoffrey C. Haines; New York: Arno, 1975).

Harold Mattingly, *Roman Coins from the Earliest Times to the Fall of the Western Republic* (2d ed.; London: Methuen, 1960).

C. H. V. Sutherland, *Ancient Numismatics: A Brief Introduction* (New York: American Numismatic Society, 1958).

Karl Christ, *Antike Numismatik: Einführung und Bibliographie* (Darmstadt: Wissenschaftliche Buchgesellschaft, 1967; reprint 1972).

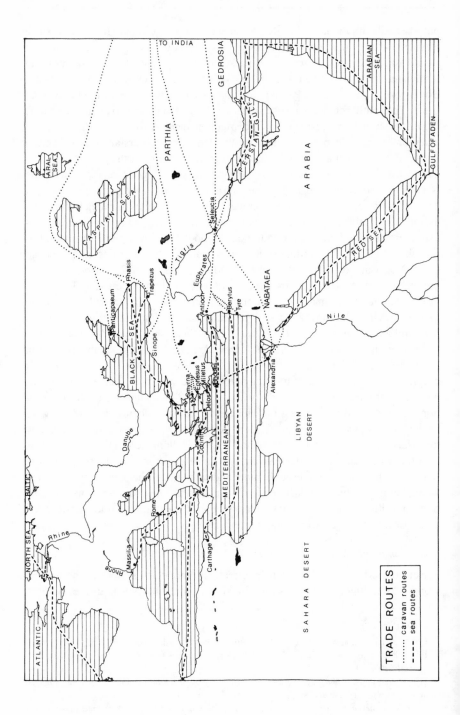

TRADE ROUTES
..... caravan routes
- - - sea routes

uniform standard of coinage. Alexander made silver the currency of his whole empire and introduced the Attic standard for all his mints. From the beginning there was no shortage of minted silver and, with the exception of the period of the wars of Diadochi, the supply of silver remained stable through most of the Hellenistic era. Shortages towards the end of the period resulted from a decrease in the output of silver mines, an increase in hoarding, and a drain of money to Rome. Access to the Spanish silver mines brought a fresh and steady supply of silver to the Roman empire for several hundred years.

Money was minted by each state, city, and league as soon as it could claim political independence. But monetary policies were determined by large kingdoms and by a few independent and commercially influential cities. The Attic silver standard was used everywhere except Egypt; in the later years of Ptolemy I Soter, the weight of silver coins was decreased and the standard reduced to become almost identical with that used previously by the Phoenician states, where silver was minted for use in all Ptolemaic possessions outside Egypt. The Ptolemies also minted gold. For use in Egypt itself, they minted copper as regular currency; the Egyptians were accustomed to copper money. Egypt thus had a currency system based on three metals: gold, used exclusively for the export/import trade and foreign subsidies; silver, for the Ptolemaic possessions overseas; and copper, for domestic use. The Ptolemies enforced the exclusive use of their own currency within their realm. Other currencies, especially gold, were rigorously excluded from the inland market.

The monetary arrangements decreed by Alexander were left unchanged in the Seleucid empire. The Attic standard was retained. Gold, silver, and copper coins were minted and circulated freely, though the Seleucids did not have a three-metal system like the Ptolemies; the issue of gold coinage was soon halted, to be resumed only on special occasions. Copper was used in the local markets. A number of cities, certainly the Greek cities of Asia Minor, were granted the privilege to mint their own copper coins, though other rights to strike coinage were not given until the time of Antiochos IV Epiphanes. Antiochos delegated the royal rights to mint silver to several cities, and later on even independent issues were permitted. Foreign currencies were by policy not legal tender within the Seleucid realm, but more and more exceptions were made. In addition, there was a kind of international currency existing side by side with the Seleucid gold and silver coins: the posthumous coins of Philip II, Alexander, and Lysimachos, which were minted following the same standard everywhere in the Hellenistic world outside of Egypt.

Roman coinage appeared relatively late in the commerce of the Mediterranean world. In addition to the cast pieces of bronze that had been used as money in central Italy for centuries, Rome began to strike its own silver coins at the beginning of the 3d century BCE, imitating the standard of the drachma of Magna Graecia. During the Second Carthaginian War, Rome issued a silver denarius roughly equivalent to the Sicilian drachma and the Punic half-shekel. This coinage became standard for all of Italy and Sicily; local coinages were discontinued. Augustus established a three-metal system, which remained in effect as the currency for the whole empire well into the 3d century CE. While gold coins were issued during the Roman republic only as special strikings, Augustus made the *aureus*, valued at twenty-five silver denarii, a standard part of the currency. One silver denarius was valued at sixteen *asses*. These *asses* were minted from copper, the intermediate values *sestertius* (= 4 *asses*) and *dupondius* (= 2 *asses*) from an alloy of copper and tin. Alongside this imperial currency there existed provincial currencies supervised by the emperor and—especially in the Greek east—local coinages of copper money, and occasionally even silver drachmas. The imperial issues were devoted entirely to state propaganda. The coins announced government programs, significant political events (such as the conquest of a new province), the virtues of the emperor, and his benefactions. The numerous representations of deities and of temples on Roman coins are extremely important for the history of religions in the Roman period.

MONETARY SYSTEMS

Greek coins
1 talent = 60 minas
  1 mina = 50 staters (gold)
    1 stater = 2 drachmas (silver)
      1 drachma = 6 obols (bronze)

Roman Coins
1 aureus (gold) = 25 denarii (silver)
  1 denarius = 4 sestertii
    1 sestertius = 2 dupondii
      1 dupondius = 2 asses
        1 ass = 4 quadrants

Relation of Greek and Roman coins: 1 drachma = 1 denarius

(d) Banking

Banks were an important factor in the economy of the Greco-Roman world. Still, most people preferred to keep their money in private hoards and to turn to a friend or a business associate for a loan rather than to a bank. Sources about banking in the ancient world are scattered and uneven in their reliability.

In earlier times, the treasuries of temples and of kings were the only banking facilities, and were designed to serve not the public but the interests of their owners. A temple bank would accumulate various types of income primarily in order to finance major festivals or building projects. Royal treasuries were agencies closely connected with taxation. The Hellenistic period, however, saw the expansion of banks owned by the cities that still had the right to strike money and private banks. Municipal banks usually collected tax money on behalf of the city and channeled the funds for its expenditures. Private bankers, whose role evolved from the practice of money-changing, became important for trade and commerce.

Continuing the business of changing currencies (foreign currencies were often not recognized as legal tender and had to be changed into local currency), private banks became international monetary clearinghouses. In addition, they kept ac-

Bibliography to §2.7d

Wesley E. Thompson, "Insurance and Banking," in Grant and Kitzinger, *Civilization*, 2. 829–36.

Inscription from Library of Pantaenus in Athens
The marble fragment with this inscription was apparently a part of a herm that was standing at the entrance
to the Library of Pantaenus, built ca. 100 CE in the
southeast corner of the Athenian Agora:
> "No book shall be carried out, because we have
> sworn it. (The library) shall be open from the first
> hour to the sixth hour."

counts and deposits for their customers (short- and long-term deposits with or without interest), made transfers, handled remittances, and gave loans to businessmen for the financing of such enterprises as the shipment of goods. Occasionally bankers might also give loans to set up a new business. In Roman times, private bankers were also used as intermediaries for major payments, because their records could be useful as evidence in court.

Athens was always the leading banking center of the ancient world; most of its banking business was in the hands of private persons, who were often foreigners. But banks also existed in every commercial city, in important port cities through which Mediterranean trade flowed, and in the cities situated along caravan routes. Since caravans transported their goods over a limited distance, these banks were responsible for equipping and financing new caravans to allow the further transport of goods.

In some places temple treasuries functioned as banking facilities. The temple of Apollo on Delos is the best-known example. Its wealth attracted the attention of the Ptolemies, who used it as one of their central banks and made Delos the capital of the island league they controlled. Later on, Rhodos, Macedonia, and Rome also used the Delian temple treasury. Temple banks were usually not concerned with money-changing (Jerusalem seems to have been an exception) or commercial loans and transactions. Their primary use was as repositories and safe deposits of large sums of money. Temple banks might also give real-estate loans, sometimes in perpetuity. The role of these banks arose from the notion that everything owned by a temple was inviolate.

The Ptolemies developed a unique banking system in Egypt. It was centralized like the rest of the economy. The royal bank was leased out to private businessmen who managed it as the central state bank, with branches everywhere in the country. These branch offices may not always have been distinct from the local offices of the royal administration. These banks used written documentation exclusively instead of oral agreements, and since they were all part of one centralized system, payment by check or transfer through remittance became the regular practice for money transactions. Some of these elements were taken over by the Roman banking system. The most important Roman contribution to banking, however, was the introduction of fully developed double-entry bookkeeping.

EDUCATION, LANGUAGE
AND LITERATURE

1. Basic Features of Cultural and Intellectual Life

(a) The Public Character of Cultural and Intellectual Life

Schools were the foundation of public cultural and intellectual life. Their development is related to the establishment of democratic rule in the major cities. Knowledge and activities that had been the privilege of special classes, namely music, gymnastics, and letters, became democratized. The public school made these privileged arts accessible to every citizen. Primary schools were the responsibility of the city administration. Gymnasia, even if they were sponsored by private associations, were viewed as a public institutions. The Ionic cities of Asia Minor were the first to develop a three-tiered school system. In the primary schools, where teachers were paid by the city, children were instructed in reading and writing, music, and athletics from the age of seven to fourteen. In a number of cases, there were also schools for girls, and coeducation for boys and girls is attested. The methods of instruction were simple: one started by learning the alphabet and proceeded to reading and writing words and sentences. Rote learning played a significant role. Not much changed in the Roman period; it was certainly no advantage when teachers on this level came to be paid privately in the later period.

The next stage of schooling was instruction by a grammarian paid by the parents. He gave instruction in grammar and introduced students to the poets, reading primarily Homer and Euripides. This did not change for many centuries. The predominant position of the poets in school instruction was critically discussed by Plutarch in the 1st century CE (*Quomodo adolescens poetas audire debet*). In their fifteenth (or seventeenth) year the young men went to the gymnasium for one or two years, the so-called *ephebia* for athletic and preliminary military training.

The major cities (Rhodos, Pergamon, Alexandria, Athens, and others) had rhetorical schools financed through public funds or private foundations. Usually this instruction was private, paid by the student or his parents. Education in rhetoric and philosophy, was open only to those who had completed their training in the gymnasium. Schools of philosophy competed with those of rhetoric, but the latter were more popular and more significant for all public careers.

The focus of Greek intellectual life was oral communication, although written books became more accessible. The goal of rhetoric was to persuade one's opponents and the masses, even to coerce; successful deception might win high praise. At the same time, education in rhetoric marked a change from repetition of myth and tradition to their critical analysis. The development of literature came to the aid of rhetoric: new ethnographic and historical writings, such as those of Herodotos and Thukydides, mediated a knowledge of the past and of people that was based on observation. The foundation for rhetorical education had been laid by the Athenian Sophists of the 5th and 4th century BCE, who for the first time had systematically investigated the character of knowledge, the function of moral values, and the problem of language itself, insofar as these related to the art of rhetoric. Their contribution determined the rhetorical curriculum for the following centuries and for the liberal arts until today.

A formal education in rhetoric, which could last as long as five years, would lead to a career in politics, law, or public administration. It included no specific preparation for those professions. Instead, its concern was rhetorical theory, study of the classical orators, and practical exercises in public speaking, along with the study of philosophy, geography, and history—though only to the extent that these subjects might prove useful. After completing this education, students would receive their professional training in the form of an apprenticeship in a lawyer's office or in an administrative agency.

During the 3d century BCE the influx into Italy of Greek slaves, including household slaves better educated than their masters, began to be felt in Roman society. In the houses of the upper classes, the first language Roman children would learn might be Greek, since many of the nurses were Greeks. Education in schools replaced the traditional family-based educational system. As early as the close of the 3d century BCE, Greek teachers of rhetoric settled in Rome. By the imperial period, education in Greek rhetoric had become the accepted form of higher education in Roman society. The language of instruction was Greek or bilingual (Greek and Latin) throughout the imperial period. Certain moral standards for such professions found general acceptance, due to the influence of Stoic philosophy (see §4.1d). Christian writers later established the same criteria for ecclesiastical offices: moral qualifications and rhetorical (or philosophical) training were presupposed as a matter of course.

With the production and sale of books in greater quantities (§2.6e), literary works became increasingly available to the general public. Hand-in-hand with

Bibliography to §3

Werner Jaeger, *Paideia: The Ideals of Greek Culture*, vol. 3 (2d ed.; Oxford: Oxford University Press, 1965).

Paul Wendland, *Die hellenistisch-römische Kultur in ihren Beziehungen zum Judentum und Christentum* (4th ed. with bibliography by Heinrich Dörrie; HNT 1/2–3; Tübingen: Mohr/ Siebeck, 1972). Since its 3d edition of 1912, a classic in the study of Hellenistic culture and Christianity.

Bibliography to §3.1

M. L. Clarke, *Higher Education in the Ancient World* (London: Routledge, 1971).

Henri-Irénée Marrou, *A History of Education in Antiquity* (London: Sheed & Ward, 1956; reprint 1981).

Idem, "Education and Rhetoric," in Finley, *Legacy*, 185–201.

Carolyn Dewald, "Greek Education and Rhetoric," in Grant and Kitzinger, *Civilization*, 2. 1077–1107.

this development came the establishment of public libraries. Originally libraries had been the private property of the rich; acquiring large numbers of books presupposed considerable wealth. The first public libraries were established by the Hellenistic kings in Pella, Alexandria, and Pergamon. The Roman emperors followed this example: Augustus founded the Palatine Library, and Hadrian built a famous library in Athens. More important for the public were the city libraries, which became common during the Roman period, financed through public funds or private donations such as the Library of Pantainos in Athens and the Library of Kelsos in Ephesos. Smaller libraries were found in the gymnasia and the schools. In both east and west the same works constituted the standard holdings: the Classical Greek authors, with the poets—especially Homer and Euripides— more fully represented than prose writers and philosophers; textbooks; florilegia; and compendia (not always of high quality).

The Classical poets were available for reading everywhere. But they could also be heard: in the theaters poetry became accessible to the illiterate public as well as to the educated reader. The tradition of the Theater of Dionysos, with fixed annual dates for the competitive presentation of tragedies and comedies, had long been a famous institution of Classical Athens. Although Alexandria still arranged for such competitions at certain dates every year, the theaters of most Hellenistic cities did not continue this tradition. Instead there were irregular yet frequent performances of the Classical plays. Euripides' tragedies must have been performed again and again. New tragedies and comedies were offered on occasion, as well as mimes. In the Roman period, pantomimes, sometimes of Classical tragedies, were especially popular. Greek tragedies in Latin translation were performed in Rome as early as the 3d century BCE. Theaters built for these performances reproduced the classical Greek architecture, though initially only in temporary wooden structures. Comedies written by Roman poets were at first but adaptations of plays from the New Comedy of Athens, published in Latin translation with the addition of some typically Roman features. Roman tragedies were also closely tied to their Greek predecessors (§3.4b; 6.4b).

Many cities also had an odeion, built as independent structure, or as part of other buildings, such as the auditorium of the large gymnasium in Pergamon, which was used for public lectures and for competitions of poets, orators, and musicians. But the stoa, a covered colonnade (*portico*), was the preferred spot for lectures and discussions. The most important philosophical movement of this period, Stoicism, was founded not in a private house or in the sacred district of a temple, but in the Stoa Poikile in Athens, where the Phoenician Zeno presented his teachings in public (§4.1d). When he died, Athens mourned the death of not merely a philosopher, but a well-known and esteemed honorary citizen, whose moral integrity was admired by all. Christian missionaries inherited this spirit and emphasized the public character of their message and the messenger's moral integrity (cf. 2 Cor 4:1–4). Sectarian seclusion fit poorly with the educational policy in the Hellenistic city, which insisted on the public character of education. Christian sectarians violated this principle as much as the emperor Domitian, who expelled from Rome those who taught philosophy publicly.

Plastic and graphic arts in the life of the city were also public. The original setting for painting and sculpture was in the realm of sacred places, especially temples and tombs. The Classical period had already secularized these arts, though sacred art continued to exist. In the Hellenistic period, the primacy of the commonwealth over the private sphere is striking. Theaters, agoras, public buildings, gymnasia, libraries, and temple precincts, were settings where works of art could be found. Hundreds of statues could be seen in such places, and numerous pictures were displayed in stoas and picture galleries. Rarely did the cities have to pay for works of art; they were donated by the rulers, by private associations, or by wealthy citizens. It is characteristic of the spirit of the city that people who were perfectly capable of maintaining private collections would instead donate large sums of money to their cities, not only for athletic games, grain supplies, and useful buildings, but also for artistic decorations and statuary. Inscriptions often state explicitly that a building was given "together with all its works of art," and the donors even paid for the statues erected in recognition of their benefactions. The flowering of architecture in the Hellenistic cities of the east testifies to the public spirit of the time. With few exceptions, private houses remained comparatively modest. Building activity was concentrated instead on the erection of temples, administrative buildings, public places, and theaters.

Even the modern viewer is impressed by the way in which Hellenistic sculpture presents human beings in their own particular individualities. The Classical tendency towards idealization receded, giving place to a more clearly expressed individualism. A merchant from Delos, the priest of a Near-Eastern cult, a bearded philosopher, a dying Celtic warrior, even the heads of kings and rulers on their coins—all appear before our eyes as personalities. To be sure, this did not go so far as the brutal realism of the Roman period. What is presented is the individual instance in which character, conviction, and life experience become transparent in the features of the face, challenging even the modern viewer to engage in a dialogue about the meaning of human life. Alongside these sculptures one must also read the inscriptions, both honorary and funerary in nature, which—in spite of many clichés—speak of the works and virtues, not only of the great and mighty, but also of untold numbers of ordinary citizens. Whatever these people had done and experienced—their faith, their fate, and the power of the gods who determined their lives—all this was visibly present for each inhabitant of a Hellenistic city in hundreds of examples.

Much of this spirit continued into the Roman period, along with some profound changes. In competition with public art treasures, private collections grew quickly in the luxurious villas of the rich. After a renewed tendency towards idealization in the early imperial period, interest in individualistic expression grew again in the plastic arts, culminating in the grim and sometimes grotesque realism of the 3d century CE. The Roman period also brought a revival in the mass production of copies of famous works of Classical art. Large works of architecture often testify to the power of an individual rather than to the public spirit. Nonetheless, an obligation of art to the public can still be found in the Roman period in the proliferation of magnificent baths, aesthetically pleasing public and sacred places, fantastic waterworks, and sculpture-lined fora.

(b) The International Character of Cultural Life

Although the Hellenistic world was divided into several independent kingdoms and a number of city-states, its cultural life was unified and international. Once the whole realm became politically united under Roman rule, Hellenistic culture became the culture of the world. Greek education had already begun to extend its influence beyond the Hellenistic kingdoms and cities, and Rome came under its influence as early as the 3d century BCE. Individual national elements did not disappear, but assumed a new role as contributors to the dominant Greek culture. Indigenous cultural traditions within the reach of Hellenistic influence maintained their strength and vitality, but they lost the ideological justification for preserving traditional forms of expression. Of course there were circles that resisted the influence of Hellenism. A good example of this sort of resistance is the Maccabean revolt. But even here, only a small portion of the Jewish people offered resistance to the spread of Hellenism, while most Jews became Hellenized and found divine inspiration in the Greek translation of their scriptures. Christianity became a Hellenistic movement through and through, largely because Judaism had already shown the way.

Whatever individual nations could claim as their heritage was transformed into a contribution to the world culture of Hellenism. This is true for all areas of cultural and intellectual activity, for craftsmanship as well as for fine arts, literature, and religion. The process was encouraged by the natural curiosity of the Greeks about foreign cultures. The kings furthered the process by energetically promoting indigenous cultural traditions and religions for internal political reasons, with the result that such traditions were revived in Greek dress and contributed even more readily to the new international culture. Books written in Greek were published on such subjects as Babylonian, Egyptian, and Jewish history, religion, wisdom, and science. Mosaics by Syrian artists can be found on the island of Delos in the Aegean Sea; paintings by Greek artists were introduced to Rome; and artistically decorated glazed vases with Parthian motifs were exported from Syria to all parts of the Mediterranean world.

Stoic philosophy appropriately mapped the horizons of this new world culture. The Stoics taught that the world was but one large polis in which people from all nations were citizens with equal rights, that all the gods of different nations represented one and the same divine providence, and that the moral principles of all people should recognize no distinctions of ethnicity or social status. Wandering philosophers proclaiming such teachings were soon joined by wandering missionaries preaching religious messages addressed to everyone. The milieu of Hellenism provided a fertile ground in which religions once rooted in the tradition of individual nations and bound to particular holy

Bibliography to §3.1b

Edward Alexander Parsons, *The Alexandrian Library, Glory of the Hellenic World: Its Rise, Antiquities, and Destructions* (New York: American Elsevier, 1952; reprint 1967).
Fraser, *Alexandria*, 1. 305-35.

places could be transformed into missionary movements claiming to be world religions.

Hellenistic literature no longer saw human beings as belonging to a particular state or city; rather, these became accidental environments in which people happened to live. To be sure, people were still obligated to serve their place of residence, and the community spirit of the residents of these cities is documented in many impressive monuments. The Hellenistic rulers promoted first of all the interests of their own countries and capital cities, where they gave considerable support to literature, the arts, and science. But not rarely great sums of money were spent in support of Greek symbols of cultural unity for the entire Hellenistic-Roman world. Antiochos IV Epiphanes of Syria donated funds to resume the building of the monumental temple of Zeus Olympios in Athens. The Pergamene kings, jealously concerned with furthering the fame of their capital city Pergamon as an international center of culture and intellectual life, donated several buildings in Athens, most notably the Stoas of Attalos and of Eumenes. Private donations by wealthy citizens were often made for the benefit of the cities and sanctuaries of Greece: the Leonidaion in Olympia, for example, which was donated and built by the architect Leonidas from Naxos. Roman emperors emulated these examples, especially Hadrian. Among private benefactors, no one could compare with Herodes Atticus. Magnificent buildings in Athens, Corinth, Delphi, Olympia, and other cities testify to the generosity of this famous rhetorician of the 2d century CE, who is said to have been the wealthiest person in antiquity. The donation by the Christian merchant Marcion of Sinope of 200,000 sestertii to the Roman church is typical of the spirit of Hellenism that was still alive in the Roman period.

Athens was the symbol of cultural and intellectual life. Even in the Roman period it was still considered the cultural capital of the world. Luke, the author of the Book of Acts, could not imagine the career of the famous apostle Paul without a visit in Athens and a speech presented to the dignified and famous Council of the Areopagites (Acts 17). Hellenistic rulers had contributed to the beauty of Athens by donating several buildings; Roman emperors spent large sums of money to enhance the city's splendor and fame. Nero renovated the Theater of Dionysos Eleutherios; Hadrian completed the immense Temple of Zeus Olympios and donated a large library building; Augustus' friend Agrippa gave a new odeion, built in the center of the agora, and Herodes Atticus built another odeion on the slopes of the Acropolis. Athens became in effect a museum, but retained its significance as the seat of the philosophical schools: the Stoic school, founded at the beginning of the Hellenistic period; the "academic" school of Plato in the garden of the hero Akademos; Arostotle's Lyceum; and the Garden of the Epicureans. Students from all parts of the ancient world would flock to Athens to study philosophy, even as late as the early Byzantine period.

Rivaling Athens was Alexandria, the Ptolemaic capital. Its fame as a center of culture, scholarship, and science was renewed under Augustus; this city, where Plotinos, the founder of Neoplatonism, received his education, is also remembered as the birthplace of Christian theology. The Museum of Alexandria, founded before 280 BCE by Ptolemy I Soter, was the first institution in the history of humankind specifically dedicated to scientific research. Scholars, poets, and artists, called to the Museum by the Ptolemies, lived in a community organized as a religious association under the direction of a priest appointed by the king. Since the king provided their full support, the members were free to devote all their time to study and research. Significant were new poetic works of the 3d century BCE and important achievements in textual interpretation and the production of definitive editions of Classical literary works. Advancements were also made in geography, astronomy, medicine, and other sciences. Attached to the Museum was the Alexandrian library, magnificently built and richly endowed, with its 400,000 volumes the largest library of antiquity. The Museum was destroyed in 269/70 or 273 CE by either Zenobia or Aurelian; afterwards its scholars apparently moved to the Sarapeion and used its library until it in turn was burned by the Christian Patriarch Theophilos in 389 CE.

In the 3d century BCE, Pergamon began to compete with Alexandria as a cultural capital; though it never achieved the same significance, Pergamon influenced Roman art and architecture far more than Alexandria did. More important for the cultural and intellectual life of the Hellenistic and Roman periods was Rhodos. Freed from Persian rule by Alexander the Great, the island republic remained independent, and though conquered and destroyed by Cassius in 42 BCE, it became a free ally of Rome in the imperial period. Rhodos was the home of an important school of sculpture which, among other works, produced the famous statue of Laocoon, now in the Vatican Museums. Beginning in the 2d century BCE, it could boast one of the most famous schools of rhetoric. Rhodos was also the residence of renowned scholars and philosophers, such as Apollonios, poet, scholar, and former librarian at Alexandria, and the Stoic philosophers Panaitios and Poseidonios. Many Romans, including Cicero, Lucretius, Caesar, and Tiberius, came to study in Rhodos in the 1st century BCE.

The international character of education is documented not only in the tendency of students to enroll in schools of philosophy and rhetoric far away from their home cities, but also in the fact that leading scholars and philosophers came from countries that had only recently been drawn into the realm of Greek cultural influence. Among the heads of the philosophical schools in Athens, many came either from Greek families residing in Asia Minor or elsewhere in the east, or from Hellenized Near Eastern families. Foreign origins are most striking among the leading Stoic philosophers: the founder of Stoicism, Zeno, was a Phoenician from Cyprus; his successor, Kleanthes, a Greek from Assos in the Troad (Asia Minor); the next head of the school, Chrysippos, came from Soloi in Cilicia. Then came Zeno from Tarsos, and Diogenes from Seleukia on the Tigris; Panaitios was the offspring of a wealthy Rhodian family. Poseidonios' home was Apamea in Syria. But also the Academician Karneades, for example, was a North African from Cyrene, and Antiochos came from the Phoenician port city of Ashkelon. It would be wrong, however, to search for any "foreign" elements that these men might have introduced. On the contrary, they were all "Greeks" who had no interest other than developing further the *one* Greek culture that had become the culture of the world.

2. The Language

(a) The Development of the Greek Language into Koine

Greeks spoke a number of dialect. Some dialects were limited to certain regions and, though occasionally attested in local inscriptions, no longer appear in extant literature. The important dialects or groups of dialects were the following: *Ionic,* spoken in the central section of the west coast of Asia Minor; *Attic,* closely related to Ionic, the dialect of Athens and Attika; *Aeolic,* spoken in the northern part of the west coast of Asia Minor, on Lesbos, and in Thessaly and Boiotia; *Doric,* spoken in the southern and western parts of the Peloponnesos, in the southwestern section of Asia Minor, on Crete, Rhodos, and Kos; the closely related Doric dialects of Elis, Achaia, and of central and western Greece; and finally the Arcado-Cyprian dialect of the interior of the Peloponnesos and the island of Cyprus. Macedonian is not a Greek dialect, but belongs to a different branch of the family of Greek languages.

Of these dialects only Ionic, Aeolic, Doric, and Attic occur in Greek literature: Ionic in early Greek epic (Homer), lyric poetry, and in part the early prose works from Asia Minor (Herodotos, Hippokrates); Aeolic in the lyric poetry of Lesbos (Sappho)—the lyric verse of the tragic chorus was written in Doric. The development of Attic prose began in the 5th century BCE and, due to Athens' leading position, Attic soon took a dominant role in literature as well as in commerce and diplomacy. With the assimilation of some elements from the closely related Ionic dialect (e.g., -σσ- for -ττ- in Attic, as in τάσσειν; -ϱσ- for -σσ-, as in ἄϱσεν; also ναός for νεώς), Attic was used by Alexander the Great and his successors as the official language of administration, and thus became the *lingua franca* of the Hellenistic world, the Koine, that is, the "common" language of the Hellenistic and Roman period. In the east, it soon rivaled and partly replaced Aramaic, the administrative and commercial language of the Achaemenid Persian empire. In its further development, a number of peculiar features emerged that distinguished the Koine more and more from Classical Attic prose:

1) *Phonetics:* The diphthongs disappeared from the spoken language; they survived only in writing and are often missing in inscriptions and papyri, and sometimes in early Christian literature as well. ει became *ê,* ου became *û* (later αι changed to *ä,* οι to *ê,* and ευ and αυ became *ef* and *af*), αι, ηι, and ωι became α, η, and ω (while the ι was normally retained in writing as an iota subscript). η became identical in sound with ι (as ει and later also οι). Among the

---

Bibliography to §3.2

Friedrich Blass and Albert Debrunner, *A Greek Grammar of the New Testament and Other Early Christian Literature* (trans. and rev. Robert W. Funk; Chicago: University of Chicago Press, 1961).

Bibliography to §3.2a

Robert Browning, "Greek in the Hellenistic World and the Roman Empire," in idem, *Medieval and Modern Greek* (2d ed.; Cambridge: Cambridge University Press, 1983).

Leonard R. Palmer, *The Greek Language* (Atlantic Highlands, NJ: Humanities, 1980).

consonants φ = pʰ became f, θ = tʰ changed to voiceless th, and χ = kʰ to ch (later β became v, δ a voiced th, and γ became gʰ or y).

2) *Morphology:* The so-called second Attic declension disappeared: ἵλεως became ἵλεος (both forms are still found in the New Testament). The vocative was largely replaced by the nominative (θεός for θεέ). The ending of the accusative plural of the consonantal stems of the third declension replaced the vocalic stems of this declension (ἰχθύας for ἰχθύς). The superlative of the adjective became rare with the comparative taking its place. In the conjugation of verbs, the optative fell into disuse and periphrastic constructions became more frequent. The verbs ending in -μι were assimilated to the thematic conjugation.

3) *Vocabulary:* Composite forms became more frequent, and new technical terms were coined in the various areas of specialized scientific, philosophical, religious, and administrative language. Some neologisms emerged on the basis of older Greek words, while other terms were borrowed from foreign languages. Thus the Koine contained occasional loan words from Semitic languages and from Latin, more rarely from Persian and Egyptian.

4) *Syntax:* Departures from Classical Attic usage were considerable. However, since typical features of Koine syntax appear most frequently in non-literary texts, or in writers untrained in the writing of literary prose, they simply reflect the fact that vernacular language in any case exhibits a paratactic style, brevity, anacoluthon, and solecism. Other features typical of the style of New Testament writers will be discussed below.

(b) The Language of Literature

Koine Greek as a shared language of discourse, commerce, and administration developed according to its own laws and dynamics. It was a complex phenomenon, involving the spoken vernacular of daily life as well as the technical languages of law, science, economy, and administration; the language of school and rhetoric, along with various degrees of influence from Classical literary conventions. A number of authors wrote in an "elevated Koine," a more cultivated common language. Extant sources provide considerable information about the common language of the Hellenistic and Roman periods, while the materials for the literary language, especially for the literary Koine are few, especially for the Hellenistic period. The archaizing movement of the imperial period, called Atticism, established standards for literary Greek that the written Koine was unable to meet—one of the reasons for the disappearance of much of this literature.

The Atticistic revival invoked the ideals of the Classical language and sought to establish the style of Attic literary prose as the standard for all literary production. As a conscious movement of literature, Atticism began in the 1st century BCE as a reaction against "Asianism." Asianism was a rhetorical style developed in Asia Minor in the 3d century BCE that preferred unusual syntactical constructions and phrases, overloaded sentences with resounding words, and employed sequences of abridged clauses for rhetorical effect. Opponents of Asianism advocated Classical Attic prose for its lucid, rational style in place of the bombastic pomposity of the Asian rhetoricians. To be sure, Asianism survived: it occurs in a number of inscriptions (for example, those of Antiochos of Kommagene), was

The Stoic Philosopher Chrysippus
The leading systematician of the Stoic philosophy.
Roman copy of a statue from III BCE.

taught in many second-rate rhetorical schools (Petronius in his *Satyricon* attacks the bombastic phrases that students of rhetoric had to learn), and was preferred by a number of authors. Among Christian writers, Ignatius of Antioch is a good example. Asianism also had some affect on the style of later Attic rhetoricians. But, on the whole, beginning with Cicero's polemic against the Asianists, Atticism became the predominant literary style of Greek writers in late antiquity.

The rhetor and historian Dionysios of Halikarnassos, who taught in Rome after 30 BCE, took Demosthenes as his model. In his work *On the Arrangement of Words*, he proposed that imitation of the Classical authors be the criterion of educated speech. In the 2d century CE, Herodes Atticus, wealthy patron of the arts and a leading representative of the Second Sophistic (§6.4e), became the most accomplished master of the Attic style. The text of one of his speeches is preserved; it shows such a perfect mastery of early Classical Attic prose style that some modern scholars have argued that it was composed in the 5th century BCE. Dionysios of Halikarnassos and a certain Pausanias from Syria (ca. 100 CE) composed dictionaries designed to ensure that literary vocabulary followed the diction of the Classical Attic authors. Ingenious craftsmanship and scientific precision combined in a successful archaizing movement that perpetuated a bilingualism within the Greek language that has not been overcome even today.

Some examples of a literary Koine, however, have survived. The language of the Hellenistic historians is most closely related to the vernacular. Though most of their works have been lost, extensive fragments and several complete books of the historians Polybios (ca. 200-120 BCE) and Diodoros Siculus (1st century CE) are preserved. Plutarch (45-125 CE) and the Jewish writers Philo and Josephus show some influence from the vernacular Koine. The sophist and satirist Lucian of Samosata (120-180 CE), though an admirer of Classical literature, still made extensive use of the language of his own time and ridiculed the excesses of Atticism. Other exceptions include the astrologer Vettius Valens and the philosopher Epiktetos; his lectures, as recorded by his student Arrian, are direct and uncorrupted testimony for the vernacular language of the early Christian period.

(c) Evidence for the Vernacular Koine

Abundant evidence for the vernacular language of the Hellenistic and Roman periods comes from non-literary papyri and from private inscriptions. In addition to papyri of literary texts, Egypt has yielded thousands of official documents and personal correspondence dating from the beginning of the Ptolemaic period to the Islamic invasion. Exactly how the language of these papyri relates to the actual spoken vernacular is a matter of debate. Though letter writers sometimes tried to emulate a more literary style, barbarisms often occur in documents produced by people whose native language was Egyptian. Thus not all the peculiar linguistic features of these papyri directly witness to the vernacular Koine. Technical

Bibliography to §3.2c

Eric G. Turner, *Greek Papyri: An Introduction* (Oxford: Clarendon, 1968; reprint 1980).
Horsley, "The Fiction of 'Jewish Greek,'" in idem, *New Documents*, 5. 5–40.

language is reflected in various ways. Administrative terminology is found in official documents like governmental edicts, administrative files, court records, and reports of officials and governmental agencies, but also in petitions from citizens of all classes, requests, and complaints. Private contracts of marriage and divorce, sales, rental of property, employment, loans, securities, and testaments (often written by official scribes) reflect the spoken language more directly than do official records.

Private correspondence offers the most direct access to the vernacular. Letters are preserved from people from all walks of life: husbands away on business write to their wives at home; a son serving as a soldier writes to his parents; a father admonishes his children; slaves and free citizens, men and women, young and old, rich and poor speak in these letters. A number of magical papyri have also been discovered. As a source for the religious language of the time they are of inestimable value. They also demonstrate the degree to which terms from non-Greek religions (including Judaism), transcribed or translated, had been incorporated within the language of the Koine.

During the decades following the first discoveries of papyri at the end of the 19th century, much of this material was sorted and collected by philologists and New Testament scholars seeking to elucidate the language of early Christian literature and was absorbed by standard New Testament dictionaries like Walter Bauer's and grammars like those of Blass-Debrunner and Moulton. The rich materials discovered in more recent decades have not yet been explored systematically from the perspective of the language of early Christianity, though G. H. R. Horsley has made important studies.

While the papyri, found in Egypt, provide a geographically limited picture of the vernacular language, private inscriptions are preserved from throughout the Greco-Roman world, most abundantly from mainland Greece, the Greek isles, western Anatolia, and Italy. Most of these inscriptions are on stone; a few remain on wood, metal, ostraca, and in mosaics. Like the official inscriptions, many private inscriptions represent publications of records written on papyrus. They include contracts, business documents, bills, and testaments. Of particular interest for the language of early Christian literature are inscriptions containing dedications, curses, votives, reports of miraculous healings, dreams and visions, or those that speak of pilgrimages and generally about the life and death of human beings. Many inscriptions use traditional formulas and clichés, and do not necessarily reflect thoughts and beliefs of individuals, they nonetheless testify to the conventions of language describing such events as birth, death, consecration, and healing and thus reveal common usage and terminology. What was said about the papyri applies to these inscriptions: a systematic investigation from the perspective of the history of early-Christian language, with particular attention to local differences, is still needed.

While nonliterary papyri and inscriptions are primary witnesses for the conventions of the vernacular, evidence for the literary Koine exists not only in such writers as Polybios and Epiktetos, but also in the extensive corpus of Jewish writings in the Greek language from the Hellenistic and Roman periods. Many of these writings are Greek translations of Hebrew or Aramaic originals, such as most of Israel's Bible and some of the pseudepigrapha of the Old Testament (for example, the *Testaments of the Twelve Patriarchs* and the *Psalms of Solomon*), which frequently follow the Hebrew original very closely, so that their Greek contains numerous Semitisms in syntax and vocabulary. These writings strongly influenced the religious language of Hellenistic Judaism and Christianity. More important for understanding of the literary Koine are translations of Hebrew books that follow the original less slavishly and, of course, Jewish literature originally written in Greek. This latter group includes the Wisdom of Solomon, the 2d, 3d, and 4th Books of Maccabees, and, outside of the Septuagint, the Jewish *Sibylline Books, Joseph and Aseneth,* the *Letter of Aristeas,* and others (§5.3b, d). Of particular importance are the fragments of Jewish writers that were collected by Alexander Polyhistor in the 1st century BCE (preserved in Eusebios *Praep. Ev.* 9.17-39) and the poetic version of Jewish sayings preserved under the pseudonym Phokylides. Some of these writings reflect a higher Koine, influenced by the conventions of Attic prose—varying with the author's literary education—but taken as a whole, these writings witness to the vernacular language as it was spoken and written by people who knew very little about the conventions of refined literary style.

(d) The Language of Early Christian Writings and the Koine

Ancient Christian writers wrote in the language of their time, the Greek Koine. Until the beginning of this century scholars called this language "Biblical Greek." The differences between New Testament (and Septuagintal) Greek on the one hand and Classical Greek on the other have been well known for some time. Some distinct features of these writings indeed result from the close relationship of the New Testament to the Holy Scriptures of Israel and to the language and literature of Greek-speaking Jews (see §3.2e). However, taken as a whole, the Greek of early Christian literature belongs to the ongoing development of Greek as a living language from the beginning of the Hellenistic period to the language of the Greek people today, the "Demotic." Indeed, New Testament Greek seems to share some features with modern Demotic, while it has very little connection to the artificial repristination of the language of Attic prose in the literature and rhetoric of the Roman imperial period.

Within this general framework the language of the various authors of early Christian writings exhibits a considerable range of differences. Next to elements of the vernacular, one finds the technical language of popular philosophy, rhetoric, historiography, and the occasional influence of Classical Attic prose. The

Bibliography to §3.2d

Walter Bauer, "An Introduction to the Lexicon of the Greek New Testament," in idem, *A Greek-English Lexicon of the New Testament and Other Early Christian Literature* (2d ed. by F. Wilbur Gingrich and Frederick W. Danker; Chicago: University of Chicago Press, 1979) xi–xxviii.

James W. Voelz, "The Language of the New Testament," *ANRW* 2.25.2 (1984) 893–977.

Horsley, "The Greek Documentary Evidence and NT Lexical Study: Some Soundings," in idem, *New Documents,* 5. 67–94.

Epistle to the Hebrews has more affinities to Attic prose than any other writing of the New Testament. The skillful periodization and hypotactic construction of its sentences reveal that its author had benefited from a good literary education, though the author does use words that a strict Atticist would not permit. Otherwise the New Testament is dominated by the vernacular Koine. To be sure, neither Paul, nor Luke, nor the authors of the Pastoral Epistles or 2 Peter lacked a Greek education. The author of 2 Peter, for example, attempts to write a more elevated Greek—though his style is less refined than that of the author of Hebrews.

Luke, the author of the Third Gospel and of the Acts of the Apostles, relies more heavily on literary models than do the authors of other New Testament books. He is quite familiar with the literary Koine, the conversational and literary language of educated Greeks that was also used by Hellenistic historians. The prologue to his books (Luke 1:1-4) displays knowledge of literary conventions. Luke replaces Aramaic and Latin loan words wherever they appear in his main source, the Gospel of Mark, with Greek terms better suited for literary tastes. Thus, Luke writes διάβολος for σατανᾶς, διδάσκαλος for ῥαββί/ῥαββουνί, φόρος for κῆνσος/*census*, ἑκαντόνταρχος for κεντυρίων/*centurio*. In composing his gospel, Luke restyles Mark's simple paratactic sentence structures into participial and relative clauses. In the Acts of the Apostles, Luke demonstrates in his composing of speeches, choice of language, and grammatical style that he is alert to the level of education of the speaker (e.g., in the use the optative, a mood that had disappeared in the vernacular language).

The author of *1 Clement* makes abundant use of terms and phrases that derive from the literary language. The same is true of the Pastoral Epistles. In the writings of the apologist Justin Martyr (middle of the 2d century), and shortly afterwards in the *Apology* of Athenagoras, the use of a higher Koine style, influenced by Atticism, has become a matter of course. The *Epistle to Diognetos,* an apology written about 200 CE, shows a higher than average standard in its employment of literary prose. Clement of Alexandria, writing at about the same time, is a master of prose style. His command of literary language is so complete that he can afford to disregard the strict rules of Atticism. In his writings the expressive power of Greek prose once more reaches heights that the rigid stringency of Atticism was unable to achieve. Henceforth Christian authors employed a prose style in which the strict rules of Atticism are somewhat relaxed; in a number of writers a closer proximity to the spoken vernacular Greek language repeatedly appears, due most likely to the influence of the Christian sermon, designed, of course, to address the common people.

These examples, however, only mark the end of a long development that began with Luke and the Epistle to the Hebrews. Most New Testament writings, unlike Luke, did not cross the threshold between vernacular and literary language. Paul dwells wholly in the world of the vernacular, though he uses the common language of his time in a masterly and skillful way. He can employ dependent clauses and draws on a comparatively large vocabulary, which he uses with conscious purpose. He also controls a variety of stylistic techniques, such as wordplay and paronomasia. These skills derive from Paul's rhetorical education, his training in the debating style of the Cynic-Stoic diatribe, and the preaching style of the Hellenistic synagogue. It would be quite mistaken to ascribe the peculiar features of Paul's language to his temperament and to the depths of his religious experience. Rather, he uses such features as ellipsis and anacoluthon deliberately as stylistic devices.

Like the Pauline letters, the Gospels of Matthew, Mark, and John, the Revelation of John, and most of the Catholic Epistles (with the exception of 2 Peter) also use the vernacular. This is the case as well in the writings of the Apostolic Fathers and in apocryphal writings of the early Christian period. The writings most closely related to the inartistic language of the uneducated common people are the Gospel of Mark, the Revelation of John, the *Shepherd of Hermas,* and the *Teaching of the Twelve Apostles* (the so-called *Didache*). Paratactic syntax prevails; there are no optatives; and periphrastic forms of the verb are frequent (for example, Mark 13:25 ἔσονται πίπτοντες, appropriately corrected to πεσοῦν-ται in Matt 24:29; examples of periphrastic verbs do also occur in the Lukan writings, but this is due to Semitic or "biblicistic" influence; see below). Loan words from Semitic languages and Latin are used as naturally as in contemporary vernacular Greek. In Mark, the signs of vulgar Koine are so flagrant that its language could not appeal to the semi-educated middle classes: Matthew, even though himself writing in an unpretentious Koine style, had to correct numerous expressions and sentences of the Gospel of Mark in order to produce tolerable and intelligible Greek sentences. Not unlike Paul, Matthew succeeds in producing a literary style that stays as close as possible to the spoken language, while still avoiding the awkwardness and clumsiness of an uneducated style.

The Gospel of John occupies a special position. The language of this book is no doubt simple and normal Koine Greek. All the linguistic peculiarities of this book, also occur in other writers who use Koine Greek, such as Epiktetos. If the language and style of the Fourth Gospel still seem different from other books of the New Testament, it is due to the simplicity of the author's stylistic devices, their limited range, and their frequent repetition. There may also be a greater proximity to the world of Semitic languages, but the question of how the New Testament writings relate to the Semitic languages is not easily answered and deserves special treatment.

(e) The New Testament and the Semitic Languages

All books of the New Testament were originally written in Greek; not a single early Christian Greek writing can be shown to have been translated from Hebrew

Bibliography to §3.2e

Joseph A. Fitzmyer, *A Wandering Aramean: Collected Aramaic Essays* (SBLMS 25; Missoula, MT : Scholars Press, 1979).

Matthew Black, *An Aramaic Approach to the Gospels and Acts* (3d ed.; Oxford: Clarendon, 1967; reprint 1971).

Idem, "The Biblical Languages," in *Cambridge History of the Bible* 1. 1–11.

Raymond A. Martin, *Syntactical Evidence of Semitic Sources in Greek Documents* (SBLSCS 3; Cambridge, MA: Society of Biblical Literature, 1974).

Moisés Silva, "Semantic Borrowing in the New Testament," *NTS* 22 (1975/76) 104-10.

Max Wilcox, "Semitisms in the New Testament," *ANRW* 2.25.2 (1984) 978-1029.

or Aramaic. It is necessary to keep this in mind when discussing the difficult and much disputed problem of Semitic influences on New Testament language. There certainly are Semitisms in the New Testament, the Apostolic Fathers, and the Apocrypha. Some writings contain more Semitisms than others, but on the whole their number is relatively high; this is indisputable. Difficulties arise in the determination of specific instances and of their type and origin. It is therefore necessary to clarify the character and type of the different Semitisms in early Christian literature.

1) *Hebraisms*. Semitisms resulting from a translation from Hebrew into Greek must properly be called Hebraisms. In the New Testament they occur only in quotations of a Greek translation from the Hebrew Bible. Christian authors normally quote from the Septuagint, sometimes from other sources, and occasionally from the translation efforts of scribal traditions (as is the case for most biblical quotations in the Gospel of Matthew). Hebraisms occur both in explicit quotations as well as in allusions, phrases derived from the Hebrew Bible that the author included in his own sentences without quoting explicitly. They appear quite naturally, even in authors who write a good literate Greek style, and prove no more than that the author knew, quoted, and used a collection of Greek documents translated from Hebrew.

2) *Aramaisms*. Semitisms can arise when a particular text is translated into Greek from Aramaic, that is, from the vernacular language of the non-Hellenized populations of Syria and Palestine. They can also occur when an author is writing in an Aramaic-speaking environment, or when an earlier tradition used in a New Testament writing was formulated in such an environment. Aramaisms are most frequent in the gospels, because Jesus, his disciples, and the members of the earliest Palestinian churches spoke Aramaic. Everything that derives from Jesus or from the tradition of the earliest Christian community, or even from later Aramaic-speaking churches, must have been translated into Greek at some time before being incorporated into an early Christian writing. Such translations occurred at an early stage of transmission in the oral tradition before the sources of the extant gospels were composed. Those who translated these traditions indeed may not have been native Greek speakers. Since translations must have existed several decades before the writing of the extant gospels, most of the original Aramaisms were probably replaced by more appropriate Greek terms and phrases in the course of the use of such materials in Greek-speaking communities. Only the Gospel of Mark seems to have used Greek sources that were straightforward translations of Aramaic originals. It is also possible that the source for the miracle stories in the Gospel of John was directly translated from an Aramaic writing. Aramaisms, furthermore, are found in those liturgical traditions that were fixed at an early date, for example, in the Greek version of the Lord's Prayer.

3) *Biblicisms*. Early Christianity inherited from Israel not only its Bible, but also a religious language deeply influenced by that Bible. This inheritance was mediated to Christianity primarily through Hellenistic Judaism and the synagogue, which used in its worship language that was influenced by the Greek version of the Bible, namely, the Septuagint (one can therefore speak of "Sep-

tuagintisms"). Such biblicisms—ultimately Hebraisms, since they derive from the Hebrew Bible—can still be found in later products of ancient Christian literature, since the Greek Bible of Hellenistic Judaism remained the Bible of the Christians. Modern English abounds with such "biblical" language as well, often in phrases taken from the King James Version.

Among early Christian writings, Paul's letters are remarkably free of biblicisms, while in the Lukan writings, composed several decades after the letters of Paul, biblicisms occur frequently, especially in the Acts of the Apostles. Because it is difficult to distinguish Luke's biblicisms from Semitisms that might derive from the use of a source translated from Aramaic, some scholars proposed the unlikely hypothesis of such a source for Acts 1-12. Biblicisms are especially frequent in those Christian authors who are influenced by the preaching style of the synagogue, such as 1 Peter and *1 Clement*. They also occur wherever Jewish methods of exegesis of the Greek Bible were adopted and continued. Both elements, closely related to each other in any case, are visible in *1 Clement* and in the *Epistle of Barnabas*.

4) *Bilingualisms*. Many Semitisms derive from a Greek vernacular that was formed in a bilingual milieu. Pagans and Christians, as well as Jews who spoke Greek, Aramaic, or both languages, were living closely together in many cities of Syria and Palestine. In such environments influences from another language are more quickly absorbed in colloquial and commercial speech than in the literary conventions of language. Some of these Semitisms are semantic borrowings deriving from the general language milieu, such as the use of θάλασσα not only for the "sea" or "ocean," but also for "lake," since the Aramaic ימאא is used for both. Others derive ultimately from the Hebrew Bible. To these belong such expressions as πρόσωπον λανβάνειν = "to show partiality" and πρόσωπον θαυμάζειν = "to flatter." Quite a few theological terms were perfectly good Greek words, but were used more frequently and took on different meanings due to the significance of their Hebrew equivalents: for example, ἄγγελος = "angel" (not "messenger"), δόξα = "glory" (not "opinion"), σπλάγχνα = "love," "mercy" (not "bowels," "guts").

Semitisms of this kind may have arisen in Christian communities in which many members spoke Greek as well as Aramaic. The earliest Christian church in Antioch certainly was such a bilingual community. Galilee itself had a considerable number of Greek-speaking residents, while even in Jerusalem we hear not only of the Aramaic-speaking community of the disciples and followers of Jesus, but also the "Hellenists," that is, Greek-speaking Jewish Christians. Many Semitisms in the Gospel of John can be explained on the same basis: the gospel, or its sources, were composed in a bilingual community of Palestine or Syria. It is not easy to draw a clear distinction between common colloquial Greek and features that derive from Aramaic influences. Some peculiarities which are quite possible in Greek, though rare, occur more frequently when analogous features in Aramaic (or Hebrew) favor such usage. This no doubt explains the striking increase of the Greek instrumental dative with the preposition ἐν (= ב) and the preference for the paratactic καί (= ו) in early Christian writings.

5) *Loan words* from Hebrew and Aramaic appear for various reasons. Semitic

words like βύσσος = the fine linen called "byssus," and μνᾶ = "mina," a monetary unit of 100 drachmas, were well established in Greek commercial language. Other foreign words probably derived from direct contact of the two languages in bilingual communities, such as the address ῥαββί = "rabbi" for a teacher. Liturgy tends to preserve special terms and phrases borrowed from a foreign language, such as the well-known μαράνα θά = מָרַנָא תָא = "Lord come!" (1 Cor 16:22; *Did.* 10.6) or "Hosanna" and "Amen," which have been preserved from their original Hebrew via Greek and Latin in the liturgical usage of modern languages. The Gospel of Mark quotes ἐφφαθά (transcription of the Aramaic אֶתְפְּתַח = "be open!" Mark 7:34) and ταλιθά κοῦμ (transcription of טְלִיתָא קוּם = "young girl, arise!" Mark 5:41). Numerous parallels to the use of such foreign words and formulas can be found in the magical papyri and in Gnostic writings.

3. THE SCIENCES

(a) Presuppositions and Beginnings

In the countries and cities settled by Greeks, scientific thinking began as early as the 6th century BCE. Colonization widened the horizons of their experience, although Egyptian and Babylonian influences had already been felt in the pre-Classical period and made a substantial contribution. The Greeks' knowledge about other countries and people was reflected in story, myth, and legend. Indeed, such stories helped inspire the epic of Homer's *Odyssey*. The Ionian cities of Asia Minor opened the doors to a more scientific view of the world in almost all areas of thought. Philosophical endeavor played an important role, marking a transition from legend and myth to a scientific assessment of experience. Plato's

Bibliography to §3.3: Texts

Morris R. Cohen and I. E. Drabkin, *A Source Book in Greek Science* (Cambridge, MA: Harvard University Press, 1948; reprint 1969).

Bibliography to §3.3: Studies

Rudolf Pfeiffer, *History of Classical Scholarship from the Beginnings to the End of the Hellenistic Age* (Oxford: Clarendon, 1968).

G. E. R. Lloyd, "Hellenistic Science," in *CambAncHist* 7 (2d ed.) 321–52.

Idem, *Greek Science after Aristotle* (New York: Norton, 1973).

Yvon Garlan, "War and Siegecraft," in *CambAncHist* 7 (2d ed.) 353–59.

O. Neugebauer, *The Exact Sciences in Antiquity* (2d ed.; Providence: Brown University Press, 1957; reprint 1970).

George Sarton, *A History of Science: Hellenistic Science and Culture in the Last Three Centuries B.C.* (Cambridge, MA: Harvard University Press, 1959).

Bibliography to §3.3a

M. Cary and E. H. Warmington, *The Ancient Explorers* (2d ed.; Baltimore, MD: Penguin, 1963).

Lionel Casson, *The Ancient Mariners: Seafarers and Sea Fighters of the Mediterranean in Ancient Times* (2d ed.; Princeton, NJ: Princeton University Press, 1991).

Walter Woodburn Hyde, *Ancient Greek Mariners* (New York: Oxford University Press, 1947).

Samuel Sambursky, *The Physical World of the Greeks* (London: Routledge, 1956).

explicit criticism of myth demanded a scientific approach to understanding the world. Thus philosophy provided a theoretical basis for a view of the world that was mathematically exact.

Ethnography as a scholarly discipline began very early. The exploration of the Black Sea and the Mediterranean, an endeavor first reflected in the *Odyssey* and the legend of the Argonauts, called for a more systematic, that is, scientific, account. Phoenician, and before long Greek, explorers began to sail into the Atlantic Ocean. Carthaginian ships reached the British Isles in the 5th century BCE. Some time between 322 and 313 BCE, the Greek Pytheas of Massilia (Marseilles) sailed into the North Sea and perhaps to the island of "Thule" six days north of Britain (Iceland, the Shetland Isles, or Norway?) and brought back a report that in those northern regions the sun never sets during the summer solstice. Euthymenes, also from Massilia, sailed down the west coast of Africa and reached the mouth of the Senegal or Niger river as early as the 6th century BCE. Skylax, from Karia in Asia Minor, under the commission of the Persian king, took a ship as far as the Cabul and Indus rivers and continued his journey back home along the shores of Persia and Arabia into the Red Sea (519– 516 BCE).

Such sea travels created a literary genre called *periploi* ("circumnavigations"), which described foreign countries from the perspective of ships sailing along their coasts with information about routes and distances; sailors used them as handbooks. They were soon taken up by geographers and ethnographers as sources for their own writings, a process that marks the transition from handbook to science. The oldest known ethnographer is Hekataios of Miletos (ca. 560–480 BCE), who reportedly introduced a schematic division of zones for his maps of the world. Beginning with Herodotos (ca. 484–430), interest turned to describing foreign peoples and their customs and habits (νόμοι) as well as the character of their lands (φύσις τῆς χώρας). The beginnings of medical science are closely related to the interest in ethnography. In the 5th century BCE Hippokrates and other members of the Koan school of medicine discussed the connection between the physical features of particular countries and the physiological characteristics of their populations.

Scientific astronomy began in the 4th century BCE. The spherical form of the earth had been discovered in the preceding century. Heraklides of Pontus, a student of Plato, suggested in his dialogues that the earth turns on its axis; he also discussed the possibility that some planets circle the sun. Eudoxos of Knidos (ca. 391–338), another student of Plato's Academy and head of a school on Kyzikos and later in Athens, was—next to Aristotle—the most important scholar with universal interests. The tractate *Eudoxi ars astronomica,* though not written by him, uses many of his insights; it also reinforced the older opinion that the sun, moon, and planets travel around the earth in concentric spheres. Eudoxos made a systematic assessment of the mathematical insights of the Eleatic school and the Pythagoreans and developed theories that enabled Euklid (in Alexandria from 306–283) to write his *Elements,* which became the standard textbook of mathematics and geometry in antiquity. Practical insights from mathematics and physics, such as the law of leverage, were also beginning to be applied by builders of simple machines and military equipment.

Scientific work reached its climax with the natural scientist and philosopher Aristotle, son of a physician from Stagira on the Chalkidike. Like other important scholars of his time, Aristotle studied at the Academy of Plato. For several years he taught in Mysia in Asia Minor, at Mytilene on Lesbos, and at the Macedonian court of Philip II in Pella. In 335 Aristotle moved to Athens and founded his own school in a gymnasium known as the Lyceum. He organized an extensive research program covering many fields. In addition to most of the natural sciences, his research included the fields of politics and history, for which his school assembled extensive source materials; as many as 158 different constitutions of cities and states were collected and compared. Aristotle's own contributions were most significant in the fields of meteorology, botany, and zoology. He supplemented existing collections of zoological materials, added many valuable observations, and created a system of classification; his insights remained unequaled until the beginning of modern natural science. In the field of botany, all that the ancient world had known were casual descriptions of plants useful for the pharmacological interests of medicine. Aristotle's student Theophrastos set up a classification system for all plants, described their structures, and collected materials that physicians, travelers, and authors of agricultural books contributed. With these works, scholarship in the field of biology had already reached its apex at the beginning of the Hellenistic period.

(b) The Golden Age of Scholarship in the Hellenistic Period.

The widening horizons of human experience through Alexander's conquests had their fullest impact in the two following centuries. Near Eastern influences had deep and lasting effects. Hellenistic kings, especially the Ptolemies, were generous supporters of scholarship, along with several cities, especially Rhodos.

Members of the school of Aristotle (the Peripatetics) continued the research begun in the previous generation. Next to Theophrastos, Eudemos of Rhodos was the most distinguished scholar of this school. In addition to the fields of inquiry already mentioned, Peripatetic research was devoted to anthropology, hydrology, mineralogy, musical theory (Aristoxenos being the first musicologist), and the history of science (natural philosophy, geometry, and astronomy). An important result of this interest in the history of scholarship was the creation of biographies of important and famous people of the past (§3.4d). Inspite of the decline of this school, it remained an important center for studies in political science, history of science, and biography.

The work of Archimedes of Syracuse, born in 287 BCE, marks the high point of ancient mathematics. A large number of the mathematical calculations and geometric discoveries that modern knowledge owes to antiquity were made by Archimedes. He calculated that the relationship between the circumference and the diameter of the circle, designated by the Greek letter π, was a number

Bibliography to §3.3b

Fraser, *Alexandria*, 1. 336–479, 520–53.
G. E. R. Lloyd, "Science and Mathematics," in Finley, *Legacy*, 256–300.
Thomas L. Heath, ed. and trans., *Greek Astronomy* (New York: Dutton, 1932).

between 3 10/70 and 3 10/71 = 3.1408 and 3.1428; the number assumed today is 3.1416. He discovered the relation between the content of a sphere and its corresponding cylinder. The insight that a body in water loses as much of its weight as the weight of the water it replaces is still known as the "Archimedean Principle." He also experimented with practical applications of mathematical and physical scientific results, inventing the differential pulley and the "Archimedean Screw," which could be used for water pumps on boats and for irrigation. Archimedes also constructed the defense machinery that Syracuse used successfully for a number of years to withstand a Roman siege. It was no accident that he was slain in 212 by Roman soldiers invading Syracuse.

The most ingenious astronomic discovery of the Hellenistic period was made at its very inception: the anticipation of the Copernican universe in the heliocentric system of Aristarchos of Samos (first half of the 3d century BCE). He taught that the sun was about three hundred times the size of the earth, that the earth and planets move in circles around the sun, and that the earth rotates on its own axis. He thus satisfied Plato's call for a demonstration that the apparent loops in the courses of the planets were actually circles. But Aristarchos' theories did not prevail; the Stoic Kleanthes even accused him of blaspheming the gods.

Babylonian astronomy made an essential contribution. Copious Babylonian materials were published in Greek translation during the 3d century BCE; but the systematization of Babylonian observations was a Greek contribution. It is unclear, whether the most important astronomer of antiquity, Hipparchos of Nicea, who taught mostly in Rhodos from 160 to 125 BCE, depended on Babylonian calculations. His most significant discovery was the procession of the equinoxes. He also calculated the exact length of the year (his result differs from modern calculations only by 6 minutes and 26 seconds), and determined that the lunar revolution lasts 29 days, 12 hours, 44 minutes, and 2½ seconds—differing by less than a second from modern calculations—and created a catalogue of 800 fixed stars, arranged according to three degrees of brightness.

According the first-century BCE scholar Poseidonios, the diameter of the sun was 39½ times that of the earth (actually 109 times the diameter of the earth). Poseidonios calculated the distance of the sun from the earth to be 6,545 times the earth's diameter (actually 11,741 times the earth's diameter).

The proposition that the earth is spherical generated the principles for a new scientific geography. Significant incentives came from Alexander the Great, who had employed geodetic surveyors immediately after his conquests. This established a purely geographical discipline quite different from the older science of ethnography, which was primarily concerned with the description of peoples, climate, plants, and animals. The new goal was to draw accurate maps of the countries and of the earth. Eratosthenes, librarian in Alexandria from 246 BCE who also wrote philosophical and mathematical works and a history of comedy, designed a system for cartographic survey of all known countries. He recognized that all the oceans of the world are connected and that the inhabited earth he knew—Europe, Asia, and Africa—must therefore be one huge island. In his calculations of the circumference of the earth, Eratosthenes erred by only 300 km. The astronomer Hipparchos later criticized Eratosthenes' cartographic endeavor and argued that observers in various spots should first establish the longitude and latitude of as many places as possible. Only a small part of these grand designs was actually accomplished, but many sites were actually plotted, as can be seen from the materials collected by Ptolemy (§3.3c).

In the field of medicine, progress was made primarily in anatomy, especially by the physicians Herophilos and Erasistratos, who worked in Alexandria during the 3d century BCE and were able to use human corpses for dissection. (A later report says that they also made vivisection of criminals condemned to death.) Hierophilos discovered the nervous system of the human body, and perhaps also the principle of blood circulation; the traditional assumption was that the arteries transported air, an error that prevailed in later times.

Philology became a scientific discipline during the Hellenistic period, especially in consolidating grammar and editing texts. Several generations of scholars in Alexandria participated in this process, most notably Aristarchos of Samothrake (ca. 216–144 BCE). Incentives for codifying grammar came from Stoic philosophy, which undertook the first classification of letters into vowels and consonants and suggested a doctrine of inflections and tenses. Aristarchos systematically elaborated the patterns of inflections, established paradigms for conjugations and declensions, and prepared a list of irregular verbs. His student Dionysios Thrax collected the results of these efforts and edited a handbook that remained definitive throughout antiquity.

The second major task for the Alexandrian philologists was the systematic edition of classical texts: collection and comparison of manuscripts, emendation, and new publication. To facilitate this work, commentaries, monographs, and concordances were produced. Alexandria played a leading role from the beginnings of scientific philology in the 3d and 2d centuries BCE until its decline in the 3d century CE. Christian scholars like Origen, Lucian of Antioch, and Eusebios of Caesarea, who produced learned works on the Bible, were able to take their starting point from this tradition of philological scholarship.

On the other hand, a different branch of philology, namely etymology, eagerly pursued by many, never reached the same level of scientific clarity. From the time of Homer, attempts had been made to explain certain words etymologically. Poets, sophists, and Homeric interpreters vied with each other in this art. Despite Plato's criticism of etymologists who wanted to define the true essence of things denoted by words, such efforts continued unabated among grammarians and philosophers, especially the Stoics. Philoxenos of Alexandria (1st century BCE) tried to establish a scientific base for etymology: he claimed that monosyllables were the roots of all words. Despite such efforts, such as Aristarchos' principle of analogy, according to which Homeric texts should be interpreted solely through other Homeric texts, ancient philology never advanced beyond the elementary stages of scholarship.

(c) The Later Developments in the Roman Period

Even an unbiased observer cannot help but see the developments of the Roman period as a decline in scholarship and science. Creative research came to an end in the 1st century BCE. Its place was taken by encyclopedias and collections of

the results of scholarly work of former generations and by uncritical popularizations written solely for entertainment. Superstitious opinions became widespread
again, and views were revived that had been shown to be inaccurate by the
scholars of the Hellenistic period.

In mathematics no new discoveries were made during the Roman imperial
period, but the achievements of previous mathematical scholarship were preserved and passed on through compendia. In astronomy the Alexandrian scholar
Ptolemy (ca. 100–170 CE) wrote a comprehensive collection of all ancient astronomical achievements, which is preserved in Arabic under the title "Almagest"
("al" is the Arabic article, "magest" is derived from the Greek title *Megist[e
Syntaxis]*). This work also contains some of Ptolemy's own insights, which are
often inferior to those of his predecessors. Already during the Hellenistic period,
zoologists had shown an increasing interest in the strange and curious phenomena of the animal kingdom. There had also been studies of the intelligence of such
species as poisonous animals. On the whole, anecdotes prevailed over scientific
inquiry.

Even geography and ethnography were subject to such interests. The curiosity
about the peculiarities and oddities of other nations produced some historical
information and paradoxography but little ethnographic scholarship. There must
have been voluminous collections of these materials. Historians and geographers
like Polybios and Strabo used them and contributed new materials, but did not
always evaluate their information critically. Some of these writings simply
wanted to entertain. This led to the production of books that indiscriminately
collected whatever reportage was available about foreign countries, serious information as well as amusing stories, authentic reports along with completely unre-
liable tales. The Hellenistic romance derived much of its material from such
sources.

Only medical scholarship reached new heights during the Roman imperial
period, although the physician's position in society declined. The major cultic
and healing establishments of the god Asklepios (§4.3d) from the Classical and
Hellenistic periods continued to flourish. Yet the public health services that had
employed trained physicians declined. Late Hellenism saw a division of medicine into several sects, whose endless quarrels resemble those of the philosophical schools. Dogmatism often prevailed over scientific investigation. At the
beginning of the Roman imperial period, medical handbooks collecting the insights and knowledge of the older period were replaced by uncritical popularizations about medicine, pharmacology, and diet with a rapid growth in quackery
and magic and an increase of specialists among practicing physicians who catered to the tastes of a spoiled urban upper class.

In view of this general deterioration in medical services, the achievements of
the great physicians of the imperial period are all the more remarkable. Their
medical observations and scholarly works enriched medical science considerably. Rufus of Ephesos (beginning of the 2d century CE) collected and clarified the
anatomical insights of his predecessors, and his careful descriptions of pathological symptoms contributed considerably to the progress of internal medicine. His
contemporary Soranus Medicus published works on gynecology and infant care

that were the best antiquity achieved in this field. Among his other prolific literary productions, Soranus' lost book *On the Soul* became the source for Tertullian's *De anima*. The most important physician was Galen of Pergamon (129–199 CE). His numerous medical books were based on his wide experience as a practicing physician and on his endeavors in medical research, and they summarize the knowledge of antiquity for most areas of medical science. In every instance he uses his own judgment, which often surpasses that of his predecessors. Galen's books were the last truly great medical works from ancient times, and also constitute the final triumph of ancient scholarship in the natural sciences. They continued to be authoritative for medical praxis and theory until the end of the Middle Ages.

4. LITERATURE

(a) Presuppositions

In the Hellenistic period, the broader understanding of the world extended to literary works, in which new subjects, forms, and traditions emerged. The connection of the Greek literary inheritance to the world of the Orient became visible in many ways. Eastern subject matter could appear in Greek literary genres, for example the drama *Exodus* by the Jewish tragedian Ezekiel. Greeks in turn included in their literary works many narratives, topics, and subjects that reflected the experiences of other people. Hellenized foreigners also began to contribute to the development of Greek literature: Iamboulos, the author of one of the oldest Hellenistic romances, came from Syria; the Syrian Lucian of Samosata was one of the most productive Greek writers of the Roman period; Babrius, a Roman by birth, court poet of a certain king Alexander (descendent of

Bibliography to §3.4

Albin Lesky, *A History of Greek Literature* (New York: Crowell, 1966).

Patricia E. Easterling and Bernard M. W. Knox, eds., *The Cambridge History of Classical Literature*, vol. 1: *Greek Literature* (Cambridge: Cambridge University Press, 1985).

Albrecht Dihle, *Griechische Literaturgeschichte von Homer bis zum Hellenismus* (2d ed.; München: Beck, 1991).

Bibliography to §3.4a: Texts

Euripides: Greek texts and English translations by A. S. Way in LCL. Most convenient edition.

E. R. Dodds, ed., *Euripides' Bacchae* (2d ed.; Oxford: Oxford University Press, 1960). Introduction, Greek text, and commentary.

Bibliography to §3.4a: Studies

Gilbert Murray, *Euripides and His Age* (2d ed.; London: Oxford University Press, 1955).

G. M. A Grube, *The Drama of Euripides* (2d ed.; New York: Barnes and Noble, 1941; reprint 1961).

Charles Segal, *Dionysiac Poetics and Euripides' Bacchae* (Princeton, NJ: Princeton University Press, 1982).

Harvey Yunis, *A New Creed: Fundamental Religious Beliefs in the Athenian Polis and Euripidean Drama* (Hyp. 91; Göttingen: Vandenhoeck & Ruprecht, 1988).

Bernard W. M. Knox, "Euripides," in Easterling and idem, *Greek Literature*, 316–39.

Herod the Great) in Cetis of Cilicia, put the fables of Aesop into Greek verse. Numerous writers, such as the Babylonian priest Berossos, the Egyptian priest Manetho, and the Jewish author Josephus, wrote in Greek about the history and traditions of their own people.

As Greek and Near Eastern elements became inextricably mixed in literary works, the quantity and variety of writings increased. The strict forms of Classical Greek literature were dissolved as Greek literature of the Hellenistic and Roman periods surpassed in its variety, quantity, and influence anything known in preceding centuries or in the subsequent period down to the invention of the printing press. An enormous number of people wrote a great deal about a vast number of topics, much of which is lost. Educated readers might restrict their reading to Classical authors and to philosophical and scientific literature; but there was also a broader public, able to read and hungry to be entertained. Writers are found not only at the courts of the great kings, but also as poets and historians of every petty prince; authors from remote Hellenistic towns could hope to find a public that would honor them and perhaps even read their books.

One aspect of book production in the Hellenistic and Roman periods was the writing and distribution of books designed for private use. Philosophical schools and the Museum in Alexandria produced collections of materials that were primarily designed to be used by scholars, while religious communities cultivated their own literatures, as is visible in many examples from Jewish and Christian writings. Some of these works were written for particular occasions, for example, letters that were only published at a later date; other writings were intended for distribution among community members, although some of these books might also have been written for a broader public. The forms and genres of such literature vary with the peculiar traditions of a religion. But even these writings should not be separated from the general history of Hellenistic literature. As these religions became Hellenized, the literary culture of Hellenism strongly influenced the formation of the specific literatures of religious communities.

In view of the diversity and multiformity of Hellenistic literature, it is not possible to describe all its important features. Even so, this literature exhibits a certain coherence, since it is basically connected to the traditions of Classical Greece and it expresses fundamental cultural insights and currents that give it some cohesiveness. As Hellenism also shaped the culture of the Roman period, a continuous development of literature extends even into areas where Greek was not the primary spoken language. The following survey is limited to those features that are significant for the understanding of early Christianity, but it must begin with one particular precursor of Hellenistic literature, namely, the last great dramatist of the Classical period, Euripides.

Although Euripides wrote in the second half of the 5th century BCE (he died in 407/6), Hellenistic literature and indeed the whole spirit of Hellenism can hardly be discussed without him. Its subjects, motifs, and problems were more decisively influenced by Euripides than by anyone else. Living in a period in which signs of cultural disintegration became visible, Euripides was the first to recognize and portray the characteristic predicament of human existence, which was to become such a dominant element in the human sensibilities of the following centuries. With this insight Euripides marks the threshold of a new epoch.

Euripides, however, would be misunderstood as an advocate of reason in the fight against superstition, as an innovator or a revolutionary. Although he was influenced by the Sophists, his insights do not belong to any particular philosophical school. His influence stems from his radically new characterization of human life; human beings with all their judicious thoughts and with all their passions are, as individuals, ultimately left isolated and helpless. This human predicament does not permit the reconciliation of opposites, nor can the existing political and religious structures (which for him, of course, are the institutions of the Greek polis) provide solutions. One might say that Euripides, in the midst of the Peloponnesian War, saw more clearly than any of his contemporaries that the Greek polis, even in its greatest moments, offered no safeguard against chaos. Humanity was threatened by powers far greater than could be managed by even a well ordered commonwealth, indeed more ominous than the best constitution might have imagined.

The greatness and impotence of humanity are equally bound to fate—here again Euripides anticipates a basic insight of Hellenism. Not that there were no longer any gods and mysterious powers in the world; on the contrary, human beings, even as they plan and devise rational solutions, are subject to such powers, whether they be called gods, or chance, or fate, or given a particular name, such as Dionysos. Though one can recognize these powers, they cannot be made to answer to human calculations. To encounter them may well be one's doom. Even if humans are willing to acknowledge and worship such powers, they cannot claim to be their equals; harmony with such powers is not allotted to the human race. A deity may even force someone into its realm of sovereignty, though this can lead to destruction, as Dionysos destroys Pentheus, the king of Thebes (*Bacchae*). This view of human existence points ahead to some of the central questions that would occupy Hellenistic literature for many centuries and become its theme in numerous variations.

(b) Drama, Comedy, and Poetry

The tradition of Classical Greek tragedy was continued in the Hellenistic period. The Ptolemaic kings of Egypt especially encouraged the cultivation of this genre. The second Ptolemy arranged dramatic contests in Alexandria. But

Bibliography to §3.4b: Texts

Eric Walter Handley, *The Dyskolos of Menander* (Cambridge, MA: Harvard University Press, 1965).

Fragments of Menander: Greek texts with English translations by F. C. Allinson in LCL.

Callimachus: Greek text and English translation of hymns and epigrams by A. W. Mair, fragments by C. A. Trypanis in LCL (2 vols.).

E. V. Rieu, trans., *Apollonius: The Voyage of the Argo* (2d ed.; Baltimore: Penguin, 1971).

A. S. F. Gow, ed., *Theocriti Bucolici Graeci* (OCT; Oxford: Clarendon, 1952).

almost nothing of the rich dramatic poetry (more than fifty dramatists are known from the 3d century BCE) has been preserved and only a few fragments, totaling just several dozen lines, have survived. From the following century only two tragedies are known in fragments; one of these is the drama *Exodus* of the Jewish tragedian Ezekiel. In Latin, however, Classical tragedy experienced a remarkable revival among the playwrights of the 2d century BCE in Rome (§6.4b).

In the early imperial period it was still fashionable to try one's hand at writing a tragedy; even Caesar and Augustus attempted it. Yet public performances of tragedies became less frequent. Romans preferred to listen to readings of favorite sections and excerpts from Classical Greek tragedies. Pantomimes were the most popular theatrical genre, and one might watch a pantomime show incorporating a complete tragedy of Euripides with dance and music, but without the words.

The spirit of Hellenism is more directly mirrored in the New Comedy of Athens. During the time of Alexander's Successors, comedy experienced a revival in that city, which had once been the foremost power in Greece. The most important poet, and the only one whose work is at least partially preserved, was Menander (342/41–293/92). It is due to his view of the political situation that New Comedy does not share the concerns of Aristophanes' comedies. Menander presupposes that the individual no longer wields political power and focuses on the particulars of the human situation. The persons who appear in his comedy are no longer mere types, as in the Old Attic Comedy, but individual personalities. Topics and characters are derived from the milieu of the ordinary classes: citizens, their wives and daughters, craftsmen, farmers, slaves, travelers, all seen along with their personal and social problems. They are shown as individuals who in their own way try to cope with the adversities of their social situation,

Idem, *The Greek Bucolic Poets: Translation with Brief Notes* (Cambridge: Cambridge University Press, 1953).

Walter George Headlam and Alfred D. Knox, trans., *Herodas: The Mimes and Fragments* (Cambridge: Cambridge University Press, 1922). Greek text and English translation.

Herondas: Greek text and English translation by A. D. Knox in LCL (Choliambics).

Anthologia Palatina (Greek Anthology): Text and English translation by W. R. Paton in LCL (5 vols.).

F. L. Lucas, ed. and trans., *A Greek Garland: A Selection from the Palatine Anthology* (2d ed.; London: Cohen & West, 1949).

Bibliography to §3.4b: Studies

T. B. L. Webster, *Hellenistic Poetry and Art* (New York: Barnes and Noble, 1964).

Fraser, *Alexandria,* 1. 553–674, 719–93.

E. A. Barber, "Alexandrian Literature," in *CambAncHist* 7 (1st ed.) 249–83.

Peter D. Arnott, "Drama," in Grant and Kitzinger, *Civilization,* 3. 1477–93.

Sander Goldberg, *The Making of Menander's Comedy* (Berkeley, CA: University of California Press, 1980).

E. W. Handley, "Menander and the New Comedy," in Easterling and Knox, *Greek Literature,* 414–25.

Anthony W. Bulloch, "Hellenistic Poetry," in Easterling and Knox, *Greek Literature,* 541–621.

Bryan Hainsworth, "Epic Poetry," in Grant and Kitzinger, *Civilization,* 3. 1417–35.

Konrat Ziegler, *Das hellenistische Epos* (2d ed; Leipzig: Teubner, 1966).

Joseph Russo, "Greek Lyric and Elegiac Poetry," in Grant and Kitzinger, *Civilization,* 3. 1437–54.

constantly threatened by poverty and malice as well as unpredictable fate. Greed and a desire for money, or at least for a few material possessions that would secure one's existence, often seem to be the only impulses in the lives of these characters. But in the midst of all this, Menander tries to uncover vestiges of genuine humanity, visible in the ability to forgive and to be reconciled. Humaneness, Menander insists, is a general human possibility, open equally to Greeks and to barbarians, to free people and slaves.

New Comedy extended its influence beyond Athens, but it is difficult to judge how broadly it affected other areas. The names of more than seventy authors of comedies are known, and some of them are said to have written more than a hundred comedies; many of them were not Athenians. At the beginning of the Roman imperial period, New Comedy, together with its Roman successors, was pushed aside by mimes and pantomimes. Paul quotes a maxim ("Bad company destroys good morals") from one of Menander's comedies in 1 Cor 15:33, and the wall paintings of the Slope Houses in Ephesos demonstrate that these comedies were still popular.

The demand for entertainment was filled by the mime plays, which dominated the theater everywhere in the later Hellenistic and the Roman periods. Developed out of some ancient forms of dance, probably connected with cultic rites, and strongly influenced by New Comedy, the mime became the most popular form of dramatic performance. Troupes of mimes went from town to town, giving solo or group performances on quickly improvised stages in the marketplace. They spoke the language of the people while presenting ancient subjects in modern improvisations, along with dance, music, acrobatic performances, and juggling tricks in farcical skits. Occasionally kings would hire companies of mimes, and rich people invited them into their homes.

Naturally very little of this repertory is preserved in written form. But the fragments of the *Mimiambi* of the Koan poet Herondas (3d century BCE) give a taste of the contents and subjects of these theatrical performances. Characteristic titles include "The Bawd," "The Pimp," "The Schoolmaster," "The Female Worshipers," "The Jealous Mistress," "The Private Conversation." Like New Comedy, the mimes put the individual from the middle and lower classes, people without political ambition, on center stage. Daily life and its all too ordinary predicaments are presented to the audience in all their licit and illicit variety. Right and wrong might be illustrated in situations not normally discussed in polite society. True and false friendships are discussed in relationships that cross social boundaries. The mimes mirror the realities of everyday life: one could find a reflection of one's true self, and the audience was able to commiserate with or laugh at itself. But the mimes did not allow their audiences to transcend the limitations of banal everyday experience and recognize their true identity in experiences in the realm of unique and extraordinary events.

Poetry had its golden age under the patronage of the second Ptolemy in Alexandria. Most important was Kallimachos (born shortly before the year 300 BCE), author of the Alexandrian library catalogue, of the first known encyclopedia, and of geographical, mythological, and polemical writings. Epigrams and hymns are preserved from his poetic works (the quotation in Tit 1:12 is adapted from his *Hymn to Zeus*) as well as large fragments of his major work the *Aitia*. He uses mythological traditions in these works in a manner characteristic of the spirit of Hellenism. Kallimachos' poetry divorces religious customs and festivals as well as their legends from their original cultic settings. However, rationalistic criticism of mythology is equally absent; rather, his refined and elegant poetry represents mythology positively in artistic form. Occasional references to the Ptolemaic king simply acknowledge his divinity, not as an expression of faith in royal divinity, but as a piece of court poetry recognizing its patron, though without flattery. Neither the ancient religion with its cults, nor the criticism of myth by the Sophists and Plato seems to be a live issue. Kallimachos instead rejuvenates myth by resuming the poetic tradition of Hesiod and the *Homeric Hymns*. Kallimachos' poetry deeply influenced Roman poets such as Ovid and Virgil.

The outstanding bucolic poet of Hellenism was Kallimachos' contemporary Theokritos. He began his career in Syracuse, then moved to Alexandria—yet apparently without any formal connection to its Museum and library—and later to Kos. For the celebration of the victory of Ptolemy Philadelphos in the First Syrian War he wrote a hymn praising the king and his sister-wife as "savior gods." His great achievements are works that were later called *Eidyllia* = "small poems" (not "idylls" in the modern sense), in which he describes pastoral topics and scenes with genuine enthusiasm for nature and reproduces realistic dialogues about everyday events in the lives of shepherds. Some of his poems are in fact "Mimes," vignettes of action and conversation that also depict city life and, like the *mimiambi* of Herondas, describe characters that are drawn mostly from the lower classes.

The Alexandrian Apollonios, called the Rhodian because he later (after 246/45 BCE) moved to Rhodos, was Kallimachos' student. Among poems and philological works he wrote the *Argonautica,* the only surviving Greek epic composed between Homer and the *Dionysiaca* of Nonnos in the 5th century CE. It is a typically Hellenistic work, reflecting intensive study of sources and incorporating geographical and antiquarian knowledge accumulated by the Alexandrian scholars. In a manner characteristic of the Alexandrian school, the *Argonautica* demonstrates a pronounced interest in etiologies, psychological analysis of its characters, and descriptions of nature, together with sometimes rather dry travel narratives. Several of the elements that became constitutive parts of the Greek romance were already present in this epic, and yet it also influenced the Latin epic poetry of Virgil.

The epigram, popular among these poets, mirrors the soul of Hellenism. Its original setting was lamentation for the dead, praising a deceased person's virtues. It might be inscribed on a commemorative herm, and could also appear in votive inscriptions. Detached from their cultic setting epigrams became brief elegies that were read on all sorts of occasions, such as a symposium. Themes emphasizing heroic greatness had almost completely disappeared; instead one sang the praise of individual joy and love. There are also elegiac descriptions of a craft or profession, of artistic works, and of impressions of nature.

The didactic poem was one of several other popular genres. The Hellenistic world considered it great art to versify the most eccentric subjects. Specialized scientific prose literature from such areas of medicine, zoology, and astronomy became the subjects of poetic works. The less poets understood of the subject matter, the more they could be sure of public admiration.

(c) Historiography

The Hellenistic period was unusually productive in the field of historiography. But although hundreds of fragments have survived from universal histories, local histories, autobiographies, and historical monographs, major portions are extant only from the works of Polybios and Diodoros Siculus. Somewhat better preserved are the works of the Greek historians from the Roman imperial period: almost all the books written by the Jewish historian Josephus and large parts of the histories of Dionysios of Halikarnassos, Arrian, Dio Cassius, and Herodian (§6.4d).

The beginning of the Hellenistic period marks a decisive innovation: histories were written by men of affairs who themselves had participated in the events they described. Writers belonging to the generation that had personally known Alexander the Great produced—not without political designs—well-informed reports based on their own experience or on reliable sources such as diaries and original documents. Among these works was a history of Alexander written by King Ptolemy I of Egypt, and the report of Alexander's admiral Nearchos about his sailing expedition from India through the Arabian Sea and the Persian Gulf to the Euphrates. Both works are preserved in part by Arrian.

Hieronymos of Kardia, a friend and associate of the Diadoch Eumenes, wrote a history of the Diadochi covering the period from the death of Alexander to the

Bibliography to §3.4c: Texts

Felix Jacoby, *Die Fragmente der griechischen Historiker* (15 vols.; reprint Leiden: Brill, 1954–1964).
Polybios: Greek text and English translation by W. R. Paton in LCL (6 vols.).
Diodoros Siculus: Greek text and English translation by C. H. Oldfather et al. in LCL (12 vols.).

Bibliography to §3.4c: Studies

Fraser, *Alexandria*, 1. 495–519.
Arnaldo Momigliano, *Essays in Ancient and Modern Historiography* (Oxford: Blackwell, 1977).
Idem, "History and Biography," in Finley, *Legacy,* 155–84.
Idem, *The Classical Foundations of Modern Historiography* (Sather Classical Lectures 54; Berkeley and Los Angeles, CA: University of California Press, 1990).
Stephen Usher, "Greek Historiography and Biography," in Grant and Kitzinger, *Civilization,* 3. 1525–40.
Charles H. Talbert, "Biographies of Philosophers and Rulers as Instruments of Religious Propaganda in Mediterranean Antiquity," *ANRW* 2.16.2 (1978) 1619–51.
Henry R. Immerwahr and W. R. Connor, "Historiography," in Easterling and Knox, *Greek Literature*, 426–71.
Kurt von Fritz, "Aristotle's Contribution to the Practice and Theory of Historiography," in *University of California Publications in Philosophy* 28.3 (Berkeley and Los Angeles, CA: University of California Press, 1958) 113–38.
T. R. Glover, "Polybius," in *CambAncHist* 8 (1st ed.) 1–24.
Martin Dibelius, "The Speeches in Acts and Ancient Historiography," in idem, *Studies in the Acts of the Apostles* (ed. Heinrich Greeven; London: SCM, 1956; and reprints) 138–85.

death of Pyrrhos (273/72 BCE). This work is lost, but was used and quoted by later historians like Diodoros Siculus and Arrian. As these historians occupied important political positions, their investigation of causes, description of success and failure, and determination of trends were fashioned by writers who had a vested interest in historical developments. Also the later Hellenistic and Roman historians Polybios, Arrian, and Dio Cassius, Caesar and Tacitus, and to a certain degree also Josephus, played significant roles in the political events of their time; Livy is probably the only exception.

Polybios (born before 200 BCE, died in 129 or after 120 BCE) was the scion of an aristocratic family from Megalopolis in Arkadia. As a leading official of the Achaian league, he was deported to Rome in 167 BCE, one of a thousand exiles from leading Achaian families. During his seventeen years in Rome, Polybios had close contacts with influential political circles. His friendship with the younger Scipio dates from this period. After a brief return to Greece in the year 150, he participated in the African campaign of Scipio against Carthage and joined a naval expedition westward along the coast of North Africa. After the disastrous defeat of the Achaian league by Rome in 146 BCE, when Corinth was razed to the ground, Polybios negotiated successfully with Rome for clemency on behalf of his fellow countrymen. Later he probably participated in Scipio's Numantian war in Iberia (134–133 BCE) and traveled extensively outside of his Greek homeland.

Polybios' historical work is intimately related to his activity as a politician. When he wrote that only those who participate actively in the events of their time are capable of writing history (12.25), he accurately characterized his own political historiography, the critical search for truth through "pragmatic historiography." Moreover, history must be universal if it is to clarify the end toward which all historical developments are moving. For Polybios this destiny was Roman hegemony over the whole world (1.3–5).

Miracle stories and *paradoxa* have no place in history writing because they obscure the quest for the causes of historical events, which is the historian's most important task. In order to accomplish that task, one must inquire into the background of the political situation and of the leading political figures, by investigating countries, nations, and important individuals. Three disciplines are therefore of utmost importance for the historian: ethnography, the study of state constitutions, and biography. At the same time, Polybios knows the power of *Tyche*—whether this be chance, luck, or fate—and he is wise enough to grant a considerable margin to this most incalculable of causes. Polybios also seeks to teach morality in his historical writing, while explicitly rejecting the notion that historiography should provide entertainment for the reader (2.56). The primary source of the historian who has participated actively in the events described is the writer's own experience; next are scrutiny of other participants, written statements, letters, and speeches of politicians; and finally, documents and information from older historians, which must be critically evaluated.

No other historian of the Hellenistic period can be compared with Polybios, either in his accomplishments or his methodical treatment of sources. It is debated whether the "pragmatic" writing of history advocated by Polybios was rivaled by a school of "tragic-pathetic" historiography. Although Polybios attacks the 3d-century historian Phylarchos for his attempts to affect the feelings of his readers by vivid descriptions of terrible and tragic events, it is unlikely that there was a program of tragic-pathetic historiography. Most Hellenistic historians knew and at least subscribed to the principle of objective historiography; whether and to what degree they were successful is another matter. Rhetorical devices were often used, even by Polybios himself. Sources were not always critically evaluated. Hearsay and legendary materials were often presented as facts.

As Polybios had continued the work of the 3d-century historian Timaios (whom he attacks in book 12), Poseidonios (ca. 135–50 BCE) endeavored to continue Polybios' universal history. Little is preserved of the 52 books of his historical work, which may have extended as far as the wars of Pompey. Poseidonios sees history as guided by divine providence, a Stoic concept replacing Polybios' *Tyche*. But no longer is rule by Rome seen as history's ultimate destiny. Rather, providence balances the continuing decadence of culture and morality with an increase in social unrest and barbaric invasions. Thus the moral disintegration of the Greeks, especially the Seleucids in the east, is visited by the rise of the Parthians; and the slow demise of Rome and its inability to maintain psychological control—as the reforms of the Gracchi (§6.1d) illustrate—is met by slave insurrections and invasions by the Germanic barbarians. Their depiction as noble savages still untouched by the ills of culture reveals a lack of critical evaluation. This is also evident in his unquestioning acceptance of stories about Sicilian slaves, though this at least shows his social concern.

While Poseidonios was still writing history by investigating the causes of events, these causes were sought in the general psychological climate, no longer in specific facts or individual actions. Other historians of the later Hellenistic period were primarily collectors and compilers—however useful for their preservation of valuable information. Nikolaus of Damascus, court historian of Herod the Great, wrote a world history in 144 books, which was later used by the Jewish historian Josephus, providing rich and detailed information about that Jewish king. Alexander Polyhistor from Miletos (ca. 100–40 BCE) collected materials about the peoples of the east, including many fragments of Jewish writers; some of these are preserved by the church historian Eusebius.

The extant sections of the universal history of Diodoros Siculus (1st century BCE) are more extensive. Important sources and materials are preserved here, though Diodoros' own accomplishments as a historian are negligible. More able as a writer was Dionysios of Halikarnassos (in Rome ca. 30–8 BCE), though his history of Rome is full of admiration for its greatness and sometimes reveals a lack of critical judgment. Ten books of his history are preserved, covering Roman beginnings to the 5th century BCE. Parallel to these historical works at the end of the Hellenistic period are the beginnings of Roman historiography (see §6.4d).

Alongside these major historical works, valuable as sources, stood an extensive literary corpus dealing with various historical subjects that would satisfy even ancient standards of historiography neither in their mastery of subject matter nor in their critical intention. They were nonetheless influential in shaping the views of their contemporaries. The panegyric glorification of Alexander the Great, which began during Alexander's lifetime, deeply influenced the literary composition of the Alexander legend and romance and thus, indirectly, the image of Alexander in later antiquity. In other works about rulers of the Hellenistic period panegyrics, rhetoric, legendary imagination, and the desire to amuse the reader were the leading motifs. Didodoros Siculus often included such materials in his history. Since ethnographic interests were widespread in antiquity, uncritical reception of such information led to incorporating untrustworthy accounts about foreign countries and peoples and promoted an emphasis on anything that was curious and peculiar. This tendency corresponds to developments in other genres of literature during the time, a trend that continued well into the Roman imperial period.

(d) Biography and Aretalogy

In the countries of the east the monarchic form of government provided the cultural impetus for the development of biography. Egypt was first to develop the biography of the ruler, and soon of leading officials, according to fixed and detailed patterns that had been established since ancient times. Biographical sections of Israel's scriptures, found in the story of Moses, in the prophetic books (especially Jeremiah), and in Nehemiah used the same schemata. In Classical Greece, however, biography was not considered a genre of literature, although Homeric epic is already interested in detailing the life of its heroes, and books

---

Bibliography to §3.4d: Texts

Philo, *Life of Moses:* Greek Text and English translation by F. H. Colson in LCL (Philo, vol. 6).
Suetonius, *Lives of the Caesars:* Latin text and English translation by J. C. Rolfe in LCL (2 vols.).
Philostratus, *Life of Apollonius of Tyana:* Greek text and English translation by C. Conybeare in LCL (2 vols.).
Richard Reitzenstein, *Hellenistische Wundererzählungen* (Leipzig: Teubner, 1906 and reprints).

Bibliography to §3.4d: Studies

Arnaldo Momigliano, *The Development of Greek Biography* (2d ed.; Cambridge, MA: Harvard University Press, 1993)
Idem, "History and Biography," in Finley, *Legacy,* 155–84.
Albrecht Dihle, *Studien zur griechischen Biographie* (AAWG.PH 3,37; 2d ed.; Göttingen: Vandenhoeck & Ruprecht, 1970).
Stephen Usher, "Greek Historiography and Biography," in Grant and Kitzinger, *Civilization,* 3. 1525–40.
Duane Reed Stuart, *Epochs of Greek and Roman Biography* (Sather Classical Lectures 4; Berkeley: University of California Press, 1928).
Hans Dieter Betz, "Gottmensch II," *RAC* 12 (1983) 234–312.
Ludwig Bieler, *ΘΕΙΟΣ 'ANHP: Das Bild des "göttlichen Menschen" in Spätantike und Frühchristentum* (1935; reprint Darmstadt: Wissenschaftliche Buchgesellschaft, 1967).
Moses Hadas and Morton Smith, *Heroes and Gods: Spiritual Biographies in Antiquity* (RPS 13; New York: Harper, 1965).
Morton Smith, "Prolegomena to a Discussion of Aretalogies, Divine Men, the Gospels, and Jesus," *JBL* 90 (1971) 174–99.
David L. Tiede, *The Charismatic Figure as Miracle Worker* (SBLDS 1; Missoula, MT: University of Montana, 1972).

like Xenophon's *Cyropaedia* and Plato's *Apology of Socrates* contain biographical elements. But they are not biographies in the strict sense of the term.

Because the political and social structures of Classical Greek society did not favor an interest in the life of single individuals surpassing all others, the literary genre of biography entered Greek culture only at the beginning of the Hellenistic period. While the Near Eastern biography of the ruler was an account of a life in public office, Greek biography grew from an increasing interest in the lives of famous poets and philosophers and became an inquiry into the relationship between the works and the lives (*bioi*) of such individuals, searching for examples of correct ways of living for the wise man.

Students of Aristotle, especially Aristoxenos, who is otherwise known as the first ancient musicologist, developed these interests into an organized literary activity. Aristoxenos wrote biographies of Pythagoras, Sokrates, Plato, and others, of which unfortunately nothing is preserved. One can assume that Aristotle's philosophical views about the differentiation of virtues and the relationship between conduct (*ethos*) and character (*pathos*) were applied in these works. These biographies presented the principles of philosophical doctrines, conduct of life, and formation of character in the form of a *bios*. As was customary in the school of Aristotle, collections of relevant materials were made in preparation for writing individual biographies and for series of *vitae* of lives of poets and philosophers, as well as in the brief *vitae* that were later put at the head of editions of Classical authors. Reading the few surviving fragments of this literary activity, one is struck by its completely uncritical attitude: anecdotes, legends, and romantic glorifications predominate, as long as they illustrated exemplary conduct.

At the beginning of the Hellenistic period the personalities of several rulers made strong impressions on many people. Therefore biographies of such men proliferated, especially about Alexander the Great and several rulers of Syracuse and Macedonia. With the exception of some serious works from the hands of such historians as Polybios, these biographies show a tendency toward panegyric and romance. The later Alexander romance has its roots here. A politically oriented ruler-biography did not emerge until the 1st century CE. Even autobiographies of rulers seem to have been rare, though it is reported that autobiographies were written by Demetrios of Phaleron, governor of Athens at the end of the 4th century BCE, by Pyrrhos king of Epiros, by the Achaian politician Aratos of Sikyon, and the Egyptian king Ptolemy VIII Euergetes II.

Not the conduct of public office but interest in the significance of the human individual were the wellspring of the Hellenistic political biography. With Polybios, biography became a standard feature of the writing of history. Polybios recognized that historical developments could often be traced to an individual, who in turn was shaped by his life experience. This insight was still valid for historiography in the Roman imperial period. From this later period numerous biographies have been preserved in both Greek and Latin. They continue the tradition of the biographies of poets and philosophers, for example, in the collections of the *vitae* by Diogenes Laertius; but they also deal more frequently with the lives of important political figures. Plutarch's *Parallel Lives* and Suetonius' *Lives of the Emperors* are outstanding examples. Biographies of philosophical founders of religious movements, such as Philo's *Vita Mosis* and Philostratos' *Vita Apollonii*, were also written.

To understand the character of this biographical genre, especially its extant examples from the Roman period, yet one more important genre must be considered: the aretalogy (from the Greek word *arete* = "virtue," "powerful deed"). The origins of the aretalogy must be sought in the cultic hymns that enumerated the great acts of a particular deity. Beginning in the Hellenistic period, these hymns were recorded on stone and publicly displayed in temple precincts, soon to be joined by prose narratives of the god's miraculous acts down to the present time—thus surpassing the divine acts from the mythical past! Especially in the cults of Asklepios and of Sarapis and Isis (§4.3d), such records were used in religious propaganda and recited in public.

In the Greek mindset, however, extraordinary human gifts were not fundamentally different from divine powers manifested in current events (see §1.5b on ruler cult). One could thus praise the divine gifts and wonderful deeds of human beings as one gave praise to the gods. For this reason, aretalogy and biography became closely related in the Hellenistic period, and in the case of the divine human being, aretalogy and biography merged in the common understanding. The typical Hellenistic belief that divine powers are manifested in the great poets, philosophers, and rulers can be traced back to the end of the 4th century BCE. The Euhemeristic criticism of myth (§4.2b) had already demonstrated that some of the gods were originally human benefactors who had received divine honors for their deeds. The claim of divinity for Homer and Sokrates may simply be a hyperbolic expression of admiration for great poetic or philosophical gifts. But in the case of Pythagoras and Epikouros the borderline between a divinely gifted philosopher and the divine founder of a religious group is obliterated.

No wonder, therefore, that Hellensitic biographies incorporate miracle stories in a strikingly uncritical manner. Indeed, had some of the earliest biographies survived, it would be difficult to determine whether they were biographies or aretalogies. This becomes clear in the case of some biographies from the Roman period, especially in the presentation of the life of the divine founder of a religion. In the *Vita Mosis* of Philo of Alexandria, the materials used by the author were already aretalogical: the well-known biblical stories of the miracles connected with Moses and the Exodus. For his biography of the Neopythagorean divine man Apollonios of Tyana, Philostratos used a collection of aretalogical miracle stories. And even though Plutarch designed his biographies to emphasize the close relationship between *bios* and character, his works demonstrate that his materials were often aretalogical.

Roman biography owes its origin to Hellenistic influences. Early Roman political thought held as little interest in such matters as did the older Greek democracy. Traditionally, an official of the Roman Republic would have published an account of the conduct of his office (*commentarius*), and the Roman view of divine action through a human being was different from the Greek concept of the divine man. A divine agent might act through a human instrument, but that did not make the human instrument divine.

However, Augustus' account of his own achievements, the *Monumentum An cyranum*, is not just an account of conduct of office, it is also a record of the deeds of the divine Augustus (in the Greek edition, of the "god Augustus"), indeed it is an aretalogy of sorts. Such biographical works exhibit clear aretalogical elements, beginning with the lives of Sulla, Pompey, and Caesar, continuing with the lives of the emperors by Suetonius and the collections of the *vitae* of famous persons (*De viris illustribus*), and ending with the Christian lives of martyrs and saints. In the lives of the emperors, stories of political and military achievements stand side by side with narrations of prodigies and supernatural appearances, which signify both the greatness of the events and the divinity of the subject. In praise of the extraordinary and superhuman abilities of human beings, panegyrical features frequently appear. The Christians adopted this genre of the aretalogical biography for accounts of their founding hero, and it is not surprising that subsequent literature, especially the legends of Christian saints, is entirely dominated by miracle stories.

(e) The Romance

Modern discoveries of papyri have demonstrated that the beginnings of the Greek romance, once dated to the later Roman period, are as old as the 2d

Bibliography to §3.4e: Texts

B. P. Reardon, ed., *Collected Ancient Greek Novels* (Berkeley, CA: University of California Press, 1989).

Moses, Hadas, ed. and trans., *Three Greek Romances, Translated with an Introduction* (Indianapolis: Bobbs–Merill, 1964; reprint 1984).

Achilles Tatius: Greek text and English translation by S. Gaselee in LCL.

Longus: Greek text and English translation by J. M. Edmonds in LCL.

Otto Schönberger, ed., *Longos: Hirtengeschichten von Daphnis und Chloe: Griechisch und deutsch* (SQAW 6; Berlin: Akademie–Verlag, 1960; reprinted 1989).

Helmut van Thiel, ed., *Leben und Taten Alexanders von Makedonien* (TF 13; 2d ed.; Darmstadt: Wissenschaftliche Buchgesellschaft, 1983). Greek text of Manuscript L and German translation.

Bibliography to §3.4e: Studies

Erwin Rohde, *Der griechische Roman und seine Vorläufer* (4th ed.; Hildesheim: Olms, 1966). The classic study of the Greek romance, first published 1876.

Rudolf Helm, *Der antike Roman* (Studien zur Altertumswissenschaft 4; 2d. ed.; Göttingen: Vandenhoeck & Ruprecht, 1956).

Ben Edwin Perry, *The Ancient Romances: A Literary-Historical Account of their Origins* (Sather Classical Lectures 37; Berkeley and Los Angeles, CA: University of California Press, 1967).

B. P. Reardon, *Courants littéraires grecs des IIe et IIIe siècles après J.-C.* (Paris: Les Belles Lettres, 1971) 309–403.

Tomas Hägg, *The Novel in Antiquity* (Berkeley, CA: University of California Press, 1983).

Idem, *Narrative Technique in Ancient Greek Romances: Studies of Chariton, Xenophon Ephesius, and Achilles Tatius* (Uppsala: Almquist & Wiskells, 1971).

G. Anderson, *Ancient Fiction: The Novel in the Greco-Roman World* (Totowa, NJ: Barnes & Noble, 1984).

E. L. Bowie, "The Greek Novel," in Easterling and Knox, *Greek Literature*, 683–99.

John J. Winkler, "The Novel," in Grant and Kitzinger, *Civilization*, 3. 1563-72.

Alexander Scobie, *Aspects of the Ancient Romance and its Heritage: Essays on Apuleius, Petronius, and the Greek Romances* (BKP 30; Meisenheim am Glan: Hain, 1969).

century BCE and are a typical expression of the Hellenistic view of human existence. The romance joined together in a new literary concept all the elements of human experience and the conquest of its limitations, as these found expression in various genres of Hellenistic literature. The romance takes account of the broader geographical horizons opened up through the conquests of Alexander, but it places the human individual at the center of the plot, and seeks to reconcile its heroes with the powers of fate that often seem to render life meaningless, culminating in a happy ending.

All the genres known to Greek literature reappear in the Hellenistic romance. Its interest in travel and foreign countries is derived from geography and ethnography. The frequent accounts of seafaring are drawn from the ancient *periploi*, going back as far as Homer's *Odyssey*, not passing by any chance to describe a shipwreck. The erotic motif is borrowed from Greek tragedy. Unlike comedy, romance elevates this theme, as lovers preserve their chastity to the very end; Euripides had already used the same technique. Sexual excess and erotic aberration, which are much more akin to comedy, are reserved for the secondary figures of the narrative; only the later parodists of romance (Petronius, Apuleius) ascribe such actions to the heroes of the story. From biography the romance drew descriptions of the wonderful origins of hero and heroine and of their exemplary moral conduct. The presentation of virtue and character and their relation to the conduct of life and to acts of providence are taken from philosophical biography.

Many elements are borrowed from aretalogy, paradoxography, and the popularizations of ethnography, zoology, and pharmacology, which so strongly emphasized whatever was curious and peculiar. Thus one finds miracles and *paradoxa*, demons and magic, appearances of dead people, talking animals, amazingly swift travel by ship, strange countries and peoples, crevasses in the earth opening up unexpectedly, and even the hailing of hero and heroine as divine. Religious and moralizing speeches by the hero, overcoming of dangers and persecutions, divine commands, oracles and dreams—all features that can also be found in inferior historiography—are genuine elements of the romance.

There are, finally, numerous motifs and considerable materials that the romances drew from popular storytelling. Such storytelling is rarely found in other literary works, so it is difficult to characterize it accurately. But there is no question that such oral narrative traditions were widespread, full of legends, fables, riddles, and anecdotes. A particularly rich tradition of storytelling existed in Ionia, whose influence can be seen in Herodotos' writings. A collection of such stories from the Hellenistic period, called the *Milesiaca,* mostly of somewhat dubious erotic character, was gathered by Aristides of Miletos. The collection was translated into Latin by Sisenna, and according to Plutarch (*Crassus* 32), many Roman officers kept a copy in their luggage. The writers of romance frequently availed themselves of a large treasury of popular stories.

Reinhold Merkelbach, *Die Quellen des griechischen Alexanderromans* (Zet. 9; München: Beck, 1954).

Otto Weinreich, *Der griechische Liebesroman* (Zürich: Artemis, 1962).

Reinhold Merkelbach, *Roman und Mysterium in der Antike* (München: Beck, 1962).

In the two oldest known romances, *Ninos and Semiramis* and Iamboulos' *Commonwealth of the Sun*—both written in the 2d century BCE—the two primary features of novelistic literature are already fully developed: the erotic motif in *Ninos* and adventurous travel in the *Commonwealth of the Sun*. The extant fragment of the *Ninos* romance does not permit a reconstruction of the entire plot. But the surviving fragments of Iamboulos' romance tell enough of the story: after adventurous travels via Ethiopia, the hero arrives at mysterious islands in the southern ocean; later he returns by way of India. The central portion of the narrative concerns a utopia. For several years the hero is allowed to participate in the life of an ideal commonwealth of happy inhabitants of islands in the southern sea; they worship the sun, share their women in common, and take equal turns in both honorable and less desirable jobs.

Both basic motifs, travel and eroticism, are found together for the first time in *Chaereas and Callirhoe,* by Chariton of Aphrodisias in Asia Minor. Papyrus fragments from the 2d and 3d centuries CE show that it was written no later than the 1st century CE. The action takes place in Miletos and Persia and is set in the 5th century BCE. Various novelistic motifs appear in colorful sequence: drama, comedy, and aretalogy. Even historiography makes its contribution: Hermokrates, the Syracusan general in the Peloponnesian War, appears, as does the Persian king Artaxerxes II, who falls in love with the heroine. His court provides the setting for the climax. The latter motif is drawn from the Persian court novel, which also left its traces in Herodotos and provided the setting for Jewish writings like Daniel 1–5, Judith, and Esther, where the action is dated in the same time. *Tyche* provides the resolution and unites the lovers.

All other extant romances were written in the 2d and 3d centuries CE. The genre's popularity is shown by a number of fragments of otherwise unknown romances that are preserved in papyrus finds dated to the same period, when also most of the Christian counterparts of the romance, the apocryphal acts of the apostles, were written. In the *Ephesiaca* of Xenophon of Ephesos, the action leads the reader to Egypt and includes the Potiphar motif (cf. the Joseph story in Genesis), as well as the theme of a chaste marriage of the heroine with a poor shepherd. Both motifs had already been used by Euripides. The *Babyloniaca* of the Syrian Iamblichos lacks the travel by ship, but miraculous stories, ghosts, magic, and gruesome entanglements appear in abundance; a number of short stories are also included here.

The *Ethiopiaca* of Heliodoros of Emesa, written in the 3d century CE, is the last great romance from antiquity, distinguished by a highly artistic narrative. This work also transcends the Hellenistic perception of human existence, namely, the view that human beings are exposed to a hostile world whose powers and gods they cannot comprehend, though a favorable fate might be able to save them. In Heliodoros' work, new religious concepts derived from Neoplatonic or Neopythagorean beliefs appear. The heroine, for whom chastity is a religious requirement, learns that the cause and the final resolution of all adversities is a higher divine justice. The parallel to the Christian apocryphal acts is evident. The romance *Daphnis and Chloe* by Longus (2d century CE), which enjoyed new popularity since the Renaissance, has a special character. The travel motif is missing. Instead, the erotic motif predominates in the form of a shepherd's idyll located on the island of Lesbos and glorifying the rustic life.

The continuing popularity of the romance in the Roman world is shown by the reappearance of the genre in Latin works by Petronius and Apuleius. The former's *Satyricon* (mid-1st century CE), a work in 16 books of which sizable fragments are preserved, contains all the relevant motifs of the romance, but in parody: it is a romance turned upside down. As Odysseus was persecuted by the wrath of Poseidon, the hero here suffers from the wrath of the phallic god Priapos. The object of his erotic desire is a boy, and the motif of chastity often vies with lewd sexual adventures. The dignity of the king's court is replaced by the banquet of the uncultured nouveau-riche freedman Trimalchio. Short stories abound, in addition to a persiflage over Homer's epics and the *Pharsalia* of Lucan. Apuleius' *Metamorphoses* (ca. 170 CE) is a romance, based on a Greek work of Lucius of Patrae, that tells the adventures of a young man whose amorous adventures accidentally turn him into an ass. The travels and sufferings of this ass provide a framework for incorporating numerous stories and novels, the most famous of which is the tale of "Amor and Psyche." The resolution is provided by the intervention of the goddess Isis, as the work ends (book 11) with an autobiographical account of a conversion and initiation into the mysteries of Isis.

An attempt to understand the Hellenistic romance as a disguised mystery narrative has been made recently by Reinhold Merkelbach, who sees the erotic romances as religious and suggests that these works were written in the service of Near-Eastern mystery religions. Iamblichos' romance would present the mysteries of Mithras, Longus the mysteries of Dionysos, Xenophon those of Isis, Heliodoros the religion of Sol Invictus, and the romance of a certain Antonios Diogenes, of which only a fragment is preserved, the doctrine of the Pythagoreans. It is indisputable that the *Metamorphoses* of Apuleius, in which the hero is initiated into the mysteries of Isis, was indeed written as propaganda for the Egyptian religion (see below §4.4a). It is also evident that certain portions of the Christian romance of the Apostle Thomas (*Acts of Thomas*) are symbolic narratives of the ascent of the soul into heaven. But both cases result from a secondary adaptation of older novelistic materials in the interests of religious propaganda. It is hard to believe that romances before Apuleius, the *Acts of Thomas,* and Heliodoros were intended to convey a symbolic religious message.

The romance is indeed "religious" as it reflects the longing of human beings for an experience that transcends the misery and monotony of everyday life. It is the yearning of those for whom the future of a political community has ceased to be the object of hopes and aspirations. As a positive value, the community appears in the romance only as a utopia or an idyll (the romances of Iamboulos and Longus) or as the heavenly paradise (*Acts of Thomas*). Such views are not prophetic political messages. It is not national salvation that the romance promises; the reader would scarcely have expected a message of this sort. Rather, it fulfills the longing for a transcendent experience by describing the extraordinary events and fate of individual human beings. Historical and political matters are nothing but a backdrop. But descriptions of foreign countries and peoples are important, because the reader's imagination still wants something wonderful and exotic lying beyond the horizons of everyday life.

When the fated ordeal of the central figures of the romance reaches its climax, what emerges is not a symbolically described religious experience—religious elements are nothing but accessories—but the fulfillment of love. In all its nobility, purity, and faithful endurance, love is presented as the true goal of human experience. Romances are religious insofar as they are romantic. It is by no means rare in the history of literature that the intrinsic import of a literary genre is most clearly understood in its contemporary parodies. Petronius' *Satyricon,* describing the often risqué amorous adventures of his hero, demonstrates that the erotic motif was the very heart of the Hellenistic romance.

PHILOSOPHY AND RELIGION

1. THE PHILOSOPHICAL SCHOOLS AND PHILOSOPHICAL RELIGION

(a) The Academy and Platonism

Some time before the year 361 BCE, Plato organized his "school" as a private cult association, donating a large house and garden a few miles west of Athens that he owned to this association, named from the nearby shrine of the hero Akademos. After Plato's death (348/47 BCE), the older Academy was primarily interested in rounding out the cosmological and theological teachings of its master. Plato's successors Speusippos and Xenokrates created the "Platonic" system that is reflected in the popular Platonism of later centuries.

The demonology of these first academicians became very influential. Plato had already suggested that the *daimones* were intermediate beings, who were able to communicate with human beings on behalf of the gods. He also assumed different classes of demons, which were active either in the realms of the heavens, or in the air, or in the realm of the spirit, or in the human soul. Xenokrates (died ca. 315 BCE) added the distinction between good and evil demons, the latter haunting the sublunar realms. This concept provided philosophical legitimacy for widespread popular beliefs and thus contributed to their later propagation in philosophical and theological literature. Platonists of the Roman period, like Plutarch and the Neopythagoreans, gave a central place to this concept. Also the Christians followed suit. Justin Martyr elaborated this demonology in arguments

Bibliography to §4.1: Texts

Cornelia Johanna de Vogel, *Greek Philosophy: A Collection of Texts* (3d ed.; 3 vols.; Leiden: Brill, 1963–67).

A. A. Long and D. N. Sedley, *The Hellenistic Philosophers* (2 vols.; Cambridge: Cambridge University Press, 1987). Greek and Latin texts with translations and commentary.

Bibliography to §4.1: Introduction and Surveys

A. H. Armstrong, *An Introduction to Ancient Philosophy* (3d ed.; London: Methuen, 1977) 114–40.

Idem, ed., *Classical Mediterranean Spirituality: Egyptian, Greek, Roman* (World Spirituality 15; New York: Crossroad, 1986).

Philip Merlan, "Greek Philosophy from Plato to Plotinus," in A. H. Armstrong, *The Cambridge History of Later Greek and Early Medieval Philosophy* (Cambridge: Cambridge University Press, 1967) 11–132.

G. E. R. Lloyd, "Greek Philosophy," in Grant and Kitzinger, *Civilization,* 3. 1585–1636.

Edwin Bevan, "Hellenistic Popular Philosophy," in T. D. Bury, ed., *The Hellenistic Age* (Cambridge: Cambridge University Press, 1923).

against pagan religion: he claimed that pagan worship of gods had actually been invented by evil demons in order to create the delusion that they were the fulfillment of Old Testament prophecies. In such arguments, Christian apologists, trained in Platonic philosophy, were able to take their starting point from Xenokrates' teachings, which had already relativized the distinction between demons and gods.

The "Middle Academy" (3d and 2d century BCE) was locked in battle with the Stoics and increasingly with other philosophical schools. Controversies began with Arkesilaos, head of the Academy from 268 BCE, and continued in the next century under Karneades. In such disputes, the Platonists made recourse to the Sokrates of the earlier Platonic dialogues. As Sokrates had demonstrated to the Sophists that knowledge through sense perception was impossible, the Academy now argued against Stoic epistemology, which ascribed truth value only to those concepts that had been developed on the basis of experience, observation, and scientific insight (Epikouros had also made knowledge dependent on experience). The Academicians opposed this view with their dialectic, demonstrating that each argument could be countered with another argument and that judgment should therefore be suspended (ἐποχή or, in Sextus Empiricus, σκέψις).

The Academy thus was accused of having fallen into the skepticism of Pyrrho of Elis. Nevertheless, skepticism regarding the derivation of truth from the world as it is perceptible through the senses became very widespread in the late Hellenistic and Roman periods. Not until Philon of Larissa (first half of the 1st century

Bibliography to §4.1: Comprehensive Treatments

Eduard Zeller, *Die Philosophie der Griechen in ihrer geschichtlichen Entwicklung*, 3,1: *Die nacharistotelische Philosophie* (2 vols.; 6th ed.; Darmstadt: Wissenschaftliche Buchgesellschaft, 1963). Most comprehensive and detailed presentation, reprint of 5th edition of 1923; now often surpassed by more recent works.

W. K. C. Guthrie, *A History of Greek Philosophy* (6 vols.; Cambridge: Cambridge University Press, 1962–1981).

Frederick Coppleston, *A History of Philosophy*, vol 1: *Greece and Rome* (Westminster, MD: Newner, 1960).

A. A. Long, *Hellenistic Philosophy: Stoics, Epicureans, Sceptics* (New York: Scribner's, 1974; reprint 1985).

Bibliography to §4.1a: Texts

David G. Rice and John E. Stambaugh, *Sources for the Study of Greek Religion* (SBLSBS 14; Missoula, MT: Scholars Press, 1979) 43–48.

Bibliography to §4.1a: Studies

Philip Merlan, *From Platonism to Neoplatonism* (2d ed.; The Hague: Nijhoff, 1960).

J. Glucker, *Antiochus and the Late Academy* (Hyp. 56; Göttingen: Vandenhoeck & Ruprecht, 1978).

Mary Mills Patrick, *The Greek Sceptics* (New York: Columbia University Press, 1929).

Charlotte L. Stough, *Greek Skepticism: A Study in Epistemology* (Berkeley and Los Angeles, CA: University of California Press, 1969).

John M. Dillon, *The Middle Platonists: 80 b.c. to a.d. 220* (Ithaca, NY: Cornell University Press, 1977).

Idem, "Plutarch and Second Century Platonism," in Armstrong, *Mediterranean Spirituality*, 214–29.

BCE) did the Academy begin to move beyond skepticism; only then was this school able to overcome its radical rejection of all other philosophical schools. In Rome, Philon was the teacher of Cicero, who still shared a moderate skepticism. Philon's successor, Antiochos of Ashkelon, broke decisively with the skepticism of his predecessors and abandoned opposition to the Stoa. This corresponds on the side of the Stoa to an increasing acceptance of Platonic concepts. The philosophers of this tradition now no longer called themselves "Academicians," but "Platonists." At the same time, the Academy in Athens lost its significance; most of the important Platonists taught elsewhere. As a result Platonic thoughts and concepts were becoming more widespread and determined for many centuries the general world view of late antiquity, including the Jewish philosopher Philo and ancient Christian thinkers from Justin Martyr to St. Augustine, but this was no longer due to the success of a particular school.

Closely associated with this general dissemination of Platonism was the development of dualistic anthropological and cosmological concepts. In his demonology, Xenokrates had already taken up Plato's statements about a good and evil world soul who are responsible for the actions of good and evil demons. The Stoic philosopher Poseidonios adopted essential parts of this Platonic dualism for his own system. In his cosmology, he distinguished a celestial world above the moon, which is imperishable and immutable, and the sublunar world, which is transitory and subject to change. It was possibly also Poseidonios who developed the trichotomic anthropology, which later became widely disseminated and was utilized by Valentinian Gnosticism: the human *spirit* has its origin in the sun, receives from the intermediate world (the moon) the *soul* which animates and maintains the *body* that is provided by the sublunar world. At the point of death, the whole process is reversed: the soul leaves the body, and once the spirit has freed itself from the soul, it returns to its solar origin. These concepts reappear among later Stoic and other philosophers, including the Romans Cicero and Seneca (§6.4c, f), perhaps in direct dependence on Poseidonios.

Platonizing Stoicism became the basis of philosophical and religious reflection at the close of the Hellenistic period, especially outside the philosophical schools. This is most clearly seen in the Jewish philosopher Philo of Alexandria. His allegorical method of exegesis is Stoic, as is his interpretation of scriptural persons as symbols of virtues. His concept of God, too, has Stoic features: God is immutable and eternal, more the basic power of the cosmos than a person (of course, Philo cannot completely eliminate the individualized features of the biblical concept of God). God and Nature are identical in Philo, and the *logos,* as in Stoic philosophy, is the power permeating all things. Despite these Stoic influences, Philo's world view, and especially his anthropology, is Platonic. The visible world as perceived through the senses is not only transitory, it is also characterized with negative predicates. The soul or the spirit has its origin in the world of God. As long as it remains in the body, it is caught in the snares of earthly existence, from which it must free itself. Insight into the essence of reality is not possible through sense perception. Only the human spirit recognizes God and the *logos* and is thus liberated from the visible world through knowledge of wisdom and through exercise in virtue, overcoming the body and its passions and returning to its home, the celestial world. Not only is the visible world the cause of evil and vice, the body is also a fundamentally foreign place in contrast to the celestial home, an unsuitable garment for the divine soul. Philo's cosmology also contains a distinctly Platonic element: God created the permanent and imperishable world of ideas first, as the prototype for the visible world, which is nothing but its changing and mortal copy. But while Philo describes the *logos* according to Stoic concepts as the power governing the universe, he also sees it in the Platonic sense as the image of God according to which the human being has been created. For this reason, human beings belong to God in their true essence and are fundamentally different from the visible world. Philo, as well as the Gnostics (§6.5f) and such Christian writings as the Epistle to the Hebrews (§12.2b) testify to the victory of Platonism at the beginning of the Roman period.

(b) The Peripatetic Philosophy

Aristotle's philosophy had very little discernible effect for several centuries. Hellenistic cosmology had no use for Aristotle's concept of the "first mover" or his mechanistic picture of the course of the world. His ethics were were too closely associated with the political unit of the *polis* and were not easily applicable to a radically changed political environment. Though it is likely that several major schools (Skepsis, Alexandria, Rhodos, Athens) possessed copies of Aristotle's didactic writings, during the Hellenistic period he was best known as a biologist and natural scientist, even in Aristotle's school itself, the Lyceum or Peripatetic school. A famous story tells that Aristotle's didactic writings were hidden in a basement of a house in Skepsis (northwestern Asia Minor) for two hundred years, and that their discovery brought a momentous renewal of interest in Aristotle's logic. In any case, Andronikos of Rhodos, head of the Peripatetic school in middle of the 1st century BCE, was responsible for a new edition of these writings, which established Aristotle's significance as logician for the imperial Roman period.

After Aristotle's death, his friend and associate Theophrastos (371–287 BCE) directed the Peripatetic school. Some of his numerous writings are preserved: a famous *Inquiry into Plants* (§3.3b), the *Characters* (a description of thirty typical characters), and extensive fragments of his work *On Religion*. The primary interests of the Peripatetics are well mirrored in these works: studies in natural science, along with character studies and biographies, especially of poets and philosophers (§3.4d).

(c) Epikouros and the Epicureans

While Plato and Aristotle founded their schools, the Academy and the Lyceum, before the beginning of the Hellenistic period, the Epicureans and the Stoics first appeared in the early decades of that period. Their founders, Epikouros and Zeno, both teaching in Athens, were contemporaries. Both schools were strongly reliant on the personal conduct of life of their founders—a factor

Bibliography to §4.1b

Patrick Atherton, "Aristotle," in Armstrong, *Mediterranean Spirituality*, 121–34.

that played only a minor role in the Academy and in the Lyceum—produced typical Hellenistic philosophies. At the same time, the contrast between these two Hellenistic schools and their founders was striking. Epikouros, a well-to-do Athenian citizen, founded his school in a garden outside of the walls of the city, where his chosen friends, including women and slaves, met in seclusion, dedicated to the pursuit of happiness and to the mutual care of their souls. On the other hand, the school of the foreigner Zeno, ascetic in his personal style of life and teaching in the busiest part of the city in a hall of the Athenian Agora, where rich and poor listened to his lectures. Among them was the crown prince of Macedonia, Antigonos (Gonatas), and Persaios, a wealthy Phoenician, who later became a Macedonian general. When the resident alien Zeno died, Persaios wrote an encomium and Athens voted him a golden crown and free burial with a monument in the Kerameikos Cemetery, because he was a man "who educated the young men in virtue and morality and who gave an example through his conduct of life which was always in agreement with his teaching." But when the Athenian citizen Epikouros died, Athens refused to vote him any honors.

Epikouros (341–270 BCE) was the son of an Athenian colonist on Samos, where he founded a school that he transferred to Athens in 306 BCE. Because of its meeting place the school is often referred to as "the Garden." Reconstruction of Epikouros' teaching is difficult because all his writings are lost, with the exception of three didactic letters; writings of his students and successors are only scantily preserved.

His epistemology—he held that all sense perceptions are true—and his atomism need not be discussed here. More important for the intellectual world of Hellenism is the fact that Epikouros drew the consequences from the failure of Plato's and Aristotle's polis ethics. The polis was no longer morally constitutive; left was the individual and the world. Thus no political entity could serve as a basis for happiness and moral responsibility. Epikouros' philosophy sought to replace the lost political home of the human being with the Garden as a substitute religious society.

The Epicureans were neither irreligious nor atheistic, although both accusations were leveled against them. But the gods, whose existence Epikouros never doubted, were in no way involved in the lives of human beings. It was meaning-

Bibliography to §4.1c: Text

Cyril Bailey, *Epicurus: The Extant Remains* (Oxford: Clarendon, 1926; reprint 1970).

Bibliography to §4.1c: Studies

Elizabeth Asmis, "Philodemus' Epicureanism," *ANRW* 2.36.4 (1990) 2369–2406.

John Ferguson, "Epicureanism under the Roman Empire," *ANRW* II.36.4 (1990) 2257–2327.

Wolfgang Schmid, "Epikur," *RAC* 5 (1961) 681–819; reprinted with other essay on Epicurus in idem, *Ausgewählte philosophical schriften*

(Berlin:De Gruyter, 1984). . The best comprehensive discussion.

A. A. Long, *"Epicureans and Stoics,"* in Armstrong, *Mediterranean Spirituality*, 135–53.

J. M. Rist, *Epicurus: An Introduction* (Cambridge: Cambridge University Press, 1972).

A. J. Festugière, *Epicurus and His Gods* (Cambridge, MA: Harvard University Press, 1956).

Bernard Frischer, *The Sculpted Word: Epicureanism and Philosophical Recruitment in Ancient Greece* (Berkeley and Los Angeles, CA: University of California Press, 1982).

less to worship the gods, pointless to call upon them in distress, and useless to sacrifice to them. Such beliefs were actually not much different from those propagated by other philosophical schools. Stoics and Peripatetics also declared it disgraceful for the wise man to be dependent on divine intervention in one's personal affairs because one should be independent of all other beings and things. But while the Stoics, despite their materialistic world view, admired the working of divine power in the realities and movements of the world and of nature, the Epicureans drew the consequences from their atomistic materialism: the course of natural events is determined by the laws that derive from the movements of atoms; hence, there is no need for either gods or a universal world reason or any spiritual realities outside the material world. The soul also belongs to this world; like the body, it is in fact nothing but the result of an accidental constellation of atoms.

It was therefore impossible for Epikouros to associate his notions of religion with any transcendent powers. Like the Stoics, he taught that life must be conducted "according to nature" in order to lead to true happiness (εὐδαιμονία). But because knowledge of "nature" cannot be derived from any metaphysical ideology, one must observe the "natural" desires of human existence, present in their purest state in the child who wants nothing but undisturbed happiness without any obligations. This established the only real value for the conduct of life: independence and imperturbability of the individual in the pursuit of happiness—all other virtues are meaningless, though vices should be avoided as they might be a hindrance on the way to happiness.

The Garden was the social and religious framework within which true happiness could be achieved through the development of the ideal of friendship. To be sure, other philosophical schools were also structured as religious associations. But among the Epicureans, this form of organization provides the basis for realizing the goals of a philosophic life. As a mystery association it supplied an environment for the religious fulfillment of its members, and the founder became a divine figure. Friendship, community, and pastoral care were understood as religious duties, while the regular common meals of the members and the memorial festivals at the birthdays of the founder, already introduced during Epikouros' lifetime, and of other distinguished members, were liturgical celebrations. These performances and duties, however, were not designed to build up community; on the contrary, the community existed in order to serve the individual to aid in the establishment of the true happiness and imperturbability of the soul.

Like all other philosophical schools of the Hellenistic period, the Epicureans subordinated all matters of common interest to that of the individual. The parallel to the mysteries is evident (§4.3e). They too were institutions into which individual human beings could be initiated in order to obtain personal salvation. But while the mysteries promised a salvation that included guarantees for a life after death, the religious goal of the Epicureans was limited strictly to the experiences of earthly life, which should become independent from all affections, from luck and misfortune, even from all desire and pleasure—in short, a kind of nihilistic harmony. In this way the wise man could prove to himself the nonexistence of all adverse experiences, including even death: since death is nothing but dissolution of not only of the body but also of the soul into the atoms from which they had been constituted, it is impossible to experience death, and there is no reason to fear it.

Epicureanism was quite influential for a time, but probably only in the educated classes. It played a considerable role in Rome during the 1st century BCE at the end of the Roman Republic. The long didactic poem of Lucretius is an important surviving witness (§6.4b). Seneca still imitated the Epicurean custom of writing pastoral letters. But Epicurean influence declined during the Roman imperial period, and in later antiquity the Epicurean teachings were little more than the target for pagan and Christian polemics against atheism.

(d) The Stoa

The Stoa was founded by Zeno, born 333/332 BCE—when Alexander the Great began his conquest of Persia—in Kition on Cyprus, a colony of Sidon, as the son of the Phoenician merchant Mnaseas (=Manasseh or Menahem). Greek, though also spoken in his home, was not his mother tongue. In 312 BCE he moved to Athens and became a student of the Cynic philosopher Krates. Ca. 300 BCE he began to give his own public lectures in the Stoa Poikile, the "Painted Stoa"—a picture gallery on the northern side of the Athenian agora, recently rediscovered in excavations by the American School of Classical Studies. The term "Stoicism" is derived from his place of teaching.

Highly respected by the Athenians, Zeno died in Athens ca. 264. His successor Kleanthes (ca. 331-232 BCE), who consolidated Zeno's teachings, came from a poor Greek family in Assos in Asia Minor. He had come to Athens with but four drachmas in his pocket and had to work hard as a hired hand in order to finance his studies. Too poor to buy papyrus, he made his lecture notes on pieces of broken pottery. His famous hymn to Zeus, the provident ruler of the universe, is preserved. After him, Chrysippos, a Hellenized Phoenician from Soloi in Cilicia (died ca. 205 BCE), was the head of the Stoa. Chrysippos is said to have written 705 books, and what we know as the system of Stoic doctrine comes from him.

From its inception, Stoic philosophy was cosmopolitan and pantheistic. Though sharing many of the Garden's presuppositions, it was violently anti-Epicurean. The problem of the polis, dominant in Aristotle's philosophy, did not exist for the Stoa. Its point of reference is not the political community, but the universe; not the gods of the polis, but the divine power of the entire world of nature. Physics is therefore the center of Stoic philosophy. But while the Epi-

Bibliography to §4.1d: Texts

Johannes von Arnim, ed., *Stoicorum Veterum Fragmenta* (4 vols.; Leipzig: Teubner, 1903–24). Max Pohlenz, ed. and trans., *Stoa und Stoiker: Die Gründer, Panaitios, Poseidonios* (Zürich: Artemis, 1950). Selections in German translations.

Bibliography to §4.1d: Studies

J. M. Rist, *Stoic Philosophy* (Cambridge: Cambridge University Press, 1969). A. A. Long, "Epicureans and Stoics," in Armstrong, *Mediterranean Spiritualiy*, 135–53.

cureans saw nature as the accidental constellation of atoms, the Stoics' central term for the understanding of nature is *logos* (= Reason). The "stuff" from which the universe is made is not dead matter, but something that is intelligent, alive, growing, and moving. "Fire" is the appropriate metaphor for universal reason, something that is material, to be sure, but a constantly creating force of change. As fire, the *logos* is not an irrational, blind force, but a rational principle, the meaningful, purposeful, and providential order of the universe. Stoics were therefore interested in science and in religion. Science demonstrated the rational order of the world; religion proved the providential care of the *logos*.

Stoicism, a philosophy with a strictly materialistic view of the world, became the main support for the Hellenistic renewal of belief in the gods and thus the basis for a new theology. Stoic monotheism rejects anthropomorphic concepts of gods (which the Epicureans maintained) and is characterized by pantheism and rationalism. God is the creative fire that permeates all things. God is also the rational principle, the *logos*, who purposefully designed the order and beauty of the world. But the Stoics did not ridicule the polytheistic beliefs of popular religion, although they thought little of purely external cultic performances. As manifestations of powers of nature the gods symbolize the wise government of the world reason, Zeus represents the heavens, Hera the air, Poseidon the water, and Dionysos the nourishing forces of growth. The stars were seen as rational beings. The different gods worshiped by the various nations were names for one and the same divine reason, normally called Zeus, the traditional highest deity of the Greeks. This Stoic view matched the syncretistic tendencies of the time and provided the desired philosophical rationale.

In their definition of the role of the human being in the world, the Stoics saw themselves as the true heirs of Sokrates (as mediated through the Cynics; see below §4.2a). This explains the preeminence of ethics in Stoic teaching: virtue is the only good that exists. But while also the Epicureans taught that the goal was to live "according to nature," the Stoics side with Sokrates' arguments against the Sophists: virtue must be independent of success and pleasure. All other goals and motivations of whatever kind—material goods, political ambitions, and especially human affections—are falsifications and perversions of human moral destiny. However, while Sokrates sought a definition of virtue that recognized the common good, respect for the rights of fellow citizens, and an active contribution to the welfare of all, the Stoics separated virtue from any political and social considerations and isolated ethics from all external and empirical motivations that were present in the social structures of the world. Rather, the divine *logos* distributes its purposes to all living beings, who all act and develop according to the share they have of the *logos* as an innate part of their being. The only goal (τέλος) of moral action is "to live in agreement" (i.e., with the *logos* = ὁμολογουμένως ζῆν), as Zeno said, or as formulated by Chrysippos: "to live in agreement with nature" (ὁμολογουμένως τῇ φύσει ζῆν). Further modifications of this *telos* formula provide an interesting index for the historical development of Stoic philosophy.

Consequences for understanding ethics are threefold: (1) The goal is not "pleasure" (Epicureans), but rationality, that is, insight into one's own *logos*/reason, which is one's true nature. (2) Recognition that a human being is "by nature" (φύσει, not θέσει) a "societal creature" (κοινωνικὸν ζῷον), though the society to which each human being belongs cannot be the polis—rather, it is the entire universe. (3) The nature, that is, the *logos* of all human beings is the same. Therefore social, ethnic, and racial distinctions are of no significance because they are not given "by nature." Yet, several problems remained unsolved. While the entire cosmos was given by nature, the Stoics did not develop ethical principles that could govern functions in a cosmopolitan society in which human beings were responsible to institutional structures. Although they could speak of the universe as "the city of gods and humanity," they did not spell out the political and social implications of this assertion, and love for all fellow human beings, no matter what their race or status, had no social consequences, because societal distinctions were not set "by nature" and therefore irrelevant. Moreover, the ideal of the philosopher who is independent of the society—even if externally bound to such hateful situations as being a slave or an emperor—remained essentially a male ideal.

"Nature" does not refer to the social world, nor even to the external physical world, although much can be learned from it, but to the true "nature" of human beings, that is, the *logos,* "reason" or "rational discernment." The normal, natural experiences of human existence, like one's physical body, health, and everything necessary for daily life, are no more than the preliminary stage of "life according to nature." Only true rational insight can tell what "nature" really is, especially the ultimate "nature" of the essence of human existence.

This view of human nature and of moral destiny required a psychology that could recognize the ultimately rational nature of the human being. Neither the established political community, nor any other external goals could provide the motivation for moral actions; such motivations would still create a dependence on external values. Even striving for such goods as friendship, family, and health remains a hindrance for the true freedom of the soul. Stoic ethics finds the tangible presence of world reason (*logos*) in the "reason" that is innate in every individual as a portion of that universal world reason (*spermatikos logos*). But the integrity of that rational human self is threatened by emotions and affections of the soul. Psychology, therefore, becomes a central and highly refined element of Stoic teaching as a doctrine of the affections (πάθος, Latin: *perturbatio, passio,* or *affectus*), which are seen as diseases of the soul. Not only desire, fear, and pleasure, but also regret, sorrow, and compassion, are pathological states, from which the wise man must free himself in order to reach the goal of imperturbability (*apatheia,* later, in Epiktetos, *ataraxia*). In their description of the affections, Stoics borrowed many terms and concepts from the medical sciences. Their view of the affections as diseases of the soul is modeled on pathological insights into the diseases of the body. The philosopher becomes a physician of the soul.

Stoic parallels to Epicurean doctrines are obvious, both in the description of the task of the philosopher and in the materialistic cosmology. The close affinity of the two bitterly feuding schools is clearly evident in their view of the ideal of the wise man, which rests on the elucidation of the appropriate moral values.

Both schools agree that it is possible to recognize evil and that, once evil is known, it can be overcome. They also agree in their definition of values as things that truly concern the individual, as distinct from those things that are a matter of indifference. As far as the content of moral values is concerned, the Stoics rejected the Aristotelian distinction between inner, physical, and external values, and did not acknowledge any hierarchy of virtues. Accepting the Platonic cardinal virtues of prudence, fortitude, temperance, and justice, they usually returned to the formal standard of "that which is according to nature." This encouraged the rise of general aphoristic rules for moral behavior, for instance, "that which is considered good at all places and at all times." In this way Stoic ethics naturally presented itself as the basis for popular moral teaching, while popular morality generally rejected the Epicurean ethics as hedonistic.

Alongside the Epicureans, the Stoics were primarily responsible for the formation and propagation of an ideal of the wise man that became characteristic for the Hellenistic period. According to Classical philosophy, the wise man gave evidence for his full possession of virtue through his actions in world and society, his fortitude in battle, his prudence in political decisions, and his temperance in dealing with others. Cynicism (§4.2a), however, had developed a new image of Sokrates, in which the wise man is distinguished through independence and frugality, and thus through withdrawal from the obligations of society. This image became determinative for both Epicureans and Stoics, both pursuing the same goal: to attain true happiness (*eudaimonia*) of the individual, who is in full harmony with himself and has therefore overcome the bondage of fate. For the Epicurean, withdrawal from society is a necessary presupposition for attaining true happiness, while for the Stoic the relationship to society remains paradoxical. He can prove his possession of true happiness even in the midst of worldly endeavors, in whatever activity his origin, education, or political position has assigned to him, whether it be that of emperor or of slave. This view is expressed in the famous phrase "as if not"—a formula that also occurs in Paul's letters, although from a Christian perspective. Thus the wise man can be actively involved in the affairs of his society, but his position and his share in it—whether he is actively working or passively suffering—do not affect his real being, since true happiness does not depend on external circumstances.

In order to present their new view of the world as one that represented whatever truth was contained in ancient traditions, the Stoics adopted and developed the allegorical method. Its primary purpose was to interpret the old myths and rituals in order to relate traditional beliefs in the gods to the new philosophy. The motivation for this sort of interpretation was a genuine reverence for the inherited religious beliefs, which explains the efforts to discover the hidden religious meanings of the writings of classical authors, especially Homer. It was in these endeavors that the allegorical method was further elaborated and refined, creating the standard hermeneutical method of antiquity, which Hellenistic-Jewish and Christian theologians would readily use later on to interpret biblical texts. The *Homeric Problems* of Pseudo-Heraklitos (1st century BCE), though not exclusively committed to Stoic philosophy, is the best surviving example of this religious allegorical interpretation of Homer as it was practiced in the schools of the time. A synopsis of the Stoic theology that was developed on the basis of allegorical interpretation of ancient myths was written by Cornutus in the 1st century CE.

The Middle Stoa began with Panaitios of Rhodos (ca. 180–110 BCE). His philosophy was characterized by a "return to the old philosophers," namely, the classical philosophy of Sokrates, Plato, and Aristotle. In his physics and cosmology, Panaitios departed from the older Stoic dogmatism and rejected the contradictions in the system of Chrysippos. Instead, he emphasized the ethical teachings for the practical conduct of life, which were heavily indebted to Plato and Aristotle. His thought strongly influenced Roman authors; his work *On Right Conduct* was used extensively in Cicero's *De officiis*.

A figure much disputed in modern scholarship was decisive for the further development of Stoicism: the historian, geographer, astronomer, and philosopher Poseidonios of Apamea, who taught in Rhodos during the first half of the 1st century BCE. His philosophy ingeniously assimilated Stoic doctrines with the general thought of late Hellenism to such a degree that it was judged unacceptable by later Stoics. At the same, he reshaped Stoic thought into a more general system that greatly influenced the general world view of the educated class of the Roman imperial period. Poseidonios adopted many elements from the pre-Socratics and from Platonic and Aristotelian philosophy, while he drew a sharp line against the Epicureans. As a consequence, Epicurean philosophy became more isolated, while the amalgamation of concepts from all other philosophical traditions was greatly encouraged. The effects are visible in many thinkers of the following centuries, whether pagan (Cicero, Plutarch), Jewish (Philo), or Christian (Justin, Clement of Alexandria), and also in the new philosophical synthesis of late antiquity, Neoplatonism.

Reconstructing Poseidonios' philosophy is problematic. Scholarship must rely completely on indirect and secondary sources and witnesses. Nevertheless, the reconstruction, however tentative, of some of his cosmological teachings is required because of their influence in the subsequent period. His view of the sun, the pure fire, as the source of the human spirit, to which the moon contributes the soul, and the earth the body, recurs in the cosmic anthropology of Gnosticism. Here, as well as in the Hermetic writings, the celestial journey of the soul or spirit is understood in a very similar way: when a human being dies, the body decays, while the soul remains for some time in the sublunar region, until it too wastes away in order to liberate the spirit, which returns to its home in the sun. With these concepts, Poseidonios created a schema which could also be used to describe the ascent of the human spirit in mystical experiences. Poseidonios also accommodated dualistic concepts that came to dominate the thought of the late Hellenistic period. Despite all efforts to maintain a Stoic monism in his cosmology, the sublunar world emerges as a realm of an inferior order. While the sun and the celestial world are identical to the pure realm of the divine, the relationship of the sublunar realm to the divine power remains ambiguous; in other words, human beings living in this realm stand in need of redemption. Naturally, the all-governing divine reason also becomes differentiated into energies of varying degrees: in mythological terms into gods, heroes, and demons, or in astrological terms into astral powers of different ranks. However influential these thoughts were in general, the Stoics of the imperial period turned their back on Poseidonios. For them, Chrysippos remained the authoritative systematician of Stoic teachings, to whom one could refer whenever necessary. While there was little interest left in cosmology among the Stoics of Roman times, Stoic ethics was now ready to conquer the world (§6.4f).

2. The Spirit of the Hellenistic Age

(a) The Cynics

Sokrates was famous for going to public places to contend with all sorts of people and to challenge them to reflect about themselves. It is this pattern of philosophizing, not any specific Socratic teaching, which Cynicism learned from Sokrates. Its founder was Antisthenes (ca. 450–365 BCE), a student of Sokrates. Antisthenes preached rigorous abstention from all pleasures and frugality, ideals that he propagated in a book about Herakles. The most famous Cynic was Antisthenes' student Diogenes of Sinope (400/390–328/232 BCE), called "the dog" (*kyon*) because of his impudence—a designation that gave this movement its name—hesitating at nothing when he wanted to demonstrate his rejection of cultural values and bourgeois convention. He slept in a barrel, rejected even the simplest utensils for eating and drinking, and wore always the same garment.

Diogenes proclaimed no specific philosophical doctrine, nor did his successors, but later Cynics were often influenced by Stoic philosophy. Their frugality and impudence were expressions of their repudiation of the conventions of society. On the positive side, they stressed natural standards of behavior, acted as pastoral counselors, and volunteered to work for the welfare of others. Cynic philosophy did not formulate and transmit doctrines, but created striking exam-

Bibliography to §4.2

E. R. Dodds, *The Greeks and the Irrational* (Berkeley and Los Angeles, CA: University of California Press, 1951).

Bibliography to §4.2a: Texts

E. N. O'Neil, ed., *Teles (The Cynic Teacher)* (SBLTT 11, Greco–Roman Religion Series 3; Missoula, MT: Scholars Press, 1977).
Gabriele Giannantoni, *Socratis et Socraticorum reliquiae* (Napoli, Italy: Bibliopolis, 1990).
Abraham J. Malherbe, *The Cynic Epistles: A Study Edition* (SBLSBS 12; Missoula, MT: Scholars Press, 1977).
Harold W. Attridge, *First-Century Cynicism in the Epistles of Heraclitus* (HTS 29; Missoula, MT: Scholars Press, 1976).

Bibliography to §4.2a: Studies

Donald R. Dudley, *A History of Cynicism from Diogenes to the 6th Century A.D.* (London, 1937).
Farraud Sayre, *The Greek Cynics* (Baltimore: Furst, 1948).
Ragnar Höistad, *Cynic Hero and King* (Uppsala: Bloms, 1948).
H. D. Rankin, *Sophists, Socrates and Cynics* (Totowa, NJ: Barnes & Noble, 1983).
Hans Dieter Betz, " Jesus and the Cynies," *JR* 74 (1994).
Abraham J. Malherbe, "Self-Definition among Epicureans and Cynics," in Meyer and Sanders, *Self-Definition in the Greco-Roman World*, 46–59.

ples for behavior, which were fixed in the form of stories, usually about its founder Diogenes. To collect these traditions, Metrokles of Maroneia created the literary genre of *chreiai*, brief anecdotes with maxims to be used as readily available rules for behavior.

The teaching of the mendicant Cynics followed no particular patterns. Some used ridicule, others chose a caring approach in order to convince and help their hearers. The *diatribê* was a Cynic creation. The original meaning of the word is "pastime," and in the 4th century BCE it was used, together with *scholê* ("leisure") to designate a philosophical school. During the 3d century BCE, diatribe as a method that sought to engage the layperson replaced the (Platonic) dialogue that addressed the philosophical colleague or student. The diatribe scorned technical language and used for its examples the vernacular language and metaphors used by the common people, even to the point of rudeness. Objections of a fictitious opponent, rhetorical questions, anecdotes, and striking quotations are typical of this style of popular oratory.

What finally emerged as the "Cynic diatribe" was not purely Cynic; absorbing elements from other philosophical schools, it affected other circles, especially the Stoics. The popular philosopher Bion of Borysthenes (3d century BCE), considered to be the founder of the diatribe style, was himself strongly influenced by Platonic and Aristotelian philosophy. The first evidence of this style appears in the fragments of an otherwise unknown philosopher named Teles, which have been preserved by Stobaios. The diatribe also influenced the literary style in the period of early Christianity and is discernible in writers such as Philo of Alexandria, Seneca, Musonius, Epiktetos, Maximus of Tyre, and, among Christian authors, especially Paul.

(b) Euhemerism

The Hellenistic period saw many theories seeking to explain the origin of belief in gods. Some of these explanations derived from earlier allegorizing of Homer's writings and from Sophistic opinions. Plato's criticism of myth, which had identified the gods with sidereal powers, became significant during the Hellenistic and Roman periods. An alternative explanation offered by the Stoics identified the gods with the forces that permeate the cosmos and saw human beings as intimately related to the gods because their ultimate nature was reason. Side by side with this pseudoscientific explanation a more popular theory viewed the gods as various classes of demons (§4.1a).

The theory about the origins of belief in the gods that found the widest reception, though it was considered by many to be the epitome of atheism, is known as Euhemerism. Its founder, Euhemeros of Messene (ca. 340–260 BCE), was disparaged as a notorious atheist, though Euhemeros' contribution to this

Bibliography to §4.2b

K. Thraede, "Euhemerismus," *RAC* 6. 887–890.

H. F. van den Meer, *Euhemerus van Messene* (Amsterdam: Vrije Universiteit te Amsterdam, 1949).

Albert Henrichs, "The Sophists and Hellenistic Religion: Prodicus as the Spiritual Father of the Isis Aretalogies," *HSCP* 88 (1984) 139–58.

theory was not as significant as was believed. The Euhemeristic explanation of myth belongs to a tradition that began with Homer, which understood the gods and their behavior, actions, and feelings in anthropomorphic terms. This interpretation was rationalistic from the very beginning. Shortly before Euhemeros, Hekataios of Abdera (ca. 350–290 BCE), the first ancient writer who described the Jews, had appropriated Egyptian concepts, in which the gods of Egypt, partially identified with Greek gods, were seen as kings from primordial times. These kings had founded states, promulgated laws, and taught people everything that was necessary for civilization and human culture. Hekataios also wrote an ethnographic utopia "About the Hyperboreans." Euhemeros drew on Hekataios, but went beyond him. In his utopian political romance, the gods Ouranos, Kronos, and Zeus (with their wives Hestia, Rhea, and Hera) are depicted as primordial kings. The Greeks had always spoken about the love affairs of the gods as if they were human amorous adventures; Euhemeros wrote about the mythical battles of the gods against the Titans as if they were court intrigues and dynastic struggles in the families of kings. Zeus is described in the image of Alexander the Great: he marches through all countries from west to east, founding kingdoms and appointing his friends as rulers, giving laws and establishing cults for his own worship—a reflection of the development of the ruler cult in the decades after Alexander.

Euhemeros simply drew the consequences from a long tradition of critical interpretation of myth; but it was he who finally dethroned the gods, removing them from those areas of experience that could not be controlled by human powers and reducing them to heroes; they were to be worshiped like divine rulers in order to secure benefactions in the same way in which one would seek rewards through the observance of the ruler cult. The world that lay outside this political theology lost its divine parents and was surrendered to the powers of the stars and to the demons. Astrology, demonology, and magical rites were only too eager to fill the place once held by the belief in gods.

(c) Astrology and Fate

Plato had already stated that the stars are divine beings. Even before Plato, the Pythagoreans had accepted similar eastern astrological beliefs. But such opinions were foreign to the tradition of Greek religious thought. The gods of Greece had nothing in common with the stars; worship of the sun was not practiced, and

Bibliography to §4.2c: Studies

Franz Cumont, *Astrology and Religion among the Greeks and the Romans* (New York and London: Putnam's, 1912).

Franz Boll, Karl Bezold, and Wilhelm Gundel, *Sternglaube und Sterndeutung: Die Geschichte und das Wesen der Astrologie* (5th ed.; Darmstadt: Wissenschaftliche Buchgesellschaft, 1966).

O. Neugebauer and H. B. van Hoesen, *Greek Horoscopes* (MAPS 48; Philadelphia, PA: American Philosophical Society, 1959).

Hans Georg Gundel, *Weltbild und Astrologie in den griechischen Zauberpapyri* (München: Beck, 1968).

Wilhelm Gundel and Hans Georg Gundel, *Astrologumena: Die astrologische Literatur in der Antike und ihre Geschichte* (Wiesbaden: Steiner, 1966).

Helios was not personalized in the same way as other gods. The notion that the fixed stars, sun, moon, and planets were powerful deities who determine the fate of nations, war and peace, the growth of the fruits of the field, and the health and fertility of domestic animals has its origin in Mesopotamia. The horoscope for human individuals was found there for the first time at the end of the 5th century BCE, whereas the horoscope for a city or nation is much older.

The Greeks learned about these astrological beliefs in the 4th century BCE. While Eudoxos of Knidos, the most significant mathematician of his time (ca. 400–347 BCE), and Theophrastos, Aristotle's student and successor, rejected such beliefs in the power of the stars, they spread quickly in the Greek-speaking world during the following century, together with advances in astronomical science (§3.3b). Zeno, the founder of Stoic philosophy, seems to have been influenced by Babylonian astrology. Berossos, a Babylonian priest, gave an extensive description of astrology in his history of Babylon, which was published in Greek and dedicated to King Antiochos I of Syria. As a consequence of these successful advances, astrology became so firmly established that the protest of Karneades, head of the Academy in the 2d century BCE, came too late, and Panaitios sought in vain to liberate Stoic philosophy from its entanglement with astrology. The new belief in the stars was there to stay.

The victory was won by Babylonian astrology in concert with Greek science and the new philosophical religion of Hellenism. Alexandria, the city in which Greek sciences, and especially astronomy, made their most spectacular advances, was also the birthplace of systematic and scientific astrological endeavors. New systems for the determination of astrological fate were developed with the aid of the most modern insights and advanced mathematical methods, because the scientific discoveries of the Hellenistic astronomers were far superior to those of their Babylonian predecessors. There was no awareness of a possible conflict between astronomy and astrology. The leading astronomer, Hipparchos of Nicea (§3.3.b), working in Alexandria briefly during the 2d century BCE, was firmly persuaded of the truth of astrological ideas. Mathematics and mysticism were by no means mutually exclusive. The same century also produced the best known handbook of astrology, published under the pseudonyms "Nechepso and Petosiris," and a similar work claiming to be written by Hermes Trismegistos—a name that later became significant as the authority for the Hermetic literature (§6.5f). These works, which have little relation to Egyptian traditions, were written by Greek scientists on the basis of their own research, which in turn relied on Babylonian astrology.

Astrology, appearing from the beginning as a consistent scientific system, was successful because it provided the framework for a new philosophico-religious interpretation of the world. The religion of city gods could survive in this form only so long as these gods were experienced as effective patrons and protectors of political, social, and personal life. However, the mobility of the populations, the widening of the geographical horizons, and the universalization of economics, politics, and sciences could no longer be satisfied by "local" deities. Even though the rulers of the Hellenistic kingdoms used the ancient city cults and their gods in the service of their universal policies, this did not necessarily result in a new understanding of these gods as universal deities. Popularized philosophy and its ally astrology pointed in new directions.

Stoicism, the most important universalistic philosophy, made recourse to universally valid astrological concepts in formulating its cosmology. Astrology provided the framework in which the old gods made their reappearance as universal powers. Zeus, once the ruler of Mt. Olympos, was transformed into the planet "Jupiter," the radiant lord of heaven, as soon as he was identified with the Babylonian healer god Marduk and rediscovered as the brightest planet. Aphrodite became "Venus" (= Ishtar), Ares was "Mars" (= Nergal, the Babylonian god of death), and Hermes became "Mercury" (= Ninurtu, the Babylonian god of wisdom). The days of the week were now determined by five planets, sun, and moon. This was a product of the Greek spirit, as is demonstrated by the dominant position of the sun, which agrees with the opinion of Greek science and its heliocentric view of the cosmos, whereas in Babylon the moon was a more important power of fate.

The universalization of the Greek gods, which gave the sun a central place, was the basis for the later Roman development that made the "Invincible Sun" (*Sol Invictus*) the most powerful symbol of paganism in its fight against Christianity. It was Poseidonios who declared that the sun as pure fire was the origin of all reason and of all "spirits," and ultimately the source of all power. The popularization of such ideas, however, took place during the Roman period.

The astrological world view, with its concepts of universal law and power, provided an apt image of the new, larger world in which human beings had to learn to live, and gave them some concept of the powers with which they had to reckon. But this world view also had a negative side, which conjured up a ghost that could not be exorcised: *Heimarmenê*. The term is derived from μείϛομαι ("to receive one's portion"), which shares the root of the Homeric term μοῖϛα ("lot" or "fate"). Classical tragedy had instead spoken about *Anankê*, the incalculable "necessity" and powerful mystery of human life that appeared in love, guilt, calamity, and death in order to demand its due. Aristotle had defined *Anankê* as "that which is contrary to the movement of free choice" (*Metaphysics* 4.5; p. 1015a, 20ff). But "necessity" does not render human life meaningless or absurd; it only prevents human beings from calculating their lives in advance. Thus it provides opportunity for true experiences of life, which are full of mystery; it demands that one remain true to one's humanity, without revealing whether success or despair will determine the end.

In Hellenism, however, Heimarmene became a power that determined human life like a mathematical calculation. She was the highest god with final power over everything, the fate written in the stars and running its course as inevitably as the courses of the stars. A characteristic description of Babylonian astrology and of the concept of Heimarmene appears in Philo of Alexandria (*Migr. Abr.* 179):

These men imagined that the visible universe [i.e., the earth and the stars] was the only thing which existed and that it was either itself god or contained god in itself as the soul of the universe. And they made fate (*heimarmenê*) and necessity (*anankê*) into gods, thus filling human life with much impiety; because they teach that outside of the visible phenomena [of the cosmos] there is no agent causative of anything whatsoever, but the sun and moon and the other bodies of heaven determine by their circuits the good as well as its opposite for every being.

There is no room for freedom, because the astrological view of the world delivers everyone into the hands of fate. The authorities and relationships of the social structures of human life were not even discussed as a realm in which freedom is possible yet limited. Human beings had been taken out of their inherited social structures, and Hellenistic philosophy was unable to determine either the realm of human freedom or moral responsibility in their social and political dimensions. The view of the world under the sign of Heimarmene did not reckon with political structures, but only with sidereal and physical/natural laws. Coins of the emperors and military standards later exhibited astrological symbols—even the ruling political power was subject to the law of the stars.

The confrontation of the human individual with the sidereal powers, immutable and knowing no mercy although their designs could be calculated, favored the spread of astrological determinism. Because they were powers of material and physical characteristics, magic that could influence such powers invaded all realms of life. One needed a magician to be successful in an erotic adventure, one chose the most opportune "hour" for a banquet according to astrological handbooks, and one made important political decisions only after consulting an astrologer. It was futile to argue with fate, but one could at least arrange one's plans accordingly. As the belief in astrology and Heimarmene reached its climax in the Roman imperial period, the new religions of salvation, such as Mithraism and Christianity, were compelled to come to terms with it.

(d) Orphism and Concepts of Afterlife

The origins of Orphism and the Thracian singer Orpheus, whose followers placed him in the time before Homer, remain enigmatic. Orphism becomes

Bibliography to §4.2d: Texts

Apostolos N. Athanassakis, ed., *The Orphic Hymns* (SBLTT 12; Missoula, MT: Scholars Press, 1977).

Bibliography to §4.2d: Studies

W. K. C. Guthrie, *Orpheus and Greek Religion: A Study of the Orphic Movement* (2d. ed.; London: Methuen, 1952; reprint: Princeton, NJ: Princeton University Press, 1993).
Martin P. Nilsson, "Early Orphism and Kindred Religious Movements," *HTR* 28 (1935) 181–230.
Arthur D. Nock, "Orphism or Popular Philosophy?" in idem, *Essays*, 1. 503-15.
M. L. West, *The Orphic Poems* (Oxford: Clarendon, 1983).
Larry J. Alderink, *Creation and Salvation in Ancient Orphism* (American Classical Studies 8; Chico, CA: Scholars Press, 1981).
Robert Garland, *The Greek Way of Death* (Ithaca, NY: Cornell University Press, 1985).
Emily Vermeule, "The Afterlife: Greece," in Grant and Kitzinger, *Civilization*, 2. 987–06.
John A. North, "The Afterlife: Rome," in Grant and Kitzinger, *Civilization*, 2. 997–1007.

clearly visible for the first time in mythical writings produced in the archaic period. Following the examples of the mythic poems of Hesiod, Greek authors produced a great number of theogonies in poetic language, all written between 600 and 500 BCE. They were not homogeneous and appropriated large amounts of Near Eastern mythical traditions, as Hesiod had done earlier (about 700 BCE). The close relationship of Hesiod's *Theogony* to Anatolian myths about Kumarbi and the monster Ullikummi (preserved through Hittite texts) and with the Babylonian creation myth *Enuma Elish* (ca. 1500 BCE) is evident. Later these myths became known once more in the Greek world, the latter through the Babylonian priest Berossos (3d century BCE), the former through the Phoenician Philon of Byblos (64–141 CE) in his *Phoenician History.* These instances of the appropriation of Near Eastern mythic materials are clearly attested in literary works, but other similar contacts with the east cannot be excluded. Such contacts inspired the mythic poetry of the 6th century BCE and were renewed in the Hellenistic period.

Orphic circles apparently had a considerable share in such mythopoetics, though one should not overestimate their role. Several theogonies of the 6th century BCE were Orphic works. Most influential was a work called *Hieroi Logoi,* to which references appear as early as Herodotos and as late as the Neoplatonists. Orphic conventicles must have existed at least that early and especially influenced the lower classes. Orphic priests offered religiously edifying books for sale and invited participation in Orphic rites ("mysteries"). Orphic myths and mysticism also seem to have influenced the Greek mysteries (§4.3e–f). Fully established Orphic mysteries are first attested in the 3d century BCE. The heartland of Orphism was Magna Graecia, the ancient seat of the Pythagorean school (which, however, no longer existed in the early Hellenistic period; see §6.5d). It is possible that the remnants of the Pythagorean sect were absorbed by the Orphic circles. Orphic hymns are also attested for the eastern Greek world.

A monotheistic tendency is characteristic for the theology of Orphism. The formula "there is *one* god," appearing in a famous quotation from Xenophanes, was widespread in later centuries and appears in an Orphic text from the 3d century BCE. On the other hand, polytheistic speculations of the older Orphic theogonies were maintained in a modified form. Kronos occupies the first position, coming into being out of the primordial principles of water and mud. He creates Aither and Chaos, and in them the world egg, out of which rises Phanes, the Orphic creator god, a winged androgynous figure with animal heads, who is sometimes identified with Dionysos and called Protogonos. Other divine entities come into being in the course of creation, some of which are identified with traditional deities, others designated as powers like Heimarmene and Ananke. Other versions and variants of this myth exist. Central for most of these is the story that the Titans overcame Dionysos and began to devour him; Zeus, enraged, burned the Titans with his thunderbolt, and human beings emerged out of the smoke of the conflagration, uniting in their nature the divinity of Dionysos as well as the evil of the Titans. Whether versions of such Orphic myths influenced Gnostic mythology, or whether the latter derived from analogous appropriations of Near Eastern myths, deserves further investigation.

Orphism was profoundly influential through its doctrine of the transmigration of souls and its conceptions of the underworld and of punishment after death, which developed in close connection with popular beliefs. The common opinion of the Hellenistic period was that after death the soul would find itself in a shadow life without true consciousness, although life after death could also be understood as "bodily" existence. Various ancient beliefs lived on with respect to the cult of the dead, rites of burial, and related magical practices and came into new flowering in Hellenistic times. Meals for the dead were a widespread custom, continuing in the Christian meals at the graves of martyrs. A closely associated belief was that the dead who had received a good lot would be able to enjoy an everlasting banquet of food and wine. It was also customary to bring food and wine to be poured out over the graves or into pipes stuck into the ground. Curse tablets were put on the graves, and the dead person was charged with carrying out the curse.

It was assumed that the souls of persons who had suffered a violent death, or were left unburied, were still haunting the neighborhood of their corpses: through magic they could be summoned and be made serviceable. Cases of necromancy are reported. One ascribed the sad fate of the souls after death to drinking from the well of Forgetting (Λήθη). This Hellenistic concept is new as compared to its Classical equivalent, which knew about the "House of Lethe"; drinking from the well of Remembrance (Μνημοσύνη) resulted into transfer to a life among the gods and heroes. Particularly the Orphics used this Classical concept. They put small gold sheets into the graves, with inscriptions admonishing the dead person to avoid the well of Lethe and to drink from the well of Remembrance.

All this reflects an increasingly widespread belief that the dead would receive punishment for their evil deeds, or go to a place of lasting bliss and joy, or even become heroes and commune with the gods. These beliefs in no way suggest a bodiless afterlife of the soul, but imagine a full reconstitution of human life. Funerary inscriptions, to be sure, only rarely give evidence for such beliefs. In most instances one finds only clichés expressing the loss of a beloved wife, husband, or child. Belief in a blessed afterlife is more clearly presented in vase paintings from Magna Graecia, in the wall paintings of Macedonian tombs with pictures of the judges of the dead, and, continuing into the Roman period, in the numerous buildings and donations that maintain and promote the cult of the heroized dead. The teachings of the Orphics, and later of the Neopythagoreans, served as catalysts for forming and expanding belief in immortality.

In spite of the astrological world view, the Orphics maintained their older concept of a place of punishment in the depths of the earth (Tartaros) and of the fields of the blessed in the far west. This belief lived on among most of the common people. Attempts to adjust such beliefs to the astrological world view, which transferred the place of punishment to the southernmost sky on the other side of the earth, never found general acceptance. Rather, the Orphic doctrine became the foundation for the descriptions of hell that were widespread as early as the Hellenistic period and are abundantly attested in the Roman period among pagans (Virgil, Plutarch, Lucian of Samosata), Jews (*1 Enoch*), and Christians (*Apocalypse of Peter, Acts of Thomas*). Plato was the first to use the Orphic doctrine of punishment in the afterlife in the context of a discussion of justice and retribution. It is completely in the Greek tradition when in the 2d century CE the pagan mocker Lucian competes with Christian preachers in gruesome descriptions of punishment in hell. Both also demonstrate that those centuries were unable to establish the idea of justice in the political order and, therefore, had to rely almost completely on the concept of just reward and fitting punishment in afterlife. Here, aspects of an earlier mythical view of the world were preserved, regardless of advances toward more adequate scientific insights. The idea of justice could not be abandoned. There was no place for it in the scientific view of the world, which was essentially materialistic. The world view of astrology could speak about powers and forces, but it was dominated by the concept of fate. Thus there was no choice but to cling to the old mythic descriptions of hellfire and punishment, which provided an asylum for the idea of justice—though only in a gruesome fashion.

3. The Development of Greek Religion

(a) "Syncretism"

The Hellenistic period has been characterized as the time of religious syncretism. In order to clarify the meaning of this term, recourse to the original

Bibliography to §4.3: Texts

Rice and Stambaugh, *Sources for Greek Religion.*
John Ferguson, *Greek and Roman Religion: A Sourcebook* (Noyes Classical Studies; Park Ridge, NJ: Noyes Press).
Kraemer, *Maenads, Martyrs,* passim.

Bibliography to §4.3: Studies

Nilsson, *Griechische Religion* 2.
Martin P. Nilsson, *Greek Piety* (Oxford: Clarendon, 1948).
Walter Burkert, *Greek Religion* (Cambridge, MA: Harvard University Press, 1985).
Idem, *Homo Necans: The Anthropology of Ancient Greek Sacrificial Ritual and Myth* (Berkeley, CA: University of California Press, 1983). These two works are the most important comprehensive discussions of Greek religion from the beginnings down to the Hellenistic period.
Idem, *The Orientalizing Revolution: Near Eastern Influence on Greek Culture in the Early Archaic Age* (Cambridge: Harvard University, 1992).
A. J. Festugière, *Personal Religion among the Greeks* (Sather Classical Lectures 26: Berkeley and Los Angeles, CA: University of California Press, 1954).
Louise Bruit Zaidman and Pauline Schmitt Pantel, *Religion in the Greek City* (trans. Paul Cartledge; Cambridge: Cambridge University Press, 1992).
Patricia E. Easterling and John V. Muir, eds., *Greek Religion and Society* (Cambridge: Cambridge University Press, 1985).
Erika Simon, *Die Götter der Griechen* (2d ed.; München: Hirmer, 1980). Presents numerous illustrations.
L. H. Martin, *Hellenistic Religion: An Introduction* (New York: Oxford University Press, 1987).
Susan Guettel Cole, "Greek Cults," in Grant and Kitzinger, *Civilization,* 2. 887-908.
John Ferguson, "Divinities," ibid., 2. 847–60.
Michael H. Jameson, "Sacrifice and Ritual: Greece," ibid., 2. 959–79.

Bibliography to §4.3a

Arthur D. Nock, "ΣΥΝΝΑΟΣ ΘΕΟΣ," in idem, *Essays,* 1. 202–51.

meaning of the word yields little: "syncretism" (συγκρητισμός) designated the federation of Cretan cities that had previously fought each other. In modern times the term was misunderstood as a derivative of the verb συγκεράννυμι = "to mix together" and was thus used to describe the mixing of religions, especially Greek and Near Eastern religions. "Mixture," however, poorly characterizes the encounter of these religious traditions and its results, an encounter that began much earlier and was intensified through the greater mobility of the population at the beginning of the Hellenistic period, with the result that Greeks and other peoples lived side by side, all with their own religious traditions. But merely mixing populations did not result in religious syncretism. The real causes were spiritual and psychological, rooted on the one hand in the dominant position of the Greeks, which necessarily led to an expansion of Greek culture, and on the other hand in the natural fascination of the Greek mind with anything novel and foreign. This resulted in a number of quite different developments, all in their own way syncretistic phenomena.

Originally the religions of the Greeks as well as of Near Eastern peoples were local cults, firmly established by a state, city, or nation. Their deities were bound to particular places, like a shrine, a sacred grove, or a mountain. But this view was changing, due to the influence of philosophy and enlightenment, as well as the mobility of the population. Greek gods were brought to the east, sometimes literally carried in the form of a statue or another sacred object, to become gods of the new Greek cities. As the Hellenistic kings sought to strengthen the Greek element in their countries, this development was officially encouraged. On the other hand, eastern deities and their cults were brought to the west by slaves, merchants, sailors, and soldiers. Immigrants established their gods first through the founding of religious associations that gave their ancient gods recognition and a new home.

In this way the Greeks who went east founded such sanctuaries as the famous temple of Apollo at Daphne near Antioch. Even before this time eastern gods had become established in the west. Slaves from Asia, for example, who worked the Laurian mines in Attika, had already brought the Asian god Men to Greece in pre-Hellenistic times. Political and trade relations with Thrace had established the Thracian goddess Bendis in Athens as early as ca. 430 BCE. Even earlier the Asian Great Mother had come to Greece and was officially recognized by many Greek cities. Such transplantation of deities was not really something new, and there is no reason to call it syncretistic. Some other elements, then, must be present in the movement of a cult in order to make it a syncretistic process.

One such element is the identification or combination of deities of different origins, even though this too was nothing new in the history of Greek religion. The Artemis of Ephesos as well as goddesses called by this Greek name in other cities of Asia Minor (Sardis, Smyrna, Perge) were Asian fertility goddesses, whose cult statues show that they had little in common with the hunting Greek virgin goddess. But the Hellenistic period witnessed an explosion of such combinations of different deities. The process normally began with the adoption of a Greek name for the newly imported deity. On Delos, for example, an association

of merchants and ship owners from Berytos (Beirut) in Phoenicia called themselves Poseidoniasts and named their Phoenician sea god Poseidon. The Greek gods
were also associated with eastern deities: on Kos existed an association of Zeus
and (the Syrian) Astarte. Finally, Greek gods, especially Zeus, received eastern
surnames; this was often the case when a Near Eastern cult that had been
officially recognized by a Hellenistic king (e.g., Zeus Keraunios, Zeus
Sabazios). Ethnography and philosophy had already prepared the way for this
identification of Greek and Near Eastern deities. Greek and Roman gods were
also identified at an early date (Zeus = Jupiter, Aphrodite = Venus, Athena =
Minerva, etc.). As a result, the Roman gods assumed Greek features and adopted
Greek mythology, although they had originally been divinities of different
character.

Another important factor in the syncretistic process was the mutual permeation
of various elements of the different religions. One can observe the following
phenomena. First, eastern religions were Hellenized. Rites and practices of the
eastern deities were usually preserved, but their myths and cult legends were
translated into Greek, which also supplied Greek concepts along with the language. Or the presentation of a Near Eastern god could be Hellenized: Melqart of
Phoenician Tyre, who was already associated with the Thasian Herakles-
Melkathros, now appears on coins from Tyre with Herakles' club and lions skin.
Second, concepts growing out of the general Hellenistic religious experience
invaded all religions, whether of Greek or of eastern origin (e.g., the one god of
heaven who rules over the all). Elements of the new world view were accepted
everywhere: astrology, popularized Platonism, belief in miracles, and emphasis
on the salvation of the individual human being. Third, ancient concepts that had
become separated from their original local tradition were reinterpreted to fit the
new world culture. Rites that were originally connected with the fertility of the
land migrated into the cities and were presented in terms of a spiritualized
understanding of salvation. In this context, the popularization of the enlightenment, criticism of myth, and Stoic theology became very effective because their
allegorical interpretation of myths, rites, and customs as spiritual statements of
universal significance had already prepared the way.

A final syncretistic phenomenon was the creation of a new religion out of
Greek and non-Greek elements. This was the case in the formation of the cult of
Sarapis (§4.4a), but this example is not really typical. Syncretism in its very
essence was not the result of artificial manipulations, but an unmonitored historical development. It was a response to the encounter of two opposing forces: first,
the constraints that arise from inherited traditions, dignified by a long history;
and second, the need to enter into conversation with a new culture and its spirit.
The artificial creation of a new religion harmonizes these opposing forces and
hence avoids any creative conflict. Indeed the history of the Sarapis cult demonstrates that it failed to incorporate its traditional Egyptian constituency and that
only the subsequent syncretistic amalgamation of the Egyptian Isis gave this cult
its appeal and strength. No single religion of the Hellenistic and Roman periods
was spared. The religion of Israel was also drawn into that process, despite a
revolt of the pious in the Maccabean uprising against the Hellenizers. Christiani-

ty began as a sect with missionary ambitions within an already Hellenized Jewish religion, but it did not simply emerge out of the preaching of the Jewish prophet Jesus. Rather, Christianity, probably more than any other religion of its time, adapted itself to a variety of cultural and religious currents and appropriated numerous foreign elements until it was ready to succeed as a world religion— thoroughly syncretistic in every way.

(b) The Older Gods and Their Cults.

At the beginning of the Hellenistic period the established cults were generally thought to be continuing with undiminished strength; that this fiction was maintained until late antiquity contributed to their final demise. Not only the ancient Greek cultic establishments, but also those of the Asian, Syrian, and Egyptian gods, rooted in their local traditions, enjoyed recognition among large parts of the populations. They could also count on the support of the new rulers, who made no attempts to Hellenize eastern cults but granted benefactions to established temples and shrines, a policy that was continued by the Romans. The initiative for Hellenization usually came from some of the cult's followers, and only in exceptional cases from the kings. To be sure, the worship of the inherited deities in Greece was no longer naively taken as a matter of course, thanks to the criticism of myth that had begun during the Classical period.

From the time of Alexander the Great, the gods of the once independent cities and states had lost political influence in foreign affairs. The political power of the central sanctuaries of the political leagues (amphictyonies) had come to an end in the west as well as in the east. The superpower politics of the Near Eastern empires from the time of the Assyrians to the Persians had long since led to the result that, for example, the Yahweh sanctuary of the Israelite amphictyony was first transformed into the royal sanctuary in Jerusalem and later, under priestly leadership, into the recognized cult of a client state of no political significance. The numerous temple states of Syria and Asia Minor, often the centers of large estates, owed their existence to similar developments. In the rare instance, in which such a client state achieved political independence, the existing cult might assume new political functions. The well-known history of the Jewish temple state demonstrates this well. But it also exemplifies that the direction of the

Bibliography to §4.3b: Texts

Rice and Stambaugh, *Sources for Greek Religion*, passim.

Franciszek Sokolowski, *Lois sacrés des cités grecques* (Paris: Boccard, 1969)

Bibliography to §4.3b: Studies

Burkert, *Greek Religion*, 119–89.

Lewis Richard Farnell, *The Cults of the Greek States* (5 vols.; Oxford: Clarendon, 1896–1907; reprint New Rochelle, NY: Caratzas, 1977).

Jon D. Mikalson, *Athenian Popular Religion* (Chapel Hill, NC: University of North Carolina Press, 1983.

Michael H. Jameson, "Sacrifice and Ritual: Greece," in Grant and Kitzinger, *Civilization*, 2. 959–79.

Martin P. Nilsson, *Greek Popular Religion* (LHR NS 1; New York: Columbia University Press, 1940).

religious developments that had taken place in the meantime could not be easily reversed: the defenders of the tradition, who had fought in the Maccabean revolt for political and religious freedom, seceded from the temple cult at the very moment that it regained its old position as the state cult of Judea (§5.1c, d), while large portions of diaspora Judaism maintained only formal ties at best with the temple in Jerusalem.

This loss of function of the cult of a traditional deity as a state cult demanded religious and liturgical reform—a frequent phenomenon in the early Hellenistic period. Typical features appear in the reform of the Yahweh cult in Jerusalem under Nehemiah and Ezra; although taking place before the Hellenistic period, it can serve as an example. Attempts to adjust to the situation of a small client state had to be made in the east earlier than in the Greek countries. Two problems required attention. First, the regulation and sanctioning of religious rites needed a new basis in order to maintain continuity with a very ancient tradition, since it was now impossible to appeal to the immediate past, when the temple had been a royal sanctuary imitating the royal cults of the great empires. Second, the sacral revenues had to be established, since the altered political situation required a new determination of the relationship of public revenue to the income and expenditures of the temple.

Once financially secure sanctuaries could no longer count on regular income, nor could they rely on regular payments from the new government. On the other hand, even cities and petty states were quite able to extort large sums of money from a well-functioning temple cult. Nor did the kings of the Hellenistic empires consider it below their dignity to avail themselves of the opportunity to plunder a temple treasury (Antiochos III was slain when he attempted to rob a temple). Along these lines, then, the cultic law that Ezra introduced (the Priestly Code) gave first place to the procedures to be followed in the temple sacrifices, and painstakingly detailed rules and regulations for participating in rites and religious festivals. Ezra's law also pays attention to the fact that Jewish authorities in Jerusalem did not have the right to collect taxes and duties (see Ezra 4:13, 20; 7:24). The Persian king donated some capital for new equipment in the temple (Ezra 7:15ff.; cf. Neh 5:14ff.; 7:70ff.). But since such funds could not serve as a lasting financial basis, regular income was fixed in the form of payment for ritual services, first fruits, tithes, and revenues from the temple estates, collected by specially appointed officials (Neh 12:44). It was also determined with great precision which persons would be entitled to benefit from these revenues (Neh 11:19ff.; 12:1ff.).

In the reforms of many Greek temples at the beginning of the Hellenistic period one finds the same recourse to ancient laws in the regulations for sacrificial procedures and in the fixing of calendars for festivals and sacrifices (*fasti*). Special attention is given to securing the financial base for the various activities of the temple. The reforms of Lykourgos, the secretary for financial and cultural affairs in Athens from 338–326 BCE, are well known. He initiated financial reforms not only for the temples in Athens, but also for other sanctuaries under the city's control, such as the temple of the healer Amphiaraos in Oropos and the mystery sanctuary in Eleusis; new equipment was bought and festivals were reorganized. Similar reforms are known from other Greek cities. New rules were also issued for ritual purity and fasts during the preparation of sacrifices, entering of temples, and participation in festivals.

Renewed activity in the building of temples demonstrates that the old cults of established divinities in many parts of the Hellenistic world flourished during this period. In addition to some major architectural projects in Greece, several monumental building programs were initiated in Asia Minor and on the Greek islands, where the economic situation was better than in Greece itself. The temple of the Ephesian Artemis, which had been destroyed by fire (as it is said, on the night in which Alexander the Great was born), was rebuilt magnificently, as also the Apollo temple at Didyma, both of which had immense proportions. In Pergamon, the kings built the huge altar of Zeus, decorated with elaborate reliefs. On the island of Kos, the Asklepieion was redesigned as a large complex erected on four terraces. Some building activities were financed by Hellenistic kings, even outside of their own territories, such as the temple of Zeus Olympios in Athens, for which building activities were resumed, after an interval of more than four hundred years, with donations from the Syrian king Antiochos IV Epiphanes. The Roman emperors resumed this policy. Thus, from the 1st century BCE, neglected sanctuaries of the old gods arose again in impressive splendor, both in the Greek countries and elsewhere, such as the temple of Jupiter in Baalbek (Lebanon). The magnificent reconstruction of the temple of Jerusalem by Herod the Great also testifies to this interest in the cult of the old gods.

The continuing life and vitality of the old cults are also seen in the numerous festivals and games, which were multiplied and reorganized. Occasions for such festivals were numerous: the celebration of the anniversary of a sanctuary's dedication (cf. the Christian celebrations of the dedication of a church), the honoring of a king or emperor, or the resumption of an old religious tradition that had fallen into disuse. These festivals may have lacked religious depth, but they nevertheless demonstrate the continuing acceptance of the old cults by large portions of the populations. Whenever there was a special procession, or the anniversary of a temple dedication with sacrificial meals and special markets— parts of such celebrations, as were school vacations for children and a free day for slaves—visitors came from the surrounding country and even from far away. Popular piety, fun for the masses, religious devotion expressed in hymns and prayers, and political propaganda were inseparably mixed at such occasions, whether it was the festival of Apollo in Didyma or the feast of Tabernacles in Jerusalem.

The Roman imperial period brought some basic changes. Augustus began an era of imperial support for Greek cults that reached its climax under the phil-hellene emperor Hadrian. But there is also evidence for a decline of the old religions. The number of sacral inscriptions drastically decreases during the Roman period. Especially in Athens, the city in which the most magnificent cultic buildings were erected, the visible presence of splendid temples did little but create the impression that this city was only a museum of Classical greatness. The increase of cult officials for the Ephesian Artemis and the building of several miles of a covered processional way in the 2d century CE is perhaps already a reaction against the increasing popularity of new religions, especially the Egyptian cult and Christianity. The more the old traditions were subsidized by the government, the more the cultic activities of the temples were estranged from the religious consciousness of a majority of the population.

Not much seems to have changed by occasional reforms and increasing acceptance of Near Eastern rites and concepts or by introduction of rites borrowed from the mysteries. Among these innovations was the introduction of lamps, which were customary in Near Eastern cults, to take the place of the traditional Greek torches, first as votive offerings, later also as cultic implements. The burning of incense was introduced everywhere as a special form of sacrifice. Following the example of the Egyptian and other eastern cults, daily worship became customary, especially in the much visited temples and healing sanctuaries, such as those of Asklepios. As the number of worship services increased, blood sacrifices were restricted to special festive occasions and disappeared almost completely from the daily service and liturgy; by the beginning of the Roman period, hymns, prayers, incense, and lamps came to constitute the daily ritual. On special occasions sermons were preached. In its last phase, the cult of the old gods was, in some of its external features, not much different from the forms of worship that had developed in the new propaganda religions, in the diaspora synagogues of Judaism, and in Christianity.

There are three aspects in which the early Roman imperial period cannot be characterized as a time of decline for the worship of the old gods. In rural areas the cults of the local deities continued with their traditional strength. The sanctuaries of the healing deities, especially Asklepios, reached the height of their popularity only in the first and second centuries of the common era. And Greek gods that had "mysteries," in particular Demeter and Dionysos, continued to receive not only imperial but also popular support. Side by side with the new deities from the east, whose worship had been spreading from the beginning of the Hellenistic period—Sarapis and Isis, the Great Mother and Attis, Mithras and Sol Invictus, Judaism and Christianity—three Greek gods thus remained among the most widely worshiped deities: Asklepios, Dionysos, and Demeter.

(c) The Oracles

Oracles had always been a significant factor in Greek religion. Oracular predictions were received in various forms: by dreams (characteristic of the Asklepios sanctuaries), by the god's speaking through a human medium (as the

Bibliography to §4.3c: Texts
Rice and Stambaugh, *Sources for Greek Religion*, 93–106.

Bibliography to §4.3c: Studies
Burkert, *Greek Religion*, 114–18.
John Pollard and John Ferguson, "Divination and Oracles," in Grant and Kitzinger, *Civilization*, 2. 941–58.
Simon Price, "Delphi and Divination," in Easterling and Muir, *Greek Religion and Society*, 128–154.
H. W. Parke and D. E. W. Wormell, *The Delphic Oracle* (2 vols.; Oxford: Blackwell, 1956).

Pythia in Delphi and the Sibyls) or even through animals (as the doves of Zeus in the sacred tree of Dodona), by a journey into the underworld (as in the Oracle of the Dead at Ephyra and the Oracle of Trophonios at Lebadeia), or by some manipulation like the casting of lots. Although Apollo became the most important deity of oracles, many other gods were consulted for oracles. The Oracle of Zeus at Dodona in Epiros boasted of being the most ancient Greek oracle; Olympia's early prominence as a national sanctuary was based on its successful activity as a political oracle; and the sanctuary of Melikertes/Palaimon in Isthmia counted a "prophet" (*mantis*) among its cultic officials.

The political significance of the oracles, mostly sanctuaries of Apollo, diminished in the Hellenistic period. That was especially true with respect to Delphi, once the political and religious center of the amphictyony of the Greek states and the place to which delegations were sent for confirmation of plans to found new colonies or for approval of new state constitutions. But the oracles continued to be highly esteemed by the Hellenistic kings and later by the Roman emperors, as is evident from the numerous buildings donated by them to such sanctuaries as Delphi and Klaros. The oracles of Apollo at Klaros and Didyma in Asia Minor rose to new political importance during the Roman imperial period. Otherwise, the oracles became more focused on the regulation of sacral, legal, and personal matters. Inquiries were made about the proper time for religious festivals, votive offerings, donations, and all sorts of matters that were significant for states, municipalities, and communities. Oracles also functioned as guarantors of legal transactions, as is demonstrated by the numerous documents of manumission of slaves that were publicly displayed on the retaining wall of the temple of Apollo at Delphi.

A different kind of prophecy assumed great significance during the Hellenistic period: the Sibyl. In their ancient form, the Sibyls were prophetic women of early times, known only through legend, who resided in different places and uttered ecstatic predictions, mostly of doom, whether or not any prophecy had been requested. (The oracles, on the other hand, required a specific request, and their answers were given only at predetermined times.) In the later period, "Sibylline oracles" were prophecies found in books that were published and circulated under the name of a famous ancient Sibyl (e.g., the Sibyl of Erythrai in Asia Minor and the Sibyl of Cumae in Italy). These books predicted fatal turns in the history of world and nations and, in general, maintained a critical position over against the dominant Greek and Roman culture. The Sibylline books that are still preserved, though written in Greek, reflect the critical undercurrent of the anti-Greek and anti-Roman sentiments of the eastern countries, including many traditions of Near Eastern origin. In addition to the Greek Sibyls, a Chaldean (Babylonian) Sibyl claimed authority. Jews and Christians appropriated such books and used them in order to propagate their own apocalyptic predictions

Joseph Fontenrose, *The Delphic Oracle* (Berkeley, CA: University of California Press, 1978). Includes a catalogue of oracular responses in translation.

H. W. Parke, *The Oracles of Zeus: Dodona, Olympia, Ammon* (Cambridge, MA: Harvard University Press, 1967).

of doom, as well as their image of a better world to come, all in the dress of an established Greek genre of religious literature.

In spite of an increased popularity and renewed prosperity of several older oracle sanctuaries, Delphi became more and more a mere tourist center; Plutarch complained that in Delphi many requests for oracles were motivated by frivolity, curiosity, or ignoble and selfish interests. Since the success of an oracle depended to a large degree on its ability to respond to the tastes of the time, Delphi's handicap was its awareness of its own dignified ancient tradition. An oracle of Apollo that adapted itself to the demands of a new time, both in its formal manipulations and in its theological attitude, was the oracle in Klaros (near Kolophon, between Smyrna and Ephesos). Several traditions indicate that Klaros appropriated the monotheistic concepts of the philosophers, that it was not opposed to syncretism (according to a preserved oracle from Klaros, IAO [= Yahweh?] is the highest god), and that it initiated visiting delegations or their leaders into a mystery cult. Such innovations, even more than the fact that some of Klaros' published predictions have been found to be correct, were the basis for this oracle's popularity throughout the Greco-Roman world. From all of Asia Minor, but also from Macedonia, Dalmatia, Sardinia, and as far away as Britain, requests were sent to Klaros, as numerous surviving inscriptions indicate.

Other oracles tried to meet the demands raised by belief in mysteries and miracles halfway by adapting their procedures. Complicated rites of initiation are known through the report of Pausanias (2d century CE) for the oracle of the chthonic deity Trophonios near Lebadeia in Boiotia. After several days of purification, the sacrifice of a ram, drinking from the well of forgetting and remembering (in order to forget the past and remember what was about to be experienced), the initiate descended into the adyton, the innermost sanctuary, was dragged down into a cave through a small opening, through which he was to be pushed out again after his journey through the underworld; then he was set on the throne of remembrance, and priests would question him about his experience; The answers were recorded and interpreted by the priests. Similar procedures were used by other oracles; underground chambers (adyta) have been found in a number of sanctuaries of Apollo.

A tractate by Lucian of Samosata reports the manipulations of the prophet Alexander of Abunoteichos (2nd century CE), who established in his oracle sanctuary a flourishing business with prophecies, healings, and advice in religious guise. Whoever wanted it could also be initiated into a mystery cult. The story of Alexander illustrates that many of the flourishing oracles of the Roman period had little interest in the political affairs of the states and cities; they catered to people seeking the aid of supernatural powers for their personal endeavors. Alexander, according to Lucian's report a fraud, was successful because enough people were willing to entrust their needs and anxieties to any institution or person claiming to control divine and otherworldly powers. These oracles of the Roman period were as different from the ancient oracles as the miracle-working θεῖος ἀνήρ, the "divine man," differed from the Cynic or Stoic wandering philosopher of previous centuries. What mattered was a representation of the divine on the religious market in order to satisfy the desires and needs of human beings who no longer had a secure home in the world. Like the "divine man," the oracles also moved closer to magic and occultism.

(d) Asklepios

Asklepios, son of Apollo and the human Koronis, married to a human with sons and daughters, and classified as a "hero" in Homer and Pindar, was nevertheless worshiped as a god in temples (not in tombs) throughout the Greek and Roman world. His origins are said to have been in Trikka in Thessaly, where he had been a local healing deity, like other healing deities and heroes of the Greek world (e.g., Amphiaraos in Oropos and Amynos in Athens). The center for the expansion of his cult, however, became Epidauros in the Peloponnesos, where his sanctuary stood in the immediate neighborhood of that of his father Apollo Maleatas.

Beginning in the 6th century BCE, the god was brought from Epidauros to many other places in the Greek world. Among these was Athens, where a sanctuary was established on the south slope of the Akropolis during a plague at the end of the 4th century BCE. Opposed by the powerful priestly family of the Kerykes and ridiculed by Aristophanes, the god was first accepted by the poet Sophokles and honored in the last words of Sokrates, as reported in Plato's *Phaedo*. The Asklepieion of Pergamon, which was to achieve fame during the Roman period, was also founded from Epidauros. Messene, in the southern Peloponnesos, where the sanctuary of the god was built in the center of the agora, soon emerged as another independent center of the god's origin. But the Asklepios sanctuary of Kos, perhaps founded by Trikka of Thessaly, soon challenged the claims of Epidauros. Kos was the home of the great Greek physician Hippokrates and the place where the guild, or family, of the Asclepiads, the healers who were sons of Asklepios, came into being. In the Roman period, there is evidence for over 300 Asklepios sanctuaries, striking proof for the successful propaganda of Epidauros, Kos, and other leading Asklepieia. The expansion of this cult was the result of methodical propaganda aided, no doubt, by favorable circumstances rooted in the general religious mood of the time.

Many factors contributed to the popularity of Asklepios. The sanctuaries continued earlier traditions of local healing deities, to whom one brought sacrifices either regularly or on special occasions, and who were consulted by people in the event of sickness or calamity. Successful cures were recorded and, originally

Bibliography to §4.3d: Texts

Emma J. and Ludwig Edelstein, *Asclepius: A Collection and Interpretation of the Testimonies* (2 vols.; Baltimore, MD: Johns Hopkins University Press, 1945).

Rice and Stambaugh, *Sources for Greek Religion*, 69–80.

Bibliography to §4.3d: Studies

Mabel Lang, *Cure and Cult in Ancient Corinth* (Corinth Notes 1; Princeton, NJ: American School of Classical Studies in Athens, 1977).

Robert Garland, "Asklepios and His Sacred Snake," in idem, *Introducing New Gods: The Politics of Athenian Religion* (Ithaca, NY: Cornell University Press, 1992) 116–35.

Lewis R. Farnell, *Greek Hero Cults and Ideas of Immortality* (Oxford: Clarendon, 1921).

Votive Monument with a Healing Scene

On the right, a patient enters making a vow. The next scene (center right) shows the same patient dreaming that the god appears in the form of a snake healing his wounded shoulder. On the left the god appears as the physician applying medical treatment. The votive is offered by Archimos to the god Amphiaraos, a healer god who is much like Asklepios.

preserved on wooden votive tablets, later "published" in the from of inscriptions on stone or votive reliefs, set up on high columns so that they wre visible to everyone. Larger sanctuaries employed aretalogists to tell the great deeds of the god. Accounts of miracles ("arelalogies") were widely distributed and very popular. Larger sanctuaries, such as Epidauros, Kos, and Pergamon, organized extensive health-spa services that provided opportunites for both spiritual and physical healing. Despite tensions between miracle healers and physicians, the development of Asklepios sanctuaries was closely connected with the beginnings of scientific medicine. Votive reliefs display scenes of miraculous cures as well as surgical instruments. A votive relief from the Amphiaraon near Athens depicts an incubation scene with the god appearing in the form of a snake side by side with a scene of medical treatment, where the god appears as a physician.

The major Asklepieia were often situated outside of a major city and, within their sacred districts, maintained whatever facilities were required for a long stay. In addition to one or two Asklepios temples, as well as temples for Apollo, Artemis, and Asklepios' daughter Hygieia, there were baths—including hot baths in the Roman period—a library, a theater, often a gymnasium and a stadium, rooms for medical treatment, an *abaton* (the sacred room in which the god appeared to the patient in a healing dream), and a guest house (the *katagogion;* in Epidauros it had 160 rooms!). The healings ranged from dream and miracle healings to psychosomatic cures (with baths, exercises, lectures, and readings) and methodical medical treatment. Surgical instruments have been found in the excavation of several Asklepios sanctuaries, and medical schools were connected to several of these healing establishments (Kos, Pergamon). Conditions and practices would differ, and the priests would emphasize that one should rather trust the healing powers of the god than the methods of medicine. But for the thousands of people who visited these sanctuaries, the difference between scientific medicine and miraculous healings, methodical cures and instructions received in a dream or vision, was rarely obvious. They praised the god for any kind of healing and contributed to his glory with votive offerings and donations. Votive reliefs, or the gift of a small bronze snake or of a pair of ears, symbolizing the god who hears prayers, emphasize the religious aspect of the experience, even if the actual cure was accomplished by medical treatment.

The cult of Asklepios was concerned with the individual human being, in medical treatment as well as in its ritual preparation. What the god pronounced in the dream was addressed to the needs of the individual. This involved a personal relationship with the god, enhanced through daily worship that was deepened even further through a mystery initiation, although our knowledge about mysteries is limited because the use of certain chambers and underground passageways that have been discovered in some sanctuaries remains unknown. Yet, the worship of Asklepios parallels the Greek mysteries in one other respect: it demanded of those who entered the sanctuaries for the purpose of healing that they be "pure," which was understood not only as a cultic but also as a moral requirement. Cases are reported in which certain persons were rejected because their conduct of life did not meet this requirement.

Among the Greek gods, Asklepios was the most humane god. He was the

"Savior" (σωτήρ), benefactor, and friend of human beings. The humane features of the god are clearly expressed in many statues: his loving care, compassion, and knowledge of human suffering. Many stories of his healing miracles demonstrate not only his miraculous powers, but also his sympathy, forbearing, and good will, especially for the poor and socially disadvantaged. Though care is required in ascribing features of the Christian image of God to pagan deities, it is obvious that the humaneness in the divine image, which Asklepios reflects more than any other god, expresses a deep desire of the time, to which Christianity responded, and which was not without influence on the Christian image of God.

(e) The Greek Mysteries (Eleusis and Samothrake)

Beginning in the 5th century BCE, the term "mysteries" (μυστήρια, from the Greek verb μύειν = "to initiate") was used for the sacred rites in the cult of Demeter, of the Kabiroi, and of some other deities. The word ὄργια ("orgies" = ritual actions) was also used, especially in the cult of Dionysos. The more general term τελετή simply means "initiation." The Demeter and Kore cult at Eleusis was the most significant for the development of the Greek and Hellenistic concepts of "mysteries." The mystery cult of the Kabiroi, the Great Gods of Samothrake, was also famous, as were the mysteries at Phlya in Attika, of the Great Goddess of Megalopolis, of Despoina at Lykosoura in Arkadia, the mysteries at Andania in Messenia, and elsewhere. However, it is not always possible to obtain literary and/or archaeological evidence for an organized mystery cult before the Classical period of Greece. Much of the building activity at these centers dates from the Hellenistic or the Roman period. The organization or reform of several mysteries in the Hellenistic period was accomplished under the auspices of Eleusis. Even for Eleusis, there are good reasons to doubt the existence of an organized mystery cult before the 8th or 7th century BCE.

Bibliography to §4.3e: Texts
Rice and Stambaugh, *Sources for Greek Religion*, 169–216.
Meyer, *Mysteries Sourcebook*, 16–59.

Bibliography to §4.3e: Studies
Walter Burkert, *Ancient Mystery Cults* (Cambridge, MA: Harvard University Press, 1987).
George E. Mylonas, *Eleusis and the Eleusinian Mysteries* (Princeton, NJ: Princeton University Press, 1961).
G. D'Alviella, *The Mysteries of Eleusis: The Secret Rites and Rituals of the Classical Greek Mystery Tradition* (Wellingborough: Aquarian Press, 1981).
Larry J. Alderink, "The Eleusinian Mysteries in Roman Imperial Times," *ANRW* 2.18.2 (1989) 1457–98.
Kevin Clinton, "The Eleusinian Mysteries: Roman Initiates and Benefactors Second Century B.C. to A.D. 267," *ANRW* 2.18.2 (1989) 1499–1539.
Idem, Myth and Cult: *The Iconography of the Eleusinian Mysteries* (Stockholm: Svenske Institutet i Athens, 1992).
Susan G. Cole, *Theoi Megaloi: The Cult of the Great Gods at Samothrace* (EPRO 96; Leiden: Brill, 1984).
Idem, "The Mysteries of Samothrace during the Roman Period," *ANRW* 2.18.2 (1989) 1564–98.
Karl Lehmann, *Samothrace: A Guide to the Excavations and Museum* (2d ed.; Locust Valley, NY: Augustin, 1960).

Telesterion at Eleusis
Seats of the western part of the Telesterion, the large
assembly hall for the Eleusinian Mysteries; in its largest form, it measured 180 by 170 feet, and its ceiling
was supported by 42 columns.

The institution of mysteries derives from ancient social structures (clan or family) that predate the Greek polis. Worship in the Greek polis is a public affair for all citizens; mysteries are secret and bring the initiate into a special group that is not identical with a city's social and political structure and may also include women, slaves, and foreigners. The sociological component of mysteries is the secret society, whose members alone have knowledge of the rites, which cannot be communicated publicly. While worship of the gods of the city is usually connected with the benefactions of the deity for the public good (social and political order, defense of the city, protection of its laws), the meaning of mysteries lies in the interpretation of agricultural and fertility symbols, often related to sexuality, which take the initiates into a realm beyond political and social function and promise individual fulfillment that may reach even beyond the boundary of death.

Mysteries also possess sacred stories (ἱεροὶ λόγοι) that tell of the fate of the deity, often of the god's suffering and even death. This sort of story establishes a new relationship with the deity and intimacy with the fate of the gods, thus taking the initiate into personal experiences of the realm beyond the tangible reality of mortal life and its social context—but it is not clear how these stories are related to the performance of the ritual. What mysteries normally do not accomplish, however, is a creation of a new community that is committed to alternative moral, social, and political values (the only exception is perhaps the Bacchus revolution that threatened Rome at the beginning of the 2d century BCE, see §4.3f).

The goddess Demeter, though of Minoan origin, was the most Greek of all deities, deeply rooted in the religious beliefs of the people. She was known in many places of the Greek world (though less frequently in the Greek parts of Asia Minor) and worshiped in sanctuaries equipped with temples and altars. Her cult was connected with the growth of the fruit of the field; she was the "Mother of Grain," not, as is sometimes assumed, "Mother Earth." Her primary festival was the feast of sowing in the late fall, the *Thesmophoria,* to which in most cases only women were admitted. The sanctuary of Demeter at Eleusis, thirty kilometers west of Athens, demonstrates in the character of its central building that it differed fundamentally from an ordinary Greek temple. Instead of a normal Greek temple, surrounded by colonnades and with a comparatively small central cella, "the house of the god," the Demeter sanctuary in Eleusis had the dimensions of an assembly hall as early as the late archaic period (the first assembly hall was built by Peisistratos in the second half of the 6th century BCE). Later this hall, called the *Telesterion,* was expanded even further so that it could provide room for several thousand people. And here, both men and women participated in her cult.

The cult legend (*hieros logos*) of the Eleusinian Demeter is the only archaic Greek cult legend still preserved in one of the *Homeric Hymns* (7th century BCE). It contains an etiological section that mentions some of the elements of the *Thesmophoria* (fasting, drinking of barley water, the so-called *kykeon*). What follows is the specific myth of the Eleusinian mysteries: the daughter of Demeter, Kore-Persephone, had been carried off by the god of the underworld, Hades-Pluto, for his bride. Demeter searched for her daughter, but unable to find her arrived at Eleusis and withdrew in sorrow to fast. As a result, the grain would no longer grow, and all people were faced with death by starvation, until Zeus intervened and forced Hades to release Demeter's daughter. Henceforth Persephone (her married name) would spend two-thirds of the year with her mother and one-third in the underworld. Fruitfulness returns to the earth. Triptolemos, the king of Eleusis, often depicted riding on the chariot of Demeter drawn by winged snakes, brought the ear of wheat to all people.

The relationship of this legend to the actual performance of the ritual is not clear. Thousands were initiated, but the secrets of the rites are revealed only in allusions in literary texts and iconographic materials. Among the descriptions by Christian writers, the oldest, found in Clement of Alexandria (*Protrepticus* 2.29) who was probably born in Athens, must be treated with caution. Repeated accusations by the Christians that obscenities were part of the ritual are not convincing; nor is it likely that the rite of Eleusis presented a performance of a "sacred marriage" (*hieros gamos*). One must therefore be content with a few general statements about the ritual.

The initiation took place in several stages, and each stage included "demonstrations," "actions," and "words." The first stage was a sacrifice and usually took place at the Eleusinion in Athens; before the sacrifice each initiate bathed with a piglet in the sea. The second stage always took place in the month of Boedromion (in the fall) and consisted of purification, fasting, and a day-long procession from Athens to Eleusis along the Sacred Way, accompanied by ecstatic dancing and rhythmic shouts. The final stage was celebrated at night inside the Telesterion, into which each initiate was guided by a previously initiated mystagogue. Details of the various acts before entering the Telesterion and inside this great hall remain uncertain. But the high point of the ceremony was the showing of an ear of wheat by the "hierophant" (the priest who shows a holy object, the highest-ranking official). The ear of wheat may have been illuminated by torches or fire or by the rising sun shining through a hole in the roof of the building.

The roots of this mystery cult in agricultural symbolism and the connection of its actions with the myth of Demeter and Kore are evident. However, as early as the Classical period and certainly during later times, the enactment of the divine mysteries of nature, which caused the fruits of the field to grow year after year, was understood as a representation of sorrow over the loss and joy at the reunion, terror of death and hope of immortality. In the words of Sophokles: "Thrice blessed are those mortals who have seen the mysteries and go to Hades; for them alone is there life, but for all others there is evil" (*Triptolemus*, frg. 19). Cicero after his initiation told Atticus that in Eleusis we recognize "the true foundations of life" and receive the conviction "that we can live with joy . . . and die with a better hope" (*De legibus* 2.38). Although many other sanctuaries celebrated secret or public rites connected with the growth of the fruits of the field, using various cult legends of Indo-European or Mediterranean origin, Eleusis appears to have stood apart in understanding these rites as symbols of death and its conquest.

In the course of time Eleusis deeply influenced other Greek mysteries and became their epitome. Its influence remained strong during the imperial period, at which time it came to assume worldwide significance. Many Romans were initiated, among them several Roman emperors: Augustus was initiated together with the Indian Zarmaros, who later burned himself publicly in Athens; Hadrian was consecrated twice; also initiated were Antoninus Pius, Marcus Aurelius, and Commodus. Nero never went to Eleusis—he knew that as a rumored matricide he was not welcome there—and the famous Neopythagorean miracle worker Apollonios of Tyana had difficulties with Eleusis because he was a magician. Eleusis also resisted syncretistic tendencies for a long time. Iakchos-Dionysos was not received among the Eleusinian gods until the 4th century CE, near the end of the history of this celebrated mystery cult (it was destroyed in the 5th century CE), and only at that time could a Mithras priest become the hierophant.

The mystery cult of the Kabiroi was also famous. Cult centers existed in the Classical period on Lemnos and at Thebes in Boiotia, the latter beginning in the 6th century BCE and continuing into the Roman imperial period. The most popular mystery cult of the Kabiroi was that on the island of Samothrake, which had its roots in the pre-Greek period. The origin and meaning of the name "Kabiros," who also appears as the protecting hero of Thessaloniki and Philippi, is not known. A female deity, perhaps of Phrygian origin and resembling Kybele, and her two male consorts are worshiped as "the Great Gods of Samothrake." The two main buildings in the sanctuary of Samothrake are assembly halls, an Anaktoron and a Hieron, the former built in the late Classical period and rebuilt in Roman times, the latter from the Hellenistic period. Both buildings were designed to initiate large groups of people, the Hieron perhaps for the higher stage of initiation. Different from Eleusis, whose cult could not be exported, Samothrake engaged in systematic propaganda and missionary activity. Eleusis influenced other places only insofar as its priests and theologians served as advisors for the institution and reform of cults elsewhere, as the Eumolpid Timotheus assisted in the organization of the Sarapis cult in Alexandria (§4.4a). The missionary activity of the Samothrakian priests transplanted the cult of the Kabiroi to other cities, especially to Ionia and the islands of the Aegean Sea.

The so-called "Hellenistic mystery religions" will be discussed later. But it is important to note here that "mysteries" are a Greek phenomenon, and that mystery sanctuaries were widely established and distributed over Greece well before the Hellenistic period brought a new influx of Near Eastern cults. Whatever the "oriental" heritage of these new cults, their appearance as mystery religions is a Greek rather than a Near Eastern feature.

(f) Dionysos

However dignified, respected, and influential the mysteries of Demeter and Kore or of the Great Gods of Samothrake may have been, the most important

Bibliography to §4.3f: Texts
Rice and Stambaugh, *Sources for Greek Religion*, 195–209.
Meyer, *Mysteries Sourcebook*, 63–109.

Bibliography to §4.3f: Studies
Burkert, *Greek Religion*, 161–66, 290–95.
Idem, *Mystery Cults*, passim.

Greek mystery religion was always that of Dionysos. This god was not a new-comer to Greek religion, as was once believed, but a Greek deity attested already in Mycenean times and common to Athenians and Ionians even before the Ionian migrations of the 11th century BCE. His name has been interpreted as "Son of Zeus," from whose thigh he is born, but the second half of the name remains an enigma. Influences from Phrygia and Lydia (his mother becomes the Phrygian goddess of the earth, Semele), even from the Semitic world (the "thyrsos" that he carries as his scepter), may have shaped the god's image as it appears in the Classical period.

Dionysos is a god of fertility and of the fruits of the field, especially the fruit tree and the vine. He appears in various forms and shapes: a child carried in the arm of his mentor Silenus, a young man with almost female features, or a bearded old man. His festivals are also of various types. They may center around festive drinking of wine, or consist of goat or bull sacrifices and processions carrying a huge phallus, or feature groups of frenzied women running into the wooded mountains in mid-winter to eat raw flesh of wild animals. This *omophagia* was doubtless a sacramental meal in which one sought to become one with the god, who was believed to appear as a wild animal. Even a Dionysos ritual that was an orderly festival of the city of Athens culminated in the ritual of a *hieros gamos* of the god with the wife of the Royal Archon.

Dionysos' appearance, in whatever form, is always connected with intoxication and madness, and also with the gift of wine that brings joy and relief from the evils of the day. Although the iconographic depiction of the god, his arrival on a carriage drawn by panthers, his company of maenads and ithyphallic satyrs (though the god himself is never portrayed as ithyphallic), surrounded by vines and bunches of grapes, and his marriage to Ariadne, remains fixed from archaic to Roman times, Dionysos is never the same, never domesticated, but remains the revolutionary god, the deity of private associations rather than of political establishments, and the granter of individual blessings and immortality through his mysteries.

Dionysos' popularity, evident as early as the 6th century BCE, continues unabated into the Roman period. Next to Asklepios, he was the most widely worshiped god of the Greek world. Both gods were more significant than the Olympian gods for the religious life of the people in the Greek-speaking world and also among the Romans and many of their subjects. Mysteries of Dionysos are fre-

Thomas H. Carpenter and Christopher A. Faraone (eds.), *Masks of Dionysus* (Ithaca: Cornell University Press, 1993).

Martin P. Nilsson, *The Dionysiac Mysteries of the Hellenistic and Roman Age* (Lund: Gleerup, 1957; reprint New York: Arno, 1975).

Marcel Detienne, *Dionysos at Large* (Cambridge, MA: Harvard University Press, 1989).

Albert Henrichs, "Greek and Roman Glimpses of Dionysos," in Caroline Houser, ed., *Dionysos and His Circle: Ancient through Modern* (Cambridge, MA: Fogg Art Museum, Harvard University, 1979) 1–11.

Idem, "Changing Dionysiac Identities," in: Meyer and Sanders, *Self-Definition 3*, 137–60.

Susan Guettel Cole, "New Evidence for Mysteries of Dionysos," *GRBS* 21 (1980) 223–38.

Gilded Bronze Crater from Derveni (Macedonia)
This large crater from the early Hellenistic period was used as a funerary urn. It shows Dionysos and Ariadne and various scenes with Maenads and Satyrs (III BCE).

quently attested in the Hellenistic period for the cities of Asia Minor and the islands. Although men were never permitted to participate in the orgies of the Bacchante women, they ocupy the offices of priest, hierophant, and *dadouchos* (torch bearer). Priests and priestesses lead the *thiasoi* of the participants in the mysteries. In Egypt the expansion of the cult of Dionysos was supported by the religious policies of Ptolemy IV Philometor (later 3d and early 2d century BCE; see §1.5c).

In Asia Minor, where the cult has more of a public than mystery character, Dionysos was worshiped as the official god of the Attalid kingdom under the title *kathegemon* (= "founder"—a designation later understood as "founder and creator of the whole universe"). He also assumed the features of the Anatolian god Sabazios, whose cult had been introduced in Pergamon by the wife of Attalos I. On the silver coins that were minted by the kings of Pergamon (called *kistophoroi*) one can see a snake creeping out of a basket, surrounded by wreaths of ivy— a combination of the cult symbols of both gods. The popularity of Dionysos in Asia Minor also appears during the late Roman republic: Mithridates of Pontus, rising up against Rome as the liberator of the Greeks, called himself "Dionysos" (§6.1d); and Marc Antony, then the ruler of the east, was celebrated as the "New Dionysos" together with Kleopatra, the "New Isis" (§6.1e). Centuries later, the temple of Dionysos in Pergamon was rebuilt for another "New Dionysos": the Roman emperor Caracalla.

Where the cult of Dionysos was accepted by the state and publicly promoted, it was not just a mystery cult; but neither does it appear as a strictly regulated state religion. Public celebrations exhibited the typical "Dionysian" features: processions with sileni and dancers, women as bacchantes and young men as satyrs and Pans, mimes and jugglers, public performances of pantomimes, Bacchantian dances and theatrical performances. All these things were part of Dionysian festivals, which could last several days, and in which men and women, young and old, and people of all classes participated. In such contexts, at least, the associations of the Dionysiac initiates were public institutions rather than mystery clubs.

While the public cult was chiefly the form of Dionysos religion practiced in Asia Minor, the Dionysos mystery cult, pregnant with profound religious concepts, comes into view in Italy as early as the 5th century BCE. At home among the Greeks of southern Italy the religion of Dionysos was connected with Orphic concepts stressing a religious orientation towards a better afterlife. What terrified the Romans so much at the beginning of the 2d century BCE was a mystery cult of Dionysos/Bakchos of considerable missionary strength and revolutionary potential. The famous *Senatus consultum de Bacchanalibus* from the year 186 BCE gives evidence of severe measures taken by the Roman state against these widespread mysteries. The Senate correctly evaluated the revolutionary potential of this movement that threatened the existing structures of the state by the rise of "another people," who, with their leadership of women and their disregard for established class distinctions, were about to establish not just a new religion, but a new state. Punishments were quick; 6,000 are said to have been executed. For centuries this decree informed the judgment of Roman officialdom with respect to private religious associations like Christianity, which held secret meetings that were not accessible to the public.

After that traumatic event, Dionysos (Bacchic) mysteries in the Roman world stayed within the confines of individual religious gratification. The rites and religious concepts of these mysteries are not fully known. They were probably not the same everywhere and may have been influenced by other mystery cults. Although temples of Dionysos existed everywhere, usually in the neighborhood of the theaters, mysteries were celebrated in private homes. It is likely that the Villa Item in Pompeii and the House of the Masks on Delos were such house sanctuaries. The celebrations included common meals and the drinking of wine—Dionysos was, after all, the god of the vine. The myth of Dionysos' dying and revivification was widely known and may have served as the basis for the hope of immortality: note the frequency of Dionysiac motifs in funerary contexts, especially sarcophagi. This is not simply the spiritualization of an older cult of vegetation, but a representation of Orphic concepts that served to interpret myths and rites of Dionysian origin. Specifically eastern influences cannot be presupposed. Explaining the wall frescoes in the Villa Item at Pompeii is difficult: a naked boy who reads from a scroll (an Orphic text?), the *liknon* (a kind of winnowing fan with a phallus in it); a dark winged figure with a scourge striking a kneeling women with bared back (a representation of the punishment in the underworld?); the view into a mirror (recognition of the immortal self?); a dancing maenad. The rites may have included the experience of horror and pain as well as of redemption and ecstasy. There also seem to have been observances of ritual purity and rules of abstention.

The assumption that these mysteries were essentially a preoccupation of the upper classes is certainly false, at least for the Hellenistic period. The people against whom Rome intervened in the *Senatus consultum* did not belong to the upper classes. On the other hand, in the Roman period these mysteries were also popular among the affluent population; as poor people could not afford frescoes and mosaics in their houses, much less is known about them. The belief in immortality, which these mysteries mediated, was serious, and the mysteries of Dionysos were revolutionary insofar as they provided an assurance of the value of life for the individual even beyond death, reagrdless of the privileges of social status and political power. It is uncertain, however, how this movement's religious impact contributed to the renewal of spiritual life—in spite of the great popularity of Dionysos' festivals and mystery celebrations.

4. The New Religions

(a) Sarapis and Isis

The cult of the Egyptian gods became the most thoroughly Hellenized eastern religion of the Hellenistic and Roman periods. Its basis was a complex develop-

Bibliography to §4.4: Bibliography

Bruce M. Metzger, "A Classified Bibliography of the Greco-Roman Mystery Religions 1924–1973 with a supplement 1974–1977," *ANRW* 2.17.3 (1984) 1259–1423.

Bibliography to §4.4: Studies

Nilsson, *Griechische Religion*, 2. 622–67.

ment of Egyptian cults and myths, in which a number of Egyptian gods were involved: Isis, Osiris, Apis, Horus, Anubis, and Seth. Each of these divine figures had different functions in the various Egyptian cult centers. Most significant was the myth of Isis and Osiris which, in its final form, was not an Egyptian but a Hellenistic product.

Isis, the mother of Horus—the mythic representation of the living Pharaoh— was the goddess of the royal throne. Osiris, originally the god of the shepherds of

A. J. Festugière, *Études de religion grecque et hellénistique* (Paris: Vrin, 1972).

Arthur Darby Nock, *Conversion The Old and the New in Religion from Alexander the Great to Augustine of Hippo* (London: Oxford University Press, 1933; reprint: Brown Classics in Judaica; Lanham, MD, and London: University Press of America, 1988). A very readable and instructive introduction.

Richard Reitzenstein, *Hellenistic Mystery Religions: Their Basic Ideas and Significance* (Pittsburgh Theological Monograph Series 15; Pittsburgh: Pickwick, 1978). Translation of a most provocative and controversial monograph, 3d German ed., 1927.

Franz Cumont, *The Oriental Religions in Roman Paganism* (New York: Dover, 1956). English translation of a classic monograph, now outdated in many respects.

Edwin Bevan, *Later Greek Religion* (London: Dent; New York: Dutton, 1927).

Bibliography to §4.4a: Literature

J. Leclant, *Inventaire bibliographique des Isiaca* (3 vols; EPRO 18.1–3; Leiden: Brill, 1972– 1985).

Bibliography to §4.4a: Texts

Ladislau Vidman, *Sylloge inscriptionum religionis Isiacae et Serapiacae* (Berlin: De Gruyter, 1969).

Meyer, *Mysteries Sourcebook* , 157–96.

Yves Grandjean, *Une nouvelle arétalogie d'Isis à Maronée* (EPRO 49; Leiden: Brill, 1975).

Helmut Engelmann, *The Delian Aretalogy of Sarapis* (EPRO 44; Leiden Brill, 1975).

J. Gwyn Griffiths, *Apuleius of Madaurus: The Isis Book (Metamorphoses, Book XI): Introduction, Translation, and Commentary* (EPRO 39; Leiden: Brill, 1975).

John Gwyn Griffiths, *Plutarch's de Iside et Osiride* (Cardiff: University of Wales, 1970).

Bibliography to §4.4a: Studies

Ladislav Vidman, *Isis und Sarapis bei den Griechen und Römern: Epigraphische Studien zu den Trägern des ägyptischen Kultes* (Berlin: De Gruyter, 1970).

Friedrich Solmsen, *Isis among the Greeks and Romans* (Martin Classical Lectures 25; Cambridge, MA:Harvard University Press, 1979).

Wilhelm Hornbostel, *Sarapis: Studien zur Überlieferungsgeschichte, den Erscheinungsformen und Wandlungen der Gestalt eines Gottess* (EPRO 32; Leiden: Brill, 1973).

Regina Salditt-Trapmann, *Tempel der ägyptischen Götter in Griechenland und an der Westküste Kleinasiens* (EPRO 15; Leiden: Brill, 1970).

Françoise Dunand, *Le culte d'Isis dans le bassin oriental de la Méditerannée* (3 vols.; EPRO 26; Leiden: Brill, 1973).

Pierre Roussel, *Les cultes égyptiennes à Délos du IIIe au Ier siècle avant J.-C.* (Nancy: Berger-Levrault, 1916).

John E. Stambaugh, *Sarapis under the Early Ptolemies* (EPRO 25; Leiden: Brill, 1972).

Sharon K. Heyob, *The Cult of Isis among Women in the Greco-Roman World* (EPRO 51; Leiden: Brill, 1975)

Robert A. Wild, *Water in the Cultic Worship of Isis and Sarapis* (EPRO 87; Leiden: Brill, 1981).

Idem, "The Known Isis-Sarapis Sanctuaries from the Roman Period," *ANRW* 2.17.4 (1984) 1739–1851.

Bust of Sarapis

The God wears the "Kalathos" (a basket for fruits) as a symbol of fertility. The "globe" supporting the bust has been interpreted as the universe, thus signifying Sarapis's rule over the whole world. Roman copy of a Hellenistic work (ultimately, all known statues of Sarapis are copies of the famous cult statue of Sarapis in Alexandria).

the Nile's eastern delta, became the mythic embodiment of its fertile lands, which flooded every year and were thus restored to new life. His enemy was Seth, the god of the desert. At the same time, Osiris was the god of the dead, and in this function he was identified with the dead Pharaoh, representing the life of the king in the world of the dead. In this role he is closely associated with Anubis, the jackal-faced protector of the graveyard, who defends the Pharaoh's corpse, that is, Osiris, against Seth. Osiris was connected with Isis in the throne mythology: Isis was the mother of Horus, the living king, and Osiris, the dead king, was her husband and the father of Horus.

In its classical form, the myth relates a battle in which Seth kills his twin brother Osiris, cuts his corpse into pieces, and throws them into the Nile; in a later Greek version the dragon Typhon dismembers the corpse and persecutes Isis and her child. Together with Nephthys, Seth's wife, Isis mourns for Osiris; both goddesses search for him, and upon finding the pieces of his corpse they fit them together again. Isis revives his phallus, becomes pregnant and gives birth to Horus or Harpokrates (= Horus as a child), often represented sitting in her lap or being nursed by her (= *Isis lactans*), or as a boy with a cornucopia in his left arm and his right hand raised to his mouth. Anubis buries Osiris, who becomes king of the realm of the dead while Horus rules over the living.

Isis was already known to Herodotos and was first identified with Demeter. But no Greek cult of Isis is known before the Hellenistic period. She began her triumphal procession through the Hellenistic world only in the entourage of Sarapis—the syncretistic creation of Hellenism. The sacred bull Apis was worshiped in Memphis long before the Ptolemies came to Egypt. The dead bull was believed to become Osiris, while the soul of the dying Osiris, on the other hand, was united with the living Apis. From this close connection of Osiris and Apis resulted the composite name Osorapis. The first Ptolemy brought the corpse of Alexander from Memphis to his new capital Alexandria and transferred the Osorapis cult to Alexandria, making it the central cult of his realm. But now this Egyptian god received Greek features. The god's statue is said to have been made by the famous Greek sculptor Bryaxis (who had worked on the famous Mausoleum, the tomb of king Mausolos of Halikarnassos), though it may have been made earlier for a different purpose. It has features of both Zeus and Hades and has no similarity with the traditional images of Egyptian deities. The Eumolpid Timotheus, a well-known Eleusinian priest (see §4.3e) and author of numerous theological books, advised the king about how to institute the new cult and arrange its ritual. The name Osorapis was Hellenized to Sarapis. The cult and ritual followed Greek patterns, though they also contained some Egyptian elements, which may have assumed renewed significance in later centuries.

The motivations and intentions that determined the creation of this new cult have been discussed repeatedly. Was the first Ptolemy trying to create a new religion that would appeal to his Greek and Egyptian subjects alike, and thus unite the two peoples of his kingdom? That is unlikely, because there is no evidence that the first Ptolemies pursued such policies. Although the Alexandrian temple of Sarapis became the state sanctuary, the Egyptians did not accept this new god, instead continuing the traditional forms of the cult of the Apis bull.

Perhaps, Ptolemy I Soter created Sarapis with its most important sanctuary in the capital Alexandria as the god of the Greek and Macedonian populations of his entire of his realm, which at the time also included southern Syria and Palestine, Cyprus, parts of western and southern Anatolia, and several Greek islands. However, we know of no attempts by the Ptolemies to establish the Sarapis cult elsewhere as the leading religion of their empire, even though they generously supported the his cult in Alexandria itself.

The most important motivation for the cult's creation may have been that the Ptolemies needed to legitimate themselves as the heirs of the Pharaohs by adopting an Egyptian deity as their dynastic god. Establishing a connection to the cult of Osiris-Apis at the old capital of Memphis, and an official transfer of the god to the new capital Alexandria would prove this point. They could not simply accept any Egyptian god without substantial modifications, because they were, after all, too closely identified with their Greek heritage. Thus the Hellenization of an Egyptian god was the only alternative.

The lasting significance of this Greco-Egyptian cult lies outside of any political aims and belongs to the realm of religious history. It was not the figure of Sarapis (although his cult spread quickly) but the overwhelming impact of the Hellenized Isis that finally brought victory. She came with Sarapis' entourage, never as Sarapis' wife, but sometimes called his sister. If ever a deity of that time was on the way to becoming the central figure of a world religion, it was Isis— not as the goddess of the throne of Pharaoh and the wife of Osiris, but as the mistress of heaven, the mother of the All, the ruler of the underworld, who united in her person everything that was significant for the religious expectations of the time.

Egyptian elements aided Isis' development into a universal deity. As the Egyptian Hathor, Isis was the goddess of heaven in the shape of a cow (whence the image of the cow that, according to Apuleius, was carried before Isis in her procession); as the wife of the dead Osiris, Isis can be identified with Persephone, the wife of Hades, who in turn is identified with Sarapis. Many of the attributes of the goddess are Egyptian: her dress and headdress, the sistrum (a metal rattle used as a musical instrument), and her companion Anubis with his jackal's head. But her overall appearance is Greek. Greek artists created her image, which expresses beauty, dignity, harmony, and benevolence. Sometimes she also takes on the features of Aphrodite. Particularly effective was her representation as a mother goddess, affectionately holding the child Harpokrates to her breast. Mary, the mother and goddess of heaven in Christianity, with the Christ-child on her lap, is artistically speaking a copy of Isis. Features of Isis also appear in the birth story of the messiah in Revelation 12: the woman who is dressed with the sun and stands on the moon with the zodiac on her head, who is pregnant and must flee the dragon (Typhon) with her newborn child.

The most characteristic descriptions of Isis appear in the Isis aretalogies, the genuine creed of the Isis religion, that have been preserved in different versions. Here Isis presents herself with the formula "I am Isis" (ἐγώ εἰμι Ἶσις) and, in the short sentences that follow, describes her position and power, identifies herself with other deities, and claims their accomplishments for herself. The aretalogies show the influence of cosmological and astrological concepts as well as a strong tendency toward universality and monotheism. The following excerpts from an inscription at Kyme give a sense of the typical claims made:

I am Isis, the mistress of every land . . .
I gave and ordained laws for human beings, that no one can change.
I am eldest daughter of Kronos.
I am wife and sister of Osiris.
I am she who finds fruit for human beings . . .
I am she that is called goddess by women . . .
I divided the earth from the heaven.
I showed the paths of the stars . . .
I devised business in the sea.
I made strong the right . . .
I revealed my mysteries to human beings . . .
I made an end to murders . . .
I overcome Fate.
Fate harkens to me.
Hail, O Egypt, that nourished me!
(Trans. F. C. Grant, *Hellenistic Religion*, 131–33, adapted).

Names of other deities are sometimes adopted and their works become the works of the one and only god Isis, ruler of the universe. She has promulgated the laws of all people, given them speech and taught the art of writing, and instructed them in the cultivation of the land. She protects marriage, gives safety to the sailors on the high seas, sets the laws for the proper circuit of the stars and, as the sun, she illumines the whole world. She even has power over fate.

In the processions and public services of the cult of Isis, Egyptian rites and cultic vessels predominate, though there is no uniformity from one place to another. Initiation into the Isis mysteries, though also incorporating Egyptian elements, continues the tradition of Greek mystery cults, especially Eleusis, and is not a typically "oriental" phenomenon. The 2d-century CE African writer Apuleius (*Metamorphoses* 11) gives a number of details, but does not tell us what actually happened in the sanctuary during the initiation itself. Apuleius writes about the preparations, instruction given in a dream about the date of the initiation, the purchase of the vessels and garments that were required—the initiation was by no means inexpensive!—and about a period of fasting and a bath for purification. The initiation itself is described only by allusions: the initiate came to the limits of death and to the threshold of Proserpina, he was led through all the elements, saw the sun shine in the middle of the night, and beheld the gods above and below and worshiped them. On the morning after the initiation he was presented to the people dressed with twelve stoles symbolizing the zodiac, a precious garment of the highest god; a crown of palm leaves arranged so as to indicate the rays of the sun. Having overcome all the powers, the initiate has attained identity with the highest heavenly deity; being no longer part of the transitory earthly domain, he is now one with the eternal world of pure spirit and appears as the sun, surrounded by his rays.

It is, of course, not of great consequence to find out what was actually seen in the adyton of the temple. Preparatory fasting and the skill of the priests, who were quite capable of manipulating images, symbols, torches, and lamps, could easily produce the desired effects. Important is the interpretation: the rite obviously symbolized the experience of death and rebirth, but not in the form of participation in the fate of the deity: the myth of Isis and Osiris does not suit such an understanding. To be sure, Osiris died and became lord of the realm of the dead, and Osiris himself can be called "initiate" (μύστης), but it is never said that he rose from the dead. Moreover, Osiris does not play a role in the initiation described by Apuleius; the text speaks about Proserpina (i.e., Isis) as the mistress of Hades.

What are the benefits for the one who came to her threshold on a journey that symbolizes not just death, but the heavenly journey of the soul (*Himmelsreise der Seele*)? The one who has thus undergone, as it were, "voluntary death" (*Metam.* 11.21) and was reborn is set on a new course of life and salvation ("quodam modo renatos ad novae reponere rursus salutis curricula"). This implies neither immortality nor resurrection from the dead, but a dying to one's former life and the possibility of a new life in the service of the goddess, in which the initiate is conscious of being united with the deity who rules the universe. This is expressed by the heavenly garments and the crown of the sun, which the initiate wears, and which sets him apart from the uninitiated. The symbolic experience of death first of all signifies a new life on earth that is radically different from the past. But the devotee of Isis receives her divine assurance: "Once you have measured out the span of your earthly life and descend to those who are in the realm below, . . . and living in the Elysian fields you will worship me as your gracious protector" (*Metam.* 11.6). Since Isis rules over everything, including Hades, those who have been initiated into her mysteries are protected even after death. The new life on earth has its counterpart in a life after death.

Parallels with Christian statements abound in these allusions to initiation into a mystery religion. The Christian understanding of baptism, as it appears in Romans 6, is informed by the same Hellenistic language and concepts of initiation: Paul also admonishes that those who have died (symbolically in baptism) should now walk in a new life. But since that new earthly human life has a natural limit, also Paul, like Apuleius, refers to the expectation that Christ will raise from the dead all those who have believed in him.

On the other hand, both the theological and the sociological differences are evident. For the Christian initiate, death and resurrection were the fate of Christ; thus they have died "with him" and they will be raised as Christ has been raised from the dead. The Christians indeed shared a fate that their god had suffered. Moreover, Christian baptism is a very cheap and simple rite, lacking the mysterious manipulations of the Greek mysteries and especially of Isis initiations. Furthermore, it incorporates the baptized into a new community, which knows no social, ethnic, and gender distinctions, and which obligates those who have been baptized to devote their lives to the well-being of that community. In contrast, initiation into the mysteries of Isis—and this also true of other mysteries—was reserved for a few privileged persons, namely, those who were able to pay the high expenses associated with the initiation. In the case of Apuleius' hero, even more initiations were required to validate the original and obtain higher stages of the mysteries, which were restricted to an even narrower circle of the truly elect. Christianity, while fully accepting the religious concepts of the mysteries, democratized the initiation and liberated it from its financial requirement. Paul's fight against several opposing groups indicates that the formation of an elitist consciousness was a danger that also faced the young Christian communities. The success of Christianity as a religion for all people would depend on the result of this fight.

Sanctuaries of the Egyptian religion from the Hellenistic and Roman periods have been found in many cities. The great variety of the excavated structures is striking. Some are small meeting houses, while others are among the largest temples ever built in the ancient world. The meeting house on Delos that is known as "Sarapeion A," dating from the Hellenistic period, devotes most of its space to activities of the members, while the "house of the god" is a small structure inside the atrium of the building. Similarly, the Isis temple from the Roman period found in Thessaloniki is an assembly hall: a small apsidal niche at its far end served as the place for the statue of the goddess. "Sarapeion C" on Delos is a large sanctuary that includes several relatively small temples, perhaps one each for Sarapis, Isis, and Harpokrates, which are grouped around a larger courtyard that is reached through a long "dromos," flanked by porches and rows of sphinxes; here too, meeting space for the worshipers is the primary architectural feature. There is no similarity to the typical Greek temple, in which the central structure of the architectural unit, the "cella," is strictly the house of the deity.

This departure from the Greek and Roman architectural norm can also be observed in the larger Sarapis/Isis sanctuaries from the Roman period. The Sarapeion of Miletos is a basilica with two interior rows of columns, resembling a Christian church more than a pagan temple. A unique structure is the so-called "Red Hall" of Pergamum, an Egyptian sanctuary built in the first half of the 2d century CE. This "temple," a huge brick structure measuring 60 by 27 meters and over 20 meters in height, was divided into an interior eastern part for the temple statue and a somewhat larger western part, accessible to the worshipers, with enough room for several hundred people. Moreover, this was only the central building of a much larger temenos, 270 meters long and 100 meters wide, equipped with a central dromos, numerous stoas, water basins, and two smaller round temples flanking the Red Hall.

While these buildings were designed to provide room for large crowds of worshipers, one may ask also whether spaces were provided in which the secret initiations for elect individuals could be held. There indeed are underground passageways in the Sarapeion of Pergamum, leading to a space under the temple statue and to other basement rooms. In the Sarapeion of Ephesos, also a very large building from the same period, the temple is equipped with an inner and an outer wall, thus creating two passageways, each with six niches. However, not all the sanctuaries of the Egyptian cult seem to have been equipped with such special structures. Rather, the most striking architectural feature is the provision of a space for a congregation to participate in the services of the cult. In this respect, the worship of Isis and Sarapis, at least in the Roman period, may have had some similarity with the service of a Jewish synagogue or a Christian church.

(b) The Magna Mater and Attis.

Kybele, the Great Mother (*Magna Mater*), mother of life for all living things, humans and animals alike, was worshiped by the Greeks as early as the archaic period. She is ultimately Kubaba, the Hittite fertility goddess from eastern Anatolia, who was adopted by the Lydians as the sister of Artemis and by the Greeks of Anatolia as the Kybele-Tyche of Smyrna, the Artemis of Perge in Pamphylia, and the Great Artemis (Diana) of the Ephesians, whose cult image is fully adorned with fertility symbols and bears no resemblance to the traditional Greek Artemis or Latin Diana (who hunts the stag with bow and arrow).

Wherever the Great Mother was accepted at an early time, her cult was domesticated and deprived of its original ecstatic features. Called simply *Meter* (μήτηρ) by the Greeks, she was sometimes identified with Rhea, the mother of Zeus, Hera, and Poseidon. In Athens, the temple of Meter served as the state archives. In Olympia, her temple from the Classical period faced the venerable temple of Hera and her cult may have been related to Hera, called the mother of the gods. (This Meter temple was later used as a temple for the imperial cult). The castration rite had disappeared—Attis, the lover of Kybele (also called Agdistis in her myth), who castrates himself in his sorrow about his infidelity, does not appear in Classical Greece. Instead of Attis, the Greeks worshiped Adonis (the lover of Aphrodite who is here identical with the Syrian Ishtar), whose cult was widespread as a symbol of the quickly passing spring time; but among the Greeks, Adonis usually had no temples but was worshiped in private rituals.

The early Hellenistic period witnessed a renewed expansion of the cult of the Mother in Greece and, indeed, very soon also in Rome. But this time she was clearly Kybele, the Phrygian Great Mother from Pessinus, the goddess flanked by two lions, who brought with her the wild and orgiastic features of her cult andalso the myth of her unfortunate lover Attis. In the east there were powerful

---

Bibliography to §4.4b: Texts

Maarten J. Vermaseren, ed., *Corpus cultus Cybelae Attidisque* (7 vols.; EPRO 50.1-7; Leiden: Brill, 1977–1989).

Meyer, *Mysteries Sourcebook*, 113–54.

Bibliography to §4.4b: Studies

Maarten J. Vermaseren, *The Legend of Attis in Greek and Roman Art* (EPRO 9; Leiden: Brill, 1966).

Idem, *Cybele and Attis: The Myth and the Cult* (London and New York: Thames & Hudson, 1977).

Hugo Hepding, *Attis, seine Mythen und sein Kult* (RVV 1; Giessen: Töpelmann, 1903; reprint Berlin: Töpelmann, 1967).

Garth Thomas "Magna Mater and Attis," *ANRW* 2.17.3 (1984) 1500–35.

G. Sfameni Gasparro, *Soteriology and Mystic Aspects in the Cult of Cybele and Attis* (EPRO 103; Leiden: Brill, 1985).

Robert Duthoy, *The Taurobolium: Its Evolution and Terminology* (EPRO 10; Leiden: Brill, 1969).

competitors: Atargatis/Ishtar in Syria, Isis in Egypt. Greece proved unreceptive to the cult, but the west accepted her quickly. The Great Mother was officially recognized in Rome as early as 204 BCE—the first, and for a long time the only Near Eastern cult to find such recognition. Restrictions for participating in the cult of Kybele were finally removed under the emperor Claudius, and the spring festival of the Great Mother became one of the most popular celebrations in Rome. This is the public side of the cult, which is well known.

The great spring festival lasted two weeks, March 15 to 27. On the first day, reeds were carried to the sanctuary of the goddess; the significance of this rite is not clear. On March 22, a pine tree was cut, carried to the sanctuary, erected there and decorated: the symbol of Attis, revealing an ancient tree cult. The following days were reserved for fasting to express sorrow for the death of Attis. March 24 was the *dies sanguinis:* the *galli,* a lower class of priests, cut their skins in a frenzied ecstatic dance and sprinkled the blood on the image of the goddess while the novices castrated themselves in ecstasy. A quiet day, called *hilaria,* followed. On March 27, the statue of the deity was brought to the river and washed. Nothing is known about an actual initiation rite of the *galli* after their castration. It is doubtful, however, that this act was the normal way for devotees to be initiated into the mysteries of Kybele. Priests of the higher class were not castrated, and it is quite probable that only the initiation of the novices in the order of the *galli* took place during the spring festival, whereas other rites of initiation were celebrated at other times.

There has been much speculation about the interpretation of the ritual in the mysteries of Attis and Kybele. Interpretation is mostly allegorical, and allegory would be subject to change anyway. Thus the castration could be understood as the cutting of the ears of the grain, while the bathing of the cult image of the goddess, identified with earth and with Demeter, in the river could mean that the earth must be irrigated in order to bear fruit. It is unlikely that the rites were also related to ideas of death and resurrection: Attis is never said to have risen from the dead, nor is there any indication of a holy marriage (ἱερὸς γάμος). The repulsive rite of self-castration may not even have been a part of a mystery initiation at all, but a sacrifice in which the testicles were offered to the goddess; there are reports that the testicles were cleaned and anointed and deposited in the temple. If this is the case, the actual mystery initiation of the crowd of worshipers into the cult must have had a different character.

The taurobolium, a peculiar rite of the mysteries of Kybele, would also not qualify as the normal initiation rite. Originally a bullfight, it was practiced as part of the ritual of the Great Mother and Attis during the Roman period. The evidence is late (2d and 3d century CE). Taurobolia offered on behalf of the emperor or of a special private citizen are not initiations but sacrifices that are meant to assure the benefactions of Attis for the emperor and the community. The high priest would climb into a pit, over which a bull was slaughtered; when he reemerged, the participants worshiped him as one who has died and risen again. The testicles of the bull were consecrated with certain ceremonies and offered to the goddess, perhaps as a vicarious offering for those who did not want to castrate themselves. Evidence that the taurobolium was also celebrated as a personal mystery initiation comes from the 4th century CE. The initiate, after strict fasting, went into the pit with fear and trembling as if going to his death; the blood that was poured over him accomplished expiation and granted rebirth and a new life, normally only for the period of twenty years (in one case it is said "in all eternity"); after this period the rite had to be repeated. This late understanding of the taurobolium might have developed with Christian influence.

The peculiar features of the rituals of the Great Mother and Attis gave rise to theological and mystical interpretations in which Attis played a more significant role than the Great Mother. Together with the god Men, who was also worshiped in Asia Minor, Attis became a god of heaven, and his castration was understood as an act of creation. Christian Gnostics claimed the Attis myth and used it for their own syncretistic theology and probably also in their ritual. In Hippolytos' report about the Gnostic Naassenes, a portion of their hymn to Attis is quoted:

> Be it the race of Kronos, or the blessed child of Zeus or great Rhea
>   [= Kybele];
> Hail to thee, Attis, sad message of Rhea;
> Assyrians call thee thrice-desired Adonis, all Egypt, Osiris . . .
> I will sing of Attis, the son of Rhea, . . .
> All hail! All hail!—as Pan, as Bakchos,
> As shepherd of the shining stars.

However, such Gnostic concepts may not be characteristic for the great popularity of the cult of Kybele and Attis. Rather, one must consider the impression that the orgiastic rites, festivals, and cultic celebrations made on the minds and feelings of many people. The religious fervor of the cult of the *Magna Mater* was radical and extreme. The festivals were colorful, filled with wild music from percussion instruments and raptured dance. The rites were primitive, cruel, and fascinating, although in bad taste by Greek standards. The moral demands of the religion of the Great Mother were severe and rigorous. Consciousness of sin and guilt played a significant role in addressing a depth of religious experience and psychological emotion, which the speculative theories of the religiously interested philosophers never touched.

(c) Sabazios, Men, and Others.

Sabazios is a Phrygian (and Thracian) god of vegetation. His cult spread into Lydia and Bithynia and further into Thrace and Macedonia, so that he was known to the Greeks as early as the 5th century BCE. Sabazios shows certain

Bibliography to §4.4c: Texts

P.-L. van Berg, ed., *Corpus cultus Deae Syriae* (2 vols.; EPRO 28.1–2; Leiden: Brill, 1972).

Harold W. Attridge and Robert A. Oden, eds., *The Syrian Goddess (De Dea Syria) Attributed to Lucian* (SBLTT 9, Greco-Roman Series 1; Missoula, MT: Scholars Press, 1976).

Maarten J. Vermaseren and E. N. Lane, eds., *Corpus Cultus Iovis Sabazii* (3 vols; EPRO 100.1–3; Leiden: Brill, 1983–1989).

E. N. Lane, ed., *Corpus monumentorum religionis dei Menis* (4 vols.; EPRO 19.1–4; Leiden: Brill, 1971–1978)

affinities with Dionysos, and the identification of both gods, which is occasionally found, may have ancient roots. The popularity of this god is evident in the many Sabazios hands that have been found, that is, raised hands in the form of the *benedictio Latina,* decorated with pine cones, snakes, and other symbols. Like the cult of Dionysos, the worship of Sabazios included features of mystery cults. There were apparently cultic meals which—judging from the paintings of the Vincentius tomb in Rome—symbolized the initiate's acquittal before the judge of the dead and reception into the everlasting meal of the blessed.

Syncretistic features are strong. In addition to the identification of Sabazios with Dionysos in Asia Minor, one finds occasional connections with the Great Mother, and later with Mithras, but especially frequently with Zeus and with *Hypsistos* ("The Highest God"). An identification with Yahweh, the God of Israel, is strange and not yet explained. In 139 BCE Jews were expelled from Rome, "who had tried to corrupt the Roman customs with the cult of Sabazios Jupiter" ("Ioudaeos qui Sabizi Iovis cultu Romanos inficere mores conati erant," Valerius Maximus 1.3.2). Several documents from the interior of Asia Minor speak of a monotheistic mystery cult of "God the Highest" (*Theos Hypsistos*), and it is said that the members observed the Sabbath and certain dietary laws. There are also inscriptions of cult associations called the "Sabbathists" with reliefs of banquet scenes.

It is not clear who these "Sabbathists" or "Hypsistarians" were, nor how they relate to Sabazios on the one hand or to Judaism on the other. Possibly some Jews of Asia Minor who were Hellenized to a large degree had, in organizing their congregations and in understanding their religious services as mysteries, accepted religious forms and designations that were assimilated to their pagan neighbors. Jewish features are clearly present in the evidence referred to above: the designation of God as "The Highest" appears in the Septuagint and frequently in the Hellenistic literature of Judaism (Philo and Josephus); the Sabbath celebration—a festival meal with wine—is characteristically Jewish; the *angelus bonus* on the tomb of Vincentius in Rome is certainly of Jewish origin. But it is difficult to decide whether the Sabazios/Hypsistos Sabbathists were a Jewish-syncretistic mystery cult, or a pagan religion that had borrowed from Judaism, or whether we are confronted with a simple confusion of names (Sabazios-Sabbath-Sabaoth). This latter alternative, however, is unlikely in view of the explicit mention of Jews in the report about the expulsion of Sabazios worshipers from Rome. There must have been a syncretistic group of some kind, at home in Asia Minor, with evident affinities to Judaism. Later Christian controversies with

Bibliography to §4.4c: Studies

Sherman E. Johnson, "The Present State of Sabazios Research," *ANRW* 2.17.3 (1984) 1583-1613.

Robert A. Oden, *Studies in Lucian's De Dea Syria* (HSM 15; Missoula, MT: Scholars Press, 1977).

Monika Hörig, "Dea Syria–Atargatis," *ANRW* 2.17.3 (1984) 1536–81.

Paul John Morin, "The Cult of the Dea Syria in the Greek World" (Ph.D. diss., Ohio State University, 1960).

Hand of Sabazios

Numerous hands of the god Sabazios, made of bronze or terra cotta, have been found. Decorated with snake, frog, lizard, and pine cone, they were believed to possess magical powers.

heretical groups demonstrate that Christian congregations were also influenced by the same Jewish mystery cults (see §12.2a on the Epistle to the Colossians). Among other Phrygian deities that spread in the Hellenistic period a prominent god was Men, frequently called Men Tyrannos. His cult spread over much of Asia Minor. Men was introduced to Greece in the 5th century BCE as the god of the slaves who worked the Athenian silver mines in Laurion in Attika. Men is the god of the moon, presented in Phrygian dress with the crescent moon. His name often appears with epithets that defy explanation, but he is also identified with Sabazios, later appears in Italy in the entourage of Attis and, together with Attis, was worshiped as a universal god of heaven.

The *Dea Syria,* Atargatis, was worshiped, together with the Semitic weather god Baal-Hadad, in Syrian cities like Edessa, Nisibis, Baalbek, Palmyra, Damascus, and Samosata, also in Philistine Ashkelon. Her features are related to those of the Phoenician Astarte, and as she became known in the Greek-speaking world she was identified with Kybele, the *Magna Mater.* Lucian (see §6.4g), who came from Samosata in Assyria, identified Atargatis and Hadad with Hera and Zeus. On the island of Delos, a large temple precinct of the Syrian goddess from the Hellenistic period, with a theater and special cultic and dining rooms, has been excavated. Roman legionaries brought this goddess of the sea, the earth, and the heavens to Italian ports and even to the northern regions of the Roman provinces.

(d) The Problem of the Mystery Religions

The question of the so-called "Hellenistic mystery religions" has been much debated in scholarship. In the first decades of this century, Franz Cumont and Richard Reitzenstein proposed the thesis of an oriental origin of the Hellenistic mystery religions, namely, the cults of Dionysos, Isis and Osiris, Kybele/the Great Mother, and Mithras. This proved to be a productive point of departure, resulting in a systematic publication of the available sources for these mysteries, especially in the series *Études préliminaires aux religions orientales dans l'empire romain*, edited by Maarten J. Vermaseren, and in a view that saw Christianity as only one of the many new emerging mystery religions of the Hellenistic and Roman periods.

Criticism of this hypothesis sometimes tried to defend the uniqueness of Christianity and distinguish its essential features from the general religious milieu of the time. Such apologetic concerns can be set aside here. More important are

Bibliography to §4.4d: Texts
Meyer, *Mysteries Sourcebook*, 225–53.

Bibliography to §4.4d: Bibliography
Bruce M. Metzger, "A Classified Bibliography of the Greco-Roman Mystery Religions 1924-1977," *ANRW* 2.17.3 (1984) 1259–1423.

Bibliography to §4.4d: Studies
Arthur D. Nock, "Hellenistic Mysteries and Christian Sacraments," in idem, *Essays,* 2. 791–820.

critical reflections that have questioned the concept of "Hellenistic mystery religions" and the hypothesis of their Near Eastern origins.

(1) "Mysteries" existed, of course, but in most instances, it would be inappropriate to call any of them a "religion" in the sense of a movement that required an exclusive commitment to a particular group and its rituals.

(2) Both the rites and the religious concepts of the mysteries are so diverse that it is impossible to reconstruct a theological orientation that all of them shared. Concepts common to all mysteries belong to the general religious and philosophical language of Hellenism; in other words, they are not limited to the mysteries.

(3) The thesis of an oriental, and specifically Iranian, origin of the mysteries is problematic. There are not sufficient Iranian sources from the Hellenistic and Roman periods available to support this hypothesis, nor does any mystery group claim such a derivation until the mysteries of Mithras emerge in the first century BCE. It will be shown below (§6.5c) that even this claim has no substance.

(4) The oldest mysteries known to us are not Near Eastern but Greek. Possible non-Greek origins are shrouded in the pre-Classical period. The mysteries of Dionysos may have some Thracian or Phrygian ancestry, but this god's name is attested in Greece as early as the Mycenean period. Demeter's connection with the lower world (her daughter, Kore, was the goddess of Hades as Persephone) may not be typically Greek, but her mystery cult in Eleusis was a Greek cult as early as the 8th century BCE. The Samothrakian gods, most likely of Thracian origin, had become Hellenized before the Classical period. And although the *Magna Mater* was introduced in Rome as an eastern mystery cult, her veneration had been known among the Greeks of Asia Minor as early as the late Bronze Age and was well established in Greece itself in the 6th century BCE.

As far as the Hellenistic and Roman periods are concerned, one must start with the observation that Greek practices, rituals, concepts, and stories are at the root of any Hellenistic cult or religion offering initiation rites that were not generally open to everyone. Such special rites differ from those required from every member of a political or social community, like the rites of passage in many other cultures. Rather, in addition to regular public worship and sacrifices, mysteries are offered to individuals who desire to participate for their own personal benefit. This interest in personal spiritual gain and edification became a characteristic phenomenon of the Hellenistic and especially the Roman imperial periods. The mystery sanctuary of Eleusis was originally regulated by a political power, namely the city-state of Athens, and it was indeed a civic institution. Every Athenian, provided the necessary cultic qualifications were satisfied, was invited to be initiated. But increasingly, Eleusis also attracted outsiders who sought in these rites spiritual gain for their own life and help for their anxieties about the afterlife. Several other cults of the old gods began to institute "mysteries" in order to compete in this market. Religious associations were founded, either in the context of existing cults or independently, with their organized *thiasoi*, presidents and priests, fixed dates and regular meetings.

Certainly, in most instances, religious associations were not "mystery" cults. Even if they were organized as private associations for the worship of a particular god, their purpose was usually to provide funds and management for public

The New Religions

festivals and processions, and to control the banquets held for the eating of sacrificial meals. Mysteries were even attached to the emperor cult, occasionally also to oracles. The term "mystery" may occur in the designation of these rituals. But the term itself is not necessarily a useful guide in order to determine which cult or association indeed possesses the essential features of a mystery religion.

The new religions, like the cult of Isis and Sarapis, quickly followed suit. In analogy to such existing Greek cults as Eleusis and Samothrake, they strove to give their own ceremonies a deeper meaning and a mysterious aura that would appeal to the increasing interest in personal edification and religious experience. It is not accidental that the cult of Sarapis was organized by Ptolemy I with the advice of a priest from Eleusis. Incorporation of "mysteries" could also mean that these new religions could claim equality with a standard of religious experience that had, in their perception, always existed in Greece, and which had become widespread and popular in the more recent past. Such mystery religions are, therefore, actually Hellenized Near Eastern cults. If they understood their own special secret rites, which may have been developed on the basis of Egyptian or other eastern inherited rituals, as "mysteries," this is part of their Hellenization, an *interpretatio Graeca* of their non-Greek heritage.

However, one of the characteristic marks of the genuine Greek mysteries can not be applied to these new mystery religions. The mysteries of Eleusis could never be transferred to another locality. But the new religions were all on the move, as it were. This seemed to apply already in the case of the Samothrakian mysteries of the Kabiroi, which founded new establishments on the Aegean islands and in western Asia Minor, and in the case of the cult of Dionysos, whose religious propaganda in Magna Graecia (southern Italy) is evident. Neither were the new mystery religions confined to an immovable foundation in one particular locality. This suggests further differences that characterized the mystery religions of the Hellenistic period. They may be summarized as follows, although not all these features are always present in each individual instance: (1) a firm organization with elected officials and fixed rules to which all members are subject; (2) membership obtained through rites of initiation; (3) participation in regular meetings, in which sacramental ceremonies (such as common meals) are celebrated according to set patterns; (4) the obligation to observe certain moral, sometimes also ascetic precepts (the latter are usually part of the preparation for an initiation); (5) commitment to mutual support of all members; (6) obedience to the leader of the cult or the community; (7) cultivation of traditions that were subject to arcane discipline.

We are thus dealing with a group of mostly new religious movements of non-Greek origin, that borrowed from the venerable Greek mysteries language and concepts for the interpretation of their inherited rituals. However, in their self-definition and their community organization, they do not resemble the older Greek mysteries. Insofar as they feature secret rites, to which not everyone was admitted, the term "mystery" religions is justified. However, it seems unwise to tie the term "mystery religions" theologically to the concept of "mystery." In that case it would be necessary to demonstrate not only that mystery rites of a similar character were present, but also that there were certain theological interpretations that understood such rites as providing salvation or the appropriation of immortality for the individual member. Such language and ideas are found widely in Hellenistic and Roman times, not only in circles that were directly connected with a mystery cult, and are general phenomena of the Hellenistic history of religions in general, which came to its flowering in the Roman imperial period. Judaism and Christianity shared fully in this language, but again that says nothing about their specific character as mystery religions. Rather, it demonstrates that the so-called mystery religions as well as Judaism and Christianity are typical Hellenistic religions that can not be imagined without these ideas of salvation and immortality. It must also be noted that these ideas are not typically "oriental"; they are part of the theology and world view of Hellenism, to which of course the Near East made a contribution. Eastern, that is non-Greek, features, however, are more frequently present in rites, cult myths, traditions, and names, that is, in the particular features that characterize each of these religions individually.

Information about specific religious rites and myths is usually limited. The reasons are manifold. Secret disciplines were often observed, and even if the story or myth of the group is generally known, the details of the ritual are not revealed. Written reports about these myths normally come from outsiders, while the community itself transmitted these stories in oral form. The social niveau was predominantly that of the middle class, including some members of the lower classes but rarely noble and wealthy people (see 1 Cor 1:26); therefore votive offerings and inscriptions were rare, if they were not ruled out on religious grounds. Meetings took place in private houses. Lack of information, therefore, does not prove that such religions were not widely disseminated. On the contrary, there is good reason to believe that such mystery religions were well established in many places, especially in Asia Minor and Italy.

Using the criteria enumerated above, it is still not easy to assign any of the known religions and cults to the category "mystery religions." We are dealing with a long period of time, in which various changes and developments occurred in all of these religions. Certain basic rites may have been relatively stable; but the interpretation of cult symbols and traditions was not dogmatically fixed. Differences within each of these religions, which usually lacked a central organization, were also due to differing regional conditions. All of this can be observed very well in the case of the history of early Christianity: while a common meal in remembrance of the founder was apparently generally observed, there were various forms of the words of institution for the Lord's Supper, which only a long development shaped into a single formula used everywhere; some congregations observed dietary laws, and others did not; some churches had apostles and prophets as their leaders, others a board of presbyters or a bishop or both; there was certainly no uniform interpretation of traditions and rites. Whereas some Christians celebrated the eucharist as a mystery that guaranteed immortality for each participant, others understood the common meal as a messianic banquet in expectation of the coming of the savior. One must take account of such differences to understand the Hellenistic mystery religions as a history-of-religions phenomenon.

Frustrating the effort to describe these religions or any one of them as a uniform phenomenon is the fact that a worldwide organization for any of these religions was an exception rather than the rule. Sometimes older cult centers may have exerted a certain influence, as, for example, Pessinus in Phrygia for the cult of the Great Mother, and Jerusalem for the Jews and initially also for the Christians. But such centers could have only symbolic significance in the long run. When Jerusalem was destroyed, most Christian congregations had long since become independent of Jerusalem in their organization. The development of Judaism and of Christianity in the Roman imperial period demonstrates how worldwide organizations were eventually created—processes that took several hundred years, accompanied by the exclusion of "heretical" groups that an outsider might not always be able to distinguish from "orthodox" congregations.

In view of these caveats, and using the criteria established above, it is possible to count the following among these mystery religions: the worship of Dionysos, of Men Tyrannos, Sabazios, Hypsistos, and Mithras, to a certain degree also the cults of the Great Mother, of the Egyptian gods, and of the Syrian Goddess. Of course, Christianity with its many groups and sects, some parts of diaspora Judaism, and even Rabbinic Judaism must be mentioned here. As Judaism was reconstituted at Yavneh after the destruction of Jerusalem and its temple, it was characterized by the cultivation of an oral tradition, the exact determination of moral and ritual rules, an obligation for mutual support, and a sharp delineation over against outsiders. Though these features are found in other mystery religions, it must be noted that secret rites are absent, though initiation rites are emphasized (circumcision, proselyte baptism), through which one pledged loyalty to the community.

Ritual actions through which individuals were accepted as members and which may have provided the central focus for the religious experience of the community, were widespread. While they do not appear in the context of the established worship of the old city gods, they are found in both Greek and eastern religions and eventually also infiltrated the cult of the old gods and even the emperor cult. Common and solemn meals were also practiced in semireligious associations and in philosophical communities and, of course, in Judaism and Christianity as well. The symbolic content and theological significance varied widely in these communities, but all interpretations had a number of Hellenistic concepts in common. Cosmology and belief in fate, ideas of the soul's immortality, demonology and concepts of power were the same everywhere, in popular philosophy as well as in the mystery religions, in magic as well as among those people who still worshiped the old gods. Jews and Christians were no exception. The language in which one spoke of these things was the general religio-philosophical language of Hellenism, not the special language of the mystery religions; the latter was confined to the specific terminology of ritual and liturgy and was different in each case. It was the general religious language of the time that was given to religious mystification of philosophical and scientific insights and had an almost eccentric interest in the profound and enigmatic. Once a religion like Christianity employed this sort of language, it immediately came under suspicion of being a mystery religion. Indeed, the Christians called their central cultic rite, the Lord's Supper, a *mysterion* (μυστήριον, Latin: *sacramentum*), and sometimes used the same word to designate their message.

One might ask whether the mystery religions were distinguished from other religions and philosophical circles by an appeal to the religious expectations of a particular class of the population. Since not enough is known enough about the social stratification of the members of the different religious groups, one must be satisfied with the general insight that the religious disposition of the fluctuating populations of the big cities differed considerably from those of the small towns and villages. Belief in mysteries and hope of immortality, occultism, and magic were certainly at home in all social classes of the urban populations. There were exceptions like the incorrigible mocker Lucian, people who thought that they were thorough skeptics; but otherwise, educated and literate people were just as susceptible as the middle class and the slaves. Well-educated people used magic; Cicero, who declared himself a philosophical skeptic, found courage to live and hope for (life after) death in Eleusis; and later the highly sophisticated Neoplatonic philosophers would practice theurgy with great seriousness. Writers who were committed to a mystery religion could be snobbish with respect to uneducated people who would be no match for them in their insight into secret subjects. But this does not imply that mysteries were only for the educated upper classes. The ideas and hopes propagated by the mystery religions were fundamentally unrelated to class distinctions, even if a particular religious community might appeal more specifically to one social group.

The prestige of a cult, its type of organization, and the financial requirements for initiation were more important factors than the religious message. Eleusis was ancient and famous—the right place for initiation of an emperor or senator. The Isis mysteries, as one learns from Apuleius, were expensive. The Mithras cult, with its strict military organization in the steps of initiation, was most popular among soldiers. The Christian initiation rite, baptism, was cheap and simple; but to claim that Christianity was therefore the religion of the poor and underprivileged can be easily refuted. The collection that Paul brought to Jerusalem (e.g., 1 Cor 16:1–4) was a substantial sum of money, not just a bagful of bronze coins.

As for the means of propaganda, there were differences, but they were not significant. The practices of the wandering philosophers and missionaries were the same everywhere, and the demonstration of divine power was widespread. One's choice of instruments of propaganda was a question of individual integrity and had little relation to the philosophical and religious content of the message. The philosopher Dio Chrysostom was as much aware of the danger of falsifying his message through sordid means as was the Christian apostle Paul. Of course, the intent of the propaganda would vary. One could either try to win some individuals for a strictly limited circle of initiates or one could invite the masses for an all-inclusive community. The Mithras cult appeared to address everybody, but it had a strictly structured hierarchy of adherents who, to a greater or lesser degree, were counted among the elect. The initiation into the mystery of Isis reported by Apuleius presupposed that only chosen (and wealthy) individuals could be initiated; but from Asia Minor we know Sarapis temples from the same period that offered room for large numbers of participants in religious services. In Christianity, the conflict between the Gnostic concept of the elect few and Christian universalism lasted a long time.

In spite of difficulties in precise definition, there is sufficient material to prove the wide spread of phenomena germane to the mystery religions and to the milieu in which they could thrive. Mystery religions must be seen as part of this milieu because they are intimately linked to typical Hellenistic views of human beings and their world. The cosmos has its divine order, but human beings are not granted their full share in this divine universe because they are caught in the realm of sense perception and matter, disorder and mortality, and are subject to Heimarmene, the power of fate. However, in their soul they share in the divine world; various divine forces are ready to aid in the acts of salvation, which cannot take place in the realm of the visible world which is, by definition, the cause of the dilemma. This also explains the lack of initiative for responsible political action—apart from the fact that institutions for such action were nonexistent. Whoever sought fulfillment there would either have to be a member of the aristocracy—where the concept of political action as the human destiny was still alive—or plunge into such hopeless political adventures as slave insurrections. Salvation could only come through faith in those powers that existed in a realm beyond the visible world and belonged to a more harmonious order unthreatened by transitoriness, although these powers were capable of extending their influence into this earthly realm.

The mastery of life, therefore, depended on whether one could secure the favor of those otherworldly powers and share in their benefits. The belief in power was primary, whether one saw the whole universe pervaded by the power of the Logos, with which one had to be in agreement (the Stoic view), or whether one saw good and evil demons at work everywhere and tried to secure their aid through magic and secret knowledge. Divine power was present in the spirit as opposed to matter, in the world of the stars as opposed to the sublunar world, and in the demonstrable power of new gods who represented a hitherto unknown force. This constituted the attraction of the new religions from the east. The aim was still to master earthly life and obtain guarantees that extended into the life beyond death. Only Gnosticism was more radical (§6.5f), since life in this world had become entirely irrelevant in its view; knowledge and power were thus entirely directed toward liberation from this material world, no longer toward its mastery with the aid of higher forces. It was easy for Gnosticism to invade the mystery religions; gnostic and non-gnostic writings stand side-by-side in the Hermetic mystery literature, and Gnostics and non-Gnostics existed side-by-side in Christian communities.

The visualization and concretization of the overcoming of matter, death, and fate, as it was offered by the mystery religions, quickly proved superior to abstract philosophical doctrines. The rite of initiation had two advantages: first, it could symbolize guarantees for the work of supernatural powers (divine images, lightning effects, symbolic garments, allegories); and second, it provided an opportunity to be accepted into a community of friends who possessed the same secret, that is, saving knowledge. This community might have only secondary significance, because it was primarily the power that the individual would share, which was the goal of the initiation. The purpose of the mystery rites, therefore, should not be understood as the creation of a community or a new and better world. What mattered was the appropriation of power and the securing of protection of higher authorities in the adversities of life and for the passage of the soul into a better world after death—ideas that also were widely accepted by Christianity. It was even possible to reach the same goal without the aid of an organized religion, through philosophical contemplation, for example, or in mysticism, or by submersion into a mystery book (e.g., the Hermetic literature); even magic and astrology might provide access to the realm of otherworldly powers. The mystery religions, however, offered maximal opportunities and were able to institutionalize access to these divine powers. Thus the mystery religions, and not least Christianity, were ultimately more successful.

THE PEOPLE OF ISRAEL
IN THE HELLENISTIC PERIOD

1. The History of the Israelite People
to the Roman Conquest

(a) From the Exile to Alexander the Great

After the destruction of Jerusalem in 597 and 585 BCE by Nebuchadnezzar, the king of the Neo-Babylonian empire, the upper class of the kingdom of Judah was exiled to Babylonia. In the year 539 BCE, Babylon was conquered by the Persians, and many of the exiles received permission from the Persian king Kyros to return to Jerusalem. The rebuilding of the religious commonwealth of Jerusalem in the following decades was accomplished under the influence of those who stayed behind in Babylon. The Temple of Jerusalem (the "Second Temple") was constructed during the years 520–515 BCE, and the reconstruction of the walls of the city was begun, though it was soon interrupted. It seems that those who had returned, now living under the authority of the satrap of Samaria, were involved in numerous conflicts and dealings with other Jewish and non-Jewish populations of the area.

Bibliography to §5: Texts

George W. E. Nickelsburg and Michael E. Stone, *Faith and Piety in Early Judaism: Texts and Documents* (Philadelphia: Trinity Press International, 1991).

Menahem D. Stern, *Greek and Latin Authors on Jews and Judaism: Edited with Introductions, Translations and Commentary* (3 vols.; Fontes ad res Judaicas spectantes; Jerusalem: Israel Academy of Sciences and Humanities, 1976–1984).

Hans G. Kippenberg and G. A. Wevers, *Textbuch zur neutestamentlichen Zeitgeschichte* (Grundrisse zum Neuen Testament, NTDSup 8; Göttingen: Vandenhoeck & Ruprecht, 1979).

Bibliography to §5: Introduction and Surveys

Emil Schürer, *The History of the Jewish People in the Age of Jesus Christ (175 B.C–A.D. 135)* (rev. and ed. Geza Vermes, Fergus Millar, Matthew Black, and Martin Goodman; vols. 1–3; Edinburgh: Clark, 1973–87).

W. O. E. Oesterley, *The Jews and Judaism during the Greek Period: The Background of Christianity* (London: SPCK and New York: Macmillan, 1941).

Elias J. Bickerman, *The Jews in the Greek Age* (Cambridge, MA: Harvard University Press, 1988).

Shaye J. D. Cohen, *From the Maccabees to the Mishna* (LEC; Philadelphia: Westminster, 1989).

Frederick J. Murphy, *The Religious World of Jesus: An Introduction to Second Temple Palestinian Judaism* (Nashville: Abingdon, 1991).

Gabriele Boccaccini, *Middle Judaism: Jewish Thought, 300 b.c.e. to 200 c.e.* (Minneapolis: Fortress, 1991).

Seth Schwartz, "Judaism," in Grant and Kitzinger, *Civilization*, 1009–45.

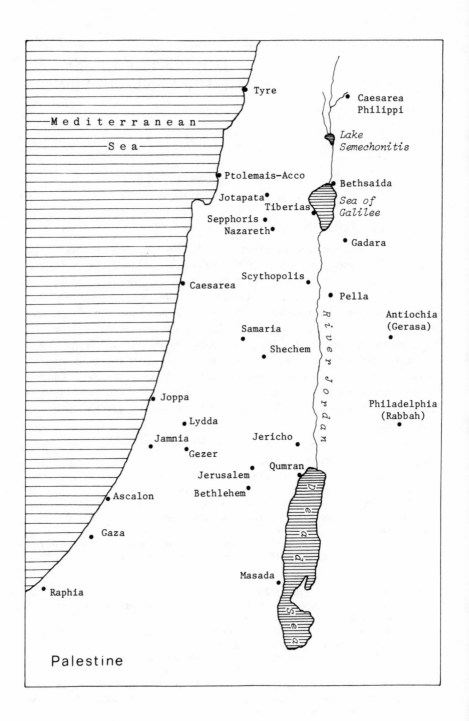

Palestine

A new turn of events came only with the arrival from Babylonia of Ezra and Nehemiah. The activities of both men must be dated in the 5th century BCE (contrary to the sequence of Chronicles, some scholars argue that Nehemiah came to Jerusalem *before* Ezra). Both men, coming with authorizations from the Persian king, were concerned with the introduction of legislation, which would preserve the particular character of the people of Israel and secure its semi-independent administration. The Persian governor was replaced by a council of elders with the high priest as the presiding officer; this council was directly responsible to the king. The high-priestly family, allied with the leading priestly families, was also charged with the supervision of justice and the regulation of cult and ritual.

Jerusalem was thus reorganized as a typical temple state like many others in the Persian realm. Although this state consisted primarily of the city of Jerusalem and a number of townships in Judea, its constitution was completely different from that of a Greek city-state: it drew its authority not from the free citizens of

Bibliography to §5: Special Topics

Arnoldo Momigliano, "Greek Culture and the Jews," in M. I. Finley, ed., *The Legacy of Greece: A New Appraisal* (Oxford: Clarendon, 1981) 325–46.

Gerhard von Rad, *Old Testament Theology* (2 vols.; New York: Harper & Row, 1965) 2. 263–315.

Martin Hengel, *Judaism and Hellenism: Studies in Their Encounter in Palestine during the Hellenistic Period* (2 vols.; Philadelphia: Fortress, 1974; reprint 1991).

Michael Edward Stone, *Scriptures, Sects, and Visions* (Philadelphia: Fortress, 1980).

Shmuel Safrai and Menahem Stern, eds., *The Jewish People in the First Century* (2 vols; CRINT 1; Philadelphia: Fortress, 1974–1976).

Sean Freyne, *Galilee from Alexander the Great to Hadrian, 323 B.C.E. to 135 C.E.: A Study of Second Temple Judaism* (University of Notre Dame Center for the Study of Judaism and Christianity in Antiquity 5; Notre Dame, IN: University of Notre Dame Press, 1980).

Pieter W. van der Horst, *Essays on the Jewish World of Early Christianity* (NTOA 14; Göttingen: Vandenhoeck & Ruprecht, 1990).

Bibliography to §5.1

Martin Noth, *The History of Israel* (2d ed.; New York: Harper & Row, 1960).

Elias Bickerman, *From Ezra to the Last of the Maccabees* (New York: Schocken, 1962).

Max Weber, *Ancient Judaism* (London: Collier-Macmillan, and new York: The Free Press, 1952; reprint: 1967).

Victor A. Tcherikover, *Hellenistic Civilization and the Jews* (New York: Atheneum, 1970).

Martin Hengel, *Jews, Greeks and Barbarians* (Philadelphia: Fortress, 1980).

W. D. Davies and Louis Finkelstein, eds., *The Cambridge History of Judaism:* vol. 1: *The Persian Period* (Cambridge: Cambridge University Press, 1984)

idem, eds., *The Cambridge History of Judaism:* vol. 2: *The Hellenistic Age* (Cambridge: Cambridge Univeristy Press, 1989)

A. Reifenberg, *Israel's History on Coins from the Maccabees to the Roman Conquest* (London: East and West Library, 1953).

Bibliography to §5.1a

Michael E. Stone and D. Satran, eds., *Emerging Judaism: Studies on the Fourth & Third Centuries B.C.E.* (Minneapolis: Fortress, 1989).

Peter J. Ackroyd, *Israel under Babylon and Persia* (London: Oxford University Press, 1970).

Jacob Neusner, *A History of the Jews in Babylon*, vol. 1: *The Parthian Period* (StPB 9; Leiden: Brill, 1965).

Frank Moore Cross, "A Reconstruction of the Jewish Restoration," *JBL* 94 (1975) 4–18.

the city and its magistrates, but from a temple, sanctioned by divine presence. The law of this state was not a civil law (albeit one with divine legitimation), but the religious law given by God, and the high priest was the highest official ("theocracy," see §4.3b). This implied that the law included sanctions designed to emphasize the religious distinctiveness of the people, such as purity regulations and the injunction against intermarriage with those who remained outside the religious community. It is likely that the legislations introduced by Ezra and Nehemiah were also accepted by those Israelites who lived in parts of Palestine that were not subject to the jurisdiction of Jerusalem, namely in Samaria, Galilee, and Transjordan, or even as far away as Elephantine in Upper Egypt, where a colony of Israelites with their own temple existed since the end of the 6th century. A letter of 419 BCE issued under the authority of Darius II requests that the colony should observe the Feast of the Unleavened Bread. The final consolidation of these laws and their amalgamation with older legal traditions in the Five Books of Moses, which was accomplished in the 4th century BCE, became valid for Israelites everywhere.

As in other parts of the Persian Empire, Greek influences increased in Palestine during the 5th and 4th centuries. Greek imports reached past the coastal cities of Phoenecia/Palestine to the inland areas of Samaria and Judea. Jewish coins imitated the Attic drachma and might bear the image of Zeus or the Athenian owl. Greek mercenaries served in many parts of the Persian realm. Also the literature of Israel from this period reveals Greek influence. Religious syncretism was probably widespread, especially among Israelite communities outside of Palestine. This is attested in the Aramaic papyri from Elephantine.

(b) Palestine under the Hellenistic Rulers

After the battle of Issus (333 BCE; see §1.2b), Palestine came under the control of Alexander the Great. His general Parmenion occupied the land and was resisted only by Samaria, which rose up again when Alexander was in Egypt (331 BCE); Alexander's army conquered the city and destroyed it. It was subsequently refounded as a Greek colony. Apparently at this time, Israelites who had been expelled from the conquered city rebuilt the ancient city of Shechem and erected a temple on Mt. Gerizim. However, there is no reason to believe that this was the occasion for the break between the Judean and Samaritan religious communities.

After the death of Alexander, Palestine eventually became part of the realm of the Ptolemies, the Macedonian rulers of Egypt. Repeated attempts by the Seleucid kings to conquer southern Syria were not successful until Antiochos III (223–187 BCE; see §1.4d). Although first beaten by Ptolemy IV Philopator at

Bibliography to §5.1b

A. Schalit, ed., *The Hellenistic Age: Political History of Jewish Palestine from 332 B.C.E. to 67 B.C.E.* (The World History of the Jewish People 6; New Brunswick, NJ: Rutgers University Press, 1972).

Raphia in southern Palestine in 217, Antiochos finally succeeded in defeating Ptolemy V Epiphanes near the sources of the Jordan in 198 at the site of the later city Caesarea Philippi. Phoenecia and Palestine became part of the Syrian kingdom. Jerusalem supported Antiochos in this war, held the Egyptian garrison in the city captive, and greeted the Seleucid king jubilantly. In turn Antiochos renewed all privileges of the temple state and granted new favors (the decree is preserved in Josephus *Ant.* 12.138–44). Good relationships between Jerusalem and the Seleucid administration persisted during the following years.

Neither the Ptolemies nor the Seleucids interfered in the internal cultural and religious activities of the people living in Palestine. However, the process of Hellenization, which began in the early Hellenistic period, affected the entire country and eventually also Jerusalem itself. The cities were the primary agents of Hellenization. The Ptolemies, though they did not sponsor the founding of cities in Egypt itself, actively supported the creation of Greek cities in their Palestinian dominions. While Samaria had already been refounded as a Greek city during the time of Alexander the Great, more Greek cities were founded in Palestine during the Ptolemaic and Seleucid periods, most of which were reconstitutions of older cities: on the Mediterranean coast, Ptolemais (formerly Akko), Yavneh, Ashkelon, and Gaza; to the south and east of the Sea of Galilee, the cities which later belonged to the "Dekapolis": Pella, Philadelphia (Rabbath-Ammon, today Amman), Gadara, Skythopolis (Beth-Shean), Seleukia in Bashan, and especially Gerasa, reconstituted by Antiochos IV as Antioch—until the late Roman empire the most magnificent city of this region. Some of the inhabitants of the new cities were Macedonians and Greeks, but Hellenized Semites predominated: Syrians, Phoenecians, Arabs, and of course also Israelites. As a consequence, Greek or Hellenized oriental cultural elements, a new style of life, and foreign cults were imported. Gods worshiped in these cities were oriental deities under Greek names (e.g., Ashtoreth as Aphrodite in Ashkelon) or Greek gods, such as Dionysos in Skythopolis, whose coins display the name Nysa, the mythological birthplace of Dionysos, as the official name of the city.

During the Ptolemaic period, southern Syria and Palestine had not been incorporated in the centralized Egyptian administration. Estates owned by the king were managed by royal officials. But large parts of the country, though economically oriented to Alexandria, remained under the semi-autonomous governance of cities, temples, and princes. Jerusalem and parts of Judea made up one of these temple states. Among the princes the wealthy Tobiads of Transjordan, traditional rivals of Jerusalem since the Persian period, were most conspicuous. The Tobiad Joseph, whose father had been the Ptolemaic army commander for Transjordan, and whose mother was a daughter of the high priest of Jerusalem, held the office of Egyptian finance minister for southern Syria for twenty-two years. Although Joseph was an Israelite, he appears as a typical Hellenistic tycoon who had accepted the Greek lifestyle as an adjunct to political and economic power. Such choices were common among upper-class Israelites. The leading priestly families of Transjordan, Jerusalem, and Samaria, closely related to each other by intermarriage, were all Hellenized. Seleucid rule, which began in the early 2d century CE, brought no basic changes. It only implied a shift of power from the pro-Ptolemaic party (led by Joseph the Tobiad) to the pro-Seleucid party in Jerusalem. Nevertheless, a crisis was soon to develop which was intricately related to the question of Hellenization.

(c) The Maccabean Revolt

The origins and causes of the Maccabean revolt are not completely clear. Jerusalem had a pro-Seleucid party well before the conquest of Palestine by Antiochos III. Its leaders included the high priest Simon (perhaps Simon the Just) as well as the older sons of the Tobiad Joseph, in other words, the most powerful families of the country. Antiochos III found a cordial welcome and gladly confirmed "the laws of the fathers," the basis of the theocratic administration and the religious life of the people. Of course, the leading circles whose "laws of the fathers" were thus guaranteed were already Hellenized. Those holding on to a more traditional form of the religion of Israel found themselves in growing opposition to these circles.

This deepening contrast between the traditional religion and accelerating Hellenization, however, was not in itself a sufficient cause for a bloody revolution. To be sure, the only (and not always reliable) source for the developments before the outbreak of open hostilities, the Second Book of Maccabees, indicates that political infighting among the leading, priestly families played a considerable role in the events preceding the revolution. However, the eruption of hostilities also coincided with the humiliation of the Syrian king Antiochos IV Epiphanes by the Romans (§1.4d) and is closely related to the financial difficulties of the Seleucids. Furthermore, elements of utopian apocalypticism, which had been developing since the time of the Exile, had found a wide acceptance (§5.2b). The second century of the Hellenistic epoch is characterized by a number of revolutionary movements in which utopian concepts play a significant role—for example, the insurrection of the adherents of "the Commonwealth of the Sun" in Pergamon (§2.3c). Social factors played a significant role. In the Maccabean revolt, the insurrection against the wealthy aristocracy was led by poor people from the countryside.

Insofar as it is possible to reconstruct the course of events which lead to the Maccabean revolt, it appears to have begun in a controversy of the pro-Syrian and pro-Egyptian parties over the high-priestly office and the control of the financial interests of the temple. After the death of the high priest Simon (after 200 BCE), who belonged to the Zadokite family (which based its claim to the office on their ancestor Zadok, the high priest of king David), Simon's son

Bibliography to §5.1c

Daniel J. Harrington, *The Maccabean Revolt: Anatomy of a Biblical Revolution* (Old Testament Studies 1; Wilmington, DE: Glazier, 1988).

Elias Bickerman, *The God of the Maccabees: Studies on the Meaning and Origin of the Maccabean Revolt* (SJLA 32; Leiden: Brill, 1972).

Onias III succeeded him. Onias leaned towards the Egyptian party and supported the youngest son of the Tobiad Joseph, who in turn used his friendship with the new high priest to employ the banking services of the temple to his advantage.

But the assassination of the Syrian king Seleukos IV in 175 BCE gave the older Tobiads and their followers the opportunity to expel Onias and to appoint Onias' brother Jason (= Joshua) as high priest in his place—all this with the knowledge and support of the new king Antiochos IV Epiphanes, from whom Jason had bought the high-priestly office. At the same time, Jason received permission from the king to reconstitute Jerusalem as a Greek city to be named Antioch. This required the appointment of a city council (boule) instead of the traditional council of elders (gerousia), the organization of an assembly of voting citizens, the building of a gymnasium, and arrangements for educating epheboi. It is not clear whether this new constitution also involved a religious reform. Jason is never accused of having set aside "the laws of the fathers," but it seems likely, judging from analogies, that this Hellenization program of a Near-Eastern city would also include the identification of the traditional oriental deity (in this case Yahweh) with a Greek god (most likely Zeus Olympios), though neither Antiochos IV nor any of his predecessors would have interfered with the established ritual and religious conventions. Had the Hellenization simply been a nominal identification of Yahweh with Zeus Olympios, a religious revolt would have been unlikely.

The turning point was Jason's expulsion. Though a member of the reform party, he was a legitimate Zadokite and thus a guarantor of "the laws of the fathers" even for the conservatives. In 172 BCE, Menelaos, brother of an officer of the temple named Simon, took Jason's place. Apparently he was more suitable in the eyes of the reformers, had the support of the Tobiads, and had offered the king an even bigger sum of money than that paid by Jason for the high-priestly office. Only now did the situation reach a crisis. It became evident that the office of the high priest must not be abused with impunity in the interests of the aristocracy. More was at stake: the high priest was the guarantor of religious law for all the people; an illegitimate high priest was a threat to the constitution of the entire commonwealth. As the resistance of the people grew, Menelaos was barely able to hold on to his office. While he was in Antioch, his brother Lysimachos, whom Menelaos had appointed as his deputy, was slain in Jerusalem. The external political developments also provided an opportunity for the "pious" to organize themselves and to form a political movement known as the Hasidim, which included the family of the Maccabees as well as those people who were later known as Essenes, and probably also the Pharisees. This new party was no longer willing to permit the aristocracy to treat the whole affair as if nothing were at stake but their rivaling claims to power.

In 169–168 Antiochos Epiphanes led two campaigns against Egypt. Returning from the first campaign, he visited his friends, the city of the new Greek polis Antioch-Jerusalem. It turned out, however, that he was more interested in the temple treasury: the financial crisis of the Seleucids had become so severe that the kings repeatedly resorted to such measures. After Antiochos had left the city, and when an attempt by Jason to reoccupy Jerusalem had failed, the enraged conservative party took possession of the city and locked up Menelaos and his partisans in the Acra, the fortified Hellenistic quarter. This action signaled the beginning of the revolt. Antiochos who had just been humiliated by the Romans—an ultimatum of the Roman senate had forced him to relinquish his Egyptian conquests—reacted promptly. He captured Jerusalem (probably through his official Apollonios), murdered or expelled the Jewish residents, and made Jerusalem a *katoikia,* that is, a city inhabited by soldiers, veterans, and other colonists (mostly Syrians). Only now did Apollonios, Antiochos' governor, begin a persecution of the faithful Jews, not for religious reasons, but in order to subdue a rebellious people. The traditional view, that the rebellion was a reaction to the religious persecution, is untenable. Only now was the temple of Yahweh (called Zeus Olympios since the reform) transformed into the cult of a superficially Hellenized Syrian god, Zeus Baal Shamayin. His sacred rock was brought into the temple, where he was worshiped together with his consorts "Athena" and "Dionysos."

Only at this time were "the laws of the fathers" annulled: they could not serve as the constitution of the Syrian-Greek citizenry of the *katoikia* Antioch-Jerusalem. The political and religious reorganization, completed with decrees of Antiochos in the year 167, legitimized the new cult and outlawed the practice of Israel's religion in Jerusalem and Judea (not, however, among Israelites elsewhere). The persecution of the faithful Judeans was a necessary consequence. It is difficult to estimate the severity of the persecution, because the information provided by the Books of the Maccabees is mostly legendary. Antiochos was correct in identifying the core of the resistance among those people who adhered most faithfully to their religion in the traditional form. He therefore forced the population to participate in the pagan cult and outlawed circumcision. Eating of pork became the test of loyalty: those who refused demonstrated that they were part of the rebellion. No doubt, many who were unwilling to deny their faith were cruelly martyred.

Those who were not apprehended by the Syrian authorities fled into the mountains of Judea in order to join the guerrillas commended by a certain Judas with the surname Maccabeus (= "the Hammer")—this is reported by 2 Macc 5:28 and 8:1. However, the First Book of the Maccabees, written by the official court historian of the Hasmoneans, gives a different account, since the later Hasmonean rulers did not descend from Judas but from his elder brother Simon. According to this version, the movement's founder was not Judas, but his and Simon's father Mattathias, a priest who descended from a certain Hasmoneus. This resistance movement appealed to the traditional values that the Hasidim had defended against the Hellenistic reformers. To gain wide support, it also exploited the resentment of the poorer classes of the population against the wealthy high-priestly families.

Leadership naturally fell to one who knew guerrilla warfare. While all Hasidim were initially united in the revolt led by Judas, the Essenes and apparently the Pharisees later broke with the heirs of the guerrilla leader, when they aspired to, and actually achieved, both political power and control of the temple. The government of Antiochos IV, on the other hand, was successful in rallying to its support all vested powers and interest groups, namely the Greek cities, the non-Jewish population of the neighboring areas, the Samaritans, and finally those in Israel who had favored Hellenization and wanted to maintain a peaceful coexistence of all people of Palestine. To this latter group belonged, of course, the Hellenized aristocracy under the leadership of the high priest Menelaos, whom Antiochos had appointed.

After four years of war, during which the guerrillas under Judas had repeated success (168–164 BCE), the Hellenized Jews of Jerusalem made a final attempt at reconciliation and succeeded in persuading Antiochos to repeal the edicts against the exercise of the traditional religion. The new decrees are preserved in 2 Macc 11:22–26. Within a specified period all those who had fled because of the persecution were permitted to return and their religious freedom was guaranteed. But it was too late: shortly after the publication of these edicts, Judas conquered Jerusalem, and the Hellenists retreated once more to the fortified Acra. Since Antiochos Epiphanes, fighting against the Parthians in the east, died in 163, his deputy Lysias, governor of the western part of the kingdom, was unable to intervene as the problem of the royal succession forced him to stay in Antioch. This gave Judas the opportunity to consolidate his power, even to humiliate his enemies beyond the borders of Judea, and to reach a compromise agreement with the new king, Antiochos V Eupator: Jerusalem's temple was officially returned to the traditional cult (162 BCE; see the document in 2 Macc 11:22–26); Menelaos was executed. The new high priest, Alkimos, probably a legitimate Zadokite, was however not recognized by Judas because of his sympathy for Hellenism.

Shortly afterwards, Antiochos V was assassinated by his cousin, Demetrios I Soter (162–150). Fortune now turned against Judas. The new king supported Alkimos, and the Hasidim in Jerusalem were now willing to accept him as high priest. Demetrios' general Bakchides defeated Judas' army; Judas himself died in battle in the year 160 BCE. Soon thereafter Alkimos also died, and the Syrian commander Bacchides offered a new compromise treaty. It was finally agreed that Judas' brother Jonathan should be established as "judge" in Michmash (near Jerusalem), but he had to promise not to interfere in the affairs of Jerusalem (157 BCE). Syrian sovereignty was established once more, but freedom of religion was guaranteed. The office of high priest, however, was left vacant.

After several years of peace (157–153), renewed fighting among the pretenders to the Syrian throne opened another period of instability. Jonathan, and later his brother Simon, took advantage of the internal problems of the Syrian kingdom and, despite of setbacks, finally achieved their goal of political independence. In 153 BCE Alexander Balas tried to gain the Syrian throne. To defend himself against this pretender, king Demetrios I sought the support of Jonathan and, in return, gave him permission to occupy Jerusalem. But soon thereafter Jonathan switched his allegiance to Alexander Balas, who rewarded him by appointing him high priest: in 152 Jonathan appeared for the first time in public in that office. After his victory over Demetrios I, Alexander Balas honored Jonathan by making him "friend of the king," and appointed him as *strategos* and governor of Judea. The foundation stone was laid for the Hasmonean state.

MACCABEES AND HASMONEANS

(all dates are BCE)

Rulers		Events	
after 200	high priest Simon dies	195	Jerusalem welcomes Antiochos III
	Onias III successor		
175	Jason high priest	175	Seleukos IV assassinated; Jerusalem reconstituted as Greek polis
172	Menelaos high priest	169	Antiochos IV takes temple treasury
168–160	Judas leader of the revolt	168–164	Maccabean revolt
		167	Jerusalem becomes "Antiochia"
		164	Antiochos IV dies
		160	Temple returned to traditional worship
152–143	Jonathan high priest		
143–134	Simon high priest	142	Expulsion of Syrian garrison from Acra Exile of "Teacher of Righteousness"
134–104	John Hyrkanos	128	Destruction of Samaritan temple on Mt. Gerizim
104	Aristoboulos		
104–78	Alexander Janneus	94	Revolt of the "Pharisees"
76–67	Alexandra		
67–65	Hyrkanos II & Aristoboulos II	65	Pompey enters Jerusalem temple

(d) The Time of the Hasmoneans

In order to achieve their goal of becoming the rulers of an independent country and bringing all of Palestine under their control, the Hasmoneans took advantage of the continuing dynastic wars in Syria and the shift of international power to Rome. Jonathan was quite successful in this respect. Even when the young son of Demetrios I, Demetrios II Nikator, overthrew Alexander Balas in 145 BCE, Jonathan was able to strengthen his position: Demetrios II awarded him with the southern districts of Samaria. Another change of allegiance, however, proved his undoing. When Diodotos Trypho rose against Demetrios II, supposedly to gain the throne for Antiochos VI, the son of Alexander Balas, he received Jonathan's support, confirmed Jonathan in his office, and appointed Jonathan's brother Simon *strategos* of the coastal district of Palestine, which resulted in the conquest the whole region from the Philistine coast to Galilee and even as far as Damascus. However, when Diodotos Trypho imprisoned Antiochos VI in order to occupy the throne himself, he also captured Jonathan and executed him. Simon, the last surviving son of Mattathias, now made a treaty with Demetrios II against Trypho, in which Demetrios recognized Simon as independent ruler of Judea, granted the Jews freedom from taxation, and permitted Simon to expel the Syrian garrison from the Acra of Jerusalem (142–141 BCE).

Synagogue of Sardes

Built in II CE in one of the wings of the gymnasium in a choice location of the city, and remodeled in V CE, the synagogue was excavated recently and restored by a Harvard-Cornell team under George M. A. Hanfmann. The entrance was at the far left through a peristyle court; between the three doors are two shrines (for the book of the Torah). On the right a monumental table, supported by two eagles, in front of an apse with rows of seats. The building measured about 200 feet (= 60 m) in length (without the court) and rose to a height of over 70 feet.

This confirmed Simon's *de facto* independence, which he used to conquer Gezer and Jaffa, thus gaining access to the Mediterranean Sea. Simon established diplomatic relations with Sparta and Rome and began to date official documents according to his regnal years. While Jonathan, like his predecessors, had been appointed high priest by the Syrian king, Simon was confirmed in this office by a great assembly of the priests, the leaders of Judea, and the elders of the country as "regent" and as "high priest forever, until a faithful prophet should arise" (140 BCE). This event seemed to be the fulfillment of all the hopes and expectations that thirty years earlier had united the conservatives, the Hasidim, and the political rebels in their fight against Antiochos IV Epiphanes. Indeed, this is exactly what the author of the First Book of Maccabees tries to communicate to his readers in the 14th chapter of his book.

However, the political and religious consequences of this step cannot be overlooked. Although the title "king" was consciously avoided in Simon's proclamation of his office, it was nevertheless a declaration of authority in the style of a Hellenistic ruler. His position was based on military power; he alone had the right to be clothed in royal purple and to wear a gold buckle; any disobedience or resistance was explicitly threatened with severe punishment. His royal accomplishments (*res gestae*) were published on bronze tablets and publicly displayed in the temple precinct as a sign of his power; the other members of his family, who had in fact fought most of the battles for independence, are scarcely mentioned in this document.

Of course, the official court history of the Hasmoneans, 1 Maccabees, does not mention that Jonathan's and Simon's high priesthoods were considered illegitimate by many because they were not from the traditional family of the Zadokites. At least one faction of the Hasidim, the Essenes, who have now become well known through the discovery of the texts from Qumran, went into exile. Under the leadership of a Zadokite priest, the "Teacher of Righteousness," they founded their own religious center at the shores of the Dead Sea. For them Simon (and perhaps already his brother Jonathan) was the "evil priest" who persecuted the "Teacher of Righteousness" (§5.2c). No wonder the decree of 1 Macc 14:44 explicitly threatens punishment for priests who disobey Simon's rule. Another faction of the Hasidim, who later became known as the Pharisees, was suppressed by Simon's successor half a century later. The Hasmoneans succeeded in the following years to make the Jewish state as powerful as it had been in the time of David and Solomon; nonetheless these groups of "the pious" remained unwilling to accept its rulers as the fulfillment of their religious hopes.

In the year 139 the throne of the Seleucid kingdom was occupied for the last time in its history by an able ruler, Antiochos VII Sidites. The new king, although willing to recognize Simon's independence, demanded that Simon withdraw from Gezer and Jaffa and accept a Syrian garrison in the Acra. Simon refused, and his sons Judas and John (Hyrkanos) defeated Antiochos' general in battle. But shortly thereafter, in 135, Simon fell prey to a conspiracy of his son-in-law Ptolemy during a drinking bout. Ptolemy also murdered Simon's wife and two of his sons, but John Hyrkanos escaped. Meanwhile, Antiochos Sidites was preparing to invade Judea with a new army. Although John Hyrkanos had prevailed over his rival Ptolemy and was recognized as his father's successor, he had to withdraw behind the walls of Jerusalem. Antiochos and John Hyrkanos reached a compromise settlement, in which the latter agreed to give up all conquests made by his father and to pay a substantial tribute. In return, Antiochos recognized Hyrkanos' independence and left the Acra in Jewish hands. When Antiochos Sidites was killed in battle against the Parthians (129), a campaign in which John Hyrkanos was obliged to participate, the danger of Syrian interference ended, since the Seleucid kingdom never regained its military power and political influence.

The following decades were characterized by a systematic conquest of the whole area of Palestine by the Hasmoneans, including the coastal district and the Greek cities. Most of the conquests were accomplished during the long reign of John Hyrkanos (135–104 BCE), some under his sons (Judas) Aristoboulos (104) and Alexander Janneus (104–78). Among the cultural and religious problems which ensued from these conquests, the fate of the Greek cities had the most momentous consequences. Hellenization of the country had once been closely linked with the founding of Greek cities. Their citizens, to be sure, were not actually Greeks in most cases, but Hellenized Phoenecians, Syrians, and others. But the concept of the free city—"free" because of its constitution and self-governance—as a center of cultural and commercial life was itself Greek. The right to education (gymnasia were among the most important institutions of these cities) and the free exercise of religion as long as the official deities had received their due recognition were also fundamentally Greek concepts.

But the kind of "Jewish" state that was propagated by the Hasmoneans could not be reconciled with the idea of the Greek city. The Maccabean revolt had rejected the attempt to reconstitute Jerusalem as a Greek city. Even the notion of cultural and religious pluralism was repulsive. The only consistent continuation of the revolt was to return the whole country to the faith in the God of Israel. This religious goal fit well with the political insight that the existence of independent cities occupying positions of economic power was irreconcilable with the interests of a small nation-state. Therefore the Hasmoneans proceeded to conquer nearly all the Greek cities in their region; only Acco-Ptolemais on the coast and Ammon-Philadelphia in Transjordan were able to remain independent.

The inhabitants of these cities were forced to emigrate or to convert to Judaism, and those who remained were deprived of their urban privileges and became subject to Hasmonean rule. This removed from the process of Hellenization its most important institution, the polis as such, although Greek elements, customs, and language continued to exist in many places. On the other hand, Hellenism was very evident in the political conduct and external manifestations of the ruling house. John Hyrkanos changed the names of his sons Judas, Mattathias, and Jonathan to Aristoboulos, Antigonos, and Alexander. Aristoboulos called himself "Philhellenos" and assumed the title "king," though only for his relations with other countries—his coins still read "John the High Priest." John Hyrkanos also employed foreign mercenaries, a typical practice of the Hellenistic kings. The Hasmonean rulers persistently pursued only two goals: enlarging the power of the Jewish state, and making all inhabitants of the country Jewish subjects, albeit by force.

At the beginning of the Maccabean War, a religious goal was predominant: to liberate the temple, the city of Jerusalem, and the land of Judea from pagan abominations. But in the hands of the Hasmoneans religion became a tool through which all inhabitants of the country could be made loyal to Jerusalem, where the ruler was at the same time the high priest. After the conquest of Idumea, all male inhabitants were compelled to be circumcised. This also happened in the conquest of Greek cities. The Samaritan capital of Shechem was also conquered, the temple on Mt. Gerizim destroyed, and the Samaritan population forced to acknowledge the religious jurisdiction of Jerusalem.

The Hasmonean hegemony produced severe reactions within some Israelite communities. The Essene literature reveals that for many people the idea of Israel as the elect people of God could no longer be reconciled with the reality of religious and political jurisdiction of the Jerusalem temple and its ruling high priest. According to Josephus (*Antiquities* 13), it would appear that also the Pharisees viewed this religious policy with ever-growing reservations. Open conflict came under the rule of Alexander Janneus, who became high priest after the short rule of his brother Aristoboulos I (104 BCE) and who continued the imperialistic policies of his father. In 94 a revolt began, apparently instigated by the Pharisees, which led to six years of civil war and to the intervention of the Syrian king Demetrios III on behalf of the revolutionaries. Janneus, finally victorious, had eight hundred leaders of the rebels publicly crucified. Josephus does not say that they were Pharisees; however, in the reign of Janneus' widow Alexandra, the Pharisees appear as the ruling party of the country. They made use of their new power by recalling those who had been exiled under Janneus and punishing his advisors.

After the death of Alexandra, Hasmonean rule disintegrated amid the intrigues and fights of her sons. Hyrkanos II, who had assumed the office of high priest, was forced by his brother Aristoboulos II to seek refuge with the Nabateans in Petra. Together with the Nabateans, and with the help of the most formidable politician of the country, the Idumean Antipater (son of the governor of Idumea and father of Herod the Great), Hyrkanos was able to defeat his brother, who was forced to barricade himself in the temple. Both sides appealed to the Roman general Pompey, who had just gained control of the eastern Mediterranean and had begun to reorganize the former kingdom of the Seleucids on Rome's behalf. With Pompey's conquest of Jerusalem came the end of the Hasmonean rule over Palestine, although several members of the family were yet to play a subordinate role in the political events and intrigues of the following decades (§6.6a, d).

(e) The Diaspora of Israel

The history of Judeans and Samaritans in Palestine is but a small segment of the history of the people of Israel in the Hellenistic period. Beginning with the Babylonian exile, a large part of the remnants of the former kingdom of Judea, lived outside of Palestine. The situation was little changed, when some of the exiled were permitted to return to Jerusalem. During the Hellenistic period, which saw substantial migrations of peoples from many nations, the proportion of Israelites living outside of Palestine grew even larger. The diaspora became increasingly important and began an independent religious and cultural development. The Babylonian diaspora was the largest in the Persian period. These Jews lived primarily in Babylon, which had been refounded by Alexander, and in Seleukia on the Tigris, founded by Seleukos I (312 BCE), which became the capital, economic center, and most populous city of the east. Hellenization of the mostly oriental inhabitants of these cities also affected the Jewish diaspora, though not to the same degree as in Alexandria. The influence of the Babylonian diaspora on the Jewish population in Palestine was considerable, even as late as the beginning of the Roman period, and so Hellenistic influences reached the Jews in Palestine even from the east. The bond between Babylon and Palestine was intimate because in both places the majority of the people spoke Aramaic, while the diaspora in Egypt, Asia Minor, and in the west used Greek as a common language. The Babylonian Jews were, as a whole, not hostile to the Seleucid and Parthian rulers. They seem to have been less positive, however, in their feelings regarding Rome.

The learned tradition of Sacred Scripture in Babylon was remarkable. In the reorganization of Judaism after the destruction of Jerusalem in 70 CE, the Babylonian text of the Hebrew Bible was accepted by the rabbis of Yavneh (now the basis of modern editions of the Masoretic text) and replaced the Palestinian text, which

Bibliography to §5.1e: Texts

Victor A. Tcherikover, *Corpus Papyrorum Judaicarum* (3 vols.; Cambridge, MA: Harvard University Press, 1957–64).

Bibliography to §5.1e: Studies

A. Thomas Kraabel, "The Diaspora Synagogue: Archaeological and Epigraphic Evidence since Sukenik," *ANRW* 2.19.1. (1979) 477–510.

J. Andrew Overman and R. S. MacLennon, eds., *Diaspora Jews and Judaism: Essays in Honor of, and in Dialogue with, A. Thomas Kraabel* (South Florida Studies in the History of Judaism 41; Atlanta, GA: Scholars Press, 1992).

Shaye J., D. Cohen, and E. S. Frerichs, eds., *Diasporas in Antiquity* (Brown Judaic Studies 288; Atlanta: Scholars Press, 1993).

Joseph Gutman, ed., *The Synagogue: Studies in Origins, Archaeology, and Architecture* (LBS New York: Ktav, 1975).

Idem, ed., *Ancient Synagogues: The State of Research* (Chico, CA: Scholars Press, 1981).

Pieter W. van der Horst, *Ancient Jewish Epitaphs: An Introductory Survey of a Millenium of Jewish Funerary Inscriptions (300 BCE–700 CE)* (Contributions to Biblical Exegesis and Theology 2; Kampen: Kok, Pharos, 1991).

Bernadette J. Brooten, *Women Leaders in the Ancient Synagogue* (BJudSt 36; Chico, CA: Scholars Press, 1982).

L. Michael White, "The Delos Synagogue Revisited," *HTR* 80 (1987) 133–60.

Erwin R. Goodenough, *The Jurisprudence of Jewish Courts in Egypt: Legal Administration by the Jews under the Early Roman Empire as Described by Philo Judaeus* (New Haven, CT: Yale University Press, 1929).

John J. Collins, *Between Athens and Jerusalem: Jewish Identity in the Hellenistic Diaspora* (New York: Crossroad, 1983).

J. N. Sevenster, *The Roots of Pagan Anti-Semitism in the Ancient World* (NovTSup 41; Leiden: Brill, 1975).

had been in use until then; the latter is preserved only as witnessed in the Greek translation of the Septuagint, the Pentateuch of the Samaritans, and the biblical manuscripts from Qumran. Later the Babylonian Talmud became the authoritative codification of the rabbinic traditions. There were also diaspora communities in other cities of the east, for example, in Edessa, Nisibis, later in Dura Europos. The diaspora in Adiabene, a district at the upper Tigris river (ancient Assyria) which was ruled by Parthian princes, may have derived from the exiles of the northern kingdom of Israel who had been brought there by the Assyrians at the end of the 7th century BCE. At the beginning of the 1st century CE, even the ruling prince and his mother converted to Judaism (Josephus *Ant.* 20.17ff).

Though the Egyptian diaspora would soon surpass the Babylonian in significance, its development was fundamentally different. One group there had forced the prophet Jeremiah to go with them; he died in Egypt. There was also an Israelite military colony in Elephantine in upper Egypt from the late 6th century BCE. In Elephantine the contrast to the Babylonian diaspora is striking. Though also here the language, as revealed by the papyrus finds, was Aramaic, these Israelites had their own temple (no Jewish temple was ever built in Babylon), their syncretism was very different from the learned cultivation of Israel's traditions in Babylon, and they may have been oriented toward Samaria rather than toward Jerusalem.

A new wave of immigrants from Israel came to Egypt after the Persian period, especially during the Ptolemaic domination of Palestine in the 3d century BCE, and created a large diaspora community in Alexandria, the cultural center of the Hellenistic world. The Ptolemies seem, on the whole, have favored such immigrations, especially as these Israelites adopted Greek as their language, occupied important functions economically and culturally, and became a vital part of the urban "Greek" constituency—as distinct from the mostly peasant Egyptian population. Even when the Seleucid rule over Palestine began in the 2d century BCE, immigration of Israelites did not come to an end. There was still a pro-Ptolemaic party in Jerusalem, and Egypt remained a refuge for its members. The story of Onias IV, son of the high priest Onias III who was overthrown in the course of the Hellenistic reforms in Jerusalem, is revealing. This younger Onias became a mercenary leader in Egyptian service during the reign of Ptolemy VI Philometor (180–145 BCE). A *katoikia* was founded for his soldiers in Leontopolis and a Jewish temple was built there. The strong position of Israelites during the reign of Philometor, and the fact that they had supported him as well as his widow, may have been the reason for the persecution under Philometor's rival Ptolemy VIII Euergetes (145–116 BCE). This persecution formed the background for the attempted pogrom which *3 Maccabees* mistakenly ascribes to Ptolemy IV. Around 100 BCE, two sons of Onias IV are reported to have been Egyptian generals.

Although later sources, both Jewish (Josephus) and Greco-Roman speak of the Egyptian and other western diaspora communities as "Jewish," it is evident that other segments of the people of Israel were involved in the formation of the diaspora as well. As seen from the outside, everyone who belonged to the religion of Israel was called a "Jew" (*Ioudaios*). But some of the extant writings that are known as "Hellenistic-Jewish" were written by people who maintained their loyalty to Samaria (see below). Moreover, the earliest synagogue in the Greek realm attested by archaeological remains, namely the synagogue on the island of Delos, was actually a Samaritan synagogue. What all these people from Israel shared was the use of a Greek translation of the Five Books of Moses, the Pentateuch, begun in Alexandria in the 3d century BCE, based on the Palestinian Hebrew, and the use of the Greek language in their prayer services. They were not ghetto communities, but were settled in various quarters of a city, though in Alexandria they were concentrated in two of the five quarters of the city. They had fully accepted the Greek language and participated in the cultural life of the city.

Alexandria may also have been the place from which the diaspora spread to other western countries, in the first instance to other Ptolemaic possessions. Important diaspora communities were founded from here in the Cyrenaica no later than the 3d century BCE, as well as on Crete and Cyprus. Since Alexandria was a significant port of transfer for exports from the east to the western Mediterranean until late antiquity, it is quite possible that the Roman diaspora also owed its beginnings to Israelites from this leading Hellenistic city.

Not as much is known about the diaspora in Syria. However, it is likely that migrations from Palestine took place during its domination by the Seleucids in the 2d century BCE, especially to its western capital Antioch. There is evidence for the presence of diaspora communities in other major cities like Apamea and Damascus, and in neighboring Cilicia (Tarsos). Jews and Samaritans also lived in the areas of Syria bordering on Palestine.

Next to Babylonia and Alexandria, the diaspora of Asia Minor assumed the greatest importance. Some of these communities along the western and southern coast of Asia Minor may have been formed by immigrants from Alexandria as early as the 3d century BCE, when the Ptolemies controlled important sections of these areas. But the earliest reliable information comes from around 200 BCE: Antiochos III settled 2,000 Jewish families from Babylonia in western Asia Minor, probably as military colonists. Beginning with the Roman conquest in the late 2d century BCE, the presence of diaspora communities can be assumed for most major cities of all districts Anatolia and also along the Black Sea. However, no epigraphical evidence is available before the Roman imperial period, and perhaps none that can be dated before the 2d century CE. Until the time after Constantine almost all Jewish inscriptions from Asia Minor use the Greek language. The only building that can be identified as a synagogue has been excavated in Sardes. This large basilica put to secondary use as a synagogue testifies eloquently to the size and social position of the community of Israelites who lived in Sardes. However, this building did not serve as a synagogue until the late 3d century CE, and most of its nearly eighty Greek inscriptions must be dated in the 4th century CE.

Little is known about the beginnings of diaspora communities in Greece and Macedonia. Most evidence comes from literary sources of the Roman imperial period, especially from the letters of the apostle Paul and from the Acts of the Apostles, which mention communities, always called "Jewish," in Corinth, Athens, Thessaloniki, and Philippi. The synagogue excavated in Stoboi in northern Macedonia is dated to the 2d or 3d century CE, and the Greek inscription found in

Corinth, "Synagogue of the Hebrews," comes from an even later period. Noteworthy is a 5th-century CE Samaritan inscription from Thessalonike.

The earliest diaspora communities in the west may have been founded in the Greek colonies of Sicily and southern Italy. The wars during Rome's expansion into the eastern Mediterranean in the 2d and 1st centuries BCE meant that Israelites from Palestine and elsewhere where brought to Rome as prisoners of war. Others would have migrated as craftsmen and merchants. The existence of a large diaspora community in Rome with probably as many as a dozen synagogues in various parts of the city (there was no "Jewish ghetto") can be assumed, though most of the archaeological evidence (synagogue buildings, inscriptions, catacombs) comes from the late 2d to the 4th century CE. The synagogue of Ostia, a building from the late 1st century CE, was not used as a synagogue until a century later.

As a development of cultural history, Hellenization affected all Israelites, whether they were Jews or Samaritans, Essenes or Pharisees, living in the diaspora or in Palestine. But in the dispersion, the effects of Hellenization were more profound. Turning Hebrew proper names into Greek, limited in Palestine to the upper classes, was common in the diaspora. Greek was known in Palestine, but it did not replace Aramaic as a commonly spoken language; religious literature continued to be written in Hebrew, while the Bible, still copied in Hebrew, was translated into Aramaic for use in synagogue services. On the other hand, the language of Israelites living in Alexandria, Asia Minor, Greece, and Rome was Greek. As late as the 3d and 4th centuries CE, almost no Hebrew and very little Latin appears in Jewish inscription from Rome. Greek readings from the Bible as well as the use of Greek as the language of liturgy became the rule in synagogue services, except in Babylon and the eastern provinces. The Greek literature produced by the Greek-speaking diaspora was very rich and diversified; unfortunately, many of these writings are lost or preserved only in fragments.

Alongside the use of the Greek language in the Bible, liturgy, preaching, and writing, Hellenistic concepts and ideas pervaded Jewish thinking and brought fundamental changes in the tradition of Israel's literary inheritance. Theological statements now became "philosophy." The Bible was understood as a writing containing deep philosophical and religious insights and was interpreted allegorically well before the time of Philo of Alexandria, just as the writings of Homer in the pagan Greek tradition. The story of the creation was seen as a cosmogony; religious rites like circumcision and the Sabbath, though usually still observed literally, were understood as symbols and reinterpreted spiritually. Traditional prayers used Stoic formulations in their translated Greek form. Genres of Greek literature were adopted for new literary productions, which were sometimes published under the pseudonym of a famous Greek author from the Classical period (§5.3d, e). In its missionary activities in the Greek-speaking world, Christianity was able to take its starting point from the Hellenization of Israel's scriptures and traditions.

Jewish and Samaritan diaspora communities also adopted Greek forms in their external appearance; they were organized as "associations." As in the case of other ethnic or religious émigré groups, these were either associations of resident aliens, who had received certain privileges pertaining to incorporation and the practice of their trade or profession, or cultic associations, like those organized by adherents of other national cults. Officers of these communities were elected by the members and their titles were borrowed from the Greek associations. Several of these offices were held by women, including including that of "president of the synagogue." Legal or business contracts were made according to Greek or Roman law, and relevant documents were always written in Greek. The hierarchical structures of authority, typical for the Jerusalem temple and its theocratic concepts, were replaced by the democratic procedures of Greek associations: decisions were made by the assembly of all voting members or by an elected council.

For Israelites living in the diaspora, there was no institutionalized super-regional authority. Insofar as Jerusalem or Samaria possessed any authority in the diaspora, it was ideal and not institutional. The fact that Jewish diaspora communities sent a temple tax to Jerusalem—we do not know whether a similar custom existed for the Samaritans—cannot be construed as evidence for a juridical authority of Jerusalem. (The attempt of the rabbis of Yavneh after 70 CE, to establish such a universal jurisdiction of the *Beth Din*—even if this did not yet become a fact during the early rabbinic period—cannot be read back into the situation before the Jewish War.) The temple tax was rather a symbol of a religious relationship to Jerusalem as the center of Israel's history of salvation. At no time did the officials of the temple have any juridical or police power over Jews living outside of the political boundaries of the Jewish state. Locally, each diaspora community had the right to decide disputes and quarrels among its members before its own court of arbitration—a right that other religious associations also exercised (cf. the constitution of the Bacchists in Athens and 1 Corinthians 5–6). Israelites in the diaspora tried to stay clear of the political affairs of Palestine—interest in self-preservation would make this necessary—and to show obedience to whatever political authority exercised power over them. This fundamental attitude was later adopted by many Christian churches (cf. Rom 13:1ff; 1 Pet 2:13ff). Practice of Israel's religion without disturbance and interference depended upon the willingness of responsible local authorities to grant certain privileges, either silently or explicitly: the observance of the Sabbath, the right to assemble, the right to slaughter their own animals, and the privilege to send money to Jerusalem. Such privileges were usually granted by the cities or by the kings and later by the Roman authorities. Only in the Roman period did the Jews try to be excused from military service in order to observe the Sabbath; in the Hellenistic period, people from Israel were frequently employed in the military and also settled in military colonies.

Members of the diaspora communities only rarely had the right of full citizenship, and they were never officially exempted from participation in the public cults of the city or state. The idea that Judaism was a *religio licita,* an officially licensed religion, is a modern construction meant to draw a comparison with unprivileged early Christianity; this concept did not exist in antiquity, either in the Hellenistic or Roman period. On the one hand, all people could practice the religion of their tradition or choice; the means of achieving recognition of a religious cult were open to everyone, whether in the form of a religious association, or in the form of a cult that was accepted among the civic cults and supervised accordingly. On the other hand, no one could possibly receive permission to scorn the deities of the city or the gods of the Roman people. It is no accident that no document is preserved that grants such a right; the claims of Jewish authors in this respect are purely apologetic. In actual practice, it was simply ignored when Jews (or Christians) failed to show up at official religious celebrations. Such nonobservance was noticed only when there were other reasons for a rise in anti-Jewish feelings among the residents of the city.

Any citizen had to acknowledge the public gods of his or her city, and there were obvious problems for anyone exercising the full rights of citizenship in remaining faithful to exclusive monotheism. In all Greek cities, however, a considerable proportion of the resident population did not possess the rights of citizenship anyway, but could nevertheless play an important part in the cities' economic and cultural life. Among the many occupations that were open to noncitizens, military service was not unknown to Jews. Residents of military colonies could own some land and work as farmers during times of peace. Others were merchants or bankers. Jewish craftsmen are rarely mentioned; perhaps established associations of craftsmen often defended their privileged membership against foreigners. Paul and his Jewish colleagues Aquila and Priscilla, however, were leather workers. Assimilated Jews are known to have held high positions in the public service. In the Roman period, Tiberius Alexander, a nephew of the Jewish philosopher Philo, was governor of Palestine for several years and later prefect of Egypt.

Despite its considerable degree of assimilation and its generally positive attitude towards the political authorities, the Jewish diaspora was repeatedly subjected to anti-Jewish actions and persecutions which found literary expression as early as the Hellenistic period. This anti-Judaism originated in the diaspora amid the clash of different cultures and religious traditions existing side by side. It did not primarily arise as a conflict between the religion of Israel and the dominant Greek culture. More significant were the tensions felt in competing with several older cultural traditions within the Hellenization process. This is already indicated in the oldest testimony of anti-Judaism, the writing of the Egyptian priest Manetho from the 3d century BCE, a work still read and known three-hundred years later, when the Jewish historian Josephus quoted from Manetho's writing and refuted it (*Contra Apionem* 1.227ff). Manetho viewed the tradition about Israel in Egypt and about the Exodus from a pro-Egyptian angle; in his writing there is no end to slander of the Israelites as lepers and barbaric desecrators of cultural and religious values. He does this, however, in a writing addressed to the Greeks, in an attempt to commend the Egyptian culture and religion with all its wisdom, piety, and justice, by appealing to ancient records. Jewish and Samaritan apologists soon began to respond in kind, and later the Christian apologists did not hesitate to compete with their Jewish counterparts, using the same methods and the same appeal to the antiquity of their own "superior tradition" and truths.

This competition of different cultures was only the framework of the rise of anti-Judaism. The immediate occasions were different in each instance and cannot be explained by one common factor. Political and economic aspects seem to have played a role alongside religious differences. Anti-Jewish polemic indicates what was offensive: strange rites such as circumcision and the observance of the Sabbath, or the Jewish refusal to worship other gods. The lack of a cult statue in the Temple of Jerusalem gave rise to the accusation of atheism and to the malicious calumny that the head of an ass was worshiped there.

The Jews insisted upon their special status and were eager to gain privileges that permitted the practice of their religion. At the same time, they wanted to be recognized members of the political communities in which they lived, but without the obligation to honor the gods of the local city or country. In such a situation an already existing anti-Judaism was likely intensified through the Hasmonean expulsion and forced Judaization of the populations of the Greek cities in Palestine. Such actions violated the ethnic and religious pluralism that was an essential foundation of the Greek city and the Hellenistic and Roman imperial world. Jews living outside of Palestine wanted to take advantage of this pluralism, while their own religious loyalty limited their participation in the life of these cities (temples, gymnasia, and public religious festivals) and their religious beliefs seemed to question the fundamental right of a pluralistic society. Therefore the situation of Israelites living in the diaspora necessarily remained precarious; the underlying conflict rendered a real solution impossible. The Hellenistic kings, and later the Roman emperors, had to intervene repeatedly to create a modus vivendi that many cities with large Jewish communities were either unwilling or unable to establish themselves.

2. DIVERSITY IN THE RELIGION OF ISRAEL

(a) The Judaic Temple, Law, and Priests (Sadducees)

The final redaction of the Pentateuch, the Five Books of Moses, was completed in the decades immediately preceding the Hellenistic conquest, incorporating the law introduced by Ezra a century earlier. The Samaritans, whose rituals and obeservances were the same as those of Jerusalem, also accepted the Pentateuch. However, we possess very little direct information about

Bibliography to §5.2: Surveys

Salo Wittmeyer Baron, *A Social and Religious History of the Jews,* vols. 1–2 (2d ed.; New York and London: Columbia University Press, 1952).

Johann Maier, *Geschichte der jüdischen Religion von der Zeit Alexanders des Großen bis zur Aufklärung* (GLB; Berlin: De Gruyter, 1972).

Bibliography to §5.2: Special Studies

Robert A. Kraft and George W. E. Nickelsburg, eds., *Early Judaism and Its Modern Interpreters* (The Bible and Its Modern Interpreters 2; Philadelphia: Fortress and Atlanta, GA: Scholars Press, 1986).

Morton Smith, *Palestinian Parties and Politics* (New York: Columbia University Press, 1971).

Marcel Simon, *Jewish Sects at the Time of Jesus* (Philadelphia: Fortress, 1967).

Samaritan cult. The following discussion is limited to Jerusalem and the area of its authority.

The rebuilding of the temple at the end of the 5th century BCE had instituted its cult as the center of the official religion; to the extent that the law involved ritual it was closely associated with the temple cult. All prescriptions of the law, cultic and otherwise, would be administered by the priests. The ultimate political authority was vested in the Persian administration, and the Persians supervised reforms in the legal and cultic administration. The case of the reforms of Ezra and Nehemiah, who functioned as Persian officials, is the best-known example. During the domination of Jerusalem by the Ptolemies in the 3d century and by the Seleucids in the early 2d century BCE, the ruling high priest was subject to the authority of the king and had to do his bidding. But within the jurisdiction of the temple state, there was no higher political authority than the temple and its priestly hierarchy.

Jerusalem and Judea were first of all a community ruled by priestly interests. The enforcement of laws of cultic purity was identical with maintaining social norms; one example is the prohibition of marriage with residents of the country who were not members of the Judaic temple community. To what degree this meant the exclusion of other Israelites such as the Samaritans is unclear. There were intermarriages between the high priests of Jerusalem and the family of the Sanballats in Samaria during the Persian period. In the early Hellenistic period, the relationships between Jerusalem and the family of the Tobiads, who ruled the country east of the Jordan, were very close.

The families from which the high priest was chosen constituted the aristocracy of the country; they were at the same time the wealthiest families, while the lower-ranking priests had only a small share of power and money. The high priests of the early Hellenistic period, though preservers of the tradition, were quite open to Hellenistic influences. The high degree of Hellenization of the Zadokite family of the Oniads was one of the factors that led to the Maccabean revolt. Those priests, however, who favored the revolt and later became supporters of the Hasmoneans, show a different theological orientation: after the disaster of the reformers' party, no one would have dared even to think about a Hellenization of the temple cult in Jerusalem.

While every Hasmonean ruler occupied the office of high priest, the name "Sadducees" appears as a designation of the priestly families who supported them and provided the high priest during the Herodian and Roman periods. The name "Sadducees" is most likely identical with "Zadokites" and thus reveals their claim to be the legitimate successors of Zadok. Ezekiel and Ezra had demanded that the descendants of Zadok, the high priest of David, should always provide the high priest (cf. Ezra 7:2; Ezek 40:45f; 43:19 etc.). The legitimacy of this claim was questioned by those who had fled to Qumran under their Zadokite

Bibliography to §5.2a

Menahem Haran, *Temples and Temple Service in Ancient Israel* (Oxford: Clarendon, 1978).
Th. A. Busink, *Der Tempel von Jerusalem von Salomo bis Herodes* (2 vols.; Leiden: Brill, 1970–1980).

leader, the "Teacher of Righteousness," protesting the illegitimate occupation of the office of high priest by the Hasmonean Simon, a descendant of a mere country priest.

In any case, these Sadducees appear as the ones wanting to guarantee the exact fulfillment of the temple and cult legislation that was codified in the written law. It was their duty to interpret the law, and they insisted that only the literal application of the law was proper. The Prophets and the Hagiographa (the "Writings") were not rejected, but neither were they recognized by this group as authoritative. The Sadducees are also depicted as rejecting the oral tradition and refusing to accept any theological ideas that could not be documented in the written law (Josephus *Ant.* 13.297 etc.). This picture fits with their appearance in the New Testament as opponents of the Pharisaic teaching of the future resurrection of the dead (Mark 12:18ff; confirmed by Josephus in *Ant.* 18.16). Hence rewards and punishments are explained only with regard to life on earth. They are the immediate result of human actions, and there is no such thing as fate (*Ant.* 13.173). This is in keeping with the statement in the Acts of the Apostles that the Sadducees denied the existence of angels and spirits (Acts 23:8).

What is preserved in these meager reports about the Sadducees—only in negative judgments from their opponents—leads to the conclusion that these priestly circles resisted without compromise any renewal born out of the spirit of Hellenism, although they had been assimilated to the culture of Hellenism in their personal style of life. Successful in their determination to exclude any reformist experiments from the established cult and as the guardians of the law of Moses, they maintained the traditional integrity of a reputable temple of the Hellenistic and Roman world. The Sadducees were also able to preserve their leading political position until the fall of Jerusalem in the Roman-Jewish War. They were scarcely aware of the fact, however, that the religious development of the Jews in Palestine as well as in the diaspora had long since passed them by and had gone in directions that were determined by the sort of foreign influences that they so meticulously tried to exclude.

(b) Apocalypticism

The apocalyptic movement became the single most important factor in the religious development of Israel in the Hellenistic period, and it was also to play a decisive role in the formation of Christianity. Apocalypticism inspired the Maccabean revolt, initiated and maintained the community of the Essenes, fueled the Roman-Jewish War and later the Bar Kokhba revolution; but it also mediated the

Bibliography to §5.2b: Introduction and Surveys

H. H. Rowley, *The Relevance of Apocalyptic: A Study of Jewish and Christian Apocalypses from Daniel to Revelation* (3d ed.; New York: Association, 1963). Together with Volz's book, a classic treament of this topic.

Paul Volz, *Die Eschatologie der jüdischen Gemeinde im neutestamentlichen Zeitalter* (2d ed.; Tübingen: Mohr/Siebeck, 1934; reprint: Hildesheim: Olms, 1966).

Paul D. Hanson, *The Dawn of Apocalyptic: The Historical and Sociological Roots of Jewish*

heritage of Israel and its prophetic tradition to John the Baptist and Jesus and their followers, and provided the essential bridge between the Old and the New Testaments. And apocalypticism remained an essential factor in movements of protest, renewal, and liberation in later forms of both Judaism and Christianity. The beginnings of apocalyptic thought predate the Hellenistic period: its origins are closely related to a fundamental change in the theological thought of Israel, which took place during the time of the exile. The fall of the kingdom of Judah and the destruction of Jerusalem in the early 6th century BCE raised fundamental doubts about the concept of historical theodicy. To be sure, the Deuteronomistic history, written during the time of the exile, did not reject the concept of theodicy in history: God is justified by historical events; it was always the guilt of Israel that led to repeated setbacks and to the final catastrophe of the nation; if Israel would only repent, God would provide new historical opportunities. However, while the author(s) of this historical work, mostly concerned with explaining the past, suggested a renewal of a history of salvation, there were others who refused to conceive of God's actions solely within the limited horizons of the nation's historical experience. History itself had become a conundrum. The Book of Job (which may be dated as early as the 6th century BCE) envisaged the revelation of God's power completely outside of the realm of history and politics. Like the nature philosophers in Ionia of this time, Job seeks to find the appearance of God not in history, but in the powers of creation and nature and in the triumph of cosmic order over chaos. Human beings are nothing compared to the power of God, who accomplished the miracle of creation and commands Behemoth and Leviathan as well as the storm and the weather.

At the same time, the prophecy of Israel turned its back upon an immanent and historical view of the future. To be sure, the prophet known as Deutero-Isaiah was still able to point to the Persian king Kyrus, that is, to an identifiable person,

Apocalyptic (rev. ed.; Philadelphia: Fortress, 1979). Deals especially with the beginnings of apocalyptic in the Exilic and post-Exilic periods.

John J. Collins, *The Apocalyptic Imagination: An Introduction to the Jewish Matrix of Christianity* (New York: Crossroad, 1984; reprint 1987).

Johann Michael Schmidt, *Die jüdische Apokalyptik: Die Geschichte ihrer Erforschung von den Anfängen bis zu den Textfunden von Qumran* (2d ed.; NeukirchenVluyn: Neukirchener Verlag, 1976).

Bibliography to §5.2b: Special Studies

Frank Moore Cross, "New Directions in the Study of Apocalyptic," *JTC* 6 (1969) 157–65

David Noel Freedman, "The Flowering of Apocalyptic," *JTC* 6 (1969) 166–74.

Hans Dieter Betz, "On the Problem of the Religio-Historical Understanding of Apocalypticism," *JTC* 6 (1969) 134–56.

Dieter Georgi, "Who is the True Prophet?" in *Christians among Jews and Gentiles: Essays in Honor of Krister Stendahl* (ed. George MacRae et. al.; Philadelphia: Fortress, 1986) 100–26.

John J. Collins, ed., *Apocalypse: The Morphology of a Genre* (Semeia 14; Missoula, MT: Scholars Press, 1979).

David Hellholm, ed., *Apocalypticism in the Mediterranean World and the Near East: Proceedings of the International Colloquium on Apocalypticism, Uppsala, August 12–17, 1979* (2d ed.; Tübingen: Mohr/Siebeck, 1989).

as the bringer of salvation appointed by God; but even here the dimensions of thought have been transformed. The Servant of God is not a representative of the people, enduring sufferings because of the guilt incurred in past history, but he is the new Moses who suffers on behalf of a new order of the world, an order that can only be described by mythological allusions. Ezekiel, whose book would become the most important inspiration for apocalyptic prophecy, depicts the new temple in mythological and cosmological dimension. Finally, the so-called apocalypses of Isaiah (24–27) and Zechariah (9–14), and the book of Trito-Isaiah, all written in the 5th or 4th century BCE, present a mythological view of the future in the form of apocalyptic theology.

The history-of-religions framework for this discovery of mythic traditions is complex. Old Canaanite myths as well as influences from the east (Babylonian and perhaps Iranian mythology) played a role. The fundamental change in theological thought made it possible to assimilate these myths and open the way for a theological reorientation that determined Israelite thought during the Hellenistic period. The most important features of apocalypticism can be characterized as follows:

(1) The concepts of chaos and creation are dominated by elements stemming from Near-Eastern mythology. Creation is understood as the result of a primordial battle against chaotic powers; Greek mythologies reveal a similar understanding of creation.

(2) Like the primordial past, also the future is viewed as a battle against chaos that will lead to a cosmic reconstitution of creation. Renewal is not expected to result from historical events, but from a dramatic and catastrophic revolution to take place in heaven as well as on earth. Astrological speculations are increasingly associated with the concept of eschatological catastrophe.

(3) The view of the cosmic and human spheres is dominated by a fundamental dualism: God and Satan, heavenly hosts of divine and satanic angels; on earth the elect of God and the men of Belial; good and evil spirits in the human heart.

(4) The view of history and especially of the present time is pessimistic. The world is no longer seen as the realm of God's rule but is under the domination of evil powers. In the ancient version of the myth of the coming of the sons of God to the daughters of men, as it appears in Genesis 6, the story is historically domesticated: it describes the increase of evil before the time of the flood so that the subsequent destruction was justified as punishment. But in apocalyptic thought this myth becomes a symbol of the rule of evil powers throughout history and in the present time.

(5) The nation and the elect people are no longer identical. Only the elect in Israel who observe the divine commandments are destined to have a share in the future bliss. Those in Israel who are faithless and disobedient will receive their due punishment.

(6) The expected turn of the events can be seen as initiated by a messianic figure, such as the anointed priest, the anointed king, or the eschatological prophet. But this messianic figure can also appear in a democratized form: the Servant of God represents the elect people of Israel as an entirety. The tasks originally attached to the office of the prophet are transferred to Israel as a

corporate figure. The "Son of man" in Daniel is such a corporate figure, representing Israel, who will become judge of the world.

(7) In comparison with God, human beings are not seen as less powerful, but as fundamentally defective: they are bound to a sinful physical body and are subject to the vicissitudes of history. Salvation cannot result from the fulfillment of human aspirations but only from the ultimate dissolution of the bonds of human life. Nevertheless, apocalyptic concepts can also appear in connection with active revolutionary movements.

(8) Beliefs in individual resurrection or immortality of the soul become widespread, as well as the closely related expectation of hell and eternal punishment, which are taken over from the Greek world (§4.2d).

(9) The theology of history is replaced by "wisdom." Knowledge of one's own situation is derived not from the political experiences of the nation's history but from insight into the human situation. Knowledge of right personal conduct in a world that is dominated by evil can be gained only from an understanding of the larger cosmic realities. "Philosophy" and "gnosis" are therefore the consistent ingredients of apocalyptic thought. Both make their appearance in Israel in the late Hellenistic and early Roman periods (see also §5.3e; 6.5f).

Very little is known about the bearers of apocalyptic theology. The writings from the Persian period, in which such ideas appear for the first time (Ezekiel, Deutero- and Trito-Isaiah, Isaiah 24–27, and Zechariah 9–14) claim to continue the prophetic office. These books were part of the literary tradition of all Israelites, whether they lived in Babylon, Jerusalem, or Alexandria. The Book of Ezekiel had a considerable influence on the reorganization of the temple cult after the exile. At this time also priestly circles accepted apocalyptic concepts that were later rejected by the Sadducees. Indeed the founders of the sect of Qumran were priests. If there were still prophetic circles during the Hellenistic era, we know no names and nothing about their institutional structures, apocalyptic books were published as a rule under the pseudonym of an ancient figure such as Enoch or Daniel. Later prophets, like John the Baptist and Jesus, do not claim to belong to any particular school of prophets.

The Hasidim, who formed the backbone of the Maccabean revolt, did not spring into existence simply on the occasion of the attempted Hellenization of the temple cult, but must have had a previous history. If they were not a firmly structured group, they were certainly connected with schools of priests and scribes, who were concerned not only with the copying of older prophetic books but also produced new apocalyptic literature. Parts of the Book of Enoch and the Temple Scroll may have been written before the Maccabean revolt, while the Book of Daniel, written during the revolt, represents the hopes and experiences of the revolutionaries. Its author does not foresee the establishment of the national state, subsequently realized by the Hasmoneans, but expects that God will usher in a new world, in which the chosen people will become rulers of nations. What was claimed as the fulfillment of hope in the new political establishment fell far short of the vision of the seer. If the movement of the Hasidim was to survive, it had to be reconstituted in opposition to the official temple cult, that is, as a sect. Henceforth apocalyptic concepts were kept alive only in sectarian movements: the Essenes, the Pharisees, and the Christians, and in a more radical form in Gnosticism, in which the rejection of history became a metaphysical principle.

(c) The Essenes

The sect of the Essenes has long been known through the reports of Philo (*Quod omn. prob. lib.* 75–91), Josephus (*Bell.* 2.119–61, etc.), and Hippolytos (*Refutatio* 9.18–28) as well as through occasional remarks in Pliny and Dio Chrysostom. The discovery of the manuscripts from the Dead Sea, and the excavation of the Essenic settlement at Khirbet Qumran during recent decades, opened a better understanding of that ancient information. No question, the sect of Qumran was identical with the Essenes mentioned in the ancient reports. Because of the rich finds of original documents, the Essenes are now better known than any other of Israel's sects or parties from that period. Publication of the still unpublished portions of the Qumran library may bring some new insights; but it is unlikely that they will fundamentally alter the knowledge gained from the texts that have been published during the last forty years.

The Essenes developed out of the circles of the Hasidim, whose protest against the Hellenization of the cult in Jerusalem led to the Maccabean insurrection (§5.1c). While they may have supported the insurrection out of protest against the appointment of a non-Zadokite high priest (Menelaos), their adherence to the

Bibliography to §5.2c: Texts

Geza Vermes, ed., *The Dead Sea Scrolls in English* (3d ed.; Sheffield: JSOT Press, 1987).
James H. Charlesworth with Frank M. Cross et al. (eds.), *The Dead Sea Scrolls: Hebrew, Aramaic, and Greek Texts with English Translations* (Tübingen: Mohr/Sïebeck, 1994).
Eduard Lohse, *Die Texte aus Qumran, hebräisch und deutsch* (2d ed.; München: Kösel, 1971).
Geza Vermes and M. D. Goodman, eds., *The Essenes: According to the Classical Sources* (Oxford Centre Textbooks 1; Sheffield: JSOT Press, 1989).
Alfred Adam and Christoph Burchard, eds., *Antike Berichte über die Essener* (KlT 182; Berlin: De Gruyter, 1972).

Bibliography to §5.2c: General Orientation and Bibliography

Joseph A. Fitzmyer, *The Dead Sea Scrolls: Major Publications and Tools for Study* (rev. ed.; SBLSBS 20: Atlanta, GA: Scholars Press, 1990).

Bibliography to §5.2c: Studies:

Frank Moore Cross, *The Ancient Library of Qumran and Modern Biblical Studies* (rev. ed.; Garden City, NY: Doubleday, 1961; reprint Grand Rapids: Baker Book House, 1980).
Idem, "The Historical Context of the Scrolls," in Hershel Shanks, ed., *Understanding the Dead Sea Scrolls* (New York: Random House, 1992) 20-32.
Geza Vermes, *The Dead Sea Scrolls: Qumran in Perspective* (rev. ed.; Philadelphia: Fortress, 1981).
Helmer Ringgren, *The Faith of Qumran* (Philadelphia: Fortress, 1963).
Hartmut Stegemann, *Die Essener, Qumran, Johannes der Täufer und Jesus: Ein Sachbuch* (Freiburg: Herder, 1994).
Bertil Gärtner, *The Temple and the Community in Qumran and the New Testament* (SNTSMS 1; Cambridge: Cambridge University Press, 1965).
Roland de Vaux, *Archaeology and the Dead Sea Scrolls* (New York: Oxford University Press, 1973).
Doron Mendels, "Hellenistic Utopia and the Essenes," *HTR* 72 (1979) 207–22.
Morton Smith, "Helios in Palestine," *Eretz-Israel* 16 (1982) 199–214.

Zadokites' claim on the office of the high priest later led to their break with the rulers in Jerusalem, when the Hasmonean Simon usurped the high-priestly office for himself and for his descendants (140 BCE; see §5.1d). What the texts of Qumran say about the "Wicked Priest" is best understood as referring to Simon and less probably to Jonathan. It is apparently Simon who is accused (especially in the *Habakkuk Commentary*) of usurping authority through violence and wickedness, of persecuting the "Righteous Teacher" who had founded the sect, of amassing riches for himself through unlawful acts, and of seducing the people into basing the commonwealth on blood and lies. Even Simon's end, his assassination during a drinking bout, is mentioned with a certain degree of satisfaction.

A building complex designed for the communal habitation of a number of persons has been excavated at the northwest corner of the Dead Sea in the immediate neighborhood of the caves in which the Dead Sea Scrolls were discovered. It was erected by the Essenes as their exile "in the desert" on the site of an older but long-since ruined Israelite fortress. According to archaeological finds, the time of the first Essenic building at this site must be dated shortly after the middle of the 2d century BCE. The establishment existed for more than two centuries. The buildings were damaged by an earthquake in 31 BCE and only repaired several decades later. The settlement was finally destroyed by the Romans during the Jewish War (68 CE). It comprised a central building 37.5 meters square with common rooms (one of these has been interpreted as a "scriptorium"), including a large banquet and assembly hall (4.5 by 22 meters). Near the main building and in the immediate surroundings were a number of cisterns with channels and reservoirs that could be used for irrigation, and that were large enough to provide several hundred people with sufficient water during the dry season. Near the main building, remnants of several other structures were found: agricultural buildings, storehouses, workshops, two mills, and one large and two smaller cemeteries with about twelve hundred graves and, oddly, carefully buried bones of animals. The manuscripts found in the nearby caves constituted the sect's library, which was hidden in the caves at the outbreak of the Roman-Jewish War.

The Essenic community understood itself as the true people of God, the renewed covenant of the last days. The establishment at the Dead Sea was designed to make it possible for the members of the community to conduct their lives according to this eschatological concept. Preservation of the cultic purity of the community was the central concern. The authority for this was the interpretation of the law, for which the community appealed to its founder, the Righteous Teacher. As a priest he possessed a legitimate authority to interpret the law.

New members of the community were required to pledge to observe everything that had been revealed to the Zadokites, the priests. (After the death of the Righteous Teacher the leadership of the community remained in the hands of the priests.) Cultic purity involved observance of the ritual commands of the law, featuring some Essenic peculiarities; among these the introduction of a solar calendar, arranged in such a way that the major festivals would never fall on a Sabbath. Of equal rank was the promise of absolute truthfulness and sincerity in one's moral conduct. All regulations and obligations were compiled in the

Manual of Discipline (1QS). This writing concerns the full members of the sect, celibate men who lived permanently at Qumran. Another document, which also contains rules for the community, the *Damascus Document* (CD; it was previously known through medieval manuscripts), seems to have been written for members of the sect who stayed in the world at large, were married, and lived like ordinary citizens.

The purity regulations belong to the basic eschatological orientation of the Essenes. Since they understood themselves as the elect, destined to play a decisive role in the battles of the end time, they had to live in constant preparedness for the war of the sons of light against the sons of darkness. Thus ritual purity, including abstinence from sexual intercourse, is part of the biblical ideology of holy war. In one of the writings from Qumran, the *War Scroll* (1QM), the formation of the last decisive eschatological battle is described in detail.

The eschatological orientation of the community appears in all aspects of its life. The Essenes not only anticipate the promised future of the true people of God, they are already these elect people and God's temple. Every new member had to assign his possessions to the community. Personal poverty and communal living represent the messianic age, which knows no difference between rich and poor. The liturgy of the common meals, regularly celebrated every day, mirrors the messianic banquet. While holy war ideology is clearly evident, there are also strong correspondences with Hellenistic utopian concepts. Retreat to a secluded place, common meals of simple food, community of goods, sharing all labor, strict moral obligations and penance for offenders, rejection of temple worship, and finally the preference for a solar over a lunar calendar are also ingredients of Iamboulos' utopian Hellenistic romance *Commonwealth of the Sun* (§3.4e).

The group's scriptural interpretation is not allegorical but eschatological; examples are preserved in the commentaries from Qumran (cf. the *Commentary on Habakkuk*, 1QHab, and the *Commentary on Nahum*, 4QNah): each scriptural passage relates to a particular event in the recent past, present, or future. The theology of the community reflects the apocalyptic concepts of the Hellenistic period, especially those of the Hasidim; Daniel is one of the books copied several times by the Essenes. The eschatological schemata are strictly dualistic: good and evil powers struggle to rule both the earthly and the heavenly realm. Light and darkness, God and Belial, the spirit of truth and the spirit of falsehood confront each other on earth as well as in the heavens. Irreconcilable enmity exists between the two; their opposition, described in mythological terms, is grounded in the primordial past. A strict determinism is closely linked with these dualistic views. The generations of the sons of light and the sons of darkness have been predetermined by God. When one enters the community, one is not converted from darkness to light; rather one is instructed about one's destiny, namely, that one already belongs to the sons of light on the basis of one's origin. This insight belongs to the secret knowledge (the "mysteries") of the wise men, in which all members of the community are instructed.

The messianic concepts are especially striking. The community expects several "messianic" ("anointed," i.e., divinely authorized) figures: the eschatological prophet, the messianic king from the house of David, and the messianic priest from the house of Aaron. The Righteous Teacher, founder of the community, is not found among the messianic figures. (The texts from Qumran do not contain any parallel to the Christian expectation of the second coming of Jesus.) Among the several messianic figures, the highest rank belongs to the anointed priest, who takes precedence over the anointed king. The center of the apocalyptic expectation is occupied not by a messianic figure but by the elect people.

Closely associated with this special insight into the future is knowledge of angels, spirits, and demons; their activity relates to the designs and deeds of human beings, those of the elect as well as those of the wicked. The divine and evil spirits and angels are not mediators between God and the human world, but powers at work in the heavenly and earthly spheres, whose actions are analogous to the eschatological events taking place in the human realm. Insofar as the term "spirit" appears in such contexts, it is not always possible to determine whether it refers to the thought of God, to an angelic figure, or to the human mind. The angels are divided into two hostile armies. On one side stand the hosts of angels led by the "prince of light" or by the "spirit of truth." Individual angels are often named, such as Michael, and it is assumed that the angelic army is hierarchically structured. Their tasks include heavenly worship as well as battle against the angels of darkness. The community of the elect participates in both of these activities; it knows both the order of battle and the angelic liturgy. Opposed to these angels is the "angel of darkness" (generally called Belial, but also the "angel of enmity" = Hebrew *mastema*) and his hosts. Belial is both the enemy of God and the tempter of the human race. His angels or spirits (the fallen angels of Genesis 6) are called the "spirits of wickedness" or the "spirits of error." They cause people to sin, and they inspire evil actions among those who belong to the realm of Belial. Sometimes Belial and his angels appear as agents of punishment.

In their angelology and demonology, the texts from Qumran remain peculiarly suspended between mythology and psychology. In keeping with the eschatological consciousness of the community, the angels are mythological cosmic powers locked in battle with each other. But they also appear in statements of individualized piety, where they are seen as helpful or seductive powers, or inclinations of the human heart. While the Essenes strove to preserve the purity of their community, the eschatological people of God, they also emphasized problems of individual piety as they arose in the context of their religious experience. The sect's Book of Hymns (*Hodayot,* 1QH) speaks about the transitoriness of human life, and about human dependence upon God's mercy. The hymns know that the human heart is but stone until God "engraves upon it events of eternity." They emphasize confidence in God's everlasting faithfulness to the pious people, which might be understood as an expression of belief in immortality. At any rate, Josephus ascribes this belief to the Essenes.

The Essenes disappeared from history after the destruction of Qumran by the Romans. The Pharisaic school, which led in rebuilding the Jewish community after the destruction of Jerusalem, did not share their special teachings. Yet Pharisaic Judaism, and Christianity to an even greater extent, carried on many elements of the apocalyptic expectations that the Essenes, in the tradition of the Hasidim, had cultivated and developed.

(d) The Pharisees

The interpretation of the word "Pharisees" is not certain. Not a self-designation of the group, but a term first used by their opponents, it may mean "those who are separated" or "separatists." We know little of their origin and development during the pre-Christian period. Since no single surviving writing can be assigned to the Pharisees with certainty (though some scholars see the *Psalms of Solomon* as Pharisaic), we are totally dependent on sources from the last decades of the 1st century CE: the gospels of the New Testament, together with the Book of Acts and the apostle Paul, who claims to have been a Pharisee himself; the reports of the Jewish historian Josephus; and the information that is preserved in the Rabbinic tradition, especially in the Mishnah. All three groups of sources are strongly biased, though in different ways.

The gospels preserve traditions that originated with Jesus' followers, whose attitudes towards the Pharisees were by no means friendly; what the author of Acts knows is historically questionable. This leaves Paul as the only reliable though not impartial witness in the New Testament. Josephus sought to demonstrate that the Pharisaic movement, as the predecessor of the reorganization of Judaism after the Jewish War, had always possessed the support of the people, and had no part in the radical political movements that had led to the insurrection against Rome. The Rabbinic traditions, fixed in written form much later, contain many Pharisaic traditions. The rabbis were certainly the heirs of the Pharisees. But the way in which the "house of Hillel" and the "house of Shammai" are opposed to each other in Rabbinic debates makes it hard to imagine that these two "houses" sprang from the same movement.

That the Pharisees were in some way descendants of the Hasidim, the primary supporters of the Maccabean revolt, seems likely. But it is difficult to establish a secure link between that movement of the 2d century BCE and the Pharisees of the 1st century CE. Josephus mentions the Pharisees as a political party at the time of John Hyrkanos (who at first supported them, *Ant.* 13.288ff.), Alexander Janneus (who persecuted them, *Bell.* 1.113; *Ant.* 13.403ff.), and his widow Alexandra (during whose time they are said to have been most influential, *Bell.* 1.107–15; *Ant.* 13.399–418; see §5.1d). If these pieces of information were reliable, the Pharisees would have been a group that did not, like the Essenes, reject the Hasmonean rulers as a matter of principle, though their involvement in the politics of the Hasmonean period seems to have been subject to changing fortunes. Under

Bibliography to §5.2d

Jacob Neusner, *From Politics to Piety: The Emergence of Pharisaic Judaism* (Englewood Cliffs, NJ: Prentice Hall, 1973).
Idem, *The Rabbinic Tradition About the Pharisees Before 70* (3 vols.; Leiden: Brill, 1971).
John Kampen, *The Hasideans and the Origins of Pharisaism: A Study in 1 and 2 Maccabees* (SBLSCS 24; Atlanta: Scholars Press, 1988).
Leo Baeck, *The Pharisees and Other Essays* (reprint with introduction by Krister Stendahl; New York: Schocken, 1960).
R. Travers Herford, *The Pharisees* (Boston, MA: Beacon, 1962)
Leo Baeck, *Paulus, die Pharisäer und das Neue Testament* (Frankfurt: Ner-Tanid, 1961).

Herod the Great, the Pharisees at first found a comfortable arrangement, but got into conflicts later because they were involved in court intrigues. Herod executed some of their leaders. But even if this information is trustworthy, it does not contribute much if anything to the understanding of the Pharisees of the 1st century CE.

At the time of the first Christian communities, the Pharisees appear as a group of laypeople, lawyers, scribes, and priests. Their primary purpose is to realize a religious goal, namely, the fulfillment of the law and the preservation of the "tradition of the fathers" under the conditions of a changed world. This is the picture conveyed by the New Testament gospels, the writings of the apostle Paul, and in general also the reports of Josephus (*Bell.* 2.162–64, 166; *Ant.* 13.12–17, 171f.). The Pharisees were not an exclusively Palestinian group, although two known names associated with them belong to Palestine: Gamaliel and Shammai. Two other Pharisees of the 1st century CE came from the diaspora: Hillel (ca. 50 BCE to 20 CE), who is said to have come from Babylon, and Paul, who belongs to the Greek-speaking diaspora (the information of Acts 22:3 that Paul studied in Jerusalem under Gamaliel is not trustworthy; see §9.1a). The assumption of a narrow geographical base for the Pharisaic movement stems from Josephus' attempt to present its history as a political movement in Palestine and from the repeated descriptions in the gospels of controversies between Jesus and the Pharisees in Galilee and Judea. If in fact there was at least a significant diaspora component, this would explain why the teaching of the Pharisees argued for a way of fulfilling the law that could *de facto* exist without the temple and its cult, why the movement became thoroughly Hellenized, and why it was quite open to popular religious ideas.

Assuming that the diaspora component was significant, and that both Paul and Rabbinic Judaism have preserved essential elements of the earlier period, the Pharisaic movement must reflect features that belong fully to the Hellenistic period, and indeed the situation of the Hellenist diaspora, although there is no external evidence to date the beginning of the movement. Apocalyptic concepts are clearly present, especially in the expectation of a coming new age, a final judgment, and the resurrection of the righteous. But the fulfillment of these promises is no longer tied to the achievement of particular political goals for Israel but to Israel's fulfillment of the law. The idea that the fate and future of human beings and of a nation should depend upon a moral and ritual fulfillment of a legal code is as much a Hellenistic concept as the presumption that such conduct can be taught.

Accordingly, the "school" and the traditions of interpretation handed down from teacher to student became the central religious institution of Pharisaic Judaism, analogous to the function of the school in the philosophical develop-ments of antiquity. It is also clear that this tradition of teaching, called the "traditions of the fathers" in Paul (Gal 1:14), had already existed over several generations by the time it made its appearance in the 1st century CE. Thus Josephus did not go wrong when he described the Pharisees as a philosophical sect. The establishment of the chains of tradition connected with particular teachers, however fictitious the Rabbinic construction of the succession of pairs of teachers may be, the cultivation of teacher-student relationships, the designation of the teaching as wisdom or philosophy—all this is typically Hellenistic. As the Rabbinic writings show, the terminology of the Pharisaic schools had also adopted many Greek philosophical terms. Paul must have debated with fellow Pharisees in Greek.

The so-called liberalism of Hillel, which became a hallmark of the Rabbinic interpretation of the law, is nothing but the successful teaching that the ancient law of Moses can be observed even under the changed conditions of a new time and new life situations—and observed to perfection (Phil 3:6). By no means did the Pharisees attempt to make the fulfillment of the law more difficult; on the contrary, their teaching, as well as the teaching of their successors (Rabbinic Judaism), wanted to make fulfillment possible—for the sake of the rule of God! Their method of interpretation, called *halakha* ("how one should walk"), consists of arguments and counter-arguments about the achievable fulfillment of each commandment under changed conditions. This hermeneutical method presupposes that ancient Scripture was written to be valid for a new time (see also 1 Cor 9:9–10). This is fully in keeping with the spirit of Hellenism; Stoic exegesis of Homer rests on similar presuppositions. In both cases, eccentricities and sophistries in interpretation were a natural consequence: one could not admit that the written record from the past could not be applied to the problems of conduct in the present, whether as a whole, or in detail. Jesus' antitheses as presented in the Sermon on the Mount ("You have heard that it was said to those of old . . . but I say to you," Matthew 5) contrast sharply with this hermeneutical method.

Another Hellenistic element of Pharisaism is its individualism. The separation of observance from the temple cult and from the immediate context of the cult community enabled the individual to fulfill the law even when living within a non-Jewish society. Anyone could learn to distinguish between clean and unclean. Such conduct could thus be credited to the individual who thus received a personal share in the righteousness of God, something originally promised only to Israel as a whole. The individual could therefore boast of fulfilling the law. Accordingly, the concepts of reward and punishment, as well as the expectation of resurrection and last judgment, also applied to the individual and thus paralleled the Greek concepts of immortality and judgment of the dead. A final Hellenistic feature of piety for which the Pharisees developed a Jewish analogy is mysticism. In our present state of knowledge it is difficult to determine how much later Rabbinic mysticism (*kabbala*), not to mention Gnosticism, are indebted to Pharisaic Judaism. In any case, Paul, a former Pharisee, refers obliquely to his own experience of the "celestial ascent of the soul" (2 Cor 12:1–4).

As for the organization of the Pharisees, the term "sect" is ill chosen. Neither Paul, reflecting on his past as a Pharisee, nor Rabbinic Judaism views obedience to the laws of the fathers as a sectarian enterprise. Pharisees met for common meals, but nothing is known about a special liturgy of such meals, nor did they have rites of initiation or rules for a common life. This distinguishes them from the Essenes. The Pharisees were an association informally bound by common interests; their only institutional tie was the common school house which, just like a philosophical school, provided instruction for the young men. After the catastrophe of the Roman-Jewish War, the reorganization of Judaism in the spirit and tradition of Pharisaism made the institution of the school its basis, and this remained characteristic for Rabbinic Judaism (§6.6f).

(e) Wisdom Theology

The experiential wisdom of Israel was a long-established predecessor of the wisdom theology of the Hellenistic period. Wisdom was an international phenomenon, and wisdom traditions existed in Israel just as among other people of antiquity. These traditions grew from the experience of many generations in various aspects of life. Family, occupations, social position, political activity, and also the observation of nature contributed to its wealth. Traditionally, gods, mythic figures, or legendary rulers of early times were considered to have been the originators and transmitters of wisdom—in Israel, Enoch and Solomon. Because of their connection to such figures, wisdom traditions often claimed divine revelation, whether in primordial times (Enoch) or in recorded history (Solomon). These figures were credited with extraordinary, even divine gifts.

The transmission of wisdom required firmly fixed traditions and relied upon the office of the wisdom teacher. In Israel, institutionalizing of the wisdom tradition in all likelihood goes back to the time of Solomon. An accumulated wealth of observations was arranged in lists, series, and onomastica, which survived for centuries and reappeared in later apocalyptic and gnostic texts, now in the context of cosmological speculations and eschatological timetables. The codification of the material originally took place for practical reasons, designed as instruction for officials, as professional information, and as general advice for ordinary people for dealing with the problems of individual and communal life. As in Greece, the emphasis in Israel was put on learning the proper proportion or measure.

After the collapse of Israel's social and political structures in the Babylonian exile, a completely new burden fell on wisdom thought. Until the time of the Deuteronomistic history, national calamities had been understood from the perspective of the history of salvation. The prophets interpreted the nation's misfortunes as the result of failures in the political and social order. The increasing conviction of the futility of such efforts demanded a new answer from the tradition of wisdom. Wisdom had not simply confirmed things everybody already knew. Rather, its task had always been to make the world intelligible, to make its order discernible, and to explain the mechanisms by which it was protected from the powers of chaos.

In wisdom, the rationale for cosmic order was found not in historical experi-

Bibliography to §5.2e

Gerhard von Rad, *Wisdom in Israel* (Nashville, TN: Abingdon, 1972).

Burton L. Mack, *Logos und Sophia: Untersuchungen zur Weisheitstheologie im hellenistischen Judentum* (SUNT 10; Göttingen: Vandenhoeck & Ruprecht, 1973).

Robert L. Wilken, ed., *Aspects of Wisdom in Judaism and Early Christianity* (University of Notre Dame Center for the Study of Judaism and Christianity in Antiquity 1; Notre Dame, IN: University of Notre Dame Press, 1975).

ence, but in contemplation of creation, of the phenomena of nature, and of the primordially determined and universally valid structures of human experience. Wisdom made recourse to a basis for knowledge that was beyond the contingencies of history. Human beings could find a point of orientation in wisdom even if the history of salvation did not hold what it promised. Like apocalypticism, its twin sister, wisdom invoked primordial time and creation. The beginnings of wisdom theology are therefore linked with the rise of apocalypticism. Even after their paths separated, connections continued to exist for a long time. In apocalypticism, the appeal to primordial time was related to the new experiences and expectations of an elect remnant of Israel. Wisdom theology, however, directed its message to the individual, and, by relating this to the Hellenistic view of the world, developed the ideal of the moral and religious human being, the wise person or philosopher.

But "wisdom" did not remain merely a method of gaining insight into the order of the universe. Personified Wisdom herself came to symbolize the plan of creation, and finally, as a mythical figure, became its mediator. Whether this transformation occurred through the reemergence of mythical undercurrents or through the hypostatization of an idea is ultimately unimportant. Attempts to prove that the figure of celestial Wisdom mirrors a Near-Eastern deity (e.g., Anat or Astarte) have failed because in each instance only a few features can be considered real parallels. Analogies to the late Egyptian-Hellenistic Isis are more convincing; she is more closely associated with wisdom and creation than other Near-Eastern deities. In Israel's theology, Wisdom was not created; instead she came out of God's mouth and existed before the beginning of creation. She also appears as consort (*syzygos*) of Yahweh. Since all things were created and sustained by her, she bears the features of the queen of heaven. She guarantees the order of the world and defends it against chaos.

As human beings try to find their way in the world, they must do more than pay attention to Wisdom's instruction. They must recognize themselves and learn about their destiny, as it can be discerned from the cosmic order. The divinely ordained destiny of the human being is no longer membership in an elect nation, but results from the creation of human beings according to the image of God; that is, it is ultimately based on humanity's divine essence. Wisdom addresses human beings about their destiny, which is as divine as their origin (cf. the Wisdom of Solomon and Philo; §5.3e, f). In this way wise and righteous people are fundamentally, and even metaphysically, distinguished from the unrighteous. Knowing their divine origin, the wise recognize the true meaning of the course of the world, which will lead them to final justification and vindication, despite the contempt and the persecution that they now endure.

A skeptical Israelite wisdom rejected this message of wisdom theology and instead emphasized the absurdity of the course of the world and the transitoriness of human existence. The Book of Ecclesiastes (Qohelet; §5.3e) is the clearest witness to this skeptical position. It is possible, of course, to observe the course of natural events, but no meaning can be found in the empty cycle of continuous return. And once one looks to the end of life and perceives the decline of human faculties in old age, it is absurd to assign a divine destiny to humans. According to this skepticism, it is impossible to relate the idea of God to the individual's experience. God can only be understood as the general power of the course of the world and of the universal fate of all human creatures.

The defense of wisdom theology against skepticism and its consequences for human morality was the uniting of wisdom with the law. What wisdom teaches became identical for Jews with that which the law demands. Thus fulfillment of the law became the path to fulfillment of humans' divine destiny. The teachings of wisdom include everything that the ancient legislation of Israel always intended. In this context the great figures of Israel's past gained new significance. They became prototypes and examples for life in service of wisdom. Their imperturbable adherence to their destiny, in spite of long delays in the confirmation of their faithfulness, is especially stressed, because this corresponds to the existence of the righteous individual in the present time.

The experience of the wise in the world is presented as timeless and generally valid; this is accomplished, for example, by elimination of individual names when reciting these examples from the history of Israel (see the Wisdom of Solomon). When Philo of Alexandria portrays the patriarchs of Israel as prototypes of the true philosopher, he is in continuity with the tradition of wisdom theology. Ultimately, the motifs of the divine origin of the wise and the obscurity of their true essence in the world—expressed in the myth of Wisdom coming into the world and finding no place in it—leads to Gnosticism (§6.5f).

Wisdom played a role in apocalyptic theology too, though the accents are set differently. Here wisdom comes only through revelation as a secret that visions, dreams, and raptures (celestial journeys) unveil. There is no link to philosophy in this version of wisdom, because in philosophy one presupposes that wisdom can be taught. Apocalyptic wisdom is couched in the language of mythology. Scientific wisdom lists are often translated into mythological narratives. The earthly and celestial topography therefore becomes thoroughly mythological. This is the inheritance from which the early Christian world view received its mythological features. Knowledge of the world no longer rests on experience and observation of nature, but derives from inspired visions of things in heaven and on earth that are inaccessible to human observation. The wise man is an inspired possessor of secrets, on the basis of which he reveals the future, instruct others about the past, and shows how both determine the present. A typical phenomenon of this concept of the wise man is expressed frequently in pseudepigraphy, when writings appear under the name of a wise man of ancient times, such as Enoch or Daniel.

(f) The Samaritans

Before its conquest by Alexander the Great, the province of Samaria (named for its capital city), the area of the tribes of Ephraim and Manasseh, was as much an Israelite country as were Judea and the Transjordan. The city of Samaria had

Bibliography to §5.2.f: Texts

John Bowman, ed., *Samaritan Documents Relating to their History, Religion and Life* (Pittsburgh Original Texts and Translation Series 2; Pittsburgh: Pickwick, 1977).

been founded by Omri (878/7–871/70 BCE) as the capital of the northern kingdom of Israel. Conquered by the Assyrians in 721 BCE, it became the capital of a smaller territory containing only the mountains of Ephraim and the land to the north as far as the valley of Jezreel. During the Babylonian and Persian periods, no major changes occurred in the administration of the province, which was still populated by large numbers of Israelites, though parts of the population had been deported by the Assyrians.

When the exiles of the southern kingdom first returned from Babylon, Jerusalem and Judea were subject to the governor of Samaria; Judea received the status of an independent province only under Nehemiah. During the Persian period there was undoubtedly some rivalry between the two provinces of Samaria and Judea. But there is also evidence of intermarriage between the high-priestly family in Jerusalem and the Sanballats, the ruling family in Samaria. Samaria and Judea also seem to have been united in matters of cult. The Israelites of Samaria accepted the reforms of Ezra and Nehemiah as well as the Five Books of Moses, which were assembled in the 4th century.

After Alexander's conquest, the history of Samaria began to deviate from Jerusalem's history. Unlike Judea, Samaria rebelled during Alexander's stay in Egypt. Alexander conquered the city upon his return, expelled the population, and founded a Macedonian military colony on the site of the old royal city of Israel. About two hundred leading citizens fled east, but were captured and killed in a cave above the Jordan; there the documents they carried with them were discovered in 1962. These Wadi Daliyeh Papyri give important information about governors of Samaria and also refer to the Persian kings Artaxerxes II (404–359 BCE) and Darius II (335–330 BCE). The rest of Samaria's population fled to the ancient site of Shechem, rebuilding a city that had lain waste for almost 400 years, as excavations have demonstrated.

This is when the Shechemite Samaritans constructed their own temple on nearby Mt. Gerizim. Even this would not necessarily have forced a disruption of religious communion with Jerusalem, because similar temples are known elsewhere, like the temple of the Tobiads in Transjordan and the temple of Onias IV

Bibliography to §5.2.f: Studies

A. D. Crown, ed., *The Samaritans* (Tübingen: Mohr/Siebeck, 1989). A manual for research on the Samaritans.

Frank Moore Cross, "Aspects of Samaritan and Jewish History in the Late Persian Period," *HTR* 59 (1966) 201–11.

R. J. Coggins, *Samaritans and Jews: The Origin of Samaritanism Reconsidered* (Atlanta: John Knox, 1975)

John Bowman, *The Samaritan Problem: Studies in the Relationship of Samaritanism, Judaism, and Early Christianity* (Pittsburgh Theological Monograph Series 4; Pittsburgh, PA: Pickwick, 1975).

Hans Gerhard Kippenberg, *Garizim und Synagoge: Traditionsgeschichtliche Untersuchungen zur samaritanischen Religion der aramäischen Periode* (RVV 30:; Berlin: De Gruyter, 1971).

Nathan Schur, *History of the Samaritans* (Beiträge zur Erforschung des Alten Testaments und des antiken Judentums 18; Frankfurt: Lang, 1989).

Alan David Crown, *A Bibliography of the Samaritans* (ATLABS 10; Metuchen, NJ: Scarecrow Press, 1984). Lists 2,806 books and articles on the Samaritans.

in Leontopolis. The final and irreparable breach between Jews and Samaritans was caused by a different event. In the year 128 BCE, the Hasmonean John Hyrkanos destroyed the temple on Mt. Gerizim; twenty years later he also conquered and destroyed the city of Samaria and annexed the entire province. At the same time, he subjected Samaria and the rest of his new Palestinian empire to the religious policies of Jerusalem. The Samaritans resisted his brutal methods of religious unification. Only after the conquest of Palestine by the Romans were they able to regain recognition as a distinct religious entity. The development of a Samaritan religious literature (Samaritan targums, and later also midrashim) began in the Hasmonean period.

This late-2d-century date for the Samaritan schism is confirmed by several other considerations. The Samaritan Pentateuch preserves a text that is closely related to the biblical manuscripts found at Qumran and to the Hebrew text that underlies the Septuagint, but that differs from the Babylonian text of the Pentateuch. Also the orthography of the Samaritan text is closely related to that found in Qumran: both show peculiarities of spelling that were established during the 2d century BCE. A further confirmation is provided by the Samaritan script. Its separate development does not begin until the 1st century BCE, as can be shown by comparison with the archaic Hebrew script used in the Pentateuch manuscripts from Qumran and on Hasmonean coins. Finally, essential aspects of Samaritan apocalypticism are closely related to the Maccabean phase of Jewish apocalyptic thought. The expectation of Moses' coming as the prophet of the last time, of the arrival of the *Taeb,* the "messiah" of the Samaritans who is expected to restore all things, as well as Samaritan angelology, belief in the last judgment, and in the resurrection of the dead are closely analogous to concurrent Jewish apocalyptic concepts. Since most of these concepts are preserved only in the rich medieval literature of the Samaritans, however, they are often overgrown with later elaborations, which makes it difficult to determine their time of origin with certainty.

The Samaritan religious community remained a vital representative of Israel's religion for many centuries, not only in Palestine but also elsewhere. There is early evidence for a Greek-speaking Samaritan diaspora. A Samaritan synagogue existed on the island of Delos in the late Hellenistic period. Some of the fragments of Greek "Jewish" literature preserved by Alexander Polyhistor may actually stem from Samaritan writings. As late as the 4th or 5th century CE an inscription from Thessalonike mentions Neapolis, the later name of Shechem (today Nablus), and records the Greek translation of the Aaronite blessing, with two lines written in Samaritan Hebrew script.

By the time of Jesus the Samaritans were rejected and despised by influential circles in Jerusalem. A number of hostile incidents between Jews and Samaritans occurred in Palestine during the Roman administration. But the insinuation that the Samaritans were semipagan, schismatic Israelites, deeply mired in syncretism, is certainly unjustified. Indeed there are no syncretistic elements in Samaritanism that are not found in Jewish sources too. It was not the Samaritan's fault that Herod the Great magnificently rebuilt Samaria as a Greco-Roman city, called the new foundation *Sebaste* in the emperor's honor and constructed a large temple to Augustus in pagan style. Nor were the Samaritans responsible for the Christian arch-heretic Simon Magus of Samaria. The Gospel of John shows quite well that the religious center of the Samaritans was not pagan Samaria, but Mt. Gerizim near Shechem, and that just like the Jews the Samaritans expected the coming of a messiah (John 4).

· The real cause of the Jews' rejection of the Samaritans lies in the separate development of the Samaritan cultic community. This divergence began well before the reorganization of Judaism took place under the leadership of the Pharisees. No wonder that the Samaritans appeared as schismatic and "unclean" in the eyes of those who shared the Rabbinic view of the observance of the law. On the other hand, this did not prevent early Christian missionaries from carrying their message to Samaria (Acts 8:1ff). Only some sectors of early Christianity shared the Pharisaic prejudice against the Samaritans (Matt 10:5), and Jesus himself did not accept it at all (Luke 10:33).

3. The Literature of Hellenistic Israel

(a) The Languages of Israel in Hellenistic Times

Hebrew, the language of Israel, continued as the language of religious literature even after the exile. Older books were copied and read in Hebrew, and new writings were composed in this language well into the Roman imperial period. Many of these books have come to light recently in their original Hebrew through

Bibliography to §5.3: Texts

R. H. Charles, ed., *The Apocrypha and Pseudepigrapha of the Old Testament* (2 vols.; Oxford: Clarendon, 1912).

James H. Charlesworth, ed., *The Old Testament Pseudepigrapha* (2 vols.; Garden City, NY: Doubleday, 1983–1985).

H. F. D. Sparks, ed., *The Apocryphal Old Testament* (New York: Clarendon, 1984).

Bibliography to §5.3: Studies

George W. E. Nickelsburg, *Jewish Literature between the Bible and the Mishnah* (Philadelphia: Fortress, 1981).

Michael E. Stone, ed., *Jewish Writings of the Second Temple Period: Apocrypha, Pseudepigrapha, Qumran, Sectarian Writings, Philo, Josephus* (CRINT 2.2; Philadelphia: Fortress, 1984). Each of these two works can be considered an indispensible introduction, handbook, and reference work; both are equippped with excellent bibliographies.

Leonard Rost, *Judaism Outside the Hebrew Canon: An Introduction to the Documents* (Nashville, TN: Abingdon, 1976).

Johann Maier and Josef Schreiner, *Literatur und Religion des Frühjudentums: Eine Einführung* (Würzburg: Echter, 1973).

Gerhard Delling and Malwin Maser, *Bibliographie zur jüdisch-hellenistischen und intertestamentarischen Literatur: 1900–1970* (2d. ed.: TU 106; Berlin: Akademie-Verlag, 1975).

James H. Charlesworth, *The Pseudepigrapha and Modern Research* (SBLSCS 7; Missoula, MT: Scholars Press, 1976).

Daniel Harrington, "Research on the Jewish Pseudepigrapha during the 1970s," *CBQ* 42 (1980) 147–59.

the discoveries of the Dead Sea Scrolls and other finds from Palestine. Hebrew continued to be the language of scholars and would occasionally be used as the official language, as on Hasmonean coins and in the letters of Bar Kokhba. This restricted use is continued in the Mishnaic Hebrew of Rabbinic Judaism.

However, the common language of Syria and Mesopotamia was Aramaic, which was also spoken and written in Palestine by Jews and Samaritans in their daily life. Like Hebrew, Aramaic belongs to the Northwest Semitic language family, spoken by the people who had begun to settle in northern Syria and along the Euphrates River in the latter half of the second millennium BCE. Together with Phoenician and Ugaritic, Aramaic formed a separate branch of Northwest Semitic. An official form of Aramaic had developed in the chancelleries of the Assyrian empire. This *lingua franca* was taken over by the Neo-Babylonians and the Persians. Known as "Imperial Aramaic," it was used and understood throughout the Persian empire, from the far eastern provinces to Egypt. But after the conquest of the Persian empire by Alexander, Aramaic took second place to Greek for administrative purposes, though it continued to be used as a business and everyday language, even during the Roman period.

Blending with many local dialects, Aramaic formed a number of derivative languages that were spoken in the later Christian period, and in some cases even today. The western Aramaic languages include the dialects spoken by the Israelites of Palestine, such as Galilean (which is the language of Jesus, and closely related to the Aramaic of the Palestinian Talmud and the later Targums), Samaritan, and the Christian Aramaic of the Melchites in Syria and Egypt. On the other hand, the language of the Babylonian Talmud, as well as Mandean and Syriac, which became the most important Christian literary language of the east, belong to the eastern branch of Aramaic. In Jewish writings of the Hellenistic period Aramaic was occasionally used instead of Hebrew, and a number of Jewish writings are preserved in translations that derive from an Aramaic original.

From the beginning of the Hellenistic period, however, Greek quickly gained ground in the successor states of Alexander's empire, especially as the language of administration, in the form of the "Koine" (§3.2a–c). Despite the survival of Aramaic, Greek also became more influential as a colloquial and business language, due to two different factors. The first was founding of Greek cities in the provinces of the east, including Palestine. The second was the significance of Greek as the language of the newly dominant culture; the study of Greek was the first step in the education of anyone who wanted to participate in the new ecumenical civilization.

Regular contact with Greek first came to the inhabitants of Palestine through the country's new cities. But the Israelites were also confronted with a new

Bibliography to §5.3a

Joseph A. Fitzmyer, *A Wandering Aramean: Collected Aramaic Essays* (SBLMS 25; Missoula, MT: Scholars Press, 1979) 29–56.

Matthew Black, *An Aramaic Approach to the Gospels and Acts* (3d ed.; Oxford: Clarendon, 1967).

Idem and David Diringer, "Language and Script," *Cambridge History of the Bible* 1. 1–29.

ecumenical culture, in which recognition for their ancestral faith depended on their learning to speak and write Greek. Not only in the diaspora, even in Palestine itself Jewish writings were composed in Greek, and Aramaic or Hebrew writings were translated into Greek. Nonetheless, in Palestine real mastery of Greek never reached beyond a relatively small educated segment of the population. The translation of Israel's literary heritage into Greek was taken up not only in Alexandria, but also in several other diaspora communities, as well as by those who had stayed behind in Palestine—a process with far-reaching consequences for ancient Christian developments.

(b) The Septuagint

The term "Septuagint" (LXX) designates the Greek translation of the Hebrew Bible. The word is derived from a legend about the origin of the translation of the Pentateuch, which is preserved in the *Epistle of Aristeas* (§5.3e[4]). It relates how Ptolemy II Philadelphos (284–247 BCE) invited seventy-two Jewish scholars from Jerusalem to translate Israel's book of laws into Greek for his library in Alexandria, a task that they accomplished in seventy-two days. A later version of this story says that through divine inspiration all the scholars produced precisely the same text independently of each other. Originally the story mentioned only the Pentateuch. This translation was based on the Alexandrian form of the Hebrew text, a branch of the Palestinian text of the Bible. In many places where the Septuagint differs from the Babylonian tradition of the Hebrew Bible (preserved in the Masoretic text), the differences stem from the translators' use of this Palestinian Hebrew text.

In the course of the 2d and 1st centuries BCE other books of the Hebrew Bible (the Prophets and the Writings) were also translated. The legend about the miraculous origin of the translation was extended to cover all the books included in the Greek collection of Israel's Scriptures. Several later books, originally written in Greek, such as the Wisdom of Solomon and *3 and 4 Maccabees,* were eventually added. These additions, as well as the inclusion of Hebrew-language books that failed to be accepted in the later Hebrew canon of Rabbinic Judaism

Bibliography to §5.3b: Text

Alfred Rahlfs, ed., *Septuaginta* (2 vols.; Stuttgart: Privilegierte Württembergische Bibelanstalt, 1935).

Göttingen Septuagint = *Septuaginta: Vetus Testamentum Graecum auctoritate Academiae Scientiarum Gottingensis editum.* Indispensible edition of the books of the Greek Bible with extensive critical apparatus. For the individual books, see the following sections.

Bibliography to §5.3b: Studies

Emanuel Tov, "Die griechischen Bibelübersetzungen," *ANRW* 2.20.1 (1987) 121–89.

Peter Walters (Peter Katz), *The Text of the Septuagint: Its Corruptions and Their Emendation* (ed. by D. G. Gooding; London: Cambridge University Press, 1973).

Peter Katz, "Septuagintal Studies in the Mid-Century," in W. D. Davies and David Daube, *The Background of the New Testament and Its Eschatology . . . in Honor of C. H. Dodd* (Cambridge: Cambridge University Press, 1964) 176–208.

Sidney Jellicoe, *The Septuagint and Modern Studies* (LBS; New York: Ktav, 1968).

(1 and 2 Maccabees, Tobit, Judith, Baruch, Ben Sira), made the Greek collection, what Christians later called their "Old Testament," larger than the Hebrew canon. Martin Luther, however, under the influence of the Renaissance belief in "Hebrew veritas," limited his translation to the Rabbinic Hebrew. Those Septuagintal books that were missing in the Hebrew canon, but were still mostly included in the Latin Vulgate of the Roman Catholic Church, Luther relegated to an appendix as "Apocrypha," that is, "books not equal to Holy Scripture, but still useful and good for reading." This judgment of the Reformation was, as we know today, only partly justified. To be sure, neither Hellenistic Judaism nor the ancient Christian churches ever made a final judgment about the canon of the Christian Old Testament. But the "Old Testament" of the ancient church, following the usage of the Hellenistic synagogue, was always the Septuagint, a collection of Israelite books that is older than the canon of Rabbinic Judaism and that included Luther's "Apocrypha" as well as other ancient Jewish writings.

It is difficult to overestimate the significance of the Greek Bible for Hellenistic Judaism. The translations were originally made for the synagogue services in the Greek diaspora—indirect testimony to the fact that as early as the 3d century BCE a knowledge of Hebrew could no longer be generally assumed among diaspora Jews. But translating the Hebrew Bible into Greek created more than a book that was useful for worship services; it also provided a basis for a fresh departure of Jewish theology in a new cultural environment. The Greek Scriptures enabled the ferment for renewal, already present in Israelite tradition and in postexilic theology, to develop further within the environs of Hellenistic culture and religion.

The Septuagint became the most significant factor in the Hellenization of Israel and enabled it to become a world religion. To be sure, some of the Greek translations are slavish renderings of Hebrew phrases and expressions. In other instances, the translators followed the Hebrew original text less closely, as in the Book of Job (though the Hebrew prototype of LXX-Job was not identical with the preserved Hebrew text). In the Book of Proverbs, where the Old Greek differs markedly from the Hebrew original, the new Greek text represents a clear shift in theology: in Prov 8:22–31, Wisdom's identity as a divine figure, issuing from God as the guarantor of a perfect creation, is present more clearly than in the Hebrew original. In exceptional cases, Greek philosophical terms played some role in the translation. But whether the translations are more literal or more independent, the Old Greek became the source for the theological language of Hellenistic Judaism and later also of ancient Christianity.

Very early one finds the Septuagint used as a basis for new written versions of the story of Israel, especially the creation and the narratives of the patriarchs and of Moses and the Exodus (§5.3d). Prototypes can be found in Hebrew and Aramaic literature. The Greek genres of literature used for these new literary productions include romance and epic as well as drama and history. Apologetic and allegorical commentaries on biblical books appear somewhat later and are fully developed in Philo of Alexandria (§5.3f); they became the prototypes for Christian biblical commentaries. The influence of the Septuagint is also visible in writings with nonbiblical subjects. The translation of the Bible into Greek made it a generally accessible, divine, and inspired book, containing ancient wisdom, deep religious truths, and political insights. It could be used as instruction for right conduct, but also as a source for magic. Jewish apologetics and propaganda could proudly claim that their sacred Scripture was a book of world culture, inferior in no way to Homer and the Greek philosophers, and superior to the ancient wisdom of Babylon and Egypt.

The history of the recensions of the Greek Bible shows that the Greek and Hebrew texts remained in contact for many centuries. Revisions of the Greek text are closely tied to the development of the Hebrew text. Later recensions show an increasing influence from the Babylonian Hebrew version. The oldest revisions are only partially known. The earliest seems to have been the proto-Lucianic recension that seeks to approximate the Greek version more closely to the Palestinian Hebrew text. It appears in some manuscripts of the Old Greek, in the quotations by Josephus, and in the Books of Samuel and Kings in the column of Origen's *Hexapla* that is designated as "Theodotion."

The proto-Theodotionic recension (also called "kai-ge" [καί γε] recension) was made in the 1st century CE. It follows the Babylonian Hebrew text, which had just gained recognition. A fragmentary Greek manuscript of the Twelve Minor Prophets, found in Palestine and dating from the 1st century BCE, belongs to this recension; it is also visible in quotations from Daniel in the New Testament, in the writings of the Christian apologist Justin Martyr, who used it for several books of the Bible; in Origen's *Hexapla* it appears under the designation "Quinta." Following these early recensions, further developments of the Greek text are visible in what are generally known as the three Jewish "translators," Theodotion, Aquila, and Symmachos. They were actually revisors, relying on earlier recensions. Theodotion continued the tradition of the proto-Theodotionic recension during the 2d century CE and made it very popular. Aquila, a proselyte from Pontus, published his "translation" in 128 CE. Building on earlier revisions, he tried to achieve greater accuracy and consistency (by constant use of the same Greek equivalents for the same Hebrew words), with the result that his Greek sentences are often nearly unintelligible. The translation of Symmachos, who is said to have been an Ebionite Christian, is distinguished by its more elegant Greek.

These revisions of the Bible's Greek text reach their apogee with the *Hexapla* of the Christian Alexandrian theologian Origen. This was a colossal work, in which various versions of the Old Testament were put side by side in six successive columns: the Hebrew text; a Greek transcription of the Hebrew; the translations of Aquila and Symmachos; Origen's own revised Greek texts, in which deviations from the Hebrew were marked according to Alexandrian text-critical methods with an asterisk (*) or obelus (÷); the sixth column contained the text of Theodotion. In additional columns (called Quinta, Sexta, and Septima, since they follow the other four translations) Origen occasionally quoted other translations known to him. Only a few remnants of this gigantic text-critical work are preserved, and its influence was limited. Origen's successors in the school of Caesarea, Pamphilos and Eusebios, attempted to put Origen's text into wider circulation. But meanwhile, Lucian (died in 312 CE), the founder of the Antiochian school, published a new text of the Septuagint. Lucian's text, which relied on an earlier recension called proto-Lucianic, was chiefly concerned with smoothening passages that were linguistically too rough. This Lucianic edition was widely disseminated and became the official text of the Old Testament in the Byzantine church.

(c) The First Book of Enoch

The *First Book of Enoch* (*Ethiopic Enoch*) is most suitable to introduce the complex variety of the Hellenistic literature of Israel. This writing is normally classified as an "apocalypse," which it no doubt is in many respects. It is, however, not a unity but a collection of various books and traditions of different genres, which came into existence over a period of about three centuries. Only the Ethiopic version has preserved most of the Enoch materials in one single book. This translates a Greek text (extensive portions are preserved) that in turn goes back to an Aramaic original. Among the Dead Sea Scrolls found at Qumran are Aramaic fragments of all parts of *1 Enoch* except the *Similitudes* (*1 Enoch* 37–71; see below), and in addition an Enochic *Book of the Giants*. The date of these fragmentary scrolls suggests that at least some sections of *1 Enoch* were written before the founding of the Qumran sect, perhaps as early as the end of the 3d century BCE. The book may be referred to in Sir 44:6, is mentioned in the *Genesis Apocryphon* and in *Jub.* 4.16–23, used in Heb 11:5–6, and explicitly mentioned in Jude 14–15.

The first part of *1 Enoch* (1–36) consists of the *Book of the Watchers*, a complex unit in itself. Its primary topic is an explanation of the flood, caused by the fallen angels, and of Enoch's role as intercessor before the throne of God. The second part depicts Enoch's two journeys to the ends of the earth. Within this section, chaps. 6–11 retell the events of Genesis 6–9. Other parts (65–67; 83–84; and 107–107) preserve mythological retellings of the events surrounding the birth of Noah, as apparently do the fragments of the *Book of the Giants* found

Bibliography to §5.3c: Text

R. H. Charles, trans., *The Book of Enoch* (1917; reprint: London: SPCK, 1982).

Michael A. Knibb, *The Ethiopic Book of Enoch: A New Edition in the Light of the Aramaic Dead Sea Fragments* (text and English translation in 2 vols.; Oxford: Oxford University Press, 1978).

J. T. Milik, ed., *The Books of Enoch, Aramaic Fragments of Qumran Cave 4* (Oxford: Clarendon, 1976).

Campbell Bonner, *The Last Chapters of Enoch in Greek* (London: Christophers, 1937; reprint: Darmstadt: Wissenschaftliche Buchgesellschaft, 1968).

Ephraim Isaac, "(Ethiopic Apocalypse of) Enoch," in James H. Charlesworth, *The Old Testament Pseudepigrapha* (2 vols.; Garden City, NY: Doubleday, 1983–85) 1. 5–89.

Siegbert Uhlig, *Das äthiopische Henochbuch* (JSHRZ 5; Gütersloh: Mohn, 1984).

Bibliography to §5.3c: Studies

James C. VanderKam, *Enoch and the Growth of the Apocalyptic Tradition* (CBQ.MS 16; Washington, DC: Catholic Biblical Association, 1984).

Michael E. Stone, "The Book of Enoch and Judaism in the Third Century b.c.e.," *CBQ* 40 (1978) 479–92.

Jonas C. Greenfield and Michael E. Stone, "The Enochic Pentateuch and the Date of the Similitudes," *HTR* 70 (1977) 51–65.

George W. E. Nickelsburg, "The Book of Enoch in Recent Research," *RSR* 7 (1981) 210–17.

at Qumran. The centrality of the account of the fallen angels of Gen 6:1–4 in *1 Enoch's* re-narrations as well as in the *Animal Apocalypse*, suggests that the authors of these sections relied on mythological materials considerably older than the "domesticated" version of the myth of the intercourse of the sons of the gods with the daughters of men in Genesis 6.

Another type of ancient Enoch material, astrological speculations, preserved in the *Book of the Luminaries* (chaps. 72–82), may have been associated with the name of Enoch at a much earlier time. This section's central focus is a solar calendar of 364 days; it must be observed lest both cosmic and moral disorder result. This concern with the solar calendar reveals a close affinity with *Jubilees* and with the Qumran sect.

Two dream visions follow, told by Enoch to his son Methuselah. The first (chaps. 83–84) is a prediction of the flood. The second vision, also called the *Animal Apocalypse* (chaps. 85–90), predicts the entire history of the world from the creation to the Maccabean revolt by describing mating, procreating, devouring, and persecuted animals of all kinds. The conclusion of the book appears in the form of an *Epistle of Enoch* (chaps.91–108), almost completely preserved in Greek; this consists of eschatological exhortations, but also incorporates an earlier tradition of different character, the *Apocalypse of Weeks* (chaps. 93 and 91.12–17), which tells the history of the world from Enoch's birth in the first week to the final judgment and the creation of a new heaven and a new earth in the tenth week.

The central portion of *1 Enoch,* comprising chaps. 38–71, is a series of *Similitudes* ending in the enthronement of Enoch as the "Son of man." This section presents visions, revelations, and predictions dealing with cosmic secrets; judgment of the world, its kings and the fallen angels; condemnation of the unrighteous; and bliss for the righteous. Because of the figure of the "Son of man" some scholars have argued that this part of *1 Enoch* is a Christian product. However, all that need be assumed is knowledge of the Book of Daniel. Moreover, allusions to historical events suggest a date in the last half of the 1st century BCE. But the *Similitudes* must have originated in circles of Judaism other than the sect of the Essenes.

(d) Ancient Books and Traditions Rewritten

Among Jewish writings that deal with history as recorded in the Bible, adaptations of the stories of creation, the patriarchs, and Moses predominate. While the

Bibliography to §5.3d (1): Texts

R. H. Charles, *The Ethiopic Version of the Hebrew Book of Jubilees Together with the Fragmentary Greek and Latin Versions* (Oxford: Clarendon, 1906).

Idem, *The Book of Jubilees* (London: SPCK, 1902)

Klaus Berger, *Das Buch der Jubiläen* (JSHRZ 2.3; Gütersloh: Mohn, 1981).

Bibliography to §5.3d (1): Studies

James C. Vanderkam, *Textual and Historical Studies in the Book of Jubilees* (HSM 14; Missoula, MT: Scholars Press, 1977).

E. Schwarz, *Identität durch Abgrenzung . . . Zugleich ein Beitrag zur Erforschung des Jubiläenbuches* (EHS.T 162; Frankfurt: Lang, 1982).

later rewriting of the story of Israel by Josephus shows a desire to give a plausible account of historical events, the Hellenistic works that retell accounts from the Pentateuch are dominated by mythological, astrological, and halakhic interests. First, they express a theological concern with the cosmic dimensions of the social and political disorders of their time; this often leads to a revival of ancient myth, as in the rewriting of the events of the flood and of the birth of Noah discussed above. Second, they try to anchor the sectarian concerns of their eschatological and speculative-mystical vision, along with their exhortations to appropriate behavior, in the cosmic realities of primordial time. Third, insofar as these works are influenced by apologetic tendencies, they try to present the primeval history of Israel as superior to that of other ancient people.

(1) The book of *Jubilees* is partially preserved in Latin, and is complete in an Ethiopic translation. Both derive from a Greek version translated from the Hebrew original. Twelve fragmentary Hebrew manuscripts of *Jubilees* have been found at Qumran. The book is a reproduction, in the style of a midrash, of Genesis 1 to Exodus 14. *Jubilees* claims inspiration because it was dictated to Moses by an "Angel of the Presence." (The framework for this situation is derived from Exodus 24.) The entire course of history, beginning with creation, is strictly arranged in periods of forty-nine years (= 1 "jubilee"). There are forty-nine jubilee periods from Adam to Moses, each again subdivided into seven-year weeks, that is, periods of seven years. A solar calendar of 364 days (= fifty-two weeks) determines the length of the year.

Expansions of the biblical narrative are mostly of halakhic character. Admonitions for proper observance of the law are mostly given by Noah and Abraham concerning the arrangement of the festal calendar according to the solar year, as well as prohibitions and regulations relating to conduct by which observant Jews must distinguish their behavior from that of the Gentiles. The biblical stories are rewritten to present the patriarchs as models for proper observance. In addition to this halakhic interest, other expansions, especially of the story of Abraham, exemplify wisdom, faith, and endurance.

The concern with calendrical matters pertaining to the position of festivals in the solar calendar (no feast must ever fall on a Sabbath), as well as the closeness to *1 Enoch* in eschatological interpolations and descriptions of the last judgment, place the book of *Jubilees* with writings related to the Essenes. The connection is confirmed by the large number of fragments found in Qumran and by the use of the book in the Damascus Document. *Jubilees* was certainly written before 100 BCE and may predate the founding of the sect of the Essenes, written to oppose the Hellenistic reforms that preceded the Maccabean uprising.

(2) *Genesis Apocryphon* (1QapGen) was found at Qumran in one badly mutilated Aramaic manuscript. This scroll, written between 50 BCE and 50 CE, permits satisfactory reconstruction of only five of its twenty columns. It narrates

Bibliography to §5.3d (2): Texts

Joseph A. Fitzmyer, *The Genesis Apocryphon of Qumran Cave I* (BibOr 18a; 2d ed.; Rome: Biblical Institute, 1971).

the events from Gen 5:28 to 15:4 (from Lamech to Abraham). Though written (or copied) at Qumran and familiar with the books of *Jubilees* and *1 Enoch,* it does not express specific sectarian elements and shows little of *Jubilees'* interest in halakha. Its primary concern is an apologetic and edifying expansion of the first book of the Bible, in which the patriarchs themselves appear as narrators; thus the first person singular prevails (cf. the *Testaments of the Twelve Patriarchs,* §5.3e [9]).

(3) *Books about Adam and Eve:* One or more books about the life and death of Adam and Eve were composed during the Hellenistic period, though evidence for their existence is indirect. A Greek book entitled *Apocalypse of Moses* is one extant recension of such an earlier work. It tells about the events recorded in Gen 4:1–25, beginning with the birth of Cain and Abel and concluding with the death and burial of Adam. Large portions of the book are occupied with Adam's deathbed account of the events of the past from the temptation to the expulsion from paradise. A longer account by Eve follows, explaining the necessity of human death but also expressing faith in the resurrection.

Several other books partially overlap with the *Apocalypse of Moses.* A Latin *Vita Adae et Evae* (also existing in a Slavonic version), an Armenian *Penitence of Adam,* both translations from a Greek original which, however, must have been different from the extant Greek *Apocalypse of Moses.* Whether the Greek text derives from a Hebrew or Aramaic original is uncertain. Despite some Christian elements in these writings, the original as well as some early revisions date from the pre-Christian period. They witness to a continuing interest in the theological meaning of the story of Adam and Eve that reappears not only in such Christian texts as Rom 5:12–21, but also in later Jewish apocalyptic texts (*2 Baruch; 4 Ezra*) and Gnostic interpretations of the first chapters of Genesis, especially evident in the *Apocalypse of Adam* from the Nag Hammadi Library (§10.5b [1]).

(4) *The Biblical Antiquities* (*Libri Philonis Judaei de initio mundi*). Though this retelling of the biblical story from Genesis to Saul was edited shortly after the catastrophe of the Jewish War in 66–70 CE, it uses earlier materials. It is

Bibliography to §5.3d (3): Texts

M. Nagel, "La Vie grecque d'Adam et d'Eve: Apocalypse de Moïse" (Dissertation Strasbourg, 1972).
J. H. Mozley, "Documents: The Vita Adae," *JTS* 20 (1929) 265–76.
L. S. A. Wells, "The Books of Adam and Eve," in Charles, *APOT* 2. 123–54.

Bibliography to §5.3d (3): Studies

George W. E. Nickelsburg, "Some Related Traditions in the Apocalypse of Adam, the Books of Adam and Eve and 1 Enoch," in Layton, *Rediscovery of Gnosticism,* 1. 515–39.

Bibliography to §5.3d (4): Texts

Daniel J. Harrington, Jaces Cazeaux, Charles Perrot, and Pierre-Maurice Bogaert, *Pseudo-Philon: Les Antiquités Bibliques* (2 vols.; SC 229–30; Paris: Cerf, 1976). Latin text with French translation and commentary.
Daniel J. Harrington, *The Hebrew Fragments of Pseudo-Philo* (Missoula, MT: Scholars Press, 1974).

preserved in Latin, but derives from a Greek translation of a Hebrew original. Frequent interpolations of legendary materials, hymns, long speeches, and homiletic pieces characterize this writing. It lacks the halakhic interest of *Jubilees* and often omits legal materials (almost all of the book of Leviticus is missing and most of Numbers and Deuteronomy). The author believes in resurrection, has a strongly developed angelology, stresses the election of Israel, and emphasizes the role of the great leader. Moses occupies a central position. Qualities of good leadership, as well as punishment for those who fail, are repeatedly demonstrated in the narration of Judges. The author's theology cannot be identified with any particular Jewish group or sect.

(5) *Poetic Fragments from Alexander Polyhistor.* Excerpts of works of Greco-Jewish authors who wrote about the figures of Genesis and the history of Israel are almost exclusively preserved in the works of (L. Cornelius) Alexander Polyhistor. Although these works have been lost, Josephus, Clement of Alexandria, and Eusebios quote a number of passages. Alexander Polyhistor was born 105 BCE in Miletus, was taken prisoner in the war with Mithridates and brought to Rome, where he remained after his manumission by Sulla until his death (ca. 50 BCE). Though his historical works, among them a book "On the Jews," were primarily uncritical collections of materials and excerpts, he did preserve valuable portions of other authors' works. Only the fragments of three Jewish poets of the Hellenistic period will be discussed here (for fragments of prose writers, classified as "historical works," see below, §5.3f [2]).

Philo the Epic Poet wrote an epic work *On Jerusalem* in Homeric style, dating

---

C. Dietzfelbinger, *Pseudo-Philo: Antiquitates Biblicae* (JSHRZ 2/2; Gütersloh: Mohn, 1975).

Bibliography to §5.3d (4): Studies

George W. E. Nickelsburg, "Good and Bad Leaders in Pseudo-Philo's *Liber Antiquitatum Biblicarum*," in idem and John J. Collins, eds., *Ideal Figures in Ancient Judaism: Profiles and Paradigms* (Chico, CA: Scholars Press, 1980) 49–65.

Bibliography to §5.3d (5):Texts

Albert Marie Denis, *Fragmenta Pseudepigraphorum quae supersunt Graeca* (PVTG; Leiden: Brill, 1970).

Carl R. Holladay, *Fragments from Hellenistic-Jewish Authors*, vol. 2: *Poets, The Epic Poets Theodotus and Philo and Ezekiel the Tragedian* (SBLTT 30; Atlanta, GA: Scholars Press, 1989).

Howard Jacobson, *The Exagoge of Ezekiel* (Cambridge: Cambridge University Press, 1983) [Introduction, Greek text, English translation and commentary].

E. Vogt and Nikolaus Walter, *Tragiker Ezechiel. Fragmente jüdisch-hellenistischer Epik. Pseudepigraphische jüdisch-hellenistische Dichtung* (JSHRZ 4/3; Gütersloh: Mohn, 1983).

Bibliography to §5.3d (5): Studies

J. Freudenthal, *Hellenistische Studien*, vol. 1: *Alexander Polyhistor und die von ihm erhaltenen Reste judäischer und samaritanischer Geschichtswerke* (Breslau: Skutsch 1875). The classical study of these fragments.

John J. Collins, "The Epic of Theodotus and the Hellenism of the Hasmoneans," *HTR* 73 (1980) 91–104. Contains extensive bibliographies.

Nikolaus Walter, "Jüdisch-hellenistische Literatur vor Philon von Alexandrien," *ANRW* 2.20.1 (1987) 67–120.

to the 2d century BCE. Though the flowery language is often obscure, the extant fragments somehow connect the promises to Abraham, Isaac, and Jacob to the holy place of God's dwelling. Jerusalem's layout and its abundant water supply are also mentioned. The poem is difficult to reconstruct, since Alexander Polyhistor interspersed quotations from it into various sections of his narrative.

The hexameter poem of *Theodotos the Epic Poet*, perhaps written in Palestine for a Greek audience, deals with the rape of Dinah and the sack of Shechem (Gen 33:18–34:31). Despite an elaborate description of Shechem's landscape, the poem is not a Samaritan product; it represents pro-Jewish propaganda glorifying the Hasmonean assault on the Samaritans.

Of the drama *Exodus* by the *Tragedian Ezekiel*, six fragments totaling 269 lines have been preserved. The plot of this drama was taken from the biblical account of the exodus from Egypt, but legendary features were added, beginning with a lengthy monologue by Moses recounting the events leading up to the beginning of the story. The extant fragments include a dream of Moses in which he sees himself enthroned on Mt. Sinai, his encounter with God at the burning bush, the destruction of the Egyptians, and a description of Elim as a paradise. It is evident that the character of Moses was central. This work is completely in keeping with the Alexandrian writing of tragedy (§3.4b) and was designed for performance. It is the only tragedy of that time (3d and 2d century BCE) of which any major fragment has been preserved.

(6) *Joseph and Aseneth.* A unique deployment of the stories about the patriarchs appears in the book *Joseph and Aseneth,* which was popular in Christian circles and therefore preserved in sixteen Greek manuscripts and a number of translations (Latin, Syriac, Armenian, Old Church Slavonic, and others). The original motif for the story, namely Joseph's marriage to a pagan woman, Pharaoh's daughter Aseneth, is Jewish; specifically Christian elements are missing. The book is an allegorical romance (§3.4e), in which the erotic motif is constitutive (the travel motif is missing). Aseneth is not just the pure virgin whose conversion from idol worship makes her fit to marry an Israelite. She represents allegorically the community of believers, perhaps those within Judaism converted to become members of the true (mystery) community of God. Turning away from the world, they are fit to receive the heavenly messenger and share in the ritual of salvation. Joseph has become a celestial, angelic figure and is called "son of God." Bread, cup, and ointment symbolize the

Bibliography to §5.3d (6): Texts

E. W. Brooks, *Joseph and Aseneth* (London: SPCK, 1918).

Marc Philonenko, *Joseph et Aséneth* (APB 13; Leiden: Brill, 1968).

Christoph Burchard, *Joseph and Aseneth (OT Pseudepigrapha* 2; Garden City, Doubleday, 1995).

Bibliography to §5.3d (6): Studies

Dieter Sänger, *Antikes Judentum und die Mysterien: Religionsgeschichtliche Untersuchungen zu Joseph und Aseneth* (WUNT 25; Tübingen: Mohr/Siebeck, 1980).

Christoph Burchard, *Untersuchungen zu Joseph und Aseneth* (WUNT 8; Tübingen: Mohr/Siebeck, 1965).

Richard I. Pervo, "Joseph and Aseneth and the Greek Novel," *SBLSP* 1976, 171–81.

sacraments of the true community, and the bread that Aseneth receives is the true bread from heaven (Manna).

(e) Literature of the Apocalyptic Movement

(1) *Daniel.* The oldest fully preserved and most influential apocalypse of the Hellenistic period was the Book of Daniel, included in the Hebrew canon among the "Writings" (not among the prophetic books). Its text appears partly in Hebrew (Dan 1:1–2:4a; 8:1–12:13) and partly in Aramaic (Dan 2:4b–7:28). It was written after the desecration of the Jewish temple by Antiochos IV Epiphanes (167 BCE) and before his death (164 BCE). The "kings of the north" are the Seleucids, the "kings of the south" the Ptolemies (Dan 11:5ff). Thus "Daniel," a Jewish sage at the Babylonian court in the 6th century BCE, was certainly not the author of the book, although some portions of Daniel 1–7 may preserve earlier Persian court stories.

Apocalyptic literature recounts, in the form of prophecy, the events of past history up to the time of writing. In this way, the traditional covenant formula is altered in characteristic fashion: the apocalypse replaces the historical introduction with a fictitious "prophetic" presentation of past history, and the announcement of curses and blessings is occupied by a visionary prediction of future events. Another typical apocalyptic element can be seen in Daniel's assimilation of mythological materials of Babylonian (astrological names of the nations and the myth of chaos) and Canaanite origin (the "Ancient of Days" is *El;* the one who is "like a son of man" is *Baal* from Canaanite mythology). This type of material is then applied to the present situation: the one "like a son of man" becomes a symbol for Israel ("the people of the holy ones of the Most High"; Dan 7:27) in his expected role as the ruler over the nations. This image expresses the eschatological vision of the Hasidic movement. A number of fragments of Daniel have been found among the manuscripts of the Essenes, to no one's surprise, since they, in contrast to the Hasmoneans, persisted in this vision.

Bibliography to §5.3e

Ithamar Gruenwald, "Jewish Apocalyptic Literature," *ANRW* 2.19.1 (1979) 89–118.

Michael E. Stone, "Apocalyptic Literature," in idem, ed., *Jewish Writings of the Second Temple Period* (CRINT 2.2; Philadelphia: Fortress, 1984) 383–441.

Devorah Dimant, "Qumran Sectarian Literature," in Michael E. Stone, ed., *Jewish Writings of the Second Temple Period* (CRINT 2.2; Philadelphia: Fortress, 1984) 483–550.

Bibliography to §5.3e (1): Text

Joseph Ziegler, ed., *Susanna: Daniel: Bel et Draco* (Göttingen Septuagint 16,2).

Bibliography to §5.3e (1): Commentary

John J. Collins, *Daniel: A Commentary on the Book of Daniel* (With an essay, "The Influence of Daniel on the New Testament" by Adela Yarbro Collins; Hermeneia; Minneapolis: Fortress, 1993).

Bibliography to §5.3e (1): Studies

John J. Collins, *The Apocalyptic Vision of the Book of Daniel* (HSM 16; Missoula, MT: Scholars Press, 1977).

C. Brekelmans, "The Sons of the Most High and Their Kingdom," *OTS* 14 (1965) 305–29.

(2) The *Assumption of Moses*, also known as the *Testament of Moses*, is preserved only in Latin translation (one single manuscript from the 6th century CE) of a Greek version that was in turn translated from a Hebrew or Aramaic original. The book is usually dated to the 1st century CE, but there is good reason to believe that it is a revision of traditions from the 2d century BCE. This apocalypse reports the last words of Moses before his ascension (which is not itself described). As in *1 Enoch* and Daniel, a sage from ancient times speaks as the authority for predictions of the last times. "Moses" first gives an account of events from his own day to the Maccabees and Herod (the latter may be an appendix to the earlier document), then predicts the coming of God to avenge and exalt Israel; no specific messianic figure is mentioned. Interpolated within this account is an anecdote of the martyrdom of a certain Taxo from the tribe of Levi together with his seven sons. The book's determinism, its emphasis on the role of Levi, and its polemic against the Hasmoneans demonstrate the affinity of this work with the writings from Qumran.

(3) The *Temple Scroll* (11QTemp) is a Hebrew document from Qumran, indeed the longest of the Dead Sea Scrolls. The scroll was written in the 1st century CE, but older fragments prove that the book was composed no later than the second half of the 2d century BCE. The speaker in this text is God himself as he addresses Moses on Mt. Sinai; thus the author of the book ascribes divine inspiration to his work. Most of the book describes the eschatological temple with its cult and festivals (cols. 3–45) and Jerusalem as the temple city (cols.45–52). A section

Bibliography to §5.3e (2): Texts

E. M. Laperrouzas, *Le Testament de Moïse* (Semitica 19; Paris: 1970). Latin Text and French translation.
J. Priest, "Testament of Moses," in: Charlesworth, *OTPseudepigrapha*, 1. 919-34.

Bibliography to §5.3e (2): Studies:

George W. E. Nickelsburg, ed., *Studies on the Testament of Moses* (SBLSCS 4; Cambridge, MA: Society of Biblical Literature, 1973).
A. Schalit, *Untersuchungen zur Assumptio Mosis* (Arbeiten zur Literatur und Geschichte des hellenistischen Judentums 17; Leiden: Brill, 1989).
Egon Brandenburger, *Himmelfahrt Moses* (JSHRZ 5/2; Gütersloh: Mohn, 1976).

Bibliography to §5.3e (3): Text

Yigael Yadin, *The Temple Scroll* (3 vols.; Jerusalem: Israel Exploration Society, 1977–1983). Hebrew Text and English translation.
Johann Maier, *The Temple Scroll: An Introduction, Translation and Commentary* (JSOTSup 34; Sheffield: JSOT Press, 1985)

Bibliography to §5.3e (3): Studies

Yigael Yadin, "The Temple Scroll: The Longest and the Most Recently Discovered Dead Sea Scroll," *BAR* 10,4 (1984) 32–49.
Idem, *The Temple Scroll: The Hidden Law of the Dead Sea Sect* (New York: Random House, 1985).
Idem et al., "The Temple Scroll," in Hershel Shanks, ed., *Understanding the Dead Sea Scrolls* (New York: Random House, 1992) 87–136.
George J. Brooke, ed., *Temple Scroll Studies: Papers Presented at the International Symposium on the Temple Scroll, Manchester, December 1987* (JSPSup 7; Sheffield: JSOT Press, 1989)

on the King's Law (cols. 56–59) and various prescriptions appear in the last part (cols. 53–56, 60–67). The primary concern of the *Temple Scroll* is halakha, regulations of sacrifices and offerings, and extensive purity regulations. These are modeled on the biblical tabernacle of the wilderness and consider Jerusalem in its entirety as the sacred district of the temple, which women are forbidden from entering. The purity rules are considerably stricter than those of the Pharisees (is a deliberate criticism of the Pharisees is implied?). The solar orientation of the temple service, the solar calendar, and the subordination of the king to the high priest make it certain that the halakha and ideology of the work are connected with the sect of the Essenes.

(4) The *War Scroll,* also known as *The War of the Sons of Light against the Sons of Darkness* (*Milhama,* 1QM) is a peculiar apocalyptic writing. Nineteen columns of this Hebrew scroll are preserved; a few lines are missing at the end of each column and the conclusion is lost. This manuscript must have been written in the 1st century CE, because its description of the battle formation of the army of the sons of light contains parallels with Roman battle formations. But discoveries of fragments in Caves 1 and 4 of Qumran suggest that the extant version is a composite document that rests on earlier works dating from the second half of the 2d century BCE. This book elaborates the topic of holy war, emphasizes the conduct of war according to the Law of Moses, and explains that a series of battles must be fought before the final victory of God. The formation of the army of the sons of light is described in great detail, including the weapons for the battle. Inserted into this description are prayers, hymns, and speeches by the priests.

(5) *Manual of Discipline* and *Damascus Document.* The organization of the Essene community as an eschatological sect—the people of the renewed covenant—resulted in the production of complex rules and regulations, the more so as one or several groups of Essenes lived in separate communities in either voluntary or imposed exile. Two documents have survived, in which these rules and regulations were codified. The *Manual of Discipline* (*Serekh hayyahad,* also

---

Bibliography to §5.3e (4): Texts: see Bibliography to §5.2c

Bibliography to §5.3e (4): Studies

Philip R. Davis, *1QM: The War Scroll from Qumran: Its Structure and History* (BibOr 32; Rome: Biblical Institute Press, 1977).

John. J. Collins, "The Mythology of the Holy War in Daniel and in the Qumran War Scroll: A Point of Transition in Jewish Apocalyptic," *VT* 25 (1975) 496–612

Bibliography to §5.3e (5): Text: see Bibliography to §5.2c

Chaim Rabin, *The Zadokite Documents* (Oxford: Clarendon, 1958)

Bibliography to §5.3e (5): Studies

A. R. C. Leany, *The Rule of Qumran and its Meaning* (London: SCM, 1966).

Lawrence H. Schiffman, *The Eschatological Community of the Dead Sea Scrolls: A Study of the Rule of the Congregation* (SBLMS 38; Atlanta: Scholars Press, 1989).

Jerome Murphy-O'Connor, "An Essene Missionary Document CD II.14–VI.1," *RB* 77 (1970) 201–29.

Idem, "La genèse littéraire de la Règle de la Communauté," *RB* 76 (1969) 528–49

called *Rule of the Community*) is the best preserved scroll from Cave 1 in Qumran, consisting of eleven columns, written in Hebrew. Numerous additional fragments of this text have been found which confirm a date of composition in the second half of the 2d century BCE. Though the writing includes materials of different character, formulated before its composition and developed during the period of its use, it is presented as the basic legislation for the community of the new covenant. In addition to liturgical instructions for the admission of new members into this all-male society, it contains regulations for the festival of the covenant renewal, and general rules for the community and its discipline. A special teaching about the two spirits, the spirit of truth to whom the sons of light belong, and the spirit of wickedness from whom the sons of darkness descend, testifies to the determinism of the sect's view of the generations of humankind. The document concludes with a hymn.

A related document, the *Rule of the Congregation* (1QSa) was found recorded on the back of the *Manual of Discipline*. It presents additional regulations and, most important, instructions for the convocation of all Israel, including women and children, for the messianic banquet in the eschatological time of salvation. In both documents, a hierarchical order is evident: "the priests the sons of Zadok" rank before the Levites and other members, just as the messianic priest of the eschatological time takes precedence over the messianic king.

The second major document is known as the *Damascus Document* or *Damascus Covenant* (CD). It was discovered in 1896 in three fragmentary manuscripts from the 10th and 12th centuries CE in the Cairo Geniza, and has been known since its publication by Solomon Schechter in 1910. But only through the manuscript discoveries at Qumran, including several fragments of the *Damascus Document* in Caves 4, 5, and 6, has it become possible to determine the book's origin. The "People of the New Covenant in the Land of Damascus," for whom this writing was composed at some time in the 2d century BCE as a community regulation, must have been Essenes. This document emphasizes that only the Zadokites have adhered faithfully to the covenant of God, and may refer to the Righteous Teacher as the group's founder.

Regulations for the religious calendar, purity, oaths, and a somewhat moderated prohibition of private poverty are similar to those in the *Manual of Discipline*. However, there are some significant differences. The community addressed in the *Damascus Document* lived outside of the establishment of Qumran ("Damascus" is perhaps a symbolic name for "exile"): married couples and children were included (there is legislation for marriage). Members were allowed to engage in business with outsiders, though also here the outside world is seen as impure. The rejection of the Jerusalem temple cult is not as radical as at Qumran. The leadership is not in the hands of the council of priests, Levites, and elders; rather responsibility for all major decisions, such as admission of new members, adjudication of legal matters, and oversight of property, is put in the hands of the "Overseer" (*Mebakker*).

(6) *Commentaries* (*Pesharim*). In interpreting the Bible, the Essenes developed a special form of commentary called *pesher*. Reading of prophetic texts as deliberately mysterious descriptions of the recent past, present, or future, all

understood as events in the eschatological process, is characteristic. The most extensive commentary of the type, in which a biblical book is interpreted verse by verse, is the *Pesher on Habakkuk* (1QpHab). Thirteen columns of a continuous interpretation of Habakkuk are preserved in a partially damaged scroll. The commentary quotes one or two sentences from the text of Habakkuk followed by a comment, usually short, introduced by: "The interpretation refers to . . ." Every statement of the prophet is in this way related to such events as the outrageous deeds of the Wicked Priest in Jerusalem, the desecration of the sanctuary, the persecution of the Righteous Teacher, and the latter's ability to interpret the Scriptures and to announce the secrets of God. Prophetic statements are frequently understood as references to present political and military events, such as the allusions to the "Kittim" (i.e., the Seleucids or the Romans).

A *Pesher on Nahum* (4QpNah), of which three columns are preserved containing commentary on Nah 2:12–3:12. Written at the end of the Hasmonean period, it makes historical references even more explicit. The comments relate to the period from one of the last Seleucid kings, Demetrios III (96–88 BCE), to the coming of the Romans. Remarkably, Demetrios and Antiochos (IV Epiphanes?) are mentioned by name. Other references to contemporary events are not as unambiguous. The "lion of wrath" who hangs people alive could be Alexander Janneus, but whether "the searchers of slippery things," who appear under the symbol Ephraim, are in fact the Pharisees remains open to question. Only a few smaller fragments remain of other *pesharim* of this type, of which most belong to commentaries on the Book of Isaiah, but fragments of *pesharim* on Hosea, Micah, Zephaniah, and the Psalms are also extant. Remains of four columns of a *Pesher on Psalm 37* (4QpPs 37) refer solely to the experiences of the community and the Righteous Teacher, and the persecutions that they suffered.

A second type of commentary arranges the biblical passages thematically. One of these documents has been published under the name *Florilegium* (4QFlor, two columns survive). Its themes are the temple and the "plant of David," both understood as eschatological symbols of the community. The discussion starts with 2 Sam 7:10–11, then proceeds to Ps 1:1 and Ps 2:1–2. Additional passages are quoted with the formula "as it is written in the book of . . ." Of a *Pesher on Melchizedek* (1QMelch) thirteen fragments of two columns survive, which demonstrate that the comments were arranged around Gen 14:18–19 and Ps 110:4— two biblical passages that also play a role in the Epistle to Hebrews and its understanding of Jesus as the high priest according to the order of Melchizedek (Heb 5:1–10; 7:1–3). The hypothesis that early Christian authors used florilegia

Bibliography to §5.3e (6): Text

Maurya P. Horgan, *Pesharim: Qumran Interpretation of Biblical Books* (CBQ.MS; Washington: Catholic Biblical Association of America, 1979).
See also Bibliography to §5.2c

Bibliography to §5.3e (6): Studies

William Hugh Brownlee, *The Midrash-Pesher Habakkuk* (SBLMS 24; Missoula, MT: Scholars Press, 1977).
Karl Elliger, *Studien zum Habakuk-Kommentar vom Toten Meer* (Tübingen: Mohr/Siebeck, 1953).

of scriptural passages finds evidence in a manuscript from Qumran called *Testimonia* (4QTest), which is preserved in its entirety. Deut 5:28–29; 18:18–19; Num 24:15–17; Deut 33:1–8, and Josh 6:26 are quoted in sequence. The topic is the coming of the messiahs of Aaron and Israel, though no explicit comments appear, except for an unexpected reference to Belial that is added to the last of these quotations.

(7) *Hymns (Hodayot)*. The sectarians of Qumran used Psalms in their liturgy, as is evident from several references to prayer and thanksgiving in their writings. Hymns are attached to the *Manual of Discipline* and the *War Scroll*. An interesting scroll of the Psalms includes several psalms beyond the ordinary 150 of the Bible (11QPs[a]). Two scrolls preserve a book with a large number of hymns which were composed by members of the Essene community: the *Thanksgiving Hymns* (*Hodayot,* 1QH). The manuscript is badly damaged and complete reconstruction is no longer possible, though seven additional fragments have been found in Caves 1 and 4. Another five fragmentary manuscripts with hymns not included in the *Hodayot* scrolls have been identified.

Many of the hymns are introduced by the formula "I praise you, Lord." Others use the first-person plural. Because the hymns in the first group speak personally about exile, persecution, and the experience of salvation, it has been suggested that the Righteous Teacher himself was their author. Despite frequent allusions to the biblical Psalms and an obvious similarity in style and phrasing, these hymns express a new religious experience. They speak of persecution by the men of wickedness, yet also of divine assistance and salvation, reflect upon the emptiness of human existence, not only in view of human bondage to sin, but also because of the transitory nature of human life; righteousness and life can only be obtained through the grace of God.

(8) *Psalms of Solomon*. This is the title of a collection of hymns, not found at Qumran, that is preserved in a number of Greek manuscripts and in Syriac and Coptic translations. Originally composed in Hebrew, possibly in Jerusalem, these hymns stem from the period 60–30 BCE, because they contain statements

Bibliography to §5.3e (7): Text

M. Delcor, *Les hymnes de Qumran (Hodayot)* (Paris: Letouzey et Ané, 1962). Hebrew text and French translation.
Bonnie Pedrotti Kittel, *The Hymns of Qumran: Translation and Commentary* (SBLDS 50; Chico, CA: Scholars Press, 1981)

Bibliography to §5.3e (7): Studies

Menahem Mansoor, *The Thanksgiving Hymns* (Grand Rapids: Eerdmans 1961).
See also Bibliography to §5.2c

Bibliography to §5.3e (8): Texts
S. Holm Nielsen, ed., *Die Psalmen Salomos* (JSHRZ 4/2; Gütersloh: Mohn, 1977)

Bibliography to §5.3e (8): Studies:

R. R. Hahn, *The Manuscript History of the Psalms of Solomon* (SBLSCS 13; Chico, CA: Scholars Press, 1982).
Joachim Schüpphaus, *Die Psalmen Salomos: Ein Zeugnis jerusalemer Theologie und Frömmigkeit in der Mitte des vorchristlichen Jahrhunderts* (ALGHL 7; Leiden Brill, 1977)

that are best understood as allusions to Pompey and to Herod the Great. As these hymns imitate the biblical Psalter, we cannot be certain about the religious circle that produced them. Although a legacy of the movement of the Hasidim, their authors do not share the typical Essenic expectation of the priestly messiah, nor do they reject the cult of the Jerusalem temple. Attempts have been made to show that the Pharisees produced the *Psalms of Solomon,* but conclusive evidence is lacking. There may have been several authors, but all of them express one and the same religious orientation, namely pietism. They exhibit the strongly stated self-confidence of the righteous person and a sharp criticism of sinners, among them foreign and native rulers as well as the impious among the people of Israel. Messianic and apocalyptic views are frequently put forward, especially in *Ps. Sol.* 17 and 18. These expectations include the coming of the messiah from David as a powerful earthly king and judgment for all ungodly people.

(9) *Testaments of the Twelve Patriarchs.* The testament literature constitutes a Hellenistic development of an earlier Israelite literary genre, the covenant formula of the Hebrew Bible. The covenant's historical introduction was replaced with the biography of an individual, thus changing what was a reminder of God's acts in national history into a narrative of the effects of virtue and vice in personal experience. The blessings and curses of the covenant formula were replaced by apocalyptic predictions. The most significant document of this genre is the *Testament of the Twelve Patriarchs,* preserved in Greek and in Armenian and Slavonic translations based upon the Greek text. Various recensions exist; their relationship is complex and cannot be discussed here. In its present form, this writing is most likely a Greek product. However, fragments of an Aramaic *Testament of*

Bibliography to §5.3e (9): Texts

Marinus de Jonge, ed., *The Testaments of the Twelve Patriarchs: A Critical Edition of the Greek Text* (PVTG 1,2; Leiden: Brill, 1978).

H. C. Kee, "Testaments of the Twelve Patriarchs," in: Charlesworth, *OTPseudepigrapha,* 1. 775–828.

J. Becker, *Die Testamente der zwölf Patriarchen* (JSHRZ 3/1; Gütersloh: Mohn, 1974)

Bibliography to §5.3e (9): Commentaries

H. W. Hollander and Marinus de Jonge: *The Testaments of the Twelve Patriarchs: A Commentary* (SVTP 8; Leiden: Brill, 1985)

Bibliography to §5.3e (9): Studies

Marinus de Jonge, *The Testaments of the Twelve Patriarchs: A Study of Their Text, Composition and Origin* (2d ed.; GTB 25; Assen: Van Gorcum, 1975).

Idem, ed., *Studies on the Testaments of the Twelve Patriarchs: Text and Interpretation* (SVTP 3; Leiden: Brill, 1975).

Idem, "The Testaments of the Twelve Patriarchs: Central Problems and Essential Viewpoints," *ANRW* 2.20.1 (1987) 359–420.

Idem, *Jewish Eschatology: Early Christian Christology and the Testaments of the Twelve Patriarchs: Collected Essays of Marinus de Jonge* (NovTSup 63; Leiden: Brill, 1991).

Dixon Slingerland, *The Testaments of the Twelve Patriarchs: A Critical History of Research* (SBLMS 21; Missoula, MT: Scholars Press, 1977).

Idem, "The Testament of Joseph: A Redaction-Critical Study," *JBL* 96 (1977) 507–16.

George W. E. Nickelsburg, ed., *Studies on the Testament of Joseph* (SBLEJL Missoula, MT: Scholars Press, 1975)

Levi and of a Hebrew *Testament of Naphthali* have been found at Qumran; though some additional small fragments in Hebrew and Aramaic have not yet been identified with certainty, in no case can any of these be seen as direct predecessors of the Greek *Testaments of the Twelve Patriarchs*. On the other hand, these finds make it difficult to consider the extant Greek text a Christian product. It is more likely that the text was composed by Hellenistic Jews, perhaps in Alexandria, and then embellished with Christian interpolations.

In these testaments, each of Jacob's sons gives admonitions to his children, introduced by an autobiographical review treating the effects of a particular vice (e.g., fornication, envy, etc.) or virtue. The exhortations consist of sermonic elaborations, followed by lists of virtues and vices. These are contrasted from the parallel perspectives of the "two ways"—the ways of life and death, good and evil, the angels of the Lord and those of Satan. A close relationship exists between these materials and the wisdom tradition and later Christian elaborations of the two ways (*Didache* 1–6; *Barnabas* 18–21). The apocalyptic element of this testament literature appears in predictions of the future, a time in which many will fall away and rebel before the final restoration. The prediction of the coming of two Messiahs, one from Levi and one from Judah, is parallel to the Essenes' expectation of a messianic priest and a messianic king.

(10) *Sibylline Oracles*. Twelve books of these oracles, written in Greek, are preserved (though numbered 1 to 14, books 9 and 10 repeat materials from the first books). In their final form they reveal the hand of a Christian redactor. However, most of their materials are pagan or Jewish and date from the Persian, Hellenistic, and Roman imperial periods. The name for such collections is derived from the Greek Sibyls: inspired prophetic women whose oracles were recorded in hexameters and gathered together in various shorter or longer collections (§4.3c). The most famous of these were three books of oracles by the Cumean Sibyl, which were kept in Rome and carefully guarded by the Senate in a vault under the Temple of Jupiter Capitolinus. After this temple burned in 83 BCE, a purified version was entrusted by Augustus to the Temple of Apollo on the Palatine in 12 BCE. These books could be consulted only on the most important occasions, and then only officially, in matters of state interest.

These procedures demonstrate the reputation of Sibylline books, the respect they were accorded, an acknowledgment of their possibly subversive content, and a fear of falsification and abuse. During the Hellenistic period, books written under the name of eastern Sibyls began to compete with the older and officially recognized collections of Greek Sibyls. Among these were products circulating under the authority of a Babylonian and a "Jewish" Sibyl. What is still preserved

Bibliography to §5.3e (10): Texts

Johannes Geffcken, *Die Oracula Sibyllina* (GCS 8; Leipzig: Hinrichs, 1902).

John J. Collins, "Sibylline Oracles," in: Charlesworth, *OTPseudepigrapha*, 1. 317–417

Bibliography to §5.3e (10): Studies

John J. Collins, *The Sibylline Oracles of Egyptian Judaism* (SBLDS 13; Missoula, MT: Scholars Press, 1974).

Idem, "The Development of the Sibylline Tradition," *ANRW* 2.20.1 (1987) 421–59.

of these earlier books in the later collection shows that these oracles indeed were politically subversive, directed against the Greek rulers of the east and later against the Roman overlords. Analogous prophecies from Egypt, of which the *Potter's Oracle* (2d century BCE) is the most famous, predict the coming of foreign rulers and many years of oppression, followed by war, chaos, and the final appearance of an eschatological liberator.

Books 3, 4, and 5, and possibly book 11 of the extant collection of *Sibylline Oracles* were either written by Israelites or adapted by them from earlier materials. They were originally directed against Greco-Macedonian rulers, predicting their final fall, some kind of cosmic catastrophe, and a final judgment with punishment and resurrection. Later, these oracles were updated to serve as anti-Roman propaganda, including apologetic motifs, arguments in favor of monotheism, and condemnations of the nations. It is difficult to distinguish between Jewish and Christian adaptations and earlier pagan materials, because much of the eschatological imagery was common. The characteristic contribution from the Israelite apocalyptic tradition appears in the view of world history as governed by a divine plan. The Jewish Sibyl argues that God is master of past, present, and future, and that he also rules the powers of nature (the worship of idols is accordingly criticized); she also proclaims a strict eschatological theodicy: the course of history runs towards final judgment and punishment of the unrighteous, while the righteous can expect to receive the reward for their deeds.

(f) The History of Israel as Reflected in Historiography and Legend

The only extant comprehensive historical works of Israelite authors were written just before and after the Hellenistic period: the Books of Chronicles, composed in Hebrew in the 4th century (revised in the 3d century BCE), and the *Antiquities* of Josephus, written at the end of the 1st century CE (§6.4d). From the Hellenistic period only a few fragments of such works survive. Other historical presentations and legendary glorifications of individual events deal with the recent past.

(1) *1 Esdras*. The Hebrew Bible includes two books dealing with the reforms of Ezra and Nehemiah, called "Ezra" and "Nehemiah." In the Septuagint and Vulgate, however, the title "Nehemiah" is never used and differently numbered books of "Esdras" appear instead. In addition, a number of apocryphal books are called either "Ezra" or "Esdras." The confusion in designations is illustrated in the following chart:

Bibliography to §5.3f: Studies

Harold W. Attridge, "Historiography," in: Michael Stone, ed., *Jewish Writings of the Second Temple Period* (CRINT 2.2; Philadelphia: Fortress, 1984) 157–84.

Bibliography to §5.3f (1): Texts

Robert Hanhart, ed., *Esdrae Liber I* (Göttingen Septuagint 8,1).
Idem, ed., *Esdrae Liber II* (Göttingen Septuagint 8,2).
Karl Friedrich Pohlmann, 3. *Esra-Buch* (JSHRZ 1/5; Gütersloh: Mohn, 1980).

Bibliography to §5.3f (1): Commentaries

Jacob M. Myers, *I and II Esdras* (AB 42; Garden City, NY: Doubleday, 1974).

	Hebrew Bible	Hebrew Bible	Paraphrase	Apocalypse
	Ezra	*Nehemiah*		*"4 Ezra"*
English Bible	Ezra	Nehemiah	1 Esdras	2 Esdras
Septuagint		2 E s d r a s	1 Esdras	
Vulgate	1 Esdras	2 Esdras	3 Esdras	4 Esdras
Later Latin	1 Esdras	3 Esdras		1–2: 2 Esdras
Mss.				3–14: 4 Esdras
				15–16: 5 Esdras

The book discussed here is "1 Esdras" of the Septuagint, appearing under the same title in the English Bible's Apocrypha (*KJV* and *NRSV*), but called "3 Esdras" in the Vulgate. This book is a Greek paraphrase of the Hebrew text of 2 Chronicles 35:1–36:21, the entire biblical Book of Ezra, and Nehemiah 7:72–8:13 (though Nehemiah himself is never mentioned). Beginning with the last years of the First Temple, it gives an account of the building of the Second Temple, and ends with a description of the activities of Ezra. The historical chronology of this book is difficult, and its purpose and date are debated. Its central concern, however, perhaps prompted by the rivalry of several Israelite temples in the 2d century BCE, is the rebuilding of the Jerusalem temple after the exile. This is evident in the interpolation of the nonbiblical Persian court narrative "Three Bodyguards of Darius" (1 Esdras 3:1–4:63). That story relates a competition among the bodyguards, arguing what is the strongest force in the world. They give speeches in turn proposing the king, wine, and woman as the strongest. As adapted by the author of 1 Esdras, however, the sequence of the first two speeches has been reversed and a fourth speech about truth has been added. This is presented by the third bodyguard, who is identified as Zerubbabel; he wins the contest and as his reward receives permission to rebuild the temple.

(2) A number of fragments of *Israel's Hellenistic Historians* have been preserved by Alexander Polyhistor (see above §5.3d[5]). The oldest of these is the

Bibliography to §5.3f (2):Texts

Albert Marie Denis, *Fragmenta Pseudepigraphorum quae supersunt Graeca* (PVTG; Leiden: Brill, 1970).

Carl R. Holladay, *Fragments from Hellenistic-Jewish Authors*, vol. 1: *Historians* (SBLTT 20; Chico, CA: Scholars Press, 1983).

Nikolaus Walter, *Fragmente jüdisch-hellenistischer Historiker* (JSHRZ 1/2, pp. 91–163; Gütersloh: Mohn, 1976) [Includes Eupolemos, Theophilos, Philo the Elder, Cleodemus Malchus, Artapanos, Ps.-Eupolemos, Ps.-Hekataios].

Idem, *Fragmente jüdisch-hellenischer Exegeten (Aristobulos, Demetrios, Aristeas)* (JSHRZ 3/2; Gütersloh: Mohn, 1975)

Bibliography to §5.3f (2): Studies

J. Freudenthal, *Hellenistische Studien*, vol. 1: *Alexander Polyhistor und die von ihm erhaltenen Reste jüdäischer und samaritanischer Geschichtswerke* (Breslau: Skutsch 1875). The classical study of these fragments.

Ben-Zion Wacholder, *Eupolemus: A Study of Judeo-Greek Literature* (Cincinnati: Hebrew Union College, 1974).

Nikolaus Walter, "Jüdisch-hellenistische Literatur vor Philon von Alexandrien," *ANRW* 2.20.1 (1987) 67–120

3d-century Alexandrian *Demetrios*. Eusebios quotes several passages from his work; its title, according to Clement of Alexandria, was *On the Kings of the Jews*. This book was an attempt to write the history of Israel from the patriarchs to the time of Ptolemy IV Philopator (222/1–204 BCE). It was composed in the style of Hellenistic historiography with particular attention to chronology.

Another Jewish historian, *Eupolemos*, was a Greek-speaking Palestinian who perhaps can be identified with Judas Maccabeus' envoy Eupolemos son of John (1 Macc 8:17). Fragments of his work, which was also entitled *On the Kings of the Jews*, are preserved in Eusebios and Clement of Alexandria. Subjects include Moses, David, Solomon, the destruction of the temple, and chronographic information. This work is more apologetically oriented than that of Demetrios. Moses appears as "the first wise man," inventor of the alphabet and founder of the sciences. Solomon is "the Great King" who erected the temple as the cultural center of an international empire with the aid of the Egyptian and Phoenician kings. These Hellenistic apologetic motifs are employed in the service of the political propaganda of the Hasmoneans.

A fragment of the work of a *Samaritan Anonymous* in Eusebios is falsely ascribed to Eupolemos; it is therefore also called *Pseudo-Eupolemos*. This fragment comes from the Greek work of a Samaritan of the early 2d century BCE (composed before the destruction of the Samaritan temple): Mt. Gerizim, the holy mountain of the Samaritans, is identified with the "Mountain of the Most High." Written on the basis of the Septuagint, this book reinterprets the biblical accounts of primeval history and the patriarchs in a more "syncretistic" fashion. Biblical figures are identified with Greek gods and heroes: Enoch is Atlas; Noah (= Nimrod) is the Babylonian Bel as well as the Greek Kronos. Abraham teaches astrology to the Phoenicians and the Egyptians and mediates oriental wisdom to the west. The tradition of Israel is seen as the link between Babylon on the one hand and Egypt and Greece on the other.

These Hellenistic motifs, appearing in Eupolemos and more strongly in the Samaritan Anonymous, also dominate the writing of *Artapanos*, an Alexandrian writer of the 3d or 2d century BCE. Two small fragments of his work about Abraham and Joseph, and a larger fragment about Moses, are preserved in Eusebios. Abraham teaches astrology to the Egyptians. Moses is depicted as the typical Hellenistic "divine man" (θεῖος ἀνήρ), a wise Egyptian prince called Mousaios (= the father of Orpheus) by the Greeks. He teaches hieroglyphics and is honored by the Egyptian priests as Hermes. He invents ships and machines for agriculture and irrigation and gives instruction about philosophy and correct religious worship. His miraculous success in warfare reveals a transition in this work from history into aretalogy (§3.4d).

Fragments of another historian are known as *Pseudo-Hekataios*. Hekataios of Abdera (§4.2b) was a Greek ethnographer who wrote in Egypt at the time of Ptolemy I, among other works a book called *Aegyptiaca*, which contained a long excursus about the Isrealites from which Diodoros Siculus quotes some passages. Two sorts of possibly Jewish fragments are preserved under the name of this author. A work *On Abraham* is quoted by Clement of Alexandria and may have been used by Josephus in the first book of his *Antiquities*. It described the migration to Egypt, the size of Israel and its population, Jerusalem and the temple, Israel's observance of the law, and finally an anecdote about the Jewish archer Mosollamus. However, citations in Josephus' *Against Apion* from a work *On the Jews* ascribed to Hekataios must belong to another historical work dealing with the Jews under Alexander the Great and his successors. Because of its positive attitude towards the Jews, it is likely to have been written by a Jewish apologist of the Hellenistic period.

(3) *1 and 2 Maccabees*. The period of the Maccabees produced several historical works. The most significant history of the revolt was written by Jason of Cyrene. Unfortunately, this five-volume Greek work, written shortly after the middle of the 2d century BCE, is lost, known only through its epitome, namely 2 Maccabees (see below). Jason was a Hellenized Jew from the diaspora, who had a good knowledge of Palestinian geography and made use of reliable sources: a biography of Judas Maccabeus, a chronology of the Seleucid kings, priestly yearbooks of Onias, Menelaos, and Jason, and documents from the temple archives in Jerusalem.

2 Maccabees, the epitome of Jason's work, written in highly literate Greek, was composed between 125 and 63 BCE. The first of the letters introducing the work (2 Macc 1:1–9) as well as the preface (2 Macc 2:19–32) were added by the epitomator; a second letter (2 Macc 1:10–2:18) was inserted by a later redactor. The historical events reported in 2 Maccabees relate the events of the years 175– 161 BCE; but there is also valuable information about the period under Seleukos IV (187–175 BCE), which forms the backdrop for the revolt. The central figure in the revolt is Judas Maccabeus, but the book remains silent about other members of his family and contains nothing that could be understood as a glorification of Hasmonean rule. Legendary materials were added, such as the narrative about the martyrdom of Eleazar and the seven brothers and their mother (8:18–31, later used by *4 Maccabees*, see §5.3g[5]), and especially the reports about the miraculous divine interventions in behalf of the temple, usually through an angel. The epitomator's chief interest is the glorification of the temple and the faithful

Bibliography to §5.3f (3): Texts

Werner Kapler, ed., *Maccabaeorum Liber I* (Göttingen Septuagint 9,1).
Robert Hanhart, ed., *Maccabaeorum Liber II* (Göttingen Septuagint 9,2).
Klaus D. Schunck, *1 Makkabäerbuch* (JSHRZ 1/4, pp. 167–285; Gütersloh, 1980).
C. Habicht, *2. Makkabäerbuch* (JSHRZ 1/3, pp. 167–285; Gütersloh, 1976).

Bibliography to §5.3f (3): Commentaries

Jonathan A. Goldstein, *1 Maccabees* (AB 41; Garden City, NY: Doubleday, 1976).
Idem, *2 Maccabees* (AB 41A; Garden City, NY: Doubleday, 1983)

Bibliography to §5.3f (3): Studies

Arnoldo Momigliano, "The Second Book of Maccabees," *Classical Philology* 70 (1975) 81-88.
Robert Doran, "The Jewish Hellenistic Historians Before Josephus," *ANRW* 2.20.1 (1987) 246– 97.
Idem, "2 Maccabees and 'Tragic History,'" *HUCA* 48 (1977) 107–14.
Idem, *Temple and Propaganda: The Character and Purpose of 2 Maccabees* (CBQMS 12; Washington, DC: Catholic Biblical Association, 1981).

observance of the law by the Jewish people, demonstrating that God richly rewards this faithfulness as he also punishes the impious without mercy. Important are also the events that form the background for the feast of the reconsecration of the temple (i.e., *Hanukkah*; 10:1–8) and the memorial festival for the victory over Nikanor (15:36–37).

1 Maccabees in part treats the same events covered by 2 Maccabees and, on the whole, uses the sources employed by Jason of Cyrene. However, it deals with a longer period, from 175 to 134 BCE, from the accession of Antiochos IV Epiphanes to the death of the Hasmonean high priest Simon. Written originally in Hebrew, but preserved only in Greek translation, it is a valuable historical source. Yet its tendentiousness should not be overlooked. 1 Maccabees is written as the court history of the Hasmonean dynasty, beginning with Judas and ending with the accession of John Hyrkanos (134 BCE). Not only is Judas Maccabeus repeatedly depicted as a pious hero, the entire Hasmonean house appears as the divinely chosen family. All its members are modeled after Israel's heroes of biblical times, while those who oppose them, whether outside or inside Israel, are described as lawless and ungodly. A number of poetic sections praising the Hasmonean leaders enhance the dynasty's status and glory.

(4) *Esther*. All the other Jewish writings dealing with events and persons after the exile are either legends concerning the temple and religious festivals, or narratives in the style of the Hellenistic romance. The Book of Esther, preserved in its original Hebrew as part of the canon, uses various legends and fairy tale motifs. There is the heroine (Esther), wife of the (Persian) king, who saves her people using her beauty as well as her intelligence; the member of a suppressed people (Mordecai), who rises to high public office; and the villain (Haman) who finally becomes a victim of his own intrigues. It has been conjectured that the names Mordecai and Esther were derived from the Babylonian gods Marduk and Ishtar, but the similarity simply wants to localize the story in the east. If there are any allusions to actual historical situations, they are merely stylistic devices used to create a suitable backdrop, just as in the Hellenistic romance.

The purpose of the book is to propagate the festival of Purim, indeed perhaps to introduce this festival, originally celebrated in the diaspora, to Palestine during the Hasmonean period—the most likely date for the composition of the book. The Greek translation of Esther added legendary features, which appear in Protestant English translations of the Apocrypha as *Additions to Esther*. They enhance the drama of the narrative but also give the entire story a more religious atmosphere (especially in the prayers of Mordecai and Esther).

(5) The Book of *Judith* is closely related to Esther. Originally written in Hebrew, it places a heroine in the center of the narrative, telling about the salvation of the people through the deeds of a beautiful woman. However, it was not included in the Jewish canon and is preserved only in Greek translation as part of the Septuagint. While Esther has a male associate in Mordecai, Judith's story focuses entirely on the victory of female power. The courage of this one

Bibliography to §5.3f (4): Text

Robert Hanhart, ed., *Esther* (Göttingen Septuagint 8,5).

woman contrasts with the despair of the entire nation and all its leading males. With cunning and sexual allure Judith not only kills Holofernes, the enemy general, but also makes a mockery of his entire army. Historical references are incidental and confusing (Holofernes is the "Persian" general of the "Assyrian" king Nebuchadnezzar!). The story's emphasis is on the faithfulness to the law, especially by observance of ritual purity, even under the most adverse circumstances. This is the piety of the Hasidim and has much in common with 2 Maccabees. However, it represents no particular religious group, but rather reflects a more widespread current, in which the temple, ritual observance, and special festivals like Hanukkah and Purim played an important role. What is new is the appearance of a social undercurrent that places the power of the pious woman over against the might of kings and armies.

(6) *Other Hellenistic Jewish Legends*. Legendary motifs embellished a number of new editions of biblical books. The story of the contest of the three bodyguards of King Darius in the Greek paraphrase of the books of Ezra and Nehemiah (*1 Esdras* in the Septuagint), has already been mentioned (§5.3g[1]). The motif of the salvation of the righteous from great distress appears in the Greek *Additions to Daniel*: the narratives of Susanna and of Daniel, Bel, and the Dragon. In the former, the piety of the woman is vindicated against her (Jewish!) enemies; in the latter, polemic against idolatry is the central motif.

Salvation of the righteous is also the theme in *3 Maccabees*, a book written in Greek about the Alexandrian Jews. The central part (chaps. 3–7) is a legendary account of events that took place in the time of Ptolemy VIII of Egypt (after 145 BCE; see §5.1e): elephants, which were intended to destroy the Jews assembled in the arena, turn against the friends of the king instead. This legend is set within the framework of the persecution of the Jews by Ptolemy IV (221–204 BCE), which leads to confusions in the historical setting. The occasion for composing the book during the 1st century BCE may have been the attempt by the Jews of Alexandria to obtain full citizenship rights. *3 Maccabees* opposes these efforts,

---

Bibliography to §5.3f (5): Texts

Robert Hanhart, ed., *Judith* (Göttingen Septuagint 8,4).

E. Zenger, *Das Buch Judit* (JSHRZ 1.6; Gütersloh: Mohn, 1981)

Bibliography to §5.3f (5): Studies

Morton S. Enslin and Solomon Zeitlin, *The Book of Judith* (JAL; Leiden: Brill, 1972).

Bibliography to §5.3f (6): Texts

Robert Hanhart, ed., *Maccabaeorum Liber III* (Göttingen Septuagint 9,3).

Moses Hadas, *The Third and Fourth Book of Maccabees* (JAL; New York: Harper, 1953).

Bibliography to §5.3f (6): Commentaries

Bibliography to §5.3f (6): Studies

Karl Friedrich Pohlmann, *Studien zum dritten Esra: Ein Beitrag zur Frage nach dem ursprünglichen Schluß des chronistischen Geschichtswerks* (Göttingen: Vandenhoeck & Ruprecht, 1970).

Victor A. Tcherikover, "The Third Book of Maccabes as a Historical Source," in *Scripta* 7, 1–26

and instead refers to the ancient vested privileges that had belonged to the Alexandrian Jews for generations.

(7) An even closer relationship to the Greek romance appears in the Book of *Tobit*. Composed ca. 200 BCE, Tobit is preserved in the Septuagint, but four fragments in Aramaic and one in Hebrew have been found at Qumran, indicating that the Greek text derives from a Semitic original. The situation of the pious Israelite as described in this book is that of the diaspora. The travel motif and the backdrop of a fictitious historical situation (Nineveh at the time of Salmanassar V and Sanherib) are typical of the romance. But there are also elements of the wisdom novel, namely, frequent exhortations and fairy-tale motifs (the gratefulness of the dead man). The purpose of the book appears in its description of the education of the pious through suffering, demonstration that prayers are heard by God, admonition to preserve one's Jewish heritage undefiled in an unfriendly gentile context, and encouragement to constant praise of the merciful God.

(g) From Wisdom to Philosophical Apologetics

(1) The Book of *Ben Sira* (*The Wisdom of Jesus the Son of Sirach;* called *Ecclesiasticus* in the Septuagint) is the most extensive Jewish wisdom book from the Hellenistic period. In the year 130 BCE the grandson of the author translated the book into Greek in Alexandria, and for a long time it was known only in this form and in Latin and Syriac translations. Parts of a Hebrew text were discovered in the Cairo Geniza, at Qumran, and at Masada, so that about two-thirds of the Hebrew text is now known. However, the textual problems are complex, because the Hebrew text seems to have been subject to changes after its initial Greek

Bibliography to §5.3d (7): Text

Robert Hanhart, ed., *Tobit* (Göttingen Septuagint 8,5)

Bibliography to §5.3g

Gerhard von Rad, *Wisdom in Israel* (Nashville: Abingdon, 1972).
Walter Baumgartner, "The Wisdom Literature," in: H. H. Rowley, ed., *The Old Testament and Modern Study* (Oxford: Clarendon, 1951) 210–37.
James M. Reese, *Hellenistic Influence on the Books of Wisdom and Its Consequences* (AnBib 41; Rome: Biblical Institute, 1970).
James L. Crenshaw, *Old Testament Wisdom: An Introduction* (Atlanta: John Knox, 1981).

Bibliography to §5.3g (1): Texts

Joseph Ziegler, ed., *Sapientia Jesu Filii Sirach* (Göttingen Septuagint 12,2).
Yigael Yadin, *The Ben Sira Scroll from Masada* (Jerusalem: Israel Exploration Society, 1965).
Georg Sauer, *Jesus Sirach (Ben Sira)* (JSHRZ 3/5; Gütersloh: Mohn, 1981)

Bibliography to §5.3g (1): Commentaries:

Patrick W. Skehan and A. A. Di Lella, *The Wisdom of Ben Sira* (AB 39; New York: Doubleday, 1987)

Bibliography to §5.3g (1): Studies

Jack T. Sanders, *Ben Sira and Demotic Wisdom* (SBLMS 28; Chico, CA: Scholars Press, 1983).
Th. Middendorp, *Die Stellung Jesu ben Siras zwischen Judentum und Hellenismus* (Leiden: Brill, 1973).
Helge Stadelmann, *Ben Sira als Schriftgelehrter* (WUNT 2.6; Tübingen: Mohr/Siebeck, 1980).

translation (preserved in the biblical uncial manuscripts and in the Vulgate); the revised Hebrew text is reflected in a later Greek translation, in the Vetus Latina, and in the Syriac translation. The author, Jesus Ben Sira, was a distinguished member of the Jerusalem aristocracy, a scribe, diplomat, and ambassador who had traveled widely. He wrote his book at the very beginning of the 2d century BCE; the high priest Simon, extolled in chap. 50, can be identified with Simon the Just, who held that office around 200 BCE.

The author of Ben Sira had a superb command of traditional wisdom, which he combined with the experiences of his own life and wrote down for the education of the young people of the upper class. In addition to five groups of wisdom sayings arranged according to particular topics, the book includes didactic poems, wisdom hymns, and psalms of thanksgiving and lament, as well as other pieces composed by the author. Wisdom for Ben Sira is not simply the sum total of human experience; rather, it must be understood as the Lord's wisdom. Through it the Lord created the world; it issues from his mouth and permeates the entire created order, including the moral world of humanity.

On the whole, the book takes a conservative stance, deeply rooted in traditional religion (wisdom is essentially the fear of the Lord), the Torah (the wisdom inherited from the fathers is identified with the law), and the established service of worship. Although the social world of Ben Sira is that of the wealthy aristocracy, he is nevertheless critical of wealth and intercedes in favor of the righteous poor. Skepticism regarding the perfection of the world is rejected; God's creation cannot be faulted; evil is exclusively the result of human evil actions. The biblical orientation of Ben Sira is also visible in his praise of the famous figures of the past as examples that should be imitated. Interest in the preservation of the tradition is combined with a relative openness towards the world and tempered by the personal experience of the teacher—just as in the ideal of citizenship propagated in the Hellenistic world by popular philosophy.

(2) The book *Qohelet* ("Ecclesiastes" of the Greek, Latin, and English Bible), written in Palestine (Jerusalem?) in Hebrew with many Aramaisms, was apparently composed shortly before the time of Ben Sira. It was accepted in the Hebrew canon while the book of Ben Sira was excluded from it; yet in its Hellenizing spirit, Qohelet reveals a more critical approach to the wisdom of Israel. The two epilogues, 12:9–11 and 12:11–14, as well as numerous "orthodox" interpolations by a later editor try to soften the book's skeptical attitude. The original author expresses radical doubts about justice in the natural order, emphasizing the inevitability of the human predicament of death. He also distances himself from the ideologies that justify the social and political order of his time. This is quite in keeping with sentiments of early Hellenistic thought, which are in evidence as early as Euripides, in New Comedy, and in epigrams and funerary inscriptions. The Book of Qohelet demonstrates that such ideas had

Bibliography to §5.3g (2)

H. L. Ginsberg, "The Structure of the Book of Kohelet," in: M. Noth and D. Winton Thomas, eds., *Wisdom in Israel and the Ancient Near East, Presented to Harold Henry Rowley* (VTSup 3; Leiden: Brill, 1955) 138-49.

invaded the educated aristocracy of Israel during the Ptolemaic period. It is exactly this skepticism that is rejected by the more conservative Ben Sira.

(3) *1 Baruch.* This Greek book, resting at least in part on a lost Hebrew original, is the oldest document of the pseudepigraphic Jeremiah-Baruch literature; the most likely date for its composition is the 2d century BCE (the *Epistle of Jeremiah* may have been written a few decades later, while *2 Baruch* and *3 Baruch* were composed after 70 CE). Its narrative introduction and prayer (1:1–3:8), as well as the concluding Zion poem (4:5–5:9), are concerned with the people's confession of sins and return to God, exemplified in the fictitious setting of the 6th-century Babylonian exile. Its central part (3:9–4:4) consists of a wisdom speech in poetic form inviting Israel to return to wisdom, that is, to the law. This poem demonstrates that in the continuing Palestinian tradition of wisdom, it was not the skepticism of Qohelet that succeeded, but the alliance between wisdom and law propagated by Ben Sira. However, while Ben Sira's teaching of wisdom is informed by a universalistic orientation, 1 Baruch makes wisdom—in the form of the Jewish law—the exclusive possession of Israel.

(4) *Epistle of Aristeas and Pseudo-Phokylides.* Wisdom books that were originally composed in Greek do not simply identify wisdom and law; rather, in an apologetic manner, they seek to demonstrate that the biblical law is fully compatible with the highest ideals of Greek morality and is the source of all true philosophy. The *Epistle of Aristeas* attempts to provide the underpinnings for the authority of the biblical law in its Greek version. Insofar as the book extols the law of Israel in its Greek translation, the argument is directed to the outsider, for at the time of the document's composition, the Alexandrian Jews had long been accustomed to the Greek translation of the law. On the other hand, the arguments that identify the biblical wisdom of the law with Greek wisdom can also be seen

Bibliography to §5.3g (3): Text

Joseph Ziegler, *Ieremias, Baruch, Threni, Epistulae Ieremiae* (Göttingen Septuagint 15).

Emmanuel Tov, *The Book of Baruch also Called 1 Baruch* (SBLTT 8; Missoula, MT: Scholars Press, 1975).

A. H. J. Gunneweg, *Das Buch Baruch—Der Brief Jeremias* (JSHRZ 3/2; Gütersloh: Mohn, 1975)

Bibliography to §5.3g (4): Text

Moses Hadas, *Aristeas to Philocrates* (JAL; New York: Harper, 1953).

Pieter W. van der Horst, *The Sentences of Pseudo-Phocylides* (Leiden: Brill, 1978).

Nikolaus Walter, *Fragmente jüdisch-hellenistischer Exegeten (Aristobulos, Demetrios, Aristeas)* (JSHRZ 3/2; Gütersloh: Mohn, 1975)

Bibliography to §5.3g (4): Studies

Elias Bickermann, "Zur Datierung des Pseudo-Aristeas," *ZNW* 29 (1930) 280–98.

Victor A. Tcherikover, "The Ideology of the Letter of Aristeas," *HTR* 51 (1958) 59–85.

Guenther Zuntz, "Aristeas Studies II: Aristeas on the Translation of the Torah," *JSS* 4 (1959) 109–26.

Naomi Janowitz, "The Rhetoric of Translation: Three Early Perspectives on Translating Torah," *HTR* 84 (1991) 129–40

Walter T. Wilson, *The Mysteries of Righteousness: The Literary Composition and Genre of the Sentences of Pseudo-Phocylides* (Tübingen: Mohr/Siebeck, 1994).

as an appeal to educated Jews to appreciate their own religious heritage while otherwise fully participating in the ways of Greek culture.

The *Epistle of Aristeas* is strongly influenced by the well-established language of the Greek Pentateuch, which argues for a date of composition well after the translation of the Septuagint. This is confirmed by a number of historical inconsistencies, which show that this book was not written, as it claims, during the time of Ptolemy II Philadelphos (284–247 BCE), but at least a century later. That the work also wants to appeal to gentiles is shown by its pseudonym Aristeas, a pagan court official of Philadelphos, in its description of Jerusalem (83–120), in the philosophical apology for the Jewish law (121–71), and finally the presentation of the wisdom of the Jewish sages in the form of a symposium (172–300). The discussions in this symposium deal with the theory and practice of kingship. Elements from Jewish wisdom are blended with numerous, and sometimes trivial, Greek proverbs, generalities, and borrowings from philosophical ethics—all to create the impression that Jewish sages dining at the king's table need not take second place to their Greek philosophical colleagues.

The *Sentences of Phokylides* is a didactic poem belonging to a higher level of intellectual achievement in Jewish apologetic wisdom. It was written in the 1st century BCE by a Jew who used the pseudonym of the Greek gnomic poet Phokylides of Miletos (6th century BCE). The 230 hexameter lines, composed in Ionic Greek but with evident influence from Hellenistic Greek, present Jewish wisdom sayings along with moral teachings from Greek gnomic poetry and popular philosophy. While some hexameters render commandments from the Decalogue and Leviticus 19 and allude to other biblical passages, there is little that could be identified as typically Jewish morality. There are no references to the Sabbath and no polemic against idol worship. Over half of the sentences can be paralleled in Greek maxims. While the purpose of this document is debated, it is best understood as moral teaching directed to the Greek world.

(5) Apart from Philo of Alexandria, only two Jewish philosophical works are attested. The first of these is a work from the first half of the 1st century CE (probably from Antioch) known as *4 Maccabees*. In essence the book is a diatribe on the power of reason, which is identical with obedience to the law. Despite this Israelite touch, reason is understood in Greek fashion as the confirmation of the cardinal virtues, namely, righteousness, prudence, mercy, and fortitude. The author uses the example of the Maccabean martyrs, Eleazar and the seven brothers and their mother (cf. 2 Maccabees; §5.3f[3]) to show how these virtues can overcome suffering and death. Other Greek concepts in this

Bibliography to §5.3g (5): Texts

Moses Hadas, *The Third and Fourth Book of Maccabees* (JAL; New York: Harper, 1953).

Nikolaus Walter, *Fragmente jüdisch-hellenistischer Exegeten (Aristobulos, Demetrios, Aristeas)* (JSHRZ 3/2; Gütersloh: Mohn, 1975)

Bibliography to §5.3g (5): Studies

Urs Breitenstein, *Beobachtungen zu Sprache, Stil und Gedankengut des Vierten Makkabäerbuchs* (Stuttgart/Basel: Schwabe, 1976).

Nikolaus Walter, *Der Toraausleger Aristobulos* (TU 86; Berlin: Akademie-Verlag, 1964)

martyrological account are the vicarious expiation for the sins of the people through suffering and the immortality of the soul. Jewish wisdom is here dissolved into Greek popular philosophy; only the use of examples from Jewish history reveals that this is a book by a Jewish author.

There can be little doubt that Jewish philosophers adopted the allegorical method for interpreting of the Bible well before Philo of Alexandria. But fragments of only one of these writers have been preserved. Eusebios quotes five large fragments of a certain Aristoboulos, who is probably identical with the "Aristoboulos . . . of the family of the anointed priests, teacher of Ptolemy the king," to whom the letter of 2 Macc 1:10–2:18 was directed (see §5.3g[3]), and may therefore be dated to the 2d century BCE. In typical apologetic fashion, Aristoboulos speaks of Moses as a prophet and teacher of ancient wisdom, thus uniting piety and philosophy in his person. Plato and Pythagoras, Homer and Hesiod are said to have borrowed from Moses. The description of the creation used Greek concepts of cosmogony and speculations with numbers but rejects mythological readings and any literal or anthropomorphic understanding of statements about God. In this respect he anticipates Philo.

(6) The *Wisdom of Solomon* (*Sapientia*) is an original Greek writing from the end of the 1st century BCE. It was included in the Septuagint, and appears in a New Testament canon lists, the *Canon Muratori,* between the letters of John and the Book of Revelation. This book occupies a special place within Jewish wisdom literature. Jewish wisdom poetry appears less Hellenized here than in other writings of this kind, although the author knew some Greek literature. The first part of the book (chaps. 1–5) essentially continues the tradition of the theological wisdom of Israel. Its interpretation of the history of Israel (10–12; 16–19) does not employ the typically Hellenistic method of allegory. In the controversy over skepticism, the author directly attacks the book of Qohelet. The typically apologetic discussion of pagan idol worship (13–15) exhibits sharp rejection without any empathy, but offers no recourse to Jewish cult and ritual.

So far, the book seems traditional in its posture and arguments. But the "Royal Speech" (6–9), an invitation to wisdom, shows strong influence by Greek philosophical concepts, though the author of *4 Maccabees* would appear to be a better philosopher. It is the overall conception of the book, together with the theologi-

Bibliography to §5.3g (6): Text

Joseph Ziegler, ed., *Sapientia Salomonis* (Göttingen Septuagint, 12,1).
Dieter Georgi, *Weisheit Salomos* (JSHRZ 3/4: Gütersloh: Mohn, 1980).

Bibliography to §5.3g (6): Commentary

David Winston, *The Wisdom of Solomon: A New Translation with Introduction and Commentary* (AB 43; Garden City, NY: Doubleday, 1979).

Bibliography to §5.3g (6): Studies

Dieter Georgi, "Der vorpaulinische Hymnus Phil. 2,6–11," in: Erich Dinkler, ed., *Zeit und Geschichte: Dankesgabe an Rudolf Bultmann zum 80. Geburtstag* (Tübingen: Mohr/ Siebeck, 1964) 262–93.
Idem, "Das Wesen der Weisheit nach der 'Weisheit Salomos'," in: Jacob Taubes, ed., *Gnosis und Politik* (München: Fink, 1984) 66–81.

cal radicalization of the concept of "Wisdom," that finally make the Wisdom of Solomon the most Hellenistic of all Jewish wisdom writings. Wisdom is not just a means by which the pious Israelite may find a convenient and faithful way to fulfill the law in a pluralistic world; wisdom is the one and only human path to God. The experience of Israel has become anonymous—all the examples from the biblical record have had their names deleted. Wisdom's existence has been taken out of its historical framework and has been ascribed to divine origin. Belief in immortality is therefore no longer an alien Greek element in a Jewish writing. Injustice, foolishness, and paganism are rejected not in favor of a Jewish concept of righteousness, but in the service of a universalistic concept of the oneness of the deity with righteousness. Within this unity the true being of the righteous person (the "soul") is concealed. With these ideas, Jewish wisdom seems to flow directly into Gnosticism.

(h) Philo of Alexandria

The learned Alexandrian philosopher Philo was the most prolific author of Hellenistic Judaism. His writings are also significant for the history of ancient philosophy: they are the first extensive corpus of philosophical writings after Aristotle to be preserved. They survive both in medieval manuscripts deriving

Bibliography to §5.3h: Text

Leopold Cohn and Paul Wendland, *Philonis Alexandri opera quae supersunt* (6 vols.; Berlin: De Gruyter, 1962).

F. H. Colson et al. in LCL (10 vols. and 2 supplementary vols.).

David Winston, ed., *Philo of Alexandria: The Contemplative Life, the Giants, and Selections: Translations and Introduction* (Classics of Western Spirituality; New York: Paulist Press, 1981).

Ronald Williamson, *Jews in the Hellenistic World: Philo* (Cambridge Commentaries on Writings of the Jewish and Christian World 200 BC to AD 200 1/2; Cambridge: Cambridge University Press, 1989).

Cartlide and Dungan, *Documents*, 253–92.

Bibliography to §5.3h: Bibliography

Earl Hilgert, "Bibliographia Philonica 1935–1981," *ANRW* 2.21.1 (1984) 47–97.

Peder Borgen, "Philo of Alexandria," in: Stone, *Jewish Writings*, 233–82.

Idem, "Philo of Alexandria: A Critical and Synthetical Survey of Research Since World War II," *ANRW* 2.21.1 (1984) 98–154.

Bibliography to §5.3h: Studies

Erwin R. Goodenough, *An Introduction to Philo Judaeus* (2d ed.; New York: Barnes & Noble, 1963).

Samuel Sandmel, *Philo of Alexandria: An Introduction* (New York: Oxford University Press, 1979).

Idem, "Philo Judaeus: an Introduction to the Man, His Writings, and His Significance," *ANRW* 2.21.1 (1984) 3–46.

Isaak Heinemann, *Philons griechische und jüdische Bildung* (Breslau: Marcus, 1932; reprint: Hildesheim: Olms, 1962).

Erwin R. Goodenough, *By Light, Light: The Mystik Gospel of Hellenistic Judaism* (New Haven: Yale University Press, 1935; reprint: Philo: Amsterdam, 1969).

Harry Austrin Wolfson, *Philo* (4th ed.; 2 vols.; Cambridge, MA: Harvard University Press, 1968). The works of Heinemann, Goodenough, and Wolfson are the three classic studies of Philo.

from the library of Caesarea and in numerous quotations by the Church Fathers. Philo belongs, strictly speaking, to the Roman imperial period. But actually he marks the endpoint of Hellenistic philosophy as well as of the development of Hellenistic Jewish apologetics.

The scattered pieces of information about Philo's life permit a reconstruction of a rough outline of his biography. Philo was born about 20 BCE in a Hellenized Jewish family of Alexandria. His education followed the patterns of Greek schooling and his parents' wealth provided the means for a training under the best teachers. Philo had an excellent command of the Greek language, was well educated in Greek philosophy and history, and could cite poets and tragedians without effort.

Much less is known about Philo's Jewish education. He certainly did not know much Hebrew; only a few Hebrew words and some etymologies of Hebrew names appear in his writings. Any suggestion that Philo also had the kind of Jewish education that could be compared to the training of later rabbinic schools is out of the question, despite occasional parallels in his writings with rabbinic exegesis. In the Greek-speaking Jewish synagogue of Alexandria he became acquainted with the regular services of the religious community and with Hellenistic Jewish scriptural interpretation and apologetics. Some formal training in these subjects explains why much that is found in Philo's writings is not original with him but an elaboration of earlier sources and traditions.

In keeping with the tradition of his family, which possessed Roman citizenship, Philo occupied leading positions in the Jewish community of Alexandria, a population perhaps in excess of 100,000. Philo's brother Alexander, whom Josephus gives the title *alabarch* (probably a high-ranking revenue officer), was one of the wealthiest men of his day. A son of Alexander, Philo's nephew Tiberius Alexander, served as the Roman governor of Palestine from 46 to 48 CE; under Nero, he became prefect of Egypt and played a decisive role in the events that led to Vespasian's proclamation as emperor. Another nephew of Philo, Marcus, was married to the daughter of the Jewish king Agrippa I. In 40 CE, Philo himself, by then an old man, became the leader of a Jewish delegation that traveled to Rome to appeal to the emperor Gaius (Caligula) on behalf of the Jews in Alexandria. The Roman prefect Flaccus had exposed them to the frenzy of the urban lower class when the Jews refused to worship the cult images of the divine emperor. Philo describes these events in his writings *Ad Flaccum* and *Legatio ad Gaium*.

These two works belong to the first of the two different genres that characterize

---

Of the numerous works on Philo, the following deserve special mention:

Wilhelm Bousset, *Jüdisch-christlicher Schulbetrieb in Alexandria und Rome* (Göttingen: Vandenhoeck & Ruprecht, 1915).

Samuel Sandmel, *Philo's Place in Judaism* (New York: Ktav, 1979).

Burton L. Mack, *Logos und Sophia: Untersuchungen zur Weisheitstheologie im hellenistischen Judentum* (Göttingen: Vandenhoeck & Ruprecht, 1973).

David Winston, *Logos and Mystical Theology in Philo of Alexandria* (Cincinnati, OH: Hebrew Union College Press, 1985).

Philo's literary production. They are apologies—unique insofar as they were occasioned by a specific historical event. It is clear that such apologetics did not arise from the mentality of a despised minority without a share in the general affairs of society. On the contrary, the Jewish community had a right to expect that all educated people would support the concerns of a philosophical world religion that was wronged by an emperor who was obviously crazy. The same optimistic attitude appears in Philo's other apologetic writings.

Philo also wrote a voluminous *Apology,* which is now lost. But two other writings are partially preserved which were originally closely connected with this *Apology: De vita contemplativa* and a book about the Essenes, of which a fragment is found in Eusebios. The significance of these works lies not only in the historical information they provide—the existence of the Therapeutai, described in *De vita contemplativa*, and of the Essenes can no longer be doubted—but also in the attraction of the ideals they propagate. The utopian concept of a common religious life that overcomes the senselessness of existence in the established social structures appeals to the yearnings of many people in antiquity. Philo here belongs to a tradition of utopia that begins with Plato, is expressed in the *Heliopolis (State of the Sun)* of Iamboulos (§3.4e), and returns in the later Neopythagorean communities, in Christianity, and in Plotinos' plans to build Platonopolis.

The rest of Philo's works are exegetical. Perhaps closely connected with the life of the religious community in Alexandria are the *Quaestiones in Genesin* and the *Quaestiones in Exodum*. Apart from a few Greek fragments, these writings are preserved only in Armenian translation. Fragments show that Philo had written similar commentaries about the books of Leviticus and Numbers. These writings briefly sketch the literal as well as the allegorical sense of each successive passage and are best understood as homiletic lectures or notes designed for use in the synagogue. They suggest that Philo occupied the position of a homilist in the Alexandrian Jewish community. These interpretations, though not different in method from his major allegorical commentaries, reveal a congenial understanding of the mindset of the average members of a congregation.

The biblical commentaries of Philo belong to two quite different corpora, the apologetic commentary and the allegorical commentary. The apologetic commentaries on the Bible are well preserved. These are not systematic theological treatments, but interpretations of the law for the educated gentile or Jewish reader. Though belonging to the category of propagandistic literature, they are at the same time a large-scale reinterpretation of the Pentateuch for Hellenistic Judaism. It is no accident that they are arranged according to the biblical formula of the covenant: (1) Previous history; this includes the books about creation, the patriarchs, and Moses. (2) Basic statement; the book about the Decalogue. (3) Legal stipulations; these are presented in Philo's writings about the individual laws. (4) Call for repentance; the book about virtues. (5) Curses and blessings; the books now combined in *De praemiis et poeniis*. An eschatological orientation appears only in the last section. However, the interpretation of the covenant is no longer concerned with Israel as a people but is addressed to the individual's place in society and the world in general.

The first book of the apologetic commentary is *De opificio mundi,* a complex interpretation of Genesis 1–2. It often follows Plato's *Timaeus* and also uses Pythagorean speculations with numbers. The first creation account of Genesis 1 is understood as the designing of the immaterial and ideal blueprint for the creation of the world and of human beings, taking place in the realm of reason, that is, within the divine Logos. To this first creation belongs the designing of the first Adam, who is both male and female, the rational archetype of empirical humanity. The second creation (Genesis 2) takes place as these archetypes are applied to matter. Thus human beings become a mixed race that partakes in both reason and body, and in which male and female are separated. The fall into sin is caused by the woman, who expresses the material aspect of humanity through her desire.

The subsequent books of the apologetic commentary deal with Abraham, Isaac, Jacob, and Joseph; only the first and the last of these books are extant. *De Abrahamo* describes the successful striving for salvation that still exists as an ideal possibility even after the fall. This consists of the right use of natural law, which is identical with the Logos-self of the human being. Sarah symbolizes wisdom and virtue; when Abraham marries her, he is no longer human but becomes a friend of God. *De Josepho* describes the ideal ruler who always follows divine guidance and who declares natural law to be the universal governor of the world and the constitution of the ideal state. This writing plainly contains advice for the Roman administration. It also became an important source for the later development of doctrines of natural law.

The climax of these biographical works of the apologetic commentary is found in the two books *De vita Mosis.* Corresponding to the Greek biographies of the time, and following earlier Jewish biographies of Moses (Artapanos, §5.3f[2]), Moses is not only prophet and priest, but also miracle worker, mystic, and mediator of divine wisdom, that is, the "divine man." His activity culminates in his legislation, which is seen as the concretization of the law of nature, which Moses applies to specific situations. The accomplishment of this task fulfills the royal mission of the greatest divine man of all times.

The treatment of the law begins with an explication of the basic statement in *De decalogo.* The Decalogue is the central formulation of the law, issued by God himself. The first five commandments (including the commandment to love one's parents) are duties having to do with God; the other five concern duties to human beings. Philo uses this division as the principle of his entire interpretation of the law. The books *De specialibus legibus* explain the individual regulations of the law. The first book begins with a long-winded treatment of the first commandment (including, for the first time, a hygienic explanation of circumcision) and then discusses the regulations for cult, ritual, priests, and sacrifices (the second commandment). The second book deals with the prohibition of oaths (the third commandment), the regulations for festivals and the Sabbath and explains the festivals as sacraments (the fourth commandment). The third and fourth books lay out—with numerous references to Greek and Roman law—the legal stipulations associated with civil and criminal law according to the last five commandments.

De virtutibus lays the foundation for ethics, as distinct from legislation, and treats Philo's four cardinal virtues: first, fortitude (ἀνδρεία); second, in great detail, kindheartedness (φιλανθρωπία); third, conversion (μετάνοια); and fourth, nobility of thought (εὐγένεια), namely, true dignity, which rests not on one's birthright but on wisdom. *De praemiis et poeniis* is not completely preserved; only chaps. 1–78 of the manuscripts belong to the original treatise. Philo begins with examples of the reward one receives for genuine striving after perfection, citing Enoch, Noah, Abraham, and other biblical heroes. The reward is mystical contemplation, the vision of God—not immortality, while the punishment for immorality is continuous fear, along with exclusion from joyful life and communion with God. The text breaks off after the examples of Cain and of the Korahites. What follows in chaps. 79–172 is a different writing: *De benedictionibus*. This is a popularizing sermon discussing the blessings for those who observe the law (peace or victory in war, prosperity, long life, health) and the curses for transgressors (famine, slavery, ill fortune, war, disease, etc.). The conclusion is eschatological: those who convert will receive the blessings, their persecutors will fall under the curse.

Philo's allegorical commentary on the Book of Genesis represents his most deeply searching and most extensive work. It is partially preserved in twenty-one books, not all of which are complete; at least nine books are lost. This is Philo's *magnum opus*. The commentary begins with the second chapter of Genesis and ends with its last chapter. A clear organizational principle cannot be found, either for the work as a whole or for the individual books. The thought progresses according to the principle of association, which often arises from allegorical interpretations of biblical sentences and words; their literal meaning is categorically presented as insufficient. In the course of the commentary, philosophical, ethical, political, scientific, and theological questions are discussed in varied sequence, and often with reference to other biblical passages. As for its literary genre, these commentaries resemble the *Stromata* ("Carpets") of Clement of Alexandria or the *Enneads* of Plotinos. Such lack of organization is characteristic of a Hellenistic fashion in religio-philosophical literature that addresses the initiated, whether Jew or Gentile—all those who had the right to call themselves "philosophers." The sheer enjoyment of speculating, reflecting, and philosophizing inspired Philo as much as did his true concern: the liberation of the spirit through contemplation, which leads to the mystical vision of God. Because of the disorganized and varied contents of this commentary, only a few essential points can be mentioned for each book.

The commentary begins with three books called *Legum allegoriae*. The first book (Gen 2:1–7) treats the difference between reason and sense perception, and between heavenly and earthly humanity. The garden, trees, and rivers of paradise are interpreted as virtues. The second book contains allegorical interpretations of the "serpent" and "nakedness," and allegorical explanations of individual terms. The third book, on Gen 3:8–19, reflects upon the human being who is called by God, and understands the curse on Adam as a judgment for various forms of craving for pleasure. The books of the allegorical commentary that follow have individual titles. *De Cherubim* (Gen 3:24 and 4:1) considers a possible explanation of the flaming sword as planetary and astral spheres, but decides that it stands for divine attributes and powers; it then explains Adam as pure reason, Eve as sense perception, and Cain as the evil intent that is borne of the two. *De sacrificiis Abelis et Caini* contains an elaborate juxtaposition of the beloved harlot, vice, and the hated lawful wife, virtue; in this context Philo offers the longest catalogue of vices ever written, listing 146 of them! The last part treats the sacrifice of the first fruits. *Quod deterius potiori insidiari soleat* (Gen 4:2–4) understands Cain and Abel as the opposite principles of self-love and love. *De posteritate Caini* offers a symbolic interpretation of the names of the offspring of Cain from Gen 4:16–25.

De gigantibus (Gen 6:1–4a) is a very important tractate. In his discussion of Gen 6:2 about the angels, demons, and the human soul, Philo offers a Platonic description of the soul's descent into the human body (chaps. 12–15). With reference to Gen 6:4 he discusses the distinction between three classes of souls, namely, the earthly, the heavenly, and the divinely born soul. *Quod Deus sit immutabilis* (Gen 6:4b–12) explains the Stoic classification of all things in nature according to ἕξις (inorganic materials), φύσις (plants), ψυχή (animals), and νοῦς (human beings). *De agricultura* and *De plantatione* use as their text Gen 9:20. The first tractate speaks about the gardener of the soul, which in turn is the shepherdess of the body, and about the relationship of reason and the desires; the second presents God as the planter of the world, the soul, and so on, and adds a moral-philosophical treatment of drinking wine and drunkenness. Prompted by Noah's drunkenness in Gen 9:21, *De ebrietate* continues this discussion and gives an allegorical interpretation to the five things that are characterized by Moses as wine: foolishness, loss of control over one's senses, gluttony, hilarity, and nakedness. Only the discussion of the first three is still preserved. *De sobrietate* explains the curses that Noah pronounced on his descendants when he awoke from his drunkenness (Gen 9:24–27).

Treatises closely related to each other follow. *De confusione linguarum* discusses basic conflicts between literal and allegorical interpretations of Gen 11:1–9. *De migratione Abrahami* presents Abraham as the archetype of the souls that follow the divine call, in a verse-by-verse exegesis of Gen 12:1–4 and 6. *Quis rerum divinarum heres*—the most extensive tractate of the allegorical commentary—interprets Gen 15:2–18 and continues the discussion of the wise person on a pilgrimage to the country of wisdom. *De congressu quaerendae eruditionis gratia* comments on Gen 16:1–6a, understanding Hagar allegorically as the encyclopedic sciences, and Sarah as the superior true wisdom. *De fuga et inventione* (Gen 16:6b–9 and 11–12) adduces examples from the Pentateuch about flight and about seeking and finding.

De mutatione nominum (Gen 17:1–5 and 15–22) uses the story of the changing of Abram's and Sarah's names to show that a literal understanding is meaningless and an allegorical understanding mandatory. The conclusion of the allegorical commentary comprises the two books *De somniis*. A preceding book on dreams is lost. The first of the two extant books interprets Jacob's dreams of the heavenly ladder (Gen 28:12–15) and of the different markings of the herd (Gen 31:11–13). The second book, poorly preserved, deals with two dreams each of Joseph, of the court baker and the cup bearer of Pharaoh, and of Pharaoh himself. Both books are largely obscure collections of allegories and expositions.

The remainder of Philo's writings are philosophical books. *De aeternitate mundi* critically discusses the Stoic doctrine of the periodic destruction of the universe. *Quod omnis probus liber sit* is also directed against the Stoics, arguing against determinism on behalf of human freedom. As examples Philo quotes Moses, the Essenes, and the Indian gymnosophist Kalanos, as well as numerous figures from the Greek tradition. *De providentia* (two books) is preserved in an Armenian translation (the only available translation is into Latin). The authenticity of this work, an important document for the history of post-Aristotelian philosophy, has been questioned. Also preserved in an Armenian version is the dialogue *Alexander,* in which Philo discusses with his nephew Tiberius Alexander whether or not animals possess reason.

Through his extensive literary activity Philo intended to transform the sacred book of the Jewish community, the Pentateuch, into a Hellenic book. By means of his apologetic and allegorical interpretation, he associated the mystical meaning of the Pentateuch, translated into philosophical language, with the ultimate goal of Greek education; at the same time, he restated the moral and legal content of the Pentateuch in Greek categories, thus perfecting what Jewish wisdom theology wanted to accomplish. The Jewish figure of heavenly Wisdom merged with the Greek philosophical idea of the Logos, which was both human reason and creator of the world. The legislation of Moses was identified with the Stoic concept of a rational order in the universe (λόγος φύσεως) and thus became the divinely authorized law of nature. From this, Philo could derive the design for a universal legislation, as well as a notion of human morality that could be described with internalized and psychological categories. World citizenship and inner striving for moral perfection in mystical contemplation are not mutually exclusive. Although the negative world view of Jewish wisdom theology reappeared in Philo in a new form, he connected this view with the cosmology of Middle Platonism. This resulted in a fundamental subordination of the earthly to the heavenly world, of the visible to the invisible, of matter to reason, and of the body to the soul. Even if Moses, as the royal legislator, fulfilled most perfectly the role of the "divine man," the real Moses for Philo was the leader into the divine mysteries and the wise man who set the soul on its way out of its earthly prison.

These Philonic thoughts had no direct relationship to the very beginnings of Christianity. But their influence began to emerge as early as the writings of the second generation, for example, in the Epistle to the Hebrews. Through the continuation of his allegorical method of scriptural interpretation and his Hellenistic-Jewish philosophy in the Alexandrian theologians Clement and Origen, Philo's work profoundly influenced the development of Christian theology and of the Christian world view as a whole.

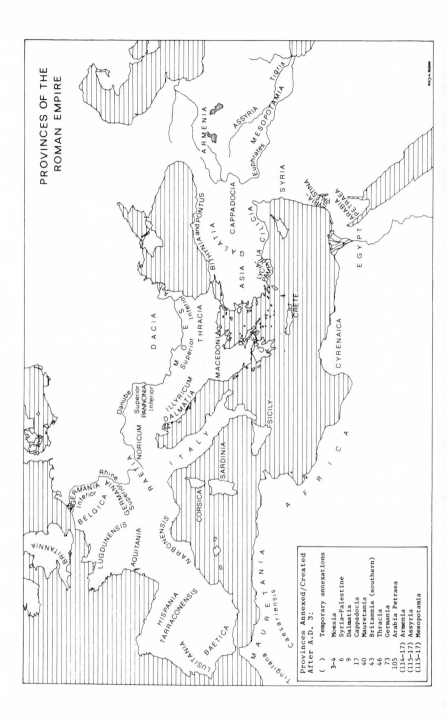

PROVINCES OF THE ROMAN EMPIRE

Provinces Annexed/Created After A.D. 3:

( ) Temporary annexations

3-4	Moesia
6	Syria-Palestine
9	Dalmatia
17	Cappadocia
40	Mauretania
43	Britannia (southern)
46	Thracia
73	Germania
105	Arabia Petraea
(114-17)	Armenia
(115-17)	Assyria
(115-17)	Mesopotamia

BRITANNIA

GERMANIA
Inferior
Rhine
BELGICA
LUGDUNENSIS
GERMANIA
Superior
AQUITANIA
NARBONENSIS
HISPANIA
TARRACONENSIS
LUSITANIA
BAETICA
MAURETANIA
Tingitana
Caesariensis
A F R I C A

RAETIA
NORICUM
VINDELICIA
Danube
PANNONIA
Superior
Inferior
ILLYRICUM
DALMATIA
I T A L Y
CORSICA
SARDINIA
SICILY

D A C I A
M
O
E
S
Superior Inferior
I A
THRACIA
MACEDONIA
CRETE
CYRENAICA

BITHYNIA and PONTUS
GALATIA
ASIA
CAPPADOCIA
LYCIA
CILICIA
PAMPHYLIA
SYRIA
PALAESTINA
ARABIA
PETRAEA
E G Y P T

ARMENIA
ASSYRIA
MESOPOTAMIA
Euphrates
Tigris

THE ROMAN EMPIRE
AS THE HEIR OF HELLENISM

1. THE DEVELOPMENT OF ROME INTO A WORLD POWER

(a) The Western Mediterranean and its Peoples

Beginning around 1000 BCE, centuries before Rome emerged as an independent city, several groups of peoples migrated into the western Mediterranean and began to found major states. The Phoenecians were the most important colonizers of the west. Established on the Syrian coast—from the beginning of the second millennium BCE—as part of the migrations of the Aramaic people, powerful Phoenecian city states, independent of each other, had prospered as trade centers (Tyre, Sidon, Ugarit, and others) for many centuries. Trade interests also brought Phoenician merchants not only to the Aegean Islands and other places of the eastern Mediterranean, but also to the west as early as the end of the second millennium BCE and as far as the southern Iberian Peninsula. The oldest western Phoenician centers of commerce included Gades (today Cádiz) and Tarshish (Tartessus; its exact location is not known) in southern Spain. Trade centers on Sardinia, Sicily, and on the coast of North Africa were added later. Pressure from the Assyrians pushed more Phoenecians to migrate from Syria and to establish the most important colony at Carthage in North Africa (founded ca. 815 BCE). By the 5th century BCE, Carthage had become the undisputed leading commercial

Bibliography to §6: Texts

R. K. Sherk, ed., *The Roman Empire: Augustus to Hadrian* (Translated Documents of Greece and Rome 6; Cambridge: Cambridge University Press, 1988).

N. Lewis and M. Reinhold, eds., *Roman Civilization: Selected Readings*, vol. 1: *The Republic and the Augustan Age;* vol. 2: *The Empire* (3d ed.; New York: Columbia University Press, 1990).

Jo-Ann Shelton, *As the Romans Did: A Sourcebook in Roman Social History* (New York: Oxford University Press, 1988).

Bibliography to §6: General Treatments

Karl Christ, *The Romans: An Introduction to their History and Civilization* (Berkeley, CA: University of California Press, 1984).

John Boardman, Jasper Griffith, and Oswyn Murray, eds., *The Oxford History of the Roman World* (Oxford and New York: Oxford University Press, 1991).

F. M. Heichelheim, C. A. Yeo and A. M. Ward, *A History of the Roman People* (2d ed.; Englewood Cliffs, NJ: Prentice Hall, 1984).

Hermann Bengtson, *Grundriß der römischen Geschichte mit Quellenkunde*, vol. 1: *Republik und Kaiserzeit bis 284 n. Chr.* (2d ed.; HAW 3,5,1; München: Beck, 1970).

Karl Christ, *Römische Geschichte: Einführung, Quellenkunde, Bibliographie* (Darmstadt: Wissenschaftliche Buchgesellschaft, 1973).

Arthur Ferrill, "Historical Summary of Rome," in Grant and Kitzinger, *Civilization*, 1. 45–85.

power of the whole western Mediterranean realm, counting the western part of the Mediterranean coast of Africa and the southern and eastern coasts of the Iberian peninsula among its possession. Its trade interests also controlled inland areas of northwest Africa.

The people ruled by the Phoenecians in southern and eastern Spain belonged to the older Mediterranean population. New cities had a relatively developed culture, with a lively exchange with the east and influences from Greece. The northern and western parts of the Iberian peninsula were occupied by Celtic tribes, while in northern Spain and southwestern France the ancient nation of the Vascones (Basques) was firmly established, speaking a language unrelated to that of any other Indo-European people. The Ligurians, an ancient Indo-European people, were living along the coasts of the western Mediterranean from the Pyrenees to the Po valley in northern Italy. Beginning in the middle of the first millennium BCE, they came under increasing pressure from Celtic tribes. On the southern French coast, the Greco-Phocean colony of Massilia (Marseilles) was founded ca. 600 BCE. The Greeks used this city as a base for their control over part of the western Mediterranean trade, founding additional colonies, and extending their influence into southern Gaul.

Indo-European tribes known as "Latins," migrated to Italy beginning about

Bibliography to §6: Special Topics

Moses Hadas, *A History of Rome from Its Origins to 529* AD *as Told by the Roman Historians* (Garden City, NY: Doubleday, 1956).

Niels Hannestad, *Roman Art and Imperial Policy* (Aarhus: Aarhus University Press, 1988).

R. Duncan Jones, *The Economy of the Roman Empire: Quantitative Studies* (2d ed.; Cambridge: Cambridge University Press, 1982).

Géza Alföldy, *The Social History of Rome* (2d ed.; Baltimore, MD: Johns Hopkins University Press, 1988).

Peter Garnsey and Richard P. Saller, *The Roman Empire: Economy, Society and Culture* (London: Duckworth, 1987).

John Ferguson, "Roman Administration," in Grant and Kitzinger, *Civilization,* 1. 649–65.

Bibliography to §6.1: Texts

R. K. Sherk, ed., *Rome and the Greek East to the Death of Augustus* (Translated Documents of Greece and Rome 4; Cambridge: Cambridge University Press, 1984).

Bibliography to §6.1: Studies

E. S. Gruen, *The Hellenistic World and the Coming of Rome* (2 vols.; Berkeley, CA: University of California Press, 1984)

A. N. Sherwin-White, *Roman Foreign Policy in the East. 168 B.C to* AD *1* (Norman, OK: University of Oklahoma Press, 1984).

Ernst Badian, *Roman Imperialism in the Late Republic* (2d ed.; Ithaca, NY: Cornell University Press, 1968).

Bibliography to §6.1a

B. H. Warmington: *Carthage* (2d ed.; New York: Praeger, 1969).

Arthur Geoffrey Woodhead, *The Greeks in the West* (APP 26; London: Thames and Hudson, 1962).

Raymond Bloch, *The Ancient Civilization of the Etruscans* (New York: Cowles, 1969).

H. H. Scullard, *The Etruscan Cities and Rome* (Ithaca, NY: Cornell University Press, 1967).

David Trump, *Central and Southern Italy before Rome* (New York: Praeger, 1967).

E. T. Salmon, *Samnium and the Samnites* (Cambridge: Cambridge University Press, 1967).

1000 BCE. They came from the regions of the Danube and Illyria and settled primarily in central Italy. These tribes, which included the ancestors of the Romans, spoke several closely related dialects, collectively called the Italic languages. Beginning around the 9th century BCE, the Etruscans migrated to Italy and, organized in several leagues of tribes and cities, ruled north-central Italy for many centuries. The question of their origin is a conundrum, though it is often assumed that they came from Asia Minor. Their language, though attested in hundreds of inscriptions written in the Greek alphabet, is still mostly undeciphered. They had a highly developed culture, dominated at first by Near-Eastern and later by Greek influences. Contact with Greece remained significant in later development of Etruscan culture; many Greek elements would be mediated to the Romans by the Etruscans.

Greek immigrants came to southern Italy and Sicily beginning in the 8th century BCE founding several colonies along the coastline and extending their influence to the inland areas. The Corinthians founded Syracuse, the Euboeans Cumae and Neapolis (Naples), the Spartans Tarentum; most of the other Greek cities of southern Italy were Achaean colonies (Sybaris, Croton). Because southern Italy was dominated by Greek culture in this period, it is often called "Magna Graecia" ("Greater Greece"). Greek expansion in Italy led to conflict with the Etruscans, yet the close cultural connection between the two peoples continued. To make things worse for the Etruscans, in the 5th century BCE Celtic tribes began to threaten their northern frontiers. A military stalemate in the 6th century gave Rome, situated between the spheres of Greek and Etruscan influence, an opportunity to shake off the Etruscan yoke.

(b) The Roman Republic

The Romans, along with rival Latin tribes like the Sabines and Samnites, were settled in central Italy at the lower course of the Tiber river. Rome's beginnings are lost in legend. According to tradition, Rome was founded 753 BCE by Romulus and Remus, and the archaeological record confirms a date in the 8th century BCE. The city was ruled and fortified by a series of kings, the last three of which at least, seem to have been Etruscans. Etruscan influence on Rome was profound. It is visible in the Latin alphabet, in architecture, metalwork, sculpture, and pottery, and in many civic and religious institutions. Urban characteristics of Rome show Etruscan influence: a fortified city with streets, sewers, temples, and administrative buildings. Furthermore, whatever appears to be "Greek" in early Rome, was mediated to the Romans by the Etruscans (including many loan-words, e.g., *triumphus* = θρίαμβος).

The expulsion of the last king, Tarquinius Superbus, in the year 510 BCE,

Bibliography to §6.1b

H. H. Scullard, *A History of the Roman World from 753–146 BC* (MHGRW 4; 3d ed.; London: Methuen, 1961).

Arnoldo Momigliano, "An Interim Report on the Origins of Rome," *JRomS* (1963) 95–121.

Pierre Grimal, ed., *Der Hellenismus und der Aufstieg Roms* (Fischer Weltgeschichte 6; Frankfurt: Fischer, 1965).

meant the liberation of Rome from Etruscan domination. The rejection of the institution of royalty persisted as an important element in the political attitudes of the Roman people. Rome's concern during the 5th and 4th centuries BCE was to preserve its independence through a steady expansion of its territory. Its internal development was marked by struggles among its classes, resulting in a political equilibrium as a semidemocratic state. After the expulsion of the kings, Rome was dominated by a few hundred families of patricians, who controlled most of the agricultural land. The heads of the patrician families constituted the Senate, which originally had the power to appoint priests and to fill public offices. The concepts of annuality and collegiality were fundamental: two consuls were elected annually to serve for one year with the power to veto each other's decisions. This characteristic structure was so elemental that it survived all later reforms. The majority of the population belonged to the class of the plebeians. During the drawn-out struggle with the patricians in the 5th and 4th centuries BCE, the plebeians were able to establish a religiously sanctioned organization of their own, and in the course of time gained access to most public offices—but not without having threatened several times to emigrate en masse.

In 367 BCE a new statute required that one of the two consuls should be a plebeian. Plebeians also gained access to other offices: they could be elected praetors, quaestors (as early as 421 BCE), and censors. Praetors were second in rank to the consuls and functioned as their deputies in the command of the army and in the administration of justice, later as provincial governors. Quaestors served under the consuls administering the several departments; they became chief financial officers in the provinces. Censors administered the citizenship and revenue files. Two aediles had always been elected from among the plebeians; they supervised certain religious events (including games), controlled the police, and maintained the streets of Rome and public places and buildings. Later, two additional aediles were appointed, the so-called curulian aediles, elected by an assembly of all classes (the *comitia centuriata*); after a period of patrician control, patricians and plebeians alternated in this office.

The tribunes had always been plebeian officials, elected by the assembly of the plebeians (the *comitia tributa*). The tribunes were powerful advocates for the plebeians, possessing veto power over any public act of the Senate or its magistrates and the right to propose laws that went into effect as soon as they were approved by the *comitia*. Any plebeian holding office received the right to become a member of the patrician class; thus the patriciate was continuously renewed (at least until the proscriptions and civil wars of the 1st century BCE) and an upper class developed that did not depend exclusively on the rights of birth.

The delicate equilibrium of the corporate Roman state was made even more complex in the 2d century BCE, when the equestrians ("knights") were established as an order separate from the senatorial order, with rights of their own, a mixture of patricians and plebeians classed by their wealth. These equestrians became a wealthy social class that soon lost its original military function. Since the senators were forbidden to enter into trade and commerce (their wealth rested on their landed estates), business and commercial enterprise became the domain of the equestrians. Admission to the equestrian class was increasingly extended to the provincial nobility, who thus gained an opportunity to participate in business and commerce, and ultimately also in public office. In the expansion of the Roman empire, the equestrians played an important role as lease-holders administering public lands and as officials in the juridical processes.

For their fight against the Etruscans, the Romans established alliances with the neighboring Latin tribes. Shortly after the conquest of the powerful Etruscan city of Veii, with which Rome had been at war for decades, the Celts invaded Italy (387 BCE). They defeated the Roman army and burned the city after the Romans had withdrawn to the Capitol. To buy their freedom and induce the Celts to withdraw, the Romans had to pay an enormous ransom. In addition to the Celts and the Etruscans, the Romans had to fight the Samnites (343–341, 327–304, 289–290 BCE) and to suppress a revolt of their Latin confederates, which forced Rome to change its relationship to its allies, resulting in a new constitution of the state. Some of the Latin cities received both the right of citizenship and the right to vote, others only the right of citizenship; still others remained dependent upon Rome as "allies"—client states.

After the final victory over the Samnites, and the last arduous battles with the Celts (285–282 BCE), Rome emerged as the master of a confederation that dominated central Italy. Immediately afterwards (280–275 BCE), the ambitious plans of the Epirote king Pyrrhos forced the Romans, for the first time, into a serious encounter with the Greek world (§1.4e). Though twice beaten by Pyrrhos, Rome emerged from the war in full control of southern Italy. Until then Rome had fought for its own independence and security, and had finally succeeded despite wars and setbacks. But now Rome saw itself confronted with a new situation. It controlled a large area with several million inhabitants, experienced an economic upturn, and had become wealthy through wars. By 270 BCE Rome had begun to issue its own silver coins in the Greek tradition of southern Italy. Rome's inheritance from Pyrrhos of a protectorate over the Greek cities of southern Italy necessitated close contact with Hellenistic culture. Prepared for this encounter through their contacts with the the Etruscans and a general fascination with Greek culture, Rome rapidly became Hellenized.

(c) The Conquest of the Roman Empire

With the control over Italy (with the exception of Sicily) Rome had become a major regional power. Parochial policies had to give way to a world-political orientation. However, why this new policy became an endeavor to conquer the whole Mediterranean world is hard to explain in spite of the appeal to possible

Bibliography to §6.1c: Texts

A. H. J. Greenidge and A. M. Clay, *Sources for Roman History 133–70* BC (2d ed. rev. by E. W. Gray; Oxford: Clarendon, 1960).

Bibliography to §6.1c: Studies

F. B. Marsh and H. H. Scullard, *A History of the Roman World from 146–70* BC (MHGRW 5; 3. ed.; London: Methuen, 1961).

P. A. Brunt, *Italian Manpower 225* BC–AD *14* (Oxford: Clarendon, 1971).

THE CONQUEST OF THE ROMAN EMPIRE

BCE	280–275	Pyrrhic War
	since 275	Domination of southern and central Italy
	264–241	First Carthaginian War
	241	Sicily Roman province
	238	Sardinia and Corsica provinces
	229	Dyrrhachium province
	222	Northern Italy province (Gallia Cisalpina)
	219	Dalmatia province
	218–201	Second Carthaginian War
	215–205	First Macedonian War
	200–197	Second Macedonian War
	195	Organization of two provinces in Spain
	191–190	War against Antiochos III of Syria
	171–168	Third Macedonian War
	148	Macedonia province
	149–146	Third Carthaginian War and War against the Achaean League
	146	Africa (Africa Proconsularis) and Achaea provinces
	133	Kingdom of Pergamon bequeathed to Rome (province Asia)
	121	Gallia Narbonensis province
	102	Cilicia province
	74	Cyrene and Bithyria provinces
	66–64	Conquest of the East by Pompey (province Syria)
	58–50	Caesar conquers Gallia
	55–54	Caesar begins conquest of Britannia
	46	Numidia province (Africa Nova)
	34–33, 14–12	Conquest of Illyria
	30	Egypt province
	29–28	Conquest of Moesia
	25	Galatia province
CE	5	Germania province
	6	Judea (later Palestine)
	17	Kappadolia
	41/42	Mauretania
	105	Arabia Felix (formerly Nabatea)
	106	Dacia
	116	Mesopotamia (never secured)

---

causes (e.g., hunger for power and military supremacy, economic interests, consciousness of a political mission). Militarily the Etruscans no longer constituted a threat, and Rome had incorporated the culture and economy of Magna Graecia into its system. The only significant rival of Rome in the western Mediterranean was Carthage, which controlled the southern and western coasts of that part of the Mediterranean Sea, as well as Corsica, Sardinia, and most of Sicily, and was not modest in its choice of methods for the defense of its trading interests. For the wars against Pyrrhos, Rome had sought the support of the Carthage, but expanding Roman economic interests and entrance into the Mediterranean as a sea power made the conflict with Carthage inevitable. The first

Carthaginian War ("Punic War"), in which Syracuse was Rome's ally, lasted from 264–241 BCE. Rome had to built its own navy for this war and its ships continued to be an important instrument for maintaining newly won acquisitions. The war ended with a division of the western Mediterranean into Roman and Carthaginian sections. Sicily, with the exception of Syracuse and other allied Greek cities, became a Roman province. This meant that, for the first time in the course of the expansion of its power, Rome used an instrument of imperialistic policy instead of its traditional policy of federation and set the pattern for future policies in consolidating newly acquired realms.

The establishment of provinces implied the exploitation of the conquered lands. The administration of a province was entrusted to a governor appointed by the Senate (praetor, later proconsul or propraetor), assisted by a quaestor. The local administrations and the lower courts remained in the control of the native authorities. But all higher courts, the administration of taxes and duties, and the military came into the hands of the Roman governor; each new governor determined the basic principles of his administrative policies and published them in an edict upon taking office. Whenever a governor intended to feather his nest through exploitation, he did not have to fear the protests of a colleague nor any restraints from the local authorities. If, on the other hand, a governor tried to prevent the exploitation of his province by Roman businessmen and lease-holders, he had to reckon that this would create powerful enemies in Rome, and the province would certainly end up with a new governor who was willing to conspire with the exploiters. Until the beginning of the imperial period, even well-meaning laws and court suits (De repetundis) were unable to cope with abusive, exploitative practices. Normally, a suit in court against a governor of a province was not brought because of the conviction that exploitation and extortion were evil. Rather, that governors would enrich themselves was taken for granted. Accusations were usually motivated by political rivalry, because governance of a province implied not only personal financial gain but also the opportunity to broaden the base of one's political power by increasing one's clientele and popularity through the financing of public projects, games, and other benefactions. It became increasingly difficult to have a successful career without a provincial command.

With the victory in the First Carthaginian War, Rome had become the major power in the western Mediterranean and from now on pursued an openly expansionist policy. It pressured Carthage into ceding Sardinia and Corsica and organized these islands as provinces (238 BCE). In behalf of the Greek cities on the Adriatic Sea, Rome conquered a part of the Illyrian coast and established the province of Dyrrhachium in 229 BCE. In order to create a bulwark against further Celtic invasions, northern Italy was conquered and became the province of Gallia Cisalpina (222 BCE). In a second Illyrian war Rome also occupied the Dalamatian coast (province of Dalmatia, 219 BCE), and thus became the unchallenged master of the Adriatic Sea. The Greeks rewarded the Romans for these wars—conducted for the protection of Greece—by admitting Rome to the Olympic Games.

However, Carthage had not forgotten the defeat it had suffered. The Carthaginian general Hamilkar, with the surname "Barkas" (= "Lightning"), had been able to crush an insurrection of mercenaries, and then began to reconquer Spain, which had slipped from its control during the previous war. His successful operation established a new power base and source of wealth in southern Spain. As a consequence, Hamilkar's party (the "Barkides"), eager to engage Rome in war once again, was able to assume power in Carthage. After Hamilkar's death (229 BCE), his son-in-law Hasdrubal, however, prevented a new war through diplomatic negotiations. A treaty with Rome determined that the river Ebro (a river in central Spain south of Saguntum, not the river that is today called Ebro) should be the dividing line between the Carthaginian and Roman spheres of interest (226 BCE). Five years later Hasdrubal was assassinated, and his brother-in-law Hannibal, the twenty-five year old son of Hamilkar, was made commander-in-chief by the army. He set out to conquer all of Spain. But when he laid siege to the Greco-Iberian city of Saguntum, north of the "Ebro," the city appealed to Rome. Roman expostulations to Carthage were of no avail; both sides had wanted war. This Second Carthaginian War became the most dangerous war of Roman history, especially since Rome had to fight the greatest military genius ever produced by the Semitic world.

Hannibal's famous crossing of the Alps (218 BCE) is well known. All Roman resistance proved in vain. The Celts in northern Italy defected, some of the Italian confederates (among them Campania) deserted Rome's cause when Hannibal dealt the Romans a crushing defeat at Cannae (216 BCE); Syracuse made an alliance with Hannibal, who also concluded a treaty with Philip V of Macedonia. The Romans, desperately held on to their last resources, appealing to their own and to the Etruscan gods with the promise of splendid games in their honor, consulting the Sibylline books, and sending a delegation to the Delphic Apollo. Capua, which had defected to Hannibal, was reconquered, and the population severely punished. Syracuse fell after a long siege; the famous scientist Archimedes, who had assisted the defenders of the city with various inventions of war machinery, found his death. But in the following year (211 BCE), two Roman expeditionary armies which had operated successfully in Spain under P. Cornelius Scipio and his brother Gnaeus Scipio were reduced by Hannibal's brother Hasdrubal; both Scipios were killed.

The course of the war took a decisive turn only when the twenty-four year old Cornelius Scipio (known as Scipio Africanus Maior) declared his willingness in 210 BCE to accept the seemingly desperate command of the battered expeditionary force in Spain as the successor of his father. Scipio Africanus Maior has been called the greatest Roman military genius before Caesar; nonetheless, his strategic ingenuity, as well as the confidence, hope, and enthusiasm which he was able to inspire among his men, are not enough to explain his success. An ancient Roman belief appeared in a new garment for the first time in Roman history: the *felicitas* of the leader and savior in a situation of greatest need. *Felicitas* was the almost supernatural ability to lead a project to a successful conclusion through insight, courage, and dexterity. The Romans recognized in Scipio's *felicitas* as the manifestation of divine intervention through the deeds of an individual. The Scipio legend, which was formed already during his lifetime, demonstrates that the Roman idea of *felicitas* had begun to merge with the Greek concept of the "divine man." Later, at the time of Caesar, this concept was developed further for propagandistic purposes under the influence of the Alexander legend. The further course of the war justified the hopes of those who had seen more in the mission of Scipio than just the appointment of another magistrate. The year 209 BCE witnessed the legendary conquest of the Punic headquarters Carthago Nova (Cartagena) in Spain; the victory over Hasdrubal at Baecula followed. Hasdrubal escaped north to join his brother in northern Italy, but was defeated by a Roman army (207 BCE). The following year saw the completion of the conquest of Spain, and a year later Scipio was elected consul. In 204 BCE Scipio went to Africa, where he campaigned successfully with the help of the Numidian prince Massinissa. Hannibal was forced to leave Italy and to return to Africa for the defense of his homeland; he was defeated by Scipio at Zama (202 BCE). In 201 Carthage accepted the conditions of the peace treaty dictated by Scipio. It lost all its Spanish possessions, had to pay a high indemnity, and was reduced to a North African petty state.

However, the Second Carthaginian War was more than a contest with Carthage. Rome did not forget that Macedonia had sided with Hannibal. This had forced the Romans to enter into treaties with Rhodos and Pergamon and with Macedonia's sworn enemy in Greece, the Aetolians. As a result, Rome could not disentangle itself from Greek affairs, even if it would have preferred to stay out of any contests with Greek states—Pyrrhos' victories in Italy had not been forgotten. The consequence was more than a century of invited and uninvited interventions into the affairs of the Hellenistic states. The individual stages in this process have already been discussed above (§1.4a–d). In the war with Macedonia 200–197 BCE, Rome was victorious at Kynos Kephalai and confined Philip V to Macedonia itself; the Roman general Flamininus declared the freedom of the Greek states and left. But when the Seleucid king Antiochos III (the Great) landed in Greece, a Roman army under the command of Scipio intervened once more; following Antiochos across the Aegean, it defeated him at Magnesia-ad-Sipylum, and deprived him of all possessions in Asia Minor. Rome made no annexations but distributed the conquered land to Pergamon and Rhodos (190 BCE). Even in 167 BCE, victorious in the war with the last Macedonian king Perseus—a war that was started without any real cause—Rome hesitated to annex Macedonia. Rather, it divided Perseus' kingdom into four independent states. Rome was now the only major Mediterranean power, and the Senate felt that intervention was mandatory whenever any other power aspired to rival Rome's status. Thus when Antiochos IV Epiphanes of Syria was about to annex Egypt in 168 BCE, a Roman ambassador confronted him with an ultimatum and forced him to withdraw, yet without any attempt to gain a foothold in Egypt.

This policy of restraint changed after the middle of the 2d century BCE. Perhaps there were circles in Rome who believed that there was no other way to get rid of the continuous unrest in the eastern Mediterranean world; with respect to Greece, they may have been right. But it is difficult to allow the same explanation in the case of other conquests. It is probably true that leading Roman politicians believed that it would be a blessing for the people in the new provinces to be ruled by Rome; thus they congratulated themselves on the increase of their beneficial and civilized rule of peace over uncivilized foreign nations. They were careful to make sure that such wars were fought for "just causes" and were favored by their gods. It was never officially admitted that financial gain and the desire of ambitious individuals to expand their personal base of power played a role. However, exactly this latter motivation explains why Rome's empire was acquired during the following century of civil war and inner-political crises.

Long-standing hate and irrational fear triggered a third war against Carthage. Hostilities were officially declared in 149 BCE because of a negligible violation of a treaty and despite Carthage's last-minute efforts to preserve the peace; Carthage was conquered three years later, and its realm incorporated as a Roman province. As the province "Africa," it became a pillar of Latin culture and the native land of "Roman" Christianity. During the same years, the Romans finally subdued restless and rebellious Greece; Corinth, the leader of the rebellion, was razed, and the Roman provinces of Macedonia and Achaea were organized (147 and 146 BCE). In 133 BCE the kingdom of Pergamon was bequeathed to Rome through the testament of the last Pergamene king, which led to the establishment of the Roman province of Asia. The first phase of the world conquest was thus concluded. Further acquisitions were directly related to the Roman civil war, which began immediately after these events.

(d) The Late Republic and the Civil War of 133–30 BCE.

EVENTS OF THE CIVIL WAR
(ALL EVENTS ARE BCE)

133	Tiberius Sempronius Gracchus elected tribune
123	Gaius Sempronius Gracchus tribune
107	Marius consul
104	Marius defeats Jugurtha of Numidia
102 & 101	Marius defeats the Cimbers and Teutones
97–87	"Social War" against the Italian allies
88–87	War against Mithradates of Pontos
88–79	Sulla consul and dictator
77	Pompey receives command of Spain
67	Pompey vanquishes the pirates
66–64	Pompey conquers the East
60	First triumvirate between Pompey, Crassus, and Caesar
58–50	Caesar conquers Gaul
49	Caesar marches upon Rome
48	Pompey killed in Egypt
48–44	Caesar dictator
44	Caesar assassinated
43	Second triumvirate between Lepidus, Marc Antony, and Octavian
31	Octavian victorious over Marc Antony at Actium
30	Marc Antony and Kleopatra commit suicide
27	Octavian accepts the title "Augustus"

The reasons for the beginning of the century-long Roman civil war are highly complex. Only a few factors can be mentioned briefly. Most significant was Rome's inability to adjust its social structures to the changing economic situation. This was the case especially in Italy itself. Here viticulture and olives had largely supplanted grain production; at the same time, more land had passed into the hands of the small upper class, which was now confronted with a growing number of dispossessed citizens and a vast army of people who had become slaves as a result of the numerous wars. Another factor was the rapid progress of Hellenization; after the conquest of Greece, Rome was left without any protection against the influx of Greek culture. The ancient Roman moral and cultural values were not well suited for the ideals of world citizenship, while the new universalistic values of Hellenism were to a certain extent considered as a threat by the champions of traditional Rome. Finally, the Roman administration was not capable of responding to the demands of ruling an empire. Rome's wars of conquest had been designed for profit; the subsequent exploitation of the provinces became a notorious problem and was a substantial obstacle to the establishment of peace. Dissatisfaction with the Roman administration and outbreaks of violence became an everyday occurrence. In addition, there were threats from the outside (e.g., the invasion of Germanic tribes) which reinforced the Roman belief that a strong army was all that was needed to solve any problems. It took several generations before Rome began to understand that the establishment of peace required a new attitude toward the conquered peoples and a fundamental reorganization of the Roman administration. Until then, the people ruled by Rome had to go through unspeakable sufferings, because Rome fought out its own problems at their expense. Only the general outlines can be indicated here, as well as particular instances which are significant for the social, cultural, and religious developments.

(1) The single event which highlighted the social grievances of Italy was the attempted *agrarian reform of the Gracchi*. Several slave insurrections had preceded the year 133 BCE, when Tiberius Sempronius Gracchus was elected tribune. He was the scion of an old patrician family: his father had been consul twice, and his sister was married to Scipio Aemilianus, the victor in the Third Carthagenian War. Although the motives for the agrarian reforms which Tiberius Gracchus proposed were already debated in antiquity, it seems likely that his thoughts were inspired by ancient Roman ideals, which had received fresh stimulus from Stoic philosophy. The increasing wealth of the patricians had enabled many of its members to buy up more land, increasing the size of their estates, for

Bibliography to §6.1d

H. H. Scullard, *From the Gracchi to Nero* (4th ed.; London: Methuen, 1976).

Ronald Syme, *The Roman Revolution* (Oxford: Oxford University Press, 1939).

Robin Saeger, ed., *The Crisis of the Roman Republic* (Cambridge: Heffer and New York: Barnes and Noble, 1969).

P. A. Brunt, *Social Conflicts in the Roman Empire* (New York: Norton, 1971).

Bibliography to §6.1d (1)

Hugh Last, "Tiberius Gracchus," and "Gaius Gracchus," in *CambAncHist,* 9. 10–101.

which they could use cheap slave labor that was abundantly available. The new agrarian laws demanded that no senator should cultivate more than 125 hectares (500 *iugera*) of publicly owned land; in addition, every senator was allowed half of this area for each of his oldest two sons. All other public lands were to be distributed to a new class of yeoman farmers. The majority of the Senate used every conceivable legal and illegal device to circumvent this reform legislation, and finally, when all else failed, did not shrink from assassinating the tribune.

Ten years later, Tiberius' brother Gaius Sempronius Gracchus was elected tribune and resumed the reforms. He succeeded with at least parts of an even more comprehensive legislation: a grain bill, which gave to every head of a household the right to buy annually a limited amount of grain at reduced prices; a bill which gave equestrians the right to staff the courts charged with the investigation of corrupt provincial governors (this law survived and had ill consequences, since senatorial governors no longer dared to take measures against the exploitation by tax farmers who were of equestrian rank); finally a law which granted full citizenship to the Latin confederates and to give Latin rights to the Italian allies. But also this reform legislation was wrecked by the cynical selfishness with which the Senate majority defended its interests. Three thousand followers of Gaius Gracchus were killed, Gaius himself, seeing no way out, requested one of his slaves to kill him (121 BCE). However, the underlying conflict caused subsequent struggles of those who supported the interests of the disenfranchised (the *Populares*) with the defenders of the inherited rights of the aristocracy (the *Optimates*).

(2) *Marius*. Outwardly, the Senate had secured its control over the affairs of the state. But it had become clear how powerful the people could be as soon as they found a leader capable of organizing them and retaining their favor. The Senate increasingly had to depend upon those who could count on the favor of the plebeians, be they true leaders or demagogues. After the fall of the Gracchi, the Senate tried to gain popular favor by imperialistic policies, establishing a province in the largely Hellenized area of southern Gaul (Gallia Narbonensis). But precisely this area and northern Italy were invaded soon thereafter by the Germanic tribes of the Cimbers and Teutones, who demolished two Roman armies which tried to stop them in 113 and 105 BCE. At the same time, Rome was involved in a drawn-out warfare with the Numidian king Jugurtha. In this situation the people forced the Senate to accept as a savior in time of need the popular general Gaius Marius, a farmer's son who had risen through the ranks of the army. Marius was elected consul in 107 BCE and—although he was a *homo novus*—against all tradition reelected six times in the following years. Marius immediately began to reform the army. Instead of drafting soldiers from the ranks of the citizens, he recruited men from the landless lower class for a sixteen- to twenty-year period of paid service with the promise of land grants for veterans. Henceforth the soldiers became "clients" of their general; they were no longer "citizens in uniform." Marius

Bibliography to §6.1d (2)

Hugh Last, "The Wars of the Age of Marius," and "Enfranchisement of Italy," in *CambAncHist*, 9. 102–210.

defeated Jugurtha, celebrating a triumph in 104 BCE, and vanquished the Cimbers and Teutones in 102 and 101 at Aquae Sextiae and Vercellae. But in the following years Marius, an excellent general but not a good politician, got into trouble when he attempted to secure land for the settlement of his veterans; he had to retire from the political scene for the time being.

(3) *Mithradates VI and Sulla.* Gaius Gracchus' attempt to secure a better legal status for Rome's Italian allies had been frustrated. The consequences were now brought home in the revolt of the allies, the so-called Social War (91–87 BCE). What the Senate was unwilling to give of its own free will, it was now forced to grant after grievous battles. The war did not end until Roman citizenship had been given to almost all of Italy south of the Po river.

In the year 88 BCE, the king of Pontos, Mithradates VI Eupator, overestimating Rome's internal difficulties, attempted to liberate Asia Minor and Greece from Roman domination. After swift victories over a Roman army and the Roman ally Bithynia, followed by the slaughter of 80,000 Italians in Asia in one single day, he went to Greece, where he was celebrated as the liberator of the Hellenes (§1.4b). Sulla, a fifty-year old undistinguished politician of the party of the Optimates, who happened to be one of the consuls of that year, was charged with the command of the war against Mithradates. While Sulla was in Capua gathering his troops, his opponents transferred the command to Marius by popular referendum. But Sulla marched upon Rome with his troops, entered the city, pushed through a suspension of all the resolutions which had been made against him, and drove his opponents out of the city. This done, he moved to Greece, where he defeated Mithradates in several battles, severely punishing his allies— among them the city of Athens.

Meanwhile, however, the tide had turned again in Rome. Marius returned from his refuge in Africa and was elected consul for the year 86 BCE. As a result of this political change, two Roman armies appeared in Greece, sent by the consul Cinna (Marius had died suddenly), ready for battle against Sulla, whom the Senate had outlawed. Most of the soldiers, however, refused to fight against Sulla and deserted to him. Sulla was also successful in Asia Minor. Mithradates capitulated, giving up all his conquests. Sulla returned to Rome as a victor and assumed absolute power, being appointed "dictator for the reconstitution of the republic" for an indefinite term. His regime began as a reign of terror. His political opponents, forty senators and sixteen hundred equestrians, were put on the proscription lists (they were outlawed and their property confiscated). The Senate was reorganized, the number of senators raised from three hundred to six hundred, and numerous reforms inaugurated in order to restore power to the Senate. In reality the senatorial administration could not function unless a strong leader like Sulla was in control, who ruled with practically regal authority. When Sulla retired voluntarily in 79 BCE (a year before his death), not a single problem had been solved, and not one of the conservative changes introduced by Sulla

Bibliography to §6.1d (3)

David Magie, *Roman Rule in Asia Minor* (2 vols.; Princeton, NJ: Princeton University Press, 1950; reprint Salem, NH: Ayer, 1988).

lasted for more than a decade. However, as Sulla had already been honored in the east as a divine man (hence he issued coins bearing his own image), there was no question after his retirement that only another "divine" leader would be able to address the persistent problems energetically.

(4) *Pompey.* This leader appeared in the person of Pompey (Gnaeus Pompeius), who came from a family that had entered the ranks of the patricians only recently. Under Sulla, who married him to his stepdaughter, Pompey had distinguished himself as an able general, and his soldiers had given him the name "Magnus." Three pressing tasks existed after Sulla's death: in Spain, Sertorius, a partisan of Marius, had created a practically independent, Romanized Iberian state; the pirates had become so strong that they seriously imperiled all Mediterranean trade; in the east, Mithradates threatened to go to war with Rome once more. In 77 BCE the Senate, though not without hesitation, gave the command for the war in Spain to Pompey, who succeeded in subjugating that country by the year 71 BCE. In his reorganization of Iberia, Pompey followed a new ideal, which suggested to the leader of the Roman empire that his actions should fulfill the expectations of the conquered people. Instead of punishment of his enemies, suppression, and exploitation, Pompey practiced clemency and granted benefactions. He was the first Roman general who tried to realize these virtues of the Hellenistic ideal of the divine ruler in his own actions. The same virtues were appeared in his subjugation of the pirates, a task with which he was charged in 67 BCE. Piracy was not a new phenomenon: it had flourished since the 3d century BCE in the eastern Mediterranean, but was held in check by the Hellenistic kings and then by Rhodos. But once the countries of the eastern Mediterranean were either ruled by Rome or had lost their military power, there was no longer any effective control. In fact, Rome's hunger for slaves was a strong economic foundation for the pirates. Moreover, king Mithradates of Pontos had strengthened their organization in order to gain allies for his fight against Rome. Protected by their rocky fastnesses on the barely accessible coasts of Crete and Cilicia, they could be rooted out only with great difficulty. Pompey, however, organized a navy with which he overcame the pirates in the western Mediterranean in only forty days and in the eastern Mediterranean in forty-nine days. He captured more than thousand vessels, followed them into their hiding places, and took twenty thousand prisoners. Yet again the generosity of Pompey exemplified the new ideal of the Roman statesman. Instead of selling the pirates into slavery, he settled them in various sections of Greece, Asia Minor, and Italy.

The war against Mithradates led Pompey to the height of his fame. In 75 BCE, the last king of Bithynia, following the example of the last ruler of Pergamon, had bequeathed his country to the Romans. Mithradates used this as an opportunity to invade Bithynia and to resume his plans for further expansion at Rome's expense. The Roman general Lucullus, who had been sent against him, was able to drive Mithradates out of Bithynia and Pontos, and also defeated the Armenian

Bibliography to §6.1d (4)

Matthias Gelzer, *Pompeius* (2d ed.; München: Bruckmann, 1959).

king Tigranes, to whom Mithradates had fled. However, Lucullus made a tactical error, when he ordered a remission of parts of the debt of the province of Asia in order to help its people to recover economically. This enraged the whole Roman equestrian class, whose economic interests he was hurting severely. When his fortunes of war also turned, Lucullus' soldiers mutinied and forced him to retreat. In this situation the Senate transferred the command to Pompey. From Crete, where he had stayed after his victory over the pirates, Pompey immediately went to Asia Minor. Mithradates, who had reorganized his forces, was quickly beaten and killed.

Cicero made a speech in support of Pompey's appointment, in which he recommended Pompey as a man whom the people of the east saw not just as someone sent by Rome, but as a god. Pompey fulfilled these expectations. Not content with his victory over Mithradates and with the appointment of the king's son as a Roman ally, he proceeded to attempt a political reorganization of all countries of the eastern Mediterranean world. Turning first against Tigranes, the king of Armenia who had incorporated Syria into his empire after the collapse of the Seleucids, and forcing him to capitulate, Pompey advanced to the east as far as Colchis (on the southeastern coast of the Black Sea), then marched into Syria and Palestine, where the two Hasmonean brothers Hyrkanos and Aristoboulos were quarreling with each other about the office of high priest. After his conquest of Jerusalem, Pompey entered into the Holy of Holies of the temple. While he appointed and confirmed vassal princes, including Hyrkanos as high priest in Jerusalem, the people of the east celebrated him as their savior and benefactor. Upon his return to Rome, he was granted a splendid triumph, though only half-heartedly. At that moment Rome considered not Pompey but rather Cicero as the savior of the fatherland. Cicero had just succeeded in uncovering and thwarting the Catiline conspiracy and had played a major role in the bloody suppression of Catiline's final desperate attempt to usurp power. Moreover, the Senate was now controlled by conservatives like Lucullus and the Younger Cato, who opposed Pompey's plans for the settlement of his veterans. Pompey found a new ally in Caesar, a younger politician who had begun to play an increasingly important role in Roman politics. Pompey and his former associate Crassus, then the wealthiest man in Rome, accepted Caesar's proposal, in which the three man agreed to manipulate the politics of the state to their mutual advantage. As the consul for the year 59 BCE, Caesar saw to it that Pompey's veterans were properly provided for.

(5) *Gaius Julius Caesar,* born in 100 BCE, belonged to an old Roman family. By origin and personal inclination, he belonged to the *Populares,* the political faction of the Gracchi, Marius, and Cinna, that had its power base in the popular

Bibliography to §6.1d (5)

Matthias Gelzer, *Caesar: Politician and Statesman* (Cambridge, MA: Harvard University Press, 1968).

J. P. V. D. Balsdon, *Julius Caesar and Rome* (New York: Atheneum, 1967).

F. E. Adcock, "From the Conference of Luca to the Rubicon," "The Civil War," and "Caesar's Dictatorship," in *CambAncHist* 9. 614–740.

assemblies. Marius was related by marriage to Caesar's parents, and Cinna's daughter became Caesar's wife; despite threats from Sulla, Caesar steadfastly refused to divorce her. Unlike his older contemporary, Pompey, who had skipped all the regular offices in his rise to power, Caesar followed the normal course after serving as an officer in the army and studying with the famous rhetor Molon in Rhodos. Although he was troubled by accusations that he had been involved in some dubious machinations (e.g., the Catilinarian conspiracy), and although his personal conduct was subject to question, Caesar managed to be appointed *pontifex maximus* in 63 BCE. This highly respected lifelong office gave him supervision of all aspects of the religion of the Roman state.

The secret pact between Pompey, Crassus, and Caesar, the "First Triumvirate," reveals that these three men had recognized the ineffectiveness of the existing political institutions. This pact would allow each of them to pursue his own aims, so long as they could count on the others' support and did nothing that would frustrate the others' pursuits. Caesar profited from the Triumvirate in two ways: he received the consulate for the year 59, and then gained the administration of the provinces of Gallia Cisalpina and Gallia Narbonensis for the five succeeding years. Caesar's consulate was filled with feverish activity. He attacked the two most pressing problems of internal Roman politics: the distribution of agricultural land in Italy and the exploitation of the provinces. His legislation regarding settlements succeeded, since 40,000 veterans and 100,000 citizens were settled on public lands during the next few years. Caesar simply ignored opposition from the Senate and had no scruples about using illegal means to achieve his ends. But when he went to Gaul in 58 BCE, he left Rome in a state of anarchy. There was continuous fighting between the *Populares,* supported by the somewhat dubious Clodius, at first tribune and then leader of a gang (acting, it was said, by arrangement with Caesar), and the conservatives in the Senate, with spokesmen like the venerable Cicero and Cato, who for their part also employed street gangs. But as long as Caesar was absent, the chaos in Rome was in his best interests.

From 58 to 51 BCE Caesar was busy with the conquest and pacification of the entire region of Gaul. As late as 52 he had to suppress an insurrection by Vercingetorix, who was supported by many Gallic tribes. But in the process of these wars Caesar fashioned the best-trained army that Rome had ever seen. Moreover, as Caesar's clients the soldiers were fiercely loyal to their patron. The Triumvirate had been renewed in 55 BCE: Caesar received another five years in Gaul, Pompey the administration of Spain, while Crassus had free rein in the east. But in 53 BCE Crassus was killed at Charrae in Mesopotamia fighting against the Parthians; his army suffered a crushing and humiliating defeat and lost several legionary standards. A year earlier, Caesar's daughter Julia, who was married to Pompey, had died in childbirth; this hastened the alienation between Caesar and Pompey. In Rome, Caesar's enemies openly pushed for his removal from office, while Pompey, serving as consul, was persuaded to join the *Optimates* in their effort to rescue the state from Caesar's ruthless ambition. The political situation reached a crisis in the debate over whether Caesar could become consul immediately after ending his tenure as governor of Gaul. When the Senate declared a state of emergency in order to prevent Caesar's election as consul, and when the hard-liners in the Senate rejected any compromise, Caesar decided to march on Rome with his army (his famous "crossing of the Rubicon," the border between the province Gallia Cisalpina and Italy).

The civil war became an open military conflict between the two most powerful men in Rome. Caesar had the better-trained army and was sure of the sympathy of large parts of the population. Pompey, acting on behalf of the Senate, claimed legal sanction for his cause and had at his disposal the immense military and economic resources of the whole empire. But Caesar moved so swiftly that Pompey had no chance to build up any resistance in Italy and had to withdraw to the east, where he was respected and even venerated, leaving behind a large fund of money and stores of unminted gold and silver. These Caesar seized, using the opportunity to propagate his own power and the status of his family with the newly minted coins. Using the mint to proclaim imperial status and achievements became standard policy from now on. Despite some initial setbacks, Caesar not only gained control of the entire west, defeating Pompey's army in Spain, he also quickly pursued Pompey and forced him to give battle at Pharsalos in Thessaly (48 BCE), where he vanquished him. Pompey fled to Egypt, but was slain on his arrival. When Caesar came to Egypt and was shown Pompey's head, he wept— the expression of an honest sentiment that well fit the new master of the world.

But the civil war was not yet finished. Caesar had to contend with internal enemies and also faced threats from the outside, especially from the Parthians and the kingdom of Pontos, which had once more risen against Rome. Egypt proved difficult; in 47 BCE Caesar installed the last of the Ptolemies, Kleopatra VII, as ruler. His liaison with Kleopatra, who bore him a son, is well known (for the events in Palestine, see §6.6a). Caesar then turned to the west, where the partisans of Pompey had gathered, first in Africa and later in Spain. In his treatment of vanquished enemies, Caesar, like Pompey before him, followed the ideal of the Hellenistic divine king: the generosity and pardon offered to his defeated enemies were rooted in this ideal as well as in his personality. However, this did not bring true reconciliation and lasting peace.

Many Roman aristocrats cherished the ideals of the republic; repeated attempts to establish for Caesar something that resembled the cultic veneration of a divine king (§6.5b) were seen as a betrayal of those ideals. Although the Senators were willing to appoint Caesar dictator for life, they balked at any constitutional change in government. This hindered a transformation of Roman domination of the world that would enable subject nations to see themselves as members of an international commonwealth, based on the *clementia* of the divine ruler. Concessions that Caesar made to other nations (including the Jews) indicate nonetheless that he had this in mind. The same direction of his thought is manifest in his plans for an ambitious military campaign into the east, in which he hoped to unite Rome with the ancient cultural centers of Mesopotamia, Persia, and India. He apparently aimed to include even the Slavic and Germanic peoples in this large commonwealth of nations. Though such plans may appear fantastic, to Caesar's republican opponents they were a genuine threat. They knew that after accomplishing such a campaign Caesar would be an invincible king and god. Caesar's assassination on the Ides of March, 44 BCE, ended both his life and his dream of a united world.

What remained were Caesar's numerous reforms. He restructered the administration, increasing the number of senators from 600 to 900 and adding a number of public offices; he resettled veterans and destitute citizens; he alleviated debts; and he reformed the calendar, establishing a system (the "Julian Calendar") that prevailed in the west for more than 1500 years. The introduction of a solar year of 365 days, with an intercalation of one additional day every four years, ended a complex tangle of the conflicting solar and lunar calendars. The new calendar also gave an unexpected boost to astrology and gave the alignment of human life with the power of the stars "official" sanction (§4.2c). With Caesar's death, the advocates of the republic, led by Brutus and Cassius, could claim that they had reestablished Rome's "freedom.' But all they had done was open the door for the return of civil war.

(e) Augustus

In his testament, Caesar had adopted his eighteen-year old grandnephew Octavius, who from then on called himself Gaius Julius Caesar Octavianus. He was known by his contemporaries as "Caesar" ("Octavian" in modern histories). Rebuffed by Marcus Antonius (= Antony), he entered into an alliance with the aging Cicero, now a mortal enemy of Antony. But perceiving Cicero's declining influence, Octavian turned to Antony once more. Antony, Marcus Lepidus, and Octavian formed a legal Triumvirate in 43 BCE, in which all three together received a mandate, limited to five years, to reconstitute the republic. Octavian was elected consul for the following year. The Senate was obliged to pronounce Julius Caesar's deification publicly.

Brutus and Cassius, the ringleaders in Caesar's murder, had meanwhile gath-

Bibliography to §6.1e: Texts

M. Reinhold, ed., *The Golden Age of Augustus* (Aspects of Antiquity; Toronto: Samuel Stevens, 1978).
Barrett, *Background,* 1–10.

Bibliography to §6.1e: Comprehensive Treatments

A. H. M. Jones, *Augustus* (London: Chatto and Windus, 1970; New York: Norton, 1971).
Mason Hammond, *The Augustan Principate* (2d. ed.; New York: Russell and Russell, 1968).
Paul Zanger, *The Power of Images in the Age of Augustus* (Ann Arbor, MI: University of Michigan Press, 1988).

Bibliography to §6.1e: Books and articles on special topics

Fergus Millar and E. Segal, eds., *Caesar Augustus: Seven Aspects* (New York: Oxford University Press, 1984) [Essays by Yavetz, Millar, Gabba, Nicolet, Eck, Bowersock, and Griffin].
K. A. Raaflaub and M. Toher, eds., *Between Republic and Empire: Interpretations of Augustus and His Principate* (Berkeley, CA: University of California Press, 1990).
Glen W. Bowersock, *Augustus and the Greek World* (Oxford: Clarendon, 1965).
Hermann Bengtson, *Marcus Antonius: Triumvir und Herrscher des Orients* (München: Beck, 1977).
F. E. Adcock, "The Achievement of Augustus," in *CambAncHist,* 10. 583–606.
See also Bibliography to §6.2

Statue of Augustus

This well-preserved statue was found in Thessaloniki. It shows Augustus with the gesture of an orator. His naked upper body, an iconographic peculiarity of Zeus, indicates his divine status.

ered an army in the east, but they were beaten by Antony at Philippi in 42 BCE; Octavian seems to have played no real role as a commander. After several shifts in their division of triumviral power, Antony emerged as ruler of the entire eastern half of the empire, with Octavian receiving Italy and Spain and Lepidus governing Africa (later, Lepidus would be eliminated so that Octavian controlled the entire western half of the empire). In 38 BCE the Triumvirate was renewed for another five years, at first without the consent of the Senate, though Octavian, who now called himself *Imperator Caesar divi filius*, secured the Senate's approval retroactively.

Antony resided primarily in the east. In 41 BCE he met Kleopatra for the first time when, summoned to give account for her actions, the queen appeared before him adorned as Isis. In the following years his relationship with Kleopatra strained Antony's marriage with Octavia, Octavian's sister, and aggravated differences with Octavian. This liaison also inspired Antony to propagate an image of himself as a ruler in the Hellenistic style, something that Rome found unacceptable. Soon after the victory over Caesar's murderers at Philippi, he had entered Ephesos as the "New Dionysos" at the head of a *thiasos*. Together with Kleopatra he later traveled through the eastern provinces as the New Dionysos united with the New Isis (or Aphrodite). The twins born from his union with Kleopatra, Alexander and Kleopatra, were worshiped as Helios and Selene.

Antony thus fully accepted the Hellenistic concept of the ruler as the manifestation of a deity. For Caesar the concept of divine kingship would have been a symbol of a united new world, bringing together the east of the Persians and Indians with the west of the Romans and Greeks. Antony, however, could not claim much military success beyond the conquest of Armenia, and he had not been fortunate in his campaigns against the Parthians. His claim to divinity was therefore not based on accomplishments and fortunate deeds. As the example of the elder Scipio demonstrates, the Romans might have accepted the Hellenistic concept of divine kingship by connecting it with the Roman concept of *felicitas;* but as it was, divine worship of this pair of rulers could only appear as a histrionic gesture.

Rome, of course, was used to having its generals receive divine recognition in the east. This by itself would not have caused problems for Antony. In order to proceed against him, Octavian had to show that these claims to divinity were part of a political design aimed at dividing the empire. The opportunity came in the last year of the Triumvirate (32 BCE), when Antony requested the Senate to confirm his donation of territories to Kleopatra and their children. When Octavian was assaulted by Sossius, one of the consuls (both consuls were Antony's partisans), he announced that he would submit documentation of Antony's treason. Both consuls fled to Antony, together with a minority of the Senate. The remaining part of the Senate, faithfully committed to Octavian, removed Antony from the Triumvirate, formally declared war on Kleopatra and gave Octavian the *imperium* for this war, authority that was confirmed by an oath of the Roman people and the western provinces.

Two aspects of Octavian's actions were significant. First, in gaining confirmation for his position he had strictly observed the existing laws and the constitution.

Second, Octavian's position was confirmed through a legal referendum and vote, not only of the urban lower classes, but of all Roman citizens of Italy. It seems that Octavian resigned as a Triumvir when Antony was deprived of his authority; after all, this had been a power that ultimately relied on the suspect office of the dictatorship. For these reasons, Octavian's propaganda presented the new *imperium*, which was later continued in the institution of the principate and was designed to establish peace after a hundred years of civil war, as based on the will of the people. On the other hand, his rival Antony had established his claim to power by means of the Hellenistic concept of the divine king, without being able to associate this with any legitimately transferred Roman *imperium*. Worse, Antony shared this divine kingship with a foreigner, and he had tried to secure future rule for the children begotten with this Egyptian woman by both Caesar and himself.

One other element gave Octavian the ideological advantage over Antony. Antony had adopted a powerful and impressive Hellenistic image to justify his rule, and he had played the part of the divine king in his public appearances. Octavian, however, had listened to the poet Virgil (and later Ovid), who expressed a vision of a coming age of peace and its new ruler in terms of a Roman recreation of Greek epic and utopian prophecy. In his *4th Eclogue* Virgil had spoken of the birth of the divine child who would bring peace and reconcile the world of human beings with the world of nature. He had also announced that the realization of eschatological hope would bring back the ideal conditions of primordial time. In his *Aeneid,* on which he had just begun to work during these years, Virgil was creating a national epic that would give new credence to the mission of the Roman people. Octavian was not only aware of these prophetic eschatological poems, he had listened to readings of portions of these works, and he consciously announced his new order of peace as their fulfillment. Fifteen years later, in the year 17 BCE, he would ask Horace to compose the festive ode for the secular celebrations (the *Carmen saeculare*) summarizing the themes of this prophecy in the form of a realized eschatology: the new age is beginning right now.

The war of Octavian against Antony thus became a war of national patriotism carried by a fresh understanding of Rome's mission, and it was a war in which Octavian had the greater fortune. His enemy's power was shattered in a naval battle at Actium (31 BCE), which his trusted general and advisor Agrippa won for him. When the victorious armies moved into Egypt, Antony and Kleopatra committed suicide (30 BCE). Octavian celebrated a splendid triumph in Rome, and after having set everything in order, he surrendered his *imperium* to the Senate at the beginning of the year 27 BCE.

Only in form, but not in essence, did Octavian restore the old republican structures. Whatever his motives and intentions may have been at that moment, the following years saw the development of a new form of government, known to us as the principate, often falsely described as an absolute monarchy. It began with a resumption of republican institutions and incorporated special honors that the Senate conferred on Octavian. Chief among these, voted already at the beginning of 27 BCE, was the title *Augustus,* an archaic sacral title that had not been tarnished by the events of the civil war. The title was chosen to express the foundations of Octavian's position in divine law as well as his *felicitas*. Henceforth, the victorious heir and adopted son of Caesar was known by the name of *Imperator Caesar divi filius Augustus*. For the next few years he was invested annually with the office of consul and received the authority *pro consule* for those provinces in which the key parts of the Roman army were stationed (Egypt, Syria, Gaul, and Spain).

It is important to understand that the subsequent reorganization of the governance of the empire did not simply consist in a transfer of monarchical power to Augustus. The term "power" is misleading anyway. What was at stake was to define certain types of "authority" (*auctoritas*), "executive oversight" (*potestas*), and the "right and responsibility to act" (*imperium*), and decide how these should be shared between the *princeps* (leading man) and the Senate. At first, Augustus tried to assert his influence on the affairs of the state by his annual reelection to the office of consul. A substantial reorganization came only after a crisis in the year 23 BCE. During a long and serious illness of Augustus, a plot by his fellow consul was uncovered. After his recovery, Augustus decided that it was not advisable to base the authority of the *princeps* on that particular office. He resigned his consulate for that year, but expanded his authority *pro consule* as an *imperium maius,* which gave him a rank higher than that of any provincial governor who held his proconsulship by the authority of the Senate. The *princeps* could intercede independently in the affairs of any province, because he now held *imperium* over the whole empire, including the city of Rome. This even included the right to maintain an army detachment (the praetorians) within the capital. In addition, Augustus assumed the authority of the tribune, which gave him the right to initiate legislation on behalf of the people. Beginning in 12 BCE, he also occupied the office of *pontifex maximus*.

Thus the actual authority of the *princeps* rested on the *imperium proconsulare* and the *imperium tribunicium*; both *imperia* were separated from the republican institutions and were specifically connected with the principate. At the same time, Augustus began to create his own administrative instruments to function alongside the Senate. These were implemented step by step as particular situations required. Among these were supervision of the grain supply, oversight of the imperial roads, and a financial administration (*fiscus* = "basket"), which existed concurrently with the senatorial state treasury and received the income due from the imperial provinces and estates. These imperial functions were carried out by a staff directly dependent on the household of the *princeps* and offered opportunities to the equestrians to fill a series of offices, opening up state service to a class that had previously been interested exclusively in its own personal enrichment (for the structures of administration, see §6.3a).

Augustus abandoned Caesar's far-reaching designs of conquest. This conformed with the mentality of a ruler whose primary concern was to preserve the peace. To be sure, Rome was at war during most of Augustus' rule, but these wars served to secure the borders. North of the Alps and in the areas of the Thracians and Illyrians, the border was moved forward to the Danube. An attempt to secure a better northern frontier along the Elbe River by conquering Germany was quickly abandoned after the defeat suffered by Varus (9 BCE), and the Roman legions remained stationed on the west bank of the Rhine. In Asia

Minor, Augustus created a number of new provinces: Galatia, Lykaonia, Paphlagonia, and Pontus. On the eastern frontier he established a number of petty vassal kingdoms; among these were the kingdom of Kommagene and the Palestinian kingdom of Herod the Great (§6.6a–b), both of which eventually became Roman provinces.

Negotiations with the Parthians brought a return of the legionary standards that had been lost in Crassus' defeat at Carrhae, as well as the liberation of Roman soldiers after 33 years of captivity. This restoration of Roman honor was celebrated with the erection of a triumphal arch—the only arch depicting a triumph without war. It is also depicted on the cuirass of Augustus' statue of Prima Porta. Egypt was brought under direct imperial administration and secured on its southern frontier. On the western African frontier, Juba II of Numidia and Mauretania became a reliable Roman vassal. Within these regions peace was securely established. For the people who had been haunted by never-ending unrest and civil war, this must have seemed a true gift from the gods. Inscriptions honored Augustus as a benefactor who had surpassed all hopes, and whose deeds had reached beyond the boasts of any future benefactors of humankind.

This peace was publicly celebrated in visible symbols. Coins depicting Augustus as the "Son of the Divinized Caesar" (*divi filius*) on their obverse show on their reverse a standing female figure and the inscription pax; signs of economic recovery appear, like the staff of Mercury, the god of merchants, and the horn of plenty. The most impressive monument symbolizing the newly established peace was the *Ara pacis,* the "Altar of Peace" on the edge of the Campus Martius, voted by the Senate in 13 BCE and dedicated four years later. Reliefs on its sides show a sacrificial procession of priests, officials, the imperial family, and other dignitaries, with Augustus himself functioning as the chief priest. Two well-preserved reliefs on the front and back of the altar show Aeneas, the founder of Rome, in the act of sacrificing, and *Tellus,* "Mother Earth," surrounded by symbols of rich vegetation and fruitfulness.

The problem of succession turned out to be difficult for Augustus, who enjoyed a very long rule (27 BCE–14 CE). The new institution of *princeps* was not a monarchy; the desire to find a successor from his family instead reflected a widely felt loyalty to his house. But Augustus had no son of his own, only a daughter, Julia, from his brief second marriage. His third and last marriage, to Livia Drusilla (who had to divorce her husband Tiberius Claudius Nero while already pregnant) remained childless. But Livia brought two sons into her marriage with Augustus: Tiberius (the later emperor) and Drusus, who was born after Livia had married Augustus. Augustus first married his daughter Julia to his nephew Marcellus; but Marcellus died young. Augustus' old comrade-in-arms and faithful friend, Agrippa, then married Julia, and Augustus adopted the two sons from that marriage, Gaius and Lucius. Though celebrated as the "Caesars, sons of Augustus and designated *principes,*" both died when they were still young men. Finally, Augustus adopted Tiberius, Livia's elder son from her first marriage, who in turn had to marry Augustus' daughter Julia, once more a widow. Tiberius, however, left Julia after a few years, and Augustus was later forced to sentence her to exile due to her immoral conduct. All subsequent emperors down to Nero descended from the

Julio-Claudian house: that is, they were either descendants of Augustus through the children of his daughter Julia (from her marriage with Agrippa), or of his wife Livia and her first husband Tiberius Claudius Nero. But a direct succession from father to son never occurred.

2. THE ROMAN EMPIRE TO THE END OF THE GOLDEN AGE

(a) The Emperors of the Julio-Claudian House

THE JULIO-CLAUDIAN HOUSE

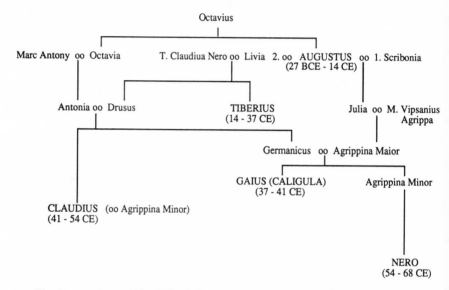

The four emperors who followed upon Augustus, members of the family of the Julians and the Claudians, belonged to ancient Roman nobility. But while Augustus possessed enough skill to surmount the tension between the new institution of the principate and the republican institutions, friction frequently occurred under his successors. The princeps, however, was always able to prevail, thanks to the various authorities with which Augustus had endowed this office. The new order proved to be stable and capable of preserving peace, although the emperors of this house were hardly extraordinary personalities.

(1) *Tiberius* (14–37 CE), fifty-six years old when he became emperor, had shown that he was a competent general and administrator. He once and for all

Bibliography to §6.2: Texts

D. Shotter, *Tiberius Caesar* (Lancaster Phamphlets; London and New York: Routledge, 1992).

D. C. Braund, *Augustus to Nero: A Source Book on Roman History, 31 BC–AD 68* (London and Sidney: Croom Helm, 1985).

B. Levick, *The Government of the Roman Empire: A Sourcebook* (Totowa, NJ: Barnes & Noble, 1985).

abandoned plans for conquering Germany, and through treaties with Armenia and Parthia secured a peace on the eastern frontier which was to last for a century. He consciously de-emphasized the power and dignity of the princeps and tried to transfer major responsibilities to the Senate—though without much success. He also did not permit divine honors for himself, and insisted that the person of the emperor should be subordinated to the office of the princeps. Nevertheless, history has not thought well of Tiberius. One of the reasons for this can be found in the lawsuits for lese majesty (*crimen laesae maiestatis*) through which a few actual and many imaginary enemies of Tiberius were condemned. Tiberius had little knowledge of human nature and was unable to draw faithful friends into his circle, as Augustus had done. The affairs of the state were instead in the hands of power-hungry sycophants. Particularly disastrous was the power which Tiberius gave to the ambitious Praetorian prefect Sejanus. He persuaded the emperor to transfer his residence to Capri (26 CE) so that he himself could establish his reign of terror undisturbed in Rome—even members of the imperial family were no longer secure! Sejanus was overthrown and executed in 31 CE, and although the new Praetorian prefect Macro was less ambitious, he was certainly not less cruel. For eleven years, the emperor never appeared in Rome, communicated with the outside world only through letters, and in the company of his astrologer Thrasyllus devoted himself exclusively to occult subjects. Tiberius' death was welcomed by all with great relief.

(2) *Caligula* (37–41). The question of the succession was difficult. Tiberius own son had been poisoned (by Sejanus?). Of the five children of Agrippa and

Bibliography to §6.2: Studies

E. T. Salmon, *A History of the Roman World from 30 BC to 138 AD* (MHGRW 6; London: Methuen, 1968).

J. P. V. D. Balsdon, *Rome: The Story of an Empire* (London: Weidenfield and Nicolson, 1970).

C. Wells, *The Roman Empire* (Stanford, CA: Stanford University Press, 1984). History of the Roman empire from 44 BCE to 234 CE.

Karl Christ, *Geschichte der römischen Kaiserzeit von Augustus bis zu Konstantin* (München: Beck, 1988).

Michael Grant, *The Roman Emperors. A Biographical Guide to the Rulers of Imperial Rome, 31 BC–AD 476* (New York: Scribner's, 1985).

Barry Baldwin, *The Roman Emperors* (Montreal: Harvest House, 1980).

Harold Mattingly, *Roman Imperial Civilization* (New York: St. Martin's, 1957).

Fergus Millar, *The Roman Near East 31 BC–AD 337* (Cambridge, MA: Harvard University Press, 1993).

Idem, *The Emperor in the Roman World* (London: Duckworth, 1977).

Idem, ed., *The Roman Empire and Its Neighbours* (2d ed.; London: Duckworth, 1981).

Bibliography to §6.2a (1)

Ernst Kornemann, *Tiberius* (Stuttgart: Kohlhammer, 1960).

Frank Burr Marsh, *The Reign of Tiberius* (London: Oxford University Press, 1931).

M. P. Charlesworth, "Tiberius," in *CambAncHist*, 10. 607–52.

Bibliography to §6.2a (2)

J. P. V. D. Balsdon, *The Emperor Gaius (Caligula)* (Oxford: Clarendon, 1934).

M. P. Charlesworth, "Gaius und Claudius," in *CambAncHist*, 10. 653–701.

J. C. Simpson, "The Cult of the Emperor Gaius," *Latomus* 40 (1981) 489–511

Augustus' daughter Julia, none was still alive. Tiberius' nephew Claudius, a sickly scholar, had been kept away from all public offices and was out of the question. This left only Gaius, great-nephew of Tiberius (two other great-nephews had become victims of Sejanus' terror), son of the popular Germanicus, and great-grandson of Augustus, who had received the nickname "Caligula" ("Little Boots") from the soldiers in his father's army camp. He was proclaimed emperor by the Praetorian prefect Macro and recognized by the Senate. After the oppressive final years of Tiberius' reign, the young emperor was greeted with great anticipation. But his reign quickly turned into a nightmare, and it became apparent that he had a deranged mind. The divinization of the late emperor, and in the east the divine worship of the ruling emperor, had become an important support for the institution of the principate. But it was a catastrophe that a ruling princeps was seriously convinced of his divinity. Caligula appeared in public in the dress and with the insignia of one god or the other, believing that he was the incarnation of Jupiter, and demanding that his statues be put up everywhere and receive divine worship—even in the synagogues of Alexandria and in the temple of Jerusalem! He lived in an incestuous marriage with his sister Drusilla and deified her after her death. In his political behavior Caligula imitated the oriental "great kings," appointing vassal kings in several Roman provinces in the east (among these Herod's grandson Agrippa I in Palestine; see §6.6d). The Jews of Alexandria, who fiercely resisted the blasphemous insanity of Caligula, were persecuted by the fanaticized plebs, and a delegation sent to Rome under the leadership of the philosopher Philo was ridiculed by Caligula. At the end, not only the leading circles of Rome but also the army had enough of this clown who claimed to be Jupiter, but nervously hid under a table at the approach of a thunderstorm. After several unsuccessful attempts on his life he was slain by officers of the imperial guard.

(3) *Claudius* (41–54). In the turmoil following the assassination of Caligula, the Praetorians accidentally found his forty-nine-year-old uncle Claudius, grandson of Augustus' wife Livia, in the imperial palace hiding behind a curtain and proclaimed him emperor. Claudius has been accused by ancient historians as lacking dignity and depending too much on his wives and freedmen. However, the record of his administration is impressive. Supported by an efficient staff of civil servants, the emperor, who was a learned historian (he had written comprehensive histories of Augustus, of Carthage, and of the Etruscans—he was one of the last Roman people who still knew Etruscan) and had studied legal matters thoroughly, conducted the affairs of the government quite well. In order to carry through several of his projects, he restructured the "imperial house" into an administration with several departments: a chancellery for military and political affairs, a treasury department, an archival administration, and a department for petitions. As heads of these departments he appointed imperial freedmen, who were mostly of Greek or oriental origin. This gave Rome for the first time a "government" which proved to have considerable stability for years to come.

Bibliography to §6.2a (3)

Arnoldo Momigliano, *Claudius* (2d. ed.; New York: Barnes & Noble, 1962).

Claudius also reorganized the financial administration, secured the corn supply for the Roman people, expanded the right of citizenship, especially to foreigners, and appointed members of the provincial nobility to the Senate. Religious reforms concerned both the established Roman cults and some recently introduced religions (e.g., the cult of Attis). In his building activity, Claudius used imperial funds for projects which would benefit general commerce: he enlarged Ostia to become Rome's primary commercial seaport, built new aqueducts, regulated the Tiber, and constructed roads (e.g., from the Adriatic Sea along the river Etsch to the Danube). Among the new cities which he founded was Colonia Agrippina (Cologne in Germany), named after his last wife, Nero's mother. In external politics he accepted Augustus' goal of securing the frontiers, though went beyond it in his conquest of a part of Britain. Provinces which Caligula had given away to vassal kings were returned to direct Roman administration (including Palestine; §6.6d–e).

What remained in the memory of history are the scandals associated with Claudius' rule. He was married to Valeria Messalina, a great-granddaughter of Augustus' sister Octavia. It is reported that Messalina publicly prostituted herself with imperial permission. When she married the consul-designate during the emperor's absence, she was done away with by Narcissus, the head of the imperial chancellery. Upon the advice of his secretary of the treasury, Claudius married his niece Agrippina (a sister of Caligula)—ambitious and hungry for power. Once persecuted, mistreated, and exiled by Tiberius, she had determined that she would never again be a member of the imperial house considered a danger to the state. Claudius had to adopt her son Lucius Domitius Ahenobarbus as Nero Claudius Caesar and to promise him his daughter Octavia in marriage, thus securing first rank in the succession for Nero, while Claudius' own son Britannicus, had to take second place. Soon, coins were issued proclaiming Agrippina as "Augusta" and her son as "crown prince." In order to obviate any unexpected turn of fate, it seems that Agrippina, together with her physician, poisoned the emperor, whose longevity might threaten her designs.

(4) The new emperor *Nero* (54–68 BCE) was greeted with enthusiasm. He gave the funerary oration for his stepfather Claudius (the philosopher Seneca, Nero's educator, had written the speech), while the Senate deified Claudius and appointed Agrippina as the priestess of the cult. The reign of this emperor, who would become the first to persecute the Christians and who brought the Jews the most catastrophic war of their history, began in great splendor. The office of the princeps had been created by Augustus because he had recognized that the immense empire could survive only if military leadership and administrative supervision were under the control of one and the same person. The princeps had to be a military leader as well as an expert administrator. Tiberius and Claudius had been equal to this task, but Nero had no inclination to prove his gifts in these

Bibliography to §6.2a (4)

Arnoldo Momigliano, "Nero," in *CambAncHist*, 10. 702–42.
B. H. Warmington, *Nero: Reality and Legend* (London: Chatto and Windus, 1969).
Michael Grant, *Nero* (London: Weidenfield and Nicolson, 1970).

endeavors. The consequences of this failure were not immediately apparent, because Nero gave the business of government to his advisors Seneca and Burrus. The Gaul Burrus, Praetorian prefect from 51 CE, was a financial expert, and it was due to his efforts that the government ran smoothly during the first years of Nero's reign. The poet and philosopher Seneca (§6.4f), a Roman nobleman from Spain, immensely rich but personally frugal as a Stoic philosopher, had been recalled from exile by Agrippina (the cause for his exile was probably a personal intrigue by Messalina) in order to assume the rhetorical education of her son Nero. Seneca wrote a treatise on generosity (*De Clementia*) designed as the governmental program for the young emperor. An ideal seemed to become reality: the greatest philosopher of his time as the guide of a young ruler had the opportunity to determine the fortunes of a state in which the generosity and magnanimity of the ruler preserved the peace within the land and with its neighbors.

Although Nero was quite open to such ideals, he had no intention to subject his immoral tastes for pleasure to the demands of the fulfillment of duty. The moral corruption of the Roman nobility had finally reached the emperor himself. Nero was convinced that neither moral considerations nor natural inhibitions should stand in the way of the satisfaction of normal and perverse sexual desires, and he felt that it was perfectly justifiable to murder even the closest members of his own family as soon as he suspected that they might stand in his way. Already in the second year of his government he had his stepbrother Britannicus (Claudius' son) poisoned. His mother Agrippina, whose image had appeared together with Nero on coins, was soon forced to withdraw from political life, and in 59 CE Nero determined that his mother also had to die; he probably feared for his own security as long as she was still alive. When Burrus died in 62 CE, Seneca had to retire from political life. Nero also repudiated his wife, Claudius' daughter Octavia, and married Poppaea, the wife of his friend Otho (who became emperor for a brief time after Nero's death). When Poppaea was pregnant for the second time, Nero killed her by kicking her in the stomach (accidentally or in drunken stupor?). In 65 CE a conspiracy was discovered, at whose head was a senator named Piso. This gave Nero an opportunity to murder all members of the imperial family who were still alive and to force several of his friends and advisors to commit suicide: Seneca, whom the conspirators might have designated as the new emperor; the writer Petronius, who had been Nero's closest advisor in his unbecoming amusements; and the poet Lucan, who had once been a flatterer of Nero, but now had to pay with his life, because he had quoted a line from one of Nero's poems in a public toilet.

In his public appearances, Nero by no means presented himself as a sinister tyrant. His enthusiasm for everything Greek combined in a peculiar way with his desire to find public approval. On his coins, his portrait—though realistically depicted with an ugly, fat face—assumes insignia from Hellenistic ruler coins: a radiate solar crown, the aegis of Zeus, and the locks of Apollo. At the same time, he is the first emperor to depict his munificence such as the distribution of money and wheat. Beginning in 59 CE, first in private, and then also in public, he gave performances as a poet, singer, and athlete. In order to enhance his popularity among the people, he arranged the most magnificent and refined but also outlandish public games. A catastrophe almost ended his career when a terrible fire broke out in Rome, raged for an entire week, and destroyed the major part of the old city. Since the rumor began to circulate that the emperor himself was the arsonist, Nero looked for a scapegoat, and he chanced upon the Christians. They were driven together and martyred in ingenious ways; some were covered with pitch and burned at night as torches in the imperial gardens. If there was any protest against such cruelties, a well-functioning system of informers was capable of discouraging any public debate. For the masses, however, Nero's government was a splendid show, although the state's finances were ruined as a consequence. In 66 CE the Parthian-appointed king Tiridates of Armenia appeared in Rome in order to receive his crown in great pomp from the hands of the Roman emperor. Nero spent large sums of money to celebrate this great result of his policies of peace. Nor did he spare any funds for the building of his "Golden House" (occupying 125 acres) and for the rebuilding of Rome, for it was Nero who gave "Eternal Rome" its architectural shape. His tour of Greece became an equally costly venture. Since the emperor wanted to compete personally in all Greek games, many had to be shifted so that all of them would take place within the same year and, against all tradition, musical contests had to be introduced to Olympia. The visit of this "Hellenophile" emperor was generally welcomed in Greece, and that he declared the "freedom" of Greece and its exemption from the payment of taxes became the foundation for the persistent belief in a "Nero redivivus" who would return as the liberator of the people. Nero returned to Rome with 1,808 victory crowns for a magnificent triumph of peace, in which he was hailed as Olympian Victor, Hercules, and Apollo. At the same time he began to gather an army, which he wanted to lead in a campaign as far as the Caucasus. But the governors of the western provinces protested. Nero lost his nerve. When even the two Praetorian prefects turned against him, he fled from the city and committed suicide in an undignified manner in a villa near Rome. His last words are reported to have been: "As what an artist do I perish!"

There was no successor left among the descendants of Augustus and Livia. The Senate had deposed Nero one day before his suicide, but was unable to solve the problem of his succession because all power lay in the hands of the troops. Heading the rebellion against Nero was Galba, the governor of Spain; thus the Senate appointed him as emperor. Galba was seventy-two years old and belonged to the Roman nobility. He was just and austere, but did not possess enough political skill to master the problems facing the state. Within six months the army stationed on the Rhine revolted and proclaimed its general Vitellius emperor. Meanwhile Galba was slain in Rome by Otho and his people, and the Senate recognized this former friend of Nero, first husband of Poppaea, and the people's favorite. But Vitellius invaded Italy; for the first time after a century of peace a battle was fought on Italian soil. Otho lost and committed suicide. Vitellius, however, quickly gambled away whatever authority he had. He was fond of good living and much too lazy to tackle any problems. There was, however, still another Roman army which had so far not intervened in the fight for Nero's succession: the army of Vespasian, occupied with the suppression of the Jewish revolt of 66 CE. On 1 July 69 the Roman prefect of Egypt, Tiberius Alexander (nephew of the Jewish philosopher Philo; see §5.3f), proclaimed Vespasian emperor. The Syrian legate Mucianus joined him two days later.

(b) The Flavian Emperors.

ROMAN EMPERORS
FROM VESPASIAN TO COMMODUS

Rulers	*Events*
69–79 Vespasian	70 Fall of Jerusalem
79–81 Titus	79 Eruption of Vesuvius
81–96 Domitian	Conquest of Britain completed
	Beginning of German Limes
	95 "philosophers" expelled
97–98 Nerva	97 *Damnatio Memoriae* of Domitian
98–117 Trajan	101–102 First Dacian War
	105–106 Second Dacian War
	115–117 Parthian War
	116 Jewish diaspora insurrection
117–138 Hadrian	132–135 Bar Kochba insurrection
138–161 Antoninus Pius	
138–161 Marcus Aurelius	162–166 Parthian War
	167 Beginning of plague
	170–174
	& 175–180 Wars with Marcomanni
180–192 Commodus	

(1) *Titus Flavius Vespasianus* was almost sixty years old when he became emperor. He descended from an equestrian family which had only recently been elevated to senatorial rank; his father had been a tax collector in Asia Minor. As a general, Vespasian had served successfully in Britain and Germany, and he had been a good proconsul of Africa. Intelligent enough not to meddle with the problems of Nero's succession, he hesitated to accept the summons to become emperor. But once he had made up his mind, he planned his moves with circumspection. First he went to Egypt, transferred the command in the Jewish War to his son Titus, and shut off the grain supply for Rome. He secured the support of the armies in Syria and Illyricum, negotiated with the Parthians to make sure that he was not attacked from the rear, and left to his supporters the actual conquest of Rome and the overthrow of Vitellius. Not until the following year (70 CE) did Vespasian himself go to Rome. Once there, however, he undertook to solve the many problems energetically. Because of the mismanagement during Nero's last years and the subsequent wars among the successors, the state's finances were

Bibliography to §6.2b

Hermann Bengtson, *Die Flavier: Vespasian, Titus, Domitian: Geschichte eines römischen Kaiserhauses* (München: Beck, 1979).

ruined. Italy had suffered severely through the civil war, and parts of Rome were demolished, with the Capitol a heap of rubble and the state archives destroyed. Insurrections in Gaul and at the lower course of the Rhine had to be crushed, and the Jewish War ended only during this year. In 71, Vespasian and his son Titus celebrated a splendid triumph, which is depicted on the Arch of Titus, preserved in Rome to this day, and also described in detail by the Jewish historian Josephus, who witnessed the event. The rebuilding of the city was supervised personally by the emperor, and the regulation of the Tiber was completed. A part of the large area that had been occupied by Nero's Golden House became the building ground for the Baths of Titus and for the "Colosseum," the largest amphitheater of the Roman world with room for 50,000 spectators. Vespasian modeled the authorities of his office as well as the symbols, through which they were propagated on coins and in sculpture, on Augustus. Extreme thriftiness, tight revenue policies, and sobriety in the conduct of the administration distinguished the years of Vespasian's rule. He was more interested in the reorganization of the patrician class and in the strengthening of the Senate than in titles of honors for his own person. The same Vespasian who is said to have worked miracles like a divine man while staying in Alexandria, and who would be remembered as one of the most successful Roman emperors, when he felt his death approaching—since the emperors could be declared gods after their death—joked: "Woe is me. I think I'm turning into a god."

(2) *Titus and Domitian.* Vespasian was followed by Titus, who ruled for only two years (79–81 CE). He continued the work of his father, but several catastrophes occurred during his reign. In 79 Mt. Vesuvius erupted and buried the cities of Pompeii and Herculaneum; a year later, a major fire destroyed parts of the city of Rome; finally a plague decimated the population. Posterity has not forgotten Titus' personal efforts as he worked for the relief of the victims, nor his integrity and clemency (famous paintings as well as Mozart's opera remember the *Clementia Titi*). This stands in sharp contrast to the judgment about his brother Domitian, whose years of (81–96 CE), however, also produced a number of positive results. The rebuilding of the city of Rome after the fire of the year 80 was continued (the ruins of the Colosseum and of the House of Domitian on the Palatine are extant witnesses); the administration was strengthened through a consolidation of the civil service; Roman rule in Germany was secured (Upper and Lower Germany became Roman provinces and the German *limes* was initiated); the conquest of Britain was completed. The arrogance of the emperor, who demanded to be addressed as "Lord and God," called forth the Senate's opposition. His severe paranoia led to a number of death sentences, which did not even exclude the members of his own family, as in the case of his cousin Flavius Clemens. Twice the "philosophers" were expelled from the city of Rome.

Some historians doubt that the Christians were also persecuted. However, during this time the apocalyptic mood seems to have intensified, so that Chris-

Bibliography to §6.2b (2)

B. W. Jones, *The Emperor Titus* (New York: St. Martin's Press, 1984).
John A. Cook, "Titus and Berenice," *ASP* 72 (1951), 162–75.

tians spoke about the coming of the antichrist (see §12.1c, on the Revelation of John); that the Christian community in Rome suffered is evident in the *First Epistle of Clement* (§12.2d). Domitian's last years became a reign of terror, and his assassination by friends and freedmen came as a relief. That is demonstrated by the *damnatio memoriae* which was executed after Domitian's death: his name was erased on all inscriptions and all his statues were removed. Thus the Flavian dynasty ended in a widespread pessimistic mood, which was intensified by the economic problems of the last years of Domitian's reign. This mood is found not only among Christians, but also in the didactic lectures of the Stoic philosopher Epictetos and in the works of the historian Tacitus (§6.4d). In spite of all this, however, the time of the Flavian emperors laid the foundation for the "golden age" of Rome. The economic upturn under the Flavians had shown that the existing order was viable and that revolutionary interventions were not needed. The decline under Domitian was not as catastrophic as it may have seemed to contemporaries. The peace with the Parthians in the east, had been maintained; Domitian had also successfully repulsed barbarian intrusions on the northern and northeastern frontier, and he was popular with the soldiers whose pay he had raised substantially. To be sure, the "Lord and God" Domitian had been an unbearable tyrant, but a more authentic princeps would have the opportunity to maintain the peace and to bring new prosperity to large parts of the population of the empire.

(c) The "Golden Age"

The decades following upon the death of Domitian saw the rule of emperors who in each case adopted their successors. This became a period of internal peace and widespread prosperity. The emperors promoted the welfare of the cities, encouraged building activity and supported it generously, and reorganized the financial and legal administration. Science, rhetoric, and philosophy enjoyed imperial favor. This period also became a time of consolidation for Christianity, which is visible in the formation of an ecclesiastical organization, the foundation of a Christian morality of the good citizen, and the institution of schools of philosophical theology.

(1) *Nerva* (96–98 CE). No plans had been made for the time after Domitian's assassination, and when it happened the best one could do was to choose Nerva, a respected senator in his sixties, who had no political following. He did his best to repair the damage of the last years of Domitian's rule: the exiles were recalled; the memory of Domitian was wiped out. Nerva also began the rebuilding of the state treasury, distributing land to the poor, and purchasing grain for the population of the capital. He encouraged building construction and gave support to the cities. But he was exclusively a man of the Senate and his political position remained insecure. In order to strengthen it and to gain the support of the

Bibliography to §6.2c

Mason Hammond, *The Antonine Monarchy* (PMAAR 19; Rome: American Academy, 1959).
Wilhelm Weber, *Rom, Herrschertum und Reich im 2. Jahrhundert* (Stuttgart und Berlin: Kohlhammer, 1937).

military, he adopted the successful army general and governor of Upper Germany, M. Ulpius Traianus, and made him co-regent. When Nerva died shortly thereafter, his deification gave all his successors the right to claim divine origin.

(2) *Trajan* (98–117) came from an originally equestrian Roman family from Spain. He was the first Roman provincial to become emperor. For two decades Trajan had been the legate of a legion and an army general and had distinguished himself in wars in Syria, Spain, and Germany. Circumspect and experienced in administrative matters, he personally concerned himself with a large number of diverse problems, for which the extant correspondence with the Younger Pliny is very instructive. His building activity in Rome and in the provinces promoted the economic upturn which had begun under Nerva. But contrary to his predecessors, Trajan returned to a policy of territorial expansion. His first target was the prosperous region of Dacia, north of the lower Danube, and adjacent to the Roman province of Moesia. In two wars (101–102 and 105–106 CE) the inhabitants were subjugated; Dacia became a Roman province and was thoroughly Romanized in a very short time, although Roman rule in Dacia lasted for less than two centuries (today's Rumanian language is derived from Latin and belongs to the Romance languages). Here, Trajan's policies of expansion were successful, and Dacian gold (one of the reasons for the annexation) as well as the new economic opportunities proved to be beneficial to the whole Roman realm. The reliefs of Trajan's Column in Rome tell about the conquest of Dacia in great detail. The Column was set between the two new libraries (Greek and Latin), which were part of the Forum of Trajan; it is the largest of the imperial fora and, together with the adjacent buildings of the Trajanic Market, gives evidence for the new wealth that was flowing into Rome as a result of the conquest.

Trajan's expansionary policy in the east was problematic and not altogether successful. For purely economic reasons Trajan first annexed the kingdom of Nabatea, east and south of the Dead Sea (106 CE), which had remained independent as a Roman client state. In its place Trajan founded the Roman province of Arabia Felix with Bostra and Petra and expanded Roman rule to the Gulf of Akabah. A fleet was stationed in the gulf which gave Rome full control of the sea trade using the routes between the Persian Gulf and Egypt, as well as the land route that passed through Nabatea. At the same time, Trajan had fortified his base for an attack upon the Parthian empire. There had been peace on the Parthian frontier since the time of Augustus: Armenia was a Roman vassal state, Kommagene (south of Kappadokia), ruled by kings who claimed both Parthian and Seleucid descent, had become part of the province of Syria in 72 CE, and northern Armenia (Armenia Minor) had been joined to the province of Kappadokia. But meanwhile, the southern part of Armenia (Armenia Maior), with its capital Tigranokerta, had come under Parthian influence. This was the signal for Trajan to declare war against the Parthians (115–117 CE). His army conquered Armenia and marched on Mesopotamia. Osrhoëne (between the upper courses of

Bibliography to §6.2c (2)

Daniel N. Schowalter, *The Emperor and the Gods: Images from the Time of Trajan* (HDR 28 Minneapolis: Fortress, 1993)

the Euphrates and Tigris), with Edessa and Nisibis, became Roman territory; Babylon, Seleukia, and the Parthian winter residence Ktesiphon fell into Roman hands. With an advance to the Persian Gulf and the conquest of Adiabene, east of the Tigris, Rome achieved its greatest territorial expansion. Three new provinces were thus added to the empire: Armenia, Mesopotamia, and Assyria. But before Trajan was able to secure these newly conquered realms, he fell ill and died. In consequence Armenia, the Osrhoëne, and Mesopotamia remained embattled for centuries, frequently afflicted by wars between Rome and its eastern enemies. The development of Christianity in these areas was not unaffected by this political situation. Trajan's eastern expansionist policies were not only the cause for the continuing instability in this area, it apparently also triggered the Jewish diaspora insurrection which began during the Parthian campaign. The revolt started in the Cyrenaica and spread to Egypt and Cyprus, but was cruelly suppressed. It may be that this insurrection speeded up the separation of Christianity from Judaism, although this process had begun much earlier (§6.6f).

(3) *Hadrian* (Publius Aelius Hadrianus, 117–138 CE), Trajan's distant relative, ward, and adopted son, also came from Spain. In the Dacian and Parthian campaigns he had been entrusted with important military assignments. But he did not continue the policies of conquest of his predecessor: Mesopotamia and Assyria were abandoned as Roman provinces, Armenia became a vassal state, and further conflicts with the Parthians were resolved through diplomatic negotiations. In the north, Hadrian sought to stabilize the Roman frontier, of which Hadrian's wall in Britain is a witness, designed as protection against Scots and Picts. In contrast to his predecessor, who had added three titles of victory celebrations to his name (Germanicus, Dacicus, Parthicus Maximus), Hadrian called himself simply *Hadrianus Augustus*. The emperor's relationship to the provinces on his coins and in sculpture is expressed in such a way that the provinces appear as "reconstituted," not as "captured." Even after the defeat of the Jews, Hadrian did not issue any victory coins. In his domestic policies, Hadrian continued to sponsor building projects. The administration was further developed in the direction of a professional civil service: the imperial freedmen were replaced by men from the equestrian class, who administered the various departments. On the basis of a reform designed by the African Salvius Julianus, Hadrian reorganized the legal system and made it more directly responsible to imperial supervision. Like Trajan, Hadrian respected the Senate, though he was never able to overcome its hostility.

Hadrian was an enthusiastic friend of Greek culture, and spent large parts of his reign traveling (121–127 and 128–134 CE), especially in the eastern parts of the empire. He involved himself personally and financially in the promotion of the welfare and beautification of the Greek cities, as well as the furthering of scholarship and education. The emperor himself was a man of wide reading in Greek literature, completely at home in the Greek language, and inspired by the scien-

Bibliography to §6.2c (3)

Stewart Perowne, *Hadrian* (London: Hodder and Stoughton, 1960).

T. D. Barnes, "Hadrian and Lucius Verus," *JRomS* 57 (1967) 65–79.

tific and religious thirst for knowledge. In Athens, he renewed the university, built a magnificent library, and completed the Temple of Zeus Olympios, which had stood partly finished for centuries: it became the largest temple ever built in Greece. Inscriptions praise Hadrian as "Olympios." In Eleusis, Hadrian was initiated into the mysteries. While Athens, where he also built a new suburb and an aqueduct and was accepted among the city's eponymous heroes, was at the center of Hadrian's benefactions, his support extended to other parts of the empire. In Thrace, his most important foundation was the city of Hadrianopolis (today Edirne in European Turkey). In Ephesus, an immense temple to the "Olympian Hadrian" and a new aquaeduct are witnesses of his imperial largess; in Pergamon, he completed a temple dedicated to Trajan, endowed a sanctuary for the Egyptian gods (one of the largest sanctuaries ever built, of which a remnant is preserved in the "Red Hall"), and financed the reconstruction of the famous Asklepieion, including its library. The most significant monument in Rome itself is the "Pantheon," architecturally the most innovative temple from antiquity: instead of the normal narrow rectangular cella, the interior is a large circular room with a vault of 42 meters in diameter and of the same height, lighted mysteriously by the rays of the sun through a central oculus. During a journey on the Nile, Hadrian's lover, a twenty-year-old Bithynian named Antinoos, drowned in the river (the statues of this beautiful young man, who was to receive divine honor in many places, are preserved in numerous copies); Hadrian founded a city at that site, Antinoopolis, in whose temple Antinoos was worshiped as a god.

Hadrian also reconstituted Jerusalem as the city of Aelia Capitolina and made preparations to build a temple for the Capitoline Jupiter on the site of the temple of Yahweh, which had been destroyed in the Jewish War. This caused the Jewish insurrection of Bar Kokhba, a revolt which also spread to other provinces. It took several years of war (132–135 CE), conducted with the utmost ferocity on both sides, to crush this insurrection. The result was the virtual annihilation of Palestinian Judaism. Hadrian died only a few years later after a debilitating disease in his villa near Rome (138 CE). Lucius Aelius, who had been adopted by Hadrian and designated his successor, had died before him. Thereupon Hadrian adopted the civil servant and lawyer Antoninus, under the condition that Antoninus in turn would adopt Lucius Aelius' son (the later emperor Verus) and his wife's nephew (the later emperor Marcus Aurelius). The Senate at first refused to grant Hadrian divine consecration, but his successor prevailed and finished the mausoleum in Rome (the Hadrianeum, now known as San Angelo).

(4) *Antoninus Pius* (138–161) belonged to a Roman family from southern Gaul. His reign is remembered as a period of uninterrupted peace and prosperity. Actually some wars along the frontiers took place: a war against the Brigantes in Britain (erection of the Antonine Wall), and campaigns against the Dacians and Parthians. However, like Hadrian, he did not add victory titles to his name;

Bibliography to §6.2c (4)

Willy Hüttel, *Antoninus Pius* (2 vols.; Prague: Calve, 1933–1936; reprint: New York: Arno, 1975).

instead, Antoninus adopted the surname "Pius." He cultivated his relationship with the Senate and supported the development of religions. Personally concerned with the details of administration, he oversaw a smooth operation of the government, strengthening the treasury department and the legal system. Extreme thriftiness (no major building projects were initiated by this emperor) went hand in hand with generous support of cities in need (Ephesus, destroyed by an earthquake, received financial aid for its reconstruction). Principate and succession by adoption, instead of election by the Senate or proclamation by the army, seemed to have become an established institution, and the Pax Augusta appeared to be a lasting reality. But this would change rapidly with his successor.

(5) *Marcus Aurelius Antoninus* (161–180 CE), adopted by Antoninus Pius as instructed by Hadrian, the philosopher on the imperial throne, possessed a comprehensive education. In addition to grammar and painting, he had studied Latin rhetoric with Fronto and Greek rhetoric with Herodes Atticus. Since 146 he had been a convert to philosophy, namely, to the Stoa which two generations before had still suffered imperial disfavor. Marcus Aurelius philosophical thoughts are preserved in his *Meditations*. Married to the Younger Faustina, daughter of Antoninus Pius, in the year 145, he was co-regent with his father-in-law since 146. After Antoninus' death he immediately promoted his adoptive brother Lucius Verus to be co-emperor (but Verus proved to be incompetent; he died in 169 CE). War began in the first year of Marcus Aurelius' reign. The Caledonians rose in Britain, while the Chatti invaded Raetia. One year later the Parthian king Vologeses III started a major offensive. The Roman legate for Syria, Avidius Cassius (himself of Syrian origin) received the command for the Parthian campaign. He was able to take Seleukia and Ktesiphon, and after a campaign into Media a peace treaty was signed (166 CE): Armenia and Osrhoëne remained in Roman hands. But the soldiers who returned from the war against the Parthians brought the plague, which raged among the population of the empire for many years. In 165 CE the Marcomanni, who had founded a strong Germanic state north of the Danube (today the Czech areas of Bohemia and Moravia), had begun to invade the Roman provinces of Noricum and Pannonia (today Austria and Hungary) and even advanced as far a northern Italy. After some initial Roman success, the war spread to the entire northern frontier, so that at times Germanic and Celtic tribes from Gaul to Illyricum were involved. The German tribes overran Moesia, Dacia, and Macedonia, and even invaded Greece, sacking Eleusis (later rebuilt by Marcus Aurelius). The repulsion of this invasion demanded many years of full effort from the emperor. In 175, shortly before the victorious conclusion of the war and while the emperor was at the point of founding two new Roman provinces north of the Danube, the Syrian legate Avidius Cassius, to whom Marcus Aurelius had entrusted the administration of

Bibliography to §6.2c (5)

Anthony Birley, *Marcus Aurelius: A Biography* (2d ed.; New Haven: Yale University Press, 1987).

J. H. Oliver, *Marcus Aurelius: Aspects of Civic and Cultural Policy in the East* (Hesperia Sup. 13; Princeton, NJ: American School of Classical Studies at Athens, 1970).

the entire east, revolted and had himself proclaimed emperor. Marcus Aurelius went into Syria immediately; but Avidius Cassus was assassinated by his own partisans before the emperor arrived in Antioch. A new invasion of the Marcomanni forced Marcus Aurelius to return to the German frontier, where he was able to secure the border (founding of Regina Castra = Regensburg), but died of the plague in Vindobona (Vienna) in 180 CE. The reliefs of the Column of Marcus Aurelius in Rome depict the wars with the Marcomanni.

(6) *Commodus*. With the death of Marcus Aurelius, the "golden age" of the Roman empire had definitely come to an end. Continual wars had consumed considerable amounts of money, the plague had taken countless lives and had accelerated the economic decline. Marcus Aurelius' son Commodus, his co-regent and successor, proved to be incompetent. Commodus was incapable of bringing any of the numerous border wars of his reign to a successful conclusion. He was governed by the Praetorian prefects and chamberlains, spent unconscionable amounts of money on games and athletic competitions, in which he loved to compete himself, and executed those who opposed him (including his own wife for adultery), supported the oriental cults, and towards the end of his life received divine worship as Hercules. In 192 conspirators had Commodus strangled in the baths by an athlete.

The subsequent 120 years, which saw the struggle of the Roman state with Christianity, belong to a new period of Roman history. Traditional historiography considers that period as the time of the decline of Rome. The image of the Roman empire no doubt changed as much as the economic situation. The pessimistic experience of the world, which became more common during the reign of Marcus Aurelius and was to dominate the following century, found its counterpart in the renewal of apocalyptic movements (Montanism), the flowering of Gnosticism, and the beginnings of speculative philosophical theology; reaction to such developments include the creation of canon of the New Testament scriptures, the codification of the early rabbinic traditions in the Mishnah, and the conclusion of ancient philosophy in Neoplatonism.

3. ADMINISTRATION AND ECONOMY

(a) Government and Administration

Augustus' new institution of the principate, in which many governmental authorities were transferred to the emperor, became the basis for the administration during the first two centuries of the imperial period. Although many significant administrative, legal, and military powers were now vested with the princeps, he had not become a monarch, but is better characterized as the chief

Bibliography to §6.3

Michael Rostovtzeff, *The Social and Economic History of the Roman Empire* (2d ed. by P. M. Fraser; 2 vols.; Oxford: Clarendon, 1957).

Ludwig Friedländer, *Roman Life and Manners under the Early Empire* (4 vols.; New York: Barnes & Noble, 1968).

executive officer and commander-in-chief of the army with certain rights to initiate legislation. The old republican institutions continued to exist, still retaining certain real authorities and enormous symbolic significance. These ancient institutions—not the emperor—represented the state, whose legal sovereign was the Roman people (*populus Romanus*). Emperors who tried to rule without the consent of the Senate rarely drew any profit from such behavior. Despotic rule by an emperor was rare, and in each instance of short duration. In the army and also in the various areas of civil service, all classes of the Roman people shared in the actual execution of power, so that an emperor could disregard the will of the people and their representatives only to his own detriment. Most emperors attached great importance to an understanding of their office as a mandate of the Roman people, and this had more than merely symbolic significance. The principate as an institution of peace and justice was upheld by a spirit that was different from earlier oriental and Hellenistic monarchies.

An essential presupposition for the reorganization of the administration was the maintenance of the classes from which public servants were recruited. The censorship thus became as permanent office of the emperor, that is, the supervision of the class membership lists for patricians and equestrians. Through the right to admit suitable men to the Senate and through the marriage laws (senators had to marry, and those who had a least three children enjoyed a privileged

Pierre Grimal, *The Civilization of Rome* (New York: Simon and Schuster, 1963).

Jerome Carcopino, *Daily Life in Ancient Rome* (New Haven, CT: Yale University Press, 1940).

Paul Veyne, *Bread and Circuses: Historical Sociology and Political Pluralism* (ed. Oswyn Murray; trans. Brian Pearce; London: Penguin, 1990).

Michael Grant, *The World of Rome* (Cleveland, OH: World, 1960).

Samuel Dill, *Roman Society from Nero to Marcus Aurelius* (London: Macmillan, 1904; reprint New York: Meridian, 1956).

Fergus Millar, *The Emperor in the Roman World (31 BC–AD 337)* (Ithaca, NY: Cornell University Press, 1977).

Ramsay MacMullen, *Soldier and Civilian in the Later Roman Empire* (Cambridge, MA: Harvard University Press, 1963).

Idem, *Enemies of the Roman Order: Treason, Unrest, and Alienation in the Empire* (Cambridge, MA: Harvard University Press, 1966).

Idem, *Roman Social Relations 50 BC–A.D. 284* (New Haven, CT: Yale University Press, 1981).

Bibliography to §6.3a

A. H. M. Jones, *Studies in Roman Government and Law* (Oxford: Blackwell, 1960).

F. H. Lawson, "Roman Law," in J. P. V. D. Balsdon, ed., *The Romans* (New York: Basic Books, 1965).

Barry Nicholas, *Introduction to Roman Law* (Cambridge: Cambridge University Press, 1952).

G. H. Stevenson, *Roman Provincial Administration* (2d ed.; Oxford: Blackwell, 1949).

J. Richardson, *Roman Provincial Administration: 227 BC to AD 117* (Inside the Ancient World; Basinstoke, UK: Macmillan Education, 1976).

H. T. F. Duckworth, "The Roman Provincial System," in Foakes Jackson and Lake, *Beginnings,* 1. 171–217.

Graham Webster, *The Roman Imperial Army of the First and Second Centuries AD* (London: Black, 1969).

G. H. Stevenson, "The Imperial Administration," and "Army and Navy," in *CambAncHist* 10. 182–238.

status) the emperors sought to keep these classes viable. The appointment of patricians from the western provinces and later also from Greece, Asia, and Syria, brought many Romans (and later also non-Romans) from other parts of the empire into the Senate.

The leadership of the army was integrated into the civil service. This prevented the formation of a professional corps of higher officers. Command positions in the army thus became the training ground for future civil servants. It was also most important that most of the legions were stationed in the border provinces: the administration of these provinces by the emperor was thus closely related to his military imperium. At first the army had twenty-five legions (reduced by Augustus from the original number of sixty), later the number was raised to thirty. Each legion had six thousand soldiers, originally recruited from the Roman citizenry. In addition there were auxiliary troops, recruited from the provinces, and a navy. Each legion comprised ten cohorts, each cohort six centuries. A legion was commanded by a legate of the senatorial class. Under him served six military tribunes, of whom the first was of senatorial rank, the others equestrians, as were also the commanders of the auxiliary troops. These officers served for only limited periods, although those of equestrian rank might serve longer. The permanent officers of the army were the centurions, who were commoners for whom this was a lifetime profession. A special part of the army was the imperial guard, the praetorians, who had developed into an elite corps which also served as a kind of military academy; senior centurions were often recruited from the praetorians. The praetorians, consisting of about four-thousand five hundred men and commanded by two prefects, were the only part of the army that was stationed on Italian soil.

In the public service career of the younger members of senatorial families, they first served in subordinate civil positions before entering the army as military tribunes for one or more years. After their return to civil service, they could advance through the offices of praetor and quaestor to the consulate. Since the consulate was required in order to advance to the higher senatorial and imperial positions, there were each year not only the two regular consuls (*ordinarii*), but also additional appointments for consuls (*suffecti*) who served during the later months of the year. The most important offices for men from the equestrian class were those of the military tribune and of the prefect and procurator. These latter posts included a number of functions, from financial administration in Rome or abroad to department head in the imperial house and to the governance of a province. Unlike the senatorial public servants, those of equestrian rank served for many years in the same position and formed the class of experienced, older professionals. But also for other classes of the population did the army serve as an instrument of social advance. Non-citizens who had served in the auxiliary troops for 25 years received with their discharge Roman citizenship. Citizens who served for 20 years and advanced to the lower ranks of the officers corps had the opportunity to advance in administrative functions after they returned home or were settled in a Roman colony.

Provincial administration was divided in such a way that the pacified provinces, not requiring a standing army, were administered by the Senate through a former consul, whose title was "proconsul" (ἀνθύπατος), and who stayed in office only for one year. These provinces included, among others, Italy, Sicily, Baetica (southern Spain), Africa, Cyrene, Achaea, Macedonia, Illyricum, Crete, Cyprus, Asia, and Bithynia. The border provinces, however, were under the direct authority of the emperor, who appointed as governor for each province a "legate" (ἡγεμών), normally of senatorial rank, who served for a longer period. The rest of Spain, Gaul, Britain, the German provinces, those along the Danube and in eastern Anatolia, Cilicia, and Syria belonged to the imperial domain. In addition, certain smaller districts were directly administered by the emperor through an equestrian "procurator" or "prefect" (in Greek also ἡγεμών or ἐπίτροπος); Judea was one of these districts. Egypt had a special status. Because of its significance, especially for Rome's grain supply, it was governed through a "prefect" of equestrian rank (senators could enter Egypt only with special imperial permission). In order to end the exploitation of the provinces, the imperial administrators received fixed salaries. The finances of each province were supervised by procurators who were directly responsible to the emperor. Estate and personal taxes were raised through his employees with the cooperation of the communities. All indirect taxes, however, were still farmed out to the highest-bidding applicant (a "publican"); this system was not abolished until late in the 2d century CE.

The Romans understood the state primarily as an order of law. Existing laws and customs among the subject people were normally respected; only those customs and traditions that seemed incompatible with a civilized administration as, for example, ritual human sacrifices, were outlawed. One important innovation in the legal system was the introduction of imperial jurisdiction. The administration of justice by the emperor and his appointed officials was added to the older courts of juries and replaced them to a large extent in serious criminal cases, such as capital punishment, and as appellate courts. Any lawsuit could be referred to the emperor, or the emperor could decide to transfer any legal proceeding to an imperial court. It was also possible for a defendant to appeal a decision of the governor's court to the emperor. This was especially important in the lawsuits *de repetundis* (charges against officials because of extortion and exploitation) and lese majesty, suits for any violation of the interests of the Roman people and their authority (*crimen laesae maiestatis populi Romani*), which included the emperor and his family. Such lawsuits, therefore, concerned not only high treason, conspiracy, and instigation to war against the Roman people, but also libel against the emperor and refusal to sacrifice in the imperial cult. Only in rare cases during the time of the principate did this result in tyranny by the imperial administration of justice. It later provided, however, the juridical bases for the persecution of the Christians. Only rarely were Christian accused of crimes against religion (practice of magic and sacrilege, e.g., theft from a temple), which did not include rejection of the emperor cult. Proceedings against the Christians varied considerably with the attitude of each emperor, because in all areas of criminal justice (and often also in civil law) the emperors influenced juridical administration through edicts and legal advice.

(b) Commerce and Trade

The economic area of the Mediterranean Sea and the countries surrounding it (§2.1–7) became a political unit through Roman rule, but the basic structures of economy and trade changed very little from the Hellenistic period (§2.2a–e; §2.7a–b). The economic centers, however, shifted to the west, and Rome became the new pivot of trade. This was due to the enormous growth in its demand for mass-consumption goods and luxury articles. Roman agriculture had shifted from the growing of grain to the production of wine and oil, which were the primary crops of the huge landed estates with its armies of agricultural slaves. As a result, Italy, and especially the city of Rome, was permanently dependent upon grain imports from Sicily, North Africa, the countries around the Black Sea, and Egypt, the "granary" of Rome. Bad harvests in those countries led several times to crises in the grain supply (this happened, e.g., under both Claudius and Nero; see Acts 11:28) and to famines in parts of the empire which also relied upon imports from the areas of grain production. The demand for luxury items greatly increased during the imperial period, with most of the imports going to Rome. As a consequence, trade with far-away areas, such as Scandinavia, Africa, and China, experienced considerable growth. Primary import items included perfumes, ointments, precious stones, incense, spices, and silk. Exotic animals were brought from central Africa and India, amber from the Baltic countries. Such trade, handled by independent merchants, was very lucrative, while trade in mass-consumption goods became so unprofitable that the emperors had to provide subsidies and management.

Supplying Rome with the necessary basic foods was also a financial problem. Rome and Italy suffered from a chronic export deficit, which was made worse by Rome's demand for expensive luxury articles, and it grew to astronomical figures under such emperors as Nero, who imported perfumes and exotic animals in large quantities for the imperial court and for public games. The imperial purse also had to finance the supplies for the army in Rome and in the provinces. Another burden was the payment of salaries for public servants, instituted at the beginning of the imperial period. Exports from Italy were unable to bring enough

Bibliography to §6.3b

A. H. M. Jones, "Rome," in *The Ancient Empires and the Economy* (Troisième conférence internationale d'histoire économique; München, 1969; Paris, 1970) 81–104.

Idem, *The Roman Economy: Studies in Ancient Economic and Administrative History* (ed. P. A. Brunt; New York: Rowan and Littlefield, 1974).

F. Oertel, "The Economic Unification of the Mediterranean Region," in *CambAncHist* 10. 383–424.

Helen Jefferson Loane, *Industry and Commerce of the City of Rome (50 BC–200 AD)* (Baltimore, MD: Johns Hopkins University Press, 1938).

A. H. Warmington, *The Commerce between the Roman Empire and India* (Cambridge: Cambridge University Press, 1928; 2d. ed. with new appendix; London: Curzon and New York: Octagon Books, 1974).

K. D. White, *Roman Farming* (London: Thames and Hudson and Ithaca, NY: Cornell University Press, 1970).

M. P. Charlesworth, *Trade-Routes and Commerce of the Roman Empire* (2d ed.; Cambridge: Cambridge University Press, 1926; reprint Chicago: Ares, 1974).

money to Rome to balance the trade deficit. Though many industrial products had at first been exported to the provinces, such as pottery and glass, the rapid economic growth also meant that formerly underdeveloped provinces were increasingly able to meet their demand through their own production. The primary source of income for the imperial treasury, of course, were taxes from the provinces. Roman citizens—the majority of the Italian population—were exempt from direct taxation. In addition, the emperors could use the income from the imperial estates in Italy and in the provinces; at the end of the Julio-Claudian dynasty all its estates became state property. When all resources still proved insufficient, the expedients of debasing the coinage and confiscating property were used to balance the imperial expenses (for the Roman monetary system, see §2.7c).

The shift in economic centers also implied changes in the trade centers and trade routes. Delos and Rhodos lost their significance as major eastern centers. But Ephesus, Antioch, and Alexandria maintained their importance as centers of reshipment because they were situated at the terminals of important trade routes from inland areas. Corinth, refounded by Caesar and quickly rebuilt, soon assumed a leading role in the trade between the eastern and western Mediterranean because merchants preferred to transfer their goods through Corinth across the Isthmus rather than taking the dangerous sea route around the Peloponnesos. (The canal through the Isthmus, begun by Nero, was never completed in antiquity.) In the western Mediterranean, Carthage had lost much of its significance. The leading center of trade here was Rome, which was directly connected with the sea through the navigable Tiber river but flourished as a seaport only after the building of the port city Ostia at the mouth of the Tiber under Claudius. A competitor was Naples and its port Puteoli. In addition to building major seaports, the emperors spent large amounts for the construction of roads. The Roman roads, which made even the most remote outpost accessible, belong to the most impressive accomplishments of antiquity. Most of them were paved and built in straight line wherever possible. In difficult terrain, obstacles were surmounted by cutting away the rock face in the mountains, building daring viaducts across deep valleys, and firm dams through swamps. Postal stations, inns, and military posts were set up at regular intervals, though it was never completely possible to eliminate the menace of highway robbery. Itineraries and maps were available to indicate the distances, the locations of inns, and major points of interest along the way. A medieval copy of such a map from the 3d century CE, known as the *Peutinger Table,* shows the entire inhabited world from Britain to India and China (the westernmost section is lost) with its network of roads, stations and distances. Carriages, often quite comfortably equipped (some of them even had beds), were the primary means of conveyance, and could be rented in many places. Thus the roads served not only military purposes, but also the travel of officials, the transportation of goods, and tourism. It has been estimated that the Roman government's mail service covered 75 km per day; messengers on horseback, using relay stations, could cover as much as 100 km per day. Soldiers were expected to march 30 km daily. Even if a normal citizen could not use the government's mail service, travel and communication were

made possible through these roads to a degree previously unparalleled in antiquity. This became a significant factor in the mission and expansion of Christianity;
it also facilitated the building of a unified ecumenical organization of Christian
churches.

(c) Social Problems

It has been said that the ultimate decline of the Roman empire was caused by
its inability to solve its social problems, which were, at least to some degree, an
inheritance from the Hellenistic period (§2.3a–g) and often a consequence of the
exploitation during Rome's late republican period. It was now brought home that
the newly conquered provinces had suffered immensely because of that exploitation, and also that only a small portion of the Roman population had benefited
from it. Thus Rome was confronted with two tasks: to provide an opportunity for
the recovery of the once wealthy provinces of the east, and to provide for the
growing masses of poor people in Rome. The first task was solved rather quickly.
The abolition of exploitation, remission of taxes and debts, stimulation of building activity (temples, administrative buildings, roads, and ports), and the establishment of secure trade routes brought about a new economic upturn in many
countries of the east, especially in the heavily populated and culturally developed
western part of Asia Minor.

The second task was never fully mastered. The expansion of the huge landed
estates in Italy had dislodged large numbers of small farmers. Together with
thousands of freedman and countless poor immigrants from other provinces, they
formed the plebs of the city of Rome. Caesar, Augustus, Claudius, and other
emperors successfully settled many veterans and displaced farmers on state-
owned properties in Italy and in the western provinces, later also in such newly
conquered provinces as Dacia. As a result, some areas experienced a slow
transition from the system of landed estates to a pattern of independent or tenant
farmers who worked small parcels of land. Such development was further enforced because of the decline in the number of slaves. But even energetic emperors did not dare to infringe upon the property rites of the owners of private estates
in Italy. The poor population of Rome constantly restored its numbers from

Bibliography to §6.3c

Ramsay MacMullen, *Roman Social Relations 50 BC to AD 284* (New Haven, CT: Yale University
    Press, 1974).
Géza Alföldy, *The Social History of Rome* (2d ed.; trans. David Braund and Frank Pollock;
    Baltimore: Johns Hopkins University Press, 1988).
J. P. V. D. Balsdon, *Romans and Aliens* (Chapel Hill, NC: University of North Carolina Press,
    1979).
Suzanne Dixon, *The Roman Family* (Baltimore, MD: Johns Hopkins University Press, 1992).
Peter Garnsey, *Social Status and Legal Privilege in the Roman Empire* (Oxford: Clarendon, 1970).
Keith R. Bradley, *Slaves and Masters in the Roman Empire: A Study in Social Control* (Tournai:
    Latomus, 1984; New York: Oxford University Press, 1987).
Keith Hopkins, *Conquerors and Slaves* (SSRH 1; Cambridge: Cambridge University Press, 1978).
Sandra R. Joshel, *Work, Identity, and Legal Status at Rome: A Study of the Occupational Inscrip-
    tions* (Norman, OK: University of Oklahoma Press, 1992).
Keith Hopkins, *Death & Renewal* (SSRH 2; Cambridge: Cambridge University Press, 1983).

Inscription of Slave Manumission from Lefkopetra

Clearly visible is one of three inscriptions cut into the face of the side support of a table, found near Lefkopetra on the road from Verria (ancient Beroea) to Kozani in Macedonia. The second inscription is visible below the first, the third (unrecognizable) is to the right. All three inscriptions record the manumission of a slave under the legal protection of the temple of the Mother of the Gods. The first inscription translates as follows:

For Good Fortune

To the Aboriginal Mother of the Gods: I, Marsidia Mamaris, according to a vow, have given a woman by the name of Tychike with any offspring which may be born to her to serve the goddess, and the goddess shall have power over her which is not to be violated. In the year 211 of Augustus, which is also 327 (= 180 CE)

uncontrollable sources despite all settlement programs. The free provision of grain for these impoverished masses remained a heavy burden for the treasury throughout the imperial period and frequently caused social unrest. Similar problems in other big cities never reached the same proportions.

One of the greatest social ills which imperial Rome inherited from the late republic was slavery (§2.3c). The military conquests of the 2d and 1st centuries BCE brought hundreds of thousands of slaves to Italy. Whenever the wars did not supply sufficient quantities of new slaves, pirates discovered that kidnapping and the slave trade were a lucrative source of income, and they knew that official Rome was unlikely to interfere. Slavery reached its peak in the last decades of the republic, when most of the slaves were employed in landed estates, industry, and the mines; the terrible lot of the agricultural slaves indeed caused a number of revolts (§2.2c). Since the educational level of many slaves was comparatively high, slaves had little difficulty finding competent leaders for such uprisings. The transplantation of many people from Greece, Asia Minor, and Syria to Italy and the western provinces because of the slave trade was an important factor in the spread of Greek culture. Educated slaves and those who mastered some craft or business had a better chance than others to be freed, and slaves of Roman citizens received Roman citizenship upon their manumission. This contributed to the growth of a class of citizens in Rome and Italy who had a Greek education. Once the pirates had been suppressed and the military conquests had come to an end, the supply of slaves dwindled. The increase in manumissions also contributed to the decline of the number of slaves, until slavery lost its economic significance at the beginning of the Byzantine period. In fact, Augustus faced already a severe problem in the rapid growth of manumissions and enacted legislation to curb its practice. The emperors themselves were the biggest slave-holders and continued to employ slaves for their estates and industrial plants, even though the economic structures were otherwise changing in favor of small-parcel farming and small workshop production. The emperors also used slaves in various branches of the administration, where they had good opportunities to advance and to occupy important official positions after their manumission.

Except for the provision of grain for Rome, there were few if any beginnings of a state welfare system. Trajan set up a fund from which orphans and children of poor citizens could receive stipends for their education. But on the whole, welfare was left to the communities and was therefore—often not to its own detriment—dependent upon the initiative of wealthy benefactors. Some cities employed physicians responsible for public health care; otherwise only members of the upper class could afford medical attention. The emperor and the very rich had private physicians. Common people often had no other choice but to visit somewhat questionable wandering physicians, miracle workers, magicians, and astrologers, who were also often able to deceive members of the upper class or even the emperor himself. Public hospitals did not exist. The numerous Asklepios sanctuaries which experienced a new flowering fulfilled an important function as health spas and outpatient clinics, but they were not regular hospitals, which existed only for the army and sometimes on estates employing many slaves. Care for the aged was left to their families. Beginnings of regular care for the aged can be found in the Christian institution of older widows, who could not remarry, and were thus cared for by the community. The establishment of alms-houses, orphanages, and hospitals is owed to the first Christian emperors and is due to the direct influence of the Christian churches.

(d) The Cities in the Roman Empire

The cities were the political and economic backbone of the Roman empire. One might even define the empire as a league of cities with Rome as its leader. Urbanization was the explicit policy of many emperors, especially of Augustus and Vespasian. Existing cities, especially in the east, were reconstituted, received special privileges, and were given financial support in emergency situations (e.g., after the destruction by an earthquake). Some cities, such as Rhodos and Tarsos, were recognized as "free allied cities," which implied that they had the right to levy their own taxes and were immune from imperial taxation, and they could govern themselves according to their own laws. Older cities, such as Damascus and Gerasa, were sometimes rebuilt according to the Roman city plan or were completely reconstituted as Roman colonies. Caesar had already refounded Corinth as *Colonia Laus Julia Corinthiensis;* Philippi, through the settlement of veterans under Augustus, became *Colonia Augusta Julia Philippensium.* A *colonia* was privileged with the *ius Italicum,* which meant that its agricultural land was not subject to taxation.

In addition to the older Greek colonies in the west, all situated on the coasts (§1.1a), the Romans founded cities primarily in the inland areas of Spain (Italica), Gaul (Nîmes, Geneva, Nyon, Lyon, Paris), Germany (Cologne, Mainz, Trier, Augsburg), Austria (Carnuntum), and Britain (Colchester, Lincoln, London, York). Some of these cities were founded on the basis of military camps, while others developed out of trade centers. In Spain and Africa, Roman cities usually comprised new foundations of older Punic cities. The typical Roman city was laid out as a large square or rectangle, surrounded by walls. All streets within this area followed a regular plan and met at right angles. One central road, usually running from east to west (*decumanus*), was crossed by another main

Bibliography to §6.3d

Pierre Grimal, *Roman Cities: Together with a Descriptive Catalogue of Roman Cities by G. Michael Woloch* (Wisconsin Studies in Classics; Madison, WI: University of Wisconsin Press, 1983).

John E. Stambaugh, *The Ancient Roman City* (Baltimore, MD: Johns Hopkins University Press, 1988).

Richard Tomlinson, *From Mycenae to Constantinople: The Evolution of the Ancient City* (London: Routledge, 1992). See esp. chapters 11 (Rome) and 12 (Pompeii).

Anthony D. Macro, "The Cities of Asia Minor under the Roman Imperium," *ANRW* 2.7.2. (1980) 658–97.

A. H. M. Jones, *The Cities of the Eastern Roman Provinces* (2d ed.; Oxford: Clarendon, 1971).

P. A. Brunt, "The Roman Mob," in M. I. Finley, ed., *Studies in Ancient Society* (London: Routledge and Kegan Paul, 1974) 74–102.

Clarence L. Lee, "Social Unrest and Primitive Christianity," in Stephen Benko and John J. O'Rourke, *The Catacombs and the Colosseum* (Valley Forge, PA: Judson, 1971) 121–38.

road running north-south (*cardo*). This is always found in the cities that developed from a camp.

Corresponding to the Greek city (§2.5.a–b), the Roman city always controlled its surrounding countryside. Its chief source of wealth lay in its agricultural lands, which were essential for the food supply of the city's population and provided most of the income for the aristocracy. The city government was considered the privilege of this land-owning aristocracy, even if its members lived on estates outside of the city proper. The Roman imperial administration discouraged the older Greek democratic city government in which administrative offices were open to all free citizens. In Roman colonies membership in the aristocracy was strictly controlled: the class of the *decuriones,* normally a hundred citizens, formed the city council, was responsible for the election of administrators from its own ranks, the confirmation of laws, and taxation. Such leadership insured stability within the patronage system: the ruling aristocrats, among them often Roman families who had settled in the province, had their patrons in Rome to whom they could appeal; the patron was assured of the support and loyalty of the provincial clients. In older Greek cities, the traditional names of offices were preserved (*archon, strategos, prytannis,* scribe), while Roman titles were used in the Roman colonies (two man called *duoviri* were the highest officials under whom others served as quaestors and aediles).

All other classes, whether free citizens, freedmen, aliens, or slaves, were excluded from participation in the government and administration of their cities. Merchants, businessmen and craftsmen might accumulate considerable wealth— though even the richest could not compare with the wealthier owners of agricultural estates—but they still could not be found among the decurions of the Roman city. The older Greek cities preserved structures which allowed for a greater participation of the citizens of the "middle class," but among the Roman cities, there were few exceptions, among them Ostia, the port city of Rome, and Palmyra, the wealthy caravan city of Syria. These cities possessed very little agricultural land but derived most of their livelihood from trade; thus merchants were dominating the upper class. Normally, the decurions did not work in trade and industry; however, this principle was often violated, either openly or in such a way that a manufacturing plant of a shipping agency owned by a decurion would be run by a freedman or slave as agent and manager. But in all instances, the actual heartbeat of the city was its trade, business, and manufacturing industry.

Beginning with Augustus, the Roman emperors made considerable efforts to revive the economic and industrial prosperity of the cities, especially in the Greek heartlands. Augustus came to Rhodos several times, the third time for more than two years (21–19 BCE), in order to supervise the reorganization of Asia Minor. The newly proclaimed Pax Augusta came to be particularly effective in the highly developed manufacturing industries of this region—with Ephesos as the "first city of Asia." Donations of wealthy citizens continued to play a significant role in the building activities and the beautification of these cities, such as those of T. Claudius Aristion in Ephesos (end of the 1st century CE), of Pantainos in Athens (ca. 100 CE), and many others elsewhere, whose benefactions are praised in numerous surviving inscriptions. Also Roman citizens who had become residents of Greek cities (e.g., the Vedii in Ephesos) are frequently attested to have donated major buildings to their host city. Thefts of art objects—Nero stole hundreds of statues from Greece and from Pergamon—were no doubt resented but did not seriously endanger these cities' growing beauty and their increasing economic well-being. Urban populations became more numerous during the 1st and 2d centuries CE, and manufacturing and trade provided employment for large numbers of people.

Overland transportation of consumer goods was very expensive. Only special industrial products were not manufactured locally: textiles from Patrai and Tarsos, for example, or glass products from Egypt, were exported even to distant areas. But, as a rule, each city had a large number of local factories. Some were small shops with few employees, others larger plants employing dozens of slaves or paid laborers. These workshops could produce all the goods needed for local consumption, while providing at the same time jobs for the majority of the city's population. Owners and workers, craftsmen and businessmen, merchants and even slaves constituted the large middle class of these cities. They were organized in associations (§2.3c), whose membership included wealthy owners of large plants, as well as humble craftsmen; free citizens as well as resident aliens, freedmen, and slaves could be found in their ranks.

During the first two centuries CE, this class was quite willing to accept the Roman order. It also maintained considerable social mobility: even slaves could, in fact, be active participants in this class and might share in its opportunities once they became freedmen. There were, to be sure, various causes of social unrest that would repeatedly lead to tumults, such as the revolt instigated by the Ephesian silversmiths described in Acts 19:23–41. Strikes by bakers and construction workers are reported from several cities. In the agricultural areas the hatred of the city, a feeling of exploitation, and the lack of patrons responsible for the welfare of rural clients contributed to unrest among farmers and farm workers. This led in the late 2d and 3d centuries to violent protests against the Roman order. But in the cities, unrest arose in the middle class, sometimes fed by the disenchantment of impoverished members of the aristocracy. The local aristocracies, together with the Roman administrators, were the only people who had control over the affairs of the city. For the members of the middle class, there were few political opportunities, and their dependence upon the munificence of the aristocracy was almost complete, often even for their supply of bread. Unrest resulted from frustration and dissatisfaction. It could be triggered by incidents that seemed to threaten the economic well-being of any group within the middle class or any of their rights, or by complaints about the quality of the games financed by members of the aristocracy. The Roman administration recognized that the associations in which most members of the middle class were organized could breed unrest and often discouraged their formation; yet in most cases it had to acknowledge their existence, though withholding official recognition. In general, an uneasy equilibrium was maintained as long as prosperity prevailed. Once the political situation changed toward the end of the 2d century CE, and continuous wars both worsened the cities' economic opportunities and increased their financial burdens, unrest became more widespread.

From the beginning, Christianity found its converts neither among the rural populations nor in the aristocracy, but in the urban middle class. Paul's description of the Corinthian church could be taken as an appropriate characterization of this class: "Not many wise, . . . not many powerful, not many of noble birth" (1 Cor 1:26). Like most of the associations, Christian churches included a few wealthy people, along with large numbers of craftsmen and working people (see 1 Thess 4:11–12) and some poor people and slaves. But these urban Christian "associations" developed a system of mutual reliance and dependence that required greater sacrifices by the rich and created more closely knit communities (see 1 Tim 6:17–19; *Hermas Sim. 1*). The further development of the structure of the churches reflects the social situation of the middle class of the city and reveals various efforts to overcome its institutions and limitations.

4. ROMAN CULTURE AND HELLENISM

(a) The Hellenization of Roman Culture

The culture of the late Roman republic and imperial Rome was so deeply affected by Hellenization that older Roman elements either disappeared or were maintained only in modified forms. Greek influences reached Rome in various ways: first, through the indirect mediation by the Etruscans, close neighbors and sometimes overlords from Rome's very beginnings; second, from the Hellenized cities and Greek colonies in Sicily and southern Italy, which already had numerous contacts with Rome in the early centuries of the Roman republic; third, through the influx of Greek education in the Roman upper classes during the time of the conquest of Greece, corresponding to a visible enthusiasm of many Greeks for the constitution and organization of the Roman state; and fourth, through the mobility of the entire population of the Hellenized eastern provinces, as immigrants came to the west as slaves, as soldiers, or in the context of trade and commerce.

Bibliography to §6.4

Albrecht, Dihle,*Greek and Latin Literature of the Roman Empire: From Augustus to Justinian* (London and New York: Routledge, 1994).

P. E. Easterling and B. M. W. Knox, eds., *The Cambridge History of Classical Literature*, vol. 1/4: *The Hellenistic Period and the Empire* (Cambridge: Cambridge University Press, 1989).

R. M. Ogilvie, *Roman Literature and Society* (Totowa, NJ: Barnes & Noble, 1980).

Eduard Norden, *Die römische Literatur* (6th ed.; Leipzig: Teubner, 1971).

Idem, *Die antike Kunstprosa* (2 vols.; 5th ed.; Darmstadt: Wissenschaftliche Buchgesellschaft, 1958) 1. 156–343.

M. L. Clark, *The Roman Mind* (Cambridge, MA: Harvard University Press, 1956).

Bibliography to §6.4a

William L. MacDonald, *The Architecture of the Roman Empire* (2 vols.; New Haven, CT: Yale University Press, 1982–84).

Roger Ling, *Roman Painting* (Cambridge: Cambridge University Press, 1991).

F. Sear, *Roman Architecture* (Ithaca, NY: Cornell University Press, 1983).

Most conspicuous was the spread of the Greek language. At the time of the late Republic, all educated Romans could speak and read Greek as well as Latin; Cicero's "mother" tongue was Greek, which he learned from his nurse. A renewed interest in the Greek language came in the 2d century CE: the emperor Marcus Aurelius, scion of a Roman family from Spain, wrote his *Meditations* in Greek. Merchants from the western provinces could converse in Greek as well as those from the east. Since the Romans accepted Greek learning not only in the field of philosophy, but also in science and technology, the Latin vocabulary was strongly influenced by Greek in areas of specialized terminology. Tractates about the construction of war machines as well as philosophical literature were read in Greek. Roman poetry, historiography, philology, philosophy, and rhetoric cannot be imagined without their Greek prototypes. Forms and methods were borrowed from the Greeks, and often topics and subject matter. Greek influences upon Roman culture were not limited to one particular period. Rather, Roman culture remained in constant juxtaposition to its Greek counterpart, which continued its own development, so that its influence was renewed time and again. Even later Roman writers and philosophers would often make recourse to older Greek models, which they deemed more important than whatever had developed meanwhile in Latin tradition and language.

In fine arts and architecture, the Augustan renaissance was at the same time a renewal of Greek influence. Imitation of Greek architecture, not unknown in the Roman republic, now became the rule. The city of Rome as it represented itself in its public buildings became more and more a Hellenistic city, with streets lined with colonnaded stoas, prostyle or peripteros temples, and theaters. In construction methods and in the practical utility of the buildings, typical Roman features are visible. The massive Greek wall constructions of dressed natural stones were replaced by walls made of rubble and cement or bricks and mortar, which were then covered with plaster or marble revetments. But even columns constructed of bricks were carefully dressed with fluted cement in order to resemble Greek marble columns. Although the Greeks knew how to construct arches, they used them only with sufficient supports on both sides, as in underground tombs, and in city gates. Roman architecture made use of the arch in many other contexts, especially to construct roofs for large interior rooms. Vaulted roofs are frequently found in characteristically Roman buildings, namely in baths with their large vaulted halls, which became very popular in all parts of the Roman empire. Roman amphitheaters were built using vaulted supports for the upper rows of seats. This method was also used for the building of free-standing theaters as well as for odeions, concert and lecture halls. Arches and vaults reappear in church architecture for the construction of roofs and domes of basilicas. Arches were also the basis for viaducts and aquaeducts which can still be found today in all areas to which Roman rule extended. On the other hand, there are numerous instances from the Roman period in which Greek materials and methods of construction were used; often earlier Greek models were copied with precision. Temples and sanctuaries built at that time, sometimes with the financial support of the imperial treasury, followed the Classic examples of dressed marble blocks. An important change, however, took place in the design of the cities' central areas. The Greek agora, on whose sides administrative buildings were placed, was normally an irregular open space to which the main streets gave free access. Only when the regular layout of the Hippodamian city plan was used, the agora became a rectangular square. But now the market became an enclosed square, the Roman forum, with entrances controlled by gates. Especially in cities founded by the Romans, the main streets no longer connected the agora with other parts of the city, but were arranged according to a strict axial system; this layout also determined the location of the most important buildings, thus imitating the pattern of the Roman military camp. Frequently, the commercial activity was relegated to special markets, while official and administrative buildings were located in another enclosed square. The tendency toward enclosed spaces is visible throughout. Major sanctuaries, originally free-standing structures accessible from all sides were surrounded by porticoes with a propylon which confronted the visitor with the façade of the temple. While the Greek theater originally consisted of two buildings, the semi-circular cavea with the seats for the spectators and the stage house, separated by two parodoi, the Romans preferred to close the spaces between stage and cavea, relegating the parodoi to tunneled side entrances, and thus creating a theater that was one single structure.

In painting and sculpture the Romans imitated the much-admired Greek prototypes. Famous Classical works of sculpture were repeatedly copied. In new creations, the Hellenistic tendency toward realistic representations was intensified and could assume almost grotesque features. Only rarely were subjects of portrait sculpture idealized as, for example, some Roman emperors. Individuality is expressed in the sculpturing of the face, while bodies and dress are dictated by set general patterns. Roman relief sculpture follows Greek patterns and appears in the Augustan period in classical refinement. It was richly developed in the numerous victory monuments and arches of the imperial period. Roman paintings were dominated by themes from Greek mythology, which were also used for the popular mosaic floors in private and public buildings. As compared to their Greek prototypes, the mannerism in the ornamentation and decoration of Roman paintings is striking. Paintings of landscapes and architecture were very popular. The frequent appearance of the mock window is noteworthy, simulating an opening in the wall through which one looks at some landscape. Buildings, especially temples, are often depicted on Roman coins and are often reliable guides to the reconstruction of buildings of which only the foundations are preserved. The classicistic austerity of the Augustan age gave way to a playful dissolution at the end of the Julio-Claudian period. However, a renewal of the Classical Greek ideals can be observed in the 2d century CE.

(b) Poetry

Latin poetic literature begins with the translation of the Odyssey and of Greek tragedies and comedies (§3.4b) in the 3d century BCE. In the following development, all Latin poetry in genre, form, and subject matter is created under the domination of the respective Greek prototypes and of Greek literary theory, that is, under the influence of a highly developed and refined theoretical system, whose demands it successfully strives to fulfill. With respect to the subjects of poetry, the Romans contributed little in mythological themes and tragic topics; everything here is Greek. However, in its reflection on the history of Rome, Latin poetry demonstrated its genuine power to reflect on the values of moral rectitude and models for political decisions. All these aspects are present in the work of the first significant Roman poet, Ennius (239–169 BCE). He came from southern Italy and, after settling in Rome, belonged to the circle of Scipio Aemilianus (§6.1c). Ennius wrote numerous tragedies (half of them are adaptations of Euripides) and comedies. In his great epic on Roman history, the *Annales,* drawing on prototypes from the epics of Homer, he introduced the Greek hexameter and made it the standard meter for all subsequent Roman epic poetry. Somewhat earlier, Plautus (who died in 184 BCE) had written over a hundred comedies in Latin closely modeled on the works of the New Comedy of Greece, both in form and topics, although they also contain some indigenous Roman elements. The comedies of the Libyan freedman Terence, written between 166 and 160 BCE, are adaptations of the famous comedies of Menander (§3.4b). The tradition that had been created by Ennius as well as further studies of Greek

Bibliography to §6.4b: Texts

George E. Duckworth, ed., *The Complete Roman Drama: All Extant Comedies of Plautus and Terence . . . in a Variety of Translations* (New York: Random House, 1942).
Plautus: Latin text and English translation by Paul Nixon in LCL (5 vols.).
Terence: Latin text and English translation by John Sargeaunt in LCL (2 vols.).
Lucretius, *De rerum natura:* Latin text and English translation by W. H. D. Rouse in LCL.
Catullus and Tibullus: Latin text and English translation by F. W. Cornish in LCL.
Horace: Latin text and English translation by H. Rushton Fairclough and C. E. Bennet in LCL (2 vols.).
Virgil, *Eclogues, Georgics,* and *Aeneid:* Latin text and English translation by H. Rushton Fairclough in LCL (2 vols.).
Propertius: Latin text and English translation by H. E. Butler in LCL.
Ovid: Latin text and English translation by J. H. Mozley et al. in LCL (6 vols.).
Lucan: *The Civil War:* Latin text and English translation by J. D. Duff in LCL.
Petronius, *Satiricon:* Latin text and English translation by Michael Heseltine in LCL.
Martial, *Epigrams:* Latin text and English translation by Walter C. A. Ker in LCL (2 vols.).
Juvenal and Persius: Latin text and English translation by George Gilbert Ramsay in LCL.

Bibliography to §6.4b: Studies

E. J. Kenney, ed., *The Cambridge History of Classical Literature,* vol. 2: *Latin Literature* (Cambridge: Cambridge University Press, 1982).
George E. Duckworth, *The Nature of Roman Comedy: A Study in Popular Entertainment* (Princeton, NJ: Princeton University Press, 1952).
Alexander Dalzell, "Lucretius," in Kenney, *Latin Literature,* 207–229.
Karl P. Harrington, *Catullus and His Influence* (New York: Longmans, Green, 1927).
Idem, "The Georgics," in Kenney, *Latin Literature,* 320–32.
J. K. Newman, *Augustus and the New Poetry* (Collection Latomus 88; Buxelles: Berchem, 1967).
R. Deryck Williams, "The Aeneid," in Kenney, *Latin Literature,* 333–69.
Philip Hardie, *Virgil's Aeneid: Cosmos and Imperium* (Oxford: Clarendon, 1986).
*J. F. D'Alton, *Horace and His Age* (New York: Russel, 1962).
E. J. Kenney, "Ovid," in idem, *Latin Literature,* 420–57.
A. G. Carrington, *Aspects of Martial's Epigrams* (Eton: Shakespeare Head, 1960).
Gilbert Highet, *Juvenal the Satirist* (Oxford: Clarendon, 1954).
J. C. Bramble, "Martial and Juvenal," in Kenney, *Latin Literature,* 597–619.

grammar and poetic and rhetorical art in Rome created the presuppositions for the work of Lucretius (97–55 BCE). His didactic poem in six books *On Nature* demonstrates that Latin poetry had become a worthy counterpart of its Greek prototypes; it also shows how the complex ideas of Epicurean philosophy (§4.1c), which Lucretius shared, could be mastered in genuine expressions in the medium of Latin.

Whereas the points of orientation for Ennius and his successors are the Classical works of Greece, the refinement and elegance in form and style that was achieved in the Alexandrian poetry of Kallimachos (§3.4b) made it possible for the so-called "modern poets" (*Neoterici*) to give expression to their yearning for new horizons of experience in the midst of the Civil War. Most of the works of this circle are lost; but many poems of Catullus (probably 84–47 CE, from a perhaps Celtic family of Verona), who belonged to this circle, are preserved. Their themes decidedly go beyond their Alexandrian prototypes. The goal is no longer the artistic poetic reproduction of any topic of human knowledge, but the expression of human desire and despair in the adverse experiences of the present. Friendship and hate, love and obscenity are felt so strongly that it is impossible not to hear the message: namely the demand for a new world in which salvation and fulfillment become a reality. The two great poets and prophets of the Augustan age, Horace and Virgil endeavored in their poetry to understand the horizons of this new world and to describe its emergence, as they saw its signs appear in the early years of Augustus.

Horace (65–8 BCE) was the son of freedman from southern Italy. Some of his earlier poems describe the doom of Rome in apocalyptic colors; he saw at that time the only salvation in the restitution of the republican order and fought at Philippi in the army of the assassins of Caesar. Received into the circle of Augustus' friend Maecenas, the indignant critic of the political situation became an inspired messenger of the new age. In his satires, odes, lyric poetry, and letters he employed manifold theological, mythological, and cultural motifs, in order to assess the legitimacy of the new age and of its ruler, as well as its possibilities for moral action and artistic perfection. In the richness of the topics explored by Horace, there is no longer any trace of rehearsing traditional themes. With his masterful command of different styles and meters Horace captures the great political concerns and topics of his time in art, philosophy, and religion as well as everyday life in its many facets. Horace became a propagandist for Augustus, and he described the aspects of eschatological fulfillment in his *Carmen saeculare* that Augustus had requested for public performance at the secular celebration of Rome in 17 BCE. But he always preserved his independence and must be understood as a poet who explored the dimensions in which the present events could be seen as the beginnings of a new age of justice and peace.

The eschatological character of these political events also dominated the work of his somewhat older contemporary Virgil (70–19 BCE). As the son of simple but well-to-do country people from Mantua in northern Italy, also Virgil, like Catullus and Horace, does not have his roots in the traditional Roman families. He received a rhetorical and philosophical education in Rome, but refused the opportunity to enter into the course of public offices. Influential people from the circle of the later Augustus restored his property that had been lost in the Civil War and enabled him to devote himself fully to his poetical work. In his first major work, the *Bucolica (Eclogues),* Virgil used the genre of the Hellenistic pastoral poem (§3.4b), but went beyond the descriptive presentation of its themes by combining them with mythological motifs in order to explore the eschatological pattern of primordial time versus end time. These poems, written ca. 40 BCE, are filled with a prophetic view which unequivocally expresses an expectation of the coming savior. The Christians afterwards understood the famous vision of the child's birth in the *Fourth Eclogue* as a prediction of Jesus' birth. Indeed these prophecies are related to the same Egyptian prophetic tradition that had already influenced the oracles of Isaiah 9 and 11—chapters that became very significant for the Christian interpretation of the birth of Jesus. The second work of Virgil, the *Georgica,* represents the genre of the Hellenistic didactic poem: materials drawn from scholarly works about agriculture appear in a poetic description. But Virgil wanted more than an artful presentation of an economically significant human occupation. His aim was to show how the human being, through mastery of the art of farming, was bound into a harmony with both nature and culture and thus with the cosmos, which fulfilled human origin and destiny. The vision of realized eschatology dominates this work, which was read to Augustus in the year of its completion (29 BCE). Virgil's final work, not completed when he died in 19 BCE, is the *Aeneid,* the masterwork of Latin epic poetry. It takes its starting point from Greek Homeric allegory, but did not simply develop it further. Rather, beginning with the destruction of Troy as a negative backdrop and the "exodus" of Aeneas, Virgil transforms the Odyssey of Aeneas into a history of salvation that finds its fulfillment in the universal mission of Rome. The reader is asked to understand that the entire course of events as well as all of its episodes follow a divinely directed plan. Prehistoric events illumine the significance of Rome's history and point to the salvific potential of the events that are experienced in this present time of realized eschatology. The epic repetition of the primordial time thus announces the presence of eschatological time.

The poets after Horace and Virgil—though still witnesses of the time of Augustus—belong to a new period. The eschatological tension is relaxed, the praise of the new order a duty fulfilled more or less willingly. Propertius (50–15 BCE) and Tibullus (48–19 BCE) were elegiac poets who primarily dealt with the topic of love. The conscious distance to the political events of the day is also evident in the work of the last great poet of this time, Ovid (43 BCE to 17 CE). He discontinued his initial political career early on—his considerable wealth allowed full devotion to his poetic calling. At first, he also wrote elegiac love poems, but with less pathos than his predecessors and with more wit and irony. A tragedy *Medea* is lost; it is a witness to the increased production of classical dramas at that time. In his next works, Ovid created didactic poems concerned with the art of love. Of the first, "About the culture of the female face," only the beginning is preserved. The second, the *Ars amatoria,* consists of two books addressed to men and one that is addressed to women. A final book concerns itself with the art of liberation from love's passion. These works are full of sometimes witty observations of details and elegant descriptions of the engagement of heart, soul, and body in erotic matters. They objectivize love as a topic of elegy and thus makes it a subject that can be taught. Ovid's next work, *Metamorphoses*—essentially finished, when he was sentenced to exile in 8 CE (the reasons are not quite clear)—is actually a collection of mostly Greek and a few Roman mythological, legendary, and historical materials, which are framed in successive chronological pictures of the history of the world. Its center is the question of the relationship of general human experience to a comprehensive view of past and present. At the end, Ovid deals with the time of Augustus, but a mythological perspective is missing, and consequently the present is no longer seen under eschatological auspices. Ovid's second narrative work, the *Fasti*, completed during the time of his exile, presents customs, legends, and religious rites in the framework of the Roman festival calendar. The last works of Ovid are mostly letters written from his exile in the barbaric surroundings of Tomis on the Black Sea. These letters express his grief due to the separation from Rome. They also contain references to the divine mission of the emperor, which sound like the repetition of a traditional court ceremonial. Hellenistic formulation of ruler worship thus enter into Latin literature for the first time, although Ovid still considered the emperor to be a human being, not a god.

Latin poetry experienced a second blossoming during the time of Nero, though this poetry no longer had any intrinsic relationship to current political events. The most significant poet of this time was Lucan, a nephew of Seneca. He was only twenty-six years old when he was executed by Nero (§6.2a). Only an unfinished epic poem about the Civil War between Pompey and Caesar, *Pharsalia,* is preserved. Because of the poet's republican bias, the two main figures of this work become antiheroes, while the staunch defender of the old republic, the younger Cato, is depicted as a hero, perishing as one who remained true to his principles. The influence of Stoic thought is visible in this work that was designed as an anti-epic written in conscious contrast to Vergil's *Aeneid.* While Lucan's political interest is reflected in his nostalgic celebration of the ideals of the republic, the work of his older contemporary Petronius, like Lucan a member of the Roman nobility, is characterized by a cynical detest of the social and political world of Rome. Pertronius was the advisor of Nero's amusements, but he nevertheless shared Lucan's fate, being commanded to commit suicide in 66 CE. His *Satyricon,* preserved only in fragments, is a parody of the erotic romance (§3.4e), but also influence of epic poetry (*Odyssey*), comedy, and the mimes is visible. The prototypes of its heroes stem from the Hellenistic romance, but they are changed into their opposites, that is, they are vulgar and perverse rather than noble and sublime. The author leads the heroes, two gay friends, through various adventures, which gives him the opportunity to characterize from an ironic distance members of all classes of the society in their vain, superstitious, greedy, and lascivious pursuits. All persons are described with masterful analysis of social ills, and they are allowed to converse in their own vulgar Latin. Many pieces of poetry are cited in the course of this prose narrative, usually in satirical criticism of contemporary literature (including the *Pharsalia* of Lucan). Petronius' contemporary Persius (34–62 CE) wrote satires in poetic form which were, however, either destroyed or revised after his early death by his teacher, the Stoic philosopher Cornutus. These satires treat critically moral and religious topics in a very difficult Latin that is full of allusions to other literature. The moral seriousness of this work soon made Persius a "classical" writer in this genre, whose work was commented on in late antiquity and still widely read in medieval times. The satirical orientation also appears among the later poets of the 1st century. Martial (ca. 40–103 CE) wrote only epigrams (his longest poem comprises a total of fifty-one lines), in which he sends festive birthday greetings, grieves about the dead, flatters the emperor (Domitian), but also attacks his contemporaries with spirited wit (using pseudonyms throughout), and lets other people see themselves as they really are. Juvenal (70–150 CE) was the last major satirical poet of Rome. His satires are merciless in their criticism and more biting than those of his predecessors, as he turns against hypocrisy and moral depravity, especially in the Roman upper classes. His power of observation makes the satires which are preserved important sources for the study of the society of his time.

(c) Cicero and Varro

The two men who determined the features of the amalgamation of Greek and Roman tradition and culture were Cicero and Varro. Both played significant roles as politicians in the last period of the republic, and their comprehensive literary works created the prototypes for many areas of cultural life in the imperial period and for centuries to come.

(1) *Cicero* (106–43 BCE), from the municipal aristocracy of Arpinum, as a Roman senator a *homo novus,* studied Greek rhetoric and philosophy, first in Rome, then in Athens (where his teacher was Antiochos of Askalon, head of the Platonic Academy), Smyrna, and Rhodos. After his return he entered on his political career, beginning as quaestor in Sicily and reaching the apex in his election as consul in the year 63 BCE and in his exposure of Catiline's conspiracy (§61.d[4]). Though Cicero was still politically active and not without influence during the later years of his life, most of his important literary works of that period were written with a clear knowledge that his own political ideal of the free republic, led by a responsible aristocracy, was at odds with the political realities— the affairs of the state were in the hands of the new power brokers Pompey and Caesar.

Bibliography to §6.4c (1): Texts

Cicero: Latin texts and English translation by various authors in LCL (numerous volumes).

Bibliography to §6.4c (1): Studies

Thomas Alan Dorey, ed., *Cicero* (New York: Basic Books, 1965).

L. P. Wilkinson, "Cicero and the Relationship of Oratory to Literature," in Kenney, *Latin Literature,* 230–67.

R. E. Smith, *Cicero the Statesman* (London: Cambridge University Press, 1966).

F. R. Colwell, *Cicero and the Roman Republic* (4th ed.; Baltimore: Penguin, 1967).

Woldemar Görler, *Untersuchungen zu Ciceros Philosophie* (Heidelberg: Winter, 1974).

A. Momigliano, "The Theological Efforts of the Roman Upper Class in the First Century BC," *CP* 79 (1984) 199–211.

Cicero's experience as an engaged politician gave him the opportunity to unite his thorough knowledge of the policies of the Roman Senate, administration, and law with the perfection of his rhetorical and literary work. For Cicero, public oratory was the most important instrument for exercising political influence, a privilege of the aristocracy, whose duty it was to direct the affairs of the state, as indeed the republic had always been guided by the persuasive words of its leaders. Serious study of Greek rhetoric had begun in Rome several generations before Cicero and rhetorical education had become the most important part of the preparation for public office. Greek teachers of rhetoric had offered instruction in Rome for many years; wealthy families sent their sons to Greece for further study. Cicero, however, saw two significant deficiencies in this course of study. Purism and formalism dominated the Latin system of rhetoric, and the adaptation of Greek rhetoric was eclectic, lacking study of fundamental disciplines, especially philosophy. Whatever could be used successfully in legal and rhetorical oratory was borrowed from the Hellenistic tradition; the result was superficiality and an oratory that was determined by the desire to be effective. Cicero demanded that the orator should have a thorough general education and include the study of philosophy. He himself had studied intensively the classical philosophers and orators (Plato, Aristotle, Xenophon, Demosthenes). His extraordinary gift for language enabled him to render into Latin in a masterly manner whatever he learned from Greek literature. It is to his credit that Latin was transformed into a language of literature and philosophy. At the same time, Cicero's works reveal a new seriousness, which contrasts with the artificiality of later Hellenistic rhetoric and is thoroughly Roman in character. Instead of formalistic purism, which had become fashionable under the influence of Atticism (§3.2b), and the subtleties of specialized knowledge, Cicero demanded discipline of language and a true knowledge of the subject matter. The orator should persuade through clarity and abstain from rhetorical tricks. Even if considerations of political expediency sometimes caused Cicero to fall short of this ideal in his speeches, his published works became the criterion for future generations. It was Cicero who forged the Latin language into a tool of precise, clear, disciplined, and augustly beautiful communication and legal and philosophical formulation, albeit at the price of separating it from the spoken vernacular of his time.

However, Cicero was not only a politician and orator, he also created for all future generations the language of Latin philosophy. In his philosophy, he was dependent upon the developments in the philosophical schools of the late Hellenistic period, in which Skepticism had led to a leveling of the different school opinions. It had become more common to think that true happiness could be found only in the retreat from the existing reality (§4.1a–d). Systematic scientific as well as dogmatic knowledge had become open to doubt, and insights merely based upon probability were seen as a satisfactory foundation for moral action. The resulting eclecticism implied that the individual was not obligated to think through an entire philosophical system and pledge allegiance to it. Rather, it was permissible to accept or reject any particular opinion of a philosophical school, according to one's own judgment and experience of usefulness. It is this philosophical universe of Hellenism that Cicero translated into Latin, thus creating not a Roman philosophical system but a precise, exact, and authentic Latin philosophical language. As a young man, Cicero had studied under the Academician Philo of Larissa, who had come to Rome after the war with Mithridates (88 BCE). Throughout his life Cicero maintained a philosophical position of a modified skepticism, according to which the probability resulting from an evaluation of alternative courses was sufficient in choosing the right and moral actions. The criterion for this selection is ultimately one's own conscience, which possesses ethical norms and knowledge of justice. As action is superior to knowledge, ethics is the primary subject of Cicero's philosophy. He rejected only the opinions of the Epicureans, while his own inclinations were toward the more popular Stoicism which was distinguished by its practical applicability. A life according to nature is, therefore, based not on a strictly philosophical definition of nature, but on those things which a more general understanding called "natural." The "law of nature," for Cicero, corresponds to the divine order of the world, to wise legislation, and to the healthy moral conscience. The final arbiter in decisions of a life according to nature is thus, again, one's own ability of discernment, implanted in the human soul, whose divine origin Cicero never doubted. But equally important—and in contrast to late Hellenistic philosophy—is the criterion of the political utility of one's action. Cicero had serious reservations regarding the system of Stoic ethics insofar as its consistent application would lead to an alienation from political responsibility. The eclecticism which characterizes all of Cicero's philosophical writings demonstrates that he never intended to create a philosophical system. It is precisely for this reason that he was able, on the basis of his immense knowledge, comprehensive studies, extensive literary activity, and his masterful control of the Latin language, to present the study of Greek philosophy to the Roman world as useful and profitable, and thus to point a way to the *Interpretatio Romana* of the Greek tradition.

(2) *Varro.* As Cicero created a criterion for future generations in the Romanization of Greek rhetoric and philosophy, his somewhat older contemporary and friend M. Terentius Varro (116–27 BCE) could boast of similar accomplishments in the areas of cultural history and the encyclopedic sciences. Varro's philosophical position was the same as Cicero's, an eclecticist who granted some position of truth to all philosophical schools and emphasized the superiority of virtue over all other goods. The primary accomplishment of Varro, however, was his brilliant mastery of scientific knowledge, which enabled him to recreate the entire Greek scientific tradition in new Roman dress. Among his works, comprising

Bibliography to §6.4c (2): Texts

Varro, *De lingua Latina:* Latin text and English translation by Roland G. Kent in LCL (2 vols.).
Varro, *Three Books on Agriculture* in Cato and Varro, Latin texts and English translation by William Davis Hooper in LCL.
Burkhard Cordanus, ed., *Varro Logistoricus über die Götterverehrung (Curio de cultu deorum)* (Würzburg: Triltsch, 1960). Edition and interpretation of Fragments.

Bibliography to §6.4c (2): Studies

Nicholas Horsfall, "Prose and Mime," in Kenney, *Latin Literature,* 286–90 (on Varro).
Jens Erik Skydsgaard, *Varro the Scholar* (Hafniae: Munksgaard, 1968).

more than fifty titles (only a small portion is preserved), are treatises on philology and grammar (twenty-five books on the Latin language), investigations in literary theory, the science of agriculture, number theory, systems of education, rhetoric, philosophy, civil law, geography, chronology, and biography. His great encyclopedic work is a comprehensive presentation of the history, culture, and constitution of the Roman people, *Antiquitates rerum humanorum et divinarum,* in forty-one books, with an epitome of nine books. This became the basic encyclopedia of the history of culture and theology for the Roman world and influenced St. Augustine very deeply four centuries later. Varro's scientific universality compelled the Roman world to use the traditional Greek criteria of scientific and philosophical assessment for all areas of human experience.

(d) The Writing of History

(1) *From Cato to Sallust.* Roman historiography began in the 3d century BCE with works in the Greek language. They were produced by members of the aristocracy, who sought to present, often from a partisan perspective, a positive image of Rome in general and of their own political pursuits to the Hellenistic world (Greek works of that time also frequently dealt with Roman history; see §3.4e). The first history in Latin was written by the elder Cato (234–149 BCE), who described in his ambitious work the historical traditions of Rome together with those of the Italian tribes and cities. In typical Hellenistic fashion, Cato often invents speeches of the primary actors which reflect upon the significance of the events. Cato was followed by the "older annalists." The model for their works, often written by leading Roman politicians, was the table erected annually by the pontifex maximus, listing all the unusual events of each year. The annalists emphasize exemplary events and figures of the Roman past, which are extolled in order to promote a family's history, but also treat contemporary events in the interests of political propaganda or moral education.

All these older works are lost, though much of their information has been absorbed by later Roman historians. Substantial portions of Roman histories are preserved from the last decades of the republic and the time of Augustus. The most important of these works come from the hand of Caesar. He used as a model for his presentation of contemporary history the "commentary," that is, the

Bibliography to §6.4d

M. L. W. Laistner, *The Greater Roman Historians* (Berkeley, CA: University of California Press, 1947).

Thomas Alan Dorey, ed., *Latin Historians* (London: Routledge and Kegan Paul, 1966).

Bibliography to §6.4d (1): Texts

Selected Works of Sallust: Latin text and English translation by J. C. Rolfe in LCL.

Caesar, *The Gallic War:* Latin text and English translation by H. J. Edwards in LCL.

Caesar, *The Civil Wars:* Latin text and English translation by A. G. Preskett in LCL.

Caesar, *The Alexandrian, African and Spanish Wars:* Latin text and English translation by A. G. Way in LCL.

Bibliography to §6.4d (1): Studies

Franz Bömer, "Der Commentarius," *Hermes* 81 (1953) 210–50.

Ronald Syme, *Sallust* (Berkeley,CA: University of California Press, 1964).

notebook of a magistrate about his official actions. In Caesar's employment of this genre the influence of the Hellenistic *hypomnema* (memoir of a leading political personality) is visible as well as the typically Roman intention to advertise one's own political astuteness and mission. His commentaries on the Gallic War and the Civil War are historical works which renounce unnecessary elaborations and were written with a masterly command of Latin prose. They reveal a rhetorical training for which utmost brevity and pregnancy are the most important instruments of persuasion—to persuade others is exactly what Caesar sought to accomplish. Their strength derives from their use of objective presentation as an instrument of political propaganda. Next to Caesar, the most influential historian was Sallust, Ceasar's partisan and contemporary (86–34 BCE). In addition to historical monographs on the Jugurthan and Catilinarian wars, he wrote a history of the first half of his century, placing a single personality in the center of each chapter. Sallust not only described the sequence of events in the history of the state and its people, he also sought to educate. As he was convinced that the affairs of Rome had become hopelessly corrupt and understood his own work as a contribution to its regeneration, he wanted to communicate a judgment about success and failure, justice and injustice, of the actions of the leading individuals. The works of Caesar and Sallust overcame the purely chronographic historiography and replaced it with a view of history that understood the past on the basis of the political commitment of the present, unafraid of making the contemporary historical experience its primary subject.

(2) *Livy.* The only major work of Latin historiography from the time of the Augustan renaissance which is at least partially preserved is *Ab urbe condita* of Titus Livius (59 BCE–17CE). Like many writers of his time (such as Virgil), he came from northern Italy. That Livy was not a politician was a new phenomenon in Latin historiography. Livy's work, written during a period of forty years, originally comprised 142 books, of which about a quarter is preserved; there are also epitomes and tables of content for the lost books. About half of the books were devoted to the time from the founding of Rome to the 2d century BCE; the second half dealt with the events from the time of the Gracchi to Augustus. In its external form, Livy's work renewed the tradition of the Roman annalists, but in language and style he was dependent upon Cicero, and thus achieved a high level in the art of historical narrative. Livy, who was deeply committed to the republican ideals of Rome, intended to describe the ancient history of Rome as the model for the renewal under Augustus. In this respect Livy wrote in the interest of politics. To which degree he was actually in agreement with the reforms of Augustus, who was his patron, is difficult to know; the latest books of his work are not preserved. The effect of his work, however, was the preservation of the

Bibliography to §6.4d (2): Texts

Livy, *Ab urbe condita:* Latin text and English translation by B. O. Foster et al. in LCL (14 vols.).

Bibliography to §6.4d (2): Studies

P. G. Walsh, *Livy: His Historical Aims and Methods* (Cambride: Cambridge University Press, 1961).

R. M. Ogilvie, "Livy," in Kenney, *Latin Literature*, 458–66.

ideals of the republican ideology as they were visible in the ancient greatness of Rome. Apart from Livy, nothing is preserved of the diversified historical literature from that time (about the non-Roman historians, see §3.4c). Even the universal history in 44 books of Trogus Pompeius, a Celtic freedman of Pompey and contemporary of Livy, is preserved only in the form of an epitome that remained very popular into the Middle Ages. It shows that Trogus, beginning with the archaic history of Assyria and Egypt, presented the history of other nations in such a way that all lines of development pointed to the realization of Roman rule over the whole world. The decades following after Augustus produced no significant historians. Possibly the history of Alexander of Curtius Rufus should be dated to the end of the Julio-Claudian period (some scholars would rather date this work to the 2d century CE). The work belongs to a time that was interested in the example of Alexander the Great, who is presented in a novelistic fashion that lacks critical investigation of sources.

(3) *Josephus*. A renewal of historiography begins at the end of the 1st century CE, but non-Roman authors also had a share in this renewal. Greek and Roman historians from now on belong to the same culture, and their interest is no longer dominated by concern for Roman history. This renewal was once more inspired by political and propagandistic interests. Among the "barbarians" who published historical and ethnographic materials from their own cultures in Greek writings, the Jewish historian Flavius Josephus occupies a special position. Josephus' autobiographical *Life* provides detailed information about his career. He was born in 37/38 CE as a descendant from the priestly nobility of Jerusalem. With respect to

Bibliography to §6.4d (3): Texts

Josephus, *The Jewish War:* Greek text and English translation by H. St. J. Thackeray in LCL (3 vols.).

Josephus, *Antiquities:* Greek text and English translation by Ralph Marcus et al. in LCL (9 vols.).

Josephus, *Life* and *Against Apion:* Greek text and English translation by H. St. J. Thackeray in LCL.

Bibliography to §6.4d (3):

Shaye J. D. Cohen, *Josephus in Galilee and Rome: His Vita and Development as a Historian* (Columbia Studies in the Classical Tradition 8; Leiden: Brill, 1979).

Harold W. Attridge, *The Interpretation of Biblical History in the Antiquities Judaicae of Flavius Josephus* (HDR 7; Missoula: Scholars Press, 1976).

Idem, "Josephus and His Works," in: Stone, *Jewish Writings,* 158–232.

Louis H. Feldmann, "Flavius Josephus Revisited: the Man, His Writings, and His Significance," *ANRW* 2.21.2 (1984) 763–862.

Rebecca Gray, *Prophetic Figures in Late Second Temple Jewish Palestine: The Evidence from Josephus* (Oxford: Oxford University, 1993).

Horst R. Moehring, "Joseph Ben Matthia and Flavius Josephus: the Jewish Prophet and Roman Historian," *ANRW* 2.21.2 (1984) 864–944.

Seth Schwartz, *Josephus and Judean Politics* (Columbia Studies in the Classical Tradition 18; Leiden: Brill, 1990).

T. Rajak, *Josephus: The Historian and His Society* (Philadelphia: Fortress, 1984).

Otto Betz, Klaus Haacker, and Martin Hengel, eds., *Josephus-Studien: Otto Michel zum 70. Geburtstag* (Göttingen: Vandenhoeck & Ruprecht, 1974).

Louis H. Feldman, *Josephus and Modern Scholarship (1937–1980)* (Berlin: De Gruyter, 1984). Comprehensive annotated bibliography.

his political role, he could not be compared with men like Polybios and Caesar, but he was not a minor figure in the significant events of his time and his own people. In 64 CE Josephus went to Rome for negotiations with the Roman authorities; after returning to his home country he become embroiled in the beginnings of the Jewish War. Unfortunately, because the accounts of his activities in his earlier and later works are contradictory, his exact position in the first years of the war is not clear. However, he was a man of affairs, ranking high in the aristocracy that initially supported the revolt, and he had been appointed by Jerusalem's priestly leaders of the revolt as army commander in Galilee, who was responsible for strengthening the resistance and fortifying the fastnesses in that part of the country. Forced to capitulate to the Romans, he prophesied in the Roman army camp that Vespasian would become emperor and was released when this prophecy became true. He remained in the camp as an advisor of Titus until the fall of Jerusalem. Later he lived in Rome on an imperial pension and as a member of the Flavian household. He probably died shortly after the year 100 CE.

His earlier work about the *Jewish War,* written in his native Aramaic, is lost. In the preserved Greek work on this topic, Josephus tries to illuminate the background and causes of the war, beginning with the description of the conflict of the Jews with Antiochos IV and dealing in detail with the difficulties, which the Roman procurators had created, before the war began. The major part of the work is devoted to the events in which Josephus himself had participated. While this first work is a defense of the Jews, his later major work, the *Jewish Antiquities,* is apologetic in a more general sense. This attempt to write a universal history of the Jewish people from the beginnings to his own time reveals the major shortcoming of Josephus' writing of history, something he shared with other historians: an uncritical use of source materials. Of course, for the early times of Israel's history his only source was the biblical narrative; only for the later period could he consult additional sources, and those which he preserved are often very valuable. But throughout he also admits questionable miraculous and paradoxological accounts. That political and cultural apologetic was the motive for Josephus' writing reflects the attitude of the time. The failure of the principate of the 1st century CE is contrasted to the greatness and dignity of more ancient times, and the attractiveness of the moral sense of a barbaric people is an important factor in such a comparison of the past and present.

(4) *Tacitus.* In this respect the closeness of Josephus to his younger contempo-

Bibliography to §6.4d (4): Texts

Tacitus, *Annals* and *Histories:* Latin text and English translation by Clifford H. Moore and John Jackson in LCL.

Tacitus, *Dialogus, Agricola,* and *Germania:* Latin text and English translation by William Peteron in LCL.

Bibliography to §6.4d (4): Studies

Ronald Syme, *Tacitus* (2 vols.; Oxford: Clarendon, 1958)

Thomas Alan Dorey, ed., *Tacitus* (London: Routledge and Kegan Paul, 1969).

F. R. D. Goodyear, "History and Biography (Early Principate)," in Kenney, *Latin Literature,* 639–66.

rary P. Cornelius Tacitus (born in 55 CE) is remarkable. Otherwise, the differences are striking. Tacitus was the most distinguished orator of his time, Roman senator, consul and proconsul, and belonged to the politically experienced Roman elite, against whose polished Latin prose the Greek style of the freedman Josephus would not survive a comparison. But Tacitus shares with Josephus an insight into the failures of the institutions of the imperial constitution of the Roman rule, as well as an admission of its necessity. However, while Josephus criticized the mismanagement of the Roman administration of Palestine, Tacitus censures the entire imperial history of the 1st century CE, which comes to a head in the disaster of Domitian's tyrannical rule. The two major works of Tacitus (both only partially preserved), the *Histories* and the *Annals,* deal with this period. Motivated by political engagement and moral protest, Tacitus devotes himself to recent history. Throughout, careful study of sources and archival materials form the base of his accounts, though never does he rest long on the recounting of facts and procedures. Tacitus shows how the people as a whole have unlearned political awareness and watchfulness. His major interest, however, lies in the drawing of vignettes of the stories of individuals—be it the emperors themselves or other persons involved in the events—whose actions and sufferings are evaluated psychologically and morally. History thus becomes a mirror that shows how the seemingly unavoidable corruption of individual persons by the imperial system leads to a betrayal of a moral nobility, for which the criteria are drawn from the Roman republic. The contradiction between these ideals from the past and the events and experiences from the time of the empire puts a characteristically pessimistic stamp upon Tacitus' works. The purpose and objectives of another of his works, the *Germania,* probably should be seen in analogy to the criticism of recent history in his two major works: there the criticism was based upon the ideals of the past; in the *Germania* these ideals are presented by way of describing the virtues of a barbaric nation.

(5) *Arrian and Dio Cassius.* Greek historiography experienced a late renaissance during the 2d and 3d centuries CE in the works of the two Bithynians Arrian and Dio Cassius. Flavius Arrianos (ca. 90–170 CE), a student of the Stoic philosopher Epictetus, to whom we owe the transcripts of Epictetus' discourses, came from Nikomedia in Bithynia. He was a politician and public servant of Rome under Hadrian (in 130 CE he was suffect consul). His published monographs and ethnographic works (e.g., a description of the coasts of the Black Sea) employ his own observations and experiences. Through his major historical work, the *Anabasis*—the first critical historical work about Alexander for four hundred years—he became famous as a historian of Alexander the Great. In contradistinction to the Alexander romance which was widespread at that time,

Bibliography to §6.4d (5): Texts

Arrian, *Anabasis of Alexander* and *Indica:* Greek text and English translation by E. Iliff Robson in LCL (2 vols.).

Dio Cassius, *Roman History:* Greek text and English translation by Ernest Carey in LCL (9 vols.).

Bibliography to §6.4d (5): Studies

Fergus Millar, *A Study of Cassius Dio* (Oxford: Clarendon, 1964).

Arrian restricted himself to the critical use of ancient sources: the works of Ptolemy I, Alexander's general and later the first Macedonian ruler of Egypt, Aristoboulos of Kassandrcia, and the diary of Alexander's admiral Nearchos. To Arrian, who was himself a general and politician, these works appeared as particularly trustworthy. His critical judgment and his style of presentation in a clear Atticistic Greek, for which he had taken Xenophon as his model, have secured Arrian's reputation until today as the writer who has preserved the most reliable material about Alexander the Great.

Dio Cassius (who died after 230 CE) from Nicea in Bithynia occupied a number of high-ranking government positions and was consul as the colleague of the emperor in 229 CE. His Roman history in 80 books (of which those about the imperial period are preserved) extended from the beginnings to his own time and was written on the basis of many years of collecting materials and sources. It became the standard Roman history for the Greek-speaking world in subsequent centuries. The reliability of his work is debated. Dio Cassius was largely dependent upon Latin annalists, inserted numerous long speeches, and showed independent judgment only in the treatment of his own period. On the other hand, his work demonstrates that even in the later imperial period a politically engaged historian was capable of writing a historical work which overcame the pedestrian repetition of information and sources that characterized most of his predecessors.

(e) Rhetoric and the Second Sophistic

(1) *Quintilian.* In the realm of the Latin language, Cicero (§6.4c) continued to be the master of rhetoric. But Cicero's ideal that rhetoric was the art of the statesman had lost its meaning in the imperial period. After the end of the republic little room was left for its function. Instead, rhetoric became the subject of state-supported schooling and higher education. The greatest Roman master of rhetoric after Cicero was not a politician but a professor, Quintilian (35–100 CE). Patronized by Vespasian and Domitian, he became the first teacher of the Roman school who received a regular salary from the state. He was famous and widely recognized already during his lifetime (among his students was the younger Pliny) and wrote the last great textbook of rhetoric that antiquity produced. In the 12 books of his *Institutio oratoria* Quintilian sought to reestablish the unity of the

Bibliography to §6.4e

George Kennedy, *The Art of Rhetoric in the Roman World 300 B.C–300* AD (Princeton, NJ: Princeton University Press, 1972).

F. R. D. Goodyear, "Rhetoric and Scholarship," in Kenney, *Latin Literature*, 674–82.

Martin L. Clarke, *Rhetoric at Rome: A Historical Survey* (Londen: Cohen and West, 1966).

Jochen Bleiken, *Der Preis des Aelius Aristeides auf das römische Weltreich* (NAWG.PH 1966.7; Göttingen: Vandenhoeck & Ruprecht, 1966).

Bibliography to §6.4e (1): Texts

Qunitilian, *Institutio Oratoria:* Latin Text and English translation by H. E. Butler in LCL (4 vols.).

Helmut Rahn, ed., *Marcus Fabius Quintilianus: Ausbildung des Redners* (TF 2; 2 vols.; Darmstadt: Wissenschaftliche Buchgesellschaft, 1972).

wise man and the statesman. With this renewal of the ancient Sophistic ideal, Quintilian was one of the pioneers of the Second Sophistic (see below). He emphasized that eloquence grants to everybody who seriously studies rhetoric the opportunity not only to serve the state as politician, lawyer, and public servant, but also to be successful as a writer or historian, and to achieve fame and wealth in any case. This explains Quintilian's scornful rejection of the philosophers, for whom theoretical knowledge and moral education was an end in itself, and who had therefore withdrawn from the public into the gymnasia and the schools. But he also criticizes the deterioration of the rhetorical art itself, in public as well as in the language of the philosophers (here he most likely had Seneca in mind, but could not criticize the greatly admired man directly), and calls for a return to the principles of rhetoric that had been established by Cicero.

Indeed, due to the impact of Nero's tyranny, whose victims included the philosopher Seneca, young people from the Roman upper classes had withdrawn from the regular course of public service and from the appropriate rhetorical education; instead, they attended the philosophical schools. Quintilian accused them of supposing that virtue could be learned through reflection about their own selves, and of fearing the demanding course of studies which a rhetorical education required. Philosophy and rhetoric belonged together, and the former could not be pursued without the latter. Philosophical tradition could function only as part of the rhetorical education. Indeed rhetoric could not simply be a tool of public utility, but the orator needed a fundamental grounding in literature, grammar, law, and philosophy in order to be a leader of society. Once more the Greek ideals of education were renewed, and this fresh appreciation for the Greek cultural heritage reflects the general attitude of the Roman upper classes which prevailed until the time of Antoninus Pius. Marcus Aurelius was the first emperor who turned away from rhetoric to philosophy. The Second Sophistic was largely based upon the attitudes which appear in Quintilian. Quintilian himself, however, was then no longer influential, because the Second Sophistic drew its concepts not from Cicero but from older Greek ideals.

(2) *Fronto*. In the 2d century, M. Cornelius Fronto (ca. 100–175 CE) from Cirta in Numidia was the most famous teacher of Latin rhetoric in Rome. Some of his letters are preserved, while is speeches are lost. He became politically influential during the time of Hadrian; Antoninus Pius appointed him as the teacher of the future emperors Marcus Aurelius and Verus. Characteristic for his style is a pronounced archaism. Plautus and the elder Cato rather than Cicero are recommended as sources for proper vocabulary. He rejected not only the "modernizing" language of Seneca, but philosophy as a whole, especially the Stoics. But he was not spared the experience that his student Marcus Aurelius, still a young man, pledged his allegiance to the Stoic philosophy of the former slave Epiktetos.

(3) *Second Sophistic*. During this time, Greek rhetoric experienced a renewal analogous to the archaism of Latin rhetoric. This movement was already known in antiquity as the Second Sophistic. It began in the famous educational centers

Bibliography to §6.4e (2): Text
Fronto, *Letters:* Latin Text and English Translation by C. R. Haines in LCL (2 vols.).

of western Asia Minor as a reflection upon the ideal of the politically active wise man, once taught by the old sophists of Athens, but was also influenced by renewed interest in the Greek of classical Athens, interest which had grown during the two preceding centuries (§3.2b). The goal of this movement was to achieve perfect mastery of he classical Attic style of rhetoric. Highly praised for his virtuosity and purity in this Attic prose was the one-time philosopher and orator Dion of Prusa of the time of Trajan; he was therefore later given the surname Chrysostomos ("Gold-mouth"; see below §6.4h).

The most famous advocate of this movement became Herodes Atticus (101–177 CE) from Marathon near Athens, heir of a family that had received Roman citizenship already in the early 1st century CE. He was immensely rich—a wealth which he generously used for various bequests, especially for building projects in Greece—and also politically active, an activity that was enhanced by the fact that his wife Regilla was related to Faustina, wife of the emperor Antoninus Pius, whom he also served as the teacher of Marcus Aurelius in Greek rhetoric. His rhetorical ideals were continued by his students, including Hadrian of Tyre (113–193 CE). A contemporary, Lollianus from Ephesus, also an orator and politician, represented the same ideals of Atticism as the incumbent of the chair of rhetoric in Athens.

The most accomplished student of Herodes, however, was Aelius Aristeides (ca. 115–185 CE), from a respected family of Pergamon. Under his name 55 speeches (not all of them genuine) and two rhetorical treatises are persevered. Aelius was devoted to the Greek healing god Asklepios, in whose sanctuary in Pergamon he repeatedly sought healing for his ailments. Six so-called "Sacred Speeches" give detailed accounts of his dream visions and treatments and his intimate personal relationship with the god. His other speeches, which soon became respected models for "classical" Greek rhetoric, treat such topics as the greatness of classical Greece as the foundation of culture and the universal peace and well-being that Rome had established especially for the Greek and Roman people. Although the Second Sophistic exerted immense influence upon all subsequent Greek prose writings, Hermogenes (160–225 CE), belonging to the next generation of orators, demonstrated that now also rhetoric was ready to abandon the ideal of political engagement and withdraw into self-reliant educational activity—without, however, making its peace with philosophy.

(f) The Stoics of the Imperial Period

(1) *Seneca.* During the 2d century CE the emperors founded endowed chairs for all four philosophical schools. But the Romans made substantial contribu-

Bibliography to §6.4e (3)

Glen W. Bowersock, *Greek Sophists in the Roman Empire* (Oxford: Clarendon, 1969).

E. L. Bowie, "Greeks and Their Past in the Second Sophistic," in M. I. Finley, *Studies in Ancient Society* (London: Routledge and Kegan Paul, 1974), 166–209.

Bibliography to §6.4f: Texts

F. Hazlitt and H. Hazlitt, eds., *The Wisdom of the Stoics: Selections from Seneca, Epictetus and Marcus Aurelius* (Lanham, MD: University Press of America, 1984).

tions only to Stoic philosophy. Its concentration upon ethical teaching made Stoicism the typical Roman philosophical movement. This was visible already in Cicero and reached its apex in L. Annaeus Seneca (4 BCE–65 CE; see §6.2a), son of a rhetoric teacher from Spain and the first of his family to obtain senatorial rank. Most of his works, except for his forensic speeches, are preserved: *Quaestiones naturales*, a discussion of various natural phenomena; *Dialogi*, short diatribes discussing the right moral attitude and conduct in the manifold situations of life; a corpus of 124 *Letters to Lucilius*, tractates of moral philosophy in the form of letters, which treat a rich variety of topics, including questions of school philosophy; *De clementia*, a "mirror for princes" addressed to the young emperor Nero; and *De beneficiis*, describing how benefactions to others are a documentation of the activity of the divine spirit that governs the human world.

Seneca was not an original thinker, but reflects the ideas and concepts of Stoic philosophers of the late Hellenistic period, especially those of Poseidonios. But he designs Stoic theology, in particular the concept of God, entirely in the interests of his moral doctrine. As providence, highest reason, and father of humankind, God made his will identical with the moral law. By fulfilling this law and purging oneself from all affections, one becomes identical with the deity. The refinement of the psychological language for the guidance of the soul in this process is striking in Seneca's writings, who connects these thoughts with a "Platonic" anthropology: only the soul is truly human and capable of equality with God; the body is the soul's prison, physical experiences are nothing but agonies, and the duties of political life unwelcome necessities. Philosophy can free the soul from this bondage because even relationships to fellow human beings are not established by political structures, but only through the moral values which are the property of the soul. Friendship, loyalty, and general love of humanity also include the slave and therefore break all social conventions.

(2) *Musonius and Epiktetos.* The standard form of Stoic philosophy of that time is represented by the Italian provincial nobleman C. Musonius Rufus (ca. 30–100 CE), who was the teacher of Epiktetos and of Dion of Prusa (§6.4h). Although he taught in Rome (except for several periods of exile), he spoke and

Abraham J. Malherbe, *Moral Exhortation: A Greco-Roman Sourcebook* (LEC 4; Philadelphia: Westminster, 1986).

Bibliography to §6.4f: Studies

J. M. Rist, *Stoic Philosophy* (London: Cambridge University Press, 1969).

Max Pohlenz, *Die Stoa: Geschichte einer geistigen Bewegung* (2 vols.; 2d ed.; Göttingen: Vandenhoeck & Ruprecht, 1959).

Bibliography to §6.4f (1): Texts

Seneca, *Epistulae morales:* Latin text and English translation by Richard M. Gummore in LCL (3 vols.).

Seneca, *Moral Essays:* Latin text and English translation by John W. Basore in LCL (3 vols.).

Bibliography to §6.4f (1): Studies

Arnoldo Momigliano, "Seneca between Political and Contemplative Life," in *Quarto contributo all storia degli classici e del mundo antico* (Rome: Edizione di storie e letterature, 1969) 239–56.

wrote in Greek. What is preserved of his teaching shows that the theoretical basis of Stoic philosophy was presupposed but not discussed. All topics are concerned with very practical questions, like marriage, children, money, personal conduct. He called for detachment from all political, social, and personal circumstances in order to gain inner freedom. The ethical norms which are derived from this inner freedom regulate relations with all beings and things and replace the external political and social norms of behavior.

Epiktetos (ca. 55–135 CE) from the Phrygian city Hierapolis, the only non-Roman among the leading Stoics of the imperial period, was a slave of a friend of Nero when he took lessons from Musonius Rufus with the permission of his master. After his manumission, he taught in Rome until he was expelled, together with other philosophers, by the emperor Domitian in 89 CE and founded his school in Nikopolis in western Greece. Epiktetos' student Arrian (§6.4d) transcribed and published the lectures of his teacher (*Dissertations*), which exhibit the perfection of Stoic philosophy in its concentration upon ethical teaching in the form of the diatribe. Also here the classical doctrines of Stoic dogmatics are presupposed in their main outlines, but not further investigated. Epiktetos emphasized the universality of the deity, whose herald is the philosopher proclaiming: the human spirit is divine; whoever recognizes this will become a god. This recognition can be realized only in the practical conduct of one's life, which requires the establishment of inner freedom as detachment from all external experiences and as the surrender of all attempts to change one's personal situation or the existing social conditions. Everything that one is forced to do or to suffer according to one's social position must be done "as if it is not." Neither the lowliest work as a slave, nor the most honorable political office affects the dignity and divinity of the human spirit. Epiktetos knew only one single obligation: the general love of human beings. They are all brothers and sisters, who must be be treated with equal love and respect.

(3) *Marcus Aurelius.* Born in 121 CE and emperor 161–180 CE, Marcus Aurelius (§6.2c) received an excellent rhetorical education (§6.4e) designed to prepare him for the highest office in the empire. But when he was twenty-five years old, he turned to philosophy. His philosophical *Meditations* were written during his later years which were marked by changing fortunes of war, constantly deteriorating political and economic conditions, and personal calamities in his

---

Bibliography to §6.4f (2): Texts

Cora E. Lutz, ed., *Musonius Rufus "the Roman Socrates"* (New Haven, CT: Yale University Press, 1947).

Epictetus, *Dissertations:* Greek text and English translation by W. A. Oldfather in LCL (2 vols.). N. White, trans., *The Handbook of Epictetus* (Indianapolis, IN: Hackett, 1983).

Bibliography to §6.4f (2): Studies

P. W. van der Horst, "Musonius Rufus and the New Testament," *NovT* 16 (1974) 306–15.
Rudolf Bultmann, "Das religiöse Moment in der ethischen Unterweisung des Epiktet und das Neue Testament," *ZNW* 13 (1912) 97–110, 177–91.

Bibliography to §6.4f (3): Texts

Marcus Aurelius: Greek text and English translation by C. R. Haines in LCL.

family. Among all the Roman emperors there was none as highly educated and none as deeply committed to justice and veracity as Marcus Aurelius. His guiding star was the former Phrygian slave Epiktetos. Like Epiktetos, Marcus Aurelius emphasized the rule of the whole world by divine providence, but had an even more radical conception of the mutability, inconstancy, and transitoriness of all things, especially of the human body. Faced with all this, a human being has no choice but to submit to the divine will, even if this will brings forth what seems to be evil and ill-fated. Reflecting upon their true selves, human beings can recognize that they are of God's family and therefore free to show love, clemency, and kindness to all other people. For him, the emperor, this required actions which were directed to the welfare of the whole world and which could not be discouraged by ill fortune. The *Meditations*, written in Greek, pointing the way to the unity of faithfulness to oneself, fulfillment of duty, and submission to the divinely ordered fate, even came to favor among Christians (whom the emperor deeply despised) and gave consolation to many troubled souls.

(g) The Philosophical Marketplace.

During the imperial period, especially in the 2d century CE, the philosophical schools attempted to recover their classical ancestry. The Peripatetics wrote commentaries on Aristotle, the Stoics produced interpretations of Chrysippos, and the Platonist Albinos composed an epitome of Plato's philosophy. The real life of "philosophy," however, had left the schools and had gone into the marketplace and onto the streets of the cities. Many people called themselves "philosophers": it was difficult to know whether a man offering his wisdom on the street was a god, a magician, an apostle of a new religion, or a true sage. The army of the wandering missionaries and philosophers became legion. Competing with each other, they advertised their art in order to attract disciples, outdid each other in demonstrations of power, and were by no means disinclined to draw money out of people's pockets. Such missionaries competed even within the same religious movement, as can be seen in the earliest Christian missionary efforts. Wherever Paul went, he was soon confronted with other Christian preachers who tried to outdo him with their performances. Much information about these marketplace philosophers comes to us only through their more educated literary opponents, because the philosophers who went out into the streets relied on the spoken word, just as Christian wandering preachers entrusted themselves not to the written word but to the effect of their oral message. It is not accidental that there is also direct written information preserved in letters, such as those of Paul. The very fact that Paul used the medium of the written letter reveals a new element which distinguishes his mission from the normal business

Bibliography to §6.4g: Texts

Cartlidge and Dungan, *Documents,* 151–65

Bibliography to §6.4g: Studies

Dieter Georgi, *The Opponents of Paul in 2 Corinthians: A Study in Religious Propaganda in Late Antiquity* (Philadelphia: Fortress, 1985).

of the philosophical market: Paul was concerned with the organization of communities and their enduring unity—a concern that was usually not present among the wandering missionaries. On the other hand, his letters were written for reasons which are very different from the motivations for writing in the established philosophical schools. They are not didactic compositions but political instruments of propaganda and community management.

Pagan, Christian, and Jewish philosophers of this sort did not address the educated establishment, but the common people, that is, anybody they could meet on the streets. The educated Platonist Kelsos accused the Christians of squandering their message on the lowest classes of society. His Christian opponent Origen responded that the Cynic philosophers did exactly the same thing. Lucian (§6.4h), the fierce critic of all propagandists and missionaries, described Peregrinus Proteus as a Cynic philosopher who became a Christian, but later defected in order to gather followers once more as a Cynic preacher. Lucian's presentation, as well as those of Martial and Juvenal (§6.4b) and the Acts of the Apostles, demonstrate that these missionaries were by no means prudish in the choice of their instruments of propaganda. Foremost was the adroitness of public speech. Even if these preachers adhered to different schools of thought, they agreed in their criticism of the existing conditions, in their attack upon the shallowness, vanity, and corruption of the bourgeois urban life, and in their moral summons. In addition to the public speech in which one pulled out all the stops, demonstration of supernatural power was an important propaganda instrument. Miracles were performed not only by Christian missionaries, as described in the Acts of the Apostles and as Paul encounters them in the opponents of 2 Corinthians, but also by Jewish preachers, Neopythagorean philosophers, and by many other teachers, physicians, and magicians. The entire scale of miraculous deeds of power was commonly used, from magical tricks to predictions of the future, from horoscopes to the healing of diseases, even the raising of dead people. In those circles which were addressed by these philosophers of the marketplace, the power of speech and the greatness of miracle had more profound effects than the depth of rational, moral, and religious insight.

The ancient and new insights of the great philosophers were not in demand, but rather whatever could clarify the world and its powers as they affected peoples' everyday problems. Astral powers took the place of the old gods; new deities had greater attraction than critically tested philosophical doctrines; demonic forces were better explanations of the world than scientific knowledge. Simple moral rules for human behavior offered better advice than psychological insights into the motivations of human actions. The solution of the most pressing

Bibliography to §6.4h (1): Texts

Dio Chrysostom: Greek text and English translation by J. W. Cohoon in LCL (5 vols.).
Abraham J. Malherbe, *Moral Exhoratation: A Greco-Roman Sourcebook* (LEC 4; Philadelphia: Westminster, 1986).

Bibliography to §6.4h (1): Studies

C. P. Jones, *The Roman World of Dio Chrysostom* (Cambride, MA: Harvard University Press, 1978).

personal problems, even if by magical tricks, would be more readily accepted than demands for social reform. If Christianity wanted to keep its message competitive, it had to enter into a critical debate with the laws of supply and demand of the marketplace. This is well attested in the Pauline correspondence which is preserved in 2 Corinthians (§9.3d).

It was difficult to draw the line between the impostor and the serious missionary. What would most easily attract people, were occultist phenomena, visions and ecstasies, exorcisms and conjurations, miracles and magic. The magical papyri report the very diversified practices to control "power" or to receive predictions and revelations: manipulations of water or light, conjurations of dead people, spirits, and gods, and the skillful handling of the media. It could be dangerous to interfere with such operations: Acts 16:16ff reports that Paul and Silas where thrown into prison because they exorcised a spirit from a possessed slave girl, who had just proclaimed the apostles as "servants of the most high god." How grotesque such a situation could be is well described in Acts 14:8ff: it is easy for Barnabas and Paul to underscore their preaching by the performance of a miracle; but they have great difficulties in preventing the people from worshipping them as Zeus and Hermes. For missionaries to say, "We are only human beings like you," would certainly undermine their credibility. Paul's opponents in Corinth were much less scrupulous than Paul himself in using all available means of propaganda (miracles, visions, ecstasies, rhetorical tricks, letters of recommendation). That occultist practices could even invade the philosophical schools is later evident in Neoplatonism. It is reported about Iamblichos that he levitated while praying, and of Proklos that he was surrounded by a halo when he was lecturing. A philosophy like Neoplatonism, which put great value upon asceticism, esteemed mystical power highly, used magic wheels in order to speak with the gods, and knew magic rights in order to make rain, closely resembles theurgy. The difference between philosophers and "philosophers" had become obliterated.

(h) Dion of Prusa, Plutarch, Lucian

Among the representatives of popular philosophy are several figures who did not belong to a particular philosophical school, but must be distinguished from the philosophers of the marketplace because of their comprehensive education and erudition, and their literary activity. It is characteristic that they were advocates of the Greek educational tradition, that they stood for propriety and morality in the name of philosophy, and that they primarily attempted to influence the comparatively broad middle class of the cities.

(1) *Dion Cocceianus of Prusa.* Typical features of the popular wandering philosophical preacher are most clearly evident in Dion Cocceianus from the Bythinian city of Prusa, later known as Dion Chrysostomos (ca. 40–120 CE). After his rhetorical education he converted to philosophy, was a student of Musonius Rufus, was exiled from Rome by Domitian, and for many years wandered from province to province as a Cynic preacher, even as far as the outposts of Greek culture north of the Black Sea. Nerva permitted his return to Rome, where he enjoyed the favor of Trajan as a spirited defender of the ideals of

the reconstituted principate. The last years of his life he spent in his home city. Many of his speeches are preserved. Written in a simple but elegant Greek style, they belong to the most instructive testimonies for the Cynic-Stoic ideal of the conduct of life. His description of the self-sufficiency (*autarkia*) of the philosopher is in harmony with the Pauline words: "I have learned to be content in whatever state I am. I know how to be abased, and I know how to abound. In any and all circumstances I have been initiated: plenty and hunger, abundance and want" (Phil 4:11–12). According to Dion, passions, desires, and vices are obstacles on the way to morality and self-sufficiency. But the philosopher's task is not only to preach moral improvement; as a pastor and counselor he should also support people in their moral and practical problems. Dion connects a positive criticism of religion with his moral preaching. The philosopher must assist people in discovering the true meaning of the worship of the gods, which is not fully comprehended in the external adoration of divine images—although even this expresses a genuine desire of the human soul. Dion's Cynicism was not uncritical of the political situation. During the years of his exile he actively agitated against the Flavian dynasty. But he was not a political revolutionary. His goal was to regain the classical ideals of morality and education, for which he frequently cites examples. Criticism of established social and religious convention is at the same time a summons to obtain true humanity in moral freedom and in true piety. In the new rulers Nerva and Trajan, Dion saw the possibility of a return to a just world order that was in harmony with God's universal rule. He used his gift as an orator to persuade cities and their citizens to establish among themselves the harmony that could make the newly ordered government of the empire beneficial for everyone.

(2) *Plutarch.* The same basic moral and religious attitude can be found in Dion's contemporary, the learned Plutarch from Chaironeia in Boiotia (ca. 46/48–120/125 CE). But while Dion was always in touch with the general public, Plutarch loved his study in order to read and to write. He came from a noble family, studied in Athens (especially at the Academy) and traveled in Greece, Asia Minor, Egypt, and Italy. The major part of his life he spent in his home city, remaining politically active on its behalf, and in nearby Delphi where he was priest of Apollo. Plutarch was a voracious reader and a prolific writer. Though only about half of his literary work is preserved, even this fills about six thousand pages in a modern edition. Many of his writings deal with scientific,

Bibliography to §6.4h (2): Text

Plutarch, *Moralia:* Greek text and English translation by Frank Cole Babbitt et al. in LCL (15 vols.).

Plutarch, *The Lives:* Greek text and English translation by Bernadotte Perrin in LCL (11 vols.)

Bibliography to §6.4h (2): Studies

R. H. Barrow, *Plutarch and His Times* (Bloomington, IN: Indiana University Press, 1967).

Hans Dieter Betz, ed., *Plutarch's Theological Writings and Early Christian Literature* (SCHNT 3; Leiden: Brill, 1975).

Idem, ed., *Plutarch's Ethical Writings and Early Christian Literature* (SCHNT 4; Leiden: Brill, 1978).

philosophical, moral, educational, devotional, and religious subjects; these works are collected under the title *Moralia*. The other part of his literary work consists of parallel biographies (twenty-two are preserved), which treat side by side a Greek and a Roman famous person, beginning with Theseus and Romulus, juxtaposing Alexander and Caesar, Demosthenes and Cicero, and ending with personalities from the 1st century CE. The biographies want to show to both Greeks and Romans that they are compatible nations, both possessing a heritage of personalities that were accomplished in political and military as well as philosophical and ethical pursuits. The purpose of Plutarch's literary work is moral education. He wanted to be understood not as an abstract scholar, but as a friend, pastor, and physician of the soul. The moral purpose is also evident in his biographies. They are not primarily presented as examples of political activity and as movers of history, but as models of an attitude of life revealing true virtue and genuine piety; deterrent models are, of course, also described. Whether told in the form of a biography or discussed in a thematic treatise, Plutarch always has in mind the formation of life on the basis of natural gifts through education and experience at a young age and the formation of character that is documented in the conduct of life and the manner of death.

In his philosophical position, Plutarch was a Platonist, although he assimilated many Stoic and Aristotelian concepts. His plain admiration is given to Plato alone, because here does he find genuine religious attitudes and the true recognition of God. More than other writers of his time, Plutarch is a theologian, and he returns repeatedly to the question of the right interpretation of religious traditions. He is in agreement with many of his contemporaries (including the early Christian apologists) when he criticizes the view that the deity can be found in material images and in the myths of the poets. Rather, allegorical interpretation is required to comprehend the true essence of the deity, which is necessary for the investigation of the things of the world, the recognition of moral forces which assist human beings, and evil powers that threaten them. God has created the whole world and is its ordering and governing power. Nevertheless, there are two world souls in the realm between God and matter, one higher soul which is good, and a lower soul which is evil. The latter determines the lower world beneath the moon, which is subject to change and instability. The entire realm between God and humanity is occupied by demons, some with divine power, while others share the vacillating world of sense-perception. The hierarchy of the demons' world is a stepladder from the human world to God. Such views are not necessarily due to the influence of the older Academy, although the concepts of a dual world soul and demonology ultimately derive from Xenokrates (§4.1a). Plutarch simply presents a Platonic world view which was widely accepted in his day. This includes a mitigated Platonism in anthropology and cosmology, amplified by astrological concepts and the widely shared belief in demons. But although Plutarch is convinced that evil rules in the sublunar world, he does not draw the same conclusions as the contemporary Christian Gnostics. He does not turn away from the world and its social and religious institutions; on the contrary, he commends a life which finds true, spiritual happiness in the mastery of the moral demands of marriage, family, the education of children, as well as in the faithful fulfillment of the duties of religion. The Greek fathers of the ancient church, beginning with Clement of Alexandria, saw a kindred spirit in Plutarch and were fond of his writings.

(3) *Lucian* (Lukianos, ca. 120–180 CE) from Samosata was a Syrian of humble origins. He learned literary Greek only as a young man and achieved an amazing mastery of its many modes and styles. Almost all works of his rich literary production seem to be preserved; but some of the more than seventy writings of the Lucianic corpus are spurious (certainly the short version of the romance "Lucius and the Ass" and perhaps also the description of the cult of the Syrian deity). He began his rhetorical career as a traveling orator, first in Ionia and Greece, then in Italy where he became famous, and in Gaul where he became rich. Lucian represents both the general level of higher education, and also the increasing disenchantment with the once highly praised values of the Classical Greek inheritance. He is the exact antithesis of Plutarch. Lucian exhibits biting irony where Plutarch is confident; he ridicules the old gods where the Delphic priest interprets them with profundity. He did not understand his rhetorical performances as instruments of political and moral influence; rather, he merely intended to entertain his listeners with his criticism of the existing conditions, and his satirical speeches were designed to amuse the audience. Later in his life, he revoked his commitment to rhetoric and was converted to philosophy and thus also to the dialogue as the genre of his literary work. Yet while the dialogue in its classical form had been the appropriate genre of philosophical reflection, with Lucian it became a tool for presenting the absurdities of philosophy, rhetoric, religion, and morality. Instead of philosophical considerations, Lucian's dialogues offer clever and witty comedy and satire. In spite of his renunciation of rhetoric, he never became a disciple of philosophy. His nearest kin are the Cynics; Lucian loves to quote Diogenes. He also shares with the Cynics the criticism of greed, luxury, debauchery, and intemperance, but he proclaims no new moral ideal. Lucian's assaults upon the charlatanism of religious propaganda are particularly sharp; well known are his writings about the false prophet Alexander of Abunoteichos, who claimed to be Asklepios' son and founded an oracle, and about the Cynic Peregrinos Proteus, a one-time Christian missionary who immolated himself publicly in Olympia (both are historical figures, whom Lucian had actually met). An expert judge of his educated and uneducated contemporaries and a keen observer, Lucian has preserved a good deal of valuable information about the religions of his time: about the ancient cults, beliefs in Hades and the judgment of the dead, the place of punishment of the evil-doers and the reward of good deeds; the conflict between fate and providence, astrology, the migration of souls, and belief in miracles. Although Lucian rarely says

Bibliography to §6.4h (3): Text

Lucian: Greek text and Enlish translation by A. M. Harmon et al. in LCL (9 vols.).

Bibliography to §6.4h (3): Studies

C. P. Jones, *Culture and Society in Lucian* (Cambridge, MA: Harvard University Press, 1986).
Hans Dieter Betz, *Lukian von Samosata und das Neue Testament* (TU 76; Berlin: Akademie-Verlag, 1961).

anything complimentary, whether about human beings—the only exception is his presentation of the Cynic philosopher Demonax—or about the gods, or religion in general, his writings, composed in brilliant classical Greek (he had no share in the sophistry of the Atticists), are rarely boring, never edifying, always entertaining, and of incomparable value as a mirror of his time.

5. THE RELIGIONS OF THE ROMAN IMPERIAL PERIOD

(a) Roman Religion and Foreign Cults

This is not the place to attempt a reconstruction of ancient Roman religion—a difficult task anyway because most literary, epigraphical, and archaeological sources present this religion already in its Hellenized form. Some information is preserved about ancient rituals, festal calendars, and the worship of various gods and divine powers. Divinities were originally conceived of as abstract powers rather than as anthropomorphic gods. However, at an early time under Etruscan and later under Greek influence, the Roman understanding of deities became more personalized and cult statues were introduced. What remained in spite of the *Interpretatio Graeca* of the ancient religious beliefs was the fact that, for the Romans, *religio* was the exact observation of established rites on behalf of the

Bibliography to §6.5: Texts

John Ferguson, *Greek and Roman Religion: A Sourcebook* (Noyes Cassical Studies; Park Ridge, NJ: Noyes Press).

Frederick C. Grant, ed., *Ancient Roman Religion* (New York: Liberal Arts, 1957).

Bibliography to §6.5: Studies

John Ferguson, *The Religions of the Roman Empire* (Aspects of Greek and Roman Life; Ithaca, NY: Cornell University Press, 1970; reprint 1985).

Kurt Latte, *Römische Religionsgeschichte* (HAW 5/4; München: Beck, 1960).

Nilsson, *Griechische Religion 2*.

J. G. W. H. Liebeschuetz, *Continuity and Change in Roman Religion* (Oxford: Clarendon, 1979).

H. H. Scullard, *Festivals and Ceremonies of the Roman Republic* (Ithaca, NY: Cornell University Press, 1981).

Arnaldo Momigliano, "Roman Religion: The Imperial Period," in idem, *Pagans, Jews, and Christians*, 178–201.

Robin Lane Fox, *Pagans and Christians*. (New York: Knopf, 1987).

Arthur D. Nock, "Religious Developments from the Close of the Republic to the Death of Nero," *CambAncHist* 10. 465–511.

Idem, "Studies in the Greco-Roman Beliefs of the Empire," in idem, *Essays*, 1. 33–48.

Ramsey MacMullen, *Paganism in the Roman Empire* (New Haven, CT: Yale University Press, 1981).

Bibliography to §6.5a

Simon L. Guterman, *Religious Toleration and Persecution in Ancient Rome* (London: Aiglon, 1951).

Martin P. Nilsson, *The Dionysiac Mysteries of the Hellenistic and Roman Age* (Lund: Gleerup, 1957; reprint New York: Arno, 1975).

M. J. Vermaseren, *Die orientalischen Religionen im Römerreich* (EPRO 93; Leiden: Brill, 1981). Twenty essays on eastern religions in the Roman empire.

Franz Cumont, *Oriental Religions in Roman Paganism* (New York: Dover, 1956).

whole political community. The fruitfulness of the fields, undisturbed peace and successful war, prosperity and health could be achieved in no other way, because everything was dependent upon the favor of those supernatural powers.

Piety (*pietas*)—the Romans thought of themselves as the most pious people on earth—was not understood in terms of the religious experience of the individual, and mysticism was always viewed with great suspicion. Rather, piety meant the faithful observation of ritual duty because the life of the individual, as well as of the community as a whole, was permeated by divine powers, whether in birth, marriage, or death, the seasons of the year, popular assemblies, or warfare. In order to maintain the favor of the gods and to avert their curse, the most important instrument was prayer. Equally significant was the observation of signs (*omina*) from which one could learn what the gods intended to do. The *augures,* a college of priests charged with the task of making these observations (from the motion of birds in flight, the appetite of the sacred chicken, and lightning and thunder), were held in high respect. The *haruspices,* who made predictions by investigating the entrails of animals (especially the liver), had learned their art from the Etruscans, and officials entrusted with its practice were drawn from Etruscan families. Important was also the interpretation of the Sibylline Books which, together with regular sacrifices, was the task of a college of priests (the *pontifices*) appointed by the state and supervised by the *pontifex maximus.* On the other hand, magic and those religious practices which the Romans called superstition (*superstitio*) were rejected. The term "superstition" was applied to everything that was alien to Roman religious rites, and it was therefore used for foreign cults practicing religious rites that the Romans judged to be strange and undignified.

In general, however, Roman religion was open to other cults. Accepting new cults of previously unknown religious powers and including them in the official religion, or at least providing space for an altar or a temple in the city, was felt to be appropriate, in order to secure the favors of such new gods. Roman religion was syncretistic already in the oldest known form. Etruscan elements (the *haruspicia,* and the triad of the highest deities, Jupiter, Juno, and Minerva) had been accepted early. Among the Greek gods, Apollo was worshiped already in the 5th century BCE. Asklepios (*Aesculapius*) was introduced to Rome in 293 BCE in order to fight a plague. The first oriental religion recognized in Rome was the cult of the Great Mother (Kybele), accepted in 204 BCE in a critical moment of the Second Carthaginian War (but Roman citizens were never permitted to participate in its orgiastic rites).

A grave and momentous turn in the Roman attitude towards foreign religions came with the Bacchanalian scandals of 186 BCE. Although both the *senatus consultum* about the Bacchanalia as well as the report of Livy are preserved, it is not quite clear what actually happened. The cult of Dionysos (§4.3f) had spread rapidly in Etruria and in the region of the city of Rome, not as a religion seeking official recognition, but as a mystery cult attracting proselytes without official sanction. Numerous new adherents had already been won, and "temples" (i.e., probably house sanctuaries) had been founded in Rome and its environs. Initiation ceremonies were held at night, and men as well as women participated.

Through some incident the whole affair received public attention. The Senate grew suspicious, fearing immorality and conspiracy, and intervened: all "temples" were destroyed, the adherents were hunted down and many executed. The cult was not completely outlawed, but only restricted and brought under the Senate's control. Henceforth the founding of a temple would require a permit, communal treasuries would not be allowed, and not more than five persons at a time could participate in the ceremonies.

Rome would never lose its suspicion of a foreign cult which appeared as a mystery religion. A deep-seated fear of magic and witchcraft and, in fact, anything which might appear to the Romans as superstition remained. Nevertheless, the mysteries of Dionysos/Bacchus were still popular in Italy and, after the end of the Republic, gained new ground, especially in the upper classes of the population. In addition, other mystery religions were able to establish themselves in Rome, although often with difficulty. The cult of Isis (§4.4a) had been brought to Rome by Egyptian immigrants in the 1st century BCE. The Senate intervened repeatedly: Isis temples, or altars were destroyed by a *senatus consultum* in 59, 58, 53, 50, and 48 BCE. In the year 28 BCE, Augustus outlawed private house sanctuaries of Isis, and in 19 CE, Tiberius had the temple of Isis in Rome destroyed once more and the cult statue thrown into the Tiber. Finally, under Caligula, the Isis cult found permanent official recognition, and a double temple for Isis and Sarapis was built, though only on the Campus Martius outside of the *pomerium* (the old district of the city which was subject to special regulations and laws).

But even if imperial Rome was opposed to the introduction of new cults into the city of Rome, there were no official restrictions pertaining to the expansion of these religions in the provinces of the Roman empire. To be sure, in order to establish a new temple, authorization was required. However, that decision was usually left to the local authorities, which normally granted such privileges gladly, as the numerous Isis and Sarapis sanctuaries of the imperial period demonstrate. In many instances, it was only a question of the renewal of older privileges. The situation was quite different for religions which could not claim ancient privileges and did not represent the national religious tradition of one of the many peoples of the empire. Propaganda and missionary activity would make such religions even more suspicious. Private meetings in secret which were neither supervised by local authorities nor led by officially recognized priests were never welcome. The celebration of secret initiation rites, such as "mysteries" in the Isis temples, would not be suspect as long as such temples were officially sanctioned, even if the mysteries were not accessible to everybody. But Christianity did not fit the Roman concept of a legitimate religion. One had learned to acquiesce in the existence of Jewish religious communities which were established in numerous cities, though ancient sources give no evidence for the modern hypothesis that the Jews enjoyed the status of a *religio licita*. But locally the Jews had ancient privileges, even it these were not always uncontested, and they were a nation which could claim possession of a long tradition.

If Jews were suspect because they did not participate in the emperor cult, such refusal put the Christians into double jeopardy. To be sure, the Roman empire was not a police state and did not possess a worldwide network of informers (this existed only at certain periods in the city of Rome itself under emperors such as Nero). Christian itinerant missionaries were free to preach anywhere, just like other wandering preachers and philosophers of the marketplace, and their followers would normally be left unmolested. Difficulties arose if local authorities had the impression that the Christians caused unrest, or if competitors and malevolent outsiders denounced them to the magistrates. In such instances they would be brought to trial (often after long imprisonment), sentenced to corporeal punishment, and expelled from the city. For this the Pauline letters give ample testimony; in the Acts of the Apostles, such actions have been stylized to a fixed schematism of the missionary experience. Capital punishment was rarely used in such cases—otherwise Paul would probably never have made it much beyond Antioch. If Paul was indeed finally sentenced to death, that sentence was most likely based on the accusation that he had violated the sacred rights of the Jewish temple (§9.4c).

Scattered pieces of information about Christian missionaries from the first two generations of Christianity lead to the conclusion that many suffered martyrdom; but not all of these death sentences can be attributed to Roman courts (cf., e.g., Acts 12:1–2; §8.3b). The Neronian persecution of the Christians in Rome (§6.2a) was a local phenomenon and must not be considered as typical for the attitude of the Roman authorities toward the Christians. The early Christian apologists tried to argue that the Christians were not a new religious sect but the legitimate heirs of the venerable ancient tradition of Israel (§12.3a). But to a Roman official, this would not have been immediately evident. In any case, the emperor cult was to remain an unsolvable problem (see below on the further development of the relationship of Christianity to the Roman state, §12.1c; § 12.3a, d–f).

(b) The Emperor Cult

The worship of the Roman emperor is a complex phenomenon. Ideologically it combined two different elements which remained in constant tension with each other: the fully developed Hellenistic royal cult (§1.5a–d) and native Roman

Bibliography to §6.5b: Bibliography

Peter Herz, "Bibliography zum römischen Kaiserkult (1955–1975)," *ANRW* 2.16.2 (1978) 833–910.

Bibliography to §6.5b: Studies

J. Rufus Fears, *Princeps a diis electus: The Divine Election of the Emperor as a Political Concept of Rome* (PMAAR 26; Rome: American Academy, 1977).

Fritz Taeger, *CHARISMA: Studien zur Geschichte des antiken Herrscherkultes*, vol. 2: *Rom* (Stuttgart: Kohlhammer, 1960).

Lily Ross Taylor, *The Divinity of the Roman Emperor* (Middletown, CT: American Philological Association, 1931; reprint Philadelphia: Porcupine, 1975).

Ronald Mellor, *ΘΕΑ ΡΩΜΗ: The Worship of the Goddess Rome in the Greek World* (Hyp. 42; Göttingen: Vandenhoeck & Ruprecht, 1975).

Glen W. Bowersock, "The Imperial Cult: Perceptions and Persistence," in: Meyer and Sanders, *Self-Definition 3*, 171–82.

concepts of the divinely gifted extraordinary personality. Whereas the Greek east saw the ruler as the epiphany of a god, the Romans worshiped transcendent powers which, under certain circumstances might become active in exceptional human beings. Victorious Roman generals who took over the authority of government from the former Hellenistic rulers repeatedly received divine honors in the east (e.g., Sulla and Pompey); but in Rome itself great pains were taken not to treat these powerful leaders as gods. The concept of the divinity of the living emperor gained ground in Rome only very slowly and under protest. Also institutionally the cult of the Roman emperor was by no means homogenous. Official declaration by the Roman Senate of the emperors divinization after his death stood side by side with sometimes spontaneously organized local cults elsewhere in the Roman realm as well as with the imperially sanctioned provincial cults during the lifetime of an emperor. Moreover, the basic features of the worship of the emperor developed only gradually as Greek and Roman concepts met during the time of the conquest of the east and changed from one emperor to the next.

A development in the direction of a cult of the ruler may have begun with Julius Caesar, although it is unclear what Caesar's own position on this question was. During the last years of his life the Senate voted several times special honors, some resulting from Caesar's own initiative, and these may have resembled divine honors. Caesar himself was deeply conscious of his mission, but we do not know, whether and in which way he conceived of himself as a divine person. He probably believed in typical Roman fashion that his destiny belonged to his *felicitas*, that is, an impersonal power which showed itself in his deeds. However, many people in Rome believed that Caesar was planning to be pronounced both king and god. If the assassination of Caesar was intended to put an end to such intentions, it achieved the opposite because it resulted in Caesar's divinization, spontaneously enacted by the people and later sanctioned by the Senate, which officially accepted Caesar among the gods of the Roman people and erected an altar for him (later a temple was built). The popular religious beliefs which soon grew around the person of Caesar included Hellenistic concepts of the divine ruler and his charisma.

Marc Antony did not share Caesar's caution and reticence: as soon as he reached the east, he demanded to be worshiped as a divine king and in typical Hellenistic fashion identified himself with a specific deity (Dionysos). His antagonist Octavian (the later Augustus) aptly took advantage of the negative Roman

Arnaldo Momigliano, "How Roman Emperors Became Gods," in idem, *Pagans, Jews, and Christians*, 92–107.

S. R. F. Price, "Gods and Emperors: The Greek Language of the Roman Imperial Cult," *JHS* 104 (1984) 79–95.

Idem, *Rituals and Power: The Roman Imperial Cult in Asia Minor* (Cambridge: Cambridge University Press, 1984).

Duncan Fishwick, *The Imperial Cult in the Latin West* (2 vols.; EPRO 108.1–2; Leiden: Brill, 1987–1990).

Inez Scott Ryberg, *Rites of the State Religion in Roman Art* (Memoirs of the American Academy in Rome 2.2; Rome: American Academy, 1955).

Henner von Hesberg, "Archäologische Denkmäler zum römischen Kaiserkult," *ANRW* 2.16.2 (1978) 911–995.

Inscription from the Roma-Augustus Temple in Athens
The temple whose fragments are now assembled behind the Parthenon on the Acropolis was built shortly after 27 BCE. The inscription on one of the epistyle blocks records the dedication by "the priest of the Goddess Rome and the Savior Augustus."

reaction. For himself, he explored a different option, which was more congenial to his own inclinations and corresponded to traditional Roman concepts. It was, of course, to his advantage that his adopted father, Julius Caesar, had been officially elevated to divine status. It allowed Octavian to call himself "Son of the Divinized" (*divi filius*). This was not a claim to divine sonship in the Greek sense but, avoiding any mythological connotations, established his legitimate continuation of the divine destiny and mission of his adopted father Caesar. Furthermore, the title *Imperator,* which Augustus regularly used, also expressed the Roman concept that he held an office endowed with a numinous dignity; what was new was the permanent use of this title. The conferment of the name *Augustus* ("One who deserves reverence," an archaic Roman designation) by the Senate in 27 BCE elevated its bearer to a position above the level of ordinary human beings; it emphasized the superhuman dimensions of his *felicitas,* but it did not make him a god. A mythological element was introduced only insofar as divine descent was assumed for the Julian family, which claimed Aeneas, the son of Venus, as its ancestor and accordingly supported the cult of the "Ancestress Venus" (*Venus genetrix*).

As long as the official Roman emperor cult maintained the structures created by Augustus, it was not a cult of the divine person of the ruling emperor. Its predominant features were rather the cult of Roma, the city of Rome as the symbol of the divinely sanctioned rule over the nations, and of the Divus Julius (Caesar). A relationship with the living emperor was expressed in the cult of his *genius,* that is, his personal guardian deity, and of the *Lares Augusti,* the protecting deities of his house. Both practices are related to older Roman concepts. This is also the case in the worship of the powers acting through the person of the emperor as, for example, *pax* and *victoria.* Augustus, instructed no doubt by political caution, but also by a genuine understanding of the Roman mind, thus distinguished the emperor cult of Rome from that of the Hellenistic idea of the worship of the revealed god. In Rome itself, Augustus became the "God Augustus" only after his death by vote of the Senate, a divinization that most of his successors would also be granted, though there were exceptions: Caligula, Nero, and Domitian, were not elevated to membership among "the gods of the Roman people."

However, such distinctions were meaningless in the eastern provinces of the empire, and even in the west the Hellenistic concept would soon overshadow the official Roman version of the cult. Altars and temples consecrated to Augustus, as well as honorary inscriptions, differed in no way from those honoring the Olympian gods. Moreover, the worship of the emperor was soon integrated into established ancient cults. A typical example is a cult that was instituted in Athens in the early years of Augustus. A temple dedicated to the "Goddess Roma and to the Savior Augustus," that is, the goddess of the leading city and the savior of the empire, was set next to the Erechtheion on the Akropolis in which Athena Polias, the goddess of the city of Athens, and Erechtheus, the founding hero of Athens were worshiped. Also members of Augustus' family, especially his wife Livia, received divine honors. Increasingly, the provincial assemblies sought Rome's sanction for temples of imperial worship, for which a particular city was chosen as the "temple guardian" (*Neokoros*). Major cities competed for the honor of guardianship of at least one, often two or three, imperial temples. Priests and one high priest for the imperial cult for each province were appointed (epigraphical evidence shows that this office was often held by women).

Augustus' successor, Tiberius, discouraged the cult of the living emperor and did not accept divine honors for himself, just as he also tried to restore the authority of the traditional institutions of the republic. Caligula, however, went to the opposite extreme. As soon as he became emperor, he demanded to be treated and worshiped as a god. As a consequence of this request, and despite the resistance of leading Roman circles, a new invasion of ideas from the Hellenistic ruler cult took place. At the same time, Caligula triggered the first serious conflicts between the emperor cult and other religions, because he went further than identifying himself with traditional deities and manipulating his own official acceptance among the gods of the Roman state; he also demanded that his cult statue be set up in the temples of other gods everywhere in the empire, even in the Temple of Jerusalem and in Jewish synagogues (because of the prudent delaying tactics of the Syrian legate, this foolhardy demand was never carried out in Jerusalem).

After Caligula's assassination, Claudius returned to the policies of Augustus. Neither Claudius nor Nero were officially accepted among the gods of the Roman state during their lifetimes. But the Hellenistic forms of reverence for the living emperor had meanwhile become so widely accepted even in the Roman upper class that the philosopher Seneca, in a petition written in exile, addressed the emperor Claudius in terms which left no doubt that he was indeed writing to a god. To be sure, many of the terms and phrases had already become worn-out formulas. They were also used in addresses to Nero, who flattered himself with the belief that such words were seriously meant. Vespasian, however, unequivocally returned to the forms of the emperor cult which had been created by Augustus: only an emperor who had been explicitly divinized after his death became one of the gods of the state. This form of the emperor cult became authoritative under later emperors until Marcus Aurelius, with the one exception of Domitian. When he demanded to be addressed as "Lord and God" (*dominus et deus*), he not only provoked the opposition of the Senate, but also appeared to the Christians as the dreaded beast from the abyss (Revelation 13). The persecution which the Roman church suffered (in 95 CE), referred to in *1 Clement,* may have resulted from Christian refusal of worship. (It is doubtful, however, whether the consul of that year, T. Flavius Clemens, and his wife Domitilla were executed because of their Christian faith.) But even if the emperors of the 2d century CE officially were not gods walking on earth, nobody was prevented from offering divine honors to an emperor, even in public. The proconsul Pliny, who had addressed Trajan in his *Panegyricum* as "Optimus" (the title of Jupiter), placed the statue of the emperor next to those of the gods, so that renegade Christians were forced to sacrifice to the emperor. A large temple for Trajan in Pergamon was begun during the emperor's reign (finished by Hadrian). And when Hadrian had completed the building of the Temple of Zeus Olympios in Athens, delegations from many cities dedicated statues to Hadrian with inscriptions which praised Hadrian as the "Olympian" (the title of Zeus), and the Athenians made him one of the Eponymous Heroes, an honor they had already bestowed on several Hellenistic kings three centuries earlier.

The cult of the emperor was part of the official Roman state religion, it never became a new religion as such, or a substitute for religion. This was well known to all, both the advocates of the emperor cult and its opponents. As a state cult, it did not compete with other religions but served to add glory to the cult of the gods of the Roman people. No one was urged to accept the emperor cult as a replacement for a traditional religion. On the contrary, the Romans supported the veneration of all gods in their native cities and nations, and they expected that those gods would in turn lend their support to the Roman state. When inscriptions speak about the emperor as "savior" (*soter*) and announce his "appearance" (*epiphaneia*) as a "gospel" (*euangelion*) praising him as the benefactor and bringer of peace to all humankind, the religious content of these terms did not question the legitimacy of other religions. In official usage, such terminology soon became hackneyed language. Certainly, people were grateful for the establishment and preservation of peace by the emperor, and they hoped that the gods or the powers of fate would continue to enable the emperor to secure peace and prosperity. But this did not imply that this Roman empire could be the fulfillment of the religious longings and spiritual aspirations of humankind. For their religious needs, people turned to their old gods or to one of the new religions, to the missionaries of the marketplace, to the philosophers, and not rarely to the magicians and astrologers.

The Christians nevertheless got into serious conflict with the emperor cult, but this was neither designed nor understood by the Roman authorities. Had Christianity been not more than a movement that tried to satisfy the spiritual needs of people who were hungry for a genuine religious experience, there might have been occasional frictions with Rome, but no irreconcilable conflict. However, the Christian message sprang from the enthusiastic experience of faith in the coming of a new world order. To be sure, some of the tension of this faith was soon relaxed, and the expectation of the coming of Christ in the near future might often disappear altogether. Yet the Christians remained citizens of a different kingdom, which had its own political and social order, and they had pledged allegiance to their ruler, Christ the king. This remained a constant part of the Christian conviction. Although Christianity was divided into feuding factions, nonetheless Gnostics, Montanists, Marcionites, and apologists for the main stream church were all united in that allegiance. Since the belief in other Gods was already intolerable for the Christians—as heirs of the tradition of Israel, they shared this monotheism with the Jewish people—the elevation of the emperor as a god of the state, designed to serve the preservation of Roman world order and of its institutions, was not only hubris and blasphemy, but a direct challenge to Christ's sovereign authority and to the vision of a new world, implied in that sovereignty. In actual practice, most Christians were quite willing to compromise. They prayed on behalf of the emperor, they adjusted their revolutionary social goal of equality for all to the more patriarchal ideals of the Roman society, and the apologists recommended the strict Christian morality as a virtue useful for the preservation of the state. But a true Christian would likely never demonstrate his allegiance to the Roman religio-political order by sacrificing to its gods and to the emperor, as was explicitly stated already in Pliny's letter to Trajan (10.96; see §12.3d). Thus the emperor cult became the criterion by which the allegiance to Christ was tested.

(c) Mithras

Among the missionary religions which spread in the Mediterranean world during the imperial period, the cult of Mithras occupied a special place. Although Mithras appeared to be the most oriental god among the new deities, and although his cult was essentially celebrated in exclusive mystery associations— the Mithras cult was a "mystery religion" in the strict sense of the word—this god was received by the Romans without resistance and, at the end of the 3d century CE, as Sol Invictus he even became the official god of the Roman state.

The cult of Mithras appeared for the first time in the Greco-Roman world in the 1st century CE. Its origins are not known. Mithras was an Indo-Aryan god worshiped in Persia whose name meant "covenant." In the Hellenistic period the names of the rulers of Pontus, who were of Iranian origin, and of members of Iranian nobility (e.g., Mithradates, Mithrazanes, Mithropastes) point to the continued veneration of Mithras. There were sanctuaries of Mithras during that period in many places of the east, including even Egypt. The magi, a priestly cast from Media, were this religion's cult officials. However, nothing indicates that this Mithraic cult of the Hellenistic period was a mystery religion, nor that its Iranian ingredients were instrumental in the development of the Mithras mysteries of the Roman world.

One might surmise that this Iranian Mithras cult assumed the features of a mystery religion during its westward migration (§4.3e; 4.4d). It is more likely,

---

Bibliography to §6.5c: Texts

A. S. Geden, *Mithraic Sources in English* (Hastings: Chthonios, 1990).
Grant, *Hellenistic Religions*, 147–49.
Meyer, *Ancient Mysteries Sourcebook*, 199–221.

Bibliography to §6.5c: Studies

Franz Cumont, *The Mysteries of Mithra* (Chicago: Open Court, 1903). The classic work on Mithras; but its results have been challenged in recent scholarship. The following works discuss an alternate interpretation.
M. P. Speidel, *Mithras-Orion: Greek Hero and Roman Army God* (EPRO 81; Leiden: 1980).
Roger Beck, "Mithraism since Franz Cumont," *ANRW* 2.17.4 (1984) 2116–34.
Idem, *Planetary Gods and Planetary Orders in the Mysteries of Mithras* (EPRO 109; Leiden: Brill, 1988).
David Ulansey, *The Origins of the Mithraic Mysteries: Cosmology and Salvation in the Ancient World* (New York: Oxford University Press, 1989).

Other important Literature on Mithras:

Leroy A. Campbell, *Mithraic Iconography and Ideology* (EPRO 11; Leiden: Brill, 1968).
Robert Duthoy, *The Taurobolium* (EPRO 10; Leiden: Brill, 1969).
Gaston H. Halsberghe, *The Cult of Sol Invictus* (EPRO 23; Leiden: Brill, 1972).
M. J. Vermaseren, *Mithras: Geschichte eines Kultes* (UB 33; Stuttgart: Kohlhammer, 1965).

however, that the mystery cult of Mithras is a new development which used names derived from the Iranian lore of Mithras for a new cult that was in its essence created on the basis of Hellenistic astrology. Astrological features pervade the entire symbolism of the story of Mithras and of the designations for the various ranks of initiates. Little information is available in ancient literature; an interpretation must rely almost exclusively upon the numerous pictorial representations. Mithras is born from a rock on 25 December (the day of the winter solstice); shepherds bring gifts. While hunting Mithras meets the bull, overcomes it, and carries it into a cave, where he kills the bull with a short sword (astrologically = *Perseus* and *Taurus*). From its blood and semen grows new life; but a snake (= *Drago*) tries to drink the blood and a scorpion (= *Scorpio*) poisons the semen. The sun, the planets, and the four winds witness the sacrifice; Mithras meets the sun (= *Helios/Sol*), both eat the meat and drink the bull's blood and make a covenant: Sol kneels before Mithras, receives the accolade, and they shake hands. It is not known how this cult legend was related to the performances of the mystery celebrations, which were held in small underground chambers with room for not more than twenty persons, the "cave," whose vault represents the sky with the zodiac. Some of these "caves" had holes which allowed the sun to illuminate the cult image on certain important days of the calendar. The initiation consisted of seven steps, related perhaps to an allegorical interpretation of the seven planets—contrary to traditional astrology which included sun and moon in the "Seven," these two often appear side by side with the seven stars. In spite of such inconsistencies the "Seven" correspond to the strictly hierarchical organization of the membership: "Raven" (*korax*), "Bee's nymph" (*nymphus*), "Soldier" (*miles*), "Lion" (*leo*), "Persian" (*persa*), "Sun-runner" (*heliodromos*), "Father" (*pater*). The initiate is called "reborn" and through an oath he becomes a soldier of Mithras. Military discipline and subordination are mirrored in the mystery cult's organization. A "Father" has to preside over the initiation of any of the higher ranks of initiation and also at the consecration of every new "cave." This explains why there is such amazing uniformity in all the Mithras sanctuaries throughout the Roman world. Moreover, a reference to the world of nature is evident in the ranks of higher mysteries of Mithras, which are related to the elements of the cosmos (fire, water, air). Mithras is also depicted as the master of the four seasons and as a gardener who furthers the fruitfulness of the fields. Ears of wheat sprout from the tail of the slaughtered bull.

At the beginning of the Roman imperial period, Mithraic mysteries existed in many parts of the empire. According to Plutarch, Cilician pirates settled by Pompey (§6.1d[4]) in the west propagated the cult in the western provinces. Evidence for a widespread dissemination, however, does not appear until the late 1st century BCE. No doubt, however, the worship of Mithras was the most important, most influential, and best organized mystery cult of the time—even as late as the 4th century CE, when the emperor Julian, himself a Mithras initiate, wrote his hymn to King Helios. Sanctuaries of Mithras (*Mithrea*) have been discovered almost everywhere, especially in the border provinces from the *Limes* in Germany to Africa and Mesopotamia (Dura Europos). Few were found in the interior provinces; however, in the city of Rome there where probably as many as one hundred Mithrea, and as many as sixteen were discovered in Rome's port city of Ostia. They are found wherever the Roman armies were stationed and where merchants were active. Only men were initiated into these mysteries of soldiers, sailors, and merchants. Membership was by no means limited to the lower classes, but regions with little mobility of the population and places where the old family structures had survived were less likely to open their doors to Mithras.

The history of the Mithraic religion reveals that Rome's official policies were quite able to accommodate a widely propagated mystery cult. But it is not possible to define in legal terms why the cult of Mithras was accepted, whereas the Christians were persecuted. An important reason was probably the fact that influential parts of the population—which increasingly included the army—were initiated into the mysteries of Mithras. Adamantly seclusive, this cult nevertheless had room for people who worshiped other gods; in fact, their statues have been found in Mithras caves. During a period in which the army expanded its role in determining the fate of the empire, the ruling classes of Rome accepted a religion of the soldiers that did not challenge the militarized authority structures of the state, while the rejection of these structures and of their ideology by the Christians made them highly suspect.

(d) Neo-Pythagoreanism

The Pythagorean movement made a new appearance in the late Hellenistic period. The Pythagoreans of the Classical period had based their teachings upon Pythagoras, philosopher, mathematician, and founder of a religious order, who was born on the island of Samos ca. 570/560 BCE. After travels to Babylon and Egypt, Pythagoras was active in Kroton in lower Italy from about 525/520 BCE. There he founded an order whose members had to live according to strict and partly ascetic rules. Pythagoras may have created this order not only for esoteric religious purposes, but also as an instrument of political power. This is reflected in its organization, which was divided into "politicians" and "theoreticians"— probably identical with the later distinction between "hearers" and "mathematicians." After some initial success in several cities of southern Italy, where the Pythagoreans became the primary support for the ruling aristocracies, the order

Bibliography to §6.5d: Texts

Holger Thesleff, ed., *The Pythagorean Writings of the Hellenistic Period* (Åbo: Åbo Akademi, 1965).

R. Navon, ed., *The Pyhthagorean Writings: Hellenistic Texts from the 1st Cent.* BC–*3d Cent.* AD *on Life, Morality, Knowledge, and the World* (Great Works of Philosophy 3; Kew Gardens, NY: Selene Books, 1986).

Philostratos, *The Life of Apollonius of Tyana:* Greek texts and English translation by F. C. Conybeare in LCL (2 vols.).

R. J. Penella, ed., *The Letters of Apollonius of Tyana: A Critical Text with Prolegomena, Translation, and Commentary* (Mn.Suppl. 56; Leiden: Brill, 1979).

Cartlidge and Dungan, *Documents*, 205–42.

Bibliography to §6.5d: Studies

Ewen Lyall Bowie, "Apollonius of Tyana: Tradition and Reality," *ANRW* 2.16.2 (1978) 1652–99.

Eikki Koskenniemi, *Apollonios von Tyana in der Neutestamentlichen Exegese* (WUNT 2.61; Tübingen; Mohr/Siebeck, 1994).

experienced catastrophic setbacks in the democratic revolutions of the 5th century BCE. If there was a short-lived recovery, it did not have much effect. In any case, at the beginning of the Hellenistic period the Pythagoreans had ceased to exist. The later Neo-Pythagoreans were not a direct continuation of the old Pythagoreans. The pseudo-Pythagorean writings from the early Hellenistic period are pure fictions which belong to no particular school.

The Neo-Pythagoreans emerged as a new movement without strictly organized schools or groups, and their doctrines were only partially Pythagorean. Orphic concepts (§4.2d) were frequently appropriated. Whatever one might point to as specifically Pythagorean inheritance could have been learned without difficulty from Aristotle, because he (or one of his students) had collected the precepts of Pythagoras, the so-called *Akousmata* (the ancient Pythagoreans never fixed the teachings of their master in writing, but transmitted them orallly). According to Aristotle's material, the Pythagorean tradition consisted of scientific definitions, wisdom sayings, and rules for conduct. The latter contained laws which, due to the doctrine of the transmigration of souls, required a predominantly though not exclusively vegetarian diet; there were also rules for ritual purity (such as the need to wear white garments and no shoes when entering a temple, or the prohibition of the cremation of a corpse). Insofar as the Neo-Pythagoreans assumed a life according to these rules, they would indeed have continued the ancient Pythagorean tradition. The symbolism of numbers developed by the Neo-Pythagoreans, most characteristic of their interests, is also an inheritance of the mathematical endeavors of the old school. In their philosophical orientation, which was by no means uniform, the Neo-Pythagoreans were eclectic, although primarily Platonists. They combined a Platonic dualism with the doctrine of the immortality of the soul and a very realistic belief in demons. To this point it would be difficult to distinguish them from Platonists of their time. The Delphic priest Plutarch, the Jewish biblical scholar Philo, and the Christian apologist Justin all shared these beliefs, and Philo and Plutarch moreover were as interested in number symbolism as the Neo-Pythagoreans. What distinguished them from other philosophers was their appropriation of certain religious undercurrents, especially concepts which derive from Orphism, such that Orphic and Neo-Pythagorean concepts cannot always be differentiated (as, e.g., in views about the fate of the soul after death). All this the Neo-Pythagoreans combined into an ideal of a conduct in which the power and superiority of the human self are visibly presented in the life of the philosopher. Since these philosophers often went from place to place as wandering preachers, they became a major factor in the propagation of a popularized Orphism and Platonism.

The best example for the ideal life of the Pythagorean philosopher is Philostratos' biography of the magician, ascetic, and wandering teacher *Apollonios of Tyana* (he lived in the 1st century CE; the work was written over a century later on the basis of older materials). The picture which Philostratos draws is idealized because all the features of a life agreeing with the Pythagorean principles of conduct are mirrored in this biography of Apollonios. Indeed, the genre of biography was far superior to that of a theoretical and systematic tractate about Pythagorean teaching: to act charitably toward friends and toward the common-

wealth, always knowing how to give others good advice; to know how to worship the gods, not through sacrifices and festivals, but through turning away from
the world of sense perception; to recognize demons and to drive them away; to
give account to oneself every day for of all one's deeds; never to depart from
righteousness, and always to trust the guidance of one's *daimonion*.

In Philostratos' work, Apollonios appears as the incarnation of the Pythagorean ideal. Dressed in a priestly garment of linen, he travels through many
lands, always faithful to his calling of serving the deity and doing good to human
beings. He never eats meat, lest he should destroy some living thing; he never
takes a bath but frequently fasts. He drives out demons, heals the sick, predicts
the future, and gives his advice where it is welcome and where it is not wanted—
thus he does not always make friends. In many ways, this fulfills contemporary
expectations very well. People were only too willing to believe in the presence of
divine power and to be impressed by mysterious knowledge about the workings
of supernatural powers. The asceticism and rigorous morality of the Pythagorean
philosopher embodied a human greatness which transcended the limitations of
everyday life, and opened a view into a possibility of existence which was more
just than most dealings in a world full of injustice. The biography of Apollonios,
as well as the many biographies of Pythagoras, which were produced at that
time, could satisfy such expectations precisely because they are religious legends
of saints. As distinct from Plutarch's parallel biographies, such legends do not
intend to provide examples for moral decision-making, but reveal insights into
deeper connections of human existence with divine powers and invisible demonic energies. What the Neo-Pythagoreans proclaimed was not a philosophy, but
rather a religion that would satisfy the longings of the individual for insights into
the divine world and immortality.

(e) Astrology and Magic

Astrology, discovered in the Greek-speaking world at the beginnings of the
Hellenistic period, strengthened beliefs in fate (§4.2c), but the new world view
which it offered did not reach broad circles of the population until the late
Hellenistic period. In the beginning, astrology was a religion of the upper,
educated classes. Horoscopes were expensive because they required comprehensive scientific investigations. But the introduction of the Julian solar calendar

Bibliography to §6.5e: Texts

Karl Preisendanz, *Papyri Graeci Magicae* (2d ed. by Albert Henrichs; Stuttgart: Teubner, 1973–
    1974)

Hans Dieter Betz, ed., *The Greek Magical Papyri in Translation. Including the Demotic Spells.*
    Vol. 1: *Texts* (2d ed.; Chicago: University of Chicago Press, 1992).

Georg Luck, *Arcana Mundi: Magic and the Occult in the Greek and Roman World: A Collection of
    Ancient Texts Translated, Annotated and Introduced* (Baltimore, MD: Johns Hopkins Univer-
    sity Press, 1985).

Bibliography to §6.5e: Studies

Franz Cumont, *Astrology and Religion Among the Greeks and Romans* (New York and London,
    Putnam's, 1912).

cleared the way for a more general dissemination of astrological concepts. Astrology was successful because it offered an opportunity to comprehend the laws of the universe by means of a system that seemed scientifically valid. Since the political, social, and economic horizons of human experience had become so much wider, people welcomed a revision of the traditional image of the cosmos, with the flat disc of the earth inhabited by human beings, the vaulted roof of the sky with the mansions of the gods above it, and the underworld below. Astronomy and astrology together made this revision possible: the earth became a sphere at the center of the constantly changing sublunar world; the place of the dead, resuming older oriental concepts, was transferred to the upper regions of the air or to the moon. The realm of sun and fixed stars, of light and the gods, of fire and spirit, lay in immeasurable distances beyond the orbits of the planets. Even if human beings were exposed to the mostly evil powers of the terrestrial world, they could be assured of their kinship with higher celestial regions. The human spirit belonged to the sun and the stars. Whoever learned to understand the laws of the universe could calculate the adverse powers of the lower regions and thus break the spells of the planets, which sought to block one's entrance to the august celestial realms above, the true home of the human self. After all, such knowledge might even prove useful for the mastery of the various everyday situations of human life.

Astrology did not enter the Hellenistic and Roman world as pseudo-religious quackery, but as scientifically approved insight into the true essence of the universe, legitimized by leading scholars and systematized by learned philosophers. The reorganization of the world of the eastern Mediterranean and the establishment of peace after the long decades of civil war by Augustus went hand in hand with the introduction of the Julian calendar. This was the solar calendar designed by Julius Caesar on the basis of scientific astronomy, and it is essentially the calendar still in use today (it was adjusted in the "Gregorian" calendar, introduced by Pope Gregor XIII in the year 1582). The average citizen was probably not always conscious of the fact that this calendar was the result of strictly astronomical computations. Indeed its introduction was as much expedited by religious beliefs concerning the sun, as the naming of the days of the week according to the planets ruling the first hour of each day was promoted by astrological superstitions. The propagation of the festival of the New Year also rested on astrological beliefs.

At the beginning of the 1st century CE everybody was acquainted with astrolo-

Fritz Graf, *La magic dans l'antiquité gréco-romaine* (Paris: Les Belles Lettres, 1994).

Frederick H. Cramer, *Astrology in Roman Law and Politics* (MAPS 37; Philadelphia: American Philosophical Society, 1954).

Hans Dieter Betz, *Hellenismus und Urchristentum* (vol. 1; Tübingen: Mohr/Siebeck, 1990).

O. Neugebauer and H. B. van Hoesen, *Greek Horoscopes* (MAPS 48; Philadelphia: American Philosophical Society, 1959).

Christopher A. Faraone and Dirk Obbink, eds., *Magika Hiera: Ancient Greek Magic and Religion* (New York: Oxford University Press, 1990).

John G. Gager, ed., *Curse Tablets and Binding Spells from the Ancient World* (New York: Oxford University Press, 1992)

gy, and consciousness of the difference between astrology and scientific astronomy was lost. Astrological symbols appeared widely in everyday life. Popularized astrological writings, easily accessible, made it possible to obtain information about favorable and unfavorable days and hours. Enough is preserved of these writings to form an image of their contents: predictions for each day according to the rising and setting of planets and stars, predictions based on the position of the sun and the moon in the zodiac, lunar calendars with information about each day of the lunar month, explanations for the occurrence of earthquakes and thunderstorms, and, finally, character portraits and behavior patterns for individuals according to the planets which determined the hour of their birth or conception. But even without reading such books it would have been difficult to avoid the influence of astrological symbols. The orbits of planets, signs of the zodiac, and displays of the months and seasons could be seen frequently on the walls and doorposts of houses and in the mosaics decorating the floors of private, public, and religious buildings (including Jewish synagogues). Augustus issued coins with the sign of the Capricorn, under which he was born. The legions received ensigns with the zodiacal signs of the month of the current emperor's birth.

Inevitably the images of the old and new gods would also be transformed according to these astrological concepts. Several copies of the statue of the Ephesian Artemis from the Roman period show the goddess with a necklace made of the twelve signs of the zodiac. Gods were often presented with the radiate crown of the sun. But in addition to this new understanding of the gods according to astrological concepts, cosmic powers were sometimes personified—evidence that this new world view did not conceive of the universe as a mindless mechanism. The gods of the new religions represented astrological powers (for Isis and Sarapis, see §4.4a; for Mithras, see §6.5c), and oriental prototypes gave rise to the god Aion, a personification of eternity and infinity and the ruler of cosmic time. He stands next to the transcendent highest god as a second deity and embodies the continuous movement of the All, the revolution of the stars, of becoming and passing away, birth, death, and rebirth. Therefore his symbols are the snake that constantly rejuvenates itself and the phoenix that rises from the ashes. Although there were occasional cult sites for Aion, there was no independent Aion religion. Rather, this god belongs to the general world view of that time: sometimes he was connected with other deities; in theogonies and cosmogonies he plays a role as creator. In Hermetic writings he is the first image and power of the highest god; in magical rites he is called upon as the origin of all energy. The widespread dissemination of astrological concepts is also demonstrated in Jewish and Christian writings of the period. The community of Qumran at the Dead Sea used a solar calendar, which also appears in the Book of Jubilees. Apocalyptic writings are full of numbers, symbols, and cosmological images which are derived from astrology. When the Revelation of John (12:1ff) describes the vision of a woman who is dressed with the sun, stands on the moon, and is crowned with the twelve stars (the zodiac), it is evident that even Christianity could not escape the influence of astrological concepts in the description of mythological figures.

With astrology came its relative, magic. To be sure, magic had always existed, submerged beneath the official cults and their rites, despised yet very much in demand. Magic characteristically remains in the shadow and does not have the same public standing as religion, even though magical and religious rites might be similar. The magician is not a priest or theologian who is publicly appointed or elected; he is a craftsman. His power does not rest upon an official institution and its sanctioned tradition, but upon the rules of his craft, which have been learned from a master technician through apprenticeship and refined through practice. Religion is concerned with all those experiences of life which are significant for the political and social community; thus religion deals with war and peace, guilt and expiation, seed and harvest, family and marriage. The magician, however, has learned to master the powers which lie outside this realm, powers of nature and energies of the cosmos, good and evil demons. He controls the delimitations of human existence: conception and birth, death and underworld, but also such "frontier" experiences like disease, personal calamities, illicit amorous adventures, and travel to foreign countries.

The developments of the late Hellenistic period created a situation in which magic appeared to many people as more important and more enticing than religion. Two factors paved the way for magic. On the one hand, philosophy had renounced its allegiance to the state and its task of providing a political education; instead, it turned to nature, the cosmos, the soul, and the afterlife. On the other hand, astrology had begun its victorious advance, advertising its ability to disclose the relationship of human fate to the powers of the stars. Astrology and magic became allies, because magic had always understood its craft as an intervention into the mysterious network of the powers of nature. Things celestial and terrestrial, stars and human beings, soul and body, spirit and matter, word and sacrament, names and gods—all were seen as corresponding parts of the same "scientific" conformity to the principles of the universe. If one knew the laws of the stars, their powers and paths, and if one knew their closely related counterparts in the terrestrial realm, one could also influence the stars' powers by manipulating the cosmic energies wherever they were accessible within things under human control. In this way astrology undergirded magic's claim of being a craft which could influence the powers of the universe. If the fate of human beings was determined by the stars, and if good and evil demonic powers constantly interfered with human life, magic could make the demons subservient to human interests and outwit the dictates of fate.

The magical papyri from the Roman period as well as scattered pieces of information from other sources demonstrate that magical practice would employ whatever was available. Its unauthorized syncretism knew no limits. Since any particular cosmic power or demon might have different names in the various religions, one was forced to pronounce all of these names in order to adjure that power. Next to the names of Greek deities one finds the names of Egyptian, Jewish (e.g., Iao = Yahweh; Sabaoth) and other gods, as well as many mysterious artificial terms—and the more mysterious and outlandish the more effective they could be. The tried and trusty instruments of the craft, too numerous to recount here, were supplemented by the tools borrowed from any and all religious traditions: transcriptions of Hebrew sentences into Greek (which were then read from left to right, i.e., backwards), liturgical pieces from mystery religions, recitations of cosmogonies, manipulations borrowed from medical and scientific handbooks and combined with old magical practice or religious ritual. Because this syncretistic process was not restrained by the sanctions of religious institutions, oriental materials could infiltrate without impediment. The proportion of Jewish materials in magical papyri is striking and is certainly related to the successful activities of Jewish magicians and the wide distribution of Jewish magical books (often under the name of Solomon).

It is difficult to overestimate the diffusion and success of magic during the Roman imperial period. Several attempts were made during the 1st century BCE to expel the "Chaldeans" and sorcerers from Rome. But they returned and could be found everywhere, advertising their craft openly or covertly. It apparently was not difficult for anybody to seek out a wizard "philosopher," the priestess of a back-street cult, or a useful magical book. How else could one manage to have an admired sweetheart yield to one's desires, get rid of a political opponent, be healed from a disease which no physician could cure, or make an important business trip despite ill omens! Magicians were badly needed, if people were unwilling to give up in the face of a menacing fate. Magic quickly conquered all classes of the society, and especially people of means and public visibility could be suspected of having used magical means to achieve their ends. When in the *Acts of John* the apostle drives out the bedbugs from the inn by his magic art, and when Peter and Simon Magus outdo each other in conjuring tricks in the *Acts of Peter,* we might wonder whether the frequent accusations of magic in the religious competition of the marketplace did not have some justification. Astrology and magic had certainly taught the missionary religions that they could be successful only if they could point a way to freedom from the fate of the stars, and to mastery over demonic powers. Christian and Jewish missionary propaganda, as well as the Egyptian religion and the cult of Mithras, understood this very well. But only the Hermetic religion and Gnosticism incorporated the answer to this challenge into their religious program.

(f) Gnosticism and the Hermetic Religion

Beginning in the time of Augustus, the Roman empire offered a political program designed to guarantee the internal peace. This program was largely successful, and a long-lasting economic upturn was the consequence. The existing religions were promoted and strengthened. Political propaganda to enhance the image of the emperor was ubiquitous: statues, inscriptions, and coins were witnesses that nobody could miss; the cult of the emperor was included in the public religions everywhere with its temples, festivals, and games. Had the gods indeed decided to grant their blessings to the world of human beings, they were guaranteed through the Caesar Augustus who stood at the head of the human hierarchy and was at the same time the god-like instrument for the mediation of divine benefactions to humankind. Was this political order and, more fundamentally, was the world as such capable of making human life worth living? Philosophy had already decided to bracket this question: metaphysics was not in demand in the schools. The Romans had long since focused their interest upon the political usefulness of philosophical ethics. One could certainly turn away from this world and its busy activities, reprimand its pompous pursuits and its craving for pleasure; one could withdraw into a skeptical distance from all things or become independent in the Cynic's contentedness. Alternatively, one could join one of the new missionary movements which offered at least some answers to the personal search for meaning and provided some fellowship.

(1) *Gnosticism.* Only one religious movement, however, could claim that it was able to answer every question with one single message: Gnosticism. It knew the answer to the one central question that includes all others: what is this world in which human beings live all about? The world is the tragic product of a fateful event in the deity itself; humanity, in its very essence a part of the transcendent deity and not part of the world, is caught in the middle of this fateful event, a foreigner in a world in which it has no business whatsoever. The problem of the human being is that the world exists at all. Salvation is the world's return to nothingness so that human beings would receive the freedom to return to their divine origin. When human beings recognize their true self, the world has already lost its power and its claim upon human existence. This is *gnosis*, knowledge, recognition of one's self and, at the same time, of God, because the true self is a part of the deity. Since human beings are caught in this world, imprisoned, deluded, and blind, and since they are asleep or intoxicated, a call from the outside is needed to awaken them and to make them conscious of their true identity. To issue this call in the world is the task of the revealer, the content of

Bibliography to §6.5f (1): Texts

James M. Robinson, ed., *The Coptic Gnostic Library* (NHS; Leiden: Brill, in progress of publication: complete edition of all texts from the Nag Hammadi Library with introduction, translation, and notes).

Idem, ed., *The Nag Hammadi Library in English* (3d. ed.; San Francisco: HarperCollins, 1990).

Bentley Layton, *The Gnostic Scriptures: A New Translation with Annotations and Introductions* (Garden City, NY: Doubleday, 1987).

Walter Völker, ed., *Quellen zur Geschichte der christlichen Gnosis* (SQS 5; Tübingen: Mohr/Siebeck, 1932). Greek and Latin texts from the Church Fathers.

Foerster, *Gnosis,* vols. 1–2. English translations of Gnostic texts.

Bibliography to §6.5f (1): Introduction and Surveys

James M. Robinson, "The Coptic-Gnostic Library Today," *NTS* 14 (1967/68) 356–401.

Kurt Rudolf, "Gnosticism," *ABD* 2 (1992) 1033–1040.

Birger A. Pearson, "Nag Hammadi," *ABD* 4 (1992) 982–993.

Bibliography to §6.5f (1): Bibliography

David Scholer, *Nag Hammadi Bibliography, 1948–1969* (NHS 1; Leiden: Brill, 1971). Continued under the title "Bibliographia gnostica" in *NovT* since 1971.

Bibliography to §6.5f (1): Comprehensive Treatments

Kurt Rudolph, *Gnosis: The Nature and History of an Ancient Religion* (Edinburgh: Clark, 1983). The best and most enlightened treatment of Gnosticism.

Hans Jonas, *The Gnostic Religion* (2d rev. ed.; Boston, MA: Beacon, 1963).

Idem, *Gnosis und spätantiker Geist,* vol. 1: *The mythologische Gnosis* (FRLANT 51; 1st ed. 1934; 3d. ed.; Göttingen: Vandenhoeck & Ruprecht, 1964); vol. 2: *Von der Mythologie zur mystischen Philosophie* (FRLANT 63; 1st ed. 1954; 2d ed.; Göttingen: Vandenhoeck & Ruprecht, 1964–1993).

whose call is solely the message that human beings belong to the divine realm and are foreigners in this world. All those who bear this equality with God in themselves are able to hear this call and recognize their true selves. With this recognition they are liberated. The remainder of the Gnostic message serves to help finding one's way out of this world that is nothing but a tragic abortion. The message answers these questions: where did I come from? why am I here? how do I find my way back? Therefore the Gnostic myth speaks of the primordial divine beginning (theogony), the tragic and fateful ensnarement (cosmogony), the human imprisonment (anthropology), and the "way" of return to the reality of divine origin (eschatology).

For the historian of religion, however, this description of Gnosticism may not be satisfactory. The comparative history of religions seeks to describe developments, understand dependencies, and present new phenomena in such a way that it is possible to recognize how they are related to, or caused by, older or analogous religious concepts. Yet the new religious insight of Gnosticism cannot be derived from an older religious movement or tradition. It is futile to ask whether Gnosticism derives from Judaism or from Christianity or from Platonism. The origin of Gnosticism cannot be explained in terms of specific historical dependencies or developments. The radical novelty of the Gnostic insight makes this impossible. Nevertheless, the general question of the place of its origin cannot be put aside. Gnostic religion emerged at a period in history during which social and political identity had become problematic for many people. Previously existing political and social institutions, such as the polis or nation state, had been religiously sanctioned and were thus endowed with religious meaning. Political and religious home had been one and the same for most people. The Hellenistic discovery of the universe as the home for human beings actually confronted people with a home that was strange and unfamiliar and which could no longer be understood with the concepts drawn from familiar and traditional religious be-

Bibliography to §6.5f (1): Selected studies in chronological order

Nock, "The Milieu of Gnosticism," in idem, *Essays,* 1.144–51.

Idem, "Gnosticism," ibidem, 2. 940–59.

R. McL. Wilson, *The Gnostic Problem: A Study of the Relationship between Hellenistic Judaism and the Gnostic Heresy* (London: Mowbray, 1958).

Gershom Sholem, *Jewish Gnosticism, Merkabah Mysticism, and TalmudicTradition* (2d. ed.; New York: Jewish Theological Seminary of America, 1965).

George W. MacRae, "The Jewish Background of the Gnostic Sophia Myth," *NovT* 12 (1970) 86–101.

R. McL. Wilson, ed., *Nag Hammadi and Gnosis: Papers at the First International Congress of Coptology (Cairo, December 1976)* (NHS 14; Leiden: Brill).

Layton, *Rediscovery of Gnosticism,* vols. 1–2. Collection of papers from the 1978 Yale University Conference on Gnosticism.

A. H. B. Logan and A. J. M. Wedderburn, *The New Testament and Gnosis: Essays in Honor of Robert McL.Wilson* (Edinburgh: Clark, 1983).

Gedaliahu Guy Stroumsa, *Studies in Gnostic Mythology* (NHS 24; Leiden: Brill, 1984).

Charles W. Hedrick and Robert Hodgson Jr., eds., *Nag Hammadi, Gnosticism, and Early Christianity* (Peabody, MA: Hendrickson, 1986).

Gedaliahu Guy Stroumsa, *Savoir et salut* (Patrimoines; Paris: Cerf, 1992).

liefs. There was, to be sure, no lack of suggested solutions. The Stoics had said that people should understand themselves as citizens of the world at large and as part of the divine Logos that permeated everything. New religions proclaimed deities which were said to be rulers of the entire universe. But the dominations and jurisdictions of these deities were not identical with the political powers to which the people of the Roman empire were subject. Moreover, if one directed one's gaze to the heavens and the celestial world, one learned that the air was populated by demos who were not necessarily well-disposed toward human beings, that the planets brought more evil days than good ones, and that the stars of the zodiac pronounced an iron-clad law to which even the gods were subject. This experience of the world is the presupposition for the Gnostic religion and its message. Gnosticism thus cannot be derived from anything but the experience of the world as a foreign place and of the liberating message of the divine call through which humans were able to recognize themselves and their true being.

More precise statements can be made about the language of the Gnostic message. This is indeed the actual question in the debate about the origin of Gnosticism: in which language of the known religions of antiquity does the Gnostic message appear for the first time? Most extant Gnostic writings were composed by authors who claimed to be Christian and who usually, though not always, believed that Jesus was the one who brought the liberating message of Gnosis. That fact was known as early as the 2d century CE. In such writings Gnostic faith is interwoven so closely with Christian traditions and language that it is difficult even today to disentangle the various strands. But much in Christian Gnostic writings cannot be easily derived from Christian language and its concepts. Particularly striking are the theogonic and cosmogonic mythologies, the metaphysically based dualism, and the mythic descriptions of the revealer figure.

The apologist Hippolytos (first half of the 3d century CE) accused the Gnostic heretics of letting reprehensible doctrines from Greek philosophy mislead them into their heretical ideas. With respect to the dualism of the Gnostics, Hippolytos was right to the extent that later Gnostics did indeed present their teachings in the terms of Greek philosophy. But in older Gnostic writings mythological language and concepts predominate to such a degree that any attempt to show a philosophical derivation is doomed to fail. These mythological materials ultimately derive from the mythical traditions of the ancient Orient. We know very little, however, about the continuance and development of these traditions during the Hellenistic period. Some features of Gnostic dualism may be of Iranian origin, but our knowledge of the Persian religion during this period is so meager that the assumption of an Iranian salvation mystery as the predecessor of the Gnostic religion is nothing but a guess. It is more probable that Canaanite creation myths were used in the formation of Gnostic cosmogonies, but such a possible dependence is difficult to verify, although several Semitic terms point in this direction. Moreover sources from Israel give testimony for the reception and critical elaboration of Canaanite and other oriental mythologies. Therefore we might well ask whether the first testimonies for the development of early Gnostic imagery do not belong to the immediate neighborhood of syncretistic forms of the religion of Israel, especially in view of the pervasive presence of mythological Genesis interpretations in Gnostic documents. Further clarification can be expected from the ongoing scholarly investigation of the newly discovered documents from Nag Hammadi (§19.1b; 10..5b; 11.2a).

At least the outlines of the development of Gnostic concepts can be sketched with a considerable degree of certainty. Emphasizing the Jewish component does not involve an attempt to "derive" Gnosticism from Judaism. Accepting the Gnostic creed would always entail for Jews a radical break with their God, the creator of heaven and earth and the lord of the history of Israel. "Deriving" Gnosticism from Judaism is just as improbable as deriving it from Christianity. However, there is at least one Jewish writing that shows some close affinity to Gnosticism: the Wisdom of Solomon proclaims Gnostic theology in the framework of the legitimate wisdom tradition of Israel. To be sure, this book did not take the step of rejecting the visible creation as the work of evil powers. But it depicts the wise man as a despised stranger in the visible world, to which he does not really belong and where he abides until he recognizes the voice of wisdom in himself and thus his true divine origin (§5.3e). But others drew more radical conclusions. Whether or not they belonged to the people of Israel can be left undecided.

In any case, in the effort of elaborating this declaration of the bankruptcy of the whole creation, and especially of the creation of the human race, the first book of the Bible acted as midwife. Elements of Jewish biblical exegesis of the Hellenistic period are clearly involved. Philo of Alexandria demonstrates that one had learned to distinguish between the true and essential creation of humanity in the sphere of the divine (in Platonic terms: in the world of ideas), and the creation of the earthly human beings, who are only secondary copies of the archetype created in heaven. Philo also testifies to efforts to understand the process of the unfolding of the divine world which preceded the formation of the visible world (§5.3f). If Philo did not allow the use of astrological and mythical speculations in his description of the creation, he imposed a limitation upon himself as a Jew and as a philosopher that would not necessarily obligate others, especially not in an age of widespread recrudescence of myth. Philo is also very careful not to make any distinctions between the highest god and a creator god of lower rank, although he knows a figure who is the mediator of creation. But Plato's dialogue, *Timaeus,* in which the figure of a subordinate creator-god, the demiurge, plays a significant role, had long since become a philosophical textbook. Postexilic Judaism, after all, had learned to understand the course of the world and the nature of humanity in dualistic terms. This cosmological dualism appeared in the form of popularized Platonism, the vernacular of philosophical speculation, and also in a mythological dualism which spoke about the battle between God and Belial, between an angel of light and an angel of darkness (§5.2b–c).

Mythical concepts of wisdom, cosmogony and astrology, dualism and Genesis interpretation, law and apocalypticism, God, demiurge, angels, demons, Satan— one could come to terms with any or all of theses at random and eclectically and still remain a law-abiding Israelite, or become a Platonic philosopher, or a messianic fanatic. But to amalgamate all these elements into a new vision of the world and of salvation required a catalyst, which Gnosticism became. It seems that several of the books from the library of Nag Hammadi belong to the earliest period of mythological Gnosticism, in which Christian elements are either completely missing or were superficially introduced at a later date (§10.5b). In these works, such as the *Apocryphon of John,* one can still feel the ravenous appetite caused by this fresh Gnostic insight. The new formula made it possible to absorb just about everything and to stop short of nothing. Reading some selections of this writing causes something like giddiness. Words and terms which any rational theologian would presumably first weigh carefully are used in the predication of the father god, recited at breathtaking speed: "For the perfect one is majestic, he is pure and immeasurable greatness. He is an aeon-giving Aeon, life-giving Life, blessedness-giving Blessed One, knowledge-giving Knowledge, goodness-giving Goodness, mercy and redemption-giving Mercy, grace-giving Grace. . . . His aeon is indestructible, at rest and in silence reposing and existing prior to everything," etc. (*Apoc. John,* NHC II,1 4,1ff.).

What follows is a description of the incomprehensible movement into which god and aeons fall as the divine pleroma is generated; Greek terms (Ennoia, Pronoia, Autogenes) are connected with oriental names of gods and angels (Barbelo, Oriel, Daveithai, Pegeraadamas). Then comes the abortion of Sophia, and Yaldabaoth, the demiurge who creates the lower world according to the image of the divine aeons. At this point the author has reached the first verse of the Bible. What follows, however, is not a well-balanced exegesis of the first chapters of the Book of Genesis, but once more a description of the complicated activities of the demiurge and his aids in the creation of Adam. A very elaborate anatomical list is used here, and to each part of the human body an angel is assigned, all with names that are otherwise unknown in religious history. Sentences from Genesis 2–3 are extemporaneously but pointedly interpreted in brief remarks, stating exactly those things which a Jewish exegete would never say, such as that the highest power of the abortive creation has intercourse with Eve and begets Elohim and Yahweh. This is either plain nonsense, or else an ingenious reevaluation of the tradition, unambiguously stating that this world of earthly existence is a monstrous miscarriage. It is necessary to know this before one can hear the message which appears at the end of the book: "He who has ears, let him get up from deep sleep," and "guard yourself from the angels of poverty and the demons of chaos and all those who ensnare you."

This is only one of the possible varieties of Gnostic expression, yet is still a variant that is closely related to the language in which Gnosticism was first proclaimed. Mythological exegesis of the Book of Genesis is found repeatedly in numerous variations in Gnostic writings. Other genres are also adapted by the Gnostic message, including many which are not as offensive to traditional religion and philosophy as mythological Gnosticism. The Gnostic message was well suited for "translation," but the offer of anarchy and the rejection of meaning for this earthly life, however formulated, is always present. Gnosticism was particularly productive in the composition of songs and hymns (§10.5c). In poetic works the description of the tragic event of creation is usually passed over. As an expression of piety, the hymn is best suited for describing the relationship of the soul to the revealer in whom it has found its true self. Also here the Gnostic presuppositions are apparent: the revealer comes from a different world that is unrelated to the earthly realm, just as the redemption of the soul vanquishes all earthly powers. Sayings of Jesus were also interpreted as the call of the Gnostic revealer. Traditional apocalyptic sayings could be employed in order to designate the transitoriness of the visible world. In the further development of the Gnostic sayings tradition, statements about the creation and about the path to the heavenly home of the soul were added (see below on the *Gospel of Thomas* and the *Dialogue of the Savior*, §10.1b). In Jewish Christianity, Gnosticism seized upon the tradition of the interpretation of the law, dealing with the cosmological dimensions of the law and with the distinction between false and true pericopes; only the letter derive from the heavenly revealer who appeared in the figure of Moses (§10.4c).

(2) *Hermetic Writings.* The *Corpus Hermeticum,* mostly preserved in Greek, attempts a reconciliation of Gnosticism and philosophy. It contains more than two dozen books, in which the Greek god Hermes appears as the heavenly messenger, revealer, father, personified reason (*nous*), and especially mysta-gogue: Hermes the Thrice-Greatest (Hermes Trismegistos). Most of the tractates were probably written in the 2d century CE by different authors, whose religious and philosophical positions vary. All the tractates have in common an offer of a syncretistic pagan philosophy of religion, which is presented as revelation that can be taught. Some tractates promote philosophical Gnostic teachings (especially I *Poimandres* and XXIII *Kore Kosmou;* two Hermetic tractates have also been found among the writings from the Nag Hammadi Library: NHC VI,1 and VI,8); others engage in a controversy with Gnosticism in behalf of an eclectic philosophical religion characterized by a moderated dualism and a pantheistic world view. Mythological statements about the generation of the world, whether as an act of creation, as a physical process, or as the product of emanations, are a major focus of these writings. Astrological speculations are used in almost every instance, sometimes with great elaboration. Religious concepts were drawn from the most diverse segments of Greek religion. Jewish elements can be recognized

Bibliography to §6.5f (2): Texts

A. D. Nock and A.-J. Festugière, *Corpus Hermeticum* (4 vols.; Paris: Les Belles Lettres, 1945-54). Greek text and French translation.

Brian P. Copenhauer, *Hermetica: The Greek Corpus Hermeticum and the Latin Asclepius* (Cambridge: Cambridge University, 1992).

Bibliography to §6.5f (2): Studies

A.-J. Festugière, *La révélation d'Hermès Trismégiste* (4 vols.; Paris: Gabalda, 1959–54).

G. van Moorsel, *The Mysteries of Hermes Trismegistus* (STRT 1; Domplein, Utrecht: Kemink en zoon, 1955).

Richard Reitzenstein, *Poimandres: Studien zur griechisch-ägyptischen und frühchristlichen Literatur* (Leipzig: Teubner, 1904; reprint Darmstadt: Wissenschaftliche Buchgesellschaft, 1966).

Garth Fowden, *The Egyptian Hermes: A Historical Approach to the Late Antique Mind* (Cambridge: Cambridge University Press, 1986).

Bibliography to §6.6: Surveys

E. Mary Smallwood, *The Jews under Roman Rule* (SJLA 20; Leiden: Brill, 1976).

Jacob Neusner, *Judaism in the Beginning of Christianity* (Philadelphia: Fortress, 1984).

Salo Wittmeyer Baron, *A Social and Religious History of the Jews,* vol. 2 (New York: Columbia University Press, 1966).

(e.g., in the creation story of *Poimandres*), and Egyptian influences are present (e.g., Hermes is identified with the Egyptian god Tot).

It appears that the Hermetic writings presuppose a pagan Gnosticism which had developed not in the form of philosophical teachings, but as the message of salvation of religious groups, which were organized as mystery associations. These writings do not argue in a philosophical manner, as would be expected in writings from a philosophical school. Dialogues mirror instructions in which the mystagogue introduces the secrets of the mystery initiation, and in which the one who is to be initiated learns the proper questions and answers. This original life situation also produced many hymns, doxologies, prayers, and formulaic proclamations of revelation that are included in these writings. What appears as philosophical reflection is frequently the interpretation of religious traditions. In their present form, the Hermetic writings are designed as "reading mysteries," which are also meant to contribute to the philosophical discussion. Was there, indeed, a pagan Gnostic mystery religion, independent of Christianity? Traditional scholarship dealing with the *Corpus Hermeticum* often rejected such a conclusion. But in the light of the recently discovered Gnostic texts, a positive answer to this question should be discussed.

6. PALESTINE AND JUDAISM IN THE ROMAN PERIOD

(a) Herod the Great

In the year 63 BCE, on a Sabbath, Pompey entered the Temple of Jerusalem (§5.1d). Hyrkanos was reinstated as high priest, but from now on he was accountable to the Romans for his administration. His brother Aristoboulos was led

---

Bibliography to §6.6: Special Topics

Martin Hengel, *The 'Hellenization' of Judaea in the First Century after Christ* (Philadelphia: Trinity Press International, 1989).

Morton Smith, "Palestinian Judaism in the First Century," in Moshe Davis, ed., *Israel: Its Role in Civilization* (New York: Harper & Row, 1955).

D. A. Fiensy, *The Social History of Palestine in the Herodian Period: The Land is Mine* (Studies in the Bible and Early Christianity 20; Lewistown, NY: Mellen, 1991).

Martin Hengel, *The Zealots: Investigations into the Jewish Freedom Movement in the Period from Herod I until 70 AD* (Edinburgh: Clark, 1989).

Morton Smith, "Zealots and Sicarii: Their Origins and Relations," *HTR* 64 (1971) 1–19.

Richard A. Horsley and John S. Hanson, *Bandits, Prophets, and Messiahs: Popular Movements in the Time of Jesus* (New Voices in Biblical Studies; Minneapolis, MN: Winston, 1985).

J. S. McLaren, *Power and Politics in Palestine: The Jews and the Governing of their Land* (JSNTSup 63; Sheffield: JSOT Press, 1991).

David M. Rhoads, *Israel in Revolution: 6–74 C.E.: A Political History based on the Writings of Josephus* (Philadelphia: Fortress, 1976).

E. P. Sanders, *Judaism: Practice and Belief 63 BCE–66 CE* (London: SCM and Philadelphia: Trinity Press International, 1992).

Anthony J. Saldarini, *Pharisees, Scribes and Sadducees in Palestinian Society: A Sociological Approach* (Wilmington, DE: Glazier, 1988).

See also literature under §5, §5.1, and §5.2.

372 The Roman Empire as Heir of Hellenism §6

as a prisoner in Pompey's triumphal procession in Rome. Later he fled to Judea but was caught and poisoned by the Pompeians because they considered him a partisan of Caesar. One of his sons, Alexander (the father of Mariamne, who later became Herod's wife), was decapitated. His other son, Antigonos, escaped.

When Caesar followed Pompey to Egypt after the battle of Pharsalos (48 BCE), many cities and countries of the east that had previously supported Pompey defected to Caesar. Hyrkanos' adroit minister, the Idumean Antipater, sent troops to Egypt who rendered valuable service to Caesar (who had run into difficulties in Egypt after the murder of Pompey). Hyrkanos persuaded the powerful Jewish community of Alexandria to support the new ruler. In the following year Antigonos, son of Aristoboulos, appeared before Caesar in Syria in order to present his claims to rule in Palestine and to the office of high priest in Jerusalem. But Caesar preferred to rely on Antipater, who had served him so well in Egypt, whom he appointed administrator of Judea, with the rank of Roman procurator. Hyrkanos was confirmed in the office of high priest and received the title ethnarch. The area of Judea was enlarged and became an allied state, a status which included freedom from certain taxes. The walls of Jerusalem could be rebuilt. Antipater reorganized the administration of the country and appointed his son Phasael as governor (*strategos*) of Judea and Perea and his son Herod as governor of Galilee.

The year of Caesar's assassination (44 BCE) once more tested Antipater's political cleverness. The murderers of Caesar, Brutus and Cassius, gathering an army in the eastern provinces, demanded his support, which they readily received. But the exploitation of the country for the support of Cassius' army increased the unrest in Palestine. Antipater was poisoned in a conspiracy and the Hasmonean Antigonos invaded Galilee, but was defeated by Antipater's son Herod. However, after the battle of Philippi (42 BCE) Herod had to come to terms with the victorious Marc Antony, the new master of the east, and he succeeded in spite of the resistance of Jerusalem. But as soon as Marc Antony had gone to Egypt, the Parthians invaded Syria, and Antigonos was able to conquer Palestine with their help. Hyrkanos, the high priest, as well as Antipater's son Phasael fell into the hands of the Parthians through deceit. Phasael committed suicide and Hyrkanos had his ears cut off by his nephew Antigonos and was thus disqualified for the office of high priest. Herod, however, had seen through the treachery of the Parthians and was able to flee after making his family secure in the fortress of Masada at the Dead Sea.

Antigonos now renewed the rule of his ancestors, the Hasmonean dynasty, in Palestine and minted coins which proclaimed him as "High priest Mattathias" in Hebrew and as "King Antigonos" in Greek. But before long the Romans took measures against the Parthians in Syria. Herod, traveling to Rome, obtained the

Bibliography to §6.6a

Michael Avi-Yonah and Z. Baras, eds., *The Herodian Period* (The World History of the Jewish People 1.7; New Brunswick, NJ: Rutgers University Press, 1975).
Stewart Perowne, *The Life and Times of Herod the Great* (London: Hodder and Stoughton, 1956).
A. H. M. Jones, *The Herods of Judaea* (2d. ed.; Oxford: Clarendon, 1967).

support of the Triumvirs (Marc Antony, Octavian, and Lepidus; see §6.1e), whereupon the Senate appointed him king of Judea. As soon as the Romans had driven the Parthians out of Syria, Herod could assume his rule in Israel. Jerusalem was conquered and Antigonos killed; Herod was the master of the country. The conflict between Octavian and Antony, however, once more threatened Herod's position. He had been a favorite of Antony. When Antony, who had fled to Egypt after the battle of Actium (31 BCE), committed suicide, Herod, in an impressive and clever move, traveled to Rhodos, where Octavian was staying, and laid his crown at the feet of the victor. Octavian accepted the gesture, reinstated Herod in his rights as king of Judea, and a year later added the Palestinian coast, Samaria, and Jericho to his realm (30 BCE). On a later occasion, Herod also received the areas north and east of the Sea of Galilee. This realm he ruled until his death in 4 BCE as an absolute despot and Augustus' faithful vassal.

HERODIANS, PREFECTS, AND PROCURATORS

63BCE   Pompey enters Jerusalem Temple
63–40   Hyrkanos high priest
40–38   Antigonos high priest and king
 38–4   Herod the Great king

Judea	*Galilee*
4 BCE–6 CE Archelaos ethnarch	4 BCE–39CE Antipas tetrarch
6–41 CE Prefects:	
6–9 Coponius	
9–12 Ambibulus	
12–15 Annius Rufus	
15–26 Valerius Gratus	
26–36 Pontius Pilatus	
36–37 Marcellus	39–41 Agrippa I

Palestine

41–44   Agrippa I king
44–66   Procurators:
44–46   Fadus
46–48   Tiberius Alexander
48–52   Cumanus
53–58   Felix
58–62   Festus
62–64   Albinus
64–66   Gessius Florus
66–70 (73)   Jewish War

Herod's loyalty to Augustus and to Rome was real. He did not renew the old ideals of Hasmonean rule. In his internal policies he emulated Augustus' policies of peace. Under Augustus, Rome promoted the Greek cities, reconstituted them, and granted them various privileges. Herod followed this example in his small kingdom. In the place of the ancient northern capital of Samaria, which had been refounded by Alexander but was destroyed by the Hasmoneans, Herod established the splendid Greek city "Sebaste" ("Sebastos" is the Greek translation of Augustus) with a theater and a large temple dedicated to the emperor; only now did Samaria experience its greatest flowering. On the Palestinian coast he built a new city, entirely in the Hellenistic style, which became a significant port and later the seat of the Roman governor, and was called Caesarea in honor of Augustus Caesar. A number of other cities were reestablished or renovated. Herod's second concern was to strengthen the fortresses at the eastern border of his realm, including the fortress of Masada at the Dead Sea. Finally, Herod spent large sums for buildings in Jerusalem, most importantly for the erection of a new temple. Its foundations were enlarged (the Wailing Wall is part of these Herodian foundations), and the temple was completely rebuilt. Herod also attended to other holy shrines of Israel, like the shrine of Abraham in Mamre, though he did not neglect the pagan cults in his country: a temple for the emperor was added to the shrine of Pan at the sources of the Jordan.

Herodian architecture belongs to the very finest in design and execution in the entire Roman world, executed by the most able artisans. Herod's extensive building projects demonstrate not only that he extracted large sums of money from his country, but also that there was considerable economic growth during his long rule. After years of war and unrest, peace had finally returned to the land of Israel, and all its inhabitants, Jews as well as Samaritans and Greeks, did profit. Nevertheless, Herod never succeeded in his attempts to become reconciled with the Jewish people. The splendor and cruelty of his rule combined to establish his image as a ruthless tyrant. Although he eagerly supported the institutions of the Jewish religion, it was never forgotten that he was an Idumean and that his kingdom relied upon the favor of the Romans, whose rule remained a hated foreign dominion for the Jewish people. Neither the Pharisees nor the Sadducees seem to have supported Herod, although they had no choice but to acquiesce. The tragedies of Herod's family history contributed to his bad reputation. He had his second wife, the Hasmonean princess Mariamne, put to death because he suspected her involvement in a conspiracy against him. The former high priest Hyrkanos was murdered by Herod at the advanced age of eighty. At the end of his rule, Herod executed his two sons from his marriage with Mariamne (Alexander and Aristoboulos; 7 BCE), and shortly before his death he eliminated his oldest son Antipater (4 BCE). Thus it is not surprising that Herod was remembered as the murderer of the children of Bethlehem (Matt 2:16–18). When he died, unrest broke out in Palestine for the first time after several decades, while Rome discussed the question of his successor. Varus, the legate of Syria, had to move to Palestine with his army to suppress the insurrection. Several cities were destroyed and more than two thousand leaders of the uprising killed.

(b) Palestine under the sons of Herod

In his testament Herod had divided the land among his sons. A delegation from Jerusalem tried to persuade Augustus not to continue this hated dynasty. But Augustus decided to recognize the testament of his friend and faithful vassal. Archelaos received Judea and Samaria, which amounted to about half of the territory that his father had ruled. He was awarded the title "ethnarch," with the promise that he would later became king, if his administration went well. This, however, was not the case; Archelaos was deposed in 6 CE and exiled to Vienne in Gaul. Archelaos is the king whom Joseph is said to have feared when he came back from Egypt to Bethlehem, settling instead in Nazareth (Matt 2:22), where Antipas, another son of Herod, ruled.

Antipas was appointed "tetrarch" of Galilee and Perea, which he ruled from 4 BCE to 39 CE. He was the true son of his father; cunning and cruel but also fond of splendor, yet without true greatness. He continued his father's building program, first enlarged his capital, Sepphoris—only a few miles from Nazareth—then built a second capital on the shores of the Sea of Galilee, which he called "Tiberias" in honor of the emperor Tiberius. This city had a predominantly pagan population and, according to the accounts of all New Testament gospels, Jesus never went there. In the 2d century CE, Tiberias became the metropolis of Rabbinic Judaism. Antipas is the "Herod" mentioned in Luke 3:1; Jesus called him "this fox" (Luke 13:32). He also appears in Luke 23:6–16 as Jesus' sovereign, to whom Pilate sent Jesus for interrogation. Finally, Antipas is remembered by the New Testament and by Josephus (*Ant.* 18.116–119) as the murderer of John the Baptist. Antipas was married to a Nabatean princess; she left him, however, when she heard that Antipas intended to marry his niece Herodias (the sister of the later king Agrippa I, a granddaughter of Herod the Great and Mariamne), who was the wife of Antipas' brother Herod (Mark 6:14–19 erroneously calls her the wife of Philip). John the Baptist had publicly attacked Antipas because of this scandal, an act which cost him his head. But it also cost Antipas his kingdom, because the separation from his former wife led to a deterioration of relations with the neighboring kingdom of Nabatea. In repeated border wars, Antipas was finally beaten so badly that the Nabatean king Aretas (the same Aretas from whom Paul escaped at Damascus; 2 Cor 11:32) that the Syrian legate Vitellius had to come to his aid. This was probably the reason for his deposition and banishment to Lyon in Gaul by Caligula (39 CE), when Antipas applied to Rome to be awarded the title "king." Apparently Antipas' nephew Agrippa was involved in devising the accusations which were brought against him; Agrippa inherited his uncle's tetrarchy (§6.6d).

The third of the successors of Herod the Great was his son Philip, who became tetrarch of the areas north and east of the Sea of Galilee: Trachonitis, Gaulanitis, and Auranitis. He built his residence at the foot of Mt. Hermon and called it

Bibliography to §6.6b

Stewart Perowne, *The Later Herods* (London: Hodder and Stoughton, 1958; New York: Abingdon, 1959).

Harold W. Hoehner, *Herod Antipas* (Cambridge: Cambridge University Press, 1972).

"Caesarea" in honor of Augustus; to distinguish this city from Herod's foundation of the same name (Caesarea Maritima), it became known as Caesarea Philippi (see Mark 8:27f.). The village of Bethsaida at the northern influx of the Jordan
river into the Sea of Galilee, mentioned several times by the gospels, was
expanded into a city by Philip and called "Julia" in honor of Augustus' daughter.
Philip seems to have been a just petty prince. His wife was his grandniece
Salome, the daughter of Herodias, who asked for the head of John the Baptist
when she was at the court of Antipas. Philip died in 34 CE without leaving
an heir.

(c) Judea under Roman administration

After Archelaos had been removed from office (6 CE), Augustus administered
the districts of Judea, Samaria, and Idumea through a prefect (*praefectus cum
iure gladii;* §6.3a) who was directly responsible to the emperor, but dependent
upon the legate of Syria for military aid. This legate also remained the Roman
administrator for the coastal area from Jamnia (Yavneh) to Gaza and for the
Decapolis, the semi-independent district of the Greek cities south of the Sea of
Galilee. Quirinius (Luke 2:2) became the new legate of Syria, Coponius the first
prefect of Judea. Because Judea came under direct Roman administration in 6
CE, a "census" (ἀπογραφή) was made, that is, an establishment of tax records.
Luke used this information in order to provide a motive for the travel of Jesus'
parents from Nazareth in Galilee to Bethlehem in Judea—an improbable assumption, because Nazareth did not belong to the area of Roman taxation. This census
caused rebellions, instigated by an unidentified radical Jewish group. There is no
evidence that it was made up of "Zealots," since Josephus uses this term exclusively for the terrorists under the leadership of John of Gishala at the beginning of
the Jewish War. The seat of government for the new prefect became Caesarea
Maritima. Only during the high festival days did the prefect reside in Jerusalem;
a permanent garrison was stationed in the fortress of Antonia, situated next to the
Temple. The other fortresses of the country were also garrisoned by Roman
soldiers.

The country was divided into eleven toparchies, each headed by a Jewish or
Samaritan Sanhedrin (*synedrion*) with jurisdiction over petty lawsuits. More
important cases of sanhedrins in Judea had to be referred to the sanhedrin in
Jerusalem. The jurisdiction, however, of this central Jewish court was also
limited. Accusations involving the death penalty had to be brought before the
prefect's court. The prefect was also responsible for the collection of direct taxes,
which was accomplished through salaried officials assisted by the local sanhedrins. Indirect taxes and customs were farmed out, as was customary then, to
private tax collectors (publicans). This practice often gave rise to complaints and
unrest. The tax farmers, who collaborated voluntarily with the Roman adminis-

Bibliography to §6.6c: Texts

J.-P. Lemonon, *Pilate et le gouvernement de la Judée: Textes et monuments* (EtBib; Paris:
    Gabalda, 1981).

tration and frequently became quite wealthy, had a poor reputation (see the gospels' references to the despised publicans). The high priest was appointed by the prefect who otherwise did not interfere in the Jewish temple cult, public worship services, and the peculiarities of Jewish legal observance. The Roman soldiers were advised not to take their ensigns to Jerusalem in order to avoid unnecessary offense to Jewish sensibilities.

The first two decades of the Roman administration of Judea seem to have been relatively free of friction; no major case of unrest is known before the year 26 CE, when Pontius Pilate was sent to Judea as the fifth prefect of the district. (The title *praefectus*, not *procurator*, is attested for Pilate by an inscription found in Caesarea.) Incidents of unrest increased under his administration. He brought the Roman military ensigns into Jerusalem, but had to withdraw them because of widespread public protest. Tumults broke out when he began to build a major aquaeduct meant to improve the water supply of Jerusalem, but Pilate quelled them ruthlessly. He did not hesitate to order on-the-spot executions by his soldiers, as is evident from the incident alluded to in Luke 13:1. Similarly, in the case of Jesus, Pilate was quick in sentencing and executing a potential agitator. When Pilate proceeded recklessly and brutally against a movement of religious fanatics in Samaria, the Syrian legate Vitellius recommended that he be recalled. He had to appear in Rome to give account for his conduct of office. It seems that he was forced to commit suicide (36 CE).

(d) Agrippa I and Agrippa II

When Caligula had become emperor in 37 CE, one of his first official actions was to appoint his friend Agrippa, grandson of Herod the Great and Mariamne, as tetrarch of Abilene (a small district north of the sources of the Jordan) and of Philip's tetrarchy, which had become vacant. Two years later, Antipas was removed from his tetrarchy in Galilee, and Agrippa, probably involved in his uncle's removal, became his successor. In the same year, Caligula ordered that his statue should be placed in the Temple of Jerusalem. In 40/41 CE the Syrian legate Petronius went to Palestine in order to lend force to the emperor's order but withdrew, realizing that enforcement would lead to revolution. But before Petronius and Agrippa could persuade the emperor to withdraw his mad order, Caligula was assassinated (§6.2a). Agrippa played a significant role in the choice of Claudius as Caligula's successor, who demonstrated his gratefulness by appointing him as king over the former territories of his grandfather Herod the Great.

From 41 to 44 CE Agrippa I was king, by the grace of Rome, over the entire area of ancient Israel. In contrast to Herod the Great and his sons, Agrippa enjoyed the goodwill of the leading circles of the Jewish people, perhaps because he was a legitimate descendent of the old Hasmonean house through his grandmother Mariamne. In Jerusalem he made great efforts to appear as a pious and law-abiding Jew, promoting the Jewish religion forcefully, and taking measures against its destractors according to the will of its Jerusalem leadership (the apostle James, son of Zebedee, was executed by Agrippa, cf. Acts 12:1). In his political capital Caesarea, on the other hand, Agrippa played the role of an oriental king. A conference with other Syrian petty kings was broken up by the Syrian legate because it looked like a conspiracy. The Syrian legate also prevented Agrippa from building a third city wall around Jerusalem. What kind of plans Agrippa actually pursued remains unknown, since he died unexpectedly from some disease in 44 CE.

Agrippa left a son of the same name who was still underage. Agrippa II did not became his father's successor even when he had reached his majority. Rather, in 50 CE he received Chalkis, a small principality in the northern part of the valley between the Lebanon and Anti-Lebanon. In 53 CE he was permitted to exchange Chalkis for the former tetrarchy of Philip, also received Abilene, and later parts of Galilee along with Tiberias. In addition he was given responsibility for the supervision of the Jerusalem Temple. Agrippa II kept his realm until his death in ca. 100 CE. He did not participate in the Jewish War, but remained loyal to Rome. The author of the Book of Acts remembers him as the king Agrippa who visited with the Roman procurator Festus during the trial of Paul, and who admitted that Paul had almost persuaded him to became a Christian (Acts 25–26; esp. 26:28). At that time Agrippa was accompanied by his sister Berenike, who was said to be living in incestuous relationship with her brother, and who later became the mistress of the general and later emperor Titus.

(e) Palestine before the Fall of Jerusalem

After the death of Agrippa I, Rome organized the whole area of Palestine as a Roman province and attempted to gain firm control over this restless country. It is difficult to say whether these efforts had any success, because our primary sources for this period are the writings of the Josephus, who seeks to demonstrate that the blunders of an incompetent Roman administration were ultimately responsible for the destruction of his people. Josephus says little about those periods of the Roman administration in which peace prevailed, but his judgment may be justified for the years immediately before the outbreak of the war.

The first procurator was Fadus (44–46 CE). At the beginning of his administration he had to quell several minor rebellions with the help of the Syrian legate Cassius Longinus. He also forced the Jews to surrender the garments of the high priest, which had been in Jewish custody during the reign of Agrippa I (later they passed into the custody of Agrippa II). The insurrection of Theudas, incorrectly dated by the Book of Acts into the time before the revolt of Judas the Galilean (6 CE; see Acts 5:36), occurred under Fadus' administration. Theudas, the leader of a messianic-prophetic movement, was executed. Fadus' successor was Tiberius Alexander (46–48 CE), nephew of the philosopher Philo (he later became prefect of Egypt; see §5.3f). After him Cumanus became procurator (48 CE).

Bibliography to §6.6e: Studies

Martin Goodman, *The Ruling Class of Judaea: The Origins of the Jewish Revolt Against Rome* AD *66–70* (Cambridge: Cambridge University Press, 1987).

G. Cornfeld with B. Mazar and P. L. Maier, eds., *The Jewish War: Newly Translated with Extensive Commentary and Archaeological Background Illustrations* (Grand Rapids: Zondervan, 1982).

See also Bibliography to §6.6: Special Topics

In the year 51, a Jewish pilgrim to Jerusalem who dared to travel through Samaria was murdered. The Jewish leaders in Jerusalem demanded strict punishment of the guilty persons from Cumanus. When Cumanus did not comply, the Jews themselves took a punitive expedition into Samaria, burned several villages and massacred the population. Now Cumanus became active, taking measures against the more recent troublemakers, namely, the Jews. This brought the intervention of the Syrian legate Quadratus, who feared that the conflict might become more widespread. Quadratus sent all the leaders of all parties to Rome to defend their causes: Cumanus and the leaders of the Jews and of the Samaritans. The negotiations apparently took place in Rome during the summer and fall of the year 52 CE. As a result, the high priest Jonathan and the powerful imperial secretary Pallas agreed that the Jews would return unpunished, if they petitioned the emperor to send Pallas' brother Felix, a freedman, to Palestine as a procurator. This turned out to be a disastrous move. It was only through the favor of the powerful Pallas that a former slave could be appointed to an office that was traditionally reserved for a member of the equestrian class.

Since Felix was probably appointed in the fall, he could hardly have assumed the duties of his office before the spring of 53 CE. Due to Felix' incompetence, the years of his administration were filled with disturbances and tumults. The Sicarii made their first appearance, revolutionaries who carried daggers under their clothing and used every opportunity to assassinate people suspected of collaboration with Rome. Felix cruelly suppressed a religious uprising involving a huge crowd of people who went into the wilderness to await the coming of the messiah, and an insurrection under the "Egyptian prophet." Among the disturbances which were quelled by the Jewish authorities in collaboration with the Roman administration was a tumult in the Temple caused by the apostle Paul, who had been recognized there and was accused of having brought a gentile into the Temple. The procurator also intervened and Paul was arrested (§9.4b–c).

The dating of the end of Felix's term is problematic, which implies that an important date for of Paul's chronology also remains uncertain. Acts 24:27 speaks of a period of two years Paul's imprisonment in Caesarea after which Felix was replaced by Festus. If Festus came into office as late as the year 60 CE, the imprisonment of Paul in the Palestinian capital could be dated to 58–60 CE. This date seems to be corroborated by Josephus, who has very little to tell about the period of Festus' administration, except that he died in office in 62; thus he apparently was procurator for only a very short period. However, several scholars have understood the "two years" of Acts 24:27 to refer to the time of Felix's procuratorship, arguing that in Luke's source this time period was not connected with Paul's imprisonment. In connection with this hypothesis, one must also mention Josephus' report (*Ant.* 19.182) that the Jewish authorities had accused Felix before Nero, but that the intervention of his brother Pallas, at that time still in good standing with Nero, saved him from punishment, although he was removed from his office as procurator of Palestine. Tacitus (*Ann.* 13.15) says that Pallas fell out of favor with Nero shortly before the murder of Britannicus in December of the year 55. Thus, this hypothesis concludes, Felix's replacement by Festus and Pallas' intervention on behalf of his brother must be dated no later than the fall of the year 55. Felix's administration would then be limited to the two years beginning in 53, and Paul's imprisonment could be dated as early as the summer of 55, followed by his trial before Festus and journey to Rome the following spring.

This combination of various data seems ingenious, but the difficulties which arise for the Pauline chronology are considerable. Moreover, the immensely rich Pallas probably did not lose all his influence, even though he fell out of favor with Nero. Thus he was certainly able to intervene on behalf of his brother at some later date; Nero did not put him to death until 62. As will be argued below (§9.1c; 9.3b–c; 9.4b–c), the internal chronology of the Pauline mission suggests a somewhat later date for his arrest in Jerusalem. On the other hand, the administration of Festus should not be calculated as too short a period. It probably covered at least the years from 58 to 62. The competent Burrus still held the reins of the Roman government at the end of the 50s, and the appointment of an able procurator for the restless province of Palestine is probable during those years of Nero's rule. That Festus was a qualified and prudent administrator may have been the reason for Josephus' silence about the years of his procuratorship.

Festus died in 62 while still in office, causing a vacancy which was used by the leaders of the Jewish community to do away with some unwelcome people. The Jewish sanhedrin in Jerusalem did not have the legal authority of passing a death sentence. Even the sentence of death for Jesus did not come from the sanhedrin, but from the court of the Roman prefect. The martyrdom of Stephen seems to be an exception; but Luke's sources told of a case of lynching by a mob, not of an orderly execution by the Jewish authorities (§8.3b). The execution of Jesus' brother James, however, took place during the vacancy after the death of Festus. Perhaps it was this event which prompted the Christian community of Jerusalem to emigrate to Pella, a city of the Decapolis which fell under the direct administration of the Syrian legate.

Albinus, sent from Rome as Festus' successor, was procurator from 62–64. According to Josephus, he was incredibly corrupt, and his successor Gessius Florus (64–66) was even worse. His incompetence created a situation that provided every opportunity for the anti-Roman elements in the country to incite further unrest and steer a course that would result in war with Rome. A feud between the Jewish and Greek parts of the population of Caesarea in 66 opened the hostilities of the Jewish War. Was the procurator reluctant to interfere? Did he simply not know what to do? It was the kind of conflict which could have been settled easily with a little good will on all sides: construction work on a lot next to the synagogue had obstructed part of the synagogue's entrance. It remains inexplicable why Gessius Florus went to Jerusalem shortly afterwards and seized some of the Temple's treasure—the situation was tense enough without such an action. When the population of Jerusalem protested, he permitted his soldiers to plunder the city. But Gessius Florus had to give way to the fury of the people and withdrew to Caesarea. Open rebellion was now a fact, and Josephus describes the events in such a way that the reader can have no doubt: the stupidity and brutality of the Roman procurator was responsible for the actual outbreak of hostilities.

Josephus thereby has indeed pointed to one important factor which brought the beginning of the war. During the last years of Nero's rule the once well-functioning Roman administration had been severely impaired. Incompetent and disreputable lackeys had received responsible positions; supervision and control by the emperor and his advisors had virtually ceased to exist. The behavior of Gessius Florus is to that extent a typical product of the late-Neronian period. Nevertheless, it is necessary to reflect upon the reasons for the outbreak of the Jewish War. The repeated messianic disturbances, including the activities of Jesus, prove that eschatological aspirations and hopes were by no means dead among the people, but had considerable influence upon wide circles of the population. In some instances the lower classes may have been those most prepared to follow the call of a messianic prophet. But at the beginning of the Jewish War, a radical political-eschatological spirit also took hold of the younger generation of the upper classes. The leader of the rebellion which threw Gessius Florus out of Jerusalem was the son of the high priest. Josephus, also a member of the upper class, tries to emphasize his own wisdom and insight, but he cannot deny that he himself, just thirty years old, belonged to the aristocratic leaders of the rebellion; in the organization of the military resistance he became the commanding general of the Galilean army.

The whole summer of the year 66, while the Romans did nothing, was filled with negotiations in which the elders of the people, led by the high priest and supported by Agrippa II, tried to persuade the rebels to come around to a negotiated peace. But when the king's three thousand mounted soldiers, brought in to lend force to Agrippa's and the high priest's position, were driven out of Jerusalem, the Syrian legate Cestius Gallus decided to intervene (autumn of 66). He appeared before Jerusalem, but the rebels now were in control of the city. Cestius Gallus was not prepared for such strong resistance and, unable to seize Jerusalem, he withdrew. His army was attacked by the rebels on its retreat and suffered heavy casualties. The legate himself escaped only with great difficulty. These events demonstrate that the Romans had to cope with more than the simple indignation of the people caused by the incompetence of a procurator; rather, they were confronted with a movement that was inspired by revolutionary messianic ideas and that had the allegiance of large parts of the population.

Characteristic for the political messianism of the rebellion was the appearance of a group which Josephus calls "Zealots." They cannot be related to any other messianic movement of an earlier period. Josephus' remarks about the Zealots of the Jewish War reveal that they subscribed to a religious ideology which was more radical than the ideas of the young aristocratic leaders of the rebellion's first year. Josephus himself soon discovered that it was difficult to come to terms with one of the leaders of these Zealots, when he tried to build up the military organization of the Jewish resistance in Galilee: John of Gishala frequently frustrated his plans and also tried to persuade the leaders in Jerusalem to remove Josephus as commander-in-chief. Meanwhile, however, Nero had come to understand that something had to be done about the rebellion in Palestine. While he was spending his time in Greece winning one contest after the other in the various Greek games, Nero entrusted the suppression of the rebellion to the experienced general Vespasian. During the winter of 66/67 Vespasian gathered three legions and various auxiliary troops; he started the campaign in the spring of 67. Galilee was his first target. After a siege of several weeks Josephus had to submit to the conquest of his main fortress Jotapata. He surrendered himself to the Romans and, as a valuable prisoner and advisor, was kept in the camp of Vespasian, whom he prophesied that he would some day become emperor. John of Gishala, the leader of the Zealots, managed to escape to Jerusalem, were he gained the upper hand among the Jewish commanders.

While Jerusalem was dominated henceforth by often bloody feuds between the radical and moderate factions, Vespasian conquered the major part of the country by the spring of 68—including Qumran, the seat of the Essenic community, which had joined the rebels. But the death of Nero in the summer of 68 and the struggle for his succession (§6.2a) brought a delay. A radical group of Zealots led by Simon bar Giora managed to force their way into Jerusalem, and John of Gishala was compelled to share the command with this new leader. Vespasian began the siege of Jerusalem in the spring of 69, though the continuing disturbance about Nero's succession interrupted the Roman war efforts once more. This gave another respite to the revolutionaries which, however, was spent with internal quarrels. In the summer of that year, Vespasian was proclaimed emperor and left the war in Judea to his son Titus, who now commanded four well-trained legions. The siege proper started in the spring of 70. By September, the several parts of Jerusalem had been conquered in succession. The Temple went up in flames, though this was not intended by the conquerors; the treasures, however, were saved and subsequently carried in the triumph of Titus as still depicted on the Arch of Titus in Rome. The last fortress, Masada, was not conquered until 73. When the defenders of Masada committed suicide in the face of their hopeless situation, the dream of political messianism was buried—at least for the time being. Jerusalem later became the Roman city of Aelia Capitolina, and no Jew was permitted to set foot in it. The Samaritan capital Shechem became Neapolis (Nablus). Those among the Pharisees who had not been compromised by the war gathered in the coastal city of Yavneh (Jamnia), attempting to built a new form of Judaism without the Temple and its priestly establishment. As Rabbinic Judaism, it proved capable of outlasting the centuries.

(f) Judaism after the Conquest of Jerusalem

(1) *Sources and Beginnings.* Almost no direct sources are preserved for the history of Judaism from the last part of the 1st through the 2d century CE. The oldest Rabbinic tradition (the Mishnah and the older *midrashim;* see below) were not committed to writing until about 200 CE. These traditions are typically

---

Bibliography to §6.6f: Surveys and general works

Jean Juster, *Les Juifs dans l'empire romaine* (2 vols.; Paris: Geuthner, 1914; reprint 1965).

George Foot Moore, *Judaism in the First Centuries of the Christian Era: The Age of the Tannaim* (3 vols; Cambridge, MA: Harvard University Press, 1927–1930; reprint 1966–1967).

Michael Avi-Yonah, *Geschichte der Juden im Zeitalter des Talmuds* (Berlin: De Gruyter, 1962).

Johann Maier, *Geschichte der jüdischen Religion* (GLB; Berlin: De Gruyter, 1972).

Jacob Neusner, *Early Rabbinic Judaism: Historical Studies in Religion, Literature and Art* (SJLA 13; Leiden: Brill, 1975).

embedded in later school discussions and blended with legendary materials. Moreover, these writings show no interest in the historical situations of the traditions they preserve, but emphasize solely their legal value. As for the later Jewish apocalyptic writings (*4 Ezra* and *2 Baruch,* both from the end of the 1st century CE), it is quite uncertain in what way they relate to Rabbinic Judaism. The sparse information of the historians is anything but impartial; this is also true of Josephus' work the *Jewish Antiquities,* with its clearly pro-Pharisaic bent. Many interesting insights seem to be offered by inscriptions and synagogues, of which many have been excavated quite recently, especially in Galilee. However, none of these synagogues can be dated to the 1st or 2d century CE but were built between the 3d and 5th centuries CE (on the diaspora synagogues and inscriptions, see below §6.6f[4]).

Many problems exist with identifying the predecessors of Rabbinic Judaism. There is no doubt, to be sure, that this particular new form of the continuation of the traditions of Israel developed out of the movement of the Pharisees (§5.2d). But this statement describes its predecessors both too narrowly and too vaguely. The assumption of a succession of five pairs of rabbis extending from Simon the Just (who was high priest ca 200 BCE; see §5.1b) down to Hillel and Shammai at

Bibliography to §6.6f: Special Topics

Saul Lieberman, *Greek in Jewish Palestine* (New York: Jewish Theological Seminary of America, 1942; reprint New York: Feldheim, 1965).

Idem, *Hellenism in Jewish Palestine: Studies in the Literary Transmission, Beliefs, and Manners of Palestine in the I. Century* BCE–*IV. Century* CE (New York: The Jewish Theological Seminary of America, 1962).

Idem, "How much Greek in Jewish Palestine?" in Henry Fischel, ed., *Essays in Greco-Roman and Related Talmudic Literature* (New York: Ktav, 1977) 325-343.

Bibliography to §6.6f (1): Texts

P. S. Alexander, ed. and trans, *Textual Sources for the Study of Judaism* (Textual Sources for the Study of Religion; Totowa, NJ: Barnes & Noble, 1984).

B. M. Metzger, "The Fourth Book of Ezra," in Charlesworth, *OTPseudepigrapha,* 1. 517–59.

J. Schreiner, *Das 4. Buch Esra* (JSHRZ 5,3; Gütersloh: Mohn, 1981).

A. F. J. Klijn, "2 (Syriac Apocalypse of) Baruch," in: Charlesworth, *OTPseudepigrapha,* 1. 615–52.

Idem, *Die syrische Baruch-Apokalypse* (JSHRZ 5/2; Gütersloh: Mohn, 1976).

U. B. Müller, *Die griechische Esra-Apokalypse* (JSHRZ 5/2; Gütersloh: Mohn, 1976).

B. Philonenko-Sayar and M. Philonenko, *Die Apokalypse Abrahams* (JSHRZ 5/5; Gütersloh: Mohn, 1982).

Bibliography to §6.6f (1): Commentaries

Michael E. Stone, *Fourth Ezra: A Commentary on the Book of Fourth Ezra* (Hermeneia; Minneapolis: Fortress, 1990).

Bibliography to §6.6f (1): Studies

Frederick J. Murphy, *Structure and Meaning of Second Baruch* (SBLDS 78; Atlanta: Scholars Press, 1985).

Egon Brandenburger, *Die Verborgenheit Gottes im Weltgeschehen: Das literarische und theologische Problem des 4. Esrabuches* (AThANT 68; Zürich: Theologischer Verlag 1981).

Wolfgang Harnisch, *Verhängnis und Verheißung der Geschichte: Untersuchungen zum Zeit- und Geschichtsverständnis im 4. Buch Esra und in der syrischen Baruchapokalypse* (FRLANT 97; Göttingen: Vandenhoeck & Ruprecht, 1969).

the beginning of the 1st century CE is entirely fictitious and explains very little. The fiction of the "Great Synagogue" that is said to have existed from the time of Ezra in the 5th century BCE adds nothing.

The two most significant developments of the Hellenistic period, which form the fundamental presuppositions for the emergence of Rabbinic Judaism, were movement of the Bible (especially the five books of Moses) into the center of Jewish life and the democratization of learning. This affected almost all circles of Judaism, including the diaspora. Only the Sadducees stood aside from this process. With their literalistic interpretation of the law, they were guardians of the ancient religious institutions (temple, sacrifices; see §5.2a), controlled by a priestly elite. During the Roman period, the Sadducees also bore the political responsibility through their control over the Jerusalem sanhedrin, which was chaired by the high priest. But outside of Jerusalem, especially in the diaspora outside of Palestine, Jews had long since learned to adjust their religion to new situations, and to solve moral, legal, and ritual questions on the basis of the ancient biblical texts by using new methods of exegesis. Thus a new tradition of interpretation was developed in the synagogues that was no longer controlled by the priests.

Certain traditions of this interpretation were already fixed in the early 1st century CE. But there was no uniformity, not even within the Pharisaic movement itself, to which Paul belonged as much as Hillel and Shammai. The sanhedrin in Jerusalem, controlled by the high priest, could not possibly have been interested as an institution in the creation of a unified tradition of interpretation. Its immediate concern, like that of the many local sanhedrins that were established in the districts of Palestine, was the task of fiscal and legal administration, for which it was accountable to the Roman authorities. The Sadducees were primarily interested in the law insofar as it concerned matters related to the temple, but not in novel alternatives of biblical interpretation for those Jews who lived not only in areas as distant as Galilee but even as far away as Babylon and Rome. It has been much disputed whether there was also, in addition to the official Jerusalem sanhedrin, a private Pharisaic sanhedrin, widely recognized by Aramaic-speaking Jews. The later rabbinic sanhedrin of Yavneh could then be seen as a continuation of this older Pharisaic institution, not as the successor of the official Jerusalem sanhedrin.

But the hypothesis of such a Pharisaic sanhedrin is burdened with too many difficulties. An obvious problem arises from the fact that the rabbis of Yavneh did not use the term "sanhedrin," but spoke of the "law court" (*Beth Din*) headed by a president (*Nasi*) and a vice-president (*Ab Beth Din*). It was organized like a school, not like a political institution. Moreover, the leading Pharisees of Jerusalem would have been members of two sanhedrins, since they certainly belonged to the official sanhedrin. But, most of all, this hypothesis underestimates the creative power of the synagogue, which simultaneously was the center of a religious association, a law court, a school house, the base for religious propaganda, and the place of worship and prayer (§5.1e).

In spite of its significance, the synagogue was not capable of creating a worldwide unity of Judaism; it was a long road to that unity even after the founding of the *Beth Din* of Yavneh. For the time being, the Alexandrian philosopher Philo had just as much place in the synagogue as Hillel from Babylon, or Jesus, or Paul, or other Israelite followers of Jesus of Nazareth. However, they all had one thing in common: questions of temple ritual were secondary to interpreting the Bible for social situations that were unrelated to the temple's cult and ritual. Issues of conduct, including questions of ritual purity, were the primary concern. The often complex legal discussions of questions of conduct (*halakha*), therefore, must have begun to be formed already before the destruction of the temple, not to mention the further development of proclamation (*haggadah*), mystical biblical interpretation, and apocalyptic speculation.

(2) Hillel was certainly a historical person, but for Rabbinic Judaism and its traditions he became so much a symbol that it is impossible to identify specific teachings that can be assigned to him. "Hillel" stands for everything that would give later Rabbinic Judaism its characteristic mark of legal interpretation. Hillel came from Babylon and lived to about 20 CE. He may have studied in Jerusalem, but his exegetical principles, which together with his humaneness became determinative for Rabbinic Judaism, reveal the diaspora situation, where legislation related to the temple cult was of only academic interest. This perspective as well as his great gifts as a teacher made Hillel the father of Rabbinic Judaism—much more so than his famous exegetical rules, like the argument *a minore ad maius* and the argument from analogy. In contrast, his oft-quoted opponent Shammai became a symbol for a branch of Pharisaism more closely related to the temple. "Shammai" stands for everything that is aristocratic, severe, and nationalistic; "Hillel" represents the common people and their humbler circumstances in life. Both "Hillel" and "Shammai" are thus code words for certain types of interpretation.

Hillel's successor as head of the school, Gamaliel I (probably a son of Hillel), emerges as a more clearly identifiable personality. He belonged to the Jerusalem aristocracy and was a member of its sanhedrin, though he may have distanced himself sometimes from the prevailing opinion of that institution, as is indicated in the report of the Book of Acts 5:34–39, where Gamaliel is extolled for his wisdom and moderation. However, Gamaliel's son Simeon became the leader of the Pharisaic war party and was associated with the first government of the revolutionaries, although later he had to make room for a more radical leadership. This Pharisaic war party can be roughly identified with the Shammaites with whom Simeon, grandson of Hillel, perished in the chaos of the Jewish War.

(3) *From Yohanan ben Zakkai to Akiva.* Judaism owes its new beginnings after the Jewish War to a man who, according to tradition, was the colleague of Simeon ben Gamaliel in the leadership of the school in Jerusalem and himself a student of Hillel: Yohanan ben Zakkai. He disengaged himself from the war party at an early date. There are testimonies that he had protested against certain brutalities that were committed in the name of national liberation. Yohanan left Jerusalem in 68 CE, even before the end of the war. Risking his life, he went into the camp of Vespasian to request permission to settle in Yavneh on the coast of Palestine, in order to found a new school. In view of the increasing gravity of the

situation in Rome with Nero's succession still disputed (§6.2a–b), Vespasian would certainly welcome the establishment of a new, moderate Jewish leadership in Palestine. Other Jewish teachers who had not identified themselves with the national revolution, especially from the school of Hillel, joined Yohanan shortly before or soon after the end of the war. More Jews were forcibly settled by the Romans in this area. This made it possible to reorganize Jewish life under the leadership of Yohanan after Jerusalem had fallen.

Everyone agreed that this catastrophe was a punishment for Israel's sins; this was the opinion not only of the Christians and the Jewish apocalyptic theologians (*4 Ezra* and *2 Baruch*), but also of Yohanan ben Zakkai and his colleagues. Yohanan also knew how to respond: only the strictest fulfillment of the law could bring recovery, because disregard for the law had brought the disaster. In the effort of establishing a reliable understanding of the law with respect to rules of ritual and contact, Hillel's methods of interpretation and his principal precepts of conduct (*halakha*), which had already been practiced outside of the immediate jurisdiction of the temple and did not imply a necessary connection with it, became decisive.

It can be assumed that the most important decisions of the reorganization were made already under Yohanan. These judgments concerned liturgical as well as legal questions. The teachers of Yavneh claimed authority to make decisions in areas that previously had been the domain of the priests. This involved especially the fixing of the calendar (the solar calendar of the Essenes was rejected and the lunar calendar reconfirmed, requiring the intercalation of a thirteenth month every three years) and the determination of dates for the festivals. The important problem of "clean and unclean" was separated from the sacrificial cult of the temple—sacrifices were only of academic interest—and thus removed from priestly jurisdiction. From now on only the word of the learned court, the *Beth Din*, was valid. Maintaining ritual purity was an obligation for all members of the Jewish community. The concept of the priesthood of all believers was just as

Bibliography to §6.6f (3): Studies

Jacob Neusner, *First-Century Judaism in Crisis: Yohanan ben Zakkai and the Renaissance of Torah* (rev. ed.; New York: Ktav, 1982).

Idem, "The Formation of Rabbinic Judaism: Yavneh (Jamnia) from AD *70–100*," *ANRW* 2.19.2 (1979) 3–42.

Shaye J. D. Cohen, "The Significance of Yavneh: Pharisees, Rabbis, and the End of Jewish Sectarianism," *HUCA* 55 (1984) 27–53.

Louis Finkelstein, *Akiba: Scholar, Saint, and Martyr* (first published 1936; New York: Atheneum, 1970).

G. Alon, *The Jews in Their Land in the Talmudic Age (70–640 CE)*, vol. 1 (Jerusalem: Magnes Press, 1980).

L. J. Levine, *The Rabbinic Class of Roman Palestine in Late Antiquity* (New York: Jewish Theological Seminary of America, 1989).

Lee I. Levine, ed., *The Synagogue in Late Antiquity* (Philadelphia: American Schools of Oriental Research, 1987).

M. J. S. Chiat, *Handbook of Synagogue Architecture* (BJudSt 29; Chico, CA: Scholars Press, 1982).

strong here as in the New Testament (1 Pet 2:5). The Sadducees' interpretation of the law and their rejection of belief in the resurrection were repudiated.

The controversy between a stricter and a more pragmatic interpretation of the law continued in Yavneh. These controversies may have had their root in the presence of representatives of the Pharisaic war party at the school at Yavneh. Gamaliel II, son Simeon ben Gamaliel (I), was one of the few leaders of the war party who had escaped the massacre after the destruction of Jerusalem. He came to Yavneh in about 80 CE and was elected *Nasi* of the *Beth Din* before the death of the aged Yohanan ben Zakkai. The prestige of the family of Hillel, whose genealogy was soon traced back to David (cf. Matt 1:2–16), may have contributed to the election of Hillel's great-grandson to this position which he was able to maintain until 135, though not uncontested. The leadership of the *Beth Din* in subsequent years also remained in the hands of the descendants of Hillel. Gamaliel's son Simeon was his successor (ca. 135–175), who was in turn succeeded by his son Judah, called "the Prince" (*HaNasi;* ca. 175–220).

The period from the death of Hillel to the final redaction of the Mishnah by the patriarch Judah is called the time of the Tannaim, that is, the "transmitters" or "teachers" (derived from the Aramaic term *tena* = "to repeat," "to transmit," corresponding to the Hebrew *shanah,* from which the word Mishnah is derived). The most important teachers of this time were R. Akiva ben Joseph and R. Ishmael ben Elisha. Akiva systematized the tradition of the *halakha* in six main sections, with numerous subdivisions that are still preserved in the later redaction of the Mishnah. The *halakha* became more strictly aligned with Scripture, as the agreement of the legal decisions with the Bible was refined. At the same time, the principle of inspiration was intensified: all minutiae of Holy Scripture, to the very last letter, were deemed significant. In the revisions of the Greek Bible, the recension of Aquila, following the Hebrew text as closely as possible (§5.3b), corresponds most closely to this principle. Aquila, a contemporary of R. Akiva, was perhaps also his student. Ishmael rejected Akiva's literalism, recognizing the use of vernacular language in the Bible, and warning that details should not be emphasized too strongly. Ishmael is credited with the expansion of Hillel's seven rules of interpretation, which he modified and divided into thirteen rules that became determinative for Rabbinic Judaism.

The Roman administration did not interfere in the reorganization of Judaism, or persecute the Jews, or disturb the activities of the *Beth Din,* which sent messengers to other Jewish communities in an attempt to broaden its influence and gain general recognition for its legal and ritual decisions. This goal was not easily achieved, especially in areas where Greek (and not Aramaic) was the spoken language, and were Hebrew was not in use even as the language of liturgy and prayer. Nothing is known about the relationship of the court in Yavneh to those communities who kept the law and also confessed Christ (§10.4a–c), nor about its connection with Gnosticism, which certainly had its beginnings in the areas of Syria and Palestine. The formation of the gnostic interpretation of the Book of Genesis cannot be explained without presuming some contact with the beginnings of rabbinic exegesis (§6.5f; 10.5b). Mystical, apocalyptic, and gnostic speculations were not unknown in Yavneh, as is evident from scattered information from later rabbinic sources. The image of a court dealing exclusively with legal and halakhic questions is certainly too narrow. The revision of the materials from the first period of the Tannaim that took place in the second half of the 2d century CE apparently purged many things that were no longer acceptable after the catastrophes of the Jewish insurrections of 116–117 and 132–135 CE.

(4) *The Diaspora in the Roman Period.* Archaeological evidence indicates that the *Beth Din* did not influence many of the Greek-speaking diaspora communities. To be sure, nonliterary evidence presents notorious difficulties for interpretation, but a few data are clear. Language may have been an obstacle to expanding the influence of the *Beth Din*. Though it is unlikely that its leaders were acquainted with Greek literature, it is undeniable that Greek influences on Pharisaic and Rabbinic Judaism were considerable. Still, its language was Aramaic and its scholarly and liturgical language Hebrew. However, Jewish inscriptions from Asia Minor, Rome, and other places in the Greek-speaking diaspora are almost exclusively in Greek. This is even more remarkable when one considers that the majority of these inscriptions come from the 3d to 5th centuries of the common era. While Latin is sometimes used in inscriptions at Rome, very little Hebrew appears.

While it can be assumed that the synagogues excavated in Galilee are related to Rabbinic Judaism, the evidence from diaspora synagogues is puzzling. Were all these synagogues Jewish, or perhaps Jewish-Christian, or Samaritan? A Samaritan inscription from Thessaloniki (Greek with two lines of Hebrew in Samaritan script) demonstrates that Samaritan diaspora communities continued to exist as late as the 5th century CE. The synagogue of Dura Europos with its spectacular wall paintings belongs in the early 3d century CE; the Stoboi (northern Macedonia) synagogue as well as the synagogue of Ostia can hardly be dated earlier; and the more recently excavated wing of the bath/gymnasium complex at Sardes was not used as a synagogue until the end of the 3d century CE, with some further building and reconstruction in evidence for the 4th and 5th centuries CE. The Sardis synagogue is oriented to the west, as is also the synagogue of Ostia. Divisions for the separate seating of men and women have not been found in any of these synagogues, nor are there traces of any construction of women's balconies. Moreover, inscriptions give ample evidence for women holding various offices, including that of the president of the synagogue. The wall paintings of the synagogue of Dura Europos and of some Jewish catacombs in Rome violate the rabbinic prohibition of images as much as do the astrological symbols of the floor mosaics of Galilean synagogues. The Jewish diaspora was thriving long

Bibliography to §6.6.f (4)

A. Thomas Kraabel, "Jews in Imperial Rome: More Archaeological Evidence from an Oxford Collection," *JJS* 30 (1979) 41–58.

Idem, "The Roman Diaspora: Six Questionable Assumptions," in Geza Vermes and Jacob Neusner, eds., *Essays in Honor of Yigael Yadin* = *JJS* 33/1–2 (1982) 445–64.

See also Bibliography to §5.1e

after Constantine, but it is evident that these communities were not subject to the *Beth Din* in Galilee.

(5) *The Insurrections of the Second Century.* Despite the pacifist position of many of its leaders, and despite the principle that study of the Torah has a higher value than the national freedom of the Jewish people, the *Beth Din* never renounced the expectation of a political fulfillment of messianic beliefs. The moderate leaders of the court in Yavneh were united with the nationalists in their desire to return to Jerusalem and rebuild the temple. In the second decade of the 2d century CE the Romans seemed willing to grant that wish. But when Trajan forbade the reconstruction of the temple after a long period of negotiations, militant nationalism prevailed over rational opinion.

The insurrection of 116–117 CE began in the Cyrenaica and Egypt and spread to Palestine. The revolt's bloody suppression had consequences for the court in Yavneh. It was forced to move to Lod (Lydda), and was deprived of some important functions, such as the right to determine the calendar. In the years following this insurrection, the radical elements seemed to have gained the upper hand, while the pacifist party led by Akiva lost ground. Another insurrection broke out when Hadrian disclosed his plans to build a sanctuary for the Capitoline Jupiter on the site of the ruined temple in the course of his reconstruction of Jerusalem as "Aelia Capitolina." Within three years (132–135 CE) the Romans crushed an initially successful messianic movement, whose leader had been called "Star of Jacob" and who is remembered by the name of Bar Kokhba.

The consequences were catastrophic. Hadrian recognized the religious motivations that had triggered the revolt. In contrast to the aftermath of the Jewish War of 66–73, Rome now took measures against the very practice of the Jewish religion. Not only were Jews forbidden even to approach Jerusalem, the prohibitions included the practice of circumcision, the observance of the Sabbath and of the Jewish festivals, as well as instruction in the Torah. The aged Akiva, over ninety years old, suffered martyrdom when he refused to comply with the latter prohibition. The *Beth Din* had ceased to exist. The Jewish population had been massacred or expelled. However, the diaspora synagogues were apparently not affected by the consequences of the Bar Kokhba revolt.

The legislation against the practice of the Jewish religion was somewhat mitigated under Antoninus Pius. As soon as it became possible to reconstitute the Jewish law court, the reorganization began in Galilee, where the *Beth Din,* after several relocations, finally settled in Tiberias. Here the students of Akiva continued and further elaborated the traditions from the first period of the Tannaim. Foremost among them was R. Meir, who had studied under both Akiva and Ishmael. He became primarily responsible for the form of the Mishnah in which it was fixed in written form by the patriarch Judah ca. 200 CE. This last period of the Tannaim made the decisions which would determine the course of Rabbinic Judaism. This period also produced the oldest Rabbinic literature that is pre-

Bibliography to §6.6.f (5)

Yigael Yadin, *Bar Kochba* (New York: Random House, 1971).

served, the Mishnah, the Tannaitic *midrashim,* and the Tosefta. These will be discussed briefly below.

(6) *From the Mishnah to the Talmud.* The Mishnah is the codification of interpretations of the laws that were at first transmitted orally. These traditions often begin with the opinions of Hillel (and Shammai) and add the opinions of later teachers. The fundamental elements of these discussions were formed during the time of the reconstruction after 70 CE. During the 2d century CE written notes were also produced, that is, handbooks for private use and for the court's legal decisions. Akiva created the division of the material into six main sections: *Zeraim* ("Seeds"—on agriculture and fruits of the field); *Moed* ("Festivals"); *Nashim* ("Women"—this section also contains legislation on vows); *Nezikin* ("Damages"—civil and criminal law); *Kodashim* ("Hallowed Things"—sacrifice and ritual); *Tohoroth* ("Cleanliness"—legislation about clean and unclean). This method of division is purely systematic, but also reveals an interest in aids for memorization. Reshaped by Meir, the Mishnah was revised and edited in written form by the patriarch Judah. It became the standard collection of the legal discussions and decisions of the Tannaim, and was accepted not only in Palestine but also in Babylon, thus becoming the basis for both the Palestinian (Jerusalem) and Babylonian Talmuds.

The Early Midrashim. Alongside the legal decisions transmitted in a system-

---

Bibliography to §6.6.f (6): Texts

Herbert Danby, ed., *The Mishna* (Oxford: Clarendon, 1933, and reprints). Best available English translation.

Jacob Z. Lauterbach, *Mekilta de-Rabbi Ishmael* (3 vols.; The Schiff Library of Jewish Classics; Philadelphia: Jewish Publication Society, 1933–1935). Hebrew of the Mekilta on Exodus with English translation.

Paul Levertoff, *Midrash Sifre on Numbers* (Translations of Early Documents 3: Rabbinic texts; London: SPCK, 1926). Selections from Sifre on Numbers in English translation.

Reuven Hammer, *Sifre: A Tannaitie Commentary on the Book of Deuteronomy* (Yale Judaica Series 24; New Haven: Yale University Press, 1986).

Claude G. Montefiore and Herbert Loewe, eds., *A Rabbinic Anthology* (London: Macmillan, 1938 and reprints).

Adlin Steinsaltz, ed., *The Talmud; The Steinsaltz Edition* (New York, Random House 1989–1992). Best available English translation, in 8 vols. plus a reference guide.

Hermann Strack and Paul Billerbeck, *Kommentar zum Neuen Testament aus Talmud und Midrasch* (6 vols.; München: Beck, 1922–1969). Used judiciously it is still a valuable tool for the New Testament student.

Bibliography to §6.6.f (6): Introductions and Studies

Shmuel Safrai, ed., *The Literature of the Sages,* first part: *Oral Tora, Halakha, Mishna, Tosefta, Talmud, External Tractates* (CRINT 3.1; Philadelphia: Fortress, 1987).

Jacob Neusner, *The Modern Study of the Mishna* (Leiden: Brill, 1973).

Michael Lattke, "Haggadah," *RAC* 13 (1985) 328–60.

Idem, "Halachah," *RAC* 13 (1985) 372–402.

H. A. Fischel, *Rabbinic Literature and Greco-Roman Philosophy: A Study of Epicurea and Rhetorica in early Midrashic Writings* (SPB 21; Leiden: Brill, 1973).

Jacob Neusner, *Method and Meaning in Ancient Judaism* (Brown University, BJUDS 10; Missoula: Scholars Press, 1979). A good introduction to the purpose and function of rabbinic literature.

atized fashion, no later than the early 2d century CE legal commentaries on the individual biblical books began to be composed, beginning with the books of Exodus, Leviticus, Numbers, and Deuteronomy. The subjects and materials of these commentaries in the early period are halakhic, that is, legal, while preaching and narrative (*haggadah*) plays only a minor role in the earliest commentaries. The name for such commentary is *midrash* (= "investigation"). The oldest commentaries that are preserved are known as *Mechilta, Sifra,* and *Sifre.*

Mechilta is a commentary on Exodus, namely on Exod 12–23; 32:12–17; and 35:1–3. It has been assumed therefore that the commentary is not completely preserved. *Mechilta* also quotes opinions of later rabbis, but its basis seems to be a commentary of R. Ishmael or of his school. *Sifra* (precisely *Sifra de-Be-Rab* = "Book of the School") is a running commentary on Leviticus, interpreting almost every sentence. It originated in the school of R. Akiva, though its final redaction took place after the codification of the Mishnah. *Sifre (Sifre de-Be-Rab* = "Books of the School") designates two different works, namely a midrash on Numbers and a midrash on Deuteronomy. The former derives from the school of R. Ishmael; in *Sifre on Deuteronomy* the commentary on Deuteronomy 12–26 comes from the school of R. Akiva. In both instances the extant parts do not represent the full extent of the original commentaries.

Tosefta is the name of a second collection of halakhic materials from the Tannaitic period. The collection was made at some time in addition to the Mishnah. The origin of this collection is debated, but since the Tosefta follows the Mishnah in its divisions of materials, it could be defined as its commentary. The halakhic rules are often the same as those of the Mishnah. In some sections the Tosefta is nothing but a presentation of additional materials (*Tosefta* = "Additions"), but it often preserves independent, parallel traditions. These are particularly valuable, since the Tosefta did not share the canonical status as the Mishnah and was therefore not subject to the redaction of later editors.

Names and Places

(Bold print indicates specific discussion of frequently cited names)

Writings

Biblical, Jewish, and Early-Christian Writings

(Bold print denotes specific treatment of a writing)

Armstrong, *Mediterranean Spirituality*
  A. H. Armstrong, *Classical Mediterranean Spirituality: Egyptian, Greek, and Ro-
  man* (World Spirituality 15; New Yord: Crossroad, 1986)
Barrett, *Background*
  C. K. Barrett, ed., *The New Testament Background: Selected Documents* (London:
  SPCK, 1956; reprint: New York: Harper, 1961).
Burkert, *Mystery Cults*
  Walter Burkert, *Ancient Mystery Cults* (Cambridge, MA: Harvard University Press,
  1987).
Burkert, *Greek Religion*
  Walter Burkert, *Greek Religion* (Cambridge, MA: Harvard University Press, 1985)
Burkert, *Homo Necans*
  Walter Burkert, *Homo Necans: The Anthropology of Ancient Greek Sacrificial Ritual
  and Myth* (Berkeley, CA: University of California Press, 1983).
Calder and Keil, *Anatolian Studies*
  W. M. Calder and Josef Keil, eds., *Anatolian Studies Presented to William Hepburn
  Buckler* (Manchester: Manchester University Press, 1939).
CambAncHist 7–10
  S. A. Cook, F. E. Adcock, and M. P. Charlesworth, *The Cambridge Ancient Histo-
  ry,* vol 7: *The Hellenistic Monarchies and the Rise of Rome;* vol. 8: *Rome and
  Mediterranean 218–133 B.C.;* vol. 9: *The Roman Republic 133–44 B.C.;* vol. 10:
  The Augustan Empire 44 B.C. - A.D. 70 (New York: Macmillan, 1928–34).
Cambridge History of the Bible 1
  P. R. Ackroyd and C. F. Evans, eds., *Cambridge History of the Bible,* vol. 1: *From
  the Beginnings to Rome* (Cambridge: Cambridge University Press, 1970).
Cartlidge and Dungan, *Documents*
  David R. Cartlidge and David L. Dungan, eds., *Documents for the Study of the
  Gospels* (Philadelphia: Fortress, 1980).
Charles, *APOT*
  R. H. Charles, ed., *Apocrypha and Pseudepigrapha of the Old Testament* (Oxford:
  Clarendon, 1913).
Charlesworth, *OTPseudepigrapha*
  James H. Charlesworth, *The Old Testament Pseudepigrapha* (2 vols.; Garden City,
  NY: Doubleday, 1983–86).
Dihle, *Literature of the Empire*
  Albrecht Dihle, *Greek and Latin Literature of the Roman Empire: From Augustus to
  Justinian* (London and New York: Routledge, 1994).
Easterling and Knox, *Greek Literature*
  Patricia E. Easterling and Bernard M. W. Knox, eds., *The Cambridge History of
  Classical Literature,* vol. 1: *Greek Literature* (Cambridge: Cambridge University
  Press, 1985).
Finley, *Legacy*
  M. I. Finley, ed., *The Legacy of Greece: A New Appraisal* (Oxford: Clarendon,
  1981).
Foakes Jackson and Lake, *Beginnings*
  F. J. Foakes Jackson and Kirsopp Lake, eds., *The Beginnings of Christianity*
  (5 vols.; London: Macmillas, 1920–1933, and reprints).

Foerster, *Gnosis*
    Werner Foerster, *Gnosis: A Selection of Gnostic Texts* (Engl. trans. and ed. R. McL
    Wilson; 2 vols.; Oxford: Clarendon, 1972–1974).
Fraser, *Alexandria*
    P. M. Fraser, *Ptolemaic Alexandria* (3 vols.; Oxford: Clarendon, 1972; reprint
    1984).
Grant, *Hellenistic Religions*
    Frederick C. Grant, ed., *Hellenistic Religions: The Age of Syncretism* (The Library
    of Religion 2; New York: Liberal Arts, 1953).
Grant and Kitzinger, *Civilization*
    Michael Grant and Rachel Kitzinger, eds., *Civilization of the Ancient Mediterra-
    nean: Greece and Rome* (3 vols.; New York: Scribner's, 1988).
Horsley, *New Documents*
    G. H. R. Horsley, *New Documents Illustrating Early Christianity* (6 vols.; The An-
    cient History Document Centre; Sidney, Australia: Macquarie University, 1981–91).
Kenney, *Latin Literature*
    E. J. Kenney, ed., *The Cambridge History of Classical Latin Literature,* vol. 2: *Lat-
    in Literature* (Cambridge: Cambridge University Press, 1982).
Kraemer, *Maenads, Martyrs*
    Ross S. Kraemer, *Maenads, Martyrs, Matrons, Monastics: A Sourcebook on Wom-
    en's Religions in the Greco-Roman World* (Philadelphia: Fortress, 1988).
Kuhrt and Sherwin-White, *Hellenism in the East*
    Amélie Kuhrt and Susan Sherwin-White, *Hellenism in the East: The Interaction of
    Greek and Non-Greek Civilizations from Syria to Central Asia after Alexander* (Lon-
    don: Duckworth, 1987)
Layton, *Gnostic Scriptures*
    Bentley Layton, *The Gnostic Scriptures: A New Translation with Annotations and
    Introductions* (Garden City, NY: Doubleday, 1987).
Layton, *Nag Hammadi Codex II*
    Bentley Layton, ed., *Nag Hammadi Codex II,2–7 Together with XIII,2*, Brit. Lib.
    Or. 4926(1) and P. Oxy. 1, 654, 655* (NHS 20–21; Leiden: Brill, 1987).
Layton, *Rediscovery of Gnosticism*
    Bentley Layton, ed., *The Rediscovery of Gnosticism* (Proceedings of the Internation-
    al Conference at Yale, New Haven, 1978; NumenSup 16; 2 vols.; Leiden: Brill,
    1981–1982).
Meeks and Wilken, *Jews and Christians in Antioch*
    Wayne A. Meeks and L. Robert Wilken, *Jews and Christians in Antioch in the First
    Four Centuries of the Common Era* (SBLSBS 13; Chico, CA: Scholars Press:
    1978).
Meyer, *Mystery Sourcebook*
    Marvin W. Meyer, ed., *The Ancient Mysteries: A Sourcebook: Sacred Texts of the
    Mystery Religions of the Ancient Mediterranean World* (San Francisco: Harper &
    Row, 1987).
Meyer and Sanders, *Self-Definition 3*
    Ben F. Meyer and E. P. Sanders, eds., *Jewish and Christian Self-Definition,*vol. 3:
    Self-Definition in the Greco-Roman World (London: SCM, 1982).
Momigliano, *Pagans, Jews, and Christians*
    Arnaldo Momigiano, *On Pagans, Jews, and Christians* (Middletown, CT: Wesleyan
    University Press, 1987).
NagHamLibEngl
    James M. Robinson, ed., *The Nag Hammadi Library in English* (3d ed.; San Fran-
    cisco: Harper-Collins, 1990).
Nilsson, *Griechische Religion, 2*
    Martin P. Nilsson, *Geschichte der griechischen Religion,* vol. 2: *Die hellenistische
    Zeit* (HAW 5.2/2; 3d ed.; München: Beck, 1974).

Nock, *Essays*
  Arthur Darby Nock, *Essays on Religion and the Ancient World*, ed., Zeph Stewart
  (2 vols.; Cambridge, MA: Harvard University Press, 1972).
Rice and Stambaugh, *Sources for Greek Religion*
  D. G. Rice and J. E. Stambaugh, *Sources for the Study of Greek Religion* (SBLSBS
  14; Missoula, MT: Scholars Press, 1979).
Sanders, *Self-Definition 1*
  E. P. Sanders, ed., *Jewish and Christian Self-Definition*, vol. 1: *The Shaping of
  Christianity in the Second and Third Centuries* (Philadelphia: Fortress, 1980).
Schmitt Pantel, *History of Women*
  Pauline Schmitt Pantel, ed., *From Ancient Goddesses to Christian Saints* (A History
  of Women in the West 1; Cambridge, MA: Harvard University Press, 1992).
Shelton, *As the Romans Did*
  Jo-Ann Shelton, *As the Romans Did: A Sourcebook in Roman Social History* (New
  York: Oxford University Press, 1988).
Stone, *Jewish Writings*
  Michael Stone, ed., *Jewish Writings of the Second Temple Period* (CRINT 2.2; Phil-
  adelphia: Fortress, 1984).
Veyne, *Private Life*
  Philippè Ariès and Georges Duby, eds., *A History of Private Life,* vol. 1, ed. by
  Paul Veyne, *From Pagan Rome to Byzantium* (Cambridge, MA: Harvard University
  Press, 1987).